THE BRONZE AGE

BATMAN

the BRAVE and the BOLD

VOLUME TWO

BOB HANEY
DENNIS O'NEIL
WRITERS

JIM APARO
NICK CARDY
NEAL ADAMS
BOB BROWN
FRANK McLAUGHLIN
ARTISTS

KARL KERSCHL
COLLECTION COVER ARTIST

BATMAN created by BOB KANE with BILL FINGER

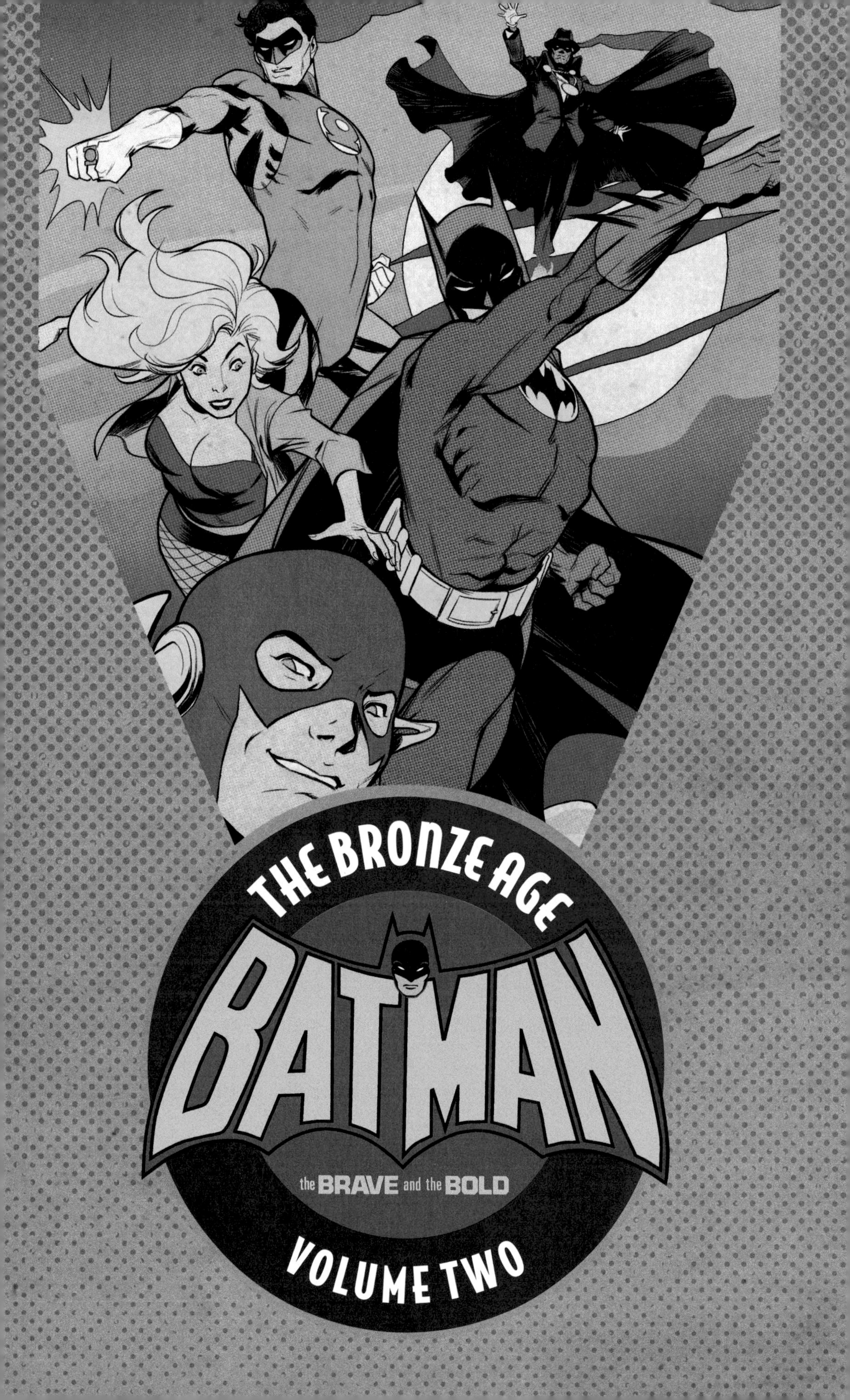

THE BRONZE AGE

BATMAN

the BRAVE and the BOLD

VOLUME TWO

GEORGE KASHDAN, MURRAY BOLTINOFF Editors – Original Series
JEB WOODARD Group Editor – Collected Editions TYLER-MARIE EVANS Editor – Collected Edition
STEVE COOK Design Director – Books DAMIAN RYLAND Publication Design

BOB HARRAS Senior VP – Editor-in-Chief, DC Comics
PAT McCALLUM Executive Editor, DC Comics

Publisher DAN DiDIO
Publisher & Chief Creative Officer JIM LEE
Executive VP – Business & Marketing Strategy, Direct to Consumer &
Global Franchise Management AMIT DESAI
VP & Executive Editor, Young Reader & Talent Development BOBBIE CHASE
Senior VP – Art, Design & Collected Editions MARK CHIARELLO
Senior VP – Sales & Trade Marketing JOHN CUNNINGHAM
VP – Business Affairs BRIAR DARDEN
Senior VP – Business Strategy, Finance & Administration ANNE DePIES
VP – Manufacturing Operations DON FALLETTI
VP – Editorial Administration & Talent Relations LAWRENCE GANEM

ALISON GILL Senior VP – Manufacturing & Operations
JASON GREENBERG VP – Business Strategy & Finance
HANK KANALZ Senior VP – Editorial Strategy & Administration
JAY KOGAN Senior VP – Legal Affairs
NICK J. NAPOLITANO VP – Manufacturing Administration
LISETTE OSTERLOH VP – Digital Marketing & Events
EDDIE SCANNELL VP – Consumer Marketing
COURTNEY SIMMONS Senior VP – Publicity & Communications
JIM (SKI) SOKOLOWSKI VP – Comic Book Specialty Sales & Trade Marketing
NANCY SPEARS VP – Mass, Book, Digital Sales & Trade Marketing
MICHELE R. WELLS VP – Content Strategy

BATMAN IN THE BRAVE AND THE BOLD: THE BRONZE AGE VOLUME 2

DC Comics, 2900 West Alameda Ave., Burbank, CA 91505
Printed by LSC Communications, Owensville, MO, USA. 12/21/18. First Printing.
ISBN: 978-1-4012-8582-1

Library of Congress Cataloging-in-Publication Data is available.

PEFC Certified
This product is from
sustainably managed
forests and controlled
sources
PEFC/29-31-337 www.pefc.org

All stories by **BOB HANEY** with art by **JIM APARO**, *unless otherwise noted.*

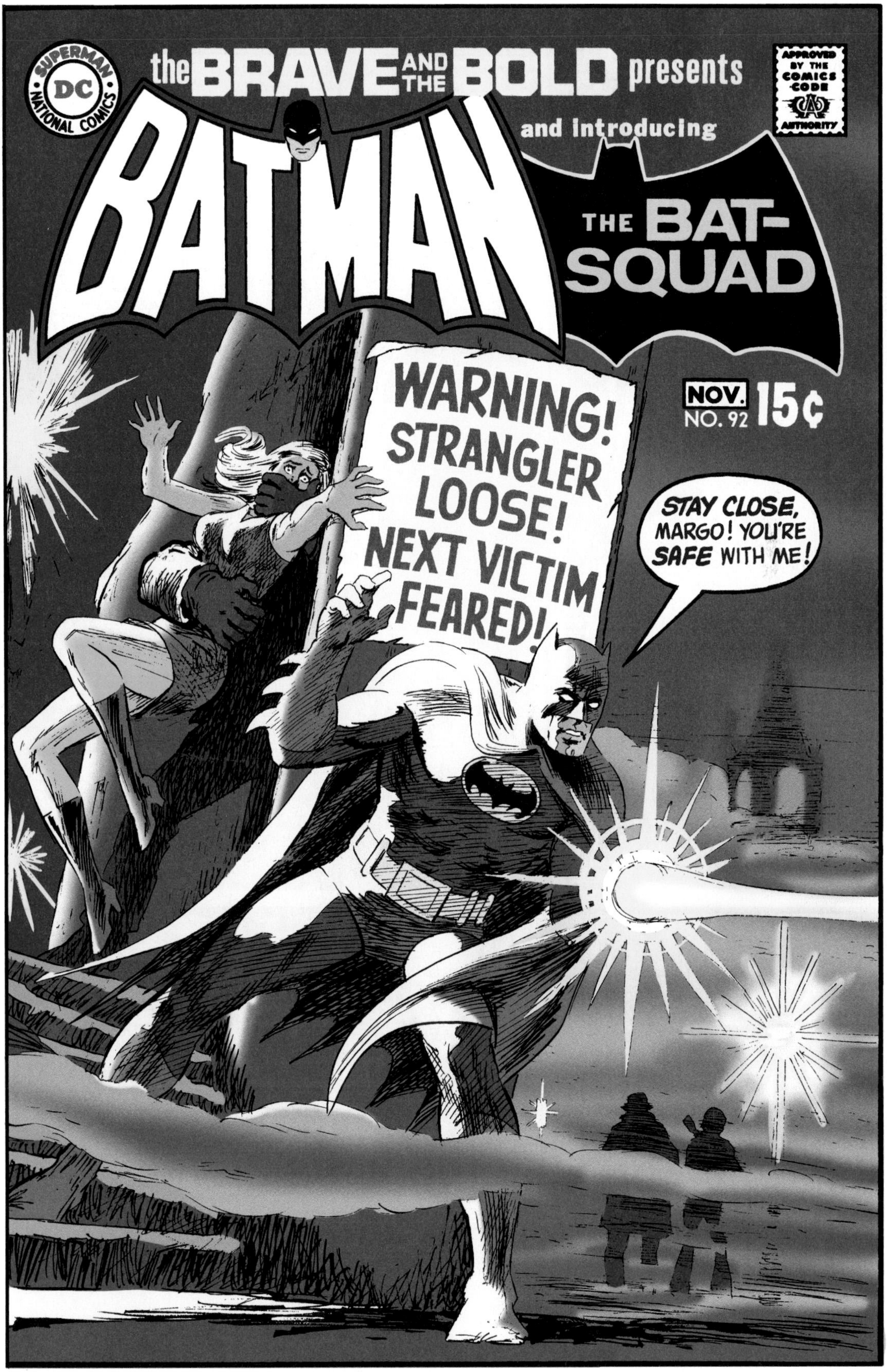
SUPERMAN DC NATIONAL COMICS
the BRAVE AND THE BOLD presents
BATMAN
and introducing
THE BAT-SQUAD
APPROVED BY THE COMICS CODE AUTHORITY
NOV. NO. 92 15¢
WARNING! STRANGLER LOOSE! NEXT VICTIM FEARED!
STAY CLOSE, MARGO! YOU'RE SAFE WITH ME!

NOW, LOVES, WE'RE GOING TO SHOOT THE BIG SCENE WHEN THE **STRANGLER** FIRST STRIKES! I WANT ABSOLUTE SILENCE...

...JUST THE MURMUR OF THE THAMES... THE FLUTTER OF THE GASLIGHT...COMPLETE REALISM...ATMOSPHERE--! GOT IT?

NEARBY, A FAMILIAR FIGURE, BRUCE WAYNE, WATCHES...

SO **THAT'S** BASIL COVENTRY, THE GENIUS DIRECTOR! I CAME HERE TO SEE IF MY INVESTMENT IN THIS MOVIE WAS IN GOOD HANDS!

HAVE NO FEAR, MR. WAYNE! BASIL'S BRILLIANT, AND "**THE SCARLET STRANGLER**" WILL BE A SMASH!

BY THE WAY, I'M MARGO CANTRELL, SCRIPT GIRL AND STAND-IN FOR THE STAR, VIVIEN TREMAINE!

AND I'M MAJOR DABNEY, A FORMER SCOTLAND YARD INSPECTOR AND TECHNICAL ADVISER! I'VE STUDIED THE REAL **SCARLET STRANGLER'S** CAREER, AND I ASSURE YOU COVENTRY'S DOING IT FULL JUSTICE!

IN FACT, THIS IS THE EXACT SPOT WHERE THE **STRANGLER** NABBED HIS FIRST VICTIM OVER 60 YEARS AGO! THIS AREA'S HARDLY CHANGED SINCE!

THE MAJOR'S RUDDY RIGHT, MR. WAYNE! I'M MICK MURDOCK... 'AVE GUITAR... WILL WANDER!

COVENTRY'S GOT ME PLAYIN' WEIRD, GROTTY MUSIC JUST TO GET THE ACTORS IN THE RIGHT MOOD! I OWE IT TO THE MAJOR 'ERE-- 'E GOT ME THE JOB!

YOU'LL DO FINE, LAD, I'M SURE, ALTHOUGH I CAN'T ABIDE THAT NOISE YOU PLAY! GIVE ME A GOOD MARCH TUNE ANYTIME...

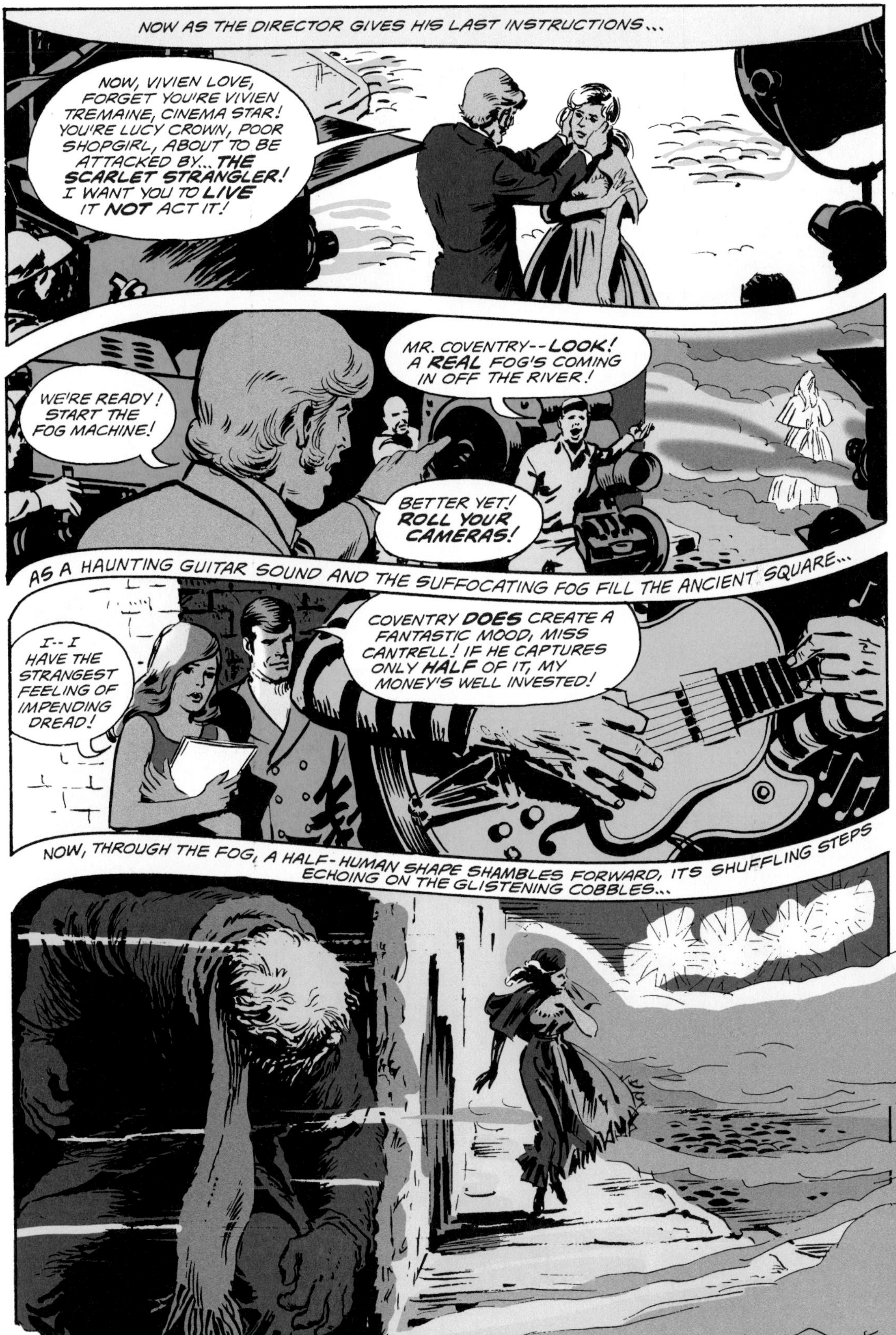
NOW AS THE DIRECTOR GIVES HIS LAST INSTRUCTIONS...
NOW, VIVIEN LOVE, FORGET YOU'RE VIVIEN TREMAINE, CINEMA STAR! YOU'RE LUCY CROWN, POOR SHOPGIRL, ABOUT TO BE ATTACKED BY... THE SCARLET STRANGLER! I WANT YOU TO LIVE IT NOT ACT IT!
WE'RE READY! START THE FOG MACHINE!
MR. COVENTRY--LOOK! A REAL FOG'S COMING IN OFF THE RIVER!
BETTER YET! ROLL YOUR CAMERAS!
AS A HAUNTING GUITAR SOUND AND THE SUFFOCATING FOG FILL THE ANCIENT SQUARE...
I-- I HAVE THE STRANGEST FEELING OF IMPENDING DREAD!
COVENTRY DOES CREATE A FANTASTIC MOOD, MISS CANTRELL! IF HE CAPTURES ONLY HALF OF IT, MY MONEY'S WELL INVESTED!
NOW, THROUGH THE FOG, A HALF-HUMAN SHAPE SHAMBLES FORWARD, ITS SHUFFLING STEPS ECHOING ON THE GLISTENING COBBLES...
2

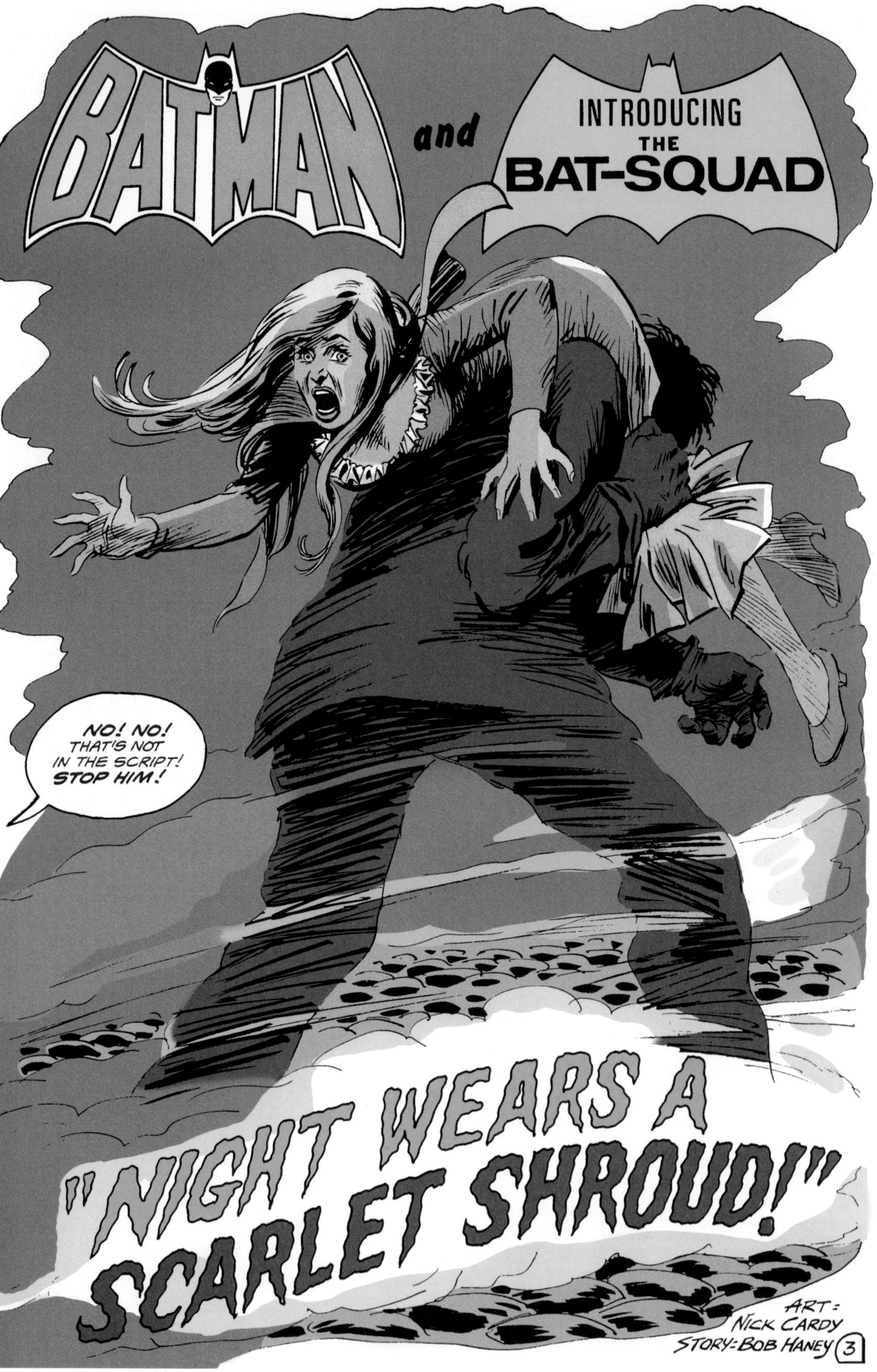
BATMAN
and
INTRODUCING THE BAT-SQUAD
NO! NO! THAT'S NOT IN THE SCRIPT! STOP HIM!
"NIGHT WEARS A SCARLET SHROUD!"
ART: NICK CARDY
STORY: BOB HANEY
3

SOMETHING AMISS HERE!

COVENTRY'S FAINTED!

MAJOR! RONALD DAWSON, THE ACTOR PLAYING THE STRANGLER-- JUST FOUND HIM IN HIS TRAILER! COME QUICKLY!

MOMENTS LATER...

GOOD HEAVENS! HE'S DEAD... STRANGLED--!

THEN WHO PLAYED THAT SCENE... WHO CARRIED OFF MISS TREMAINE?

SOUNDS LIKE BRUCE WAYNE BETTER EXIT...

... SO BATMAN CAN ENTER! FIRST, TO CONTACT THE POLICE...

...THEN TO GET SOME HELP-- AND I KNOW WHERE TO FIND IT!

BLIMEY!

JOVE! THE BATMAN, I PRESUME!

NONE OTHER! BRUCE WAYNE KNEW I WAS HERE, STUDYING BRITISH POLICE METHODS, AND CALLED ME--!

HE ALSO SAID YOU THREE MIGHT HELP ME TRACK DOWN THE CULPRIT WHO KILLED THAT ACTOR AND ABDUCTED MISS TREMAINE!

'ELP THE BLOOMIN' BATMAN? GEAR AND GROOVY!

HOW SMASHING!

AT YOUR SERVICE, SIR!

4

11

SINCE WE'LL NEED INSTANT COMMUNICATIONS IN THIS FOG, THESE FILM COMPANY WALKIE-TALKIES ARE PERFECT! I'LL CHECK WITH YOU EVERY 15 MINUTES! MISS CANTRELL, YOU GO WITH MICK FOR SAFETY!

NO NEED! I'M A KARATE BLACK BELT HOLDER-- AND NOT EASILY FRIGHTENED!

GOOD GIRL! NOW SPREAD OUT-- AND GOOD LUCK!

AS *BATMAN* AND HIS NEW-FOUND ALLIES FAN OUT-- SHORTLY, IN THE TRAILER WHERE BASIL COVENTRY WAS TAKEN...

MR. COVENTRY THE POLICE ARE HERE--

HE'S GONE!

WHILE IN THE SWIRLING, SWATHING FOG...

NOT A SIGN OF ANYTHING...HUMAN OR OTHERWISE! TIME TO CHECK ON MARGO, MICK, AND THE MAJOR!

BATMAN TO ALL-- CHECK IN, PLEASE!

MARGO TO *BATMAN*-- NOTHING YET!

MICK HERE-- QUIET AS A BLINKIN' TOMB--!

DABNEY, *BAT-CHAP!* ALL QUIET!

WEIRD...BUT THIS WHOLE MYSTERY GIVES ME THE FEELING OF TIME HAVING REVERSED ITSELF... THE PAST COMING TO LIFE AGAIN! BUT IT MUST BE THE NIGHT AND THIS BLASTED FOG!

5

SUDDENLY, LOOMING THROUGH THE MIST...

STOP!

BLIMEY! A MASKED HIGHWAYMAN! HELLP!

I'M NO ROBBER! HAVE YOU SEEN A TALL MAN... WEARING SCARLET GLOVES... CARRYING A WOMAN--?

WOT? CARRYIN' A WOMAN--? NO, GUV'NOR...

...BUT I SEEN KING EDWARD CARRYIN' HIS LAUNDRY!

NOW OUT OF MY WAY, YOU BLOOMIN' MANIAC!

DID I IMAGINE IT? THAT OLD MAN... HE DIDN'T KNOW ME... AND HE TALKED OF KING EDWARD, WHO RULED ENGLAND IN THE SCARLET STRANGLER'S TIME!

BUT BATMAN'S DOUBTS ARE INTERRUPTED BY A DIFFERENT SOUND--A SINISTER SHUFFLING...

IT'S HIM-- THE CHARACTER WHO ABDUCTED VIVIEN TREMAINE!

6

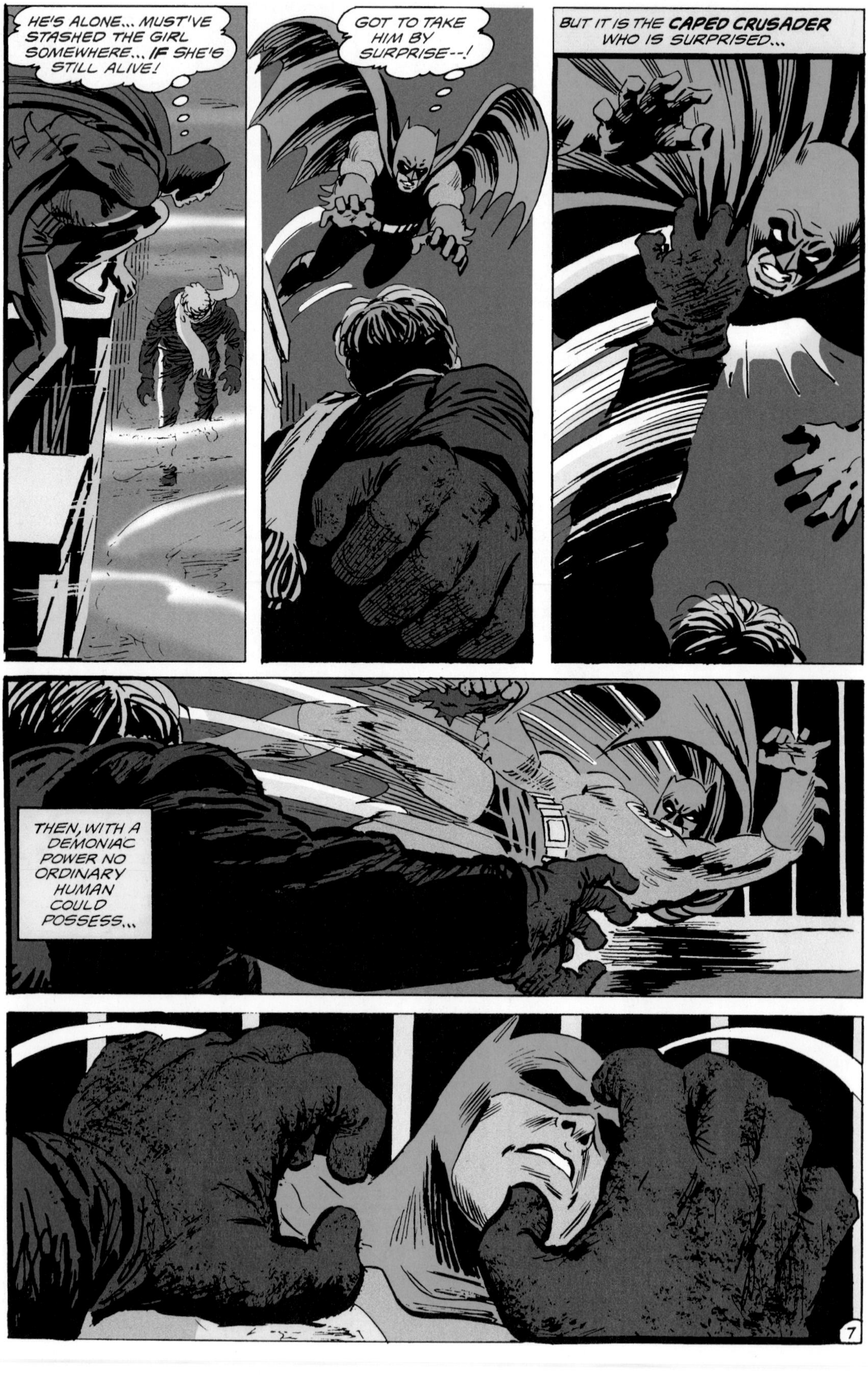
HE'S ALONE... MUST'VE STASHED THE GIRL SOMEWHERE... IF SHE'S STILL ALIVE!
GOT TO TAKE HIM BY SURPRISE--!
BUT IT IS THE CAPED CRUSADER WHO IS SURPRISED...
THEN, WITH A DEMONIAC POWER NO ORDINARY HUMAN COULD POSSESS...
7

THOK WHOK
THOK WHOK

MAJOR--?

EASY, OLD BOY! YOU'RE JUST STUNNED! WHEN I COULDN'T RAISE YOU ON THE WALKIE-TALKIE, I FOLLOWED MY OLD SCOTLAND YARD NOSE!

HELLO! WHAT'S **THAT**?

A SOUVENIR FROM TANGLING WITH THE **STRANGLER**-- OR WHOEVER HE IS...

HMMM, MOST INTERESTING! COLEOPTERA OPTHALMI CLINGING TO THE CLOTH!

COLEOPTERA--? YOU MEAN... **BEETLES**?

PRECISELY! BUT **BLIND** BEETLES...FROM LIVING FOR UNTOLD GENERATIONS IN DARK CELLARS!

THE AMAZING THING IS THEIR **MARKINGS**... THEY DIFFER FROM CELLAR TO CELLAR...NO TWO ALIKE!

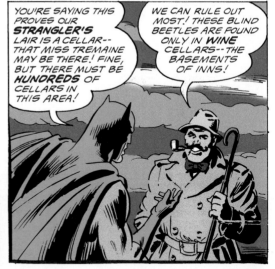

YOU'RE SAYING THIS PROVES OUR **STRANGLER'S** LAIR IS A CELLAR-- THAT MISS TREMAINE MAY BE THERE! FINE, BUT THERE MUST BE **HUNDREDS** OF CELLARS IN THIS AREA!

WE CAN RULE OUT MOST! THESE BLIND BEETLES ARE FOUND ONLY IN **WINE** CELLARS--THE BASEMENTS OF INNS!

IF I FIND THE CELLAR WITH THE SAME BEETLES, WE'VE FOUND OUR MAN-- AND PERHAPS MISS TREMAINE! I'M OFF ON THE SEARCH, OLD FELLA!

GOOD LUCK, MAJOR!

THE MAJOR'S IDEA IS A LONG SHOT-- TAKES TIME! I'VE GOT A PLAN THAT MAY WORK FASTER!

BATMAN TO MARGO! BATMAN TO MICK!

8

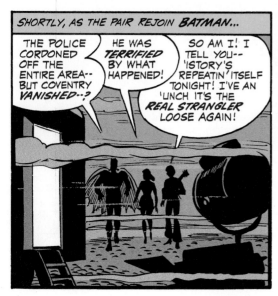

SHORTLY, AS THE PAIR REJOIN *BATMAN*...

THE POLICE CORDONED OFF THE ENTIRE AREA-- BUT COVENTRY *VANISHED*--?

HE WAS *TERRIFIED* BY WHAT HAPPENED!

SO AM I! I TELL YOU-- 'ISTORY'S REPEATIN' ITSELF TONIGHT! I'VE AN 'UNCH IT'S THE *REAL STRANGLER* LOOSE AGAIN!

HARDLY, MICK--HE LIVED 60 YEARS AGO! BUT WE'RE WASTING TIME! WE NEED A TRAP TO LURE OUR QUARRY-- AND A TRAP NEEDS BAIT-- IN THIS CASE, *YOU*, MARGO!!

YOU WERE HER STAND-IN! I'M ASKING YOU TO WEAR THIS AND BE HER STAND-IN *AGAIN*... TO LURE THE *STRANGLER* BY PLAYING LUCY CROWN!

YOU FIGURE HE'LL THINK SHE ESCAPED-- AND TRY ABDUCTING HER AGAIN!

VERY WELL, I'LL *DO* IT!

BRAVE GIRL! MICK AND I WILL BE NEAR YOU EVERY STEP-- USE YOUR WALKIE-TALKIE THE *INSTANT* HE APPEARS!

WELL, I ALWAYS WANTED TO PLAY REAL DRAMATIC PARTS...HERE'S MY CHANCE! CHEERIO, DUCKS!

I 'OPE YOU KNOW WHAT YOU'RE DOIN'! MARGO'S A CLASSY BIRD! WHAT IF SOMETHIN' 'APPENS TO HER?

NOTHING WILL-- *IF* WE STAY CLOSE TO HER! COME ON!

9

NOW, THROUGH THE COBBLED, CROOKED STREETS MOVES MARGO CANTRELL...

"SHE WALKS IN BEAUTY LIKE THE NIGHT--BUT ALL SHE MAY MEET IS AN AWFUL FRIGHT," TO REWRITE LORD BYRON'S FAMOUS LINES!

STEADY, MARGO GIRL--MUST SHOW *BATMAN* YOU'RE WORTH HIS TRUST!

THEN AS THE ENVELOPING MIST GROWS EVEN THICKER...

OOOH!

BATMAN TO MARGO...DO YOU HEAR ME? ARE YOU ALL RIGHT?

NO... NO...!

10

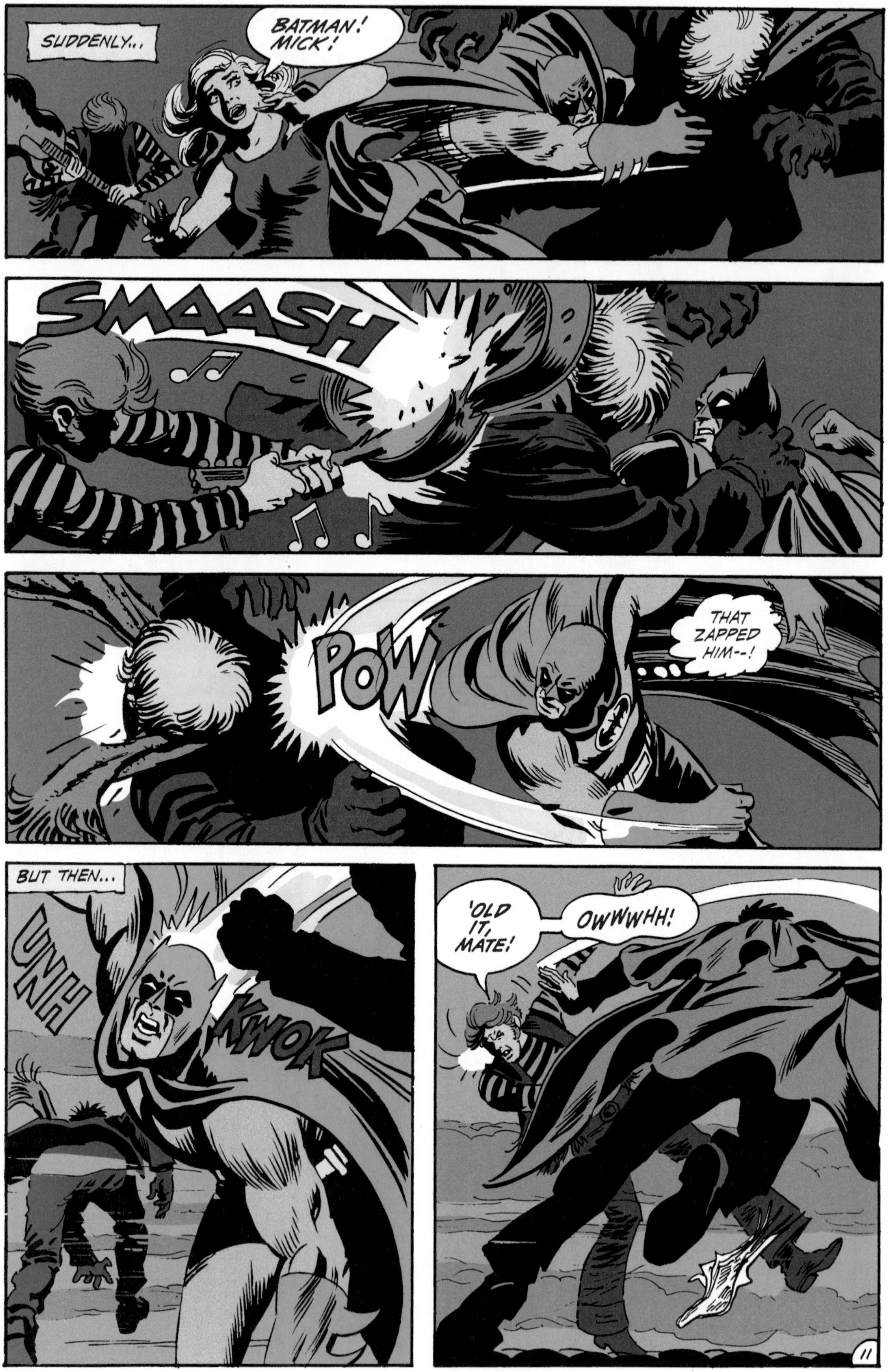
SUDDENLY...
BATMAN! MICK!
SMAASH
POW
THAT ZAPPED HIM--!
BUT THEN...
UNH
KWOK
'OLD IT, MATE!
OWWWHH!
11

FOOTSTEPS RACE AWAY...ABRUPTLY DYING TO SILENCE...

BATMAN! YOU ALL RIGHT? THANK HEAVENS YOU GOT HERE! MY BEST KARATE BLOWS HARDLY AFFECTED HIM!

I'M JUST GROGGY, MARGO! WE'RE DEALING WITH SOME KIND OF MANIAC... WITH A MADMAN'S STRENGTH! HOW'S MICK?

FAIR ENOUGH, BUT MY GUITAR'S PLAYED ITS LAST! AND WHO WAS THAT SECOND BLOKE--THE ONE WHO SLAMMED YOU AND KNOCKED ME KICKIN'?

I DON'T KNOW! WE HAD THE *STRANGLER* ON THE ROPES WHEN THAT STRANGER INTERFERED!

WHAT'S THAT? A NEWS-PAPER--?

"THE LONDON TIMES"!... JUNE 17, 1906! THAT'S THE EXACT DAY THE *STRANGLER* MADE HIS FIRST ATTACK... HERE'S THE ORIGINAL STORY!

BLIMEY! THIS *PROVES* IT--WE'RE ALL BACK IN GROTTY 1906--AND IT'S THE *GENUINE STRANGLER* WE'RE UP AGAINST!

I'D BETTER NOT MENTION THAT WEIRD OLD CABBIE--!

IT'S JUST THE FOG THAT'S GOT US ALL SPOOKED! BUT WE MUST FIND MISS TREMAINE SOON! MAYBE THE MAJOR'S DUG UP SOMETHING!

A DINGY UNDERWORLD NEST! DESERTED... AFTER CLOSING TIME! NOW TO SEE WHAT ITS CELLAR HOLDS!

HALF MOON INN

MINUTES LATER...

JOVE--THIS IS *IT!*

DABNEY TO *BATMAN!* I DO BELIEVE I'VE STRUCK IT! THE HALF MOON INN ON TINKER STREET! COME QUICKLY!

12

SOON... BLIND BEETLES WITH THE *EXACT SAME MARKINGS* AS THE OTHERS! THIS *HAS* TO BE THE PLACE--!

GREAT WORK, MAJOR!

SHHHH! I HEARD SOMETHING BEHIND THIS DOOR--! I'M GOING TO OPEN IT!

BLIMEY! IT'S 'ER--VIVIEN TREMAINE!

MISS TREMAINE... ARE YOU ALL RIGHT?

SURELY YOU ARE *MISTAKEN!* I AM LUCY CROWN, A SHOP-GIRL! I WAS GOING... TO MEET MY YOUNG MAN... WHEN A MADMAN SEIZED ME... BROUGHT ME HERE!

YOU 'EAR THAT? THIS *AIN'T* MISS TREMAINE--BUT LUCY CROWN, THE *STRANGLER'S* FIRST VICTIM! I TELL YOU... THIS IS THE RUDDY FINAL PROOF! WE *ARE* BACK IN BLOOMIN' 1906!

GET HOLD OF YOURSELF! WE *CAN'T* HAVE TRAVELED BACK IN TIME! WE *CAN'T* HAVE--!

13

BUT THAT *NEWSPAPER...* THE *STRANGLER* HIM-SELF...!

BATMAN..., THE SCRIPT SAID *NOTHING* ABOUT LUCY CROWN MEETING HER BOYFRIEND! HOW *COULD* SHE KNOW THAT UNLESS--?

SHUFF SHUFF

SHUFF

IT'S ALL CO!NCIDENCE... CAN BE EXPLAINED! MAJOR, SURELY *YOU* DON'T BELIEVE IT--?

DON'T KNOW *WHAT* TO THINK, BAT- CHAP!

HARK, WHAT'S THAT--?

BLAZES! THE *STRANGLER...* RETURNING! MICK... MARGO...TAKE CARE OF MISS TREMAINE! MAJOR-- *COME WITH ME!*

SOMEONE *ELSE* THERE!...MIGHT BE THE FELLOW WHO ATTACKED ME BEFORE--

THEN A SHAFT OF LIGHT KNIFES ACROSS THE NEWCOMER'S FACE...

STOP! THERE IS DANGER HERE FOR YOU--!

IT--IT'S-- *BASIL COVENTRY?*

BAD SHOW! THE *STRANGLER'S* SEIZED HIM!

PLEASE--! DON'T DO IT!

THE *STRANGLER'S* GOING TO HURL HIM INTO THE RIVER! *I'VE GOT TO STOP HIM--!*

14

BUT BEFORE *BATMAN* CAN REACH THE SPOT...

POW POW

AND AS THE DARK, ROILING WATERS COURSE ON THEIR WAY TO THE DISTANT SEA...

HE'S GONE... THE RIVER'S CLAIMED HIM!

I HAD NO CHOICE, OLD BOY! WHOEVER HE WAS, HE WAS A MURDERER-- ANOTHER MOMENT AND COVENTRY WOULD HAVE TAKEN HIS FINAL FADEOUT!

BY THE WAY, HADN'T WE BETTER LOOK TO COVENTRY?

JOVE! HE'S GONE--!

HE CAN'T BE FAR! YOU GO THAT WAY, MAJOR-- I'LL TAKE THIS DIRECTION!

COVENTRY!!

YOU KILLED HIM-- BUT THE PAST CANNOT DIE! THE PAST *LIVES...FOREVER!*

CRASH

⑮

22

KRAAACK!

WE'RE PLUNGING THROUGH THE FLOOR--

AND IN THE RUBBLE-FILLED CELLAR...

HE'S COMPLETELY FLIPPED OUT!

COVENTRY! STOP! THE RUBBLE IS COMING DOWN ON US!

YOU WILL NOT ESCAPE THE STRANGLER!

SUDDENLY, A GREAT, CRUSHING SHAPE SHIFTS AND ROLLS WITH THE CASCADING DEBRIS ...

KRUUSSHH!

OH, MY LEG!

YOU THINK YOU KILLED THE STRANGLER... BUT YOU DID NOT... FOR I AM HE!

HE'S COMING FOR ME AND I'M PINNED DOWN!

YES, THE STRANGLER LIVES... I NEVER DIED... TIME NEVER MOVED... YESTERDAY AND TODAY ARE THE SAME!

CAN'T HOLD HIM OFF... HELPLESS LIKE THIS!

NO, COVENTRY-- YOU'RE WRONG! YOU'RE NOT THE STRANGLER-- HE'S DEAD... YOU'RE ANOTHER MAN!

16

A *SWASTIKA!* OF COURSE, IT'S A NAZI BOMB... A DUD LEFT FROM THE WAR--!

COVENTRY! LOOK, MAN! IT'S A BOMB... FROM THE BLITZ... 1940! HOW COULD THIS BE 60 YEARS AGO? HOW COULD YOU BE THE *STRANGLER?*

WAR... BLITZ... BOMB ...YES! I SEE... OH, MY GOD-- *WHAT AM I DOING HERE?*

EASY... GET A GRIP ON YOURSELF!

WHEW! WHAT LUCK--SEEING THE BOMB SHOCKED HIM BACK TO REALITY!

THEN...

BAT-CHAP! DON'T MOVE, COVENTRY--!

MICK! MAJOR! COVENTRY'S NO THREAT NOW-- JUST GET ME OUT FROM UNDER THIS THING!

OOF! CAN'T BUDGE THIS BLEEDIN' THING... WEIGHS A *TON!*

TWO TONS, TO BE PRECISE! BY THE GREAT HARRY! WHAT'S THAT--??

TICK TICK

WHAT IS IT?

TICK TICK

VERY BAD SHOW, OLD BOY! THE STRUGGLE MUST HAVE SHIFTED THE BOMB'S CENTER OF GRAVITY! IT'S BECOME *ACTIVATED!* IT'S GOING TO *EXPLODE...* IN EXACTLY *10 MINUTES!*

17

ARE YOU **SURE**?

TICK! TICK! TICK!

NO DOUBT OF IT-- I COMMANDED A BOMB SQUAD DURING THE BLITZ! DISMANTLED MANY A BLOCKBUSTER LIKE THIS! MICK, LAD, WE MUST **DIG** TO THE ACTIVATOR!

FURIOUSLY, THE PAIR TUNNEL UNDER THE CRUSHING MISSILE...

THAT'LL DO! NOW, MICK, **YOU'RE** THE SMALLER! CRAWL TO THE ACTIVATOR-- I'LL GIVE YOU INSTRUCTIONS TO DEFUSE IT FROM HERE!

TICK TICK

MOMENTS LATER...

ALL RIGHT, LAD, YOU'LL FIND A KNOB THERE! TURN IT CLOCKWISE...THREE TURNS!

TICK TICK

GOT IT! CLOCKWISE... THREE TURNS!

NOW THERE'S A RING PIN! PULL IT OUT... **SLOWLY**!

CAN'T FIND NO BLEEDIN' RING... **WAIT**, HERE IT IS!

THE SECONDS TICK BY... SECONDS BECOME MINUTES AS THE DESPERATE DISMANTLING CONTINUES...

HOW MUCH TIME, MAJOR--?

FOUR MINUTES... 34 SECONDS!

MICK! WE MUST WORK **FASTER**!

I'M TRYIN', MAJOR, BUT THE RUBBLE'S MOVIN'--GETTIN' IN MY WAY!

NOW, LAD, THE **TOUGHEST** PART! YOU MUST UNBOLT THE METAL CAP... LOOSEN THE TWO WIRES... **BUT DON'T LET THEM TOUCH!**

TICK TICK TICK

GOT THE CAP, BUT CAN'T SEE TO UNBOLT IT... DUST IN MY EYES!

18

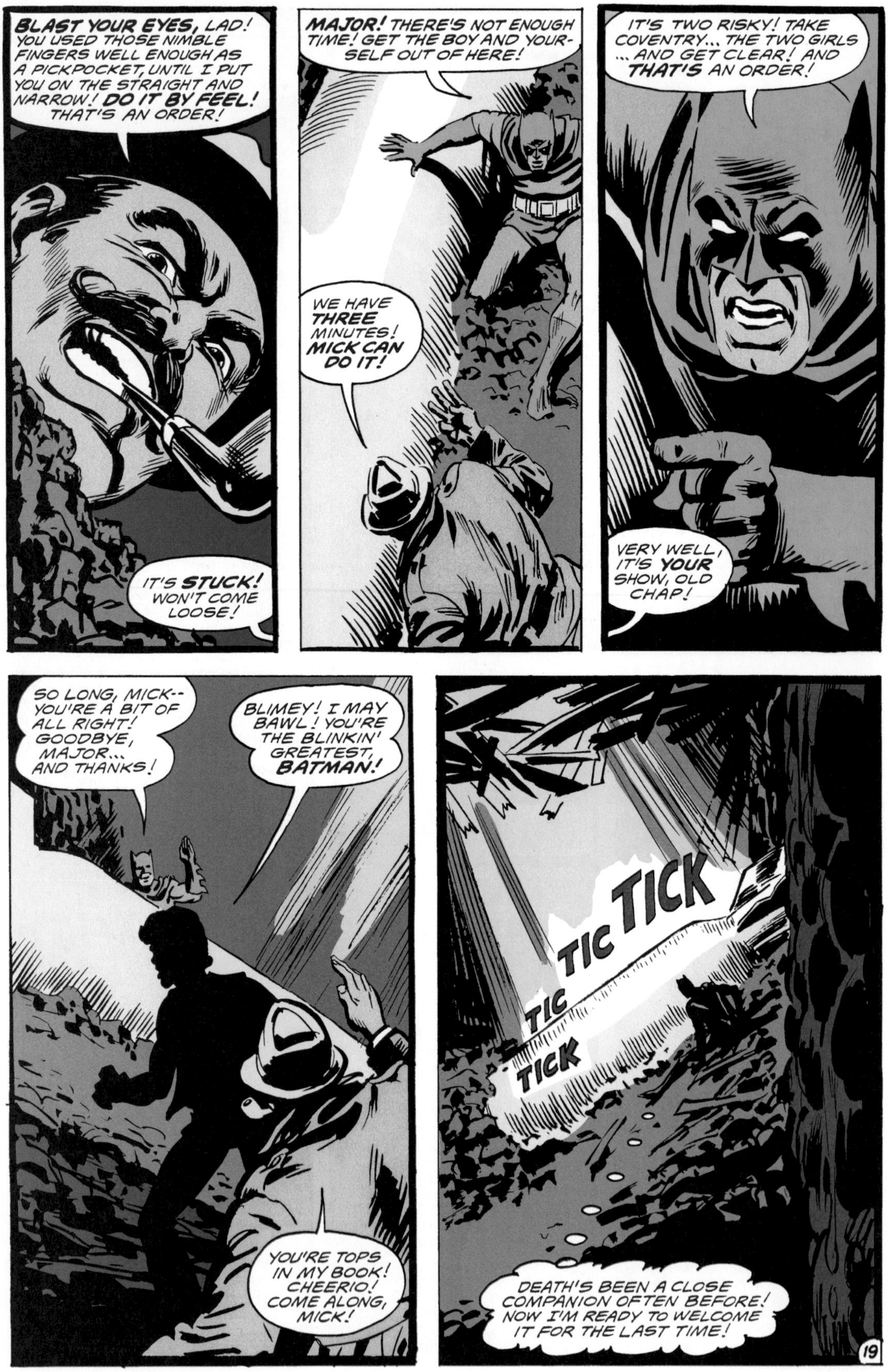
BLAST YOUR EYES, LAD! YOU USED THOSE NIMBLE FINGERS WELL ENOUGH AS A PICKPOCKET, UNTIL I PUT YOU ON THE STRAIGHT AND NARROW! DO IT BY FEEL! THAT'S AN ORDER!
IT'S STUCK! WON'T COME LOOSE!
MAJOR! THERE'S NOT ENOUGH TIME! GET THE BOY AND YOURSELF OUT OF HERE!
WE HAVE THREE MINUTES! MICK CAN DO IT!
IT'S TWO RISKY! TAKE COVENTRY... THE TWO GIRLS ...AND GET CLEAR! AND THAT'S AN ORDER!
VERY WELL, IT'S YOUR SHOW, OLD CHAP!
SO LONG, MICK-- YOU'RE A BIT OF ALL RIGHT! GOODBYE, MAJOR... AND THANKS!
BLIMEY! I MAY BAWL! YOU'RE THE BLINKIN' GREATEST, BATMAN!
YOU'RE TOPS IN MY BOOK! CHEERIO! COME ALONG, MICK!
TICK
TIC
TIC
TICK
DEATH'S BEEN A CLOSE COMPANION OFTEN BEFORE! NOW I'M READY TO WELCOME IT FOR THE LAST TIME!
19

THE LAST SECONDS TICK BY, AND A SAFE DISTANCE AWAY...

WRAAAMM

BRAVE SHOW, BAT-CHAP!

'E'S GONE! I RUDDY WELL CAN'T BELIEVE IT!

NEITHER CAN I-- SINCE I'M STILL HEARING MICK DROP HIS "AITCHES"!

BATMAN?

I'M NOT A GHOST! I WOULD BE ONE-- EXCEPT FOR OLD ARCHIMEDES! AS I WAS LYING THERE WAITING TO DIE, MY HAND TOUCHED SOME DAMP RUBBLE...

"THROUGH THE HALF-CRUMBLED WALL, I COULD HEAR THE RIVER ON THE OTHER SIDE..."

TICK TICK

IF... I CAN JUST... DIG A BIG ENOUGH HOLE...FAST ENOUGH...! THERE, THAT DOES IT!

"ARCHIMEDES FOUND, CENTURIES AGO, AN OBJECT IS LIGHTER UNDERWATER! I HELD MY BREATH AS THE RIVER WATER COVERED THAT BLOCKBUSTER..."

BOMB'S GOTTEN JUST BUOYANT ENOUGH... FOR ME TO WRIGGLE FREE! NOW TO GET OUT OF HERE... FAST!

10

ANOTHER FEW MOMENTS AND I'D HAVE BEEN THE FINAL CASUALTY OF WORLD WAR II!

MORE LIKE THE FINAL VICTIM OF THE *SCARLET STRANGLER!* I SAY, THE FOG'S LIFTING! TIME WE LIFTED THE VEIL OFF THIS WHOLE MYSTERY!

SHORTLY...

I OWE YOU ALL AN EXPLANATION-- THE *ORIGINAL STRANGLER...* A MENTALLY DERANGED KILLER...WAS MY GRAND-FATHER! A POLICE BULLET ENDED HIS CRIMINAL RAMPAGE LONG AGO!

MY *OWN* FATHER SO FEARED BECOMING LIKE HIM, HIS MIND SNAPPED AND HE WAS COMMITTED TO AN ASYLUM!

I WAS TOLD HE DIED IN A TRAIN WRECK, BY MY MOTHER WHO DIED OF GRIEF, AND I WAS RAISED BY AN UNCLE!

RECENTLY, I FOUND OUT THE TRUTH-- AND BECAME OBSESSED WITH MAKING A MOVIE ABOUT MY GRAND-FATHER, THE ORIGINAL *STRANGLER!*

MY POOR FATHER HEARD OF IT, ESCAPED FROM THE ASYLUM, AND BEGAN TO RELIVE HIS *OWN* FATHER'S TRAGIC CAREER!

IN HIS TWISTED MIND, MY FATHER *REALLY BELIEVED* HE WAS THE *STRANGLER!* IN A JEALOUS RAGE, HE KILLED RON DAWSON FOR IMPERSONATING HIM AND ABDUCTED VIVIEN BECAUSE HE TRULY THOUGHT SHE WAS LUCY CROWN, THE STRANGLER'S FIRST VICTIM!

I RECOGNIZED HIM FROM OLD PHOTOS AND FOOLISHLY TRIED TO FIND HIM BEFORE YOU OR THE POLICE DID...TO PROTECT HIM FROM HIS OWN MADNESS!

AS YOU KNOW, HE TURNED ON ME...AND *HAD* TO BE KILLED!

21

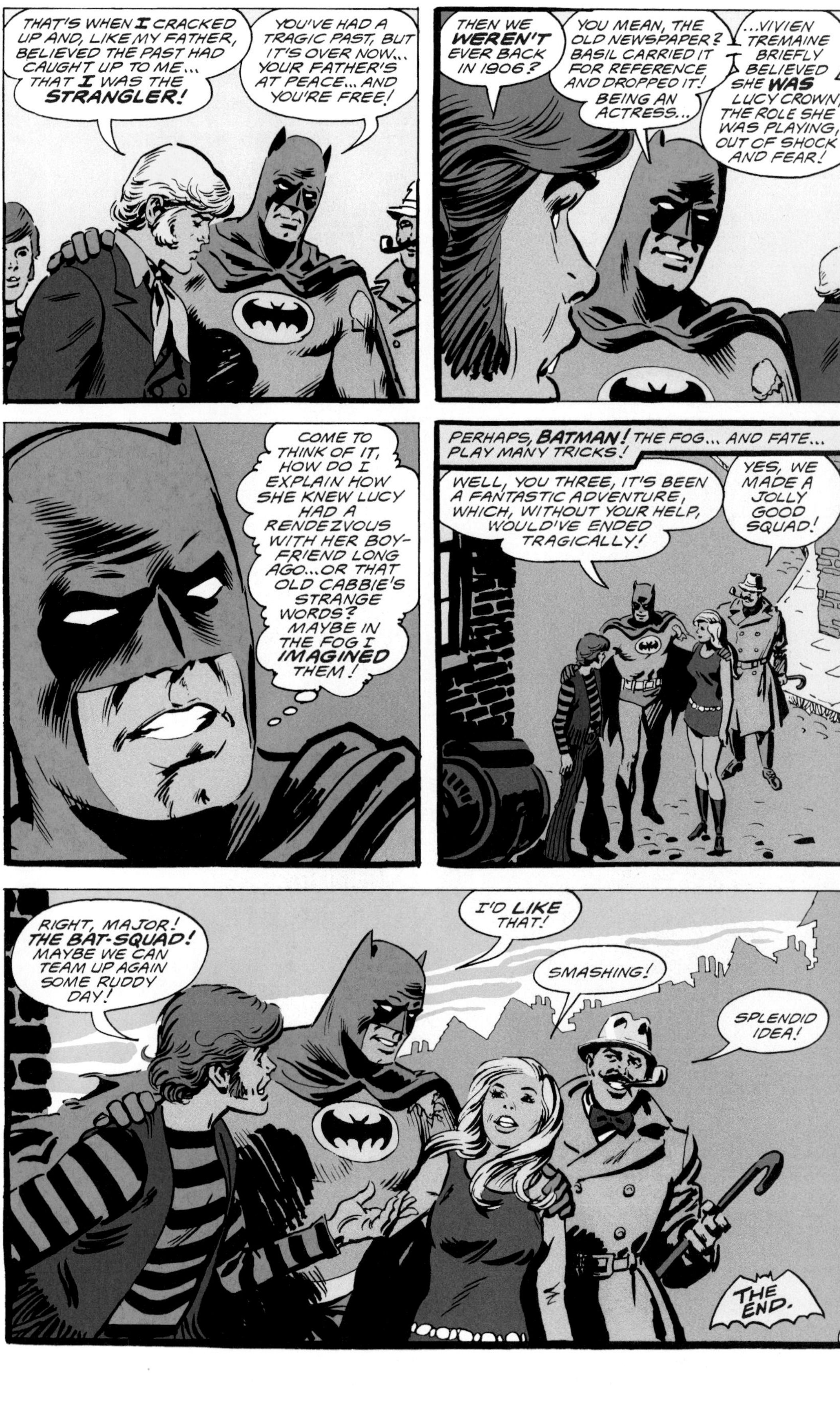
THAT'S WHEN I CRACKED UP AND, LIKE MY FATHER, BELIEVED THE PAST HAD CAUGHT UP TO ME... THAT I WAS THE STRANGLER!
YOU'VE HAD A TRAGIC PAST, BUT IT'S OVER NOW... YOUR FATHER'S AT PEACE... AND YOU'RE FREE!
THEN WE WEREN'T EVER BACK IN 1906?
YOU MEAN, THE OLD NEWSPAPER? BASIL CARRIED IT FOR REFERENCE AND DROPPED IT! BEING AN ACTRESS...
...VIVIEN TREMAINE BRIEFLY BELIEVED SHE WAS LUCY CROWN, THE ROLE SHE WAS PLAYING, OUT OF SHOCK AND FEAR!
COME TO THINK OF IT, HOW DO I EXPLAIN HOW SHE KNEW LUCY HAD A RENDEZVOUS WITH HER BOY-FRIEND LONG AGO...OR THAT OLD CABBIE'S STRANGE WORDS? MAYBE IN THE FOG I IMAGINED THEM!
PERHAPS, BATMAN! THE FOG... AND FATE... PLAY MANY TRICKS!
WELL, YOU THREE, IT'S BEEN A FANTASTIC ADVENTURE, WHICH, WITHOUT YOUR HELP, WOULD'VE ENDED TRAGICALLY!
YES, WE MADE A JOLLY GOOD SQUAD!
RIGHT, MAJOR! THE BAT-SQUAD! MAYBE WE CAN TEAM UP AGAIN SOME RUDDY DAY!
I'D LIKE THAT!
SMASHING!
SPLENDID IDEA!
THE END.
22

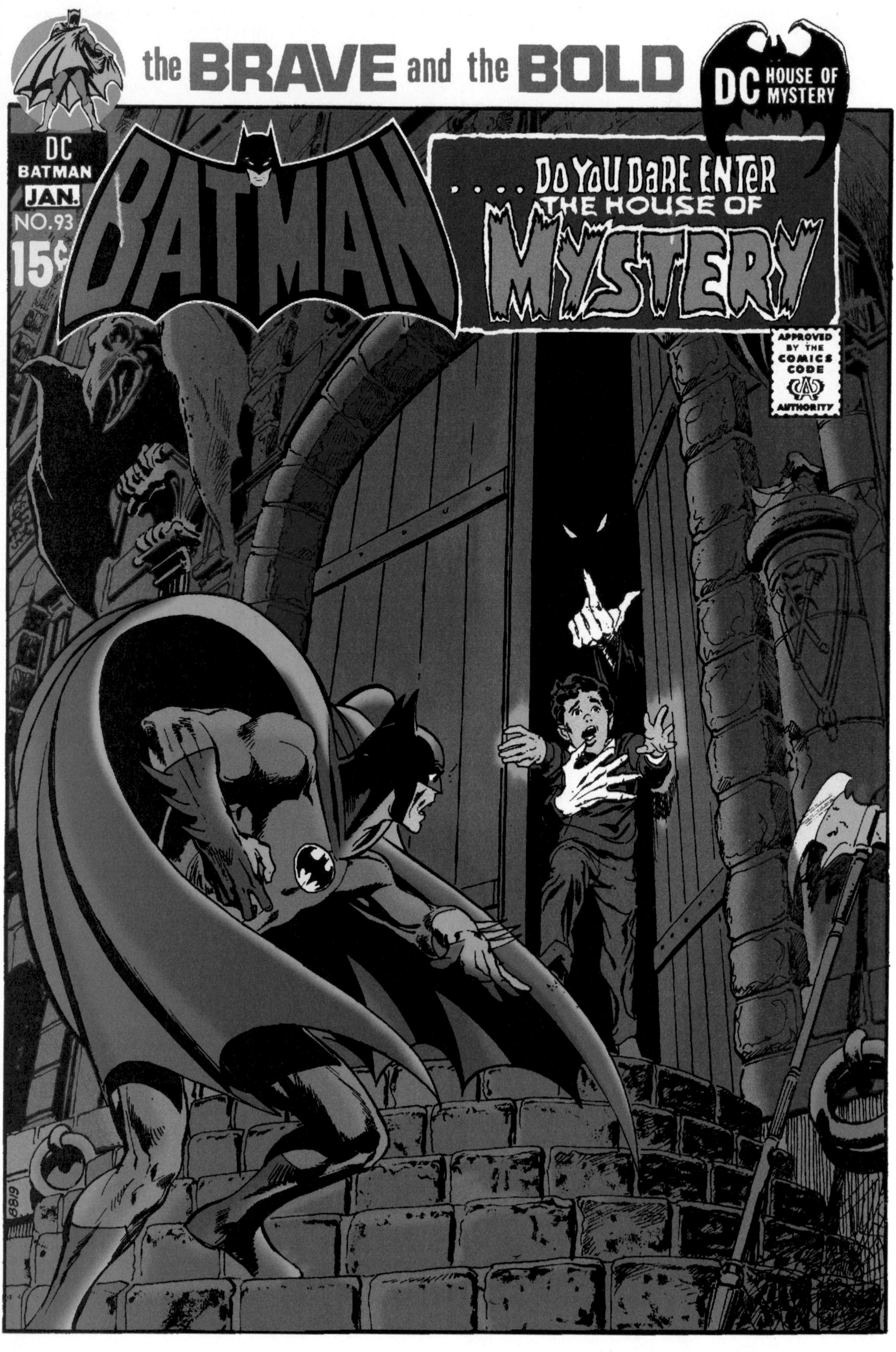
the BRAVE and the BOLD
DC HOUSE OF MYSTERY
DC BATMAN JAN. NO.93 15¢
BATMAN
. . . . DO YOU DARE ENTER THE HOUSE OF MYSTERY
APPROVED BY THE COMICS CODE AUTHORITY

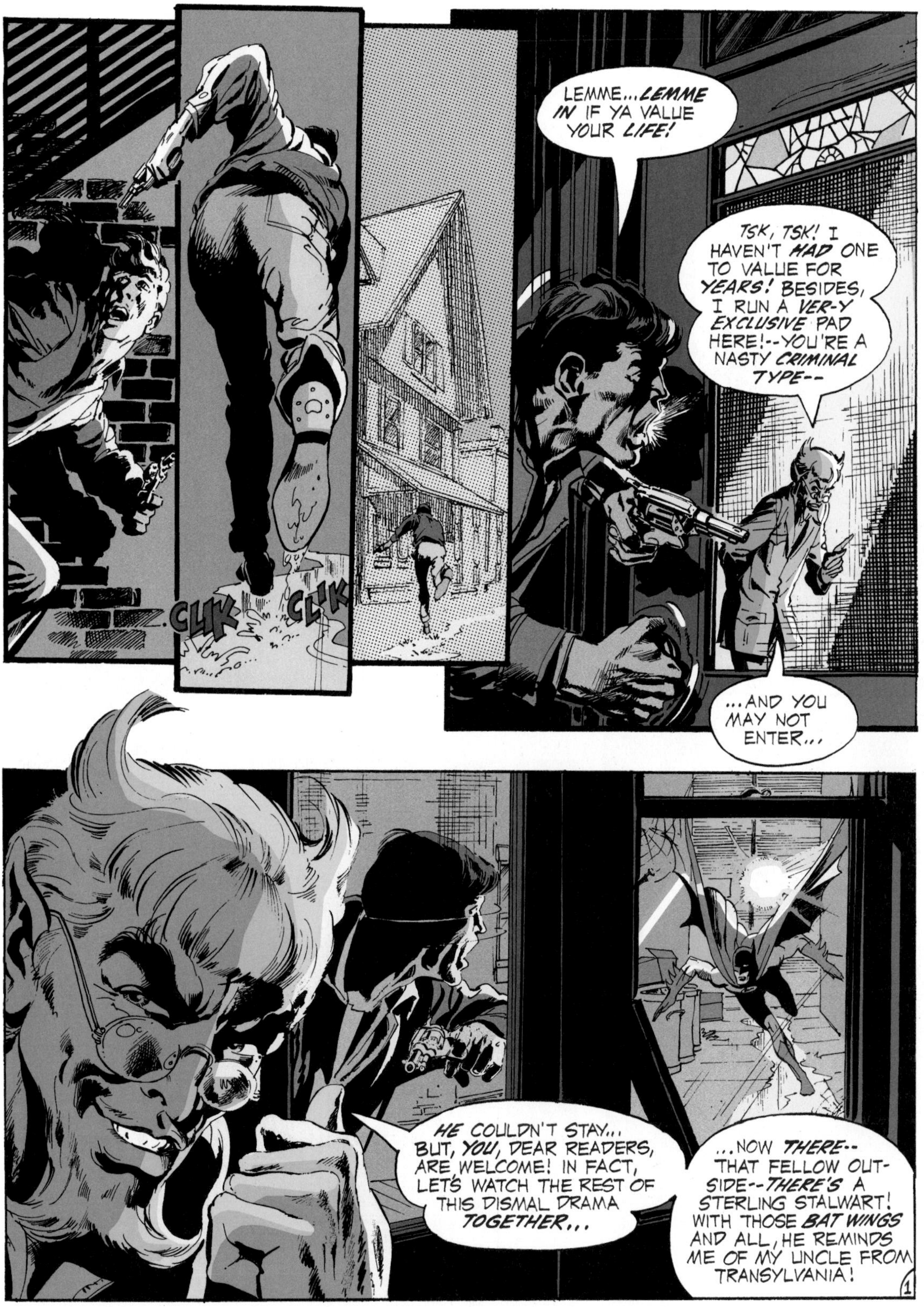
CLIK CLIK
LEMME...LEMME IN IF YA VALUE YOUR LIFE!
TSK, TSK! I HAVEN'T HAD ONE TO VALUE FOR YEARS! BESIDES, I RUN A VER-Y EXCLUSIVE PAD HERE!--YOU'RE A NASTY CRIMINAL TYPE--
...AND YOU MAY NOT ENTER...
HE COULDN'T STAY... BUT, YOU, DEAR READERS, ARE WELCOME! IN FACT, LET'S WATCH THE REST OF THIS DISMAL DRAMA TOGETHER...
...NOW THERE-- THAT FELLOW OUT-SIDE--THERE'S A STERLING STALWART! WITH THOSE BAT WINGS AND ALL, HE REMINDS ME OF MY UNCLE FROM TRANSYLVANIA!
1

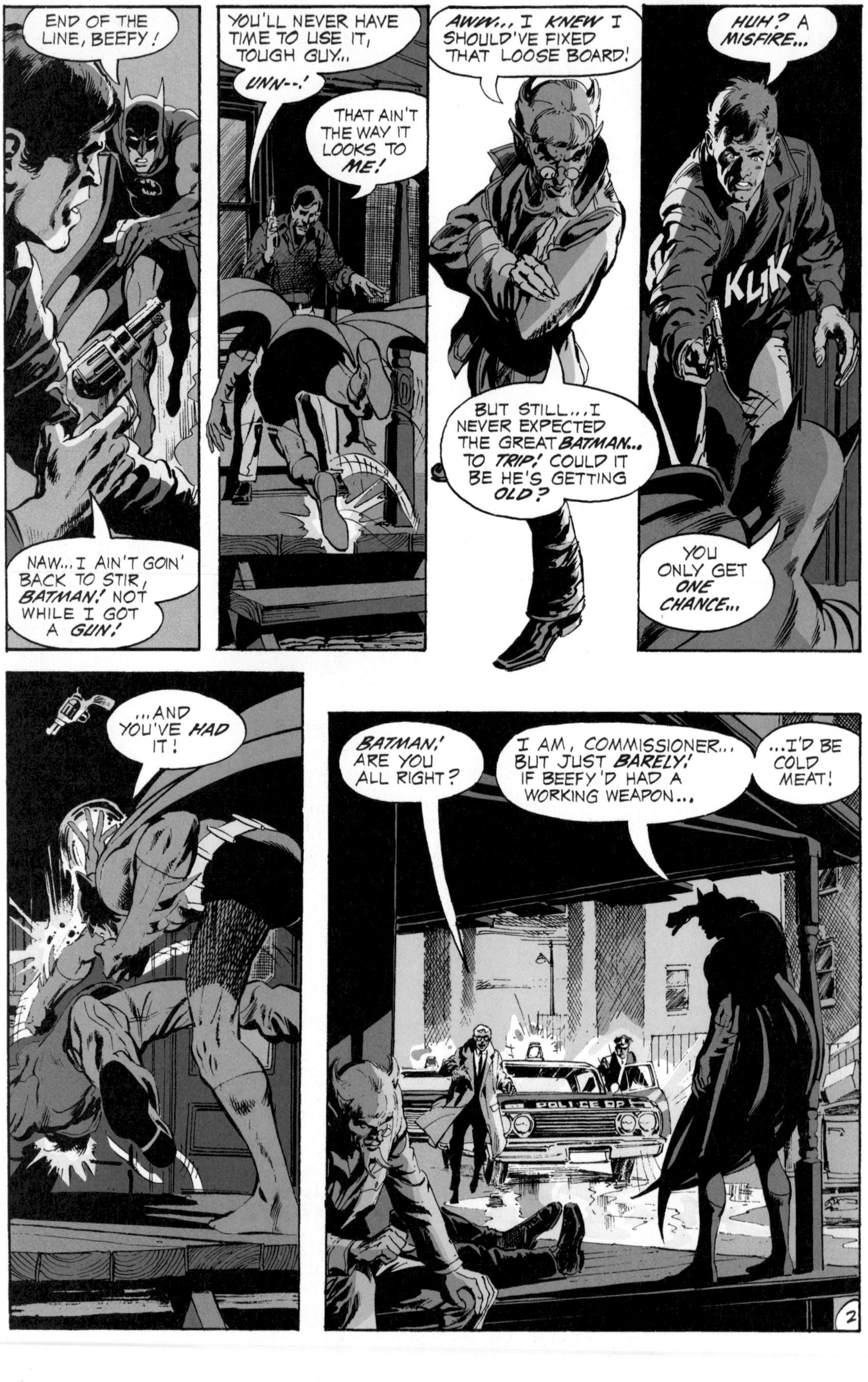

END OF THE LINE, BEEFY!
NAW... I AIN'T GOIN' BACK TO STIR, BATMAN! NOT WHILE I GOT A GUN!
YOU'LL NEVER HAVE TIME TO USE IT, TOUGH GUY...
UNN--!
THAT AIN'T THE WAY IT LOOKS TO ME!
AWW... I KNEW I SHOULD'VE FIXED THAT LOOSE BOARD!
BUT STILL... I NEVER EXPECTED THE GREAT BATMAN... TO TRIP! COULD IT BE HE'S GETTING OLD?
HUH? A MISFIRE...
KLIK
YOU ONLY GET ONE CHANCE...
...AND YOU'VE HAD IT!
BATMAN! ARE YOU ALL RIGHT?
I AM, COMMISSIONER... BUT JUST BARELY! IF BEEFY'D HAD A WORKING WEAPON...
...I'D BE COLD MEAT!
POLICE DP
2

I STUMBLED... LIKE SOME RANK AMATEUR!

AND NO WONDER! YOU HAVEN'T HAD ANY REST FOR A WEEK! FIRST THERE WAS THAT COUNTERFEITING RING... THEN THE PRISON BREAK...

EVEN A MAN WITH YOUR PHYSIQUE CAN'T TAKE THAT MUCH DANGER IN SO SHORT A TIME!

FRANKLY, BATMAN, I THINK YOUR NERVES ARE SHOT! YOU NEED A VACATION...BADLY!

I HAVE A STEAMSHIP TICKET TO IRELAND! THE LINER LEAVES AT NOON TOMORROW... WITH YOU ABOARD!

I CAN'T...THERE'S STILL SO MUCH TO DO!

IT'LL KEEP! GET ON THAT SHIP...AND DON'T SHOW YOUR COWL IN GOTHAM FOR AT LEAST A MONTH!

DON'T ARGUE! YOU'RE NO GOOD TO ME DEAD!

OKAY, OKAY... I KNOW WHEN I'M BEATEN! SEE YOU IN A FEW WEEKS!

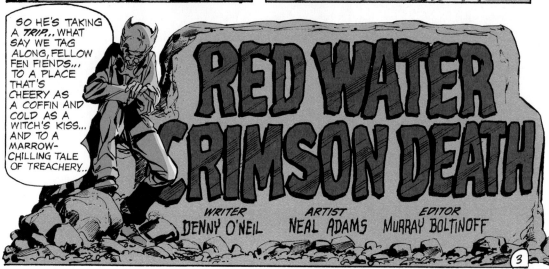

SO HE'S TAKING A TRIP...WHAT SAY WE TAG ALONG, FELLOW FEN FIENDS... TO A PLACE THAT'S CHEERY AS A COFFIN AND COLD AS A WITCH'S KISS... AND TO A MARROW-CHILLING TALE OF TREACHERY..

RED WATER CRIMSON DEATH

WRITER **DENNY O'NEIL** ARTIST **NEAL ADAMS** EDITOR **MURRAY BOLTINOFF**

3

AND HERE WE *ARE*...ALREADY ALMOST ACROSS THE ATLANTIC...

THOUGH YOU MAY NOT *RECOGNIZE* HIM, THAT HUMAN AT THE RAIL IS *BATMAN*... ALIAS *BRUCE WAYNE!*

KEEP YOUR EYE ON THAT *KID*-TYPE HUMAN, TOO! SOMETHING TELLS ME HE'LL BE *IMPORTANT* TO OUR TALE...

WE'RE NEARING THE ARIN ISLES, OFF THE NORTH COAST OF IRELAND...

...NO RADIO STATIONS, FEW TELEPHONES, AND VIRTUALLY NO CRIME!

A SETTING LIKE THAT MIGHT BE JUST WHAT I NEED TO GET MY HEAD TOGETHER!

MISTER... MY BALL!

HERE YOU ARE, SON!

MY NAME'S NOT *SON*...IT'S *SEAN!*

ATTENTION!

WE'RE ENTERING A STORM AREA... ALL PASSENGERS ARE REQUESTED TO GO TO THEIR CABINS AND STAY OFF THE DECKS UNTIL FURTHER NOTICE!

BETTER DO WHAT THE MAN SAYS, SEAN! I'LL SEE YOU LATER!

4

WE'RE IN... UGH... BRUCE'S CABIN...

A REAL BRUTE OF A BLOW OUT THERE--! SHIP'S TOSSING LIKE A SOAP BUBBLE...

GOOD LORD! THAT YOUNGSTER... ALONE, ON DECK! IF ONE OF THOSE BIG WAVES HITS...

...HE'S CERTAIN TO BE SWEPT OVER!

UNCLE... UNCLE!

YEP, JUST LIKE BRUCIE FIGURED... INTO THE DRINK!

WAVES MUST BE THIRTY FEET HIGH... THE KID MAY ALREADY BE DROWNED...

MAN... ER... MEN OVERBOARD!

NO... HE'S ALIVE... GOT TO... REACH... HIM...

SWIMMING IN THIS IS NEXT TO IMPOSSIBLE... WATER HITS LIKE A HEAVYWEIGHT!

5

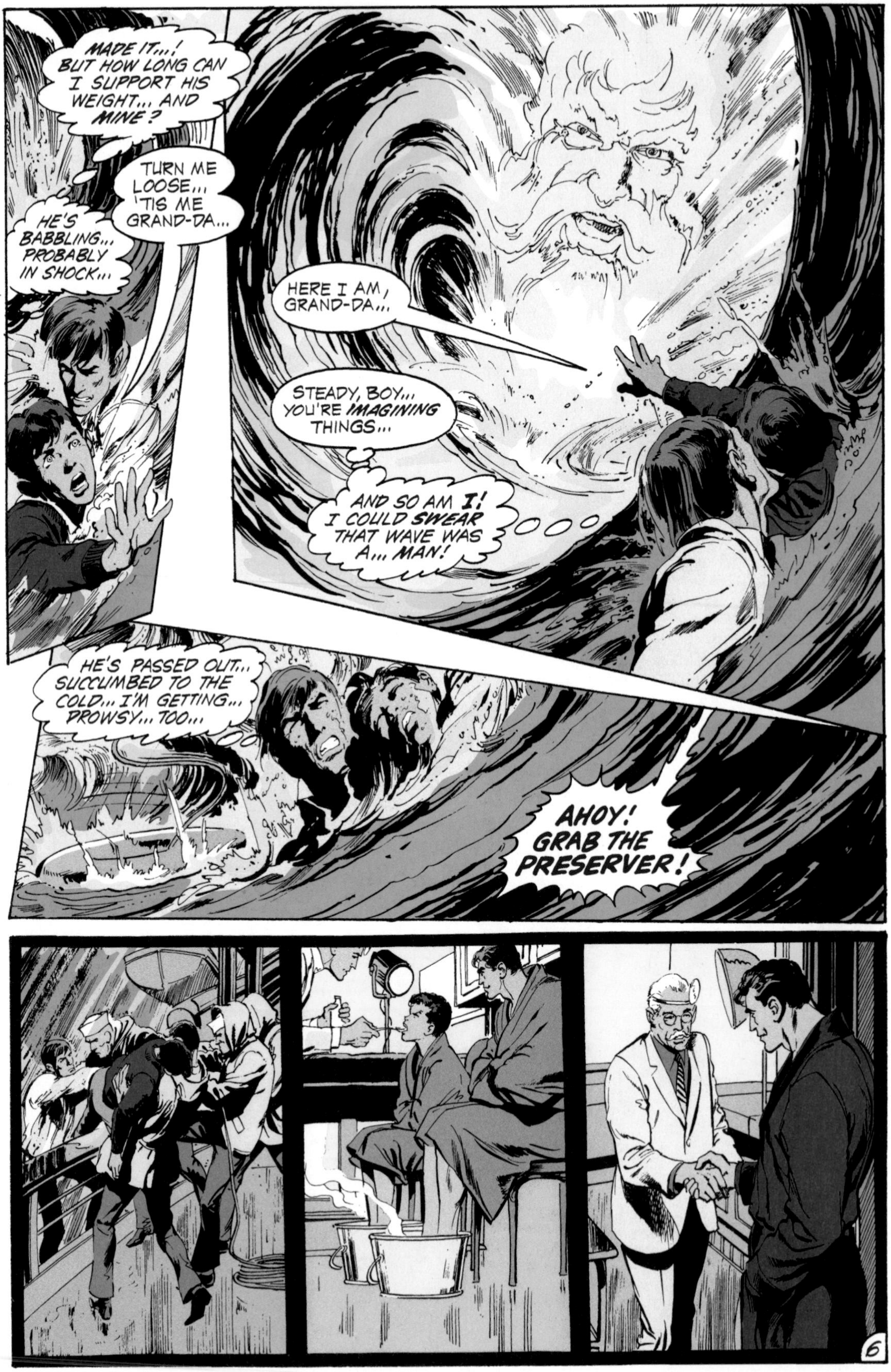
MADE IT...! BUT HOW LONG CAN I SUPPORT HIS WEIGHT... AND MINE?
TURN ME LOOSE... 'TIS ME GRAND-DA...
HE'S BABBLING... PROBABLY IN SHOCK...
HERE I AM, GRAND-DA...
STEADY, BOY... YOU'RE IMAGINING THINGS...
AND SO AM I! I COULD SWEAR THAT WAVE WAS A... MAN!
HE'S PASSED OUT... SUCCUMBED TO THE COLD... I'M GETTING... DROWSY... TOO...
AHOY! GRAB THE PRESERVER!
6

IF I WAS *WEARY* BEFORE... I'M *SHOT* NOW! THAT LITTLE DIP WAS THE FINISHING TOUCH...

MUSCLES FEEL LIKE SO MUCH SPAGHETTI... AND MY NERVES ARE JANGLING LIKE A FOUR-ALARM FIRE...

GORDON WAS *RIGHT!* I'VE *HAD* IT!

ALL I WANT NOW IS A *CLEAN* PAIR OF PAJAMAS AND ABOUT A WEEK'S SLEEP...

WHAT THE *DEVIL...?*

I *TOLD* ALFRED *NOT* TO PACK THIS! UNTIL I REGAIN MY HEALTH, THE *BATMAN* IS *DEAD!*

AND TO MAKE *CERTAIN*...I'LL GIVE HIM A BURIAL AT *SEA!*

EIGHT HOURS HAVE PASSED... GEE... I'LL BET YOU DIDN'T EVEN NOTICE! ANYWAY, THIS GLORIFIED BATHTUB HAS STOPPED...AND OUR *BRUCIE* HAS JUST ASKED THE STEWARD, *WHY!*

IT'S THE *BOY,* SIR! HE LIVES ON THAT ISLAND...

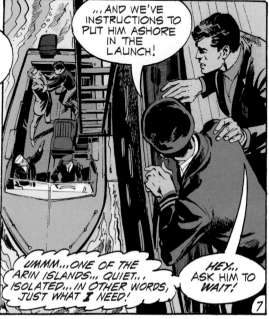

...AND WE'VE INSTRUCTIONS TO PUT HIM ASHORE IN THE LAUNCH!

UMMM...ONE OF THE ARIN ISLANDS... QUIET... ISOLATED...IN OTHER WORDS, JUST WHAT *I* NEED!

HEY... ASK HIM TO *WAIT!*

7

SO BRUCIE'S FOLLOWING THE KID... AND IN CASE YOU HAVEN'T GUESSED, *WE'RE* FOLLOWING BRUCIE...

QUICK TRIP! AND THAT'S THE DOCK OF *KENNAMORA...* WHICH, IF YOU'RE LIKE ME, YOU'VE NEVER HEARD OF BEFORE!

'TIS YOUNG *SEAN...* BACK FROM HIS TRAVELIN'!

AN' HOW WAS *AMERICA,* LAD?

'TWAS NICE! BUT IT'S GLAD I AM TO BE HOME!

WHO'S YOUR *FRIEND?*

MY NAME IS *BRUCE WAYNE!*

BRUCE SAVED MY *LIFE,* UNCLE DERRY!

THEN, THOUGH WE DON'T USUALLY TAKE TO *STRANGERS,* YOU'VE A WARM WELCOME HERE, MR. WAYNE!

YOU'LL BE STAYIN' WITH US AN' I'LL HEAR OF NO OTHER PLAN!

NOW DIG *THIS!* BRUCE WAYNE IS A *RICH GUY,* RIGHT? USED TO EATING PATÉ DE FOIE GRAS AND PHEASANT UNDER GLASS AND LIKE THAT, RIGHT! SO WHY IS HE ENJOYING PLAIN *MULLIGAN STEW?* GO FIGURE IT...

ANYWAY, LET'S SKIP THE NEXT FEW HOURS...

8

...AND CHECK IN AT SEAN'S BEDTIME!

OFF WITH YOU NOW, LAD!

AWWW... WOULDN'T YOU LET ME FINISH ME STORY?

I WOULD *NOT!* TO THE SHEETS, AN' NO COMPLAINTS!

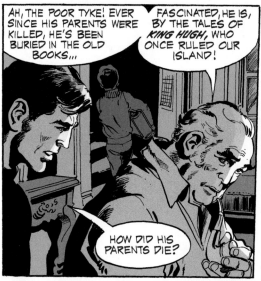

AH, THE POOR TYKE! EVER SINCE HIS PARENTS WERE KILLED, HE'S BEEN BURIED IN THE OLD BOOKS...

FASCINATED, HE IS, BY THE TALES OF *KING HUGH,* WHO ONCE RULED OUR ISLAND!

HOW DID HIS PARENTS DIE?

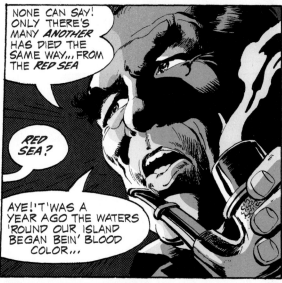

NONE CAN SAY! ONLY THERE'S MANY *ANOTHER* HAS DIED THE SAME WAY... FROM THE *RED SEA!*

RED SEA?

AYE! 'T'WAS A YEAR AGO THE WATERS 'ROUND OUR ISLAND BEGAN BEIN' BLOOD COLOR...

...KILLIN' ALIKE THE FISH AN' THE FOLK AS *ATE* THE FISH! 'TIS A *CURSE,* SOME SAY!

I HOPED A VISIT TO RELATIVES IN *YOUR* COUNTRY WOULD BRIGHTEN YOUNG SEAN! BUT IT SEEMS NOT!

I'M VERY SORRY... I'LL BE TURNING IN IF YOU DON'T MIND!

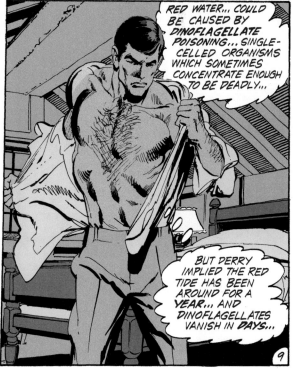

RED WATER... COULD BE CAUSED BY *DINOFLAGELLATE* POISONING... SINGLE-CELLED ORGANISMS WHICH SOMETIMES CONCENTRATE ENOUGH TO BE DEADLY...

BUT DERRY IMPLIED THE RED TIDE HAS BEEN AROUND FOR A *YEAR*... AND DINOFLAGELLATES VANISH IN *DAYS*...

9

NO, BLAST IT! I'M THINKING LIKE *BATMAN* AGAIN...

I'M *BRUCE WAYNE*...AND I'M ON *VACATION*!

ROCK-A-BYE BRUCIE

UHH...WHA...? WHO IS IT? LEMME SLEEP...

HUH...MUST HAVE BEEN *DREAMING*... THOUGHT I SAW SOME SORT OF... *WARRIOR*...

GOOD...*LORD!* MY... *COSTUME!* BUT IT'S *IMPOSSIBLE!*

ONLY ONE EXPLANATION... I'VE...I'VE GONE AROUND THE *BEND!*...I'M...*MAD!*

I'M COMING, KING HUGH...

YOU'LL HELP ME FIND ME MOM AND DAD'S KILLERS, KING...

MAD OR *NOT,* I CAN'T LET THE KID GO WANDERING AROUND IN HIS *SLEEP!*

10

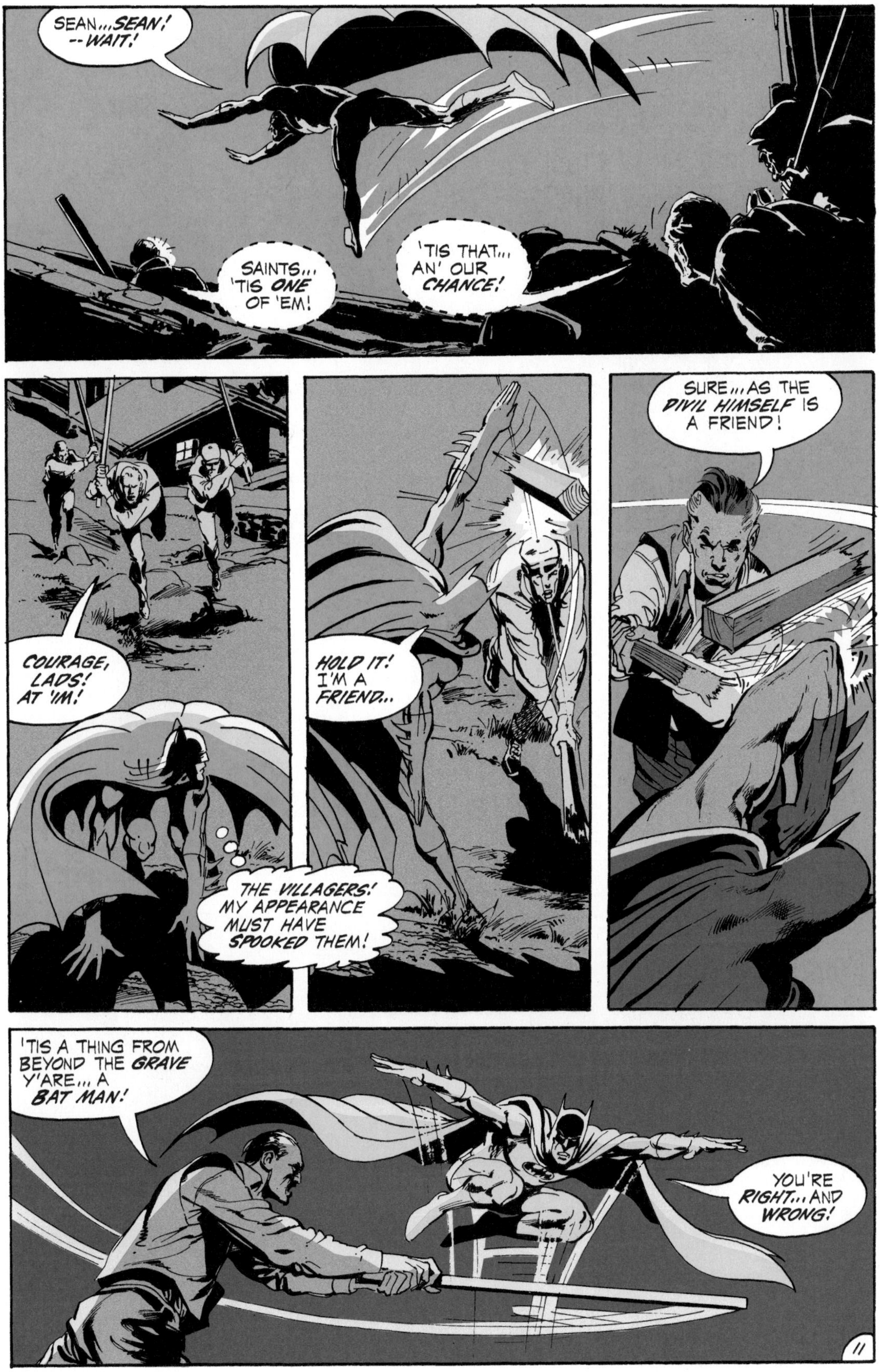
SEAN... SEAN! --WAIT!
SAINTS... 'TIS ONE OF 'EM!
'TIS THAT... AN' OUR CHANCE!
COURAGE, LADS! AT 'IM!
THE VILLAGERS! MY APPEARANCE MUST HAVE SPOOKED THEM!
HOLD IT! I'M A FRIEND...
SURE... AS THE DIVIL HIMSELF IS A FRIEND!
'TIS A THING FROM BEYOND THE GRAVE Y'ARE... A BAT MAN!
YOU'RE RIGHT... AND WRONG!
11

I'M JUST AS HUMAN AS *YOU* ARE,...I DRESS AS I DO FOR... *PERSONAL* REASONS!

I'M THINKIN' HE'S SPEAKIN' THE *TRUTH* TO US!

ARE Y' SAYIN' HE'S NOT ONE OF THEM FROM THE *CASTLE*, THEN?

WHAT CASTLE?

UP *THERE*... THE HOUSE OF *KING HUGH*, HIM DEAD THESE THREE CENTURIES, AND HIS QUARTERS EMPTY TILL A *TWELVEMONTH* AGO!

A *JUST RULER* HE WAS,...JUST AN' *GOOD!* AN' WHO CAN SAY WHY HE'S RETURNED TO *TORMENT* US?!

TORMENT??

AYE, *THAT!* BRINGIN' GHOSTS AN' BANSHEES AN' SUCH THINGS UPON US!

EVER SINCE THE TIDE TURNED RED, *EVIL* HAS HUNG AROUND KING HUGH'S PALACE, AN' NO DOUBTIN' IT!

12

GHOSTS... BANSHEES! A PACK OF *SUPERSTITION*--

OWHOOOOOOOOO...

HEAVEN PRESERVE US... THERE 'TIS!

THE *BATMAN* RAISES HIS EYES TO THE DISTANT RUIN, AND SEES...

SEAN... HE'S HEADING STRAIGHT FOR IT...

WELL... *LET* HIM! OR LET THE *VILLAGERS* GO AFTER THE KID...

...I'M SICK... IN NO CONDITION TO... TO...

13

...TO FOOL MYSELF! I'VE GOT TO GO...IT WOULD BE EASIER TO STOP *BREATHING* THAN TO DELIBERATELY LET THAT BOY GET HURT...

ANOTHER STORM BREAKING... CAN'T EVEN *SEE* SEAN THROUGH THE RAIN...

...AND HE WON'T BE ABLE TO HEAR ME *CALLING* EITHER!

THE *WRAITH*...

DOOM LIVES HERE...GO BACK...

K-RAASH

EITHER THAT THING IS *REAL*...

...OR A THREE-DIMENSIONAL HOLOGRAM PROJECTED ONTO A SCREEN FROM THE CASTLE...

...AND *THAT* SETTLES THAT!

AS I FIGURED...THERE'S NOTHING SUPERNATURAL ABOUT THE HAPPENINGS HEREABOUTS...

SEAN--! CROSSING THAT BRIDGE...!

14

GOT TO *CATCH* HIM... THERE COULD BE A *MOB* INSIDE...AND I'M NOT UP TO A MAJOR FIGHT!

THE *GATE...* FALLING! I'VE GOT MAYBE *ONE* SINGLE SECOND TO DECIDE...

...EITHER STOP AND NOT RISK GETTING SKEWERED ON THE GATE'S SPIKES...

...OR MAKE A *DIVE* FOR IT!

CHUNGGG

SO HE'S INSIDE THE *CASTLE...* AND A CASTLE IS A *HOUSE...* AND SINCE HE DOESN'T KNOW WHAT HE'S GETTING *INTO*, IT'S A *MYSTERY...*

SO, IN CASE ANY OF YOU DON'T GET IT... THE *BATMAN* IS IN THE *HOUSE OF MYSTERY!*

NOW, BACK TO OUR STORY...

AN OPEN SPACE OF 50 YARDS BETWEEN ME AND THE MAIN STRUCTURE...

IF ANYONE'S WATCHING, HE'S SURE TO SPOT ME IN THE FLASH OF LIGHTNING!

NO WAY TO CROSS UNDETECTED...!

EH...?

I DISTINCTLY FELT A TAP ON MY SHOULDER... YET THERE'S *NO ONE* HERE!

BUT THERE'S AN ENTRANCE WHICH MIGHT LEAD TO A SECRET PASSAGE...

ODD...I DIDN'T NOTICE IT BEFORE!

15

WHILE YOU WERE TURNING THE PAGES, *BATMAN* AND I WALKED ABOUT 120 FEET UNDERGROUND...

THIS PASSAGE MUST HAVE BEEN BUILT ORIGINALLY AS AN EMERGENCY EXIT...

VOICES... JUST ABOVE ME!

IMAGINE...THEM YOKELS BELIEVE THIS JOINT IS HAUNTED!

MAYBE THEY'RE *RIGHT!* I MEAN *SOMETHIN'* MESSED OUR HOLOGRAM EQUIPMENT...

SURE... THE WIND KNOCKED DOWN THE SCREEN, IS ALL!

WONDER HOW MUCH LONGER WE'LL HAFTA STAY IN THIS HOLE?

NOT MUCH! THE YOKELS *GOTTA* GIVE IN SOON AN' MOVE TO THE MAINLAND!

...THEN, THE BOSS GETS WHAT HE WANTS... A CORNER ON THE FISHIN' RIGHTS IN THESE PARTS!

YEAH...HE SAYS WITH THE ISLANDERS OUTTA THE WAY, HE STANDS TO MAKE A *FORTUNE!*

SOON'S THEY FIND THAT KID'S *BODY* IN THE MORNIN'... I'M BETTIN' THEY MOVE OUT!

I DON'T LIKE FEEDIN' POISON TO A KID... BUT A JOB'S A JOB!

YOU ROTTEN, DIRTY...!

TH...THE *BATMAN!*

16

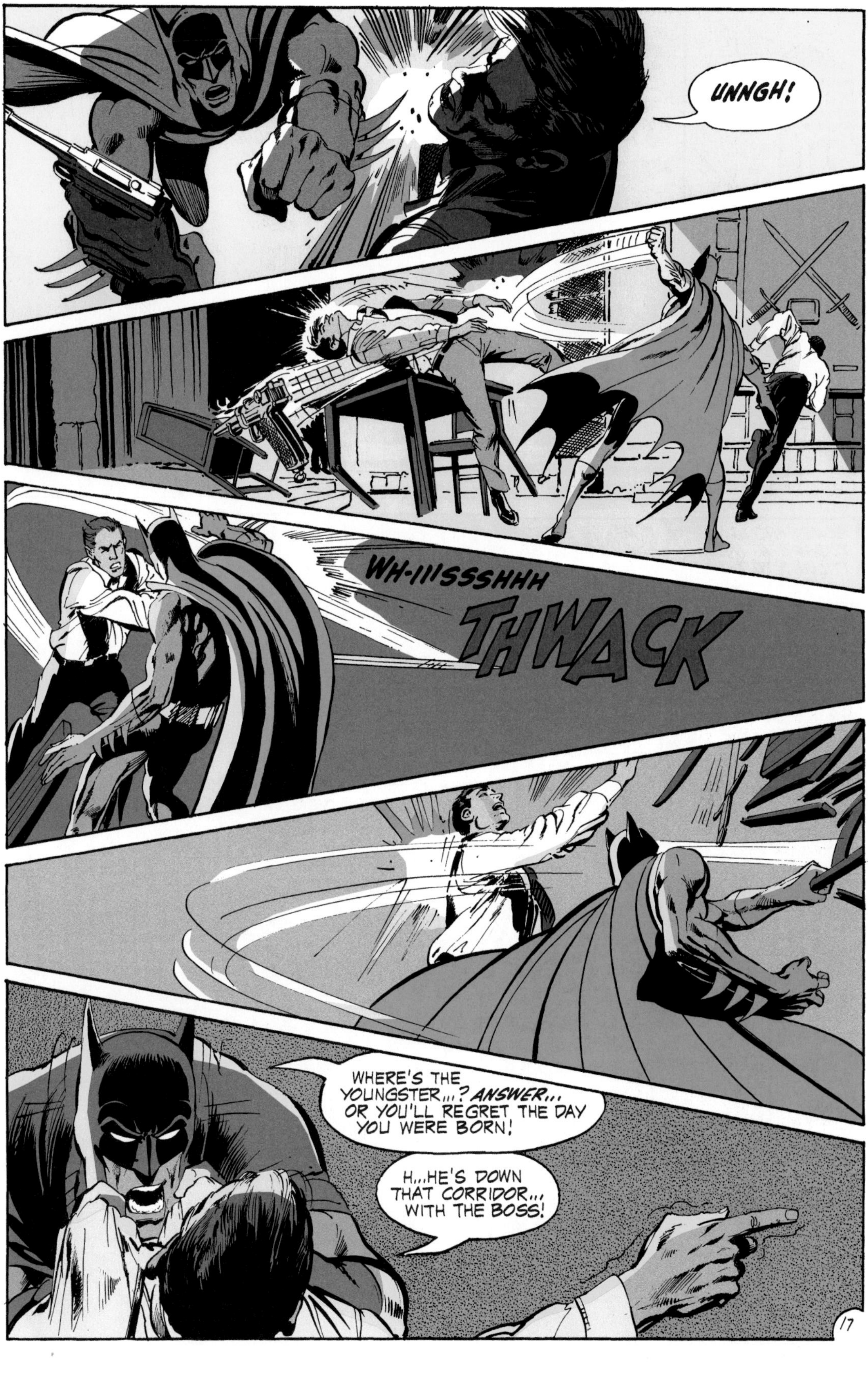
UNNGH!
WH-IIISSSHHH
THWACK
WHERE'S THE YOUNGSTER...? ANSWER... OR YOU'LL REGRET THE DAY YOU WERE BORN!
H...HE'S DOWN THAT CORRIDOR... WITH THE BOSS!
17

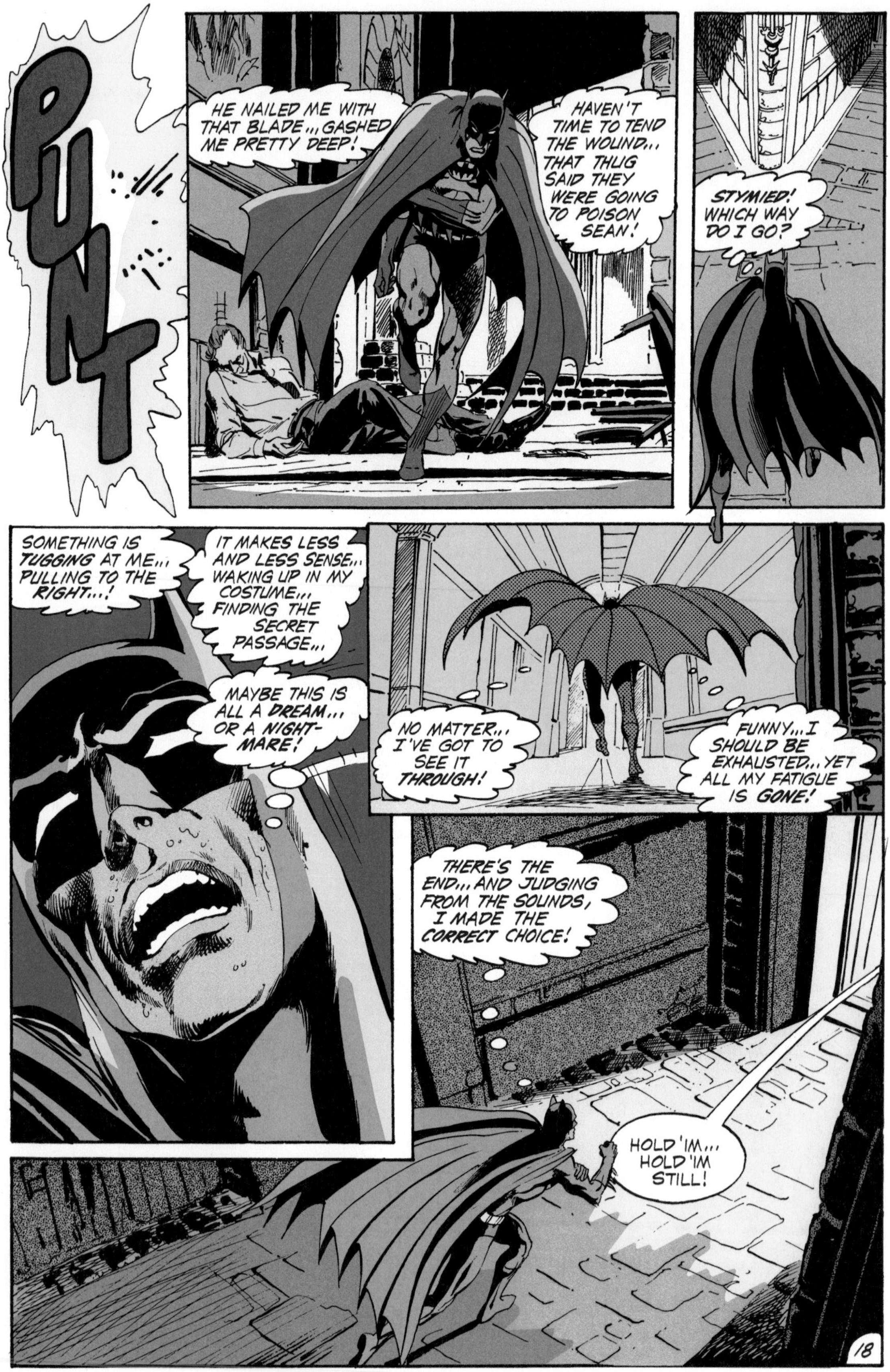
PUNT
HE NAILED ME WITH THAT BLADE... GASHED ME PRETTY DEEP!
HAVEN'T TIME TO TEND THE WOUND... THAT THUG SAID THEY WERE GOING TO POISON SEAN!
STYMIED! WHICH WAY DO I GO?
SOMETHING IS TUGGING AT ME... PULLING TO THE RIGHT...!
IT MAKES LESS AND LESS SENSE... WAKING UP IN MY COSTUME... FINDING THE SECRET PASSAGE...
MAYBE THIS IS ALL A DREAM... OR A NIGHT-MARE!
NO MATTER... I'VE GOT TO SEE IT THROUGH!
FUNNY... I SHOULD BE EXHAUSTED... YET ALL MY FATIGUE IS GONE!
THERE'S THE END... AND JUDGING FROM THE SOUNDS, I MADE THE CORRECT CHOICE!
HOLD 'IM... HOLD 'IM STILL!
18

STRUGGLING WON'T DO YOU ANY GOOD, BOY! JUST SWALLOW... AND ALL YOUR TROUBLES WILL BE OVER-- *PERMANENTLY!*

NO! DON'T DO IT, SEAN!

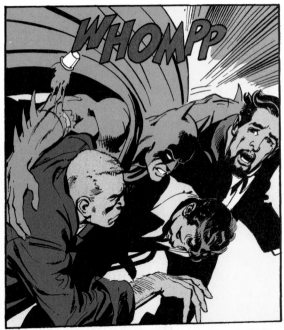

WHOMPP

ANYONE WHO WOULD VICTIMIZE A KID... IS *WORSE* THAN CONTEMPTIBLE!

I WISH I DIDN'T HAVE TO PUT YOU AWAY WITH ONE BLOW!

AND *YOU* ARE THE *BOSS*--?

INDEED! ALOYSIUS CABOT, AT YOUR SERVICE! I OWN A FISHERY.

SO I HEARD! I KNOW *EXACTLY* WHO YOU ARE... WHAT YOU'VE BEEN DOING...

...FAKING GHOSTS SO YOU COULD MANUFACTURE YOUR VILE CHEMICALS WITHOUT BEING DISTURBED... DUMPING THEM INTO THE OCEAN... *MURDERING...*

19

49

...MURDERING AND DE... DESTROYING FOR PROFIT...

OF *COURSE!* I NOTICED A *CUT* ON YOUR ARM! I FURTHER NOTICED THAT SOME OF THE *POISON* SPLASHED INTO IT!

I BELIEVE YOU'RE THE NOTORIOUS *BATMAN*...FROM AMERICA...

...WHERE YOU'LL *NEVER* RETURN... BECAUSE IN LESS THAN A MINUTE, YOU SHALL *DIE!*

...WELL, YOU'RE FIN... FINISHED...

HOWEVER, I SHALL MAKE YOU A SPORTING PROPOSITION! ONE OF THESE BEAKERS CONTAINS SIMPLE *WATER*...

...AND THE OTHER AN *ANTIDOTE* TO THE LIQUID WHICH IS KILLING YOU!

YOU HAVE TIME TO CHOOSE *ONE*... ONE *ONLY!*

...I--I CAN'T KEEP MY HEAD STRAIGHT ...FEEL SICK... DIZZY...

CAN'T *SEE* THE BEAKERS HE'S TALKING ABOUT... JUST THAT PORTRAIT ...MUST BE A PAINTING OF KING HUGH...

20

...AND IT'S POINTING TO THAT *TEST TUBE* AT THE BACK OF THE TABLE...

MADE YOUR *CHOICE* YET, *BATMAN*... YOUR *FINAL* CHOICE?

IMPOSSIBLE! HOW *COULD* YOU HAVE KNOWN THAT *BOTH* BEAKERS CONTAINED DEADLY TOXINS...THAT THE *REAL* ANTIDOTE IS IN THAT TUBE?

SOMEHOW, YOU MADE A LIFE-SAVING GUESS! NO MATTER THOUGH...

...YOU WON'T FULLY RECOVER FOR ANOTHER MINUTE! PLENTY OF TIME FOR ME TO PUT A BULLET THROUGH YOUR BRAIN...

NOTHING CAN SAVE YOU... *NOTHING!* GOODBYE--

21

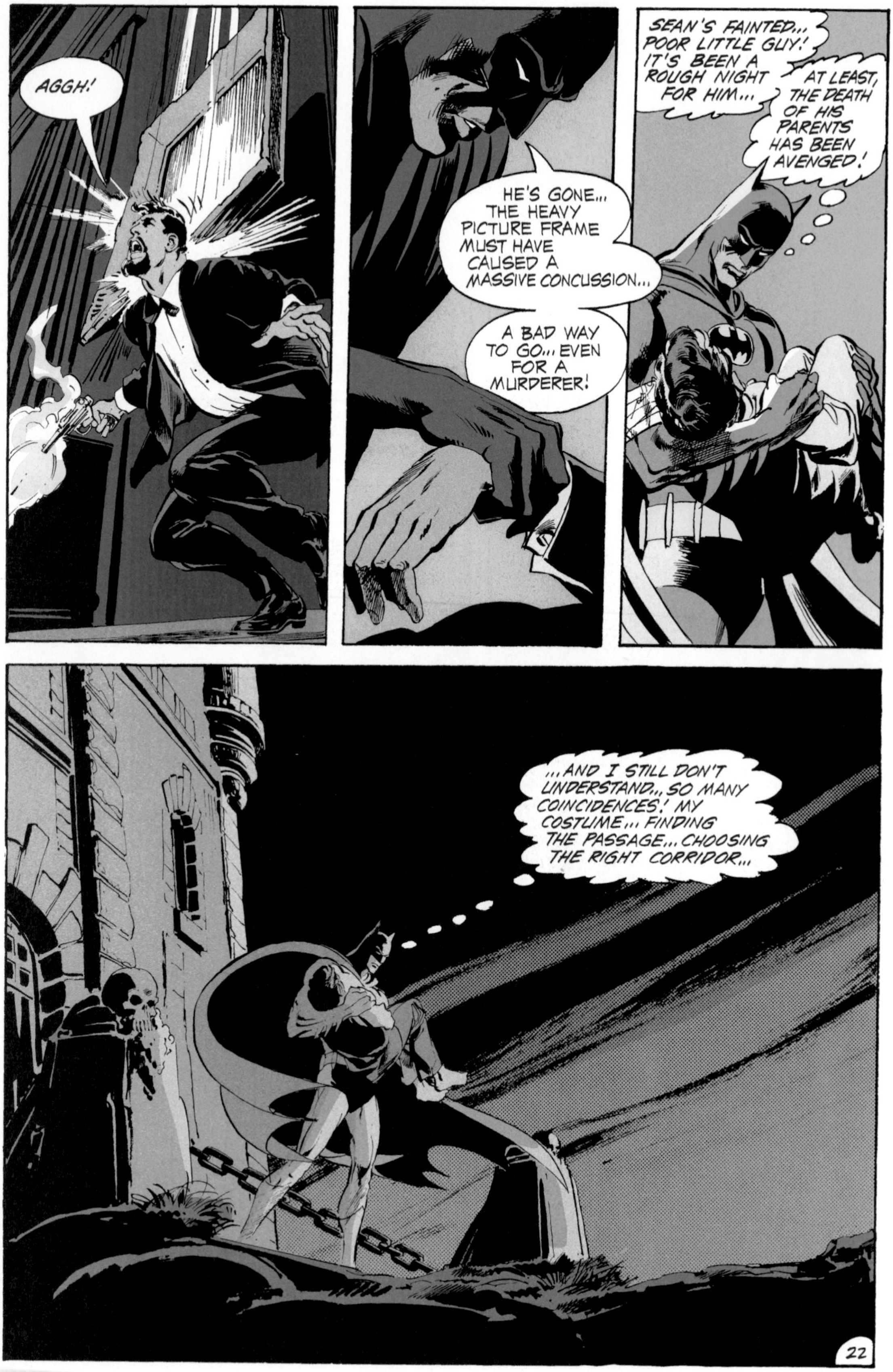

AGGH!
HE'S GONE... THE HEAVY PICTURE FRAME MUST HAVE CAUSED A MASSIVE CONCUSSION...
A BAD WAY TO GO... EVEN FOR A MURDERER!
SEAN'S FAINTED... POOR LITTLE GUY! IT'S BEEN A ROUGH NIGHT FOR HIM...
AT LEAST, THE DEATH OF HIS PARENTS HAS BEEN AVENGED!
...AND I STILL DON'T UNDERSTAND... SO MANY COINCIDENCES! MY COSTUME... FINDING THE PASSAGE... CHOOSING THE RIGHT CORRIDOR...
22

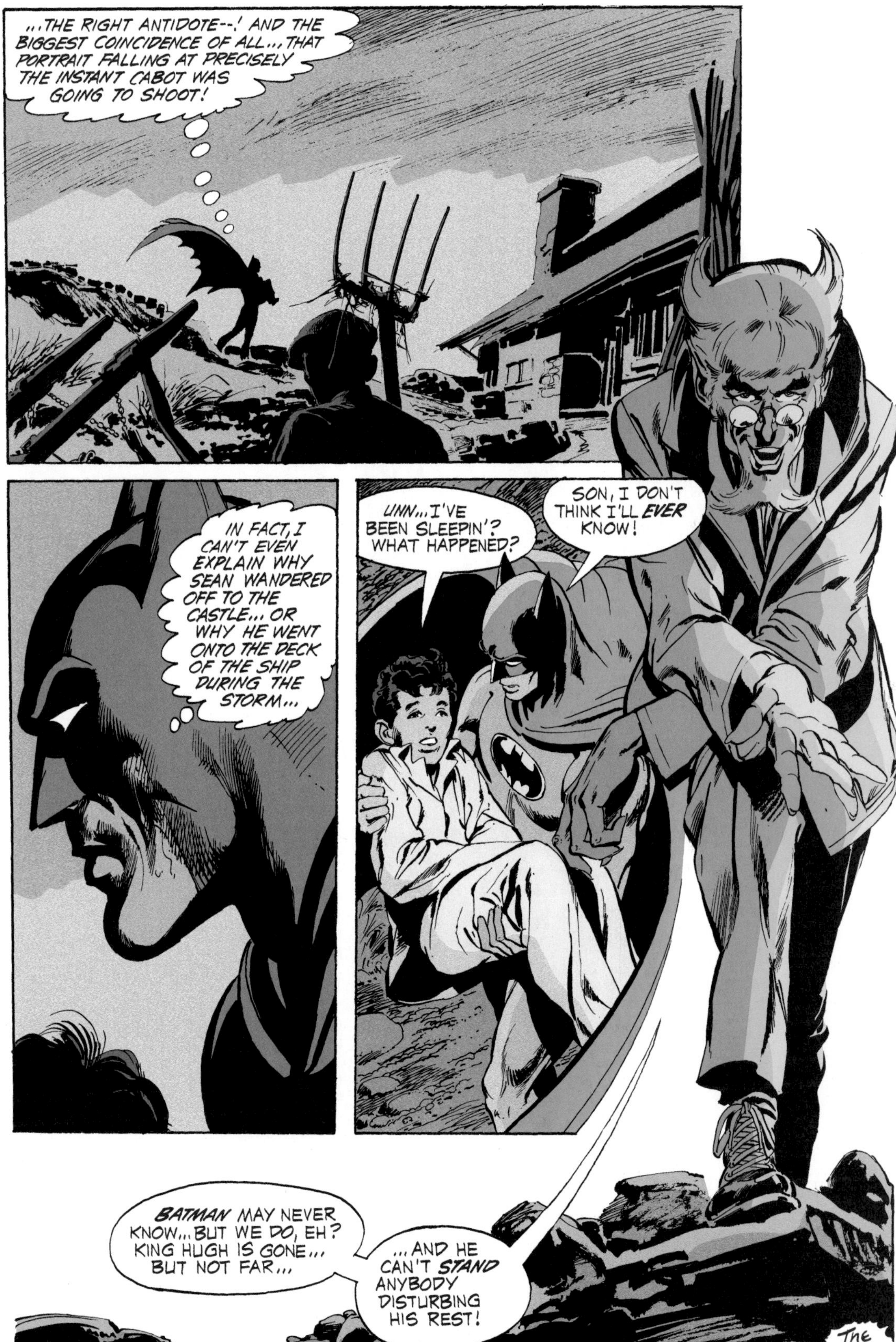
...THE RIGHT ANTIDOTE--! AND THE BIGGEST COINCIDENCE OF ALL...THAT PORTRAIT FALLING AT PRECISELY THE INSTANT CABOT WAS GOING TO SHOOT!
IN FACT, I CAN'T EVEN EXPLAIN WHY SEAN WANDERED OFF TO THE CASTLE... OR WHY HE WENT ONTO THE DECK OF THE SHIP DURING THE STORM...
UNN...I'VE BEEN SLEEPIN'? WHAT HAPPENED?
SON, I DON'T THINK I'LL EVER KNOW!
BATMAN MAY NEVER KNOW...BUT WE DO, EH? KING HUGH IS GONE... BUT NOT FAR...
...AND HE CAN'T STAND ANYBODY DISTURBING HIS REST!
23
THE END

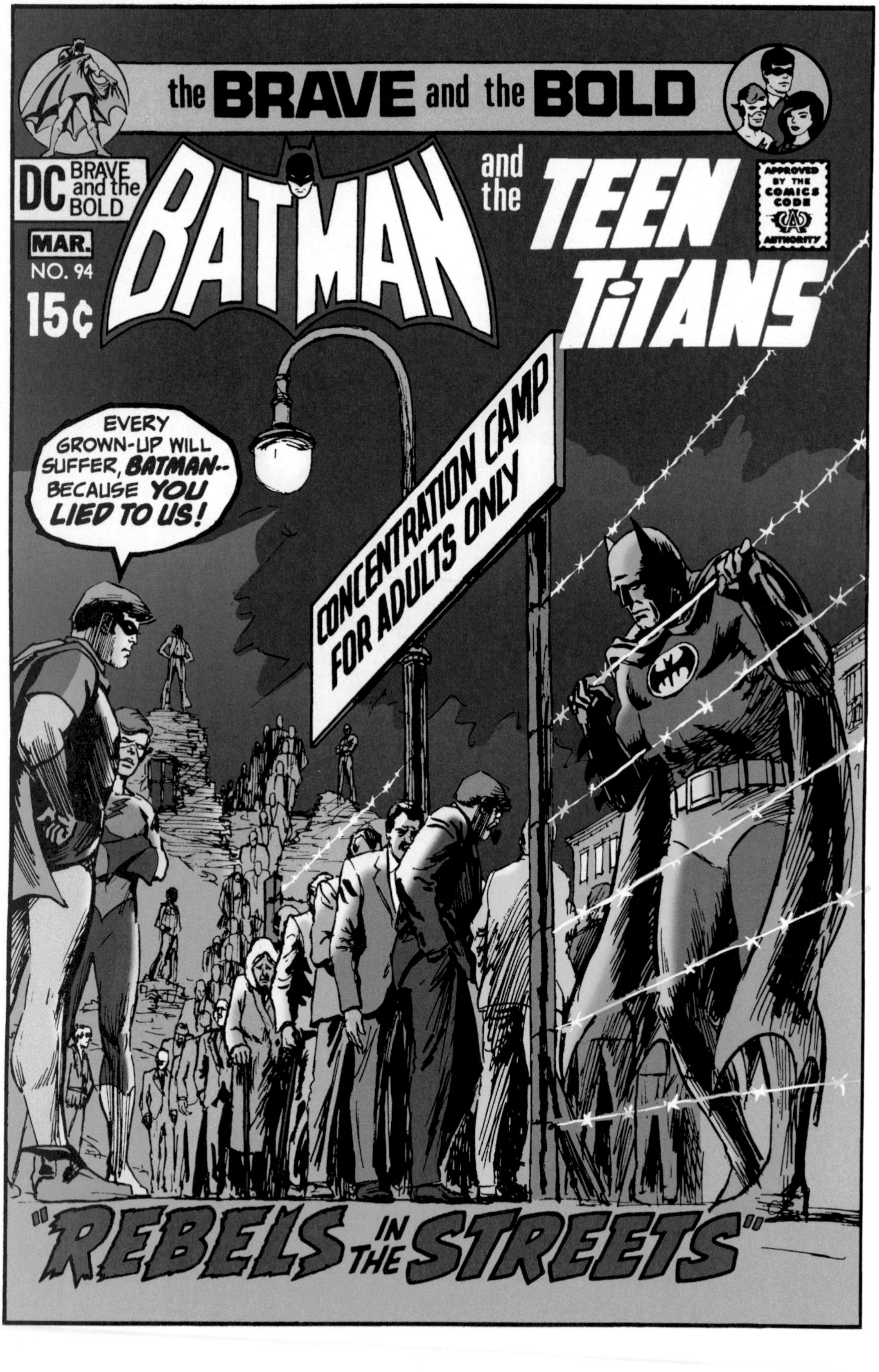
the BRAVE and the BOLD
DC BRAVE and the BOLD
MAR.
NO. 94
15¢
BATMAN
and the
TEEN TITANS
APPROVED BY THE COMICS CODE AUTHORITY
EVERY GROWN-UP WILL SUFFER, BATMAN-- BECAUSE YOU LIED TO US!
CONCENTRATION CAMP FOR ADULTS ONLY
"REBELS IN THE STREETS"

THE JULY HEAT HANGS OVER GOTHAM CITY IN A SMOTHERING SMOG -- PRESSING DOWN LIKE A HUGE IRON BLANKET...

THERE IT IS, COMMISSIONER ...*THE GHETTO!* YOU CAN SMELL AND *TASTE* IT... 10 BLOCKS AWAY!

I STILL SAY IT'S A MISTAKE TO GO IN THERE, *BATMAN!* IT'S WRONG TO DEAL WITH *THEM*...WHO-EVER THEY ARE!

I AGREE! NEVER RECOGNIZE YOUR ENEMY WHEN HE'S BLUFFING...IT GIVES HIM *CONFIDENCE!*

WHAT IF IT'S *NOT* A BLUFF, GENERAL GRAVES? I ADMIT IT'S WILD...CRAZY...BUT WHAT IF THEY REALLY CAN DO IT? *WHAT IF THEY REALLY HAVE...IT??!!*

WE, THE UNDERSIGNED, DECLARE GOTHAM CITY TO BE UNDER REVOLUTIONARY SIEGE! IF OUR DEMANDS ARE NOT MET WE SHALL DESTROY GOTHAM ENTIRELY WITH AN ATOMIC BOMB! WE ARE NOT JOKING!
DEAL WITH US...
OR DIE!
DO NOT SEND THE FUZZ.
STOPP
(SOCIETY TO OUTLAW PARENT POWER)

FOR THE HUNDREDTH TIME, *BATMAN* SCANS A CREASED, MUCH-HANDLED MESSAGE...

LET'S HOPE IT'S ONLY A *PRANK!* THE PRESIDENT'S STANDING BY IN WASHINGTON-- THE GOVERNOR'S ALERTED THE NATIONAL GUARD!

BETTER GET GOING, *BATMAN!* THAT ANONYMOUS PHONE CALL SAID ...*HIGH NOON!* IT'S *ONE MINUTE TO!*

KEEP YOUR FINGERS CROSSED, GENTLEMEN!

U.S. ARMY SIGNAL CORP

POLICE BARRICADE DO NOT CROSS

AS HE HAS COUNTLESS TIMES BEFORE, *BATMAN* WALKS INTO UNKNOWN DANGER-- BUT THIS TIME IS DIFFERENT... *SO DIFFERENT!*

DOWN STEAMING, SILENT STREETS HE MOVES, WHERE GUTTED WINDOWS STARE LIKE HOSTILE, ACCUSING EYES! SUDDENLY, SCURRYING FOOTSTEPS BEHIND, AND...

THUS *THE BATMAN* AND THE CITY HE HAS FOUGHT, BLED, AND ALMOST DIED FOR, ENTER TOGETHER INTO THEIR ULTIMATE ADVENTURE -- INTO A STRUGGLE WHERE RIGHT AND WRONG WEAR AN EQUAL FACE -- WHERE AN ENTIRE SOCIETY'S VERY SOUL AND SURVIVAL ARE THE STAKES SUPREME! COME NOW WITH THE *CAPED CRUSADER* -- AND THE *TEEN TITANS* -- INTO THE SHOCKER OF THEM ALL...

REBELS IN THE STREETS

/2

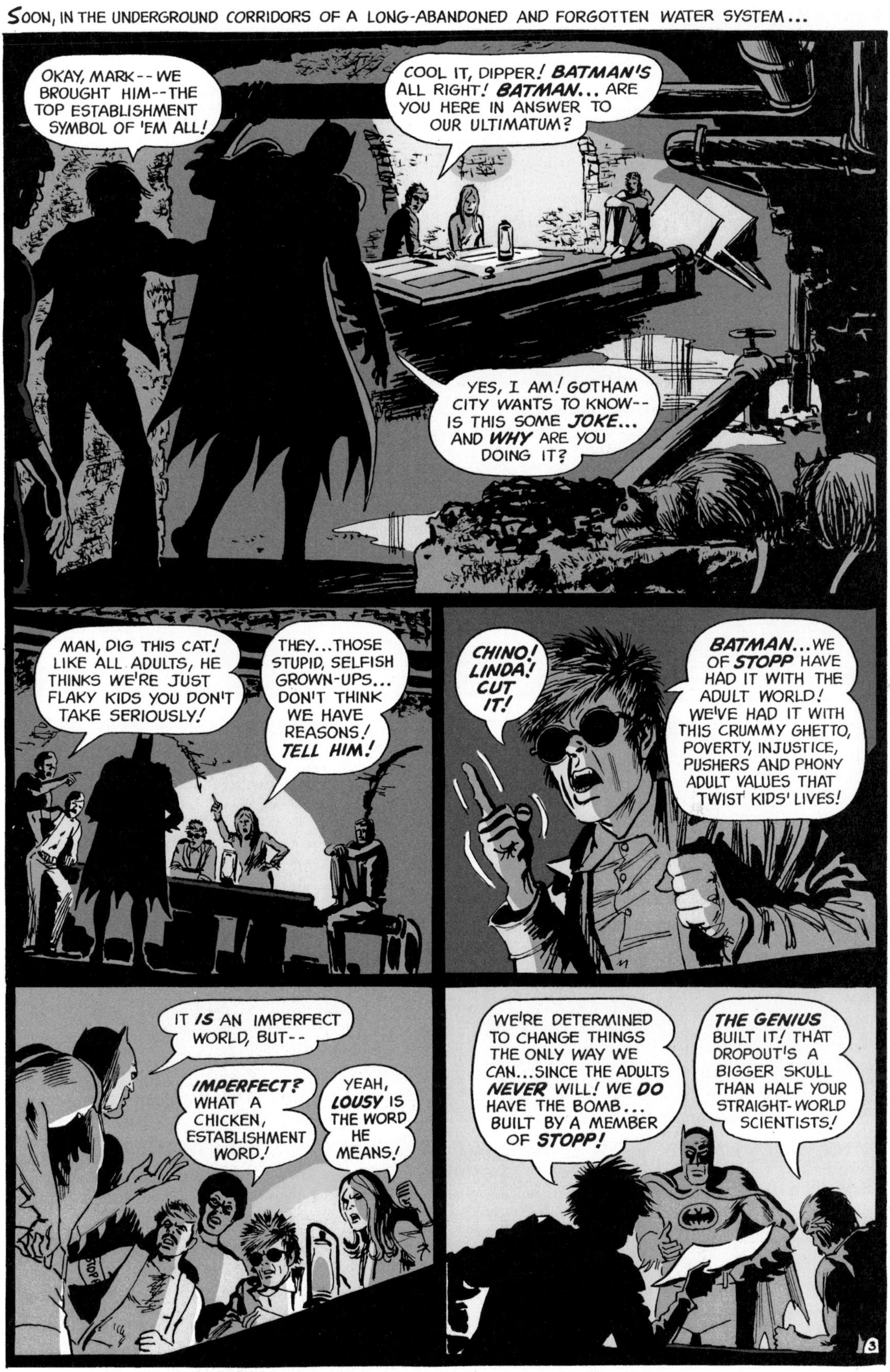
SOON, IN THE UNDERGROUND CORRIDORS OF A LONG-ABANDONED AND FORGOTTEN WATER SYSTEM...
OKAY, MARK--WE BROUGHT HIM--THE TOP ESTABLISHMENT SYMBOL OF 'EM ALL!
COOL IT, DIPPER! BATMAN'S ALL RIGHT! BATMAN... ARE YOU HERE IN ANSWER TO OUR ULTIMATUM?
YES, I AM! GOTHAM CITY WANTS TO KNOW--IS THIS SOME JOKE... AND WHY ARE YOU DOING IT?
MAN, DIG THIS CAT! LIKE ALL ADULTS, HE THINKS WE'RE JUST FLAKY KIDS YOU DON'T TAKE SERIOUSLY!
THEY...THOSE STUPID, SELFISH GROWN-UPS... DON'T THINK WE HAVE REASONS! TELL HIM!
CHINO! LINDA! CUT IT!
BATMAN...WE OF STOPP HAVE HAD IT WITH THE ADULT WORLD! WE'VE HAD IT WITH THIS CRUMMY GHETTO, POVERTY, INJUSTICE, PUSHERS AND PHONY ADULT VALUES THAT TWIST KIDS' LIVES!
IT IS AN IMPERFECT WORLD, BUT--
IMPERFECT? WHAT A CHICKEN, ESTABLISHMENT WORD!
YEAH, LOUSY IS THE WORD HE MEANS!
WE'RE DETERMINED TO CHANGE THINGS THE ONLY WAY WE CAN...SINCE THE ADULTS NEVER WILL! WE DO HAVE THE BOMB... BUILT BY A MEMBER OF STOPP!
THE GENIUS BUILT IT! THAT DROPOUT'S A BIGGER SKULL THAN HALF YOUR STRAIGHT-WORLD SCIENTISTS!
3

THOSE PLANS **PROVE** THE BOMB EXISTS! IT'S HIDDEN WHERE YOU'LL **NEVER** FIND IT! IF OUR DEMANDS AREN'T MET BY **MIDNIGHT TOMORROW**, THE BOMB **GOES OFF!**

OKAY, TAKE HIM OUT!

KIDS... JUST **KIDS**-- BUT ORGANIZED, DETERMINED... AND SO BITTER...

...MY FLESH IS CRAWLING!

HERE HE COMES! **BATMAN**... IT'S A PRANK-- **RIGHT?**

POLICE BARRICADE DO NOT CROSS

IT'S NO PRANK, AND ONLY DR. LANDAU CAN TELL JUST HOW REALLY **SERIOUS** IT IS!

GENTLEMEN, THESE PLANS ARE **FOOLPROOF!** A BOMB BUILT ON THEM **WILL** WORK...AND THIS PHOTO **PROVES** IT **HAS** BEEN BUILT!

GOOD LORD!

BLAZES! BUT HOW COULD KIDS...MAKE AN ATOMIC BOMB?

NUCLEAR MATERIALS CAN BE BOUGHT... PLANS ARE AVAILABLE IN BOOKS! THEN ALL YOU NEED ARE AN OLD BOMB CASING, DYNAMITE FOR A TRIGGER...

...AND A BRIGHT HIGH SCHOOL SCIENCE MAJOR **TO PUT IT TOGETHER!**

THEN THE CITY ACTUALLY FACES ATOMIC **BLACKMAIL!** THE PRESIDENT MUST SEND TROOPS SO WE CAN **FIND THAT BOMB!**

NO! THEY DON'T TRUST US NOW -- THROW FORCE AGAINST THEM AND THEY MIGHT EXPLODE THAT BOMB **AHEAD OF TIME!** I'LL SPEAK TO THE PRESIDENT--!

.U.S. ARMY

4

I UNDERSTAND, *BATMAN!* YOU HAVE 24 HOURS TO SOLVE THIS *YOUR* WAY--BUT AFTER THAT, I MUST TAKE DIRECT ACTION TO PROTECT THE NATION!

THANK YOU, MR. PRESIDENT!

A BOMB TICKING SOMEWHERE IN THE CITY AND WE DO NOTHING? *IT'S CRAZY!* THOSE YOUNG HOODLUMS HAVE DECLARED WAR!

THEY'RE NOT HOODLUMS--JUST KIDS, HURT AND EMBITTERED BY THE GHETTO THAT'S BEEN THEIR ONLY TEACHER! LET'S GET TO THE *BAT-LINE!*

SHORTLY, AT POLICE HEADQUARTERS...

BATMAN? THIS IS MARK! OFFICIAL REACTION, PLEASE!

WE *BELIEVE* YOU, MARK! LISTEN, I'M SYMPATHETIC TO YOUR CAUSE. IF YOUR DEMANDS ARE FAIR, I'LL HELP SEE THEM MET! TRUST ME!

OKAY--WE'LL GO ALONG! BUT I *WARN* YOU... NO ADULT TRICKS OR DOUBLE-TALK! AND ABOVE ALL, NO FUZZ IN THE GHETTO! YOU'LL RECEIVE OUR DEMANDS... *TONIGHT!*

CLICK!

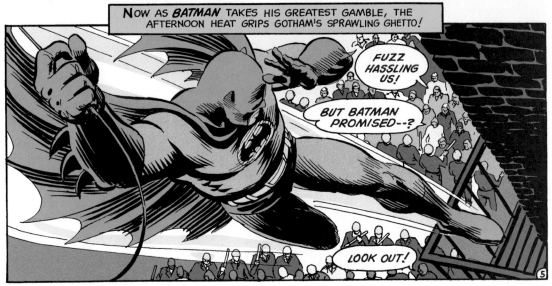

NOW AS *BATMAN* TAKES HIS GREATEST GAMBLE, THE AFTERNOON HEAT GRIPS GOTHAM'S SPRAWLING GHETTO!

FUZZ HASSLING US!

BUT BATMAN PROMISED--?

LOOK OUT!

5

SUDDENLY, A STONE IS THROWN, AN ORDER SNAPS, AND THE GHETTO BOILS OVER! THEN...

GO TO YOUR HOMES! I'LL HANDLE THE POLICE!

WHAT ABOUT THIS, CAPTAIN?

COMMISSIONER'S ORDERS! BRING IN ANY KID WEARIN' A *STOPP* ARMBAND!

QUICKLY, THE *CAPED CRUSADER* SWINGS TO POLICE HQ...

BLAST IT, COMMISSIONER--THE PRESIDENT OKAYED HANDLING IT *MY* WAY... *NO* FORCE... *NO* ROUSTING!

HE MEANT NO *GOVERNMENT* FORCE! MY DUTY IS TO *FIND* THAT BOMB ANY WAY I CAN!

BUT YOU'RE POLARIZING THE CITY... AND RUINING MY CREDIBILITY WITH THESE KIDS!

IT'S BATMAN!

KIDS? THEY'RE AN ARMY OF TRAINED REVOLUTIONARIES! NO ONE WILL TALK! THEY'RE TOUGHER THAN HARDENED CRIMINALS!

THE FINK!

YOU LIED! WE TRUSTED YOU!

OH, NO!

BIG PHONY!

AND AS THE SPECIAL *BAT-LINE* PHONE RINGS...

BATMAN? THIS IS MARK AGAIN! YOU *LIED* TO US! THAT MEANS OUR DEMANDS ARE GOING TO BE *TOUGH!*

REMEMBER, UNLESS THEY'RE MET... THE BOMB GOES OFF *AT MIDNIGHT TOMORROW!*

CLICK!

WAIT... PLEASE..!

I'M CAUGHT--BETWEEN THESE KIDS AND THE ADULTS! I NEED HELP ... *SPECIAL* HELP... AND *FAST!*

6

HELLO, *BATMAN!* AN *EMERGENCY?* LUCKY YOU CAUGHT FOUR OF US HERE! WE'LL BE THERE IN NO TIME...WITH OR WITHOUT UNIFORMS?

TWO *WITH...* TWO *WITHOUT!* STEP ON IT!!

HOURS LATER, AS DUSK FALLS OVER THE TENSE, THROBBING CITY...

HALT!

SHORTLY...

FOUND 'EM BEING HASSLED BY FUZZ, BUT MAYBE THEY'RE *SPIES!*

I'LL JUDGE THAT, CHINO! OKAY, *RAP! WHO* ARE YOU AND *WHY* WAS THE LAW AFTER YOU?

7

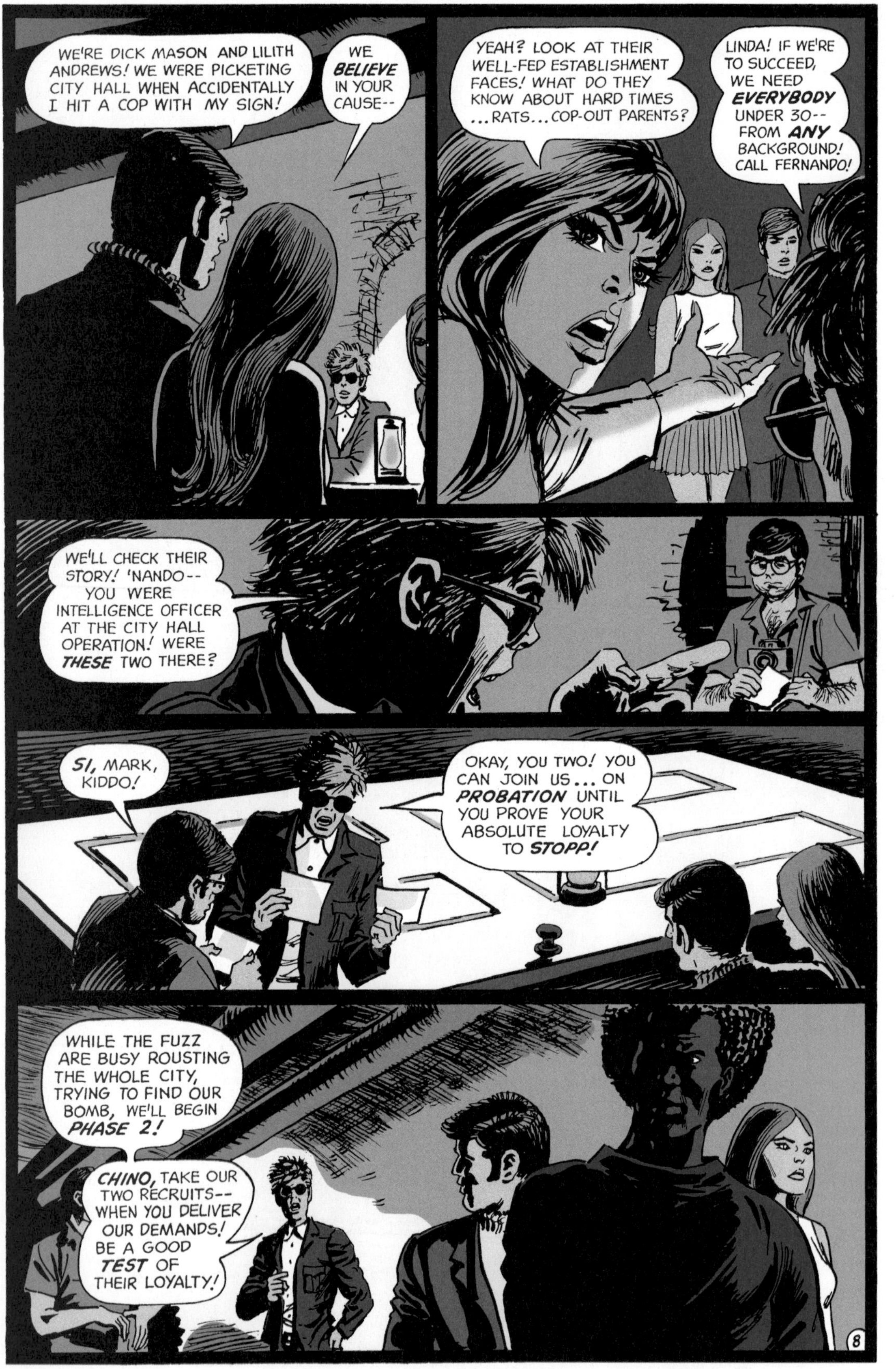
WE'RE DICK MASON AND LILITH ANDREWS! WE WERE PICKETING CITY HALL WHEN ACCIDENTALLY I HIT A COP WITH MY SIGN!
WE BELIEVE IN YOUR CAUSE--
YEAH? LOOK AT THEIR WELL-FED ESTABLISHMENT FACES! WHAT DO THEY KNOW ABOUT HARD TIMES ...RATS...COP-OUT PARENTS?
LINDA! IF WE'RE TO SUCCEED, WE NEED EVERYBODY UNDER 30-- FROM ANY BACKGROUND! CALL FERNANDO!
WE'LL CHECK THEIR STORY! 'NANDO-- YOU WERE INTELLIGENCE OFFICER AT THE CITY HALL OPERATION! WERE THESE TWO THERE?
SI, MARK, KIDDO!
OKAY, YOU TWO! YOU CAN JOIN US... ON PROBATION UNTIL YOU PROVE YOUR ABSOLUTE LOYALTY TO STOPP!
WHILE THE FUZZ ARE BUSY ROUSTING THE WHOLE CITY, TRYING TO FIND OUR BOMB, WE'LL BEGIN PHASE 2!
CHINO, TAKE OUR TWO RECRUITS-- WHEN YOU DELIVER OUR DEMANDS! BE A GOOD TEST OF THEIR LOYALTY!
8

IT'S *STAGGERING!* THE ORGANIZATION... THE DEDICATION OF THESE KIDS--!

BUT THEY BELIEVE THEY'RE *RIGHT*--AND I'M HALF IN AGREEMENT WITH THEM!

BUT THEY CAN'T CHANGE THE WORLD *THEIR* WAY! IT'S TOO RISKY! STAY CLOSE TO CHINO--PICK HIS BRAINS --WHILE I DROP BACK AND REPORT--BUT *WATCH* IT! HE'S A SUSPICIOUS GUY!

BIRDBOY TO COWLMAN! WE HAVE DONE OUR THING AND ARE BEGINNING AS ORDERED! OVER!

COWLMAN TO BIRDBOY! *EXCELLENT!* REPORT HOURLY IF POSSIBLE! BUT BE *CAREFUL!* OVER!

BEAUTIFUL! THE *TEEN TITANS* HAVE INFILTRATED *STOPP!* I HAVEN'T FOUND A CLUE TO WHERE THAT BOMB IS... *THEY* MUST DO BETTER!

BATMAN

9

NOW, THE INCOGNITO *BOY WONDER* WHISPERS AGAIN INTO HIS SECRET WRIST RADIO...

BIRDBOY TO TWINKLETOES AND BRACELETS! ON WAY TO CITY HALL! STAY CLOSE AND BACK US UP!

READ YOU LOUD AND CLEAR, BIRDBOY! OVER!

THEY MAY NEED A LITTLE HELP, *WONDER GIRL!* THAT'S *US!*

I'M RIGHT BEHIND YOU, *KID FLASH!*

MEANWHILE, AT CITY HALL...

MR. MAYOR! DEMAND MARTIAL LAW!

EVACUATE THE CITY!

BURN THE GHETTO! *SMOKE OUT* THESE TEEN TERRORISTS!

YOU FOOLS!

BATMAN!

THIS IS *MADNESS!* ONLY THE GOVERNOR CAN DECLARE MARTIAL LAW! EVACUATING THE CITY WILL CAUSE MASS PANIC! BURN THE GHETTO? HOW DO YOU KEEP A FIRE FROM CONSUMING *ALL* GOTHAM?

SOME OF YOU ARE SLUMLORDS ...WHO PROFIT FROM THE GHETTO! YOU'RE MORE RESPONSIBLE FOR GOTHAM'S PLIGHT THAN THESE KIDS--!

WHAT?

BATMAN'S WITH THEM!

10

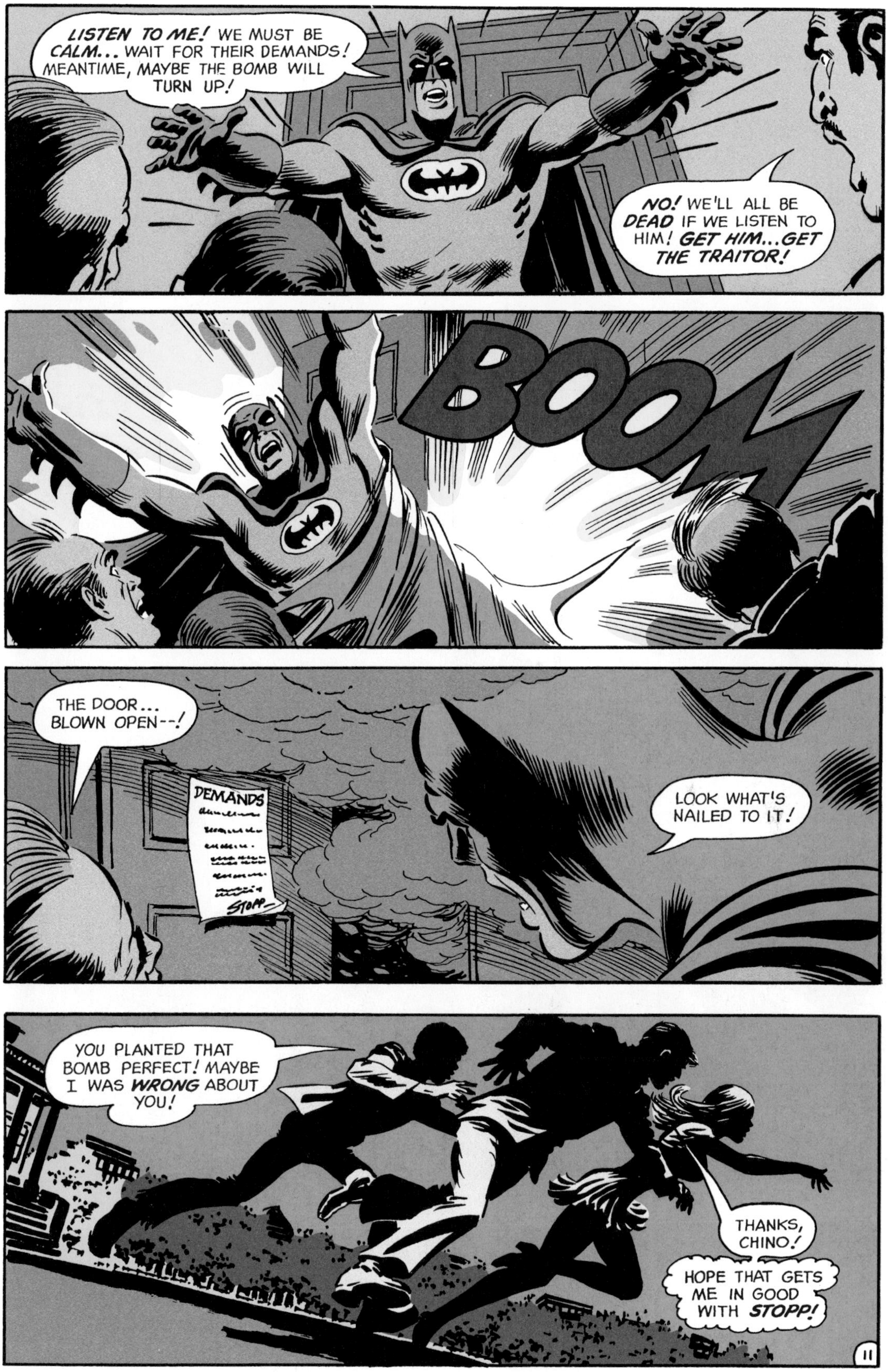
LISTEN TO ME! WE MUST BE CALM... WAIT FOR THEIR DEMANDS! MEANTIME, MAYBE THE BOMB WILL TURN UP!
NO! WE'LL ALL BE DEAD IF WE LISTEN TO HIM! GET HIM...GET THE TRAITOR!
BOOM
THE DOOR... BLOWN OPEN--!
DEMANDS
STOPP
LOOK WHAT'S NAILED TO IT!
YOU PLANTED THAT BOMB PERFECT! MAYBE I WAS WRONG ABOUT YOU!
THANKS, CHINO!
HOPE THAT GETS ME IN GOOD WITH STOPP!
11

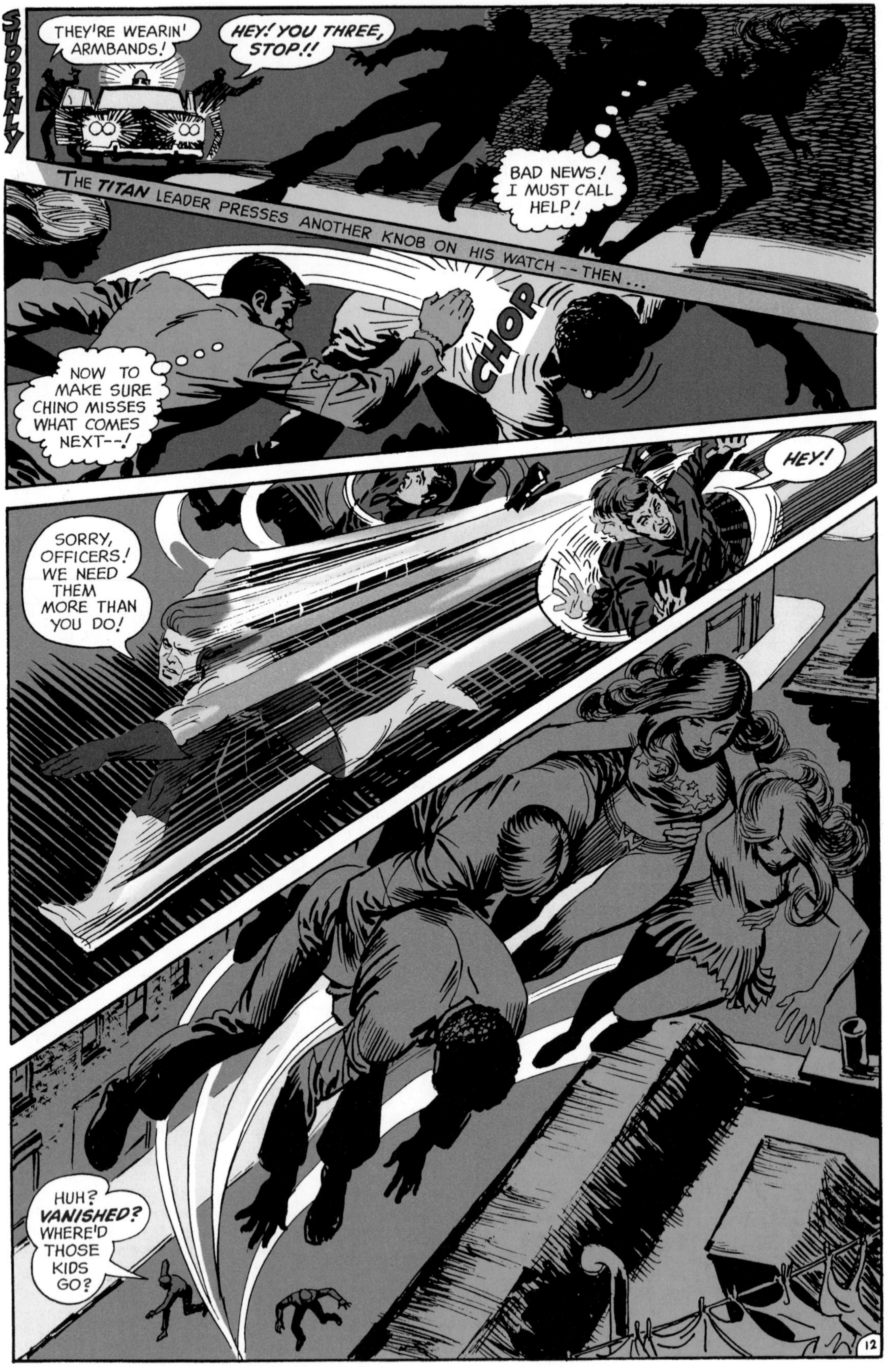
SUDDENLY
THEY'RE WEARIN' ARMBANDS!
HEY! YOU THREE, STOP!!
BAD NEWS! I MUST CALL HELP!
THE TITAN LEADER PRESSES ANOTHER KNOB ON HIS WATCH--THEN...
CHOP
NOW TO MAKE SURE CHINO MISSES WHAT COMES NEXT--!
HEY!
SORRY, OFFICERS! WE NEED THEM MORE THAN YOU DO!
HUH? VANISHED? WHERE'D THOSE KIDS GO?
12

NEVER THOUGHT *TITANS* WOULD EVADE THE POLICE -- BUT WE MUST KEEP TO *BATMAN'S* PLAN! DONNA, YOU REJOIN WALLY...WE'LL TAKE OUR MILITANT PAL ELSEWHERE!

WHILE BACK AT CITY HALL...

PROSECUTE ALL SLUMLORDS...ROUND UP ALL KNOWN PUSHERS...CLEAN UP OUR GARBAGE...CLOSE GHETTO SCHOOLS UNTIL FURTHER NOTICE...RELEASE ALL *STOPP* PRISONERS!

NO, NEVER!

BLACKMAIL!

NO COMPROMISE!

DON'T GIVE IN TO THOSE ROTTEN KIDS!

WHAT CHOICE DO WE HAVE?

HOLD IT! ARE WE ALL BLIND? MOST OF THESE DEMANDS ARE THINGS THAT SHOULD'VE BEEN DONE *LONG AGO!*

I AGREE! ABSOLUTELY RIGHT!

I ADMIT I'VE BEEN AGAINST THOSE KIDS, BUT MAYBE WE CAN DEAL WITH THEM... *MEET* SOME OF THEIR DEMANDS AND THEY'LL *TELL* US WHERE THE BOMB'S HIDDEN!

THANKS, OLD FRIEND!

13

THERE'S ONE *MORE* ITEM! THESE "ESTABLISHMENT LEADERS" BE PUT IN PREVENTIVE DETENTION TO SHOW *GOOD FAITH*--

THE MAYOR, THE CITY COUNCIL, COMMISSIONER GORDON...AND... YOURS TRULY, *BATMAN!*

WHAT?

PREPOSTEROUS!

I...I CAN'T GO ALONG WITH THAT!

WHY NOT? *I'M* WILLING! WE MUST CLOSE THE GAP WITH THESE KIDS ...*DO* SOMETHING TO SHOW THEY CAN *TRUST* US!

THIS MEETING IS *SUSPENDED!* IF ALL ELSE FAILS, WE *MAY* HONOR THESE... *ABSURD DEMANDS!* BUT NOW I ORDER COMMISSIONER GORDON AND *BATMAN TO FIND THAT BOMB!*

BUT AS THE SULTRY NIGHT GROWS OLDER...

WE'VE TURNED THE CITY INSIDE OUT... BUT NOT A *HINT* OF IT! THE *TITANS* HAVE *GOT* TO MAKE A BREAKTHROUGH!

AT THIS MOMENT IN *STOPP'S* SECRET LAIR...

WE DELIVERED THE DEMANDS, MARK BABY, BUT I DON'T KNOW *HOW* I GOT COLD-CONKED!

DON'T YOU REMEMBER, CHINO? YOU TANGLED WITH THE FUZZ...GOT HIT FROM BEHIND! LILITH AND I GRABBED YOU AND SPLIT!

14

69YOU HOT HEAD, CHINO! WHAT IF YOU'D BEEN *BUSTED* WITH WHAT YOU KNOW!

GOOD WORK, YOU TWO! NOW TO SEE IF THE CITY MEETS OUR *DEMANDS*...OR PREFERS *DESTRUCTION!*

WHAT'D YOU FIND OUT FROM CHINO?

HE, MARK, AND THE GENIUS WHO BUILT IT, AND LINDA ARE THE *ONLY* ONES WHO KNOW WHERE THE BOMB'S HIDDEN! BUT *WHO* OR *WHERE* HE IS, I COULDN'T LEARN!

SHIELD ME WHILE I CONTACT THE OTHERS!

NO LUCK, BIRDBOY...

...NOT EVEN...

...A *CLUE* TO...

...THE BOMB...

HAVE MADE EVERY TEEN SCENE IN TOWN, BIRDBOY, BUT NO *HINT* ABOUT BOMB!

WHILE AS A FAMED FIGURE FLITS ACROSS A BELOVED SKYLINE...

THE NATIONAL GUARD DEPLOYING! DAWN WILL BE HERE SOON!

15

AT NOON, THE PRESIDENT WILL SEND IN THE FBI AND THE ARMY! IT COULD BE GOTHAM'S ONLY HOPE -- OR MIGHT ALIENATE THESE KIDS FOR GOOD!

IF ONLY THE MAYOR WOULD AGREE TO *SOME* OF THEIR DEMANDS! BUT I'VE GOT ONE *LAST* HUNCH TO PLAY... THE KID WHO BUILT THE BOMB! THE ONE CHINO CALLED... *DROPOUT GENIUS!*

MAYBE I CAN TRACK DOWN THIS JUNIOR EINSTEIN THROUGH THESE SCHOOL RECORDS...

HERE--THIS COULD BE *IT!* HARVEY LOGAN...CLASS NICKNAME ...*GENIUS!* WINNER GOTHAM SCIENCE AWARD...QUIT SCHOOL ...DUE TO FAMILY HARDSHIP!

QUICKLY, THE *MASKED MANHUNTER* IS ARCING THROUGH THE NIGHT AGAIN...

IT FIGURES-- BRILLIANT KID HAS TO DROP OUT--BECOMES BITTER...TURNS HIS TALENT TO EXPLOSIVES!

THERE'S THE BUILDING ...TYPICAL RUN-DOWN HOLE!

A KNOCKING THAT WILL NOT BE DENIED...

MY SON, HARVEY? HE...HE'S IN JAIL... HE WAS ARRESTED FOR PICKETING YESTERDAY!

IN *JAIL?* THANK YOU, MRS. LOGAN-- MAYBE YOUR BOY WILL *STILL* TURN OUT TO BE A HERO!

16

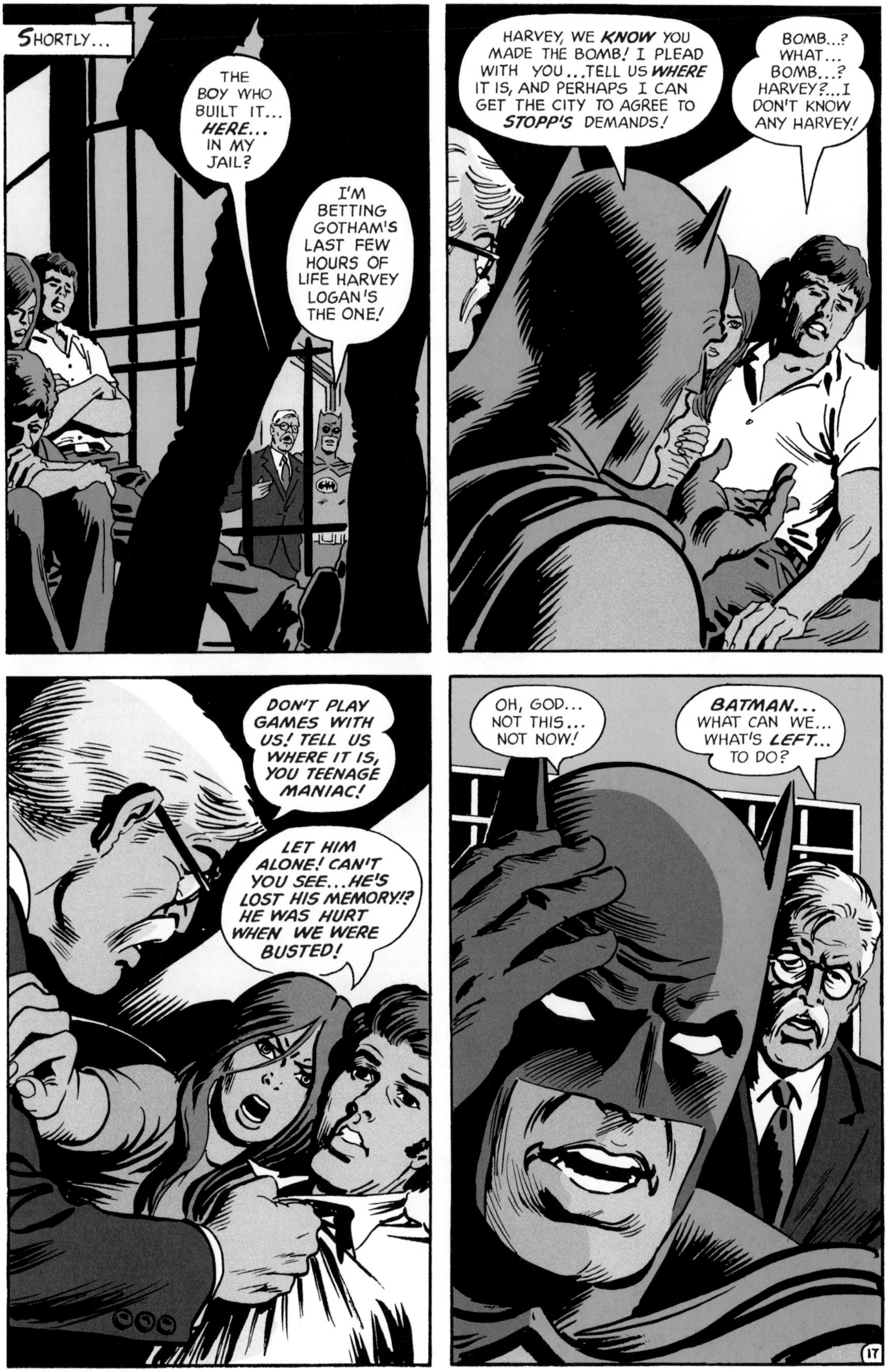
SHORTLY...
THE BOY WHO BUILT IT... HERE... IN MY JAIL?
I'M BETTING GOTHAM'S LAST FEW HOURS OF LIFE HARVEY LOGAN'S THE ONE!
HARVEY, WE KNOW YOU MADE THE BOMB! I PLEAD WITH YOU...TELL US WHERE IT IS, AND PERHAPS I CAN GET THE CITY TO AGREE TO STOPP'S DEMANDS!
BOMB...? WHAT... BOMB...? HARVEY?...I DON'T KNOW ANY HARVEY!
DON'T PLAY GAMES WITH US! TELL US WHERE IT IS, YOU TEENAGE MANIAC!
LET HIM ALONE! CAN'T YOU SEE...HE'S LOST HIS MEMORY!? HE WAS HURT WHEN WE WERE BUSTED!
OH, GOD... NOT THIS... NOT NOW!
BATMAN... WHAT CAN WE... WHAT'S LEFT... TO DO?
17

MR. MAYOR, WE'RE LICKED! BEFORE THE ARMY MOVES IN AND WE LOSE CONTROL OF GOTHAM'S DESTINY, I BEG YOU... AGREE TO *STOPP'S* DEMANDS! MAYBE IT WILL END THE BLACKMAIL!

GOTHAM OWES YOU A LOT! I GUESS WE OWE YOU THIS, TOO! ALL RIGHT, WE'LL *DO* WHAT THEY WANT!

AND AS SLEEPLESS CITIZENS TUNE IN THEIR MORNING TV...

BATMAN SPEAKING TO *STOPP!* GOTHAM CITY ACCEPTS YOUR DEMANDS! PLEASE MONITOR ALL NETWORKS FOR THE NEXT FEW HOURS!

WGC TELEVISION

AND IN THE HOURS AHEAD...

POLICE ARE ROUNDING UP SCORES OF SLUMLORDS...PUSHERS... AND GRAFTERS IN A TOTAL DRAGNET!

AN ARMY OF SANITATION MEN ARE CLEANING UP THE JUNK AND RAT-INFESTED STREETS!

... AND ALL THE *STOPP* MEMBERS ARE BEING RELEASED...

STOPP

14 PRECINCT

18

...WITH THEIR CELLS BEING OCCUPIED BY GOTHAM'S HOSTAGES INCLUDING *BATMAN* HIMSELF!

HURRAAH

WE'VE WON!

WE'VE WON!

LET'S TELL 'EM WHERE THE BOMB IS! WE WON--NO NEED TO MAKE EIGHT MILLION PEOPLE SWEAT ANY MORE!

MAN, THEY MADE US SWEAT AND KNUCKLE UNDER ALL OUR LIVES!

COME ON, CHINO-- WE'VE MADE OUR POINT! WE DON'T *REALLY* WANT TO BLOW UP EVERYTHING-- OURSELVES, TOO!

OKAY, MARK! I GUESS WE GOTTA GIVE 'EM ANOTHER CHANCE!

NO!

YOU'RE ALL FOOLS! THEY'LL *DOUBLECROSS* YOU! YOU CAN *NEVER* TRUST ADULTS! *NEVER!*

COOL DOWN, LINDA! YOU'RE OUT OF ORDER --AND CHINO AND I OUTVOTE YOU TWO TO ONE AS MEMBERS OF *STOPP'S* CENTRAL CONTROL! I'M GO-ING TO CALL THE BOMB SQUAD!

AND SHORTLY...

OF ALL THE PLACES... THE BASE OF MY STATUE!

THOSE KIDS--YOU GOTTA HAND IT TO THEM! HA! HA! IF I DON'T LAUGH, I'LL CRY!

19

73

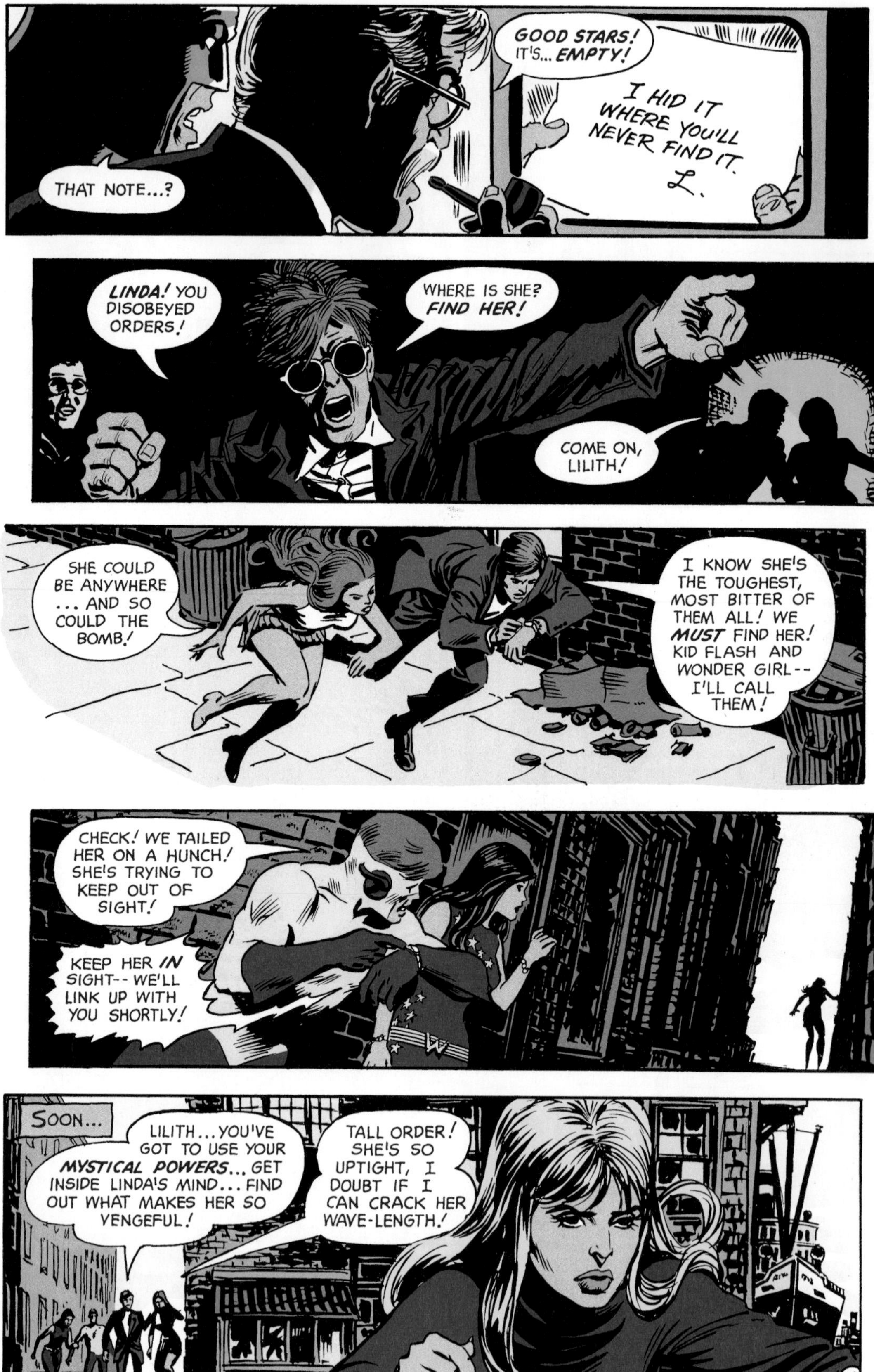

THAT NOTE...?
GOOD STARS! IT'S... EMPTY!
I HID IT WHERE YOU'LL NEVER FIND IT. L.
LINDA! YOU DISOBEYED ORDERS!
WHERE IS SHE? FIND HER!
COME ON, LILITH!
SHE COULD BE ANYWHERE ... AND SO COULD THE BOMB!
I KNOW SHE'S THE TOUGHEST, MOST BITTER OF THEM ALL! WE MUST FIND HER! KID FLASH AND WONDER GIRL-- I'LL CALL THEM!
CHECK! WE TAILED HER ON A HUNCH! SHE'S TRYING TO KEEP OUT OF SIGHT!
KEEP HER IN SIGHT-- WE'LL LINK UP WITH YOU SHORTLY!
SOON...
LILITH... YOU'VE GOT TO USE YOUR MYSTICAL POWERS... GET INSIDE LINDA'S MIND... FIND OUT WHAT MAKES HER SO VENGEFUL!
TALL ORDER! SHE'S SO UPTIGHT, I DOUBT IF I CAN CRACK HER WAVE-LENGTH!
20

SHE'S GONE INTO A *TRANCE*...

WOW! IT ALWAYS SPOOKS ME!

IF THIS DOESN'T WORK, WE'RE RIGHT BACK WHERE WE STARTED... *DOOMSDAY!*

I UNDERSTAND, MR. PRESIDENT! YOU MUST TAKE ACTION... MY TIME IS ALMOST UP! BUT THE *TITANS* ARE STILL ON THE JOB--!

SORRY, *BATMAN*, BUT AT 12 NOON, I MUST ORDER THE ARMY IN!

BLAST! TO BE SO NEAR-- AND FAIL AT THE LAST MINUTE! IF TROOPS COME IN, WHO KNOWS *WHAT'LL* HAPPEN! THE CITY COULD ERUPT... RIOTS... PANIC...

AND THE BOMB WOULD DO THE REST!

MEANTIME...

LILITH'S BEEN UNDER FOR MINUTES ...AND LINDA'S SITTING THERE LIKE A ZOMBIE!

MAYBE LILITH'S MADE CONNECTION WITH HER SUBCONSCIOUS! LOOK AT HER...THAT BOMB COULD GO OFF AND SHE'D NEVER KNOW IT!

BUT IN THE MIND OF THE CLAIRVOYANT *TITAN,* THERE IS LIFE... NOISE... PULSATING IMAGES OF THE PAST...

LINDA...YOU'LL LIVE WITH YOUR AUNT AND UNCLE UNTIL I CAN COME FOR YOU!

NO, MOMMY! I WANT TO BE WITH YOU! PLEASE!

21

BUT, LINDA... YOUR MOTHER'S COMING FOR YOU!

SHE'S SEVEN YEARS TOO LATE! TELL HER I HAVE NO MOTHER --TELL HER I'M...*DEAD!*

LILITH! YOU *OKAY?*

YES... BUT I'VE *GOT* IT-- THE KEY TO WHAT MAKES LITTLE LINDA SUCH A BITTER CHICK!

HEY, SHE'S GONNA LEAVE!

SUDDENLY...

HOLD IT!

WE TAILED YOU -- YOU'RE *NOT* WHAT YOU SAID! *YOU'RE LIARS AND SPIES!*

WE *DID* LIE, MARK-- BUT ONLY IN A GOOD CAUSE-- TO KEEP YOU COOL...KEEP YOU FROM DESTROYING GOTHAM...AND INNOCENT PEOPLE!

MAYBE LINDA'S RIGHT-- YOU SHOULDN'T TRUST *ANYBODY*-- EVEN THE *TEEN TITANS!*

NO, CHINO! YOU GOT WHAT YOU WANTED! AND WE'LL HELP YOU MAKE GOTHAM CITY STICK TO ITS PROMISES...BUT RIGHT NOW LINDA'S DOUBLE-CROSSING EVERYONE ...*YOU*...EVEN *HERSELF!*

HMMM, YOU'RE RIGHT! SHE BROKE THE FAITH! A BETTER WORLD COMES FROM COOPERATION, NOT SELFISH INDIVIDUAL ACTION!

22

WE MUST LEARN WHERE SHE STASHED THE BOMB--AND TO DO THAT, WE MUST FIND HER MOTHER, WHO LIVES SOMEWHERE IN THE GHETTO!

THIS IS *OUR* TURF! *WE'LL* FIND HER!

TIME TICKS BY TOWARDS HIGH NOON, AND A FORLORN FIGURE WANDERS AIMLESSLY...

WHO'S THAT? OH, NO, PLEASE!

LINDA...BABY--! IT'S ME...MOTHER!

I HAVE NO MOTHER! MY MOTHER LEFT ME...LEFT ME TO CRY MY HEART OUT EVERY NIGHT!

I HAD NO CHOICE! WHEN YOUR FATHER DIED--I HAD TO WORK ...THE GHETTO'S HARD ON GROWN-UPS, TOO!

WHEN I COULD, I CAME FOR YOU...BUT YOU RAN AWAY... I'VE BEEN SEARCHING FOR YEARS FOR YOU!

YOU DON'T WANT ME NOW-- YOU JUST WANT TO KNOW WHERE THE BOMB IS-- YOU'RE LIKE ALL GROWN-UPS... *PHONY!*

IF...IF YOU FEEL THAT WAY... THERE'S NOTHING LEFT TO SAY! MAYBE THIS CITY...YOU ...NONE OF US...ARE WORTH SAVING!

NO! NEVER SAY THAT! MOTHER! I...I LOVE YOU!

23

THEN, A CALM VOICE, A TALL, LITHE FIGURE STANDING NEAR...

LINDA... WHERE IS THE BOMB?

YES, I'LL TELL YOU ...NOW!

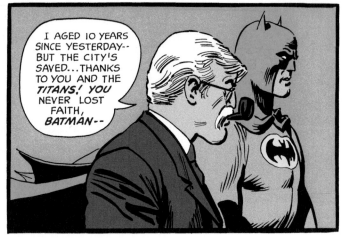

I AGED 10 YEARS SINCE YESTERDAY-- BUT THE CITY'S SAVED...THANKS TO YOU AND THE TITANS! YOU NEVER LOST FAITH, BATMAN--

NOT LONG AFTER...

DON'T LITTER GOTHAM'S STREETS

THE BOMB'S ...IN THAT? WE'D NEVER HAVE LOOKED THERE! THESE KIDS! HA! HA!

IT'LL BE FLOWN OUT TO SEA-- AND DISARMED BY EXPERTS!

(24)

I ALMOST DID SEVERAL TIMES-- BUT NOW WE MUST MAKE SURE WE BUILD A BETTER CITY... AND WORLD...SO THESE KIDS NEVER LOSE FAITH AGAIN ...EVER!

THE END

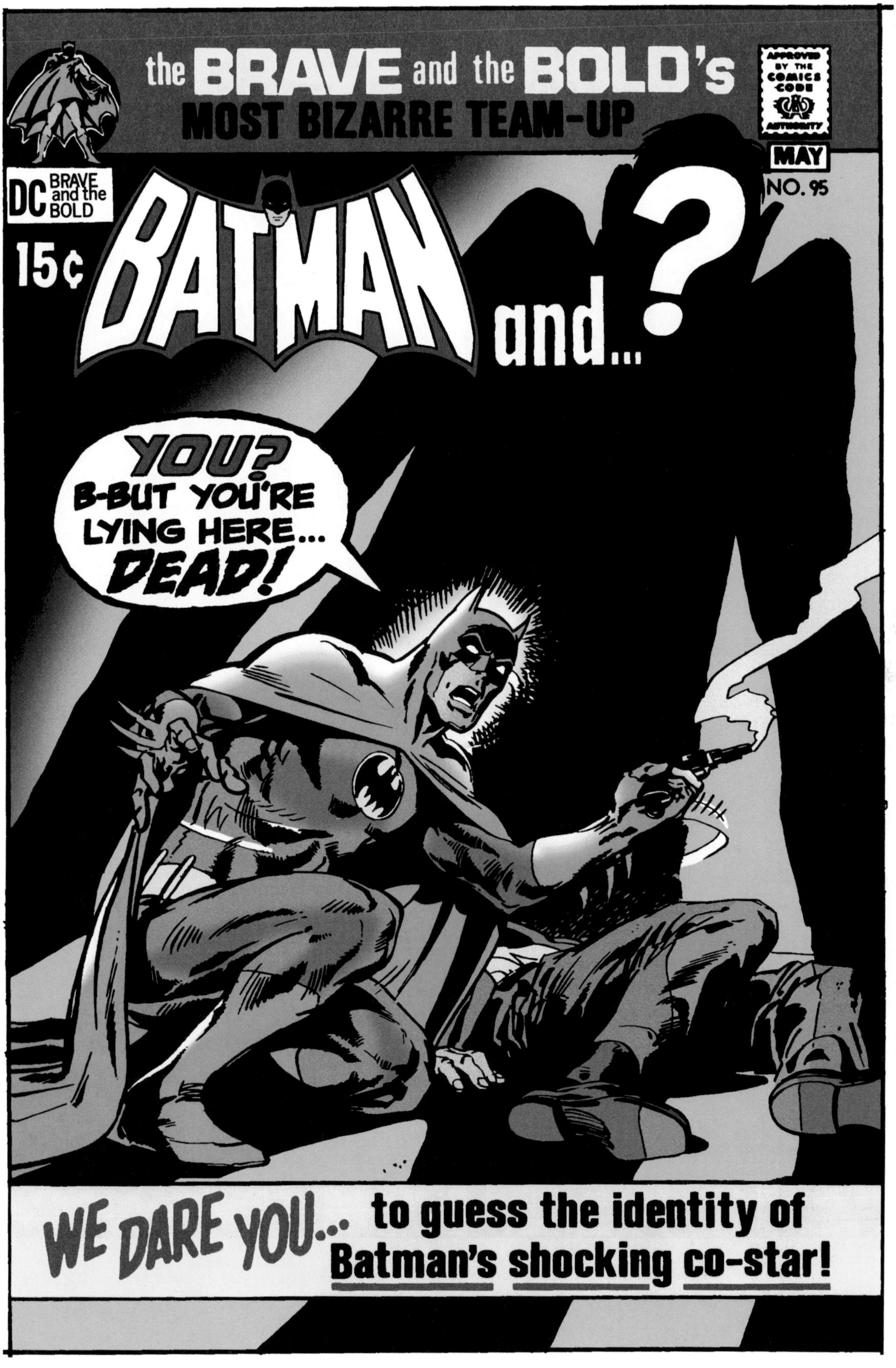

the BRAVE and the BOLD's
MOST BIZARRE TEAM-UP
APPROVED BY THE COMICS CODE AUTHORITY
MAY
DC BRAVE and the BOLD
NO. 95
15¢
BATMAN and...?
YOU? B-BUT YOU'RE LYING HERE... DEAD!
WE DARE YOU... to guess the identity of Batman's shocking co-star!

MOST TOWERING OF ALL GOTHAM CITY SKY-SCRAPERS, DWARFING EVEN THE MAJESTIC WAYNE BUILDING, IS THE *"BIG DOUBLE R"*-- HOME OF *RUBY RYDER, INC.*-- INTO WHICH A FAMED, FAMILIAR FIGURE NOW ENTERS...

BATMAN ARRIVING AT STREET LEVEL, MISS RYDER!

BATMAN IS CLEAN, MISS RYDER-- NO WEAPONS!

SAY SOMETHING-- WE MUST CHECK YOUR VOICE-PRINT!

BIG BOSS LADY TAKES NO CHANCES, EH? OKAY...

"MAIRZY DOTES AND DOEZY DOTES AND THE BLAZES WITH RUBY RYDER!"

MISS RYDER SPEAKING! STOP GAWKING AND GET BACK TO WORK, GIRLS! HE'S ONLY A *MAN!*

BUT *WHAT* A MAN, YOU BOSSY WITCH!

THAT *SPRAY*--? WHAT THE--?

MY FAVORITE MAN'S COLOGNE, *BATMAN*-- "TIGER LOVER"... I CAN'T STAND THOSE CHEAP SCENTS MOST MALES USE!

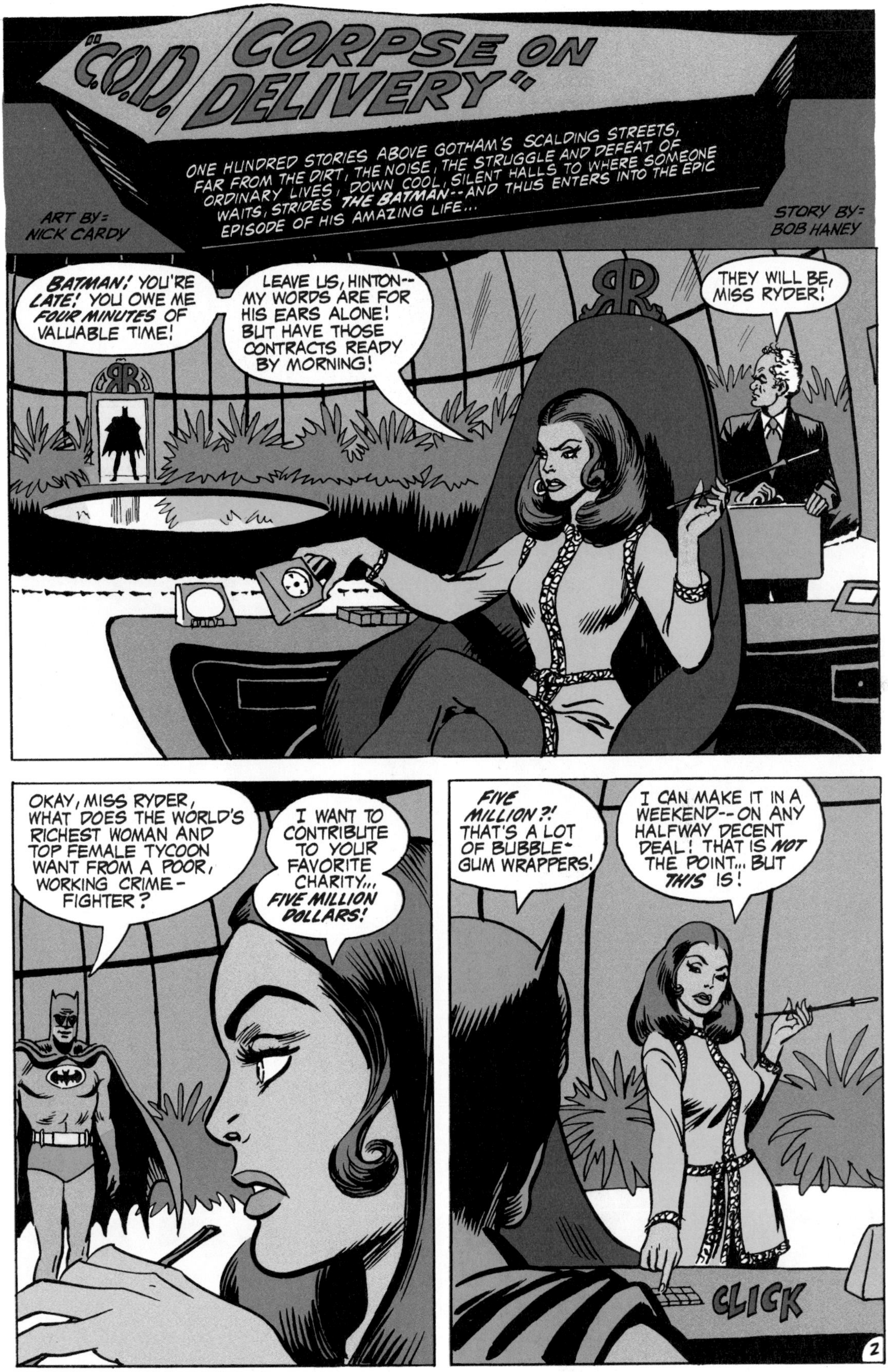
"C.O.D. CORPSE ON DELIVERY"
ONE HUNDRED STORIES ABOVE GOTHAM'S SCALDING STREETS, FAR FROM THE DIRT, THE NOISE, THE STRUGGLE AND DEFEAT OF ORDINARY LIVES, DOWN COOL, SILENT HALLS TO WHERE SOMEONE WAITS, STRIDES THE BATMAN-- AND THUS ENTERS INTO THE EPIC EPISODE OF HIS AMAZING LIFE...
ART BY: NICK CARDY
STORY BY: BOB HANEY
BATMAN! YOU'RE LATE! YOU OWE ME FOUR MINUTES OF VALUABLE TIME!
LEAVE US, HINTON-- MY WORDS ARE FOR HIS EARS ALONE! BUT HAVE THOSE CONTRACTS READY BY MORNING!
THEY WILL BE, MISS RYDER!
OKAY, MISS RYDER, WHAT DOES THE WORLD'S RICHEST WOMAN AND TOP FEMALE TYCOON WANT FROM A POOR, WORKING CRIME-FIGHTER?
I WANT TO CONTRIBUTE TO YOUR FAVORITE CHARITY... FIVE MILLION DOLLARS!
FIVE MILLION?! THAT'S A LOT OF BUBBLE-GUM WRAPPERS!
I CAN MAKE IT IN A WEEKEND-- ON ANY HALFWAY DECENT DEAL! THAT IS NOT THE POINT... BUT THIS IS!
CLICK
2

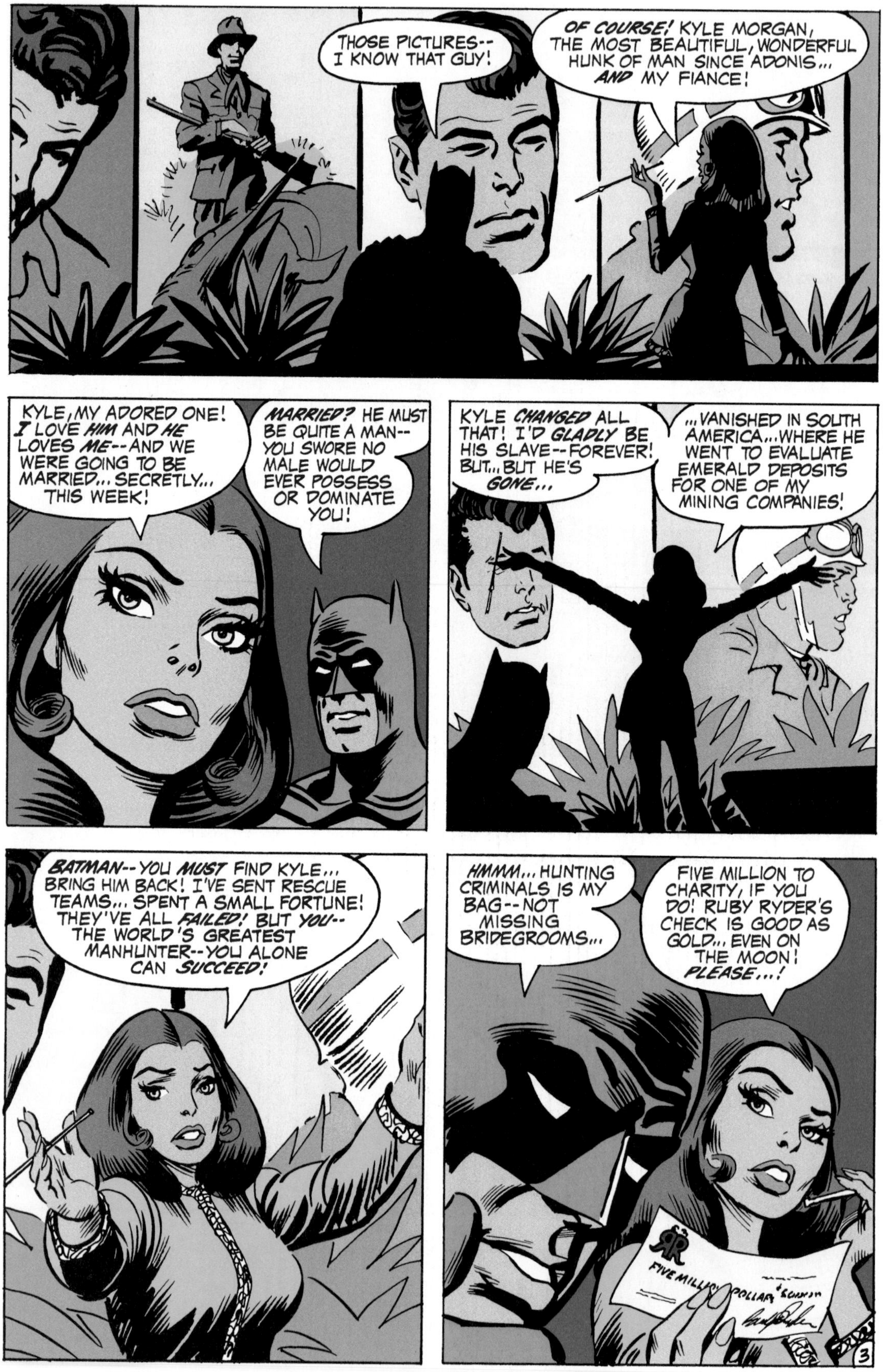
THOSE PICTURES--
I KNOW THAT GUY!
OF COURSE! KYLE MORGAN, THE MOST BEAUTIFUL, WONDERFUL HUNK OF MAN SINCE ADONIS... AND MY FIANCE!
KYLE, MY ADORED ONE! I LOVE HIM AND HE LOVES ME--AND WE WERE GOING TO BE MARRIED... SECRETLY... THIS WEEK!
MARRIED? HE MUST BE QUITE A MAN--YOU SWORE NO MALE WOULD EVER POSSESS OR DOMINATE YOU!
KYLE CHANGED ALL THAT! I'D GLADLY BE HIS SLAVE--FOREVER! BUT... BUT HE'S GONE...
...VANISHED IN SOUTH AMERICA... WHERE HE WENT TO EVALUATE EMERALD DEPOSITS FOR ONE OF MY MINING COMPANIES!
BATMAN--YOU MUST FIND KYLE... BRING HIM BACK! I'VE SENT RESCUE TEAMS... SPENT A SMALL FORTUNE! THEY'VE ALL FAILED! BUT YOU--THE WORLD'S GREATEST MANHUNTER--YOU ALONE CAN SUCCEED!
HMMM... HUNTING CRIMINALS IS MY BAG--NOT MISSING BRIDEGROOMS...
FIVE MILLION TO CHARITY, IF YOU DO! RUBY RYDER'S CHECK IS GOOD AS GOLD... EVEN ON THE MOON! PLEASE...!
3

AS *THE CAPED CRUSADER* HESITATES...

OH, MAN OF THE NIGHT... MAN OF MYSTERY... I BEG YOU... I HUMBLE MYSELF AT YOUR FEET! BRING BACK MY LOVE!

RUBY RYDER..., THE TYCOON TIGRESS BEGGING ON HER *KNEES?* WELL, OKAY... I... I'LL *DO* IT!

YOU MADE A HEARTBROKEN WOMAN SMILE AGAIN!

HINTON, MY LAWYER, WILL EXPLAIN THE DETAILS! ALL EXPENSES WILL BE PAID BY *RUBY RYDER, INC!* HURRY--AND *GOOD LUCK!*

SHORTLY--IN ANOTHER OFFICE...

WELL, HINTON, SHE PERSUADED ME! SHE'S QUITE A DAME!

MISS RYDER IS *NO* DAME! SHE IS THE WORLD'S *BEST* BUSINESS MIND--ABSOLUTELY *BRILLIANT!*--

SHE'S A *GODDESS*...A *LEGEND!* NO MAN IS GOOD ENOUGH FOR HER!

HE'S IN LOVE WITH HER! THAT DRY LAWYER'S HEART IS HUNG UP ON BIG BOSS LADY! BET *HE* HOPES I DON'T FIND LOVER-BOY IN THOSE BOONIES!

SOME TIME LATER, A STEAMING TOWN ON A *SOUTH AMERICAN RIVER*...

THIS IS WHERE MORGAN'S LAST TRACE WAS FOUND!

4

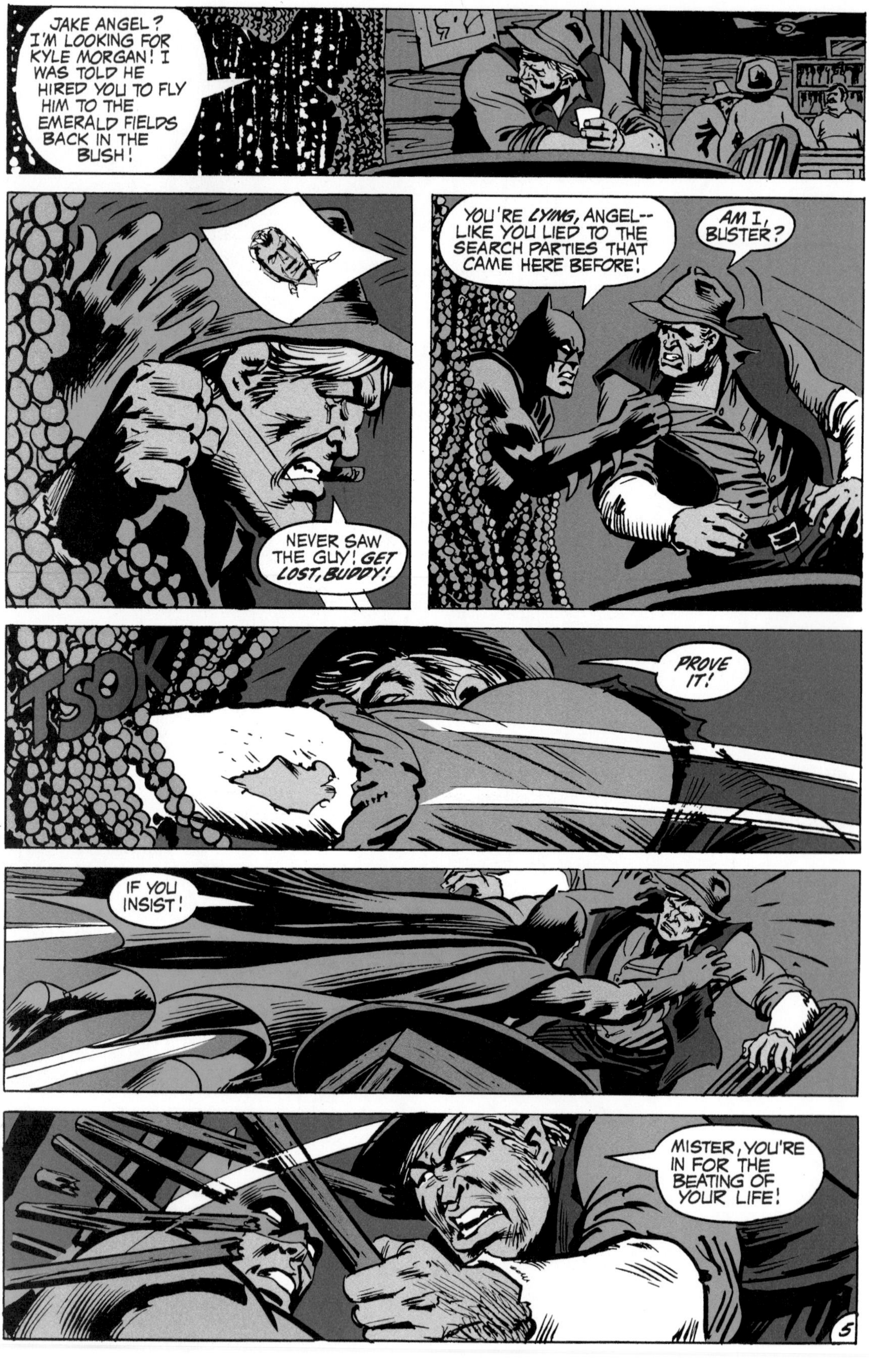
JAKE ANGEL? I'M LOOKING FOR KYLE MORGAN! I WAS TOLD HE HIRED YOU TO FLY HIM TO THE EMERALD FIELDS BACK IN THE BUSH!
NEVER SAW THE GUY! GET LOST, BUDDY!
YOU'RE LYING, ANGEL-- LIKE YOU LIED TO THE SEARCH PARTIES THAT CAME HERE BEFORE!
AM I, BUSTER?
TSOK
PROVE IT!
IF YOU INSIST!
MISTER, YOU'RE IN FOR THE BEATING OF YOUR LIFE!
5

THIS GUY'S TOUGH! BETTER PULL OUT THE STOPS!

UH....NOBODY...EVER BEAT JAKE ANGEL....IN FAIR FIGHT... BEFORE! WHAT DO YOU.... WANT, FELLA?

KYLE MORGAN! TAKE ME WHERE YOU TOOK HIM!

DOWN THERE....THAT NATIVE VILLAGE.... I DROPPED MORGAN OFF THERE.... SIX MONTHS AGO!

TAKE ME DOWN, ANGEL!

6

IN THE DEEPEST JUNGLE--OR DARKEST ALLEY--A *BATMAN'S* BEST FRIEND IS HIS UTILITY BELT!

BUT AS THE ASTOUNDED INDIANS RECOVER FROM THEIR SURPRISE...

WHEW! MY MAGIC SHOW TOOK THEIR MINDS OFF VIOLENCE!

AND THE PHOTOS TRIGGERED SOMETHING! THAT HUT?

GOOD LORD... IT...IT'S *KYLE MORGAN!*

IT'S THE END OF THE SEARCH! RUBY RYDER'S GOING TO BE WAITING AT THE CHURCH... FOREVER!

TWO DAYS LATER, AFTER A DANGEROUS DUGOUT CANOE-TRIP DOWNRIVER...

THAT BAT CHARACTER IS THE PRIZE PIECE IN THOSE HEADHUNTERS' COLLECTION BY NOW!

BUT I'M *NOT*, ANGEL--AND NEITHER IS KYLE MORGAN!

YOU?? YOU'RE... *DEAD!*

NO--BUT *YOU* WILL BE, IF YOU DON'T TAKE ME TO MORGAN! THAT PHONY SHRUNKEN HEAD ONLY FOOLED ME FOR A MINUTE! YOU FORGOT THE INDIANS LEAVE THE HAIR ITS ORIGINAL LENGTH-- *NOT* CLOSE-CROPPED!

NOW... TALK!

SOON, AT SOME ANCIENT INDIAN RUINS BEYOND THE TOWN...

THERE'S MORGAN... WHAT'S *LEFT* OF HIM!

MAN IN CAPE...NICE MAN... GOING TO TELL KYLE A STORY...

8

FEVER-- SOME TYPE I COULDN'T CURE! HE'S BEEN THAT WAY FOR MONTHS!

WHAT WAS YOUR GAME, ANGEL-- BIG RANSOM FROM RUBY RYDER? WELL, YOU'LL GET *NOTHING* NOW... AND I'M TAKING YOUR PLANE TO FLY HIM OUT OF HERE!

NO, YOU...

OOF!

YOU MIGHT SHOOT BETTER THAN YOU LIE AND FIGHT! SO--!

ANOTHER ITEM FOR THE OLD EXPENSE ACCOUNT-- ONE PLANE...TEN THOUSAND BUCKS!

COME ON, LOVER-BOY, YOU'VE GOT A DATE WITH THE WORLD'S RICHEST GIRL!

TWO DAYS LATER, AS *BATMAN*, WITH ONLY STOPS FOR FUEL, BANKS THE PLANE OVER NORTHERN MOUNTAINS...

I'M GROGGY-- BUT THERE'S BIG DOUBLE-R-- BOSS LADY'S COUNTRY ESTATE!

NOW TO DELIVER MY PACKAGE AND COLLECT THAT FIVE MILLION! HE SLEPT LIKE A BABY ALL THE WAY--MAYBE THAT MEDICINE I GAVE HIM HELPED!

9

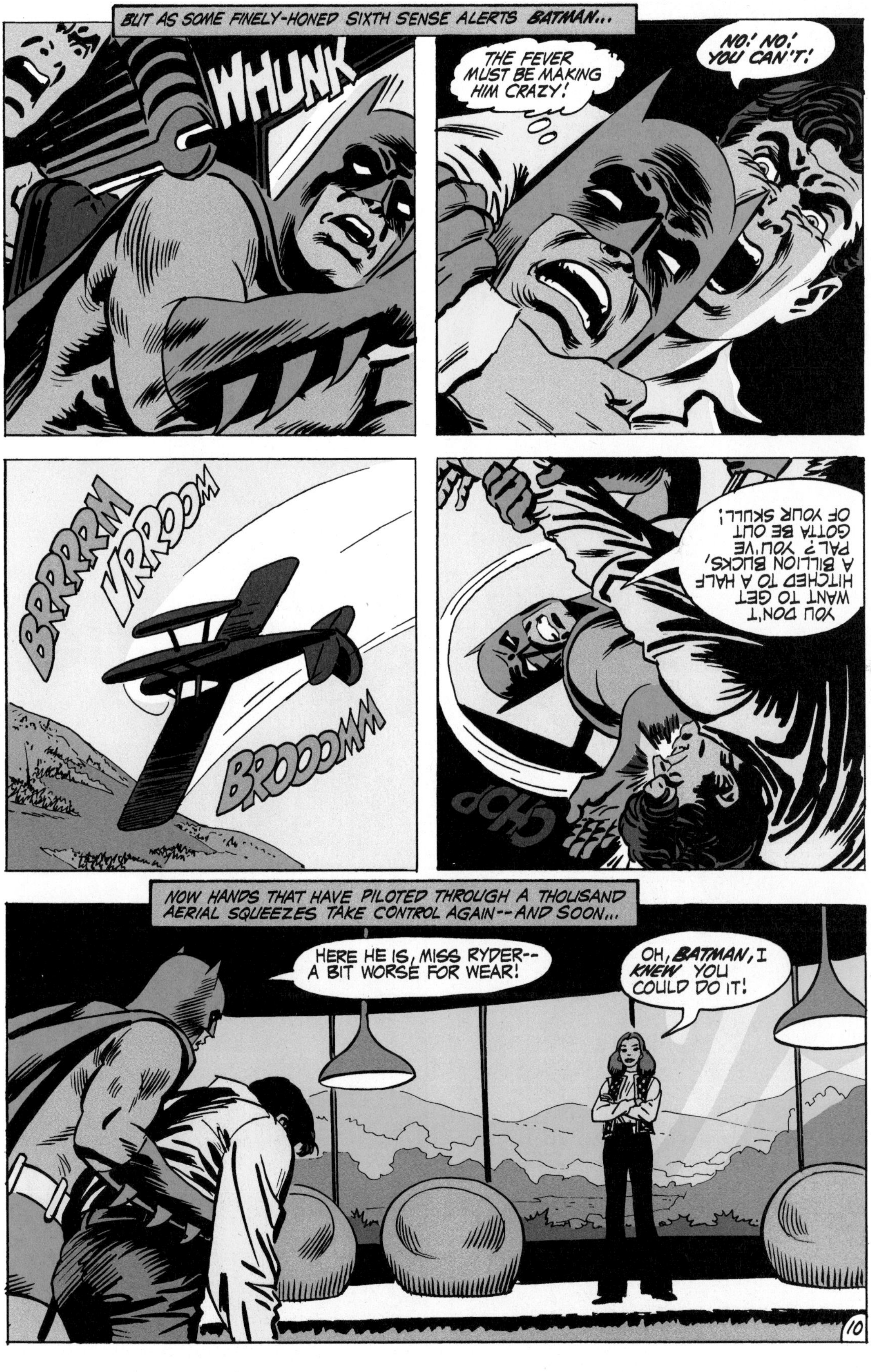
BUT AS SOME FINELY-HONED SIXTH SENSE ALERTS BATMAN...
WHUNK
THE FEVER MUST BE MAKING HIM CRAZY!
NO! NO! YOU CAN'T!
BRRRRM
VRROOM
BROOOMM
YOU DON'T WANT TO GET HITCHED TO A HALF A BILLION BUCKS, PAL? YOU'VE GOTTA BE OUT OF YOUR SKULL!
CHOP
NOW HANDS THAT HAVE PILOTED THROUGH A THOUSAND AERIAL SQUEEZES TAKE CONTROL AGAIN--AND SOON...
HERE HE IS, MISS RYDER-- A BIT WORSE FOR WEAR!
OH, BATMAN, I KNEW YOU COULD DO IT!
10

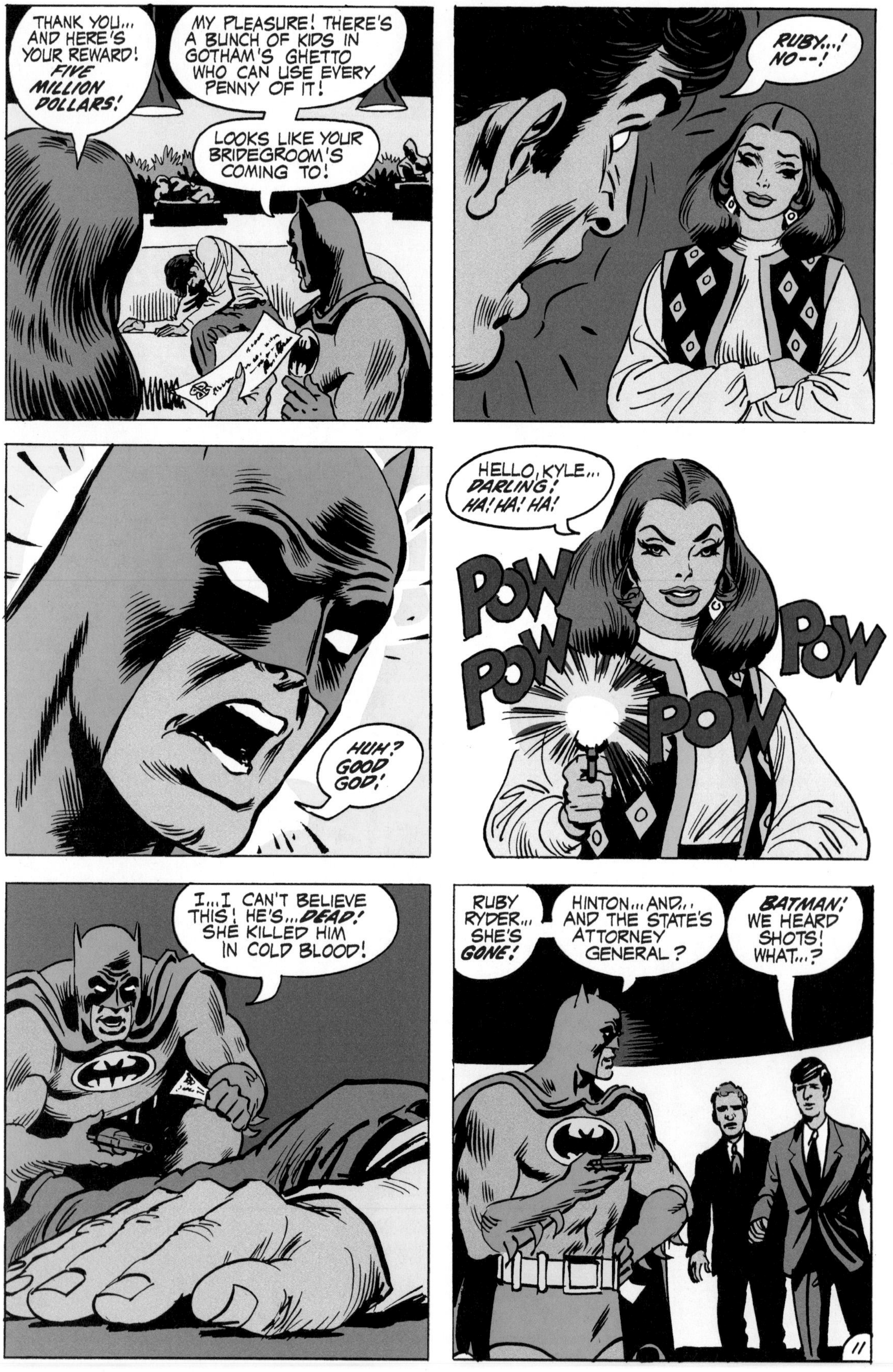

THANK YOU... AND HERE'S YOUR REWARD! FIVE MILLION DOLLARS!
MY PLEASURE! THERE'S A BUNCH OF KIDS IN GOTHAM'S GHETTO WHO CAN USE EVERY PENNY OF IT!
LOOKS LIKE YOUR BRIDEGROOM'S COMING TO!
RUBY...! NO--!
HUH? GOOD GOD!
HELLO, KYLE... DARLING! HA! HA! HA!
POW
POW
POW
POW
I... I CAN'T BELIEVE THIS! HE'S... DEAD! SHE KILLED HIM IN COLD BLOOD!
RUBY RYDER... SHE'S GONE!
HINTON... AND... AND THE STATE'S ATTORNEY GENERAL?
BATMAN! WE HEARD SHOTS! WHAT...?
11

TWO DAYS LATER, AS A SOLEMN CAVALCADE CRAWLS TOWARD THE CEMETERY...

I'D HAVE *GLADLY* PULLED THE TRIGGER MYSELF-- BUT SHE WANTED THAT PLEASURE! A WOMAN SCORNED IS MERCILESS!

A NEW MAUSOLEUM WITH HIS NAME ON IT? YOUR WITCH OF A BOSS SURE HAD THIS THING PLANNED!

YOU'RE SICK, HINTON--JUST LIKE SHE IS! I KNOW RUBY LEFT THE COUNTRY! NOW I'M PAINTED WITH THIS WHOLE MESS! MY ONLY WAY OUT IS TO FIND HER AND BRING HER BACK TO FACE JUSTICE!

AND I *AM* GOING TO GET *HER!* I'M GOING TO GET HER IF IT'S THE LAST THING I DO!

AND I'LL BE FIGHTING YOU EVERY STEP OF THE WAY, *BATMAN!* NOW, PLEASE, A LITTLE SILENCE AND RESPECT FOR THE DEAD!

THAT NIGHT, AT GOTHAM JETPORT...

THE POLICE DRAGNET IS OUT FOR *BATMAN*-- BUT *NOT* FOR *BRUCE WAYNE,* TRAVELING ON "BUSINESS" WITH A VALID PASSPORT!

WHILE IN A *SILENT SEPULCHER* IN GOTHAM CEMETERY, A COFFIN GROANS WITH THE STRAIN OF SOMETHING ALIVE ESCAPING ITS ALL-CONTAINING CONFINES!

GRRNNNNN

13

RUBY'S A REAL JET-SETTER-- THE WITCH CAN'T RESIST BEING SEEN IN ALL THE BEST PLACES!

IF I COVER ALL HER KNOWN HAUNTS, MAYBE I CAN DIG UP A CLUE TO HER WHEREABOUTS! SINCE THIS IS A MAN-HUNTING--OR WOMAN-HUNTING JOB--IT'S A JOB FOR BATMAN!

CR AAASSH

BLAZES! SOMEBODY TRIED TO CROWN ME "KING OF THE CORPSES!" OF COURSE-- HINTON'S GOONS! HE SAID HE'D BE ON MY TAIL EVERY STEP-- PROTECTING BELOVED BOSS LADY!

BUT WHO SHOVED ME CLEAR? A COCKROACH COULDN'T HIDE HERE!

ONE THING I KNOW-- THE BATMAN ROLE IS OUT! HE'S A TARGET! IT'S BRUCE WAYNE TIME AGAIN!

NOT LONG AFTER, IN A HOTEL ROOM...

SO-- THERE IS REASON TO BATMAN'S ENTRANCE AND EXITS TO THIS ROOM! THIS PASSPORT PROVES HE BORROWED THE IDENTITY OF THE AMERICAN MILLIONAIRE, BRUCE WAYNE, AS A COVER!

14

SHORTLY, VIA TRANSATLANTIC PHONE...

SO *BATMAN* IS HUNTING MISS RYDER, DISGUISED AS HIS FRIEND WAYNE? VERY WELL--INFORM ALL OPERATIVES! *GET WAYNE BEFORE HE FINDS HER!*

TWO DAYS LATER, ON THE RIVIERA...

PARIS WAS A BUST--BUT MAYBE RUBY'S PRIVATE VILLA WILL GIVE ME A SOLID CLUE TO HER WHEREABOUTS!

SUDDENLY...

AAIEE EEEEE!

ANOTHER WOULD-BE ASSASSIN... BUT SOMEONE... SOMETHING GOT HIM FIRST!? NO QUESTION OF IT... I'M BEING PROTECTED... BUT BY *WHOM*...OR *WHAT*??!!

AND WHEN A WEARY, BEWILDERED "HUNTER" RETURNS LATER...

THE VILLA WAS DESERTED-- AND I'VE RUN OUT OF LEADS ON RUBY RYDER! FOR SOME REASON, MY WAYNE COVER ISN'T WORKING...I MAY AS WELL OPERATE AS *BATMAN!*

A NOTE WITH A SMALL RUBY WRAPPED IN IT?

IT COULD MEAN ONLY *ONE* THING-- A LEAD TO RUBY RYDER! BUT HOW'D IT GET *HERE?* THE ROOM WAS LOCKED...THE WINDOW SEALED FOR AIR CONDITIONING!

JEBEL AL DIKK MARAKEECH

15

94

HINTON! HE COULD'VE LEFT THIS PHONY LEAD TO LURE ME INTO ANOTHER AMBUSH! BUT I CAN'T IGNORE IT! FINDING THAT COLD-BLOODED DAME IS MY ONLY HOPE!

DAYS LATER, IN THE MOROCCAN DESERT...

JEBEL AL DIKK... AN OLD MOUNTAIN FORTRESS-OASIS! AND IT'S OWNED BY RYDER ENTERPRISES! THAT LEAD LOOKS GOOD SO FAR! HOPE MY GUIDE ISN'T AS TREACHEROUS AS HE LOOKS--!

BUT THAT NIGHT, AS AN EXHAUSTED BATMAN SLEEPS...

NOW REARING UP FROM THE COLD SANDS, A PRESENCE, A SHAPE, A GROTESQUE THING THE MOONLIGHT CAN ONLY HINT AT...

AND WHEN THE DESERT SUN BLAZES OVER THE HORIZON...

MY MYSTERIOUS PROTECTOR WAS HERE AGAIN! BUT THOSE TRACKS... THEY'RE LIKE NOTHING HUMAN!

OR IS THIS THING THAT FOLLOWS ME REALLY SOME ULTIMATE KILLER-- SOME GRIM JEST OF RUBY RYDER?

TRAVELING ON ALONE INTO THE SHARP, COOL AIR OF THE MOUNTAINS THE MASKED MANHUNTER REACHES...

JEBEL AL DIKK! IS THIS THE TIGRESS' LAIR-- AT LAST?

16

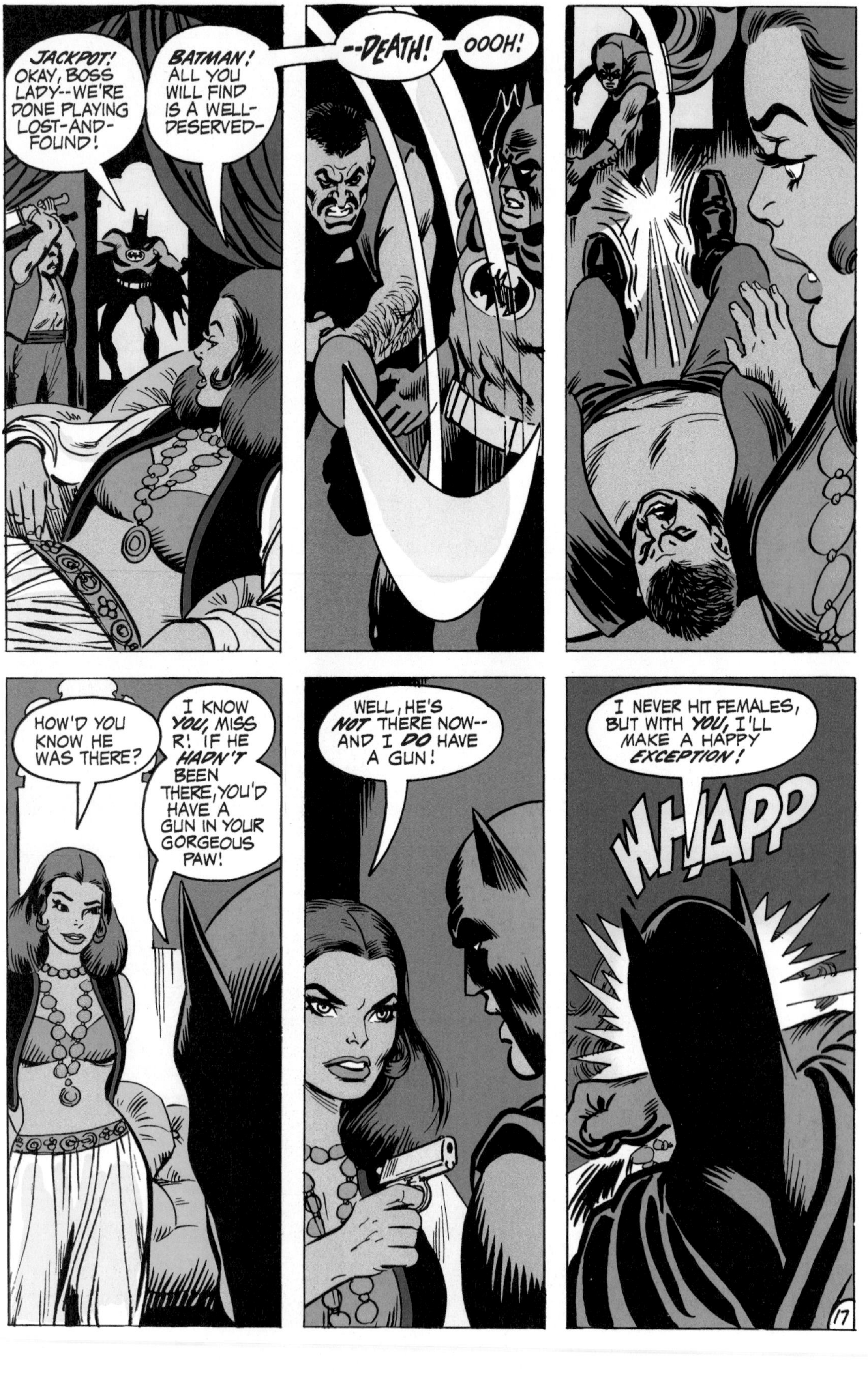
JACKPOT! OKAY, BOSS LADY--WE'RE DONE PLAYING LOST-AND-FOUND!
BATMAN! ALL YOU WILL FIND IS A WELL-DESERVED-
--DEATH!
OOOH!
HOW'D YOU KNOW HE WAS THERE?
I KNOW YOU, MISS R! IF HE HADN'T BEEN THERE, YOU'D HAVE A GUN IN YOUR GORGEOUS PAW!
WELL, HE'S NOT THERE NOW--AND I DO HAVE A GUN!
I NEVER HIT FEMALES, BUT WITH YOU, I'LL MAKE A HAPPY EXCEPTION!
WHAPP
17

FOR *BATMAN*, THE PURSUIT HAS BEEN LONG AND BIZARRE, BUT NOW FOR RUBY RYDER, JUSTICE IS SWIFT AND STRAIGHT...

MY CLIENT WAS A WOMAN *WRONGED!* KYLE MORGAN BROKE HER HEART! A WEAK, UNHAPPY FEMALE, SHE WAS TEMPORARILY DRIVEN *INSANE!*

TEMPORARY INSANITY? NONSENSE! SHE HIRED *BATMAN* TO FIND KYLE MORGAN, BRING HIM BACK TO FACE HER *REVENGE!* *BATMAN* WAS AN UNWITTING ACCOMPLICE! THIS "WEAK FEMALE" IS A VICIOUS, CUNNING *MURDERESS!*

ON THE SCALES OF JUSTICE, ALL ARE WEIGHED EQUALLY -- THE POOR AND LOWLY, THE HIGH AND MIGHTY! NOW, AFTER LONG ARGUMENTS...

WE FIND THE DEFENDANT... *GUILTY* OF MURDER IN THE FIRST DEGREE!

NO! YOU CAN'T CONDEMN *RUBY RYDER!*

HOW DOES IT FEEL, *BATMAN* -- TO SEND SUCH BEAUTY AND BRAINS TO OBLIVION?

SHE SHOT MORGAN IN COLD BLOOD....

HE *WASN'T* WHAT YOU THINK -- THERE WAS SOMETHING *WEIRD*... NOT ENTIRELY *HUMAN* ABOUT HIM!

AND AS THE MONTHS PASS...

I KEEP REMEMBERING HINTON'S WORDS -- *NOT ENTIRELY HUMAN*... AND THAT MYSTERIOUS THING THAT FOLLOWED ME ABROAD --

GOOD BLAZES... COULD IT BE --? GOT TO MOVE FAST... SO LITTLE TIME...

The Daily HUURU

RUBY RYDER LOSES APPEAL; DIES TONIGHT!

THAT NIGHT, IN STATE PRISON...

HERE SHE COMES! NOT SO CON- CEITED NOW!

YEAH, THE TIGRESS LOOKS PRETTY HUMBLE!

18

THAT GUY WITH THE STONEY FACE! HE'S THE *EXECUTIONER!*

IMAGINE-- HAVING TO PULL THE SWITCH ON A GORGEOUS DAME LIKE RUBY RYDER!

THEN, AS THE FLAMED-HAIRED BEAUTY APPROACHES DEATH'S EMBRACE...

PLEASE...I BEG YOU... LET ME *LIVE!* I'LL DO ANYTHING... GIVE EVERYTHING! I WANT TO *LIVE!*

SUDDENLY...

BATMAN!? THE DISTRICT ATTORNEY!

STOP! THIS EXECUTION IS A MOCKERY...

FOR THE MURDER VICTIM, KYLE MORGAN, IS ALIVE... AND IN THIS ROOM!

BUT MORGAN'S DEAD AND BURIED!

NOBODY HERE EVEN *LOOKS* LIKE HIM!

BATMAN'S FLIPPED!

WHA...?

THAT'S *HIM--* THE EXECUTIONER! HE'S KYLE MORGAN.... ALIAS... PLASTIC MAN!

HE'S ESCAPING!

19

OH, WHAT'S THE USE! THE GAME'S OVER!

YES, I AM *PLASTIC MAN,* THAT CLOWN I'D HOPED THE WORLD HAD LONG FORGOTTEN... AND I'M ALSO... *KYLE MORGAN!*

BATMAN, YOU WERE DEAD RIGHT!

WARDEN, THIS *REPRIEVE* IS SIGNED BY THE GOVERNOR!

AM I TO LIVE, *BATMAN?* THIS IS NO CRUEL JOKE...?

NO, RUBY! YOU CAN'T BE EXECUTED FOR A MURDER THAT *NEVER* HAPPENED!

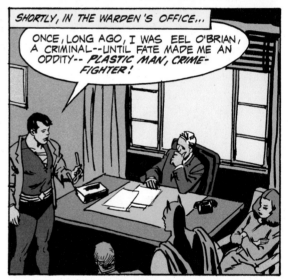

SHORTLY, IN THE WARDEN'S OFFICE...

ONCE, LONG AGO, I WAS EEL O'BRIAN, A CRIMINAL--UNTIL FATE MADE ME AN ODDITY-- *PLASTIC MAN, CRIME-FIGHTER!*

"BUT HOW I HATED BEING TRAPPED INSIDE THAT PLASTIC CLOWN! HOW I LONGED TO BE FREE...LEAD A NORMAL LIFE...KNOW A WOMAN'S LOVE..."

20

ONE DAY, THE SIMPLE SOLUTION CAME TO ME! I COULD BE *ANYONE I WANTED*!

SO I MADE MYSELF INTO A MAN NO WOMAN COULD RESIST--!

PLASTIC MAN *DIED*... KYLE MORGAN WAS *BORN*!

KYLE... IT *IS* YOU!

I MET YOU AND FELL IN LOVE! I BELIEVED YOU LOVED ME, *TOO*--BUT I SOON FOUND OUT YOU WERE CRUEL... SELFISH... POWER-MAD... LOVE MEANT *OWNING* PEOPLE--TO YOU!

"SO WHEN I WALKED OUT ON YOU, RUBY, YOU SENT *BATMAN* TO BRING ME BACK TO AVENGE YOURSELF FOR HAVING DARED SCORN YOU!"

POW

POW

I PAID JAKE ANGEL TO FAKE MY DEATH SO YOU AND THE WORLD WOULD THINK ME DEAD! BUT *BATMAN* WASN'T FOOLED--!

SO *THAT'S* WHY YOU ATTACKED ME IN THE PLANE WHEN THE FEVER WORE OFF-- YOU KNEW I WAS TAKING YOU TO FACE RUBY'S BULLETS!

LUCKILY, RUBY, YOUR RAGE CAUSED THOSE BULLETS TO HIT ONLY *PLASTIC* FLESH, NOT VITAL ORGANS! STILL, THE SHOCK MADE FEIGNING DEATH EASY! ESCAPING FROM THAT MAUSOLEUM WAS ALSO EASY!

THEN KYLE MORGAN'S "CORPSE" TRAILED ME ABROAD, SAVING ME FROM YOUR GOONS AND LEAVING THE *CRUCIAL* CLUE THAT LED TO YOUR CAPTURE!

YOU CAN'T PROVE *THAT*!

21

STILL DEFIANT? YOU WEREN'T SO HAUGHTY WITH DEATH NEAR! I TOOK THE EXECUTIONER'S PLACE TO SEE YOU *HUMBLED* FOR ONCE... *BEGGING* FOR MERCY! BUT I'D *NEVER* HAVE PULLED THE SWITCH!

I COULDN'T RISK *THAT!* ONCE I DEDUCED WHO YOU WERE, I HAD TO CONTACT THE GOVERNOR AND RUSH HERE TO STOP THE EXECUTION!

NOW THAT I KNOW WHO YOU *REALLY* ARE, I'M *RELIEVED!* IMAGINE ME, RUBY RYDER, MARRIED TO A... *FREAK!!*

YEAH, I GUESS IT WOULDN'T HAVE BEEN MANY LAUGHS!

GOOD NIGHT... AND GOODBYE, YOU... YOU... *MEN!*

MISS RYDER! YOU MAY FACE CHARGES FOR *ATTEMPTED* MURDER!

SEE MY LAWYERS-- I'LL BE TOO BUSY!

DO I SEE THOSE PLASTIC FEATURES DROOPING?

I *STILL* LOVE HER! BUT I'LL GET OVER IT! I'VE *GOT* TO--

WELL, WHAT DOES THE FUTURE HOLD FOR... *PLASTIC MAN?*

I DON'T KNOW, *BATMAN!* IN THIS WIDE, WILD WORLD OF TODAY, IS THERE ROOM FOR ME, OR AM I REALLY WHAT I FEARED--AN OUT-OF-DATE FREAK?

The End

ONLY FUTURE ISSUES OF *BRAVE* and *BOLD* WILL REVEAL *THAT!* READ IT EVER! MISS IT *NEVER!*

22

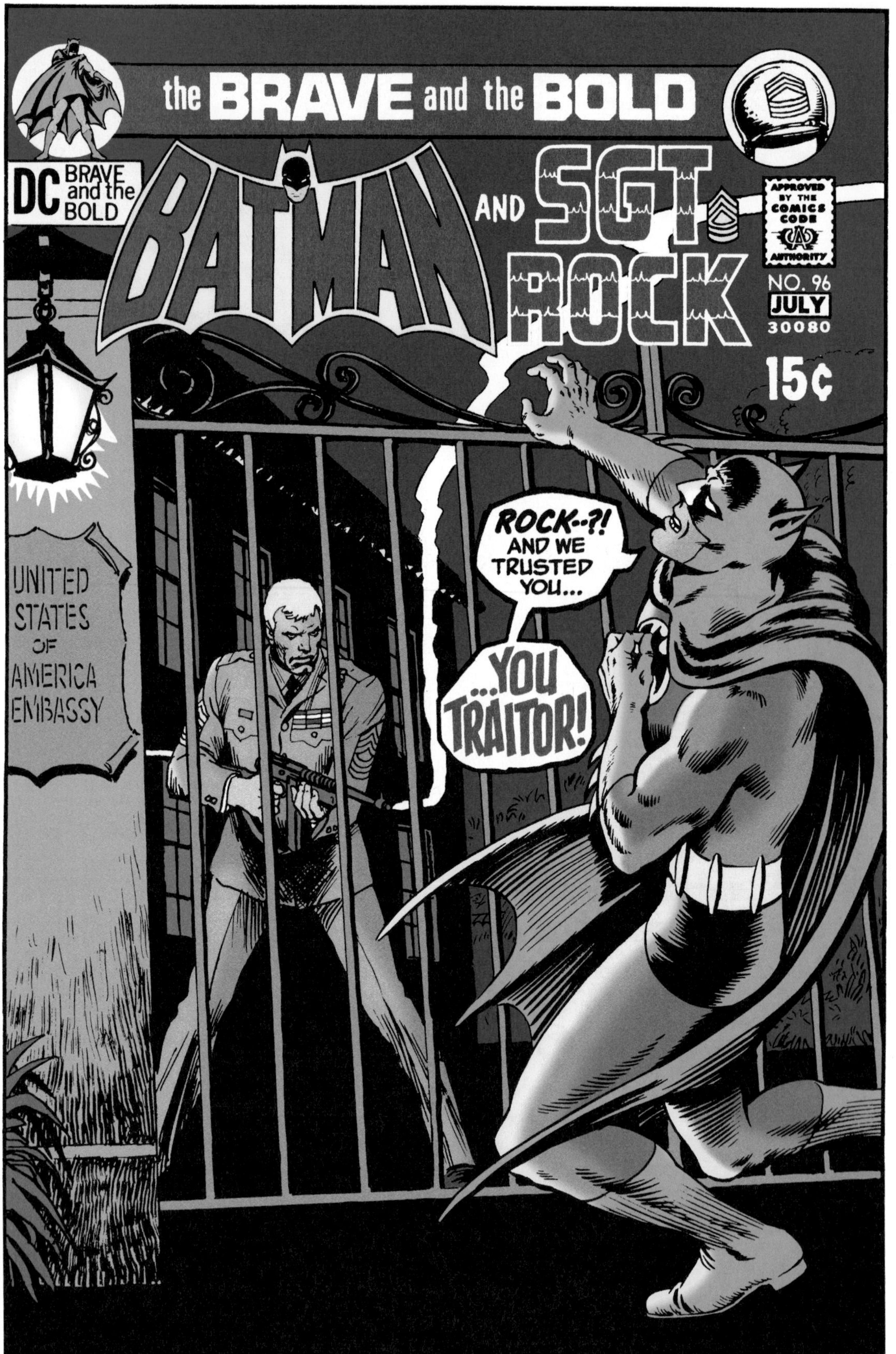
the BRAVE and the BOLD
DC BRAVE and the BOLD
BATMAN AND SGT. ROCK
APPROVED BY THE COMICS CODE AUTHORITY
NO. 96
JULY
30080
15¢
UNITED STATES OF AMERICA EMBASSY
ROCK--?! AND WE TRUSTED YOU...
...YOU TRAITOR!

THE SOFT NIGHT BATHES THE MARBLE BOULEVARDS OF A QUIET SOUTH AMERICAN CITY IN DISTORTING MOONLIGHT ...

KRRAASSHH

THE NEXT MOMENT...

A SHATTERING BURST OF AUTOMATIC FIRE --!

BUDDA-BUDDA!

AND ONCE MORE THE SOFT, DISTORTING MOONLIGHT CLOSES IN...

①

THE FOLLOWING DAY, IN WASHINGTON, D.C. ...

YOU MAY GO IN NOW, MR. WAYNE!

THE *SECRETARY OF STATE* WANTS TO SEE *ME* ON SUDDEN NOTICE! *WHY?* YOU'RE MOVING IN HIGH CIRCLES, BRUCIE-BOY!

AS THE WELL-KNOWN PLAYBOY-PHILANTHROPIST ENTERS THE IMPOSING OFFICE ...

MR. WAYNE-- GOOD OF YOU TO COME SO QUICKLY! YOU RECOGNIZE THE GENTLEMAN IN THE CHAIR...?

MR. PRES--! I...UH... DIDN'T EXPECT...

I'M HERE UNOFFICIALLY! PLEASE RELAX AND LISTEN CAREFULLY--!

YOU'VE SEEN THIS?

YES, SIR! AMBASSADOR ADAMS IS A FRIEND OF MINE! IT'S A TERRIBLE THING! ANY NEWS ON THE CASE?

HE WAS ABDUCTED BY THE *"COMPANEROS DE LA MUERTE"... THE COMPANIONS OF DEATH.*. THE TERRORIST GROUP THAT'S KIDNAPPED OTHER GOVERNMENTS' DIPLOMATS! THEIR RANSOM DEMAND WAS RECEIVED THIS MORNING--!

WE PRAY AMBASSADOR ADAMS CAN BE RANSOMED SAFELY, BUT HIS KIDNAPPING COMPLICATES *ANOTHER* PROBLEM ...

A TREATY WE'RE MAKING WITH THAT SAME GOVERNMENT-- A TREATY *VITAL* TO FREE WORLD SECURITY!

2

WE MUST APPOINT A TEMPORARY AMBASSADOR TO TAKE ADAMS' PLACE AND SIGN THE TREATY *BEFORE* THE DEADLINE! ALL OUR TOP DIPLO- MATS ARE IN CRUCIAL SITUATIONS, AND *CANNOT* BE TRANSFERRED!

THEREFORE, WITH THE CHIEF EXECUTIVE'S APPROVAL, I AM APPOINTING *YOU* TO THE POST! YOUR CREDENTIALS, *AMBASSADOR WAYNE!*

AMBASSADOR? WHY, MR. SECRETARY... THIS IS A GREAT SURPRISE ...AN *HONOR!*

AN HONOR I HOPE YOU WILL *ACCEPT!* AND TO MAKE *SURE* YOU ARE WELL PROTECTED AND HELP RESCUE AMBASSADOR ADAMS, WE ARE APPOINTING *ANOTHER* "ENVOY" TO ACCOMPANY YOU *SECRETLY--!*

B-BATMAN??!!

THIS IS THE TALE OF A WAR--*UNLIKE ANY OTHER EVER FOUGHT!* BUT JUST AS DEADLY, FOR STAKES JUST AS HIGH! THE HEADLINES DON'T TELL THE *HALF* OF IT! THE REAL AND SECRET STORY'S *HERE...NOW...* IN THE SHOCKER CALLED...

"THE STRIPED PANTS WAR!"

ART: NICK CARDY

STORY: BOB HANEY

③

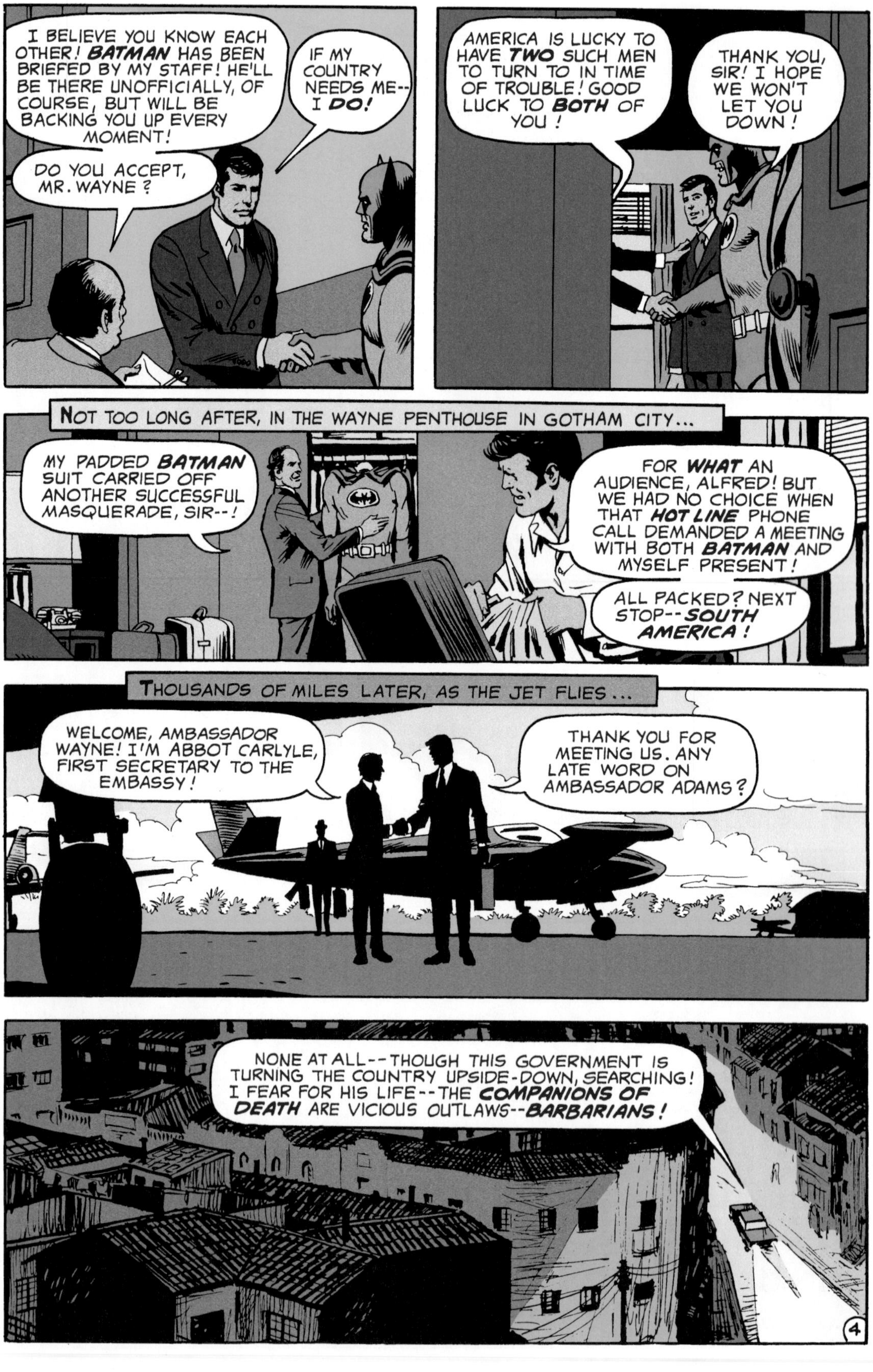
I BELIEVE YOU KNOW EACH OTHER! BATMAN HAS BEEN BRIEFED BY MY STAFF! HE'LL BE THERE UNOFFICIALLY, OF COURSE, BUT WILL BE BACKING YOU UP EVERY MOMENT!
DO YOU ACCEPT, MR. WAYNE?
IF MY COUNTRY NEEDS ME-- I DO!
AMERICA IS LUCKY TO HAVE TWO SUCH MEN TO TURN TO IN TIME OF TROUBLE! GOOD LUCK TO BOTH OF YOU!
THANK YOU, SIR! I HOPE WE WON'T LET YOU DOWN!
NOT TOO LONG AFTER, IN THE WAYNE PENTHOUSE IN GOTHAM CITY...
MY PADDED BATMAN SUIT CARRIED OFF ANOTHER SUCCESSFUL MASQUERADE, SIR--!
FOR WHAT AN AUDIENCE, ALFRED! BUT WE HAD NO CHOICE WHEN THAT HOT LINE PHONE CALL DEMANDED A MEETING WITH BOTH BATMAN AND MYSELF PRESENT!
ALL PACKED? NEXT STOP--SOUTH AMERICA!
THOUSANDS OF MILES LATER, AS THE JET FLIES...
WELCOME, AMBASSADOR WAYNE! I'M ABBOT CARLYLE, FIRST SECRETARY TO THE EMBASSY!
THANK YOU FOR MEETING US. ANY LATE WORD ON AMBASSADOR ADAMS?
NONE AT ALL--THOUGH THIS GOVERNMENT IS TURNING THE COUNTRY UPSIDE-DOWN, SEARCHING! I FEAR FOR HIS LIFE--THE COMPANIONS OF DEATH ARE VICIOUS OUTLAWS--BARBARIANS!
4

FELICIDAD, SEÑOR WAYNE! IT IS A BAD TIME FOR **BOTH** OUR COUNTRIES--!

YES, EL PRESIDENTE --BUT WHY CAN'T AMBASSADOR ADAMS BE **RANSOMED?**

THE **COMPAÑEROS DE LA MUERTE** DEMAND THE RELEASE FROM PRISON OF SEVERAL OF THEIR MEMBERS... BANDITS...ASSASSINS!

IF WE AGREE, OUR POLITICAL ENEMIES WOULD ACCUSE ME OF GIVING IN TO BLACKMAIL! THE GOVERNMENT WOULD FALL, AND CHAOS RESULT!

WE HAVE NO CHOICE BUT TO HOPE THE **POLICIA** AND THE **ARMY** CAN RESCUE SEÑOR ADAMS AND DESTROY THE **COMPAÑEROS!**

I SEE! AS YOU KNOW, **BATMAN** IS ALSO HERE--**SECRETLY!**

SI! THE GREAT **BATHOMBRE**--! WITH HIM, OUR HOPES ARE MUCH INCREASED!

YOUR EMBASSY, MR. AMBASSADOR-- THE PALACE OF THE GOVERNOR WHEN SPAIN OWNED THIS COUNTRY!

IMPRESSIVE-LOOKING PILE!

UNITED STATES OF AMERICA EMBASSY

LATER

MINUTES LATER, INSIDE...

OH, YES, OUR MILITARY ATTACHE AND CHIEF OF EMBASSY SECURITY... **SERGEANT ROCK, U.S. ARMY!**

ROCK?! YOU--?

WAYNE? **BRUCE WAYNE!?** MY OLD PLAYBOY SOJER!?

5

CAREFUL OF THE SERGEANT'S SHOULDER, MR. AMBASSADOR-- A GUILTY CONSCIENCE MUST MAKE IT HURT *TWICE* AS MUCH!

ROCK-- YOU OLD SON OF A GUN!

CARLYLE, WOULD YOU MIND LEAVING US?

INCREDIBLE, RUNNING INTO YOU AGAIN, *ROCK* -- BUT WHAT'S THE ARMY'S TOP-KICK DOING *HERE* WITH A SHOT-UP SHOULDER?

YOU KNOW, BRUCE KIDDO, *ROCK'S* A 30-YEAR MAN! EMBASSY DUTY'S A CUSHY DEAL FOR ANY OLD SOJER! NO MORE DIRTY FOXHOLES OR GETTIN' SHOT AT--!

BUT I WAS *WRONG!* I GOT NAILED GOOD, TRYIN' TO SAVE AMBASSADOR ADAMS FROM THOSE *COMPAÑERO* CREEPS AND FANCY-PANTS WON'T LET ME FORGET I *GOOFED* THE JOB!

I'M SURE YOU DID YOUR *BEST!*

YEAH, BUT WHO REMEMBERS YOUR *BEST?* SEE THESE SCARS? I GOT 'EM FIGHTIN' UNCLE SAM'S WARS! *THIS* ONE FROM A NAZI MINE IN NORTH AFRICA... *THIS* ONE, A SNIPER ON D-DAY'...

BOTH LEGS FULL OF GOODIES FROM A GOOK GRENADE IN KOREA! I'M CARRYIN' MORE SOUVENIRS THAN A RECRUIT RETURNIN' FROM HIS FIRST PATROL--!

YOU'VE GOT EVERY MEDAL IN THE BOOK TO SHOW YOUR COUNTRY'S GRATITUDE!

GRATITUDE! NOW THE ARMY SAYS I CAN'T RE-ENLIST WHEN MY HITCH IS UP NEXT MONTH! *SOME GRATITUDE!*

THERE MUST BE A REASON, *ROCK!*

6

SURE, THEY SAY IT'S BECAUSE I'M ALL *SHOT UP*--BUT I KNOW THE *REAL* REASON...I LET THE AMBASSADOR GET *SNATCHED!*

ONE FOUL-UP, AND ALL MY SCARS AND MEDALS DON'T MEAN A *THING!*

KEEP YOUR CHIN UP! THIS IS TOP-SECRET-- BUT *BATMAN'S* HERE, TOO, TO HELP FIND ADAMS!

THE *BAT GUY?* SURE, GREAT--HE WAS A BIG HELP BACK AT CHATEAUROUGE IN THE WAR!* MAYBE HE CAN HELP OLD *ROCK* AGAIN--BUT I *DOUBT* IT!

HE'S REALLY *BITTER*--BEATEN DOWN! NEVER THOUGHT I'D SEE THE *ROCK OF EASY* LIKE THIS!

*SEE *BRAVE AND THE BOLD* #84

SHORTLY...

TIME FOR *BATMAN* TO MAKE THE DIPLOMATIC SCENE! KEEP YOUR EARS AND EYES PEELED--!

I SHALL BE LIKE THE PROVERBIAL SPHINX, SIR-- SEEING AND KNOWING ALL-- SAYING NOTHING-!

MOMENTS LATER, TWILIGHT ENFOLDS THE CREATURE-OF-THE-NIGHT...

KEEP A GOOD GUARD, SOJER-- OR YOU'LL WISH YOU'D NEVER WAS BORN! WE DON'T WANT AMBASSADOR WAYNE GRABBED, *TOO!*

YESSIR, *SERGEANT ROCK,* SIR!

ROCK IN CIVVIES HURRYING AWAY SOME- WHERE... WELL, HE'S OFF DUTY!

NOW *BATMAN'S* GOT A DUTY--TO FIND WHERE THE *COMPAÑEROS* ARE HOLDING AMBASSADOR ADAMS BEFORE THEY KILL HIM ... IF THE GOVERNMENT DOESN'T MEET THEIR OUTRAGEOUS DEMANDS!

NOT LONG AFTER...

THIS IS WHERE THAT VAN RAMMED THE AMBASSADOR'S CAR...BUT *ROCK* SAID HE WAS SO BUSY TANGLING WITH THOSE THUGS, HE DIDN'T GET A GOOD LOOK AT IT!

7

NOW, A BIZARRE CRY SHATTERS THE STILLNESS OF THE DESERTED BOULEVARD...

HAH! TORO! HUH-HUHH! TORO!

WHAT IN BLAZES--? A BULLRING...AND SOMEBODY IN THERE--?

STEALTHILY, THE MASKED MANHUNTER ENTERS THE EMPTY AREA...

HUH-HAH! TORO!

WELL, I'LL BE--! A KID PRACTICING TO BE A MATADOR!

BATHOMBRE! MADRE MIA!

BUEÑAS NOCHES! PERHAPS YOU CAN HELP ME! HOW ARE YOU CALLED, AMIGO?

ANGEL... ANGEL CAMACHO!

DO YOU COME HERE OFTEN, ANGEL?

SI, EVERY NIGHT! I MUST PRACTICE IF I AM TO BECOME A GREAT TORERO!

THEN YOU WERE HERE THE NIGHT THE AMERICANO AMBASSADOR WAS TAKEN?

OH, SI! I HEARD SHOOTING AND RAN TO SEE! A BIG HOMBRE LAY WOUNDED AND A TRUCK WITH A DENT LIKE A BULL'S HORN ON IT RACING AWAY!

YOU COULD SEE A DENT AT THAT DISTANCE?

8

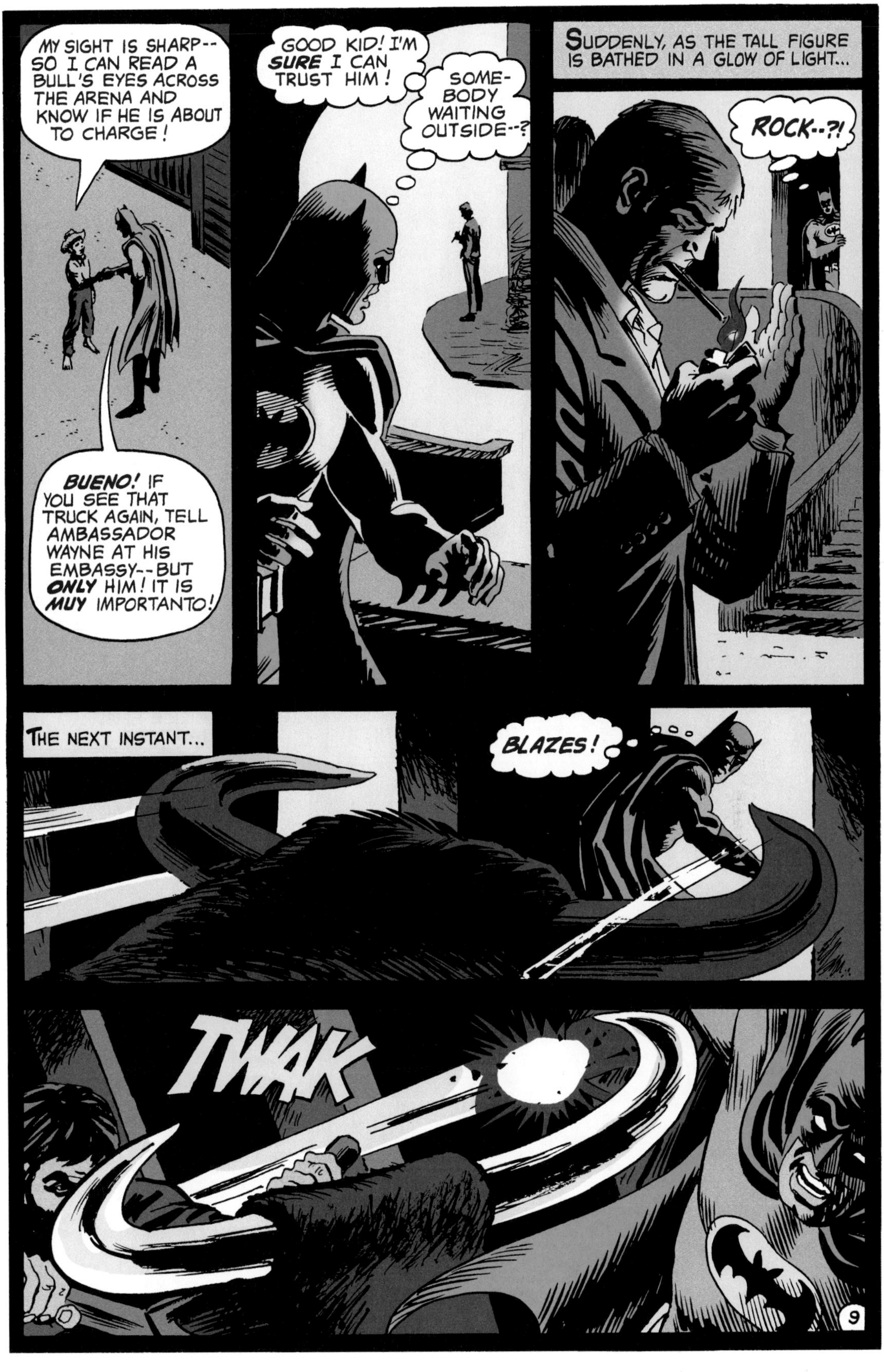
MY SIGHT IS SHARP-- SO I CAN READ A BULL'S EYES ACROSS THE ARENA AND KNOW IF HE IS ABOUT TO CHARGE!
BUENO! IF YOU SEE THAT TRUCK AGAIN, TELL AMBASSADOR WAYNE AT HIS EMBASSY--BUT ONLY HIM! IT IS MUY IMPORTANTO!
GOOD KID! I'M SURE I CAN TRUST HIM!
SOME-BODY WAITING OUTSIDE--?
SUDDENLY, AS THE TALL FIGURE IS BATHED IN A GLOW OF LIGHT...
ROCK--?!
THE NEXT INSTANT...
BLAZES!
TWAK
9

NOW NO ROARS OF TRIUMPH OR DEFEAT ECHO IN THE EMPTY ARENA--ONLY THE SILENCE OF DEATH...

SORRY ABOUT YOUR TORO RIG, ANGEL!

ES NADA! THAT I CAN FIX... WHICH IS MORE THAN I CAN SAY FOR THAT THIEF WHO STOLE IT!

NOT LONG AFTER, IN THE CENTRAL POLICE HEAD-QUARTERS...

YOUR WOULD-BE ASSASSIN, BATHOMBRE, WAS A MEMBER OF THE COMPAÑEROS! HE HAD A RECORD FOR EVERY KIND OF CRIME--!

HMMM, I WAS AFRAID OF THAT! BUT DID THAT GANG KNOW I'M HERE--OR DID THAT KILLER JUST HAPPEN BY?

AGAIN USING THE NIGHT FOR COVER, *THE CAPED CRUSADER* MOVES ACROSS THE SLEEPING CITY...

DAWN COMING -- GOT TO REACH THE EMBASSY! ONE BIG PUZZLER -- WHAT WAS *ROCK* DOING OUTSIDE THE ARENA RIGHT BEFORE THAT *COMPAÑERO* AMBUSHED ME?

THERE HE IS AGAIN -- IN THAT DOORWAY! HE'S LOOKING MY WAY --!?

SUDDENLY...

BOLAS!!

WHUNNG- A-WHUNNGG!

HIS LEGS ENTRAPPED BY THE WHIRLING BALLS, THE *MASKED MANHUNTER* TOPPLES LIKE A PAMPAS FOX...

THUD

WHAM

THE NEXT INSTANT...

WOK

WHACK

THROAT FEELS LIKE AN ELEPHANT STEPPED ON IT! THE *COMPANIONS OF DEATH* TWICE IN ONE NIGHT, THEY TRIED TO GET ME --!

THAT CLINCHES IT-- THE *COMPAÑEROS* WERE TOLD *BATMAN'S* HERE AND WERE READY FOR ME! AND THE ONLY ONE WHO KNOWS I'M HERE-- BESIDES THE AUTHORITIES-- IS A CERTAIN SIX-STRIPER NAMED *SERGEANT ROCK!*

BUT NOW AS *BATMAN* HURRIES TO RESUME HIS DIPLOMATIC IDENTITY, AT THE EMBASSY ...

HALT!

AMERICANO DOGS! EL AMBASSADOR ADAMS DIES AT NOON--UNLESS OUR DEMANDS ARE HONORED! LOS COMPAÑEROS DE LA MUERTE!

12

SHORTLY...

NOON—SO LITTLE TIME—AND I'VE GOT TO PLAY DIPLOMAT!

CARLYLE—! HAS SERGEANT ROCK RETURNED YET?

NO, MR. AMBASSADOR! HE'S LONG OVERDUE! IF YOU ASK ME, HE'S BEEN BEHAVING ODDLY OF LATE!

CAREFUL, CARLYLE! REMEMBER, ROCK'S A DECORATED HERO—!

HMMPH—WHY DID YOUR BIG HERO DRIVE AMBASSADOR ADAMS ON A DIFFERENT ROUTE THE NIGHT HE WAS ABDUCTED?

MR. WAYNE, SIR—!

I JUST FOUND THIS IN YOUR PRIVATE QUARTERS, SIR—YOUR BEDROOM HAS BEEN BUGGED!

WHAT? HAVE THE ENTIRE EMBASSY SEARCHED! WE MUST FIND THE LISTENING POST FOR THAT BUG!

AND AN IMMEDIATE SEARCH OF THE RAMBLING OLD STRUCTURE REVEALS...

MR. WAYNE, SIR, I'M AFRAID I'VE FOUND THE LISTENING POST—IN SGT. ROCK'S QUARTERS!

NOT LONG AFTER...

HUH? YOU FOUND THAT GIZMO IN ROCK'S ROOM? I NEVER SAW IT BEFORE!

LIKE YOU NEVER "SAW" BATMAN ALMOST GET KILLED TWICE LAST NIGHT? OR ARE THERE TWO AMERICAN SERGEANTS WITH MUGS LIKE UNMADE BEDS IN THESE PARTS?

ARE YOU ACCUSIN' ROCK OF BEIN A TRAITOR? WHY, YOU CRUMMY PLAYBOY—

AS AMBASSADOR, I'M IN COMMAND HERE!

COOL IT, ROCK! THAT'S AN ORDER!

13

AND, UNTIL FURTHER NOTICE, YOU'RE UNDER *HOUSE ARREST*-- DON'T LEAVE THE EMBASSY! UNDERSTOOD, SERGEANT?

UNDERSTOOD, MR. AMBASSADOR, SIR!!

HATE TO BELIEVE IT--BUT IT ALL FITS! HIS BITTERNESS AGAINST UNCLE SAM... HIS "FINGERING" *BATMAN*... THIS BUGGING DEVICE--LOOKS LIKE *ROCK'S SOLD OUT* HIS COUNTRY!

QUITE SOMETIME LATER...

I...I'M SORRY, *SERGEANT ROCK*, SIR! MY ORDERS ARE TO... NOT ALLOW YOU TO LEAVE THE EMBASSY GROUNDS!

SURE, SONNY! OLD *ROCK* UNDER- STANDS.! A GOOD SOJER *ALWAYS* FOLLOWS ORDERS... *RIGHT*?

BUT A GOOD SOJER ALSO...NEVER LETS *ANYBODY*...GET CLOSE ENOUGH...TO DO *THIS*!!

POW

I THOUGHT I TAUGHT HIM BETTER THAN *THAT!* CRUMMY RECRUITS THEY'RE SENDIN' THESE DAYS! GOOD THING OLD *ROCK'S* DONE WITH THIS MAN'S ARMY!

⒁

AND AS THE BURLY EX-BOSS OF *EASY* VANISHES...

THIS *PROVES* IT-- THE SERGEANT IS A TRAITOR--PART OF THE *COMPAÑERO* CONSPIRACY!

I'M AFRAID SO, CARLYLE! HE'S *SOLD OUT* HIS UNCLE SAM!

NOW TO TRY TO TRAIL HIM AS *BATMAN* IN HOPES HE'LL LEAD TO AMBASSADOR ADAMS *BEFORE TIME RUNS OUT--!*

AMBASSADOR WAYNE! I HAVE A MESSAGE FOR HIM!

IT'S ANGEL-- MY BULLFIGHTING PAL!

I'M WAYNE, SON! *QUE PASA?*

MY MESSAGE IS FOR YOUR EARS, *ALONE!*

THE *TRUCK*-- HE SPOTTED THE KIDNAP TRUCK HIDDEN NOT FAR FROM HERE! GOOD BOY!

TELL *BATHOMBRE* BZZZ - BZZZ - BZZZ .--.

SHORTLY, WHEN A BATTERED VAN PULLS OUT OF A GARAGE ...

THIS IS IT, ALL RIGHT-- IDENTIFYING DENT AND ALL! WONDER WHERE THEY'RE HEADING --?

QUICKLY, *BATMAN* PRODUCES A LISTENING DEVICE FROM HIS UTILITY BELT, AND...

YOU ARE READY, CARLOS?

SI! AM I NOT THE OFFICIAL *EXECUTIONER?* THE AMERICAN ADAMS DIES WHEN WE REACH THE EMBASSY!

WHAT? THE AMBASSADOR'S HIDDEN IN A FOREIGN EMBASSY!?

15

AS THE VAN PICKS UP SPEED AND MOVES ACROSS THE CITY...

NO WONDER THE ARMY AND POLICE COULDN'T FIND A TRACE OF HIM--AN EMBASSY IS *FOREIGN* SOIL AND *CAN'T* BE SEARCHED! SO THE *COMPAÑEROS* ARE WORKING WITH SOME OTHER COUNTRY--BUT *WHICH* ONE?

EMBASSY OF THE UNITED KINGDOM

BUT AS THE MINUTES GO BY...

WE'VE ALREADY PASSED A *DOZEN!* WHERE *ARE* THEY HEADING--?

YOU'LL GET THE SHOCKING ANSWER TO THAT, *BATMAN*--RIGHT NOW!!

DELIVERY FOR ZE KITCHEN, AMIGO! OUR PASSES!

HOLY HADES! HERE?! THE AMERICAN EMBASSY? I...I CAN'T BELIEVE IT!!

UNITED STATES OF AMERICA EMBASSY

OKAY-- ENTER!

AND AS THE VAN PULLS UP TO THE EMBASSY REAR DOOR...

IT'S ALMOST *NOON!* THAT GUY, CARLOS--HE'S THE ONE WHO TRIED TO GARROTE ME! MUST BE THE AMBASSADOR'S EXECUTIONER--!

WAITING A MOMENT, *THE MASKED MANHUNTER* QUICKLY FOLLOWS INTO THE EMBASSY'S LARGE, OLD KITCHEN...

FANTASTIC! A *SECRET* PASSAGEWAY BEHIND THE FIREPLACE... LEFT FROM THE DAYS WHEN THIS WAS THE GOVERNOR'S PALACE!

16

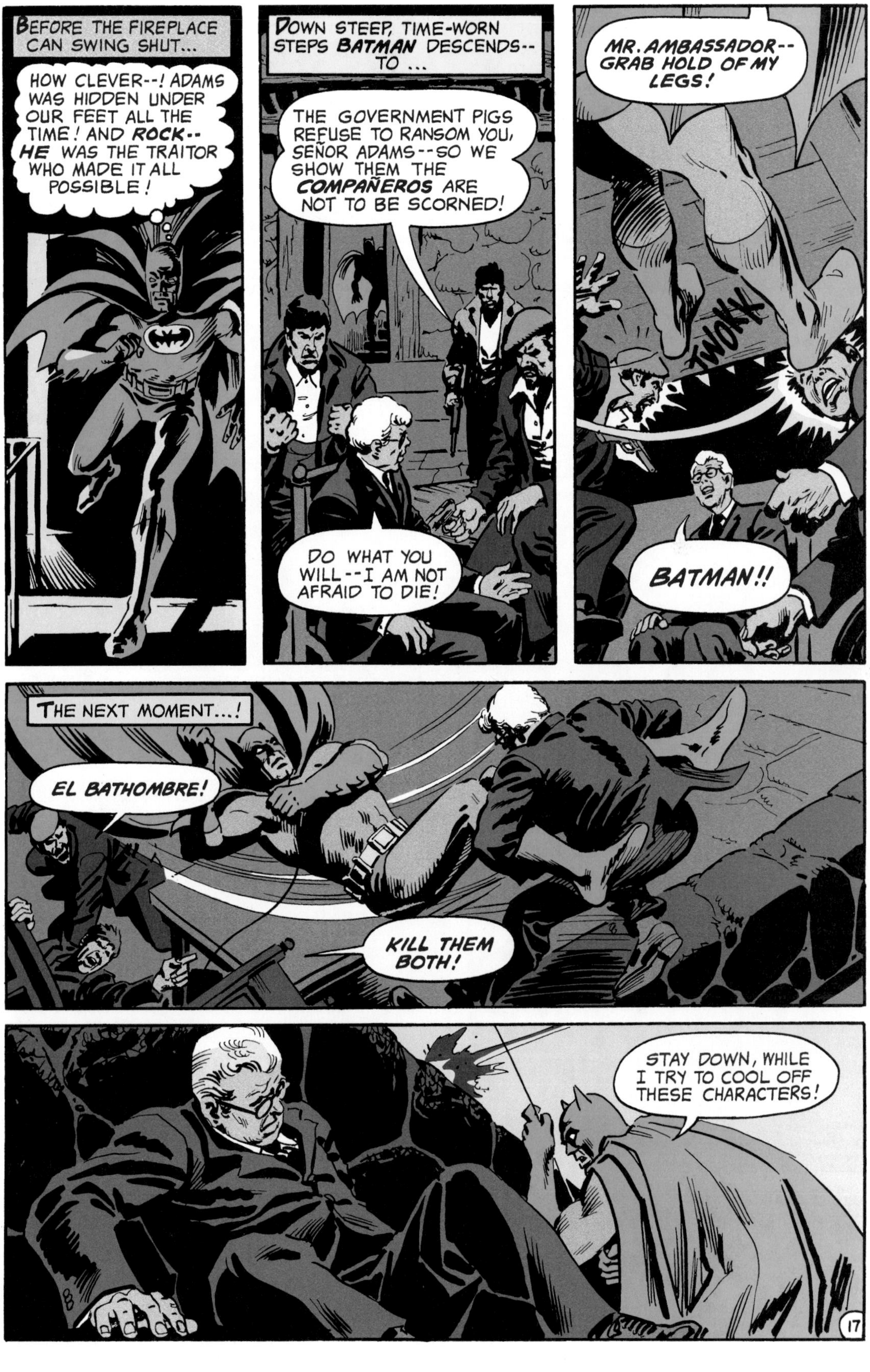
BEFORE THE FIREPLACE CAN SWING SHUT...
HOW CLEVER--! ADAMS WAS HIDDEN UNDER OUR FEET ALL THE TIME! AND ROCK-- HE WAS THE TRAITOR WHO MADE IT ALL POSSIBLE!
DOWN STEEP, TIME-WORN STEPS BATMAN DESCENDS-- TO ...
THE GOVERNMENT PIGS REFUSE TO RANSOM YOU, SEÑOR ADAMS--SO WE SHOW THEM THE COMPAÑEROS ARE NOT TO BE SCORNED!
DO WHAT YOU WILL--I AM NOT AFRAID TO DIE!
MR. AMBASSADOR-- GRAB HOLD OF MY LEGS!
TWOKK
BATMAN!!
THE NEXT MOMENT...!
EL BATHOMBRE!
KILL THEM BOTH!
STAY DOWN, WHILE I TRY TO COOL OFF THESE CHARACTERS!
17

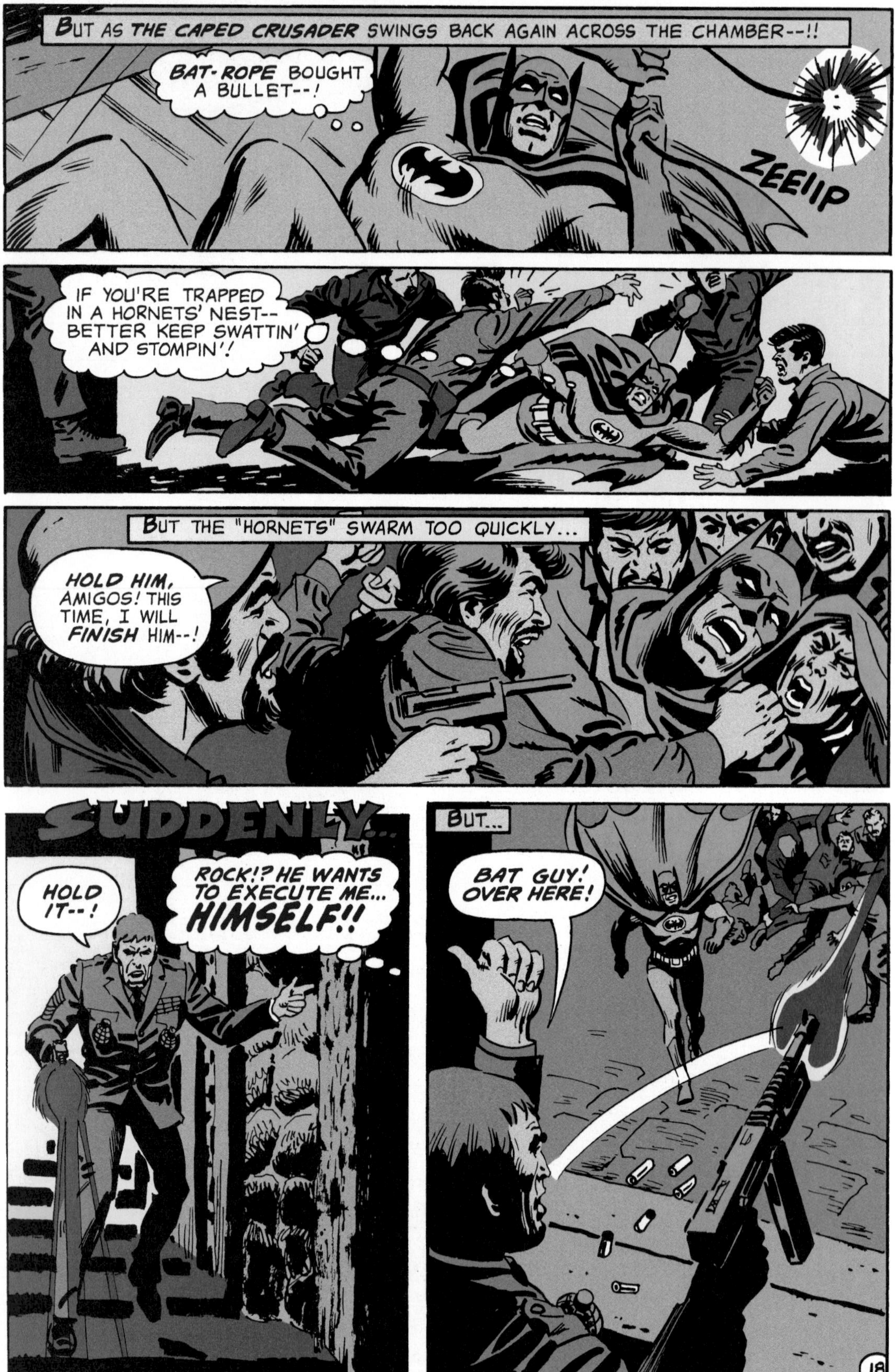

BUT AS THE CAPED CRUSADER SWINGS BACK AGAIN ACROSS THE CHAMBER--!!
BAT-ROPE BOUGHT A BULLET--!
ZEEIIP
IF YOU'RE TRAPPED IN A HORNETS' NEST-- BETTER KEEP SWATTIN' AND STOMPIN'!
BUT THE "HORNETS" SWARM TOO QUICKLY...
HOLD HIM, AMIGOS! THIS TIME, I WILL FINISH HIM--!
SUDDENLY...
HOLD IT--!
ROCK!? HE WANTS TO EXECUTE ME... HIMSELF!!
BUT...
BAT GUY! OVER HERE!
18

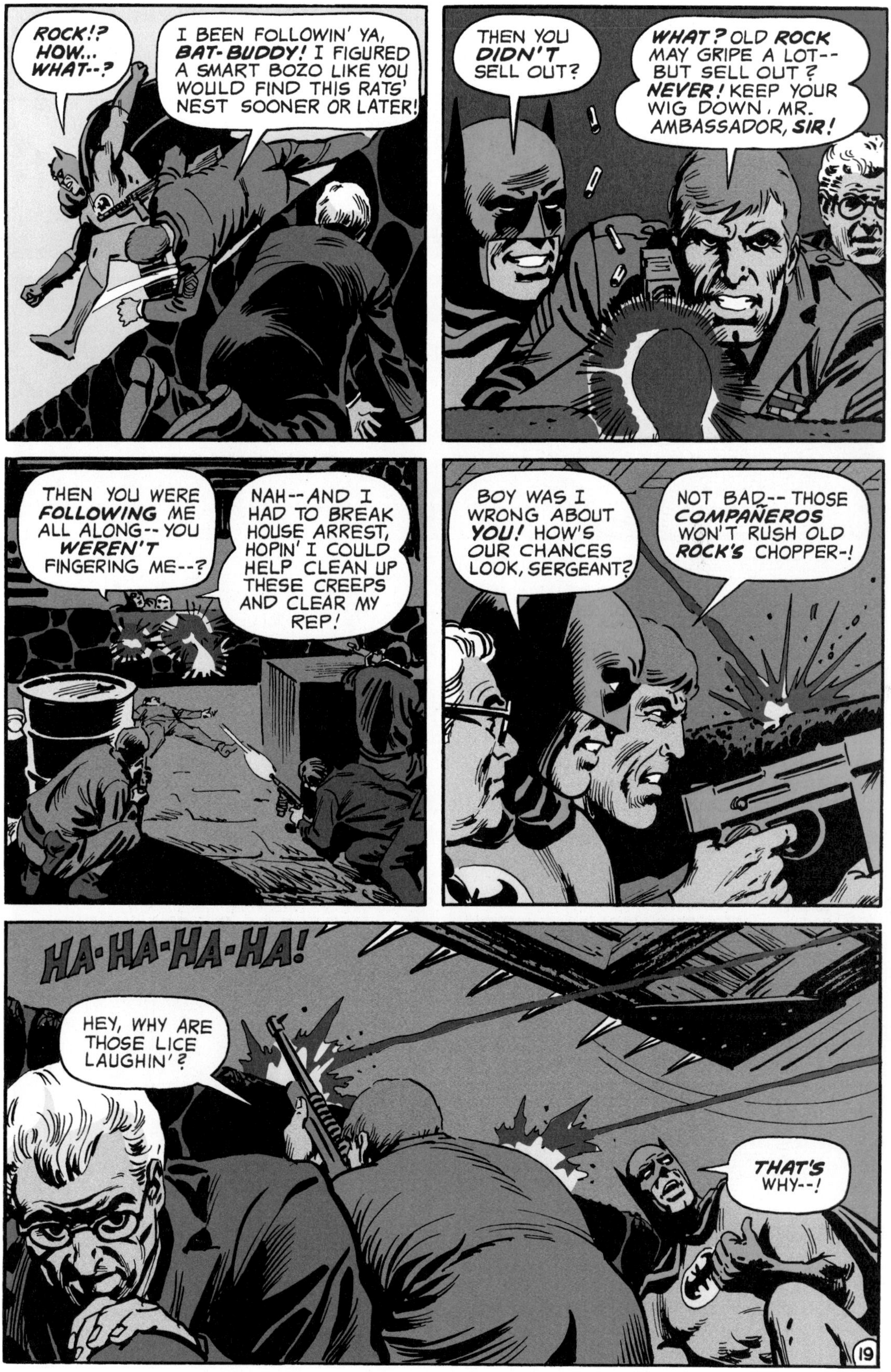
ROCK!? HOW... WHAT--?
I BEEN FOLLOWIN' YA, BAT-BUDDY! I FIGURED A SMART BOZO LIKE YOU WOULD FIND THIS RATS' NEST SOONER OR LATER!
THEN YOU DIDN'T SELL OUT?
WHAT? OLD ROCK MAY GRIPE A LOT--BUT SELL OUT? NEVER! KEEP YOUR WIG DOWN, MR. AMBASSADOR, SIR!
THEN YOU WERE FOLLOWING ME ALL ALONG--YOU WEREN'T FINGERING ME--?
NAH--AND I HAD TO BREAK HOUSE ARREST, HOPIN' I COULD HELP CLEAN UP THESE CREEPS AND CLEAR MY REP!
BOY WAS I WRONG ABOUT YOU! HOW'S OUR CHANCES LOOK, SERGEANT?
NOT BAD--THOSE COMPAÑEROS WON'T RUSH OLD ROCK'S CHOPPER-!
HA-HA-HA-HA!
HEY, WHY ARE THOSE LICE LAUGHIN'?
THAT'S WHY--!
19

As THE BIZARRE DEVICE SWINGS DOWN...

SHADES OF EDGAR ALLAN POE! MUST BE SOMETHING FROM THE OLD DAYS FOR WRINGING CONFESSIONS FROM PRISONERS!

RIGHT, MR. AMBASSADOR! IF WE RUN--THE *COMPAÑEROS* WILL *BLAST* US! IF WE *STAY*--WE'LL BE CUT TO *BITS!*

HA HA HA HA

BAT GUY! THAT OLD ELEVATOR GIZMO THERE-- IT'S GOTTA GO UP TO THE EMBASSY! TAKE THE AMBASSADOR AND BUG OUT--*I'LL* COVER YA!

AND LEAVE YOU HERE-- *ALONE?* FORGET IT, *ROCK!*

I'M RUNNIN' THIS SHOW! THE AMBASSADOR'S LIFE IS MY RESPONSIBILITY! SO TAKE 'IM AND GO! THAT'S AN ORDER, BUSTER!

THE EYES THAT HAVE FACED SO MANY ENEMIES...STIFFENED THE SPINES OF SCARED RECRUITS...CANNOT BE ARGUED WITH...

GO--GO-- GO!!

ROCK--HOLDING OFF THOSE KILLERS...TO SAVE US! AND *THAT'S* THE MAN THE ARMY WON'T LET RE-ENLIST!

20

A FEW SECONDS LATER, A DUSTY STOREROOM...

WE MADE IT, MR. AMBASSADOR-- BUT *WHERE* ARE WE?

IT'S A PART OF THE EMBASSY EVEN *I'M* NOT FAMILIAR WITH!

BUT *I* AM, GENTLEMEN! UNFORTUNATELY FOR YOU!

CARLYLE!? YOU... *YOU'RE* THE SPY-- THE *TRAITOR!*

EXACTLY! I TRIED TO MAKE HEROIC *SGT. ROCK* APPEAR TO HAVE BETRAYED DEAR UNCLE SAM-- BUT IT DOESN'T MATTER ANYMORE!

BOTH OF YOU DIE... *NOW--!*

BATMAN MEASURES THE DISTANCE BETWEEN HIMSELF AND THE GUN-- KNOWING IT IS TOO FAR, *TOO FAR!* SUDDENLY...

BLAM

ALFRED?

MR. WAYNE TOLD ME TO KEEP MY EYES AND EARS OPEN AND *YOU* KNOW I ALWAYS FOLLOW HIS ORDERS!

ROCK-- HE'S STILL DOWN THERE-- NEEDS HELP!

MR. AMBASSADOR! GET ON THE PHONE-- AUTHORIZE THE POLICE TO ENTER THE EMBASSY AND CLEAN UP THE *COMPAÑEROS!*

AT ONCE, *BATMAN!*

AT THIS MOMENT, BELOW...

GIZMO'S SO LOW I CAN'T PUT MY HEAD UP TO FIRE! ONLY ONE THING TO TRY...HANG A PINEAPPLE ON IT... *IF* I CAN!

21

LIKE A BLIND MAN TRYING TO THREAD A NEEDLE, *THE ROCK OF EASY* THRUSTS THE GRENADE IN THE PATH OF THE SLASHING, SWINGING SPIKES, AND ...

DID IT!!

*T*HE NEXT MOMENT, AS THE CONTRAPTION SWINGS OUT ABOVE THE *COMPAÑEROS*...

BLAAM

LOOK OUT!

*T*HEN SILENCE-- BROKEN BY THE VOICE OF A MAN CLOSE TO TEARS...

ROCK! ROCK!

TOO LATE--! HE DID IT... FINISHED THOSE *COMPAÑEROS*...

BUT... BOUGHT IT HIMSELF!

HEY, *BAT-BUDDY*-- DON'T GO BLOWIN' TAPS OVER ME YET! REMEMBER, OLD SOJERS NEVER DIE-- THEY JUST RE-ENLIST!

ROCK!! YOU SON OF A--!

*S*OME TIME LATER...

WELL, *ROCK*, THE TREATY WAS SIGNED THIS MORNING-- MY MISSION HERE IS OVER!

YEAH, AND THE ARMY TOOK ME BACK FOR ANOTHER HITCH-- THANKS TO YOU AND THE *BAT-GUY!*

GUESS THE GOOD GUYS WON ANOTHER ONE!

THE END

22

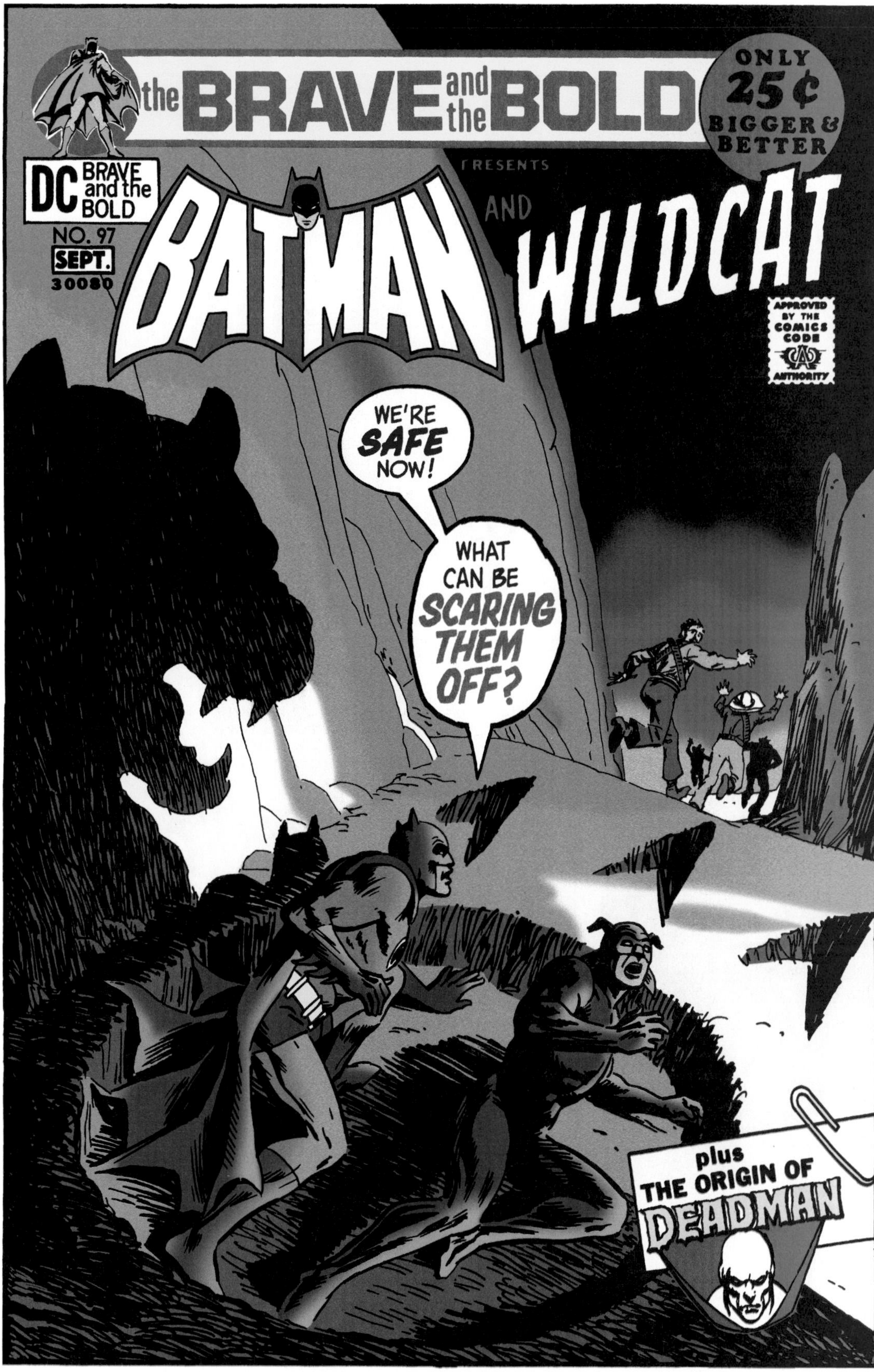

the BRAVE and the BOLD
ONLY 25¢ BIGGER & BETTER
DC BRAVE and the BOLD
NO. 97
SEPT.
30080
PRESENTS
BATMAN AND WILDCAT
APPROVED BY THE COMICS CODE AUTHORITY
WE'RE SAFE NOW!
WHAT CAN BE SCARING THEM OFF?
plus THE ORIGIN OF DEADMAN

ACAPULCO! MEXICO'S JET SET PLAYGROUND ON THE PACIFIC, WHERE ATOP TOWERING CLIFFS A SLIM FIGURE POISES...

NEARBY, TOURISTS GAPE IN AWE OF THE INTENDED DIVE, AMONG THEM A TALL MAN WHOSE TIGERISH MUSCLES RIPPLE BENEATH WELL-TAILORED CLOTH...

SUDDENLY, HIS KEEN EYES PICK OUT SOMETHING...*SOMEONE*... FARTHER DOWN THE RUGGED CLIFF FACE...

NOW AS THE LONG PACIFIC SWELL SURGES INTO THE NARROW GORGE BETWEEN THE CLIFFS...

...FILLING THE ROCKY DEFILE DEEPER...*DEEPER*... THE SLIM FIGURE *DIVES!*

BUT OFF TO ONE SIDE, FARTHER DOWN, ANOTHER FIGURE *ALSO* DIVES... *THE BATMAN!*

1

USING HIS CAPE LIKE WINGS, ANGLING HIS HURTLING BODY, STRETCHING FOR EVERY INCH OF GLIDE....

BANG

WHUNK

NOW, TWO BODIES MEET THE SEA, ONE CLEAVING IT IN PERFECT CONTROL....

THE OTHER PLUMMETING INTO IT LIKE A WOUNDED BIRD....

KER-WHOOSH!

LONG MOMENTS LATER...

WHEW! CLOSE--BUT NO CIGAR! LUCKILY THE OLD BAT-SUIT'S DRIP-DRY...BUT I'D BETTER CHANGE BACK TO BRUCE WAYNE AND THE FUN-IN-THE-SUN TOURIST BIT!

2

SHORTLY...

LUIS MERCADO... RISKING HIS YOUNG LIFE FOR A HATFUL OF PESOS... AND *PRETENDING* THAT WOULD-BE KILLER WAS NEVER THERE--?

SOON, IN THE WORKING-- CLASS QUARTER OF ACAPULCO, IN THE DINGY ALLEYS BEHIND THE GARISH, BEACHFRONT LUXURY HOTELS...

HE ALONE MUST HAVE SEEN *BATMAN* SAVE HIS LIFE--BUT HE'S IGNORING THAT, TOO! AND WHY IS ANYONE GUNNING FOR HIM? *WHY?*

WAIT A MINUTE, BRUCIE-BOY-- THAT POSTER... THAT COSTUME...IT'S *GOT* TO BE...

FIGHTING TONIGHT
EL TIGRE!

XOTOPETL ARENA

...WILDCAT??!

LUIS! HE'S BEEN JUMPED!

CORRIDA DE TOROS

NOW AS KNIVES FLASH IN THE LIMPID MEXICAN DUSK, A BRAVE BOY STANDS AT BAY--AND A MAN FROM FAR NORTHERN HAUNTS COMES FACE TO FACE WITH THE MYSTERY, THE MASTERY OF THE PAST, MEETING AN OLD ALLY, FINDING NEW FOES, AS FATE FLAUNTS *THE BATMAN* WITH...

BATMAN and WILDCAT

..."THE SMILE OF CHOCLOTAN!"

PENCILS: BOB BROWN   INKS: NICK CARDY   STORY: BOB HANEY

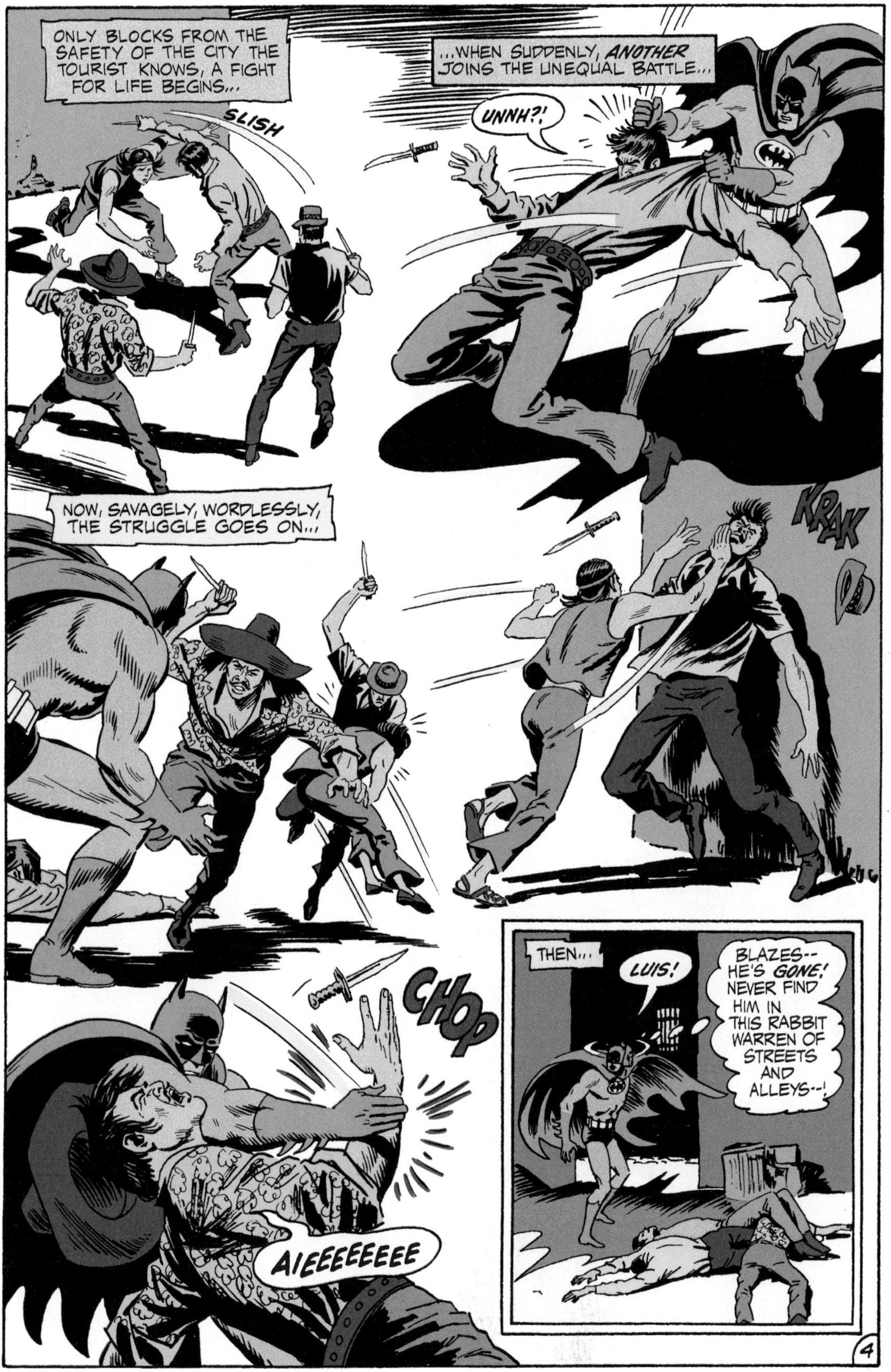
ONLY BLOCKS FROM THE SAFETY OF THE CITY THE TOURIST KNOWS, A FIGHT FOR LIFE BEGINS...
SLISH
...WHEN SUDDENLY, ANOTHER JOINS THE UNEQUAL BATTLE...
UNNH?!
NOW, SAVAGELY, WORDLESSLY, THE STRUGGLE GOES ON...
KRAK
CHOP
AIEEEEEEEE
THEN...
LUIS!
BLAZES-- HE'S GONE! NEVER FIND HIM IN THIS RABBIT WARREN OF STREETS AND ALLEYS--!
4

BUT I'VE GOT *ANOTHER* MYSTERY TO LOOK INTO, ANYWAY-- JUST WHAT IS MY OLD PAL *WILDCAT* DOING IN MEXICO FIGHTING FOR PESOS AS... *EL TIGRE?!*

EL TIGRE

NOT LONG AFTER, IN AN ANCIENT AMPHITHEATRE JUST OUTSIDE TOWN...

THESE FIGHT FANS FOREFATHERS WATCHED HUMAN SACRIFICE HERE-- HOPE THEY DON'T REVIVE THE CUSTOM...*TONIGHT!*

EL TIGRE VS. EL MACH...

THEN, AS THE FIGHTERS ARE INTRODUCED...

EL TIGRE!

YAYYYYY BRAVO OLE EL TIGRE

IT'S *WILDCAT*, ALL RIGHT... AND HIS SECOND IS *LUIS MERCADO!*

IT'S *TED GRANT* UNDER THAT COSTUME! STILL THE MASTER BOXING STYLIST--

BUT AS THE FIRST ROUND ENDS...

EL MACHETE'S CLUMSY-- BUT THAT CANE-CUTTING PUNCH OF HIS COULD CHOP TED DOWN...!

HEY! THAT GUY... SLIPPING SOMETHING INTO *WILDCAT'S* WATER--?

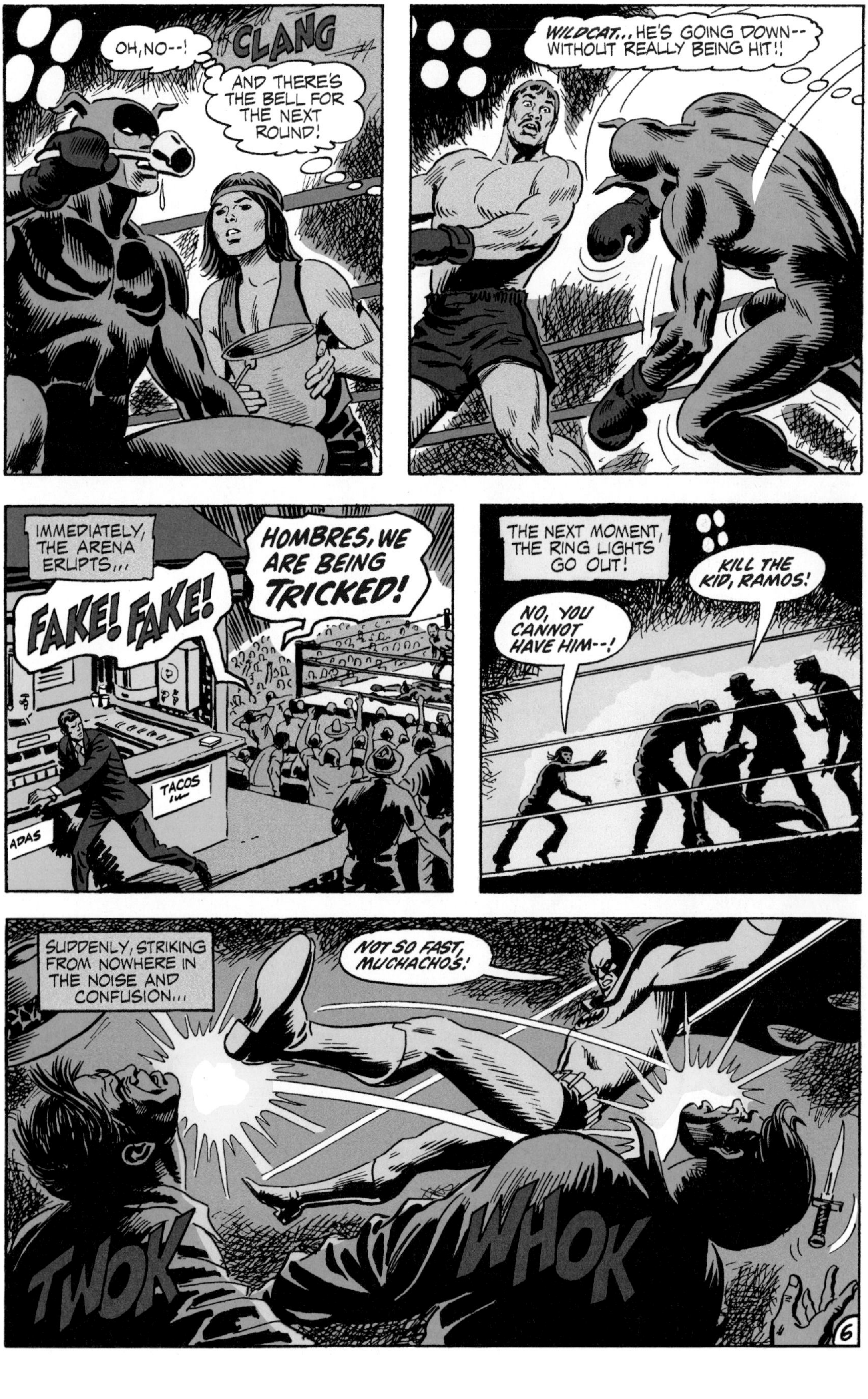
OH, NO--!
CLANG
AND THERE'S THE BELL FOR THE NEXT ROUND!
WILDCAT... HE'S GOING DOWN-- WITHOUT REALLY BEING HIT!!
IMMEDIATELY, THE ARENA ERUPTS...
HOMBRES, WE ARE BEING TRICKED!
FAKE! FAKE!
TACOS
ADAS
THE NEXT MOMENT, THE RING LIGHTS GO OUT!
KILL THE KID, RAMOS!
NO, YOU CANNOT HAVE HIM--!
SUDDENLY, STRIKING FROM NOWHERE IN THE NOISE AND CONFUSION...
NOT SO FAST, MUCHACHOS!
TWOK
WHOK
6

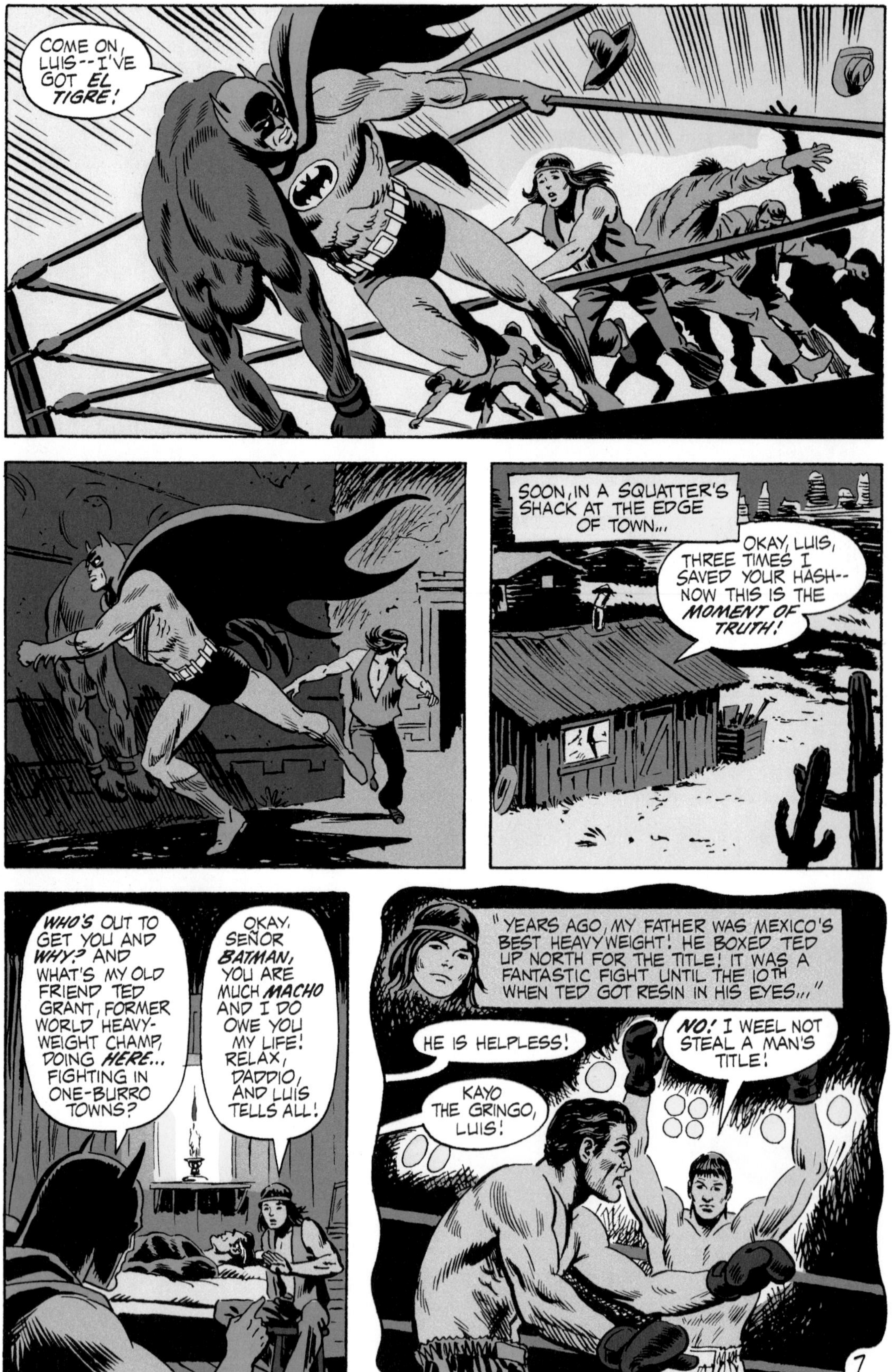
COME ON, LUIS--I'VE GOT EL TIGRE!
SOON, IN A SQUATTER'S SHACK AT THE EDGE OF TOWN...
OKAY, LUIS, THREE TIMES I SAVED YOUR HASH--NOW THIS IS THE MOMENT OF TRUTH!
WHO'S OUT TO GET YOU AND WHY? AND WHAT'S MY OLD FRIEND TED GRANT, FORMER WORLD HEAVY-WEIGHT CHAMP, DOING HERE... FIGHTING IN ONE-BURRO TOWNS?
OKAY, SEÑOR BATMAN, YOU ARE MUCH MACHO AND I DO OWE YOU MY LIFE! RELAX, DADDIO, AND LUIS TELLS ALL!
"YEARS AGO, MY FATHER WAS MEXICO'S BEST HEAVYWEIGHT! HE BOXED TED UP NORTH FOR THE TITLE! IT WAS A FANTASTIC FIGHT UNTIL THE 10TH WHEN TED GOT RESIN IN HIS EYES..."
HE IS HELPLESS!
NO! I WEEL NOT STEAL A MAN'S TITLE!
KAYO THE GRINGO, LUIS!
7

"MY FATHER WAS MUCH *MACHO*--MUCH MAN--! THE FIGHT WENT THE DISTANCE AND TED RETAINED HIS TITLE ON A DRAW DECISION! THEY BECAME GREAT FRIENDS..."

A YEAR AGO MY FATHER ASKED TED TO HELP HIM IN HIS LIFE'S GREAT DREAM... TO FIND... *CHOCLOTAN!*

CHOCLOTAN? "HE WHO *SMILES*"? THE LEGENDARY LOST GOD THAT'S MEXICO'S MOST IMPORTANT ARCHEOLOGICAL TREASURE... *IF* IT EXISTS?

IT *DOES* EXIST--BECAUSE MY FATHER AND TED *FOUND* IT!

BUT THERE IS A *CRIMINAL RING* THAT COLLECTS AND STEALS MEXICO'S ANCIENT TREASURES... AND SMUGGLES THEM TO OTHER COUNTRIES FOR *MUCHO DINERO!*

NOBODY KNOWS THE RING'S LEADER--HE IS SIMPLY CALLED *SEÑOR EL GRANDE*... *MR. BIG!* WHEN TED AND MY FATHER WENT AFTER CHOCLOTAN, HIS GOONS TRAILED THEM--!

TED'S AWAKE... SEEMS OKAY!

I GOT A CODED RADIO MESSAGE FROM THEM, SAYING THEY'D *FOUND* THE GOD... BUT NOT *WHERE!*

THEN THEY WERE AMBUSHED! MY FATHER WAS KILLED... AND TED GOT A BULLET CREASE ON THE HEAD AND *LOST HIS MEMORY!*

AMNESIA? NO WONDER HE DOESN'T KNOW ME!

SI! I FOUND HIM WANDERING IN THE MOUNTAINS! SINCE THEN, I'VE BEEN TRYING TO PROTECT HIM... HIDE HIM FROM *EL GRANDE!*

8

NOW I UNDERSTAND EVERYTHING! THOSE GOONS HAVE BEEN TRYING TO KNOCK YOU OFF--GRAB TED--MAKE HIM *LEAD* THEM TO CHOCLOTAN!

SI! THEY KNOW I WOULD NEVER BETRAY TED-- SO I AM BEST DEAD! EVIDENTLY, *EL GRANDE* IS UNAWARE TED HAS LOST HIS MEMORY!

MEANTIME, I DIVE FOR A LIVING... TED FIGHTS AS *EL TIGRE!* THE COSTUME I FOUND IN HIS BELONGINGS GAVE ME THE IDEA!

LUIS DOESN'T KNOW TED'S *OTHER* IDENTITY AS *WILDCAT!* I ONLY LEARNED IT DURING OUR FIRST JOINT ADVENTURE, WHEN HE VANISHED TILL NOW! *

*SEE *BRAVE & BOLD* #88

LUIS, I'M NOT HERE AS A TOURIST! YOUR GOVERNMENT INVITED ME TO INVESTIGATE THAT SMUGGLING RACKET! NOW HERE'S MY PROPOSITION...

WHAT SAY *WE* TEAM UP TO FIND CHOCLOTAN? IT'S THE PERFECT THING TO SMOKE OUT *EL GRANDE*-- AND IF WE DO FIND IT, WE'VE FULFILLED YOUR FATHER'S DREAM!

THE GREAT *BAT-HOMBRE* ALONG...? *BEAUTIFUL!*

THE FOLLOWING DAY...

NICE RIG! YOU MUST BE HOLDING *MUCHO* BREAD, *BAT-HOMBRE!*

I'VE GOT ENOUGH! NOW GET TED ABOARD AND LET'S GET GOING... *TO CHOCLOTAN COUNTRY!*

9

AND AS THE VEHICLE HEADS FOR THE DISTANT SIERRA MADRE...

DO YOU THINK TAKING TED BACK TO THE MOUNTAINS WILL *WORK?*

IT'S A *GAMBLE*-- BUT SOMETIMES RETURNING AN AMNESIAC TO THE PLACE HE LOST HIS MEMORY *RESTORES* IT!

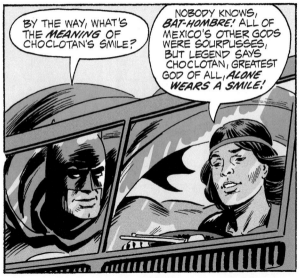

BY THE WAY, WHAT'S THE *MEANING* OF CHOCLOTAN'S SMILE?

NOBODY KNOWS, *BAT-HOMBRE!* ALL OF MEXICO'S OTHER GODS WERE SOURPUSSES, BUT LEGEND SAYS CHOCLOTAN, GREATEST GOD OF ALL, *ALONE WEARS A SMILE!*

NEXT DAY, ALONG A HIGH, ARID PLATEAU...

HOLD IT, LUIS-- WE'RE SURROUNDED!

IT'S OKAY, *BAT-HOMBRE!* THOSE VAQUEROS WON'T HURT US! IT'S DAD'S OLD FRIEND-- *EL SORDO!*

LUIS! LUIS, SON OF MY DEAR, DEAD FRIEND! WHAT MAKES YOU CROSS MY LANDS, MUCHACHO?

MY AMIGO, *BAT-HOMBRE,* AND TED GRANT-- GO WITH ME TO FIND CHOCLOTAN!

AAAH, YOU GO TO FINISH WHAT YOUR FATHER GAVE HIS LIFE FOR--! *BRAVA,* LUIS, *BRAVA!* BUT THE WAY IS LONG... THE SAME BANDIDOS WHO KILLED HIM MAY LIE IN WAIT!

10

BUT WITH *BAT-HOMBRE* I FIGURE I'VE GOT A CHANCE!

OF COURSE, BUT *I* KNOW THE *SIERRA MADRE!* LET ME COME WITH YOU... AS GUIDE AND PROTECTOR! I AM BORED WITH RANCHING AND FIESTAS!

YOU GUIDE US? I WOULD BE *HONORED!*

CHOCLOTAN MUST BE FOUND AND PUT SAFELY IN OUR COUNTRY'S MUSEUM -- A NATIONAL TREASURE FOR ALL MEXICANS TO BE PROUD OF!

SHORTLY, THE JOURNEY CONTINUES, WITH AN ADDED PASSENGER...

YOU OWN *ALL* THIS REAL ESTATE, EL SORDO?

SI--I WAS LUIS' FATHER'S FIGHT MANAGER! WE MADE MUCHO MONEY TOGETHER, AND I BOUGHT THIS RANCHO WITH MY SHARE!

THIS BOY IS LIKE A SON TO ME! I WOULD DO *ANYTHING* TO HELP HIM, EH, MUCHACHO?

NOW, KEEP YOUR EYES PEELED-- FOR ANY SIGNS OF CHOCLOTAN!

BUT AS HOURS... AND DAYS PASS...

WE'VE COME *HUNDREDS* OF MILES--BUT THOSE MOUNTAINS DON'T LOOK ANY CLOSER!

IT'S A BIG COUNTRY! I DID FIND TED IN THOSE MOUNTAINS, SO WE MUST BE IN THE RIGHT GENERAL DIRECTION!

11

IF ONLY TED WOULD REMEMBER *SOMETHING,* BUT HE'S HARDLY SAID A WORD SINCE WE STARTED! POOR GUY--JUST STARES OUT AT THE COUNTRYSIDE!

ABRUPTLY...

LUIS! HERE-- STOP HERE!

OKAY, AMIGO! WHAT IS IT?

THIS PLACE-- I *KNOW* IT! BUT UP THERE ON THE MESA... *YOU MUST GO UP THERE!*

UP *THERE?* A STICKY-FOOTED LIZARD COULDN'T SCALE THAT CLIFF!

MAYBE *I* CAN! IT'S NOT MUCH TOUGHER THAN THE ONES I CLIMB AND DIVE FROM BACK IN ACAPULCO!

BE CAREFUL, LUIS!

UP...UP THE SHEER ROCK WALL INCHES THE LITHE LUIS...

THAT KID IS ONE BRAVE HOMBRE!

SI, LIKE HIS *PADRE!*

12

AND AGONIZING MINUTES LATER...

HE *MADE* IT! NOW ALL HE HAS TO DO IS MAKE IT DOWN!

SOON, AFTER AN EQUALLY PERILOUS DESCENT...

NICE GOING, LUIS! WHAT DID YOU SEE UP THERE BESIDES A GREAT VIEW?

PLENTY! THE TRAIL TO CHOCLOTAN IS WHAT I SAW--AND WE ARE STANDING RIGHT *IN* IT!

YOU JOKE?

NO--FROM UP THERE I COULD SEE THIS DEPRESSION WE'RE IN IS A GIANT JAGUAR PRINT--DUG OUT BY ANCIENT PEOPLE, THE WORSHIPPERS OF CHOCLOTAN!

I DON'T GET IT, BUT TED'S NODDING *AGREEMENT!*

SIMPLE, *BAT-HOMBRE!* THE JAGUAR WAS CHOCLOTAN'S SYMBOL! THERE ARE OTHER GIANT PRINTS AHEAD--DUG BY HUMAN HAND--TRACKS-- *POINTING THE WAY* TO THE GOD'S LOCATION!

FANTASTICO!

TED *SENSED* WE WERE NEAR THE TRACKS--HE AND MY FATHER MUST'VE FOUND THEM BEFORE! BUT ONLY FROM HIGH UP CAN YOU SEE THEM! *THAT WAY*--TO THE MOUNTAINS WE MUST GO!

13

NOW, AS THE SEARCHERS PUSH ON, SURE OF THEIR DIRECTION....

WHAT IS IT, SORDO?

THAT *DUST*, AMIGOS! I HAVE BEEN WATCHING IT FOR SOME TIME! IT MOVES AS WE DO!

HORSES...OR A CAR! NO DOUBT OF IT, WE ARE BEING *FOLLOWED!*

YOU'VE GOT HAWK EYES, SORDO! HMM, COULD BE THE SAME *EL GRANDE* GOONS WHO JUMPED LUIS' FATHER AND TED!

AND THAT NIGHT...

FROM NOW ON, WE STAND GUARD AT NIGHT! I WILL TAKE THE FIRST WATCH! IF ANY *EL GRANDE* PISTOLEROS SHOW, I WILL FIX THEM!

SOON...

SORDO MUST BE PATROLLING BEYOND CAMP! HE'S A TOUGH OLD BUZZARD...BUT MAYBE HE CAN USE SOME HELP!

MOVING AS SILENTLY AS THE CREATURE HE IS NAMED FOR, *THE BATMAN* FLITS THROUGH THE MOON-LIT CHAPARRAL...

FRESH BOOT-PRINTS... AND UNLIKE ANY OF US ARE WEARING!

OUR PURSUERS ARE HERE--

--NOW!

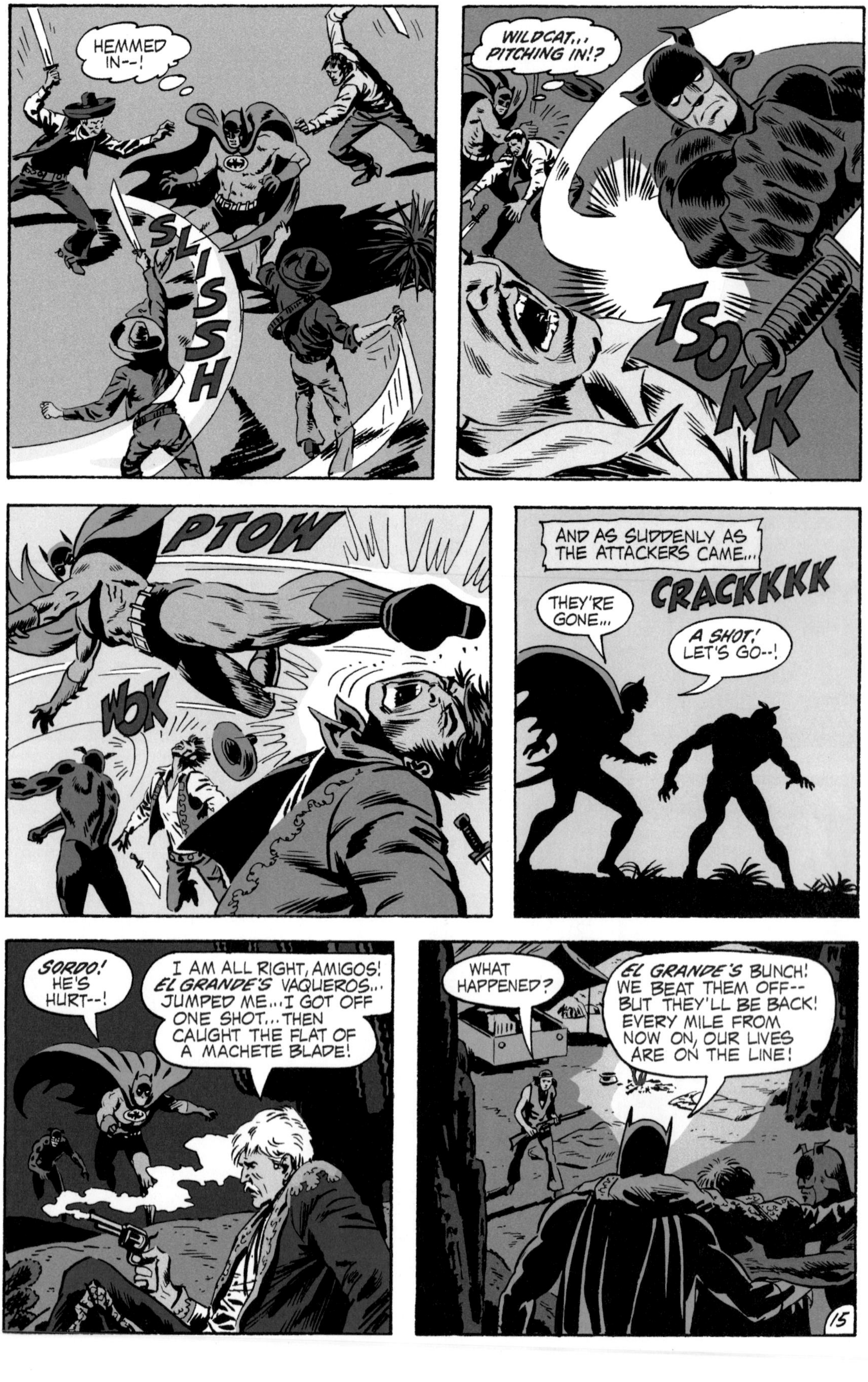
HEMMED IN--!
SLIISSH
WILDCAT... PITCHING IN!?
TSOKK
PTOW
WOK
AND AS SUDDENLY AS THE ATTACKERS CAME...
CRACKKKK
THEY'RE GONE...
A SHOT! LET'S GO--!
SORDO! HE'S HURT--!
I AM ALL RIGHT, AMIGOS! EL GRANDE'S VAQUEROS... JUMPED ME... I GOT OFF ONE SHOT... THEN CAUGHT THE FLAT OF A MACHETE BLADE!
WHAT HAPPENED?
EL GRANDE'S BUNCH! WE BEAT THEM OFF-- BUT THEY'LL BE BACK! EVERY MILE FROM NOW ON, OUR LIVES ARE ON THE LINE!
15

THANKS FOR THE HELP... *TED!*

HEARD SOMETHING... FIGURED YOU AND SORDO NEEDED THE OLD *ROCK-'EM-SOCK-'EM* OF *EL TIGRE!*

POOR GUY... STILL DOESN'T REMEMBER HE'S *WILDCAT!* HE'S SLIPPING BACK INTO HIS AMNESIAC STATE AGAIN!

THE FOLLOWING DAY, AS THEY PUSH ON...

I SEE *ANOTHER* JAGUAR PRINT... POINTING RIGHT TOWARD THE VOLCANO! *THAT'S* OUR DIRECTION!

THEN, THAT AFTERNOON...

A LAKE IN THE VOLCANO CRATER-- COULD CHOCLOTAN BE DOWN THERE-- UNDER-WATER?

TED DOESN'T SEEM TO RECOGNIZE THIS PLACE... BUT THERE'S THE *LAST* GIANT JAG PRINT... GOING RIGHT INTO THE LAKE!

GOT TO CHECK IT OUT! HERE I GO BACK INTO THE DIVING BUSINESS!

CAREFUL, LUIS!

16

DOWN...DOWN... INTO THE SINISTER, STILL WATERS PLUNGES THE BRAVE MEXICAN YOUTH...

A BIG STONE JAGUAR HEAD...BUT NOTHING ELSE! THAT *CAN'T* BE CHOCLOTAN... MUST GO UP--!

BUT WHEN HE BREAKS THE SURFACE....

TH-THEY'RE ALL GONE--?

BUT *WE* HAVE NOT GONE FAR, AMIGO! *UP HERE!*

COME JOIN THEM-- *AND NO TRICKS!* MY VAQUEROS ARE *ITCHING* TO KILL AFTER SO MANY MILES OF DUSTY TRACKING!

I...I DO NOT BELIEVE IT-- YOU...YOU, MY FATHER'S FRIEND, ARE... *EL GRANDE*... HEAD OF THE SMUGGLING RING?

SI, LUIS! MY RANCHO...THE WAY I LIVE... TAKES MUCHO DINERO! THE OLD TREASURES OF MEXICO-- WHAT ARE THEY BUT STONE AND JUNK!

IF FOREIGNERS WILL PAY SO MUCH FOR THEM, WHY SHOULDN'T SORDO PROFIT? NOW YOU HAVE LED ME TO CHOCLOTAN-- AND SEÑOR TED GRANT HERE WILL NOW TELL ME THE *EXACT* LOCATION!

HE *CAN'T!* HE HAS AMNESIA!

17

PERHAPS, BUT I THINK HE IS FAKING! SEE THIS VAQUERO? HE IS CALLED "EL BUEY"--THE OX! HE CAN FELL A BULL WITH ONE BLOW! HE SHALL *BEAT THE TRUTH* OUT OF SEÑOR GRANT!

HE DRINKS A NATIVE BREW WHICH WILL MAKE HIM NOT FEEL PAIN OR HIS FOE'S BLOWS! HERE, *EL TIGRE...* YOUR FIGHTING SUIT!

TED... NO... DON'T DO IT--!

HE HAS NO CHOICE, FOR IF HE DOES NOT--I SHALL SHOOT YOU...HIS FRIENDS... *ONE AT A TIME!*

YOU'RE *MAD,* SORDO--!

TIE THEM SO THEY CAN GET A GOOD VIEW!

NOW LET THE BATTLE COMMENCE--*EL BUEY AGAINST EL TIGRE!*

SWOOSHASOOO

SO YOU WANT TO MIX WITH ME, FELLA? I WAS ONCE THE CHAMP... SO THEY TELL ME! YOU'RE IN FOR A LICKIN'!

18

143

LIKE A MATADOR AGAINST A BRUTE OF A BULL, TED GRANT EASILY SIDESTEPS AND BEATS HIS HUGE FOE TO THE PUNCH...AGAIN...AND AGAIN...AND AGAIN!

BUT THIS IS A BULL THAT KNOWS NO PAIN--NO CAUTION--AND AS THE EX-CHAMP PUNCHES HIMSELF OUT...

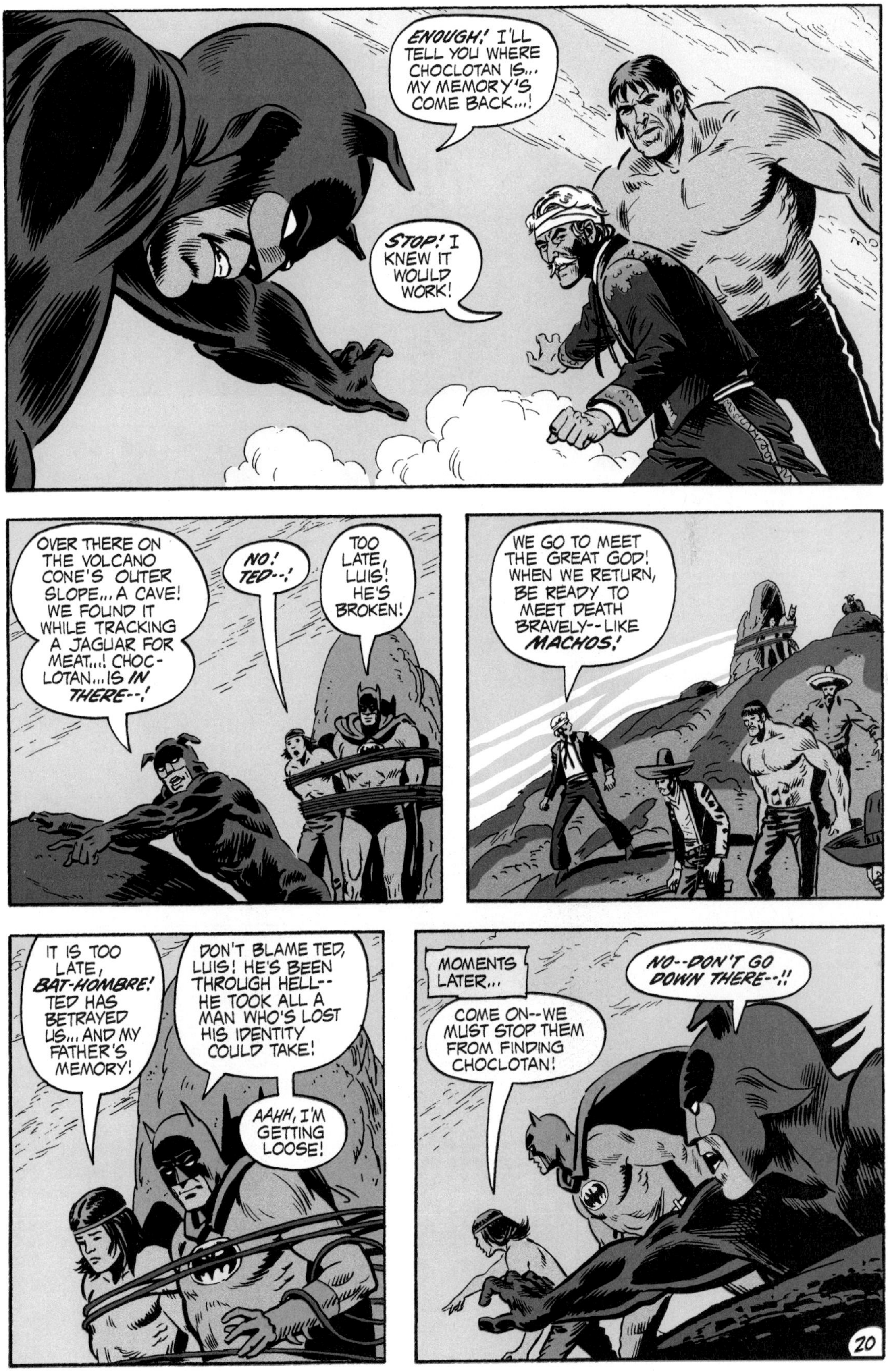
ENOUGH! I'LL TELL YOU WHERE CHOCLOTAN IS... MY MEMORY'S COME BACK...!
STOP! I KNEW IT WOULD WORK!
OVER THERE ON THE VOLCANO CONE'S OUTER SLOPE... A CAVE! WE FOUND IT WHILE TRACKING A JAGUAR FOR MEAT...! CHOC-LOTAN... IS IN THERE--!
NO! TED--!
TOO LATE, LUIS! HE'S BROKEN!
WE GO TO MEET THE GREAT GOD! WHEN WE RETURN, BE READY TO MEET DEATH BRAVELY--LIKE MACHOS!
IT IS TOO LATE, BAT-HOMBRE! TED HAS BETRAYED US... AND MY FATHER'S MEMORY!
DON'T BLAME TED, LUIS! HE'S BEEN THROUGH HELL-- HE TOOK ALL A MAN WHO'S LOST HIS IDENTITY COULD TAKE!
AAHH, I'M GETTING LOOSE!
MOMENTS LATER...
COME ON--WE MUST STOP THEM FROM FINDING CHOCLOTAN!
NO--DON'T GO DOWN THERE--!!
20

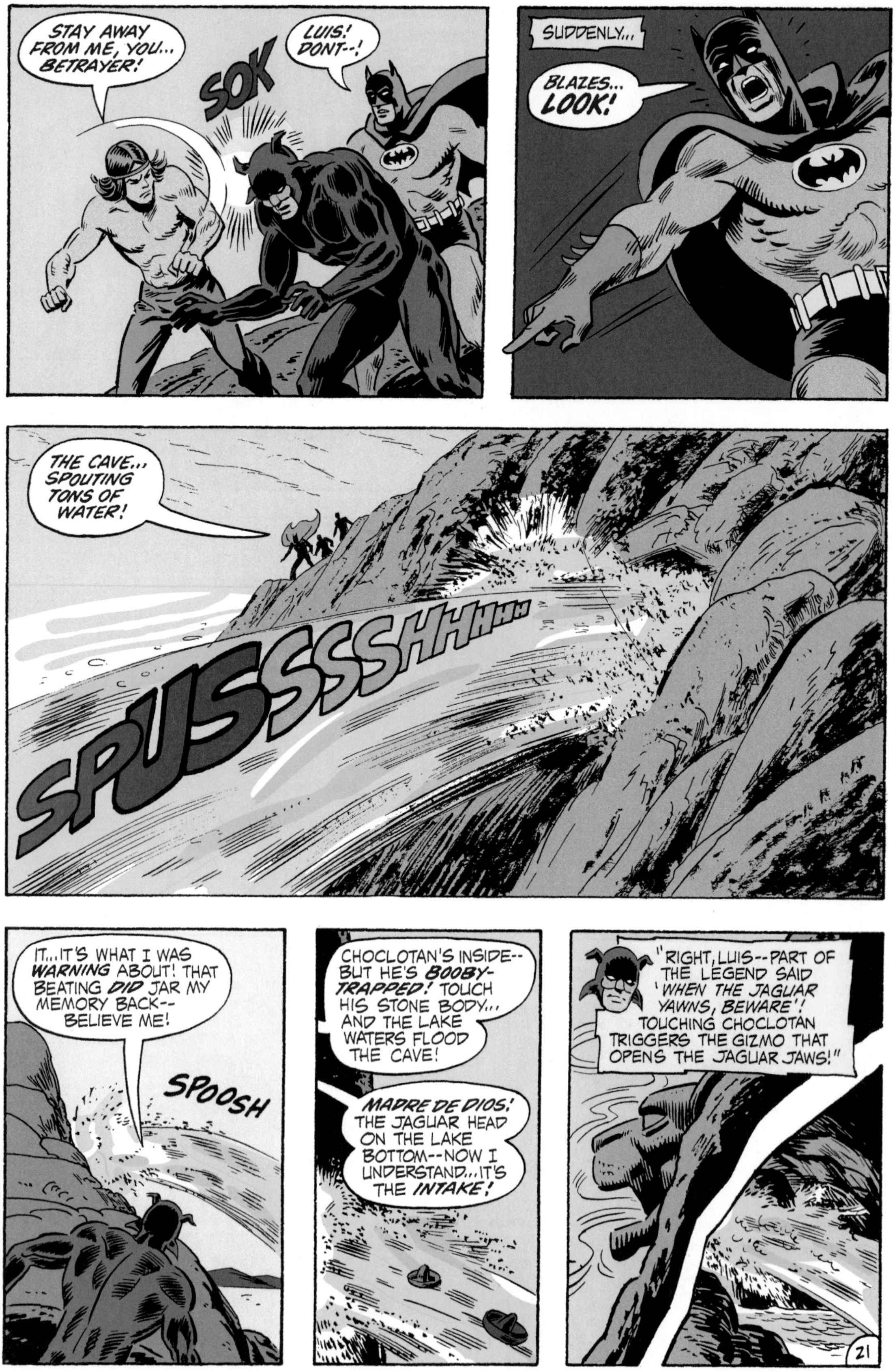
STAY AWAY FROM ME, YOU... BETRAYER!
SOK
LUIS! DONT--!
SUDDENLY...
BLAZES... LOOK!
THE CAVE... SPOUTING TONS OF WATER!
SPUSSSSSHHHHH
IT...IT'S WHAT I WAS WARNING ABOUT! THAT BEATING DID JAR MY MEMORY BACK-- BELIEVE ME!
SPOOSH
CHOCLOTAN'S INSIDE-- BUT HE'S BOOBY-TRAPPED! TOUCH HIS STONE BODY... AND THE LAKE WATERS FLOOD THE CAVE!
MADRE DE DIOS! THE JAGUAR HEAD ON THE LAKE BOTTOM--NOW I UNDERSTAND...IT'S THE INTAKE!
"RIGHT, LUIS--PART OF THE LEGEND SAID 'WHEN THE JAGUAR YAWNS, BEWARE'! TOUCHING CHOCLOTAN TRIGGERS THE GIZMO THAT OPENS THE JAGUAR JAWS!"
21

AS THE WILDLY RUSHING WATERS RECEDE...

FANTASTIC! SO YOU REALLY WERE *TRICKING* SORDO, TED?

SURE! WHEN MY MEMORY RETURNED, I RECALLED LUIS' FATHER AND I ALMOST GETTING TRAPPED! LUCKILY, WE NOTICED SEEPAGE IN THE CAVE AND CHECKED IT OUT FIRST!

MOMENTS LATER, WITHIN THE DIM CAVERN, A GREAT GLITTERING GOD GREETS THE TRIO...

IT IS HIM... *CHOCLOTAN!* MY EYES ARE HUMBLED!

MAGNIFICENT! THE SEARCH IS OVER--FOR US--AND FOR SORDO AND HIS MEN! THEY'RE GONE... ALL OF THEM!

TED... AMIGO... FORGIVE ME FOR EVER DOUBTING YOU?

FORGET IT, KIDDO! THAT AMNESIA HAD THE OLD CHAMP *DOWN* BUT NOT *OUT!* YOU BETTER THANK *BATMAN,* TOO--WITHOUT HIM, WE'D ALL HAVE TAKEN THE COUNT!

NOW CHOCLOTAN WILL BELONG TO *ALL* MEXICO... *SAFE* IN A MUSEUM!

AND NOW WE *KNOW* WHAT HIS SMILE MEANS! HE KNEW THAT ANCIENT BOOBY TRAP WOULD PRESERVE HIM TO BE MARVELED AT BY FUTURE GENERATIONS!

THE END

22

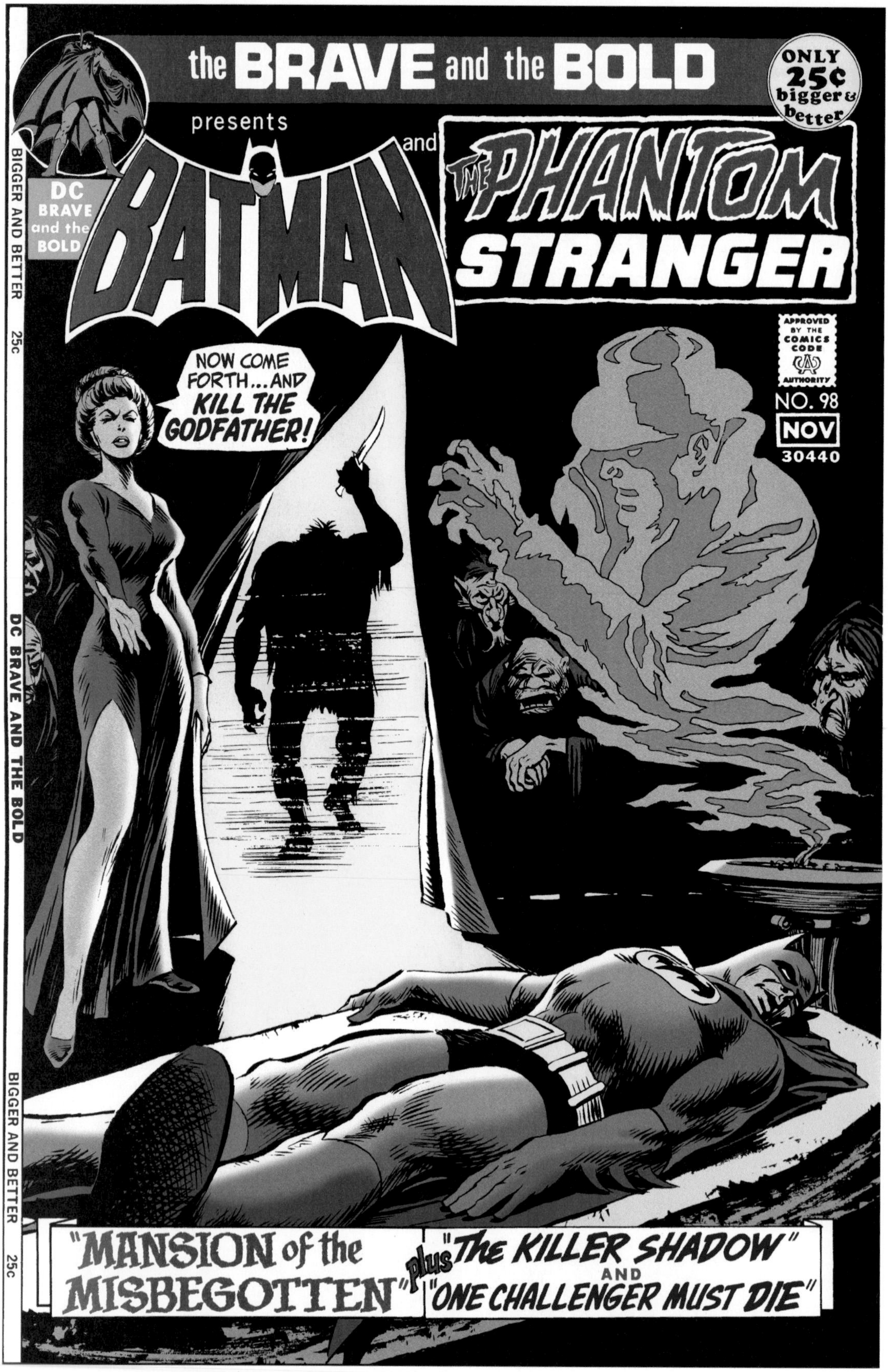
the BRAVE and the BOLD
ONLY 25¢ bigger & better
presents
BATMAN
and
THE PHANTOM STRANGER
DC BRAVE and the BOLD
BIGGER AND BETTER 25c
DC BRAVE AND THE BOLD
NOW COME FORTH... AND KILL THE GODFATHER!
APPROVED BY THE COMICS CODE AUTHORITY
NO. 98
NOV
30440
"MANSION of the MISBEGOTTEN"
plus "The KILLER SHADOW" AND "ONE CHALLENGER MUST DIE"

"MUCH EVIL HAS THIS BURNT-OUT CINDER, EARTH, ENDURED-- AND ONLY WITH EACH INNOCENT CHILD IS ITS HOPE REBORN!"

BUT THESE ARE NOT THE THOUGHTS OF A CLOAKED FIGURE WHO MOVES SILENTLY AS THE MIST TOWARD A GREAT HOUSE BULKING AGAINST THE SKY...

THE MAN OF THE NIGHT LIFTS A GREAT IRON KNOCKER ONCE... TWICE...

CLORINDA! STILL AS BEAUTIFUL AS EVER--!

BATMAN! THANK THE FATES YOU'VE COME! ROGER'S BEEN ASKING FOR YOU EVERY HOUR! COME QUICKLY!

THERE'S BIRNAM TOWERS... AND INSIDE IT, MY FRIEND ROGER BIRNAM LIES DYING!

GOD, I CAN HARDLY BELIEVE THIS DAY HAS COME!

BUT AS BATMAN'S FEET TREAD ON OLD FAMILIAR FLOORS WHERE HE'D OFTEN KNOWN HAPPY MOMENTS...

BATMAN!

LITTLE ENOCH!

IS MY DADDY GOING TO DIE? PLEASE...DON'T LET IT HAPPEN!

HOW CAN I LIE TO THE CHILD? TRUTH IS ALWAYS BEST!

REMEMBER YOUR PET BIRD GOT HURT... AND DIED? NOTHING COULD HURT IT ANY-MORE!

THAT'S WHAT *THIS* IS LIKE-- NOTHING WILL HURT YOUR DADDY ANYMORE!

THEN INTO THE DEATH CHAMBER STEPS THE *MASKED MANHUNTER*, HUMBLE BEFORE A FOE NO MORTAL CAN ESCAPE OR CONQUER...

BATMAN... OLDEST AND BEST OF FRIENDS...

YES, ROGER, I'M HERE...

I'M GOING... DOCTOR MALTHUS HAS DONE EVERYTHING... HE BROUGHT MY SON INTO THE WORLD-- BUT EVEN *HIS* GREAT SKILL CAN'T PREVENT MY LEAVING IT...

I DIE HERE IN MY BELOVED HOME WITH THE WIFE AND CHILD I ADORE AND THE MAN I ADMIRE MOST BY MY SIDE! ONE LAST REQUEST, *BATMAN*...

YES, ROGER..?

I'LL DIE HAPPY IF I KNOW *ONE* THING-- THAT IN THIS HARSH WORLD, YOU'LL PROTECT CLORINDA AND LITTLE ENOCH! *PROMISE*--?

I PROMISE! I'M ENOCH'S GODFATHER--I'D GIVE MY *OWN* LIFE FOR HIM... OR CLORINDA!

THEN I'M AT PEACE! GOODBYE, MY FRIEND... GOODBYE, MY LOVE...

FAREWELL, ROGER...

ROGER! NO!

2

MANSION OF THE MISBEGOTTEN!

STORY: **BOB HANEY** ART: **JIM APARO**

A KNOT OF MOURNERS IN A BLEAK FOREST OF STONE... A FEW WORDS OF COMFORT... AND ANOTHER MORTAL JOURNEY IS OVER...

IN MY FATHER'S HOUSE ARE MANY MANSIONS... DUST TO DUST...

THESE FRIENDS OF CLORINDA'S AND ROGER'S... ODD I NEVER MET ANY OF THEM BEFORE... BUT THEY CERTAINLY ARE GRIEF-STRICKEN!

AND AFTER THE SAD CEREMONY...

I MUST RETURN TO GOTHAM CITY, CLORINDA-- BUT YOU CAN REACH ME VIA THE *BAT-LINE*! REMEMBER, I PROMISED ROGER TO PROTECT YOU BOTH, ALWAYS!

GOODBYE, GODSON!

'BYE, *BATMAN*! I LOVE YOU!

AND SO THE *CAPED CRUSADER* PLUNGES ONCE MORE INTO THE ROLE OF CRIMEFIGHTER... UNTIL A FEW WEEKS LATER...

PARDON ME... AREN'T YOU DR. MALTHUS, THE LATE ROGER BIRNAM'S PHYSICIAN?

NO, I'M EDWARD CANTRELL, A SALESMAN OF RELIGIOUS ARTICLES!

3

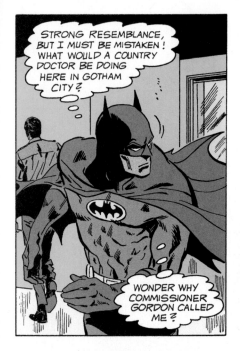

STRONG RESEMBLANCE, BUT I MUST BE MISTAKEN! WHAT WOULD A COUNTRY DOCTOR BE DOING HERE IN GOTHAM CITY?

WONDER WHY COMMISSIONER GORDON CALLED ME?

SHORTLY, IN THE MORGUE...

...FOUND THIS MORNING... AND JUST IDENTIFIED! HIT-AND-RUN VICTIM, I'D SAY, BUT MAC, HERE, HAS ANOTHER THEORY!

YOU BET I DO, COMMISSIONER-- IT WAS RITUAL MURDER!

COME ON, MAC--YOU'VE BEEN SEEING TOO MANY TV SHOWS...

HAVE I, BATMAN? THE WOUNDS-- SURE THEY LOOK LIKE A HIT-AND-RUN...

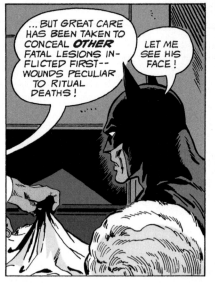

...BUT GREAT CARE HAS BEEN TAKEN TO CONCEAL OTHER FATAL LESIONS IN-FLICTED FIRST-- WOUNDS PECULIAR TO RITUAL DEATHS!

LET ME SEE HIS FACE!

YOU LOOK LIKE YOU SAW A GHOST!

MAYBE I DID, COMMISSIONER!

NO TIME TO TELL THEM I'M FAIRLY SURE THIS CORPSE WAS A MOURNER AT ROGER'S FUNERAL!

4

SHORTLY, IN A BANK...

YES, THE DECEASED DID WORK HERE FOR YEARS...QUIET...LOYAL... IN OUR AUDITING DEPARTMENT! I CAN'T *BELIEVE* THIS AWFUL THING!

YOU BETTER BELIEVE HE CHECKED HIS LAST COLUMN OF FIGURES--! QUIET...LOYAL, EH?

HARDLY A CANDIDATE FOR RITUAL MURDER!

IF YOU ASK ME, HE WAS *TOO* QUIET! IN CLEANING OUT HIS DESK, I FOUND... *THIS!*

A CHICKEN FOOT?

LATER...

YOU CALLED TO SAY SOMETHING'S *WRONG* UP THERE, CLORINDA? YOU'RE *FRIGHTENED?* OF COURSE...I'M ON MY WAY!

AND SOON, A HUNDRED MILES NORTH OF THE CITY'S CONCRETE CANYONS...

WHAT IS IT?

THERE'S *SOMEONE...SOMETHING...* IN THE HOUSE, *BATMAN!* A TERRIFYING FIGURE ...APPEARING THESE LAST FEW NIGHTS!

LAST NIGHT, ENOCH SAW IT AT THE TOP OF THE STAIRS--

OH, GOD, THERE IT IS NOW!..

BUT AS THE **MASKED MANHUNTER** LUNGES AT THE EERIE APPARITION...

UNNHH--!

BATMAN!!

A SECOND LATER...

GONE--!? DID IT **REALLY** EXIST? YET SOMETHING... SOME INVISIBLE FORCE **DID** SLAM ME BACK!

SO IT **WAS** THERE-- **YOU** SAW IT, TOO! COULD IT BE **ROGER**...RE-TURNED TO US... IN ANOTHER FORM?

KLACK KLACK

COME NOW, GRIEF AND MEMORY CAN PLAY **TRICKS** ON US! ROGER'S GONE... **FOREVER!**

WALT--!

EVENING, CLORINDA!

WELL, I'LL BE... **BATMAN!** THIS IS A GREAT HONOR, MEETING YOU! WALT HIGGINS, CHIEF CONSTABLE, AT YOUR SERVICE!

6

I CALLED WALT FOR HELP WHEN ENOCH FIRST SAW THAT *THING!* WALT, IT WAS JUST HERE *AGAIN!*

NOW, CLORINDA, YOU PROBABLY JUST IMAGINED IT! IT'S *THEM* I'M MORE WORRIED ABOUT!

THEM--?

A GROUP OF LOCAL TOWNIES! THEY'VE BEEN HARASSING AND BAD-MOUTHING CLORINDA! DID IT WHEN MR. BIRNAM WAS ALIVE! NOW HE'S DEAD, THEY'RE *REALLY* AFTER HER!

RESENTFUL OF *HER...* HER *BEAUTY...* THIS *HOUSE*--! ACCUSING HER OF ALL KINDS OF SICK THINGS! I'M NOT THE GREAT *BATMAN...* JUST A COUNTRY COP...

BUT I CAN PROTECT HER AND THE BOY JUST FINE, YOU BET!

THE WAY HE LOOKS AT HER--HE'S INFATUATED WITH HER! CAN'T BLAME HIM... CLORINDA'S A FABULOUS FEMALE!

YOU'RE IN GOOD HANDS, CLORINDA! I MUST GET BACK! NOW, DON'T WORRY... YOU'RE STILL UPSET FROM ROGER'S DEATH! IT'S ONLY NATURAL!

I SUPPOSE SO! GOODBYE, *BATMAN!*

A PHOTO OF THE MOURNERS AT ROGER'S FUNERAL? ODD IDEA!

AND SOMETHING'S *WRONG!* I *KNOW*-- THAT MURDER VICTIM I THOUGHT WAS ONE OF THEM, HE'S *NOT* IN THE PICTURE!

7

155

COULD I'VE HAD A MEMORY GOOF-- LIKE MISTAKING THAT SALESMAN FOR DR. MALTHUS?

MAYBE...BUT I'VE GOT A HUNCH I'D BETTER NOT LEAVE JUST YET...

...MAYBE I *DIDN'T* SEE THAT APPARITION, BUT THERE *WAS* A STRANGE FORCE THERE I DIDN'T WANT TO SCARE CLORINDA ABOUT--!

GOOD BLAZES! IT... *AGAIN!?*

...AND POINTING TOWARD THE *HOUSE?* WHAT'S *THAT?* MUSIC... LAUGHTER... *WEIRD* LAUGHTER--!

GONE-- JUST LIKE THE OTHER TIME!

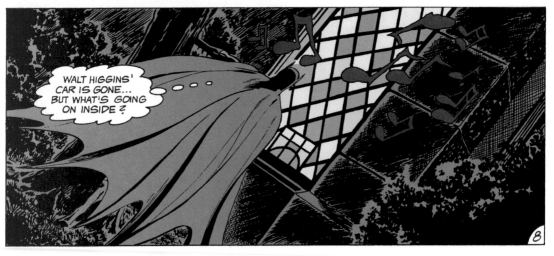

WALT HIGGINS' CAR IS GONE... BUT WHAT'S GOING ON INSIDE?

8

156

AS *BATMAN* SQUINTS THROUGH ONE OF THE PANES...

GOOD HEAVENS-- *UUGGHH!*

KRA-ACK

SOMETIME LATER, THROUGH A HAZE OF PAIN AND THROBBING, WHIRLING PINPOINTS OF LIGHT, *BATMAN* SEES...

CLORINDA... ENOCH...

OH, I FEEL SO AWFUL ABOUT THIS-- THOSE CHIMNEY POTS ARE TOPPLED BY THE SLIGHT-EST BREEZE! I *WARNED* ROGER ABOUT THEM OFTEN...

THIS ROOM... I THOUGHT I SAW--

MY FRIENDS? THEY ALL CAME TO COMFORT ME IN MY GRIEF! ROGER'S DEAD ONE MONTH TONIGHT!

LET MY FRIENDS HELP YOU, *BATMAN*... YOU NEED TO REST! YOU HAD A NASTY BLOW!

MY HEAD! YES... OF COURSE...

BATMAN, COULD YOU SIGN THIS...GIVE ME YOUR AUTOGRAPH? IT WOULD MEAN SO MUCH...

WHAT AN INCONSIDERATE THING AT THIS TIME!

IT'S ALL RIGHT, CLORINDA! I FEEL SHAKY... BUT NOT *THAT* BAD--!

OH, THANK YOU... I'LL TREASURE IT ALWAYS!

SHORTLY...

YOU REST AWHILE, I'LL GET RID OF MY GUESTS! MIND IF LITTLE ENOCH STAYS WITH YOU, HE ADORES YOU SO?

10

FEELING BETTER..?

YES, SON! YOUR BEING HERE HELPS A LOT!

SUDDENLY, A STRANGE STUPOR OVERCOMES THE *CAPED CRUSADER!*

WHAT'S... HAPPENING...TO ME..? AND WHAT'S THAT I HEAR..?

SOMEONE... AIMING A CRAZY TRIDENT...AT ME...

AGHH!

DEEPER, DEEPER INTO HIS PULSING FLESH HE FEELS THE CRUEL TINES PRESS...

SUDDENLY THE DEADLY PRESSURE CEASES.

MY GOD! IT'S MENACING ENOCH! MY LEGS-- CAN'T MOVE...TO HELP...

11

HE'S DWINDLING... *FLYING THROUGH THE KEYHOLE!*

THE NEXT AMAZING MOMENT...

IT--IT'S CHANGING FORM...TO... THE *PHANTOM STRANGER* ?!

YES, *BATMAN* IT'S YOUR OLD FRIEND YOU NOW SEE AGAIN!

PHANTOM STRANGER, THAT MYSTERIOUS MASTER OF THE OCCULT *BATMAN* FIRST MET IN *BRAVE & BOLD #89.* WHAT IS HIS MISSION HERE?

BUT... BUT I DON'T UNDERSTAND! YOU TRIED TO KILL ME WITH THAT TRIDENT!

NOT *I*-- BUT YOUR *GODSON* CERTAINLY DID!

ENOCH? PREPOSTEROUS--

BUT *TRUE*-- THAT THIS HOUSE IS A *COVEN FOR WITCHES AND WARLOCKS* ...AND CLORINDA AND LITTLE ENOCH ARE *THEIR MASTERS!*

WHAT? ...I...CAN'T MOVE...WHAT'S *WRONG* WITH ME ?

YOU GAVE A WITCH YOUR AUTOGRAPH! SHE USED IT AS A TOKEN TO HEX YOUR *BODY!* THIS COUNTER-POTION SHOULD HELP!

MOMENTS LATER...

YOU REALLY *DID* SEE THAT COVEN CELEBRATING THROUGH THE WINDOW! THAT CHIMNEY POT *DIDN'T* FALL *ACCIDENTALLY!*

YOU MEAN, SOMEONE *TOPPLED* IT ON ME ?

12

EXACTLY! TO PROTECT MYSELF FROM THE COVEN'S SPELLS I ASSUMED SPECTRAL FORM, SURROUNDING MYSELF WITH A PSYCHIC BARRIER BUT LEAVING ME VOICELESS!

AND THAT'S WHAT I SLAMMED INTO ON THE STAIRS!

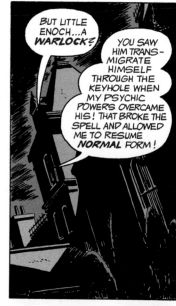

BUT LITTLE ENOCH...A WARLOCK?

YOU SAW HIM TRANS-MIGRATE HIMSELF THROUGH THE KEYHOLE WHEN MY PSYCHIC POWERS OVERCAME HIS! THAT BROKE THE SPELL AND ALLOWED ME TO RESUME NORMAL FORM!

BUT HE'S ONLY A CHILD! HOW COULD HE BE A KILLER?

WHO ELSE WAS IN THIS ROOM WITH YOU... BUT HIM? I'VE BEEN WATCHING THE COVEN FOR SOME TIME-- ENOCH'S THE EVIL GODLING THEY ALL WORSHIP!

EVERYTHING ELSE MAKES SENSE NOW! THE BANK AUDITOR REALLY WAS RITUALLY MURDERED --BUT THAT CHICKEN FOOT?

A WITCH'S WARNING HE WAS MARKED FOR DEATH...PERHAPS FOR TRYING TO LEAVE THE COVEN AND GO "STRAIGHT"!

THAT FUNERAL PHOTO... PHONIED TO ALLAY MY SUSPICIONS! AND THAT WAS DR. MALTHUS I SAW... EXCEPT HE'S PROBABLY NO DOCTOR!

OH, HE IS, KIND OF-- A WITCH DOCTOR! NO JOKE INTENDED!

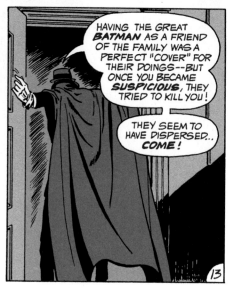

HAVING THE GREAT BATMAN AS A FRIEND OF THE FAMILY WAS A PERFECT "COVER" FOR THEIR DOINGS--BUT ONCE YOU BECAME SUSPICIOUS, THEY TRIED TO KILL YOU!

THEY SEEM TO HAVE DISPERSED... COME!

13

TO THINK POOR ROGER MARRIED TO A WITCH AND NEVER KNOWING IT! DON'T THEY FEAR YOU NOW?

IF YOU CONFRONTED HER, SHE'D *DENY* ALL!

WHO WOULD BELIEVE OUR PREPOSTEROUS STORY? THAT SHE *USED* ROGER TO FATHER HER CHILD AND PROVIDE HER WITH WEALTH AND THIS HOUSE AS A COVEN'S LAIR, AND THEN HAD HIM MURDERED?

MURDERED?

THAT'S WHY WE NEED LEGAL *PROOF* THE COVEN EXISTS -- PROOF OF THEIR CRIMES, INCLUDING ROGER'S DEATH!

THAT'S *MY* KIND OF BAG, AND I'VE GOT A PLAN HOW WE CAN *GET* THAT PROOF!

THEN, AS A MOURNFUL SOUND RIDES THE NIGHT AIR...

A CHILD CRYING! THAT'S ENOCH IN THE WINDOW!

IGNORE THAT SPAWN OF EVIL, *BATMAN!* IT COULD BE SOME TRAP! COME!

THE FOLLOWING NIGHT...

A COURT ORDER TO EXHUME ROGER BIRNAM'S BODY? YOU EXPECT FOUL PLAY, *BATMAN?*

I DON'T KNOW, WALT! BUT IT'S YOUR DUTY TO CARRY OUT THE ORDER!

HIT 'IM-- NOW!

KA-WHAM

14

THERE ARE SPECIAL PLACES--PLACES SACRED TO THE SLAVES OF EVIL --AND NOW, NEAR MIDNIGHT, A DREAD PROCESSION MARCHES WITH SLOW STEP INTO AN ABANDONED QUARRY...

ENOCH... ENOCH...ALL POWERFUL BE HIS NAME!

LET THE SACRIFICE TO HIS GREATER GLORY BE DONE!

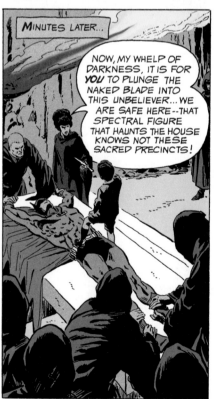

MINUTES LATER...

NOW, MY WHELP OF DARKNESS, IT IS FOR YOU TO PLUNGE THE NAKED BLADE INTO THIS UNBELIEVER... WE ARE SAFE HERE--THAT SPECTRAL FIGURE THAT HAUNTS THE HOUSE KNOWS NOT THESE SACRED PRECINCTS!

SUDDENLY, THE INERT MASKED MANHUNTER REGAINS CONSCIOUSNESS...

BLAZES!

AS THE GLITTERING BLADE STARTS ITS FATAL PLUNGE...

NO, YOU DON'T!

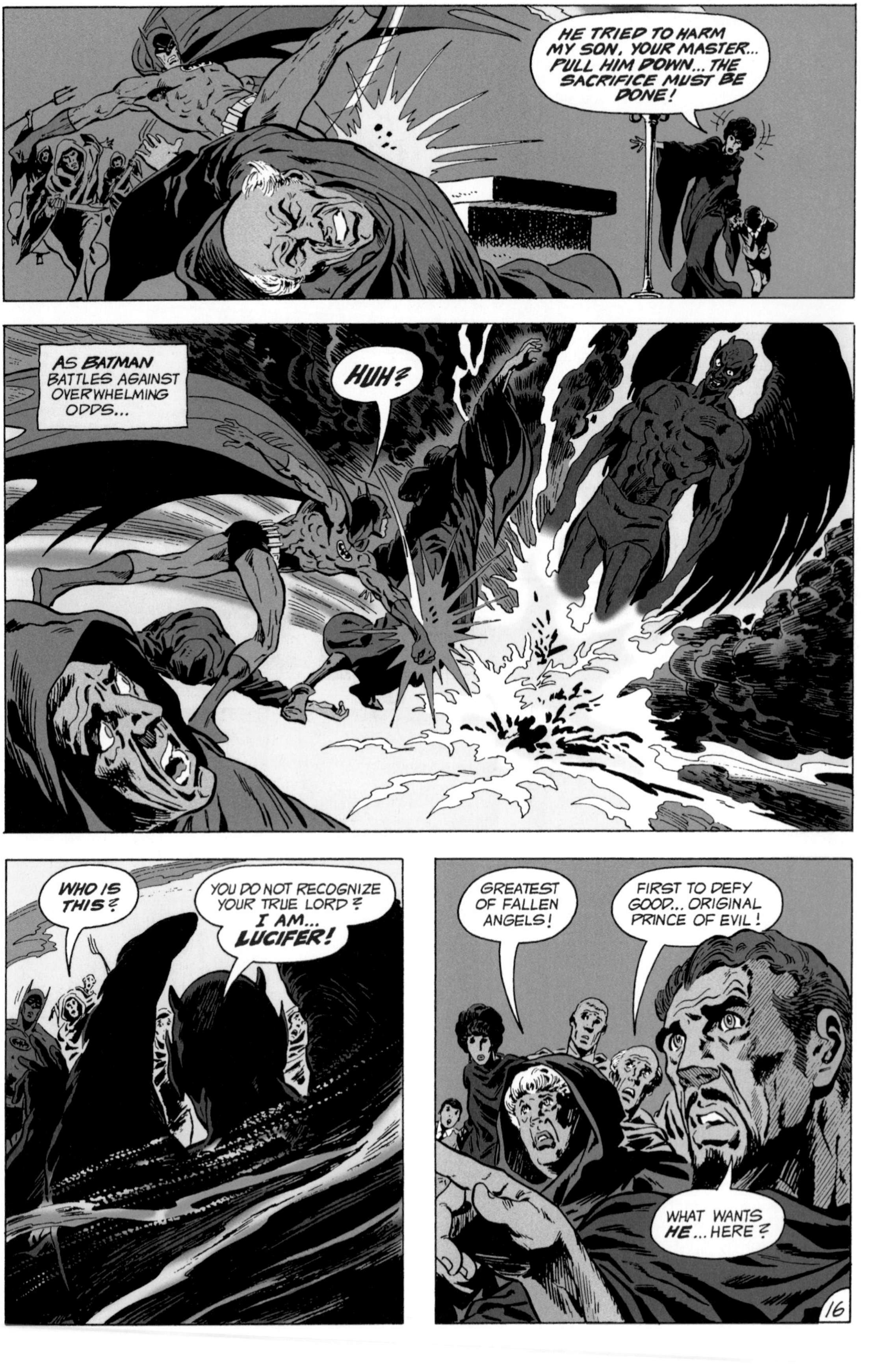
HE TRIED TO HARM MY SON, YOUR MASTER... PULL HIM DOWN... THE SACRIFICE MUST BE DONE!
AS BATMAN BATTLES AGAINST OVERWHELMING ODDS...
HUH?
WHO IS THIS?
YOU DO NOT RECOGNIZE YOUR TRUE LORD? I AM... LUCIFER!
GREATEST OF FALLEN ANGELS!
FIRST TO DEFY GOOD... ORIGINAL PRINCE OF EVIL!
WHAT WANTS HE... HERE?
16

YOUR BLASPHEMY HAS CALLED ME FORTH! A MORTAL OF *HIS* DISTINCTION IS ONLY FIT TO BE SACRIFICED BY ONE OF HIGH STATURE--*I, LUCIFER!* THUS I PREPARE HIM!

NOW I DEPART, TAKING HIM TO A PROPER, CONSECRATED DEATH!

SHORTLY, IN SHROUDING WOODS...

SO IT WAS *YOU, PHANTOM STRANGER?*

WHEN YOU DIDN'T RETURN FROM THE CEMETERY, I CHECKED OUT THE COVEN'S HAUNTS! THAT WAS A VIAL OF HARMLESS GAS I USED TO KNOCK YOU OUT! HOW ARE YOU FEELING?

FOR A GUY WHO'S BEEN SLAMMED WITH A SHOVEL AND ALMOST SACRIFICED--*NOT BAD!* BUT I KEEP SEEING THAT LOOK IN THE BOY'S EYES... *AUGGHH!*

YES, YOUR GODSON'S *PURE EVIL* -- THE MYSTIC SOURCE OF THE COVEN'S POWER!

WITHOUT HIM, THEY'D BE *POWERLESS!* WE MUST GET OUR HANDS ON ENOCH--BUT *SECRETLY!* MY FIRST PLAN TO EXHUME ROGER'S BODY FAILED BECAUSE EVEN CONSTABLE HIGGINS IS ONE OF *THEM!*

17

THE NEXT NIGHT...

THERE HE IS... PLAYING LIKE ANY ORDINARY CHILD!

BUT I KNOW DIFFERENT! *PHANTOM STRANGER* SAID THIS SACK HAD PROPERTIES TO *CANCEL* HIS WARLOCK POWERS--*I HOPE!*

WAAUGH

A FEW DAYS LATER, IN A GOTHAM HOSPITAL WARD EQUIPPED WITH A ONE-WAY WINDOW...

AS A PSYCHIATRIST, I DON'T BELIEVE IN THE *ACTUAL* POWER OF WITCHES AND WARLOCKS...

CHILDREN'S PSYCHIATRIC DIVIS

...BUT I REALIZE ANYONE WHO *HAS* SUCH POWERS WILL EXHIBIT BIZARRE BEHAVIOR!

EXACTLY, DOCTOR! IF WE CAN SHOW HIM DISPLAYING THOSE POWERS...

...PERHAPS WE CAN MAKE A *LEGAL CASE* AGAINST THE COVEN-- *TRY THEM* FOR THEIR CRIMES!

BUT WE'VE OBSERVED HIM FOR *DAYS*--AND ALL HE LOOKS IS *FRIGHTENED* BY THOSE OCCULT OBJECTS! COULD OUR THEORY BE *WRONG?*

18

166

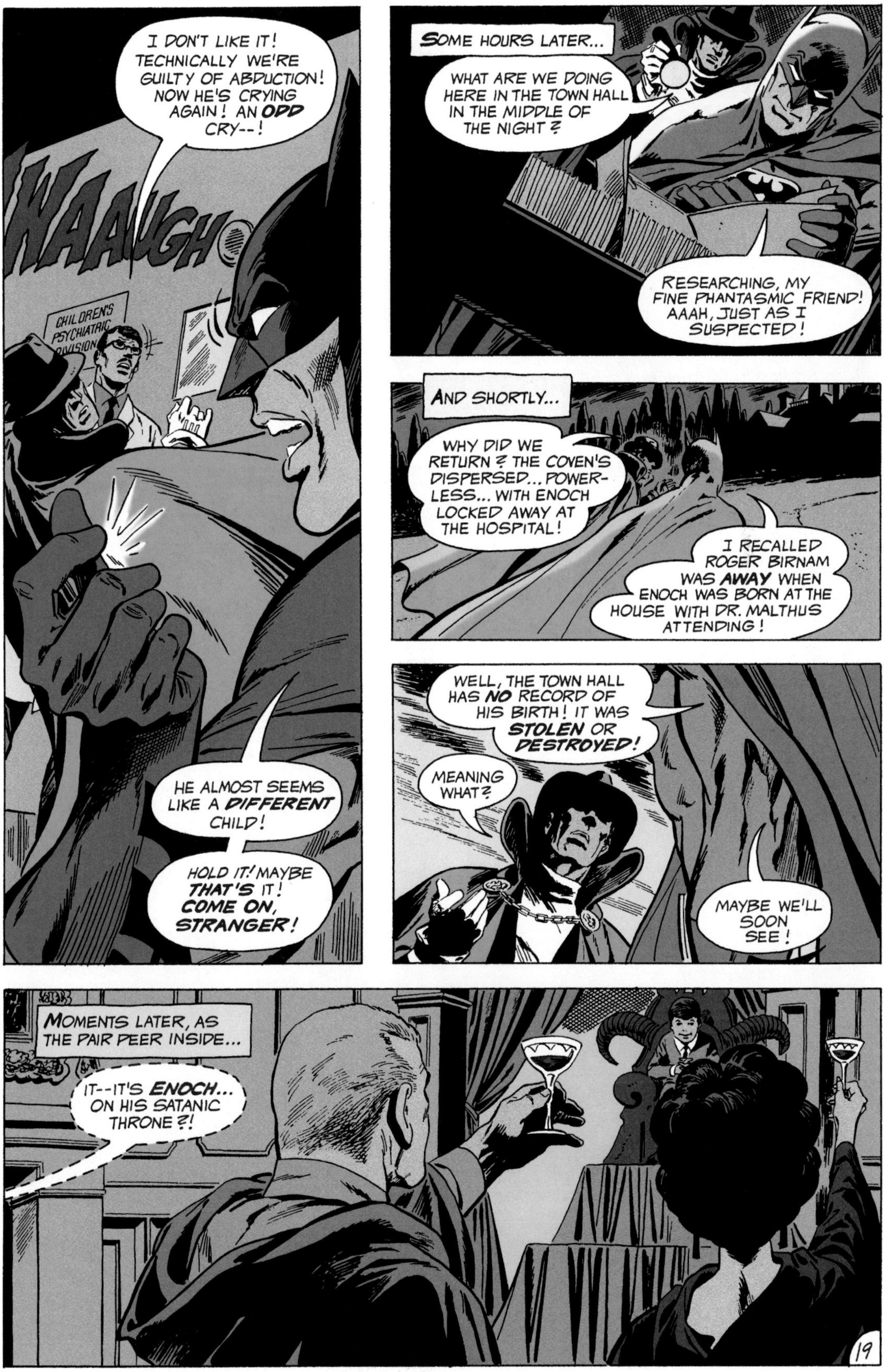
I DON'T LIKE IT! TECHNICALLY WE'RE GUILTY OF ABDUCTION! NOW HE'S CRYING AGAIN! AN ODD CRY--!
WAAAUGH
CHILDREN'S PSYCHIATRIC DIVISION
HE ALMOST SEEMS LIKE A DIFFERENT CHILD!
HOLD IT! MAYBE THAT'S IT! COME ON, STRANGER!
SOME HOURS LATER...
WHAT ARE WE DOING HERE IN THE TOWN HALL IN THE MIDDLE OF THE NIGHT?
RESEARCHING, MY FINE PHANTASMIC FRIEND! AAAH, JUST AS I SUSPECTED!
AND SHORTLY...
WHY DID WE RETURN? THE COVEN'S DISPERSED... POWERLESS... WITH ENOCH LOCKED AWAY AT THE HOSPITAL!
I RECALLED ROGER BIRNAM WAS AWAY WHEN ENOCH WAS BORN AT THE HOUSE WITH DR. MALTHUS ATTENDING!
WELL, THE TOWN HALL HAS NO RECORD OF HIS BIRTH! IT WAS STOLEN OR DESTROYED!
MEANING WHAT?
MAYBE WE'LL SOON SEE!
MOMENTS LATER, AS THE PAIR PEER INSIDE...
IT--IT'S ENOCH... ON HIS SATANIC THRONE?!
19

BUT IT **CAN'T** BE HIM!

I'LL SWEAR IT **IS**! DON'T YOU SEE, **THAT'S** WHY THE BIRTH RECORD WAS MISSING! CLORINDA DIDN'T HAVE **ONE** SON--

--BUT **TWO**! THAT CHILD BACK AT THE HOSPITAL IS ENOCH'S **TWIN BROTHER**!

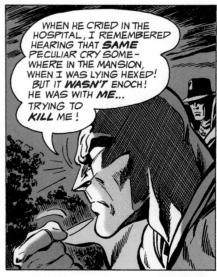

WHEN HE CRIED IN THE HOSPITAL, I REMEMBERED HEARING THAT **SAME** PECULIAR CRY SOMEWHERE IN THE MANSION, WHEN I WAS LYING HEXED! BUT IT **WASN'T** ENOCH! HE WAS WITH **ME**... TRYING TO **KILL** ME!

OF **COURSE**! THERE **HAD** TO BE ANOTHER CHILD...ONE LOCKED AWAY IN THE HOUSE BECAUSE HE WAS **GOOD**-- BORN **WITHOUT EVIL**-- THE CHILD WE HEARD CRYING IN THE TOWER!

CLORINDA MUST'VE GUESSED I'D TRY TO GRAB ENOCH, SO SHE **SWITCHED** THEM-- LEFT THE **GOOD** SON WHERE I COULD EASILY FIND HIM... AND HID ENOCH AWAY INSTEAD!

TIME TO BREAK UP THEIR GLOATING! **BACK ME UP, STRANGER**!

BATMAN--?!

20

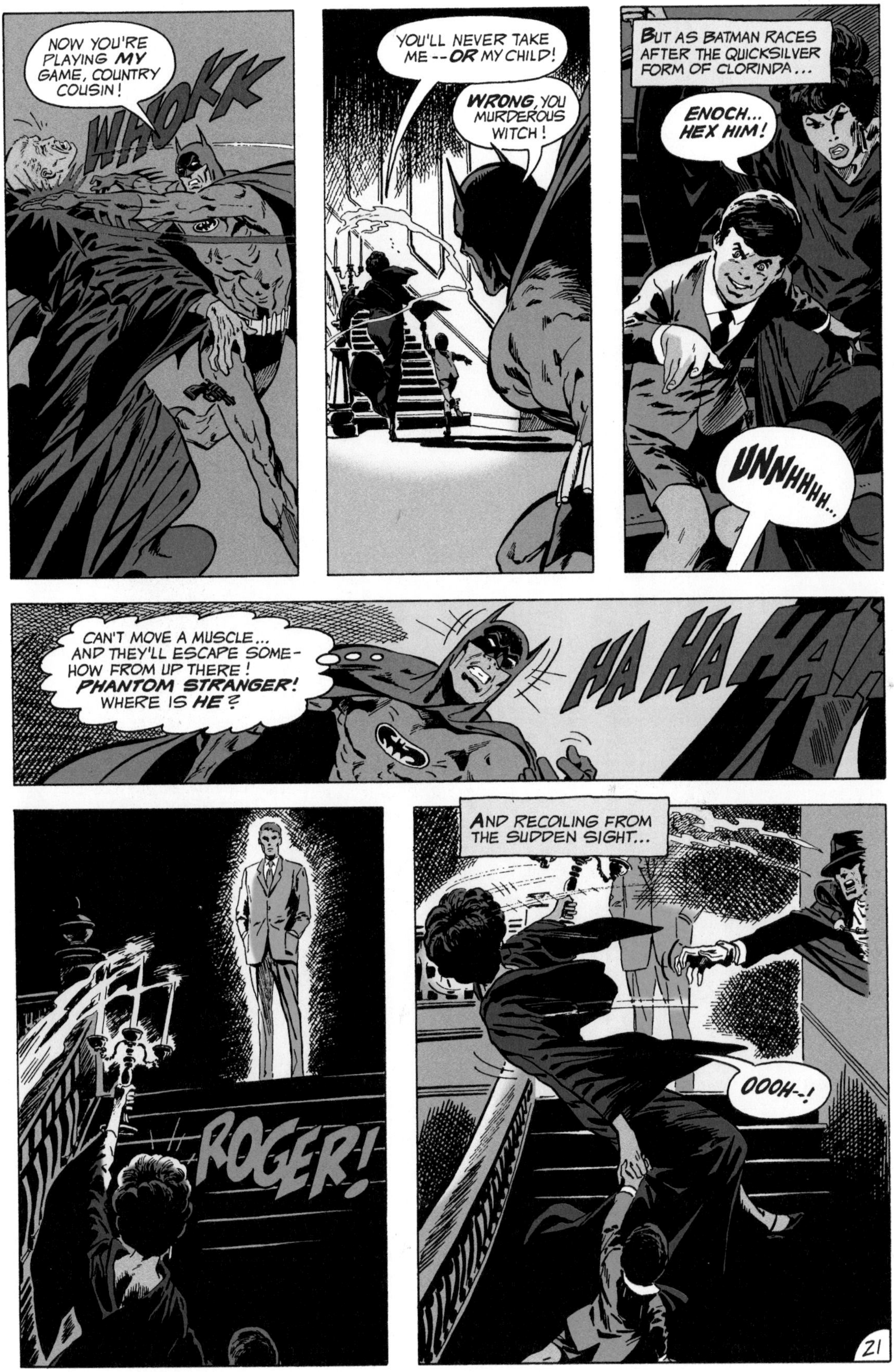
NOW YOU'RE PLAYING MY GAME, COUNTRY COUSIN!
WHOKK
YOU'LL NEVER TAKE ME -- OR MY CHILD!
WRONG, YOU MURDEROUS WITCH!
BUT AS BATMAN RACES AFTER THE QUICKSILVER FORM OF CLORINDA...
ENOCH... HEX HIM!
UNNHHHH..
CAN'T MOVE A MUSCLE... AND THEY'LL ESCAPE SOME-HOW FROM UP THERE! PHANTOM STRANGER! WHERE IS HE?
HA HA HA
ROGER!
AND RECOILING FROM THE SUDDEN SIGHT...
OOOH-!
21

WHERE *WERE* YOU?

I HAD A PSYCHIC HUNCH SHE'D TRY TO ESCAPE THIS WAY! BUT I GOT HERE TOO LATE TO PREVENT THE FALL! SORRY...

THERE--YOUR HEX IS BROKEN!

DEAD...BOTH OF THEM! THEY WERE MORTAL... FORTUNATELY!

BUT...WHAT MADE HER *FALL*?

I THINK I KNOW!

ROGER BIRNAM'S PORTRAIT...LOOKING SPECTRAL AS THE MOONLIGHT HIT IT! IT WAS THE TERROR BORN OF HER OWN GUILT THAT CAUSED HER TO FALL!

22

SO POOR ROGER AVENGED HIMSELF, IN A WAY!

WITH THE COVEN FINISHED, MY WORK HERE IS DONE! FAREWELL, *BATMAN*, UNTIL WE MEET AGAIN ON SOME OCCULT BATTLE-GROUND!

SOME TIME LATER...

I COULDN'T SAVE ENOCH FROM HIS AWFUL FATE, ROGER, OLD FRIEND, BUT I PROMISE YOU MY NEW GODSON, ROGER JR., WILL HAVE MY LOVE AND PROTECTION ...ALWAYS!

"MUCH EVIL HAS THIS BURNT OUT CINDER, EARTH, ENDURED-- AND ONLY WITH EACH INNOCENT CHILD IS ITS HOPE REBORN!"

THE END

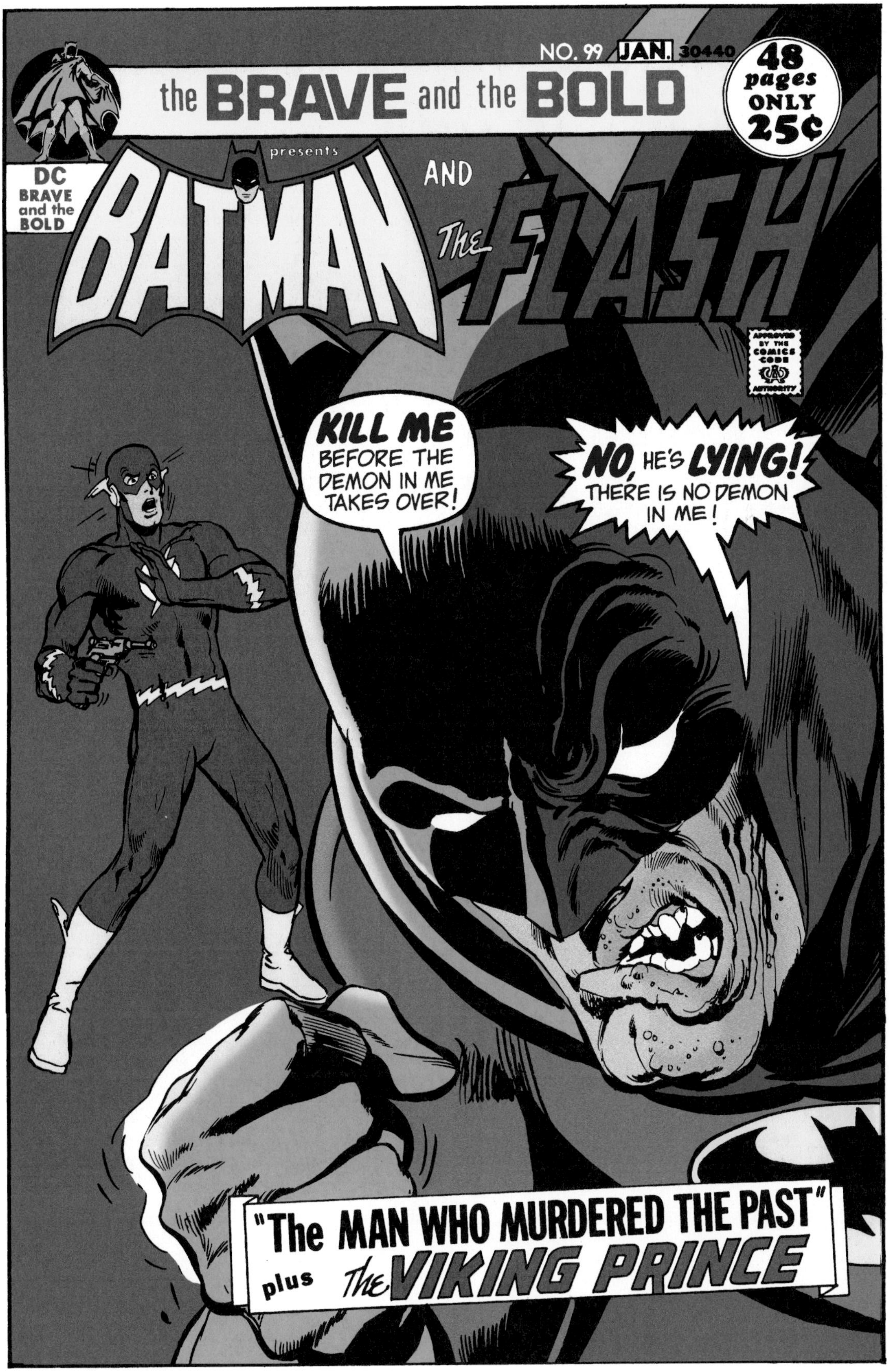
NO. 99 JAN. 30440
the BRAVE and the BOLD
48 pages ONLY 25¢
DC BRAVE and the BOLD
presents
BATMAN
AND
THE FLASH
KILL ME BEFORE THE DEMON IN ME TAKES OVER!
NO, HE'S LYING! THERE IS NO DEMON IN ME!
"The MAN WHO MURDERED THE PAST"
plus THE VIKING PRINCE

BATMAN and **The FLASH**

ON A FERRY NEARING A NEW ENGLAND ISLAND STANDS A SOMBRE FIGURE...

AFTER ALL THESE YEARS, THE ISLAND AGAIN... HAD SUCH A STRONG DESIRE TO DRIVE UP HERE FROM GOTHAM ... DIDN'T EVEN CHANGE THE OLD *BAT-SUIT!*

SHORTLY, BEFORE A WEATHERED, LONG SHUT-UP STRUCTURE...

THE WAYNE FAMILY SUMMER HOME! LOOKS THE SAME... A LITTLE OLDER... BUT THEN, SO AM I!

A GLOVED HAND INSERTS AN OLD KEY, TURNS A WELL-WORN DOOR HANDLE, AND...

MY OLD TENNIS RACKET AND FISHING ROD! DAD GAVE THEM BOTH TO ME...!

FAMILIAR THINGS...THAT TUG AT THE HEART, MAKE TIME EBB LIKE THE TIDE, UNCOVERING THE MEMORY OF SUMMERS PAST...

DAD... LOOK!

GREAT, BRUCE! A NICE BLUEFISH, OR MORE PRECISELY-- A NICE POMATOMUS SALTATRIX!

MEMORY--THAT MAGIC TRIP ANYONE CAN TAKE INSIDE HIS HEAD, AS *BATMAN,* ALIAS BRUCE WAYNE, IS DOING NOW!

BEAUTIFUL, BRUCE! NEXT YEAR, THOMAS, HE'LL BE BEATING *YOU!*

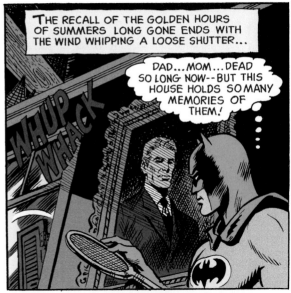

THE RECALL OF THE GOLDEN HOURS OF SUMMERS LONG GONE ENDS WITH THE WIND WHIPPING A LOOSE SHUTTER...

WHUP WHACK

DAD...MOM...DEAD SO LONG NOW--BUT THIS HOUSE HOLDS SO MANY MEMORIES OF THEM!

NOW AS A SUDDEN SUMMER SQUALL SHAKES THE OLD HOUSE, AND THE DUNE GRASSES SIGH LIKE SOULS IN TORMENT...

MORTAL REMAINS OF THOMAS AND MARTHA WAYNE

THEN, ABOVE THE DRUMMING OF THE RAIN, THE LASHING OF THE SEA AGAINST THE CLIFFS ...ANOTHER SOUND ...A STRONG MAN STIFLING A SOB...

DAD...MOM...ALL THAT'S LEFT OF THEM... THEIR ASHES!

MORTAL REMAINS OF THOMAS AND MARTHA WAYNE

AND AS THE WIND HOWLS IN DIRGE-LIKE FURY, AS IF TO TEAR THE SAD OLD HOUSE DOWN...

WHOOOOOO

QUITE A BLOW... GOT TO CLOSE THE DOOR...

BUT AS *THE BATMAN* GRASPS THE KNOB, A SHUDDER SHAKES HIS EVERY INCH, AND WITH A STRANGE STIFF-LEGGED GAIT... HE SUDDENLY LURCHES OUT INTO THE STORM!

2

NOW LET US FOLLOW THIS FAMILIAR BUT ODDLY— BEHAVING FIGURE -- LET US FOLLOW THE *MASKED MANHUNTER* AS HE LAUNCHES FORTH UPON A BIZARRE AND TERRIFYING DESTINY... AS HE BECOMES...

"The MAN WHO MURDERED THE PAST!"

REAL SOU'EASTER BLOWIN', MR. EBBS! OLD MANUEL THE PORT-A-GEE DIED IN SUCH A STORM... 50 YEARS AGO!

CAP'N JOSIAH! WHAT'S THAT COMIN'? GLORY BE! OLD MANUEL'S ...GHOST!?

STOMP
KLUMP

ART: BOB BROWN
NICK CARDY
STORY: BOB HANEY

'TIS NO GHOST, ABNER... BUT *BATMAN*--HE...HE RENTED THE OLD WAYNE HOUSE!

HO, AMIGO... SOME *RUM!* MY THIRST SHE IS *GREAT!*

BUT THAT STIFF-LEGGED WALK... LIKE OLD MANUEL'S WOODEN LEG... AND HIS VOICE AND ACCENT... THE *SAME!?*

UH...WE'VE ONLY *SODA* HERE... *BATMAN!*

3

AT THE MENTION OF HIS NAME, THE VISITOR SHUDDERS, AND...

HUH?

YOU'RE MAKING A *JOKE?* SAY, THAT WAS A PRETTY GOOD IMITATION OF OLD MANUEL THE PORTUGUESE HARPOONER! GAVE ME A SCARE!

MANUEL? *HA! HA!* MY FRIEND, BRUCE WAYNE, TOLD ME ABOUT HIM! WELL, I WAS JUST TAKING SHELTER FROM THE STORM! MUST GO NOW...

STORM'S OVER-- BUT HOW'D I GET *HERE?* AND WHY WAS I IMITATING OLD MANUEL? I NEED SLEEP... COMING BACK HERE HAS UNNERVED ME!

BUT BACK AT THE ISOLATED HOUSE, IT IS A FITFUL, RESTLESS SLEEP THAT COMES TO BRUCE *(BATMAN)* WAYNE...

DAD! MOTHER--!

WHAT A DREAM! I COULD *SWEAR* MY PARENTS WERE *HERE*... IN THIS VERY ROOM! IMPOSSIBLE, OF COURSE-- BUT THIS HOUSE IS SO FULL OF THEIR SPIRIT!

4

THE FOLLOWING DAY, AS A SPARKLING SUN SEEMS TO DISPEL THE NIGHT'S DARK CONFUSION...

HERE HE COMES... LOOKS *NORMAL* ENOUGH--!

AYE, CAP'N JOSIAH... BUT HE DIDN'T *YESTERDAY!* KEEP AN EYE ON HIM, CONSTABLE TODD!

BUT AS THE *CAPED CRUSADER* PASSES A MONUMENT TO THE TOWN'S WHALING PAST...

LOOKIT HIM STOMPIN' LIKE HE'S GOT A WOODEN LEG *AGAIN!*

HE'S SEIZIN' THE MONUMENT HARPOON!

GLORY! NOBODY EVER TOSSED A WHALIN' IRON LIKE THAT... *EXCEPTIN' OLD MANUEL THE PORT-A-GEE!*

WHIZZZ

THUNK

WHALIN' INN

I TELL YOU, CONSTABLE, THE MAN'S *POSSESSED!*

SURE IS!

OLD MANUEL WAS A DEVIL! NOW HE'S COME BACK TO POSSESS THIS *BATMAN* FELLA!

I BETTER FOLLOW HIM!

CLUMP

CLUMP

BOATING SUPPLIES

SOON, ATOP SEA-SCULPTURED CLIFFS BEYOND THE VILLAGE...

HE'S ENTERING THE ABANDONED LIGHTHOUSE? BEEN BROKEN FOR YEARS -- AND *OFF-LIMITS* TO TRESPASSERS!

U.S. GOV'T PROPERTY KEEP OUT

5

SHORTLY, ATOP THE TOWERING STRUCTURE...

HO! YOU BOTHER MANUEL?

ALL RIGHT, JUST WHAT ARE YOU UP TO?

A SUDDEN LEAP-- A POWERFUL FIST LASHES OUT...

HUH? WHERE... AM I? WHAT DID I DO?

TSOKK

NOT LONG AFTER...

ASSAULT ON AN OFFICER OF THE LAW IS A SERIOUS CHARGE! I MUST JAIL YOU UNLESS YOU PUT UP BAIL!

UH...YOUR HONOR ...I'VE NO MONEY WITH ME!

I'LL GO THE BATMAN'S BAIL!

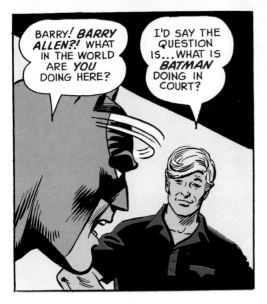

BARRY! BARRY ALLEN?! WHAT IN THE WORLD ARE YOU DOING HERE?

I'D SAY THE QUESTION IS...WHAT IS BATMAN DOING IN COURT?

CAN THIS STARTLING REUNION OF BATMAN AND THE MAN WHO IS SECRETLY THE FLASH BE STRICTLY CHANCE? SHORTLY, AS THE TWO JUSTICE LEAGUE COMRADES LEAVE...

...SO IT APPEARS I'VE TWICE BEEN POSSESSED OF THIS DEAD PORTUGUESE HARPOONER'S PERSONALITY!

HMM, I'VE HEARD OF SUCH "POSSESSIONS", BATMAN!

1ST DISTRICT COURT

6

BUT HAPPENING TO SOMEONE LIKE *YOU?* SOCKING POLICEMEN IS NOT EXACTLY YOUR THING--!

ALL I CAN FIGURE IS, RETURNING HERE, TO MY PARENTS' OLD SUMMER HOME AFTER ALL THESE YEARS HAS UPSET ME *EMOTIONALLY!* BUT I'M NOT SURE--!

BUT WHAT ABOUT *YOU?* WHAT BROUGHT *YOU* HERE?

WELL, I WAS DOING *MY* THING, AS BARRY ALLEN, POLICE SCIENTIST, WHEN MY LAB INSTRUMENTS BEGAN PICKING UP CERTAIN STRANGE VIBRATORY SIGNALS!

"WHEN I RAN SOME TESTS ON THOSE SIGNALS, THEY MADE NO SENSE..."

THEY'RE LIKE NOTHING I'VE SEEN BEFORE-- COSMIC OR INFRA-RED RAYS... OR EVEN SEISMIC TREMORS CAN'T BE CAUSING THEM!

"I RAN THE TEST FIGURES THROUGH THE COMPUTER, AND THE RESULTING PRINT-OUT CURLED MY HAIR..."

GOOD BLAZES! THEY'RE *PROBE RAYS*... FROM *ANOTHER DIMENSION*... A WORLD BEYOND OUR OWN!

I THEN PLOTTED THOSE PROBES, AND THEY ALL CONVERGED AT THE SAME SPOT-- THIS ISLAND... *THIS HOUSE!*

I CAME HERE AT ONCE, NEVER DREAMING *YOU* OWNED IT!

AMAZING! DO YOU KNOW *WHERE* THIS DIMENSION IS... OR *WHO* OR *WHAT* IS SENDING THE PROBES?

NO, BUT IT MUST BE CHECKED OUT-- I TOOK A BRIEF LEAVE OF ABSENCE FROM CENTRAL CITY'S POLICE FORCE!

7

WELL, I'M *GLAD* YOU'RE HERE... THESE POSSESSED STATES HAVE ME WORRIED! DO YOU THINK THERE'S ANY CONNECTION BETWEEN *THEM* AND THOSE *DIMENSIONAL* PROBES?

MIGHT BE SINCE THIS HOUSE SEEMS TO BE THE LOCALE OF BOTH! ONE CONNECTION WE *DON'T* WANT ANYONE TO MAKE-- YOU'VE *GOT* TO STAY IN YOUR *BATMAN* COSTUME EVERY MINUTE FROM NOW ON-- EVEN *SLEEP* IN IT!

YOU'RE *RIGHT*--IF I SUDDENLY BECAME POSSESSED AS *BRUCE WAYNE*, THESE PEOPLE WOULD KNOW I'M *ONE* AND THE *SAME* MAN!

EXACTLY! NOW, LET'S RELAX AND SEE WHAT TOMORROW BRINGS!

BUT THAT NIGHT, STRANGE DREAMS AGAIN INVADE THE MIND OF THE OLD HOUSE'S OWNER...

BRUCE, MY SON... COME!

YES, DAD--!

MOMENTS LATER, IN A LONG-LOCKED BASEMENT ROOM...

THIS ROOM... IT'S A COMPLETE LAB! I WAS NEVER ALLOWED IN HERE AS A BOY!

DAD--! HE'S *GONE!* AND I'M... *AWAKE!*

8

IT'S DAD'S HANDWRITING...

Dear God, forgive me! I have opened the door--torn away the veil between the worlds of the living and the dead...

AND AS THE PAGES REVEAL THEIR LONG-HIDDEN MEANINGS...

INCREDIBLE! THIS PROVES DAD EXPERIMENTED IN RETURNING TO LIFE AFTER DEATH!

HE WAS WORKING ON A METHOD FOR DOING JUST THAT...IN FACT, HAD SET THINGS UP FOR SUCH A RETURN, JUST BEFORE HE WAS KILLED! FANTASTIC!

WHAT A DENSE FOOL I'VE BEEN! THESE STRANGE DREAMS... OLD MANUEL POSSESSING ME... THEY CAN ONLY MEAN ONE THING!

DAD AND MOM ARE TRYING TO COME BACK NOW... TRYING TO COMMUNICATE WITH ME!

OLD MANUEL'S THE KEY-- SOMEHOW HIS SPIRIT'S MANAGED TO CROSS OVER... AND IS PREPARING THE WAY FOR MY PARENTS TO FOLLOW! I MUST MAKE SURE HE ISN'T THWARTED BY ANYONE... OR ANYTHING!

SHORTLY...

DAD...MOM...I UNDERSTAND NOW! I WANT TO MEET YOU...TALK TO YOU AGAIN, TOO! NOW I KNOW YOU HAVEN'T REALLY DIED... THAT THESE ASHES AREN'T YOUR FINAL FORM!

9

So as the great **BATMAN** succumbs to the deepest of human urges--to meet again long lost loved ones, he confides in his friend, Barry Allen...

BRUCE, I UNDERSTAND YOUR DESIRE TO... AH... CONTACT YOUR DEAD PARENTS--BUT WHAT IF IT SHOULD *FAIL*...OR *BACKFIRE* SOMEHOW?

WHAT HAVE I TO LOSE, BARRY? I LOST SO MUCH AS A CHILD... GROWING UP ALONE... THIS IS MY CHANCE TO WASH AWAY THOSE EMPTY YEARS!

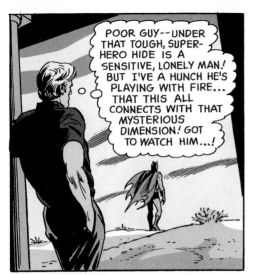

POOR GUY--UNDER THAT TOUGH, SUPER-HERO HIDE IS A SENSITIVE, LONELY MAN! BUT I'VE A HUNCH HE'S PLAYING WITH FIRE... THAT THIS ALL CONNECTS WITH THAT MYSTERIOUS DIMENSION! GOT TO WATCH HIM...!

THAT AFTERNOON...

ACCORDING TO DAD'S NOTEBOOK, THERE'S SOMETHING, AS MANUEL, I MUST DO AT THE LIGHTHOUSE-- BUT IT'S NOT CLEAR! JUST HAVE TO WAIT TILL THE OLD HARPOONER POSSESSES ME AGAIN!

DARKNESS COMES, AND WITH IT, ANOTHER BIZARRE TAKEOVER OF THE *MAN OF NIGHT*-- AND SHORTLY, DOWN THE BEACH...

HO...SO THEY PUT GUARD HERE TO STOP MANUEL!

GOV'T PROPERTY KEEP OUT

WHOK!

UN COA STA

WHILE IN THE WAYNE HOUSE, A GUEST AWAKES...

BATMAN'S BED HASN'T BEEN SLEPT IN--! AND HE'S NOWHERE AROUND!

10

NOW FROM A SPECIAL RING, A FAMILIAR CRIMSON COSTUME SPURTS, EXPANDING INSTANTANEOUSLY...

I'LL BET I KNOW *WHERE* HE IS... AND *WHY!* OLD MANUEL'S POSSESSED HIM AGAIN! BUT FIRST I BETTER BECOME "POSSESSED" MYSELF... OF *THE FLASH!*

THE NIGHT'S GHOSTLY GRAY IS STREAKED WITH A CRIMSON BLUR AS BARRY ALLEN TAKES OFF AFTER HIS FRIEND...

POLICE GUARD KAYOED...! I WAS AFRAID OF THIS...!

AND AS HE REACHES THE LIGHTHOUSE TOP IN HALF A HEARTBEAT...

YOU INTERRUPT MANUEL... *I FIX YOU!*

GOT TO "PULL" THIS... OR I'D KILL HIM!

PTOW

THEN, ANOTHER SCARLET BLUR, BEARING A LIMP BODY RAPIDLY AWAY...

VERY SHORTLY...

AS YOU SEE, CONSTABLE... *BATMAN'S* ASLEEP!

HMM, GUESS HE COULDN'T HAVE GOT BACK SO FAST...! MUST HAVE BEEN PRANKSTERS OR VANDALS ATTACKED THAT LIGHTHOUSE GUARD!

11

BUT THE NEXT MORNING...

BRUCE, I *CAN'T* KEEP COVERING YOU IF YOU CONTINUE TO BREAK THE LAW DURING THESE WEIRD STATES!

SORRY, BARRY, BUT I'VE NO CONTROL OVER WHAT I DO WHEN I'M OLD MANUEL!

I ONLY KNOW I *MUST* DO WHAT I HAVE TO... IF I'M TO SEE MY PARENTS AGAIN! THINK OF THE STAKES... *BRINGING THEM BACK!*

SURE, BUT I'M THINKING OF MY FRIEND, BRUCE WAYNE-- THE *BATMAN*...

...BECOMING AN OBSESSED *FANATIC,* AND TEMPTING FATE WITH WHO KNOWS WHAT DANGEROUS CONSEQUENCES!

STOP IT, BARRY! I'M SURE DAD'S EXPERIMENT WON'T BACK- FIRE! NOW PLEASE LET ME STUDY HIS NOTEBOOK!

CAN'T REACH *HIM!* YET, I MUST TRY TO AVERT ANY TROUBLE! HMM, THOSE DIMENSIONAL PROBES FOCUS ON THIS HOUSE!

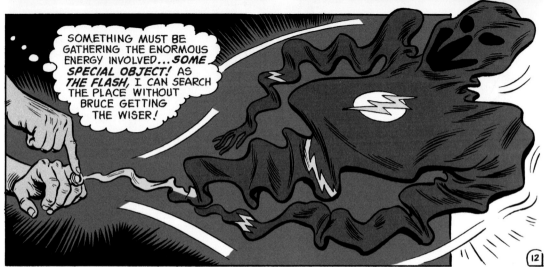

SOMETHING MUST BE GATHERING THE ENORMOUS ENERGY INVOLVED... *SOME SPECIAL OBJECT!* AS *THE FLASH,* I CAN SEARCH THE PLACE WITHOUT BRUCE GETTING THE WISER!

12

NOW, IN INSTANTS, THE *CRIMSON CANNONBALL* COVERS EVERY NOOK AND CRANNY OF THE OLD HOUSE...

NOTHING! NOTHING THAT COULD CONCEIVABLY CONCENTRATE THAT DIMENSION-BRIDGING ENERGY! YET IT MUST BE HERE...*SOMEWHERE!*

THE *DOOR!* MY CALCULATIONS SHOWED THE PROBE RAYS FOCUSED *THROUGH* IT! MAYBE I CAN USE IT TO UNLOCK THE WHOLE INCREDIBLE PROBLEM... NO PUN INTENDED!

WHAT DOES THE *MONARCH OF MOTION* MEAN? THE NEXT SECOND...

FLASH? WHAT--?!

HANG ON! WE'RE TAKING A TRIP THAT WILL *REALLY* BE A MIND-BLOWER!

YOU'RE *MAD--!*

DON'T WORRY, MY COSTUME'S AURA WILL PROTECT YOU!

13

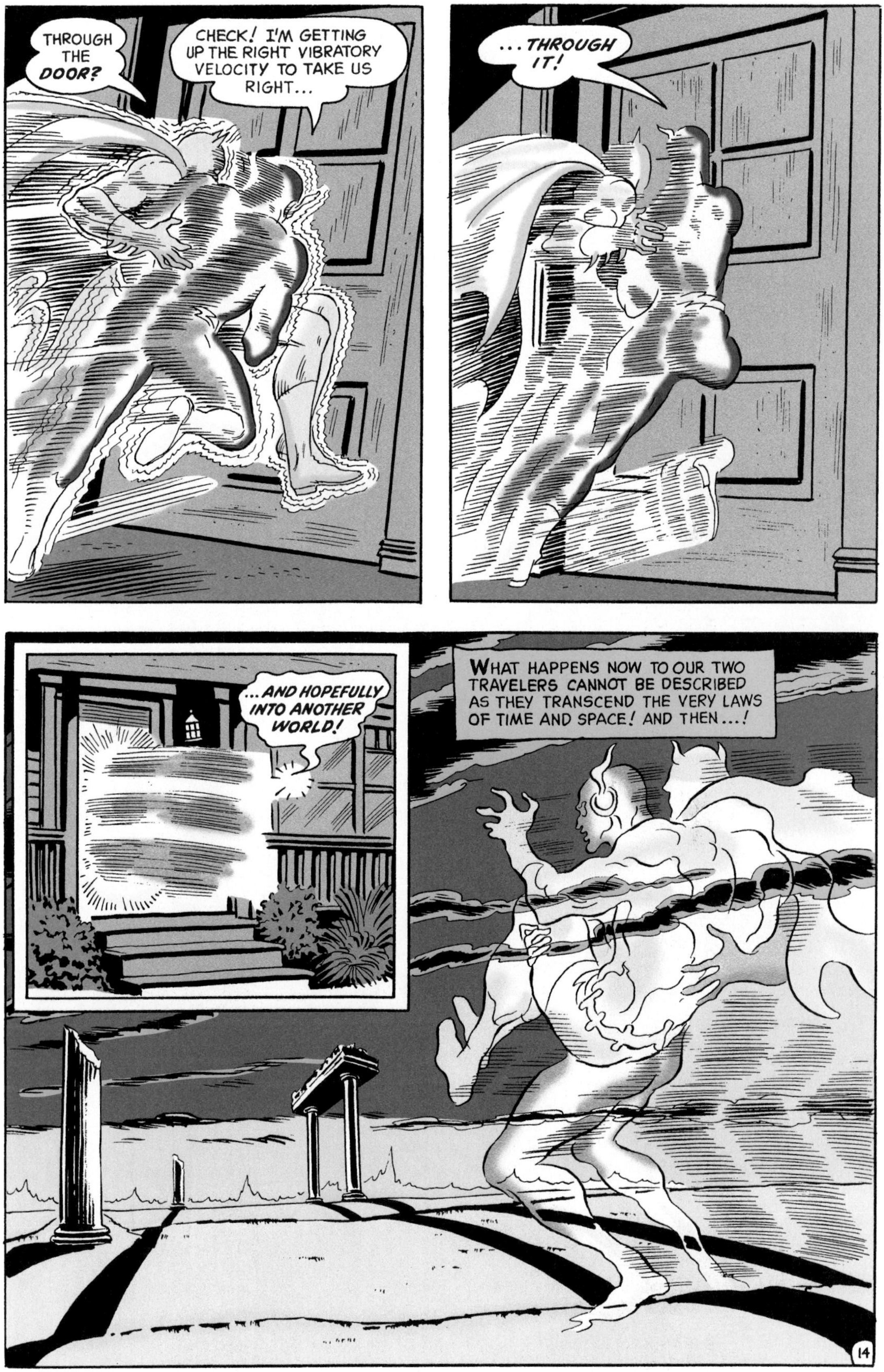
THROUGH THE DOOR?
CHECK! I'M GETTING UP THE RIGHT VIBRATORY VELOCITY TO TAKE US RIGHT...
...THROUGH IT!
...AND HOPEFULLY INTO ANOTHER WORLD!
WHAT HAPPENS NOW TO OUR TWO TRAVELERS CANNOT BE DESCRIBED AS THEY TRANSCEND THE VERY LAWS OF TIME AND SPACE! AND THEN...!
14

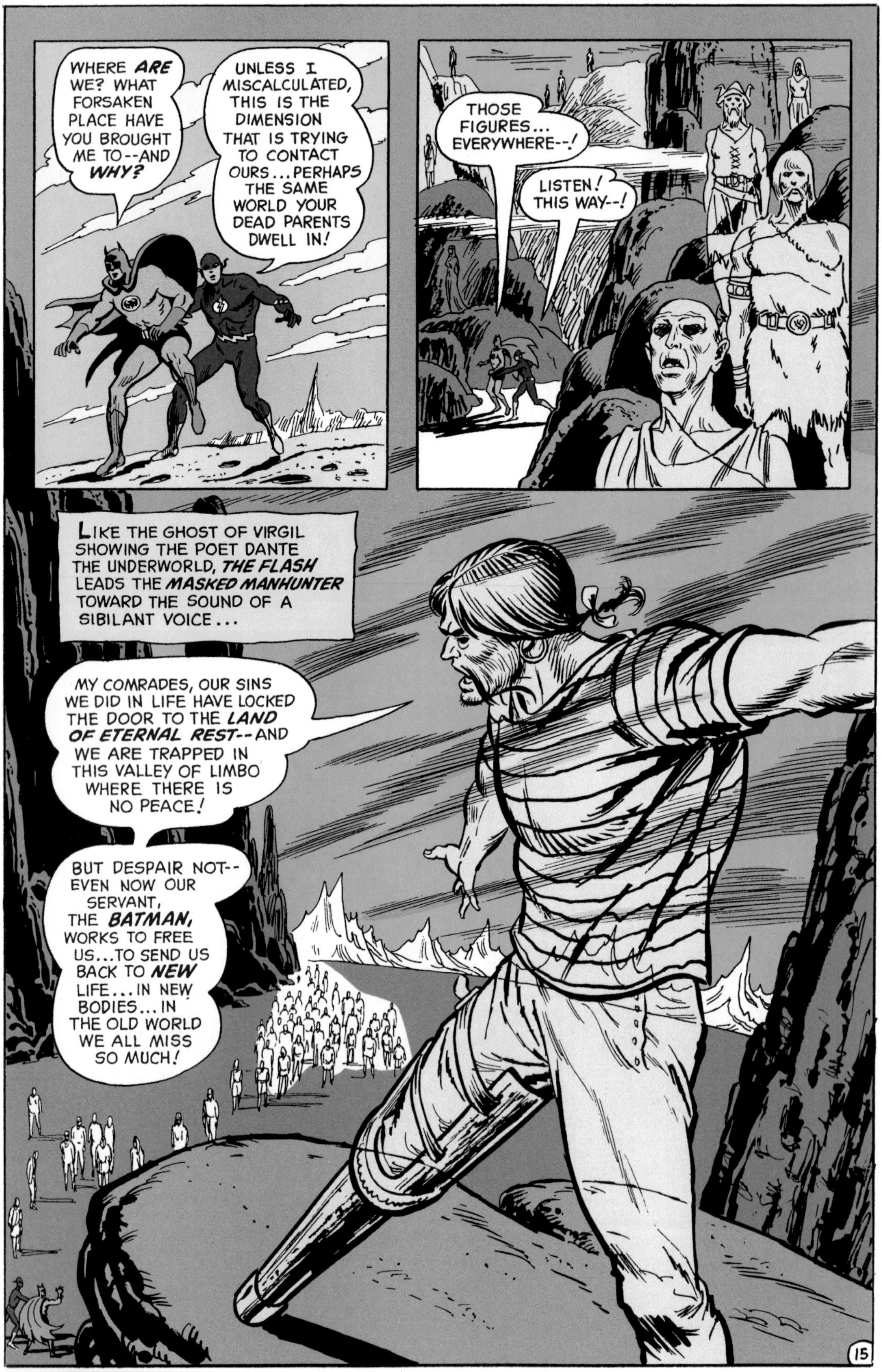
WHERE ARE WE? WHAT FORSAKEN PLACE HAVE YOU BROUGHT ME TO--AND WHY?
UNLESS I MISCALCULATED, THIS IS THE DIMENSION THAT IS TRYING TO CONTACT OURS...PERHAPS THE SAME WORLD YOUR DEAD PARENTS DWELL IN!
THOSE FIGURES... EVERYWHERE--!
LISTEN! THIS WAY--!
LIKE THE GHOST OF VIRGIL SHOWING THE POET DANTE THE UNDERWORLD, THE FLASH LEADS THE MASKED MANHUNTER TOWARD THE SOUND OF A SIBILANT VOICE...
MY COMRADES, OUR SINS WE DID IN LIFE HAVE LOCKED THE DOOR TO THE LAND OF ETERNAL REST--AND WE ARE TRAPPED IN THIS VALLEY OF LIMBO WHERE THERE IS NO PEACE!
BUT DESPAIR NOT--EVEN NOW OUR SERVANT, THE BATMAN, WORKS TO FREE US...TO SEND US BACK TO NEW LIFE...IN NEW BODIES...IN THE OLD WORLD WE ALL MISS SO MUCH!
15

HE ALONE SEEMS TO HAVE THE POWER TO CROSS OVER! THE ISLAND PEOPLE SAY HE PRACTICED DEVILISH RITES WHEN ALIVE!

OVER THERE... THOSE *OTHER* TWO! *MY PARENTS!*

AND AS THE *BATMAN* STRAINS TOWARD TWO HAUNTINGLY FAMILIAR FIGURES...

DAD! MOTHER! IT'S *ME...* BRUCE, *YOUR SON!* PLEASE... *SPEAK TO ME!* THEIR FACES SO SAD...!?

THERE--THAT FIGURE... IT *MUST* BE--

MANUEL THE PORT-A-GEE! OF COURSE...WHEN HE'S NOT POSSESSING YOU IN *OUR* WORLD, HIS SPIRIT'S HERE IN *THIS* WORLD!

LET ME GO! LET ME EMBRACE THEM... *TOUCH* THEM!

LISTEN--THEY CAN'T SEE OR HEAR US!

STOP FIGHTING ME... THE VIBRATION TIME PHASE IS ENDING! IF WE BREAK CONTACT, YOU'D BE TRAPPED HERE... *FOREVER!*

N O SOONER HAS THE *FLASH* SPOKEN THAN AGAIN THERE IS THE INDESCRIBABLE TRANSCENDING OF TIME AND SPACE -- AND...

WE'RE BACK! THANK GOD!

16

NOW WE KNOW THE TERRIBLE TRUTH... A MULTITUDE OF DEAD SOULS WAITING TO REENTER OUR WORLD AND POSSESS *LIVING* BODIES! YOU MUST GIVE UP YOUR PLANS!

GIVE UP FREEING MY PARENTS, POOR UNHAPPY SPIRITS FROM THAT HELLISH PLACE? *NO, FLASH!* I'M SURE DAD'S EXPERIMENT WILL WORK... AND BRING ONLY *THEM* BACK AS THEY WERE IN LIFE... AS THEMSELVES!

AND I *WILL* BRING THEM BACK--THE NEXT TIME OLD MANUEL POSSESSES ME! *I SWEAR IT!*

BLAST! ENTERING THAT DEAD DIMENSION DIDN'T DISCOURAGE HIM! HE'S MORE DETERMINED THAN EVER TO FULFILL THIS DANGEROUS DESTINY!

HIS NEXT POSSESSION COULD COME AT ANY MOMENT! I HAVEN'T MUCH TIME...BUT THERE'S ONE HUNCH LEFT TO PLAY!

MILES MELT TO NOTHINGNESS UNDER THE *FLASH'S* FLYING FEET-- AND IN MOMENTS...

BRUCE WAS A KID WHEN HIS PARENTS DIED! CALEB BRONSON, A FAMILY FRIEND, MADE THE FUNERAL ARRANGEMENTS!

BRUCE SAID BRONSON LIVES HERE IN BOSTON... *IF* HE'S STILL ALIVE! AS DR. WAYNE'S CLOSEST FRIEND, HE MIGHT KNOW SOMETHING ABOUT THE EXPERIMENTS!

17

AFTER SOME SWIFT SLEUTHING...

I'M IN LUCK--BRONSON'S *ALIVE*... RETIRED IN THIS REST HOME! IF HE CAN JUST TELL ME *WHAT'S* GATHERING THE DIMENSION-BRIDGING ENERGY... AND *WHERE* IT IS!

ELYSIUM REST HOME

THAT'S BRONSON, MR. ALLEN, BUT HE HAD A STROKE... CAN'T MOVE... OR SPEAK!

OH, NO! COULD I HAVE A MOMENT ALONE WITH HIM?

IN THE DIMNESS, THE OLD MAN STARES BLANKLY AS BARRY ALLEN SPEAKS SOFTLY BUT PERSISTENTLY...

NO USE! I EXPLAINED EVERYTHING TO HIM! I CAN TELL HE HEARS ME, BUT EVEN IF HE KNOWS ANYTHING... HOW CAN HE COMMUNICATE IT?

THEN, A WITHERED CLAW OF A HAND FEEBLY STRUGGLES TO MOVE...

HE'S SCRATCHING SOMETHING... ON THE ARM OF HIS WHEELCHAIR!

MEANWHILE, MILES AWAY, IN A SAD AND CRUMBLING HOUSE...

THEY DOUBLED THE LIGHTHOUSE GUARD-- SO WHEN OLD MANUEL POSSESSES ME AGAIN, I'LL REALLY HAVE TO BE ON THE BALL! TONIGHT IS THE TIME I MUST BRIDGE THE GAP BETWEEN THE WORLDS!

SO IT IS THAT A BROODING *BATMAN* WAITS FOR THE "VISITOR" HE KNOWS MUST COME--AND AS NIGHT FALLS...

18

189

SOON, WHERE SCUDDING CLOUDS OBSCURE THE MOON, AND NERVOUS MEN STAND GUARD...

SHORTLY, LIKE THE WINGED MAMMAL WHOSE NAME HE BEARS, THE POSSESSED *BATMAN* SOON SOARS TO THE TOP AND ENTERS...

A FEW MINUTES LATER, HE EXITS! BUT SUDDENLY, AS THE CLOUDS PART...

UP THERE... AGAINST THE MOON! SHOOT!

VIP

BEEOW

AND THEN, THE BIZARRE STIFF-LEGGED FIGURE VANISHES INTO THE NIGHT!

BEEIP

ZING

19

NOT LONG AFTER, AS A SCARLET BLUR ONCE MORE STREAKS OVER THE BEACH...

MAYBE NOW I HAVE THE ANSWER!

WHAT'S THAT AHEAD... *TORCHES?*

THE POLICE... AND SOME VILLAGERS!

IT WAS THAT CRAZY *BATMAN*, ALL RIGHT, CHIEF! HE GOT INTO THE LIGHTHOUSE... THEN ESCAPED USING OLD MANUEL'S FUNNY GAIT!

IT'S TIME THIS MADMAN WAS STOPPED! TERRORIZIN' THE WHOLE ISLAND...

NO TELLIN' WHAT HE MIGHT DO, POSSESSED THE WAY HE IS OF THAT DEAD DEVIL, THE PORT-A-GEE!

START SEARCHING! *WE'LL FIND HIM--!*

GOOD BLAZES! THEY'RE REALLY RILED UP -- OUT FOR *BATMAN'S* BLOOD! I'VE GOT TO FIND HIM *FIRST!*

SUDDENLY, THE NIGHT IS TORN APART BY A GREAT, STABBING BEAM...

THE LIGHTHOUSE... *IT'S WORKING?* BUT IT HASN'T FOR *YEARS!*

20

AND WHERE THE INCANDESCENT CIRCLE OF LIGHT STRIKES THE ROLLING WAVES...

GOOD LORD! IT'S... *THEM!* THE SPIRITS FROM THE DEAD WORLD! THEY'RE MOVING... TOWARD THE HOUSE! MUST GET THERE AT ONCE!

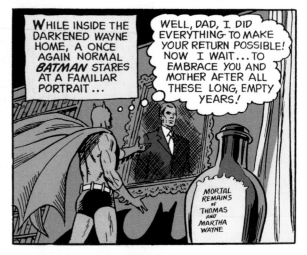

WHILE INSIDE THE DARKENED WAYNE HOME, A ONCE AGAIN NORMAL *BATMAN* STARES AT A FAMILIAR PORTRAIT...

WELL, DAD, I DID EVERYTHING TO MAKE YOUR RETURN POSSIBLE! NOW I WAIT... TO EMBRACE YOU AND MOTHER AFTER ALL THESE LONG, EMPTY YEARS!

MORTAL REMAINS OF THOMAS AND MARTHA WAYNE

FLASH!

YOU *DID* IT... RELEASED THE DEAD! A WHOLE MULTITUDE OF THEM IS APPROACHING THE HOUSE--!

NO, ONLY MY PARENTS WILL BE BROUGHT BACK!

IT DIDN'T WORK THAT WAY! I KNOW NOW WHY AS MANUEL YOU KEPT GOING TO THE LIGHT- HOUSE--*TO FIX IT!* THE BEAM'S POWER WAS NEEDED TO DRAW THE SPIRIT BEINGS FROM THE SEA!

21

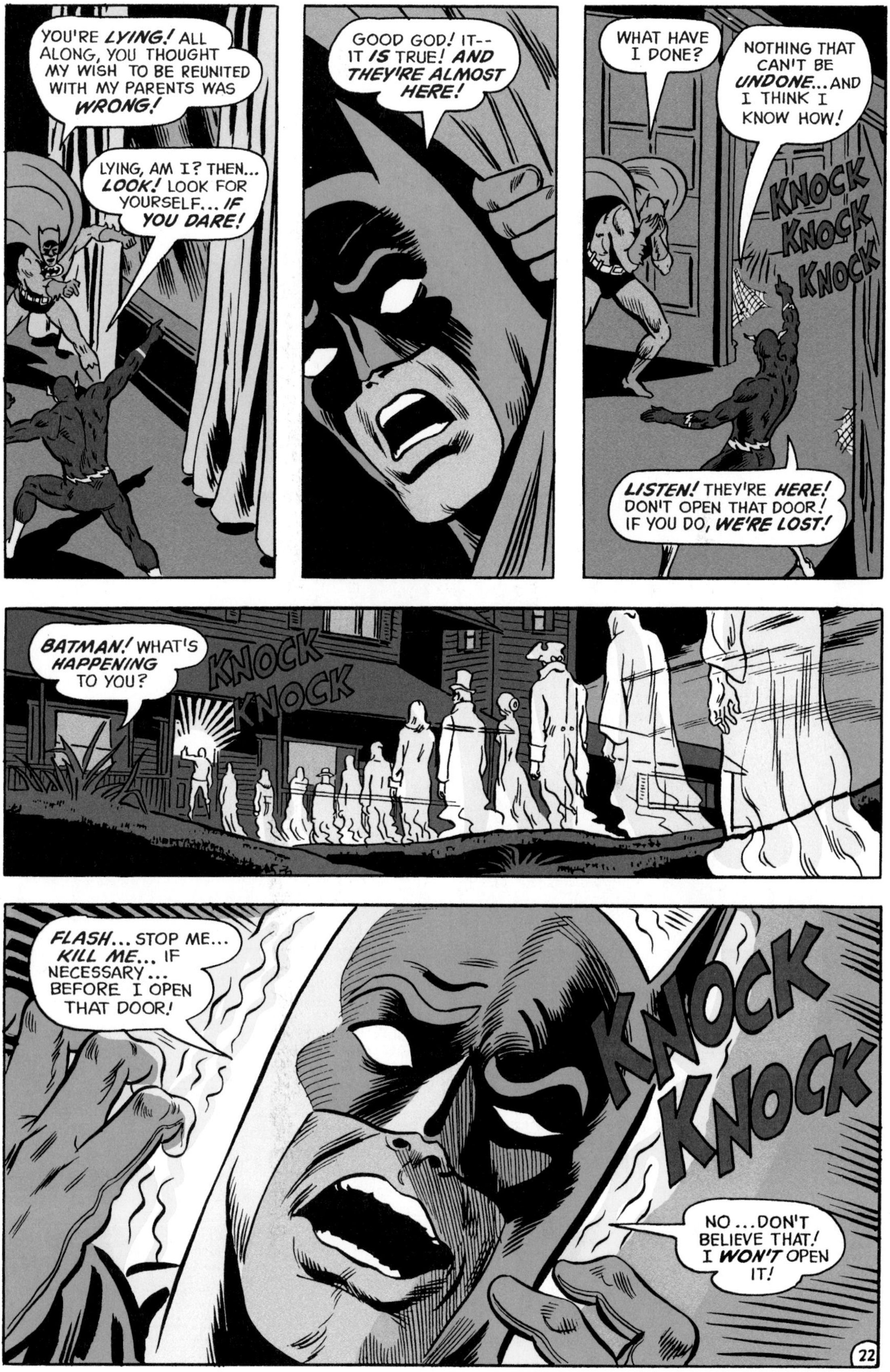
YOU'RE LYING! ALL ALONG, YOU THOUGHT MY WISH TO BE REUNITED WITH MY PARENTS WAS WRONG!
LYING, AM I? THEN... LOOK! LOOK FOR YOURSELF... IF YOU DARE!
GOOD GOD! IT-- IT IS TRUE! AND THEY'RE ALMOST HERE!
WHAT HAVE I DONE?
NOTHING THAT CAN'T BE UNDONE... AND I THINK I KNOW HOW!
KNOCK KNOCK KNOCK
LISTEN! THEY'RE HERE! DON'T OPEN THAT DOOR! IF YOU DO, WE'RE LOST!
BATMAN! WHAT'S HAPPENING TO YOU?
KNOCK KNOCK
FLASH... STOP ME... KILL ME... IF NECESSARY... BEFORE I OPEN THAT DOOR!
KNOCK KNOCK
NO... DON'T BELIEVE THAT! I WON'T OPEN IT!
22

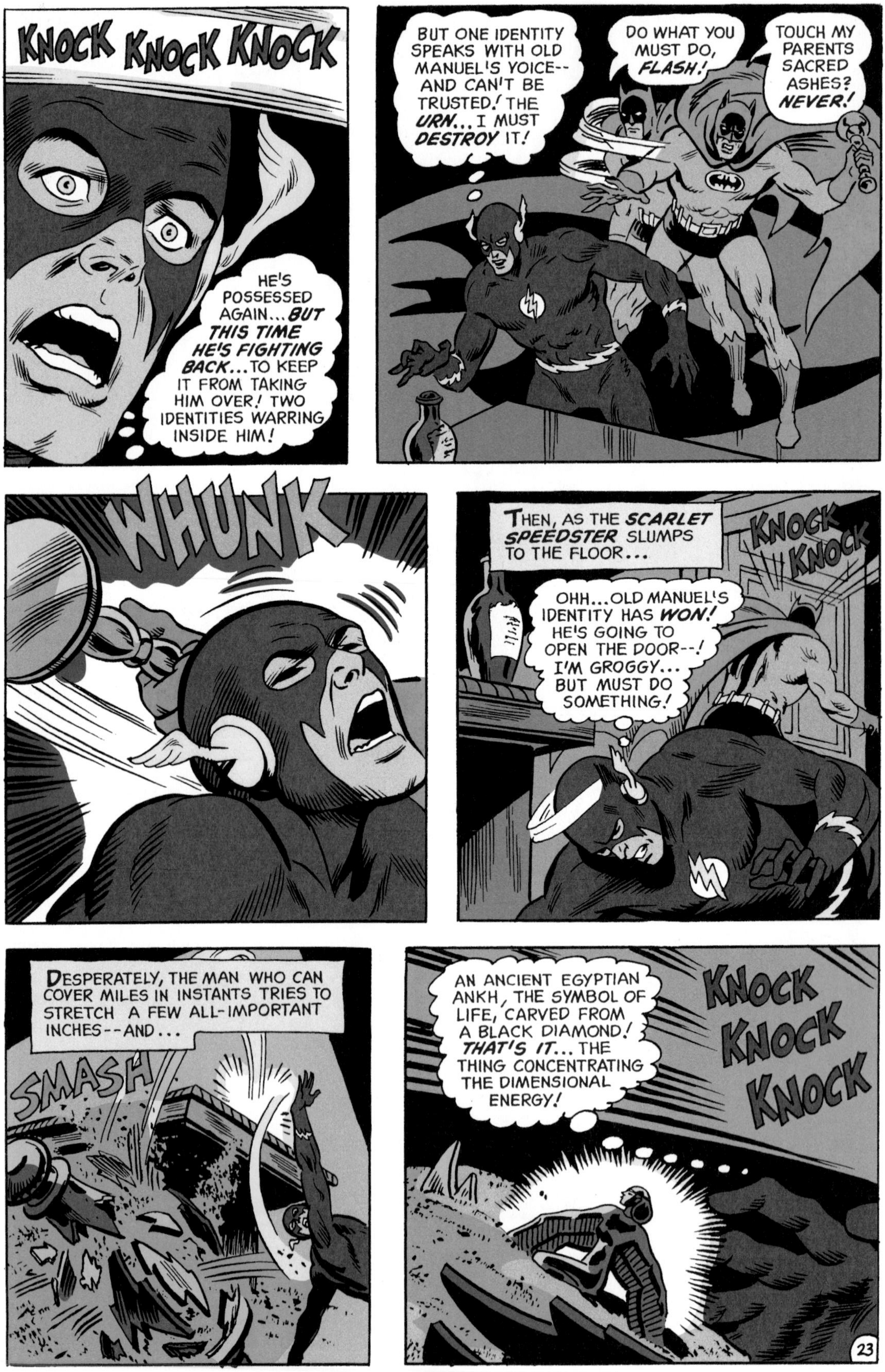
KNOCK KNOCK KNOCK
HE'S POSSESSED AGAIN... BUT THIS TIME HE'S FIGHTING BACK... TO KEEP IT FROM TAKING HIM OVER! TWO IDENTITIES WARRING INSIDE HIM!
BUT ONE IDENTITY SPEAKS WITH OLD MANUEL'S VOICE-- AND CAN'T BE TRUSTED! THE URN... I MUST DESTROY IT!
DO WHAT YOU MUST DO, FLASH!
TOUCH MY PARENTS SACRED ASHES? NEVER!
WHUNK
THEN, AS THE SCARLET SPEEDSTER SLUMPS TO THE FLOOR...
KNOCK KNOCK
OHH... OLD MANUEL'S IDENTITY HAS WON! HE'S GOING TO OPEN THE DOOR--! I'M GROGGY... BUT MUST DO SOMETHING!
DESPERATELY, THE MAN WHO CAN COVER MILES IN INSTANTS TRIES TO STRETCH A FEW ALL-IMPORTANT INCHES--AND...
SMASH
AN ANCIENT EGYPTIAN ANKH, THE SYMBOL OF LIFE, CARVED FROM A BLACK DIAMOND! THAT'S IT... THE THING CONCENTRATING THE DIMENSIONAL ENERGY!
KNOCK KNOCK KNOCK
23

AS THE KNOCKING REACHES A PERSISTENT CRESCENDO, A GAUNTLETED HAND REACHES FOR A WELL-WORN HANDLE...

KNOCK KNOCK KNOCK

HOPE... I'VE GOT ENOUGH STRENGTH... TO GIVE THIS THING A SUPER-SPEED LIFT-OFF!

SMASH

THE NEXT INSTANT, LIKE SOME TINY METEORITE IN REVERSE, THE BLACK ARTIFACT LEAVES EARTH FOREVER FOR THE STARS!

WHILE BELOW...

DAD!? MOTHER?? NO ONE... NO ONE... AT ALL!

UHHH, MY HEAD FEELS LIKE I JUST AWAKENED FROM A NIGHTMARE!

SAND? THE URN CONTAINED... SAND?

YES, SAND... AND THE ANKH--WHICH, ONCE GONE, BROKE THE ENERGY LINK BETWEEN THE TWO WORLDS AND OLD MANUEL'S POSSESSION OF YOU!

HOW CLOSE TO DISASTER I CAME! FORGIVE ME, FLASH... AND THANKS!

THANK OLD CALEB BRONSON! HE GAVE ME THE VITAL CLUE--SCRATCHING THE MESSAGE THAT THE ANKH WAS HIDDEN IN THE URN SO IT WOULD REMAIN UNDISTURBED!

24

OF COURSE! DAD KNEW EVEN *I'D* NEVER OPEN WHAT I BELIEVED CONTAINED MY OWN PARENTS' REMAINS!

BUT HE COULDN'T KNOW THE EXPERIMENT WOULD GO AWRY!

WHERE ARE MY PARENTS NOW-- STILL TRAPPED IN THAT AWFUL DIMENSION? AND *WHY?*

PERHAPS BECAUSE YOUR FATHER *DARED* TO TAMPER WITH WHAT MUST REMAIN SEPARATE--THE *LIVING* AND *DEAD* WORLDS!

I DON'T EVEN HAVE THEIR ASHES... NOW!

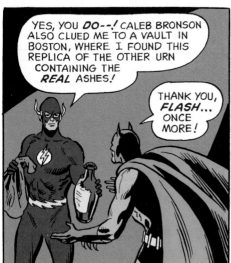

YES, YOU *DO--!* CALEB BRONSON ALSO CLUED ME TO A VAULT IN BOSTON, WHERE I FOUND THIS REPLICA OF THE OTHER URN CONTAINING THE *REAL* ASHES!

THANK YOU, *FLASH*... ONCE MORE!

AND LATER, AS AN EXHAUSTED MAN SLEEPS...

BRUCE, OUR SON... IT'S OVER! WE FAILED TO RETURN TO YOUR WORLD... BUT DESTROYING THE ANKH FREED US FROM THE NETHER WORLD! WE'VE REACHED THE LAND OF ETERNAL PEACE... AT LAST!

TIME IS MERCIFUL! THE NIGHT'S DARKNESS ONLY LASTS UNTIL A NEW DAY'S DAWNING...

THE LOCAL AUTHORITIES WENT ALONG WITH MY ESCORTING YOU OFF THE ISLAND TO SEEK PSYCHIATRIC HELP!

THAT'S ONLY *HALF* A LIE, BARRY-- I REALLY *COULD* USE A HEAD-SHRINKER AFTER *THIS* VACATION!

BUT SERIOUSLY, I'VE ALSO FOUND PEACE AT LAST! I'M NO LONGER HAUNTED BY MY ORPHANED CHILDHOOD... KILLING MY PAST BY FINALLY PUTTING THE GHOSTS OF MY PARENTS TO REST HAS FREED ME!

GOODBYE, DAD... MOM! GOODBYE, HOUSE--!

The END

25

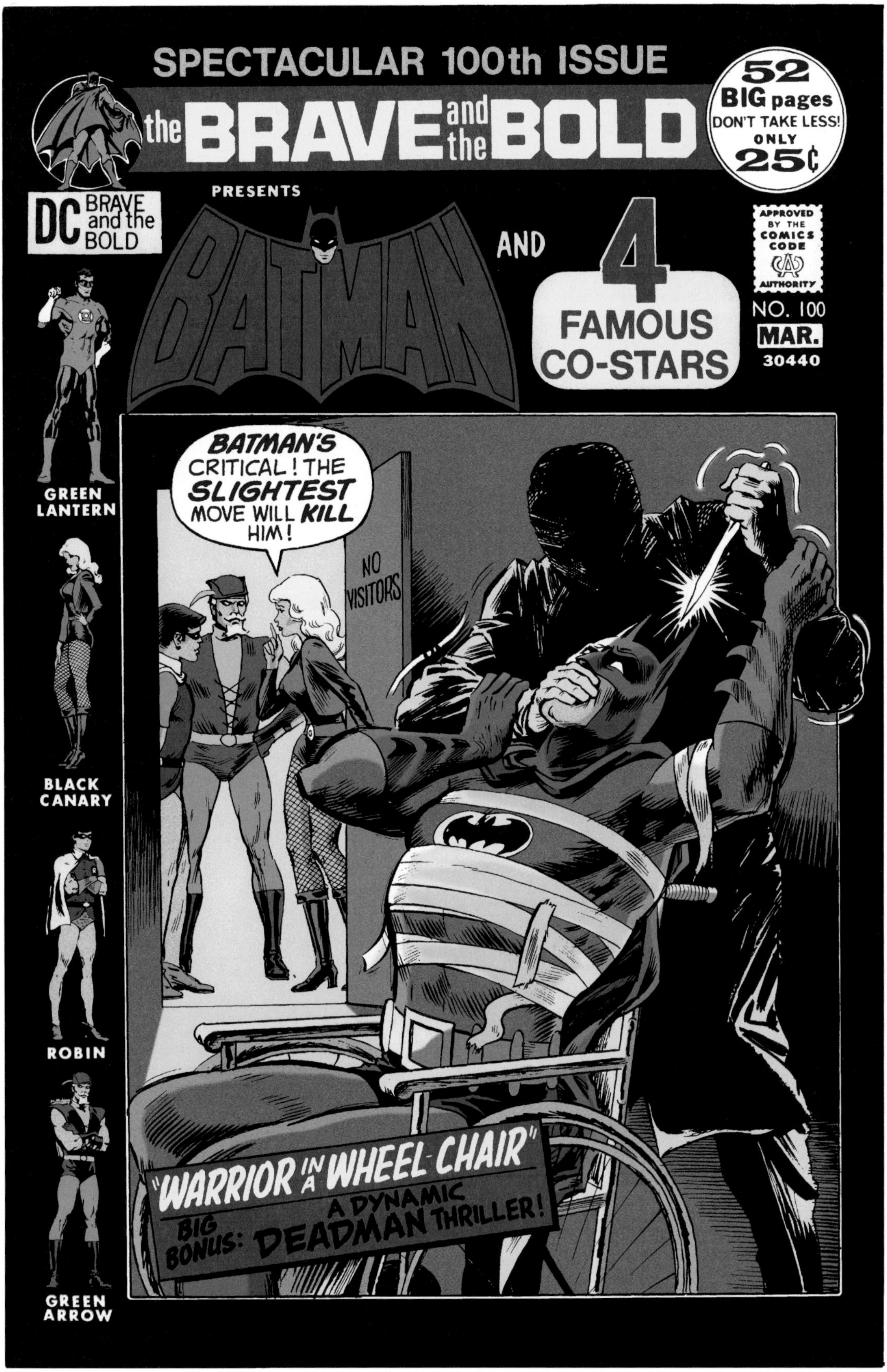
SPECTACULAR 100th ISSUE
the BRAVE and the BOLD
52 BIG pages DON'T TAKE LESS! ONLY 25¢
DC BRAVE and the BOLD
PRESENTS
BATMAN
AND
4 FAMOUS CO-STARS
APPROVED BY THE COMICS CODE AUTHORITY
NO. 100
MAR.
30440
GREEN LANTERN
BLACK CANARY
ROBIN
GREEN ARROW
BATMAN'S CRITICAL! THE SLIGHTEST MOVE WILL KILL HIM!
NO VISITORS
"WARRIOR IN A WHEEL-CHAIR"
BIG BONUS: A DYNAMIC DEADMAN THRILLER!

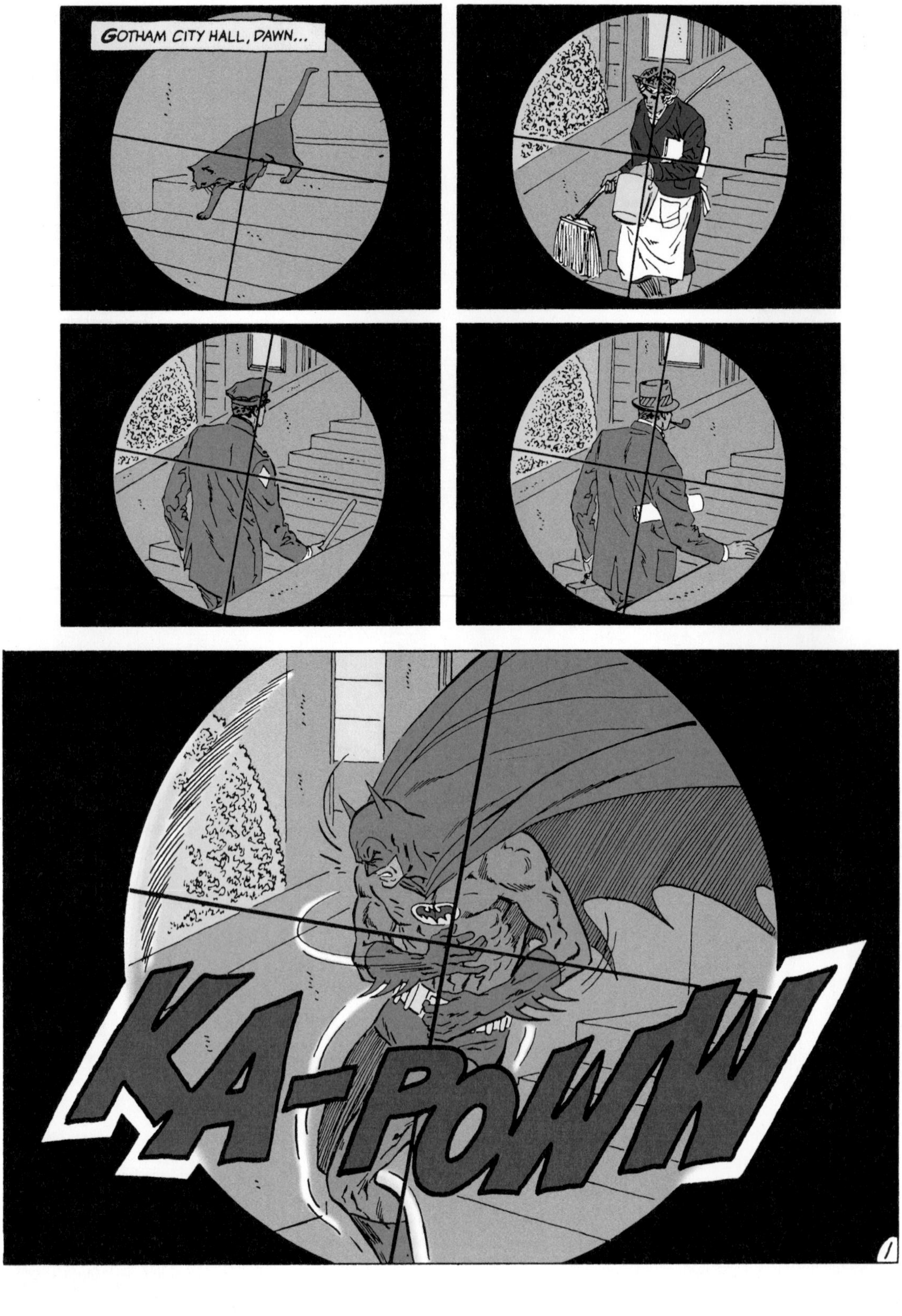
GOTHAM CITY HALL, DAWN...
KA-POWW
1

A WAIL OF AN AMBULANCE IN THE FRESH NEW DAY, A WAIL LIKE A WHOLE CITY'S ANGUISH...

VITAL SIGNS STEADY... HE'S ALIVE... THERE'S *HOPE*, COMMISSIONER!

THANK GOD! BUT A BULLET NEAR THE *HEART*, DOCTOR... CAN EVEN *BATMAN* BEAT THAT?

THEY GOT HIM AT LAST... THE WORST CRIMINAL SCUM OF ALL... THE DRUG RING... THEY CUT HIM DOWN BECAUSE THEY KNEW HE SWORE ETERNAL WAR AGAINST THEM!

GOTHAM HOSPITAL-- A CATHEDRAL OF HEALING AND PAIN... A PATIENT, MIRACULOUSLY CONSCIOUS, MERE MINUTES LATER, IS RUSHED INTO A HUSHED ROOM...

BATMAN... COMMISSIONER... AS HOSPITAL DIRECTOR, I WANT YOU TO UNDERSTAND WHAT WE'RE UP AGAINST!

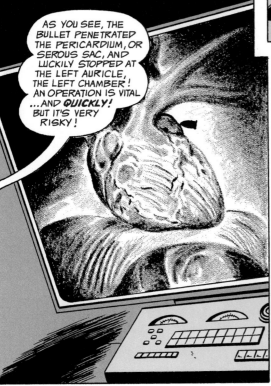

AS YOU SEE, THE BULLET PENETRATED THE PERICARDIUM, OR SEROUS SAC, AND LUCKILY STOPPED AT THE LEFT AURICLE, THE LEFT CHAMBER! AN OPERATION IS VITAL ... AND *QUICKLY!* BUT IT'S VERY RISKY!

THE ONLY SURGEON FOR THE JOB IS DR. HELLSTROM OF ZURICH! HE'S THE WORLD'S *BEST*... WITH HIM, YOU'VE GOT A *CHANCE!*

2

BUT DR. HELLSTROM COULDN'T BE HERE BY PLANE UNTIL FRIDAY--THAT'S *THREE DAYS*! MEANTIME, *BATMAN*, YOU MUST REMAIN *IMMOBILIZED*! A WRONG MOVEMENT COULD BE *FATAL*!

GOTHAM HOSPITAL

YOU HEARD HIM, *BATMAN*?

GORDON *KNOWS* WHAT I'M THINKING... THAT BY FRIDAY THE BIGGEST HEROIN SHIPMENT EVER WILL HAVE BEEN SMUGGLED INTO GOTHAM BY THE INTERNATIONAL DRUG RING...

THE ONE CRIME I'D GIVE MY WHOLE CAREER...EVEN MY *LIFE*...TO STOP...AND NOW I'M *HELPLESS*!

TUESDAY, JULY 10th, 1 P.M.-- A SUNKEN FIGURE STARES OUT AT THE CITY HE LOVES...HIS BRAIN SEETHING WITH BITTER THOUGHTS...

THE DEADLY CIRCLE--IT'S ALMOST COMPLETE! FROM THE POPPY FIELDS OF TURKEY... TO THE LABS OF MARSEILLES... TO THE BIG DEALER HERE IN GOTHAM...TO THE STREET PUSHERS... AND AT LAST TO THE KIDS WHO'LL BUY THE JUNK THAT'LL RUIN THEIR LIVES... THEIR FAMILIES...AND BREED NEW HELL IN THE STREETS!

SO BEGINS THE CROWNING SAGA OF THE *BRAVE* AND *BOLD* SERIES--THE ULTIMATE EXPERIENCE OF THIS *100th ANNIVERSARY ISSUE* -- THAT REUNITES *BATMAN* AND FOUR ALLIES AS THE *MASKED MANHUNTER*, SURVIVOR OF COUNTLESS DESPERATE COMBATS, NOW MUST FACE HIS SUPREME CHALLENGE...TO SAVE AN ENTIRE GENERATION... WHILE THREATENED BY DEATH ITSELF AS HE BECOMES...

"THE WARRIOR IN A WHEEL-CHAIR"

3

I **CAN'T** LET IT HAPPEN...I **WON'T!** I'LL STOP THAT SHIPMENT IF IT'S...

...THE LAST THING I DO...

MY GOD--!

I...I'M ALL RIGHT, ALFRED! JUST MY CHEST...ACHES...BURNS...

YOU **MUST** NOT MOVE, SIR! YOU COULD **DIE!** PLEASE, **PLEASE** DON'T LEAVE THAT CHAIR AGAIN!

I KNOW--BUT THE ONE TIME IN MY LIFE I NEED THESE HANDS...THESE LEGS...EVERY **OUNCE** AND **INCH**, EVERY FIBER OF MY BEING...I'M A **CRIPPLE!**

A **CRIPPLED** BAT DOESN'T FLY, ALFRED!

THE FAMILIAR FIGURE SINKS INTO DESPAIR BEYOND UTTERANCE...UNAWARE OF A TINY COMPANION THAT SHARES HIS HIGH PERCH...

BUT A SUDDEN BUZZING, MORE SUDDENLY STILLED PULLS THE MAN FROM HIS STUPOR...

A FLY...CAUGHT IN THE SPIDER'S WEB! AND THERE'S THE WEB-SPINNER... JUST SITTING PRETTY!

NOW HE LEISURELY CRAWLS TOWARD HIS VICTIM... AND HE DIDN'T HAVE TO BUDGE AN *INCH* TO CATCH IT!

OF COURSE, *THAT'S IT!* TO CATCH THE "FLIES" *I'M* AFTER, THE *BAT* MUST TURN *SPIDER!*

ALFRED! CALL ROBIN! I NEED HIM HERE-- *QUICKLY!*

SNAP

TUESDAY, JULY 10th, 6 P.M.

HI! I WAS STARTING BACK FROM COLLEGE TO BE HERE WITH YOU, ANYWAY, WHEN ALFRED'S CALL CAME! THE TV...I SAW THE NEWS...! MY GOD, ARE YOU *ALL RIGHT?*

I'M ALIVE, DICK! THANKS FOR COMING... ALFRED'S CALL WAS JUST INSURANCE... I'VE NO DOUBT OF YOU...I...UH...

BRUCE...BRUCE!..

DICK...

THESE TWO TOGETHER AGAIN--! NOW MAYBE GOTHAM'S KIDS HAVE BOUGHT ONE MORE CHANCE!

TUESDAY, 8 P.M., AND AS THE SETTING SUN OF A SIMMERING SUMMER NIGHT GILDS THE COBBLES--THERE COMES THE MEASURED TREAD OF A TRIO UNIQUE...

SICK FAM City

WHAT'S THE TRUE SCOOP? THE *BAT GUY'S* REALLY GOOFING OFF... AND WE'RE THE SUMMER REPLACEMENT SHOW, RIGHT?

TELL THIS BEARDED BOASTER I'M FOOL ENOUGH TO LOVE WHERE IT'S AT!

WILL DO! SURE, *BATMAN'S* GOOFING ...WITH A 30.06 SLUG A SILLY MILLIMETER FROM HIS HEART! HE NOT ONLY NEEDS US... HE NEEDS A *MIRACLE!*

OLIVER QUEEN! DINAH LANCE! HAL JORDAN! OR, TO AN ADMIRING WORLD, *GREEN ARROW, BLACK CANARY, GREEN LANTERN!* IN GOTHAM! WHY? LET'S LISTEN!

OKAY, OKAY, SO HE NEEDS US! THAT'S WHY I CAME! BUT WHY ALL THE MYSTERY--?

IT'S *BATMAN'S* TURF, *G.A.!* WE DO IT HIS WAY! WE'RE ALMOST THERE--!

SHORTLY...

THREE WRIST RADIOS STASHED IN A CAN? WHAT KIND OF PHONY CLOAK AND DAGGER STUFF--?

BATMAN HAD NO TIME TO SET THINGS UP FORMALLY! WE NEED *INSTANT* COMMUNICATION WITH HIM! HE'LL GIVE US OUR INSTRUCTIONS AS THINGS BREAK!

SPEAKING OF COMMUNICATION, THE GHETTO PUNKS BOOST THE COIN BOXES JUST TO GET BREAD FOR *JUNK!*

KLIK

CHECK, *G.A.!* BUT THEN MAYBE SO WOULD *YOU* IF THAT'S ALL THAT GAVE YOU ESCAPE FROM THE STREETS!

DON'T LECTURE *ME* ON THE DRUG PROBLEM, *LANTERN!* I'VE BEEN INTO IT WITH *SPEEDY,* MY OWN WARD!..

OH, BIG DADDY'S A REAL GENERATION-GAP VETERAN!

CUT IT! MAYBE I...I'M NOT THE BEST IMAGE THE KID COULD'VE HAD... BUT *I* DIDN'T MAKE THIS WORLD!

IN ANY CASE, WE'VE GOT A CHANCE TO STRIKE A BLOW AGAINST DOPE... RIGHT HERE IN GOTHAM... FOLLOWING *BATMAN'S* ORDERS... EXACTLY... EVERY MINUTE... NO MATTER WHAT! *RIGHT?*

RIGHT!

RIGHT ON!

6

NOW AS A SECRET FREQUENCY GOES INTO USE...

BIRDBOY TO MR. ARACHNID! COMMUNICATIONS ESTABLISHED!

THANKS, BIRDBOY!

GREEN ARROW'S A HARD CHARGER, GREEN LANTERN'S THE ANCHOR MAN... BLACK CANARY? I CAN'T FIGURE WHY WE NEED HER?

YOU WILL! NOW STAND BY! YOU'RE MY BACKSTOPPER! THE BALL GAME STARTS AT 2 A.M.!

SUDDENLY, A SPECIAL PHONE RINGS...

GORDON HERE! LISTEN, YOU CAN'T RUN THIS OPERATION ALONE!... SITTING THERE HELPLESSLY!

I'M NOT, COMMISSIONER! ROBIN, GREEN ARROW, GREEN LANTERN, BLACK CANARY-- THEY'RE MY EYES AND EARS AND LEGS!

BUT DRUG TRAFFICKING IS A POLICE MATTER...

I AGREE, BUT ONE MISSTEP BY A SINGLE DETECTIVE OR PATROLMAN, AND THE WHOLE DEAL WILL BLOW SKY-HIGH!

CAN YOU KEEP OUT-- UNTIL I NEED YOU?

WE'RE UP AGAINST THE KINGPIN OF INTERNATIONAL JUNK MERCHANTS...BELKNAP HIMSELF! AND HE'S TRICKIER THAN A COBRA ON GLASS!

THE ONLY CHANCE OF STOPPING THIS SHIPMENT--AND ANY OTHERS--IS DOING THINGS MY WAY!

7

NOW I'VE GOT TO KEEP MY OTHER COMMUNICATIONS CHANNELS OPEN AND CLEAR!

CLICK

MY CHEST... OUUHHH! PAIN LIKE A HOT IRON... MUST KEEP CALM...

GOT TO EMULATE MY WEB-SPINNING FRIEND HERE... AND WAIT... WAIT FOR THE NEXT FLY TO BUZZ INTO THE TRAP!

AT THIS MOMENT, IT IS AFTERNOON OF THE NEXT DAY IN A VILLA ON A SWISS LAKE...

THE SHIPMENT'S READY TO GO, MR. BELKNAP!

IT'S A LARGE AND IMPORTANT ONE! I HAVE SOME MISGIVINGS! BETTER RUN A *TEST* ON THE DELIVERY CHANNELS!

TUESDAY, 11 P.M.--AND A DOZING MAN AWAKES TO THE HUM OF A CITY CLOAKED IN THE HEAT OF THE NIGHT...

TIME TO START THE GAME! OLD SPIDER CAN SLEEP... HIS WEB'S DONE... BUT I'VE STILL GOT TO SPIN MINE...

THIS IS MY KEY...WITHOUT IT, I WOULDN'T EVEN BE IN THE GAME! A CODED SYSTEM OF "CONNECTIONS" THE DRUG RING USES TO GET THE SHIPMENTS INTO GOTHAM... AND INTO THE HANDS OF THE BIG DEALERS!

8

LUCKY I CAME BY IT! A DEALER THE DRUG RING SHOT OUT ON THEM GAVE IT TO ME ON HIS DEATHBED! NOW LET'S SEE IF I CRACKED THE CODE RIGHT--!

MR. ARACHNID TO ACE ARCHER--!

AND ON A DARK STREET...

ARCHER TO ARACHNID!

HERE WE GO, CHUM... HERE ARE YOUR ORDERS!..

WEDNESDAY, JULY 11th, 1:30 A.M.-- GOTHAM CITY'S MAIN POST OFFICE...

WHAT BETTER WAY TO SHIP JUNK INTO THE STATES THAN THIS WAY! CLEVER AND SIMPLE!

TWO O'CLOCK-- THERE'S THE WINDOW...AND TWO POSTAL WORKERS MAKING A PICK-UP! COULD BE IT!

THEY PICKED UP THE PACKAGES!.. BATMAN SAID TO MAKE SURE!

9

EXCUSE ME, FELLAS... BUT COULD I INSPECT THOSE--?

HUHH? THEY'RE BUGGING OUT--!

MOVE!

THE NEXT MOMENT, A SINEWY ARM FLEXES A BONE BOW OF WHIPLASH POWER-- AND...

THOK

THUD

KPOW

KPOW!

BATMAN WAS RIGHT-- PHONIES!

BLEOW

ZING

OH-OH, SOMEBODY'S GRANDMA'S FRUIT CAKE'S GOING TO HAVE A METALLIC TASTE--BUT BETTER IT THAN ME!

AGAIN THE BONE BOW BENDS--AND...

THWUNNG

10

THEN...

ONE DEAD... ONE GOT AWAY--BUT I GOT THE STUFF--A WHOLE CARTLOAD OF IT!

WHITE...FINE...MUST BE A HUNDRED "KEYS"* OF UNCUT SKEZAG HERE...WORTH MILLIONS CUT AND SOLD ON THE STREET!

IT'S NOT JUNK!.. IT'S... SUGAR!!

* KEY: 1 KILO, OR 2.2 POUNDS

WEDNESDAY JULY 11, 6 A.M., AND DAWN OF ANOTHER HOT DAY SEARS THE STREETS OF GOTHAM...

SO BELKNAP WAS RUNNING A TEST--HE EVEN SACRIFICED ONE OF HIS GOONS TO FIND OUT! NOW HE MUST GUESS I'M SPINNING A WEB FOR HIM...

BUT NOW WE KNOW THE SHIPMENT HASN'T ARRIVED YET! BUT IT COULD COME THROUGH THE NEXT CHANNEL!

WAKE UP, SPIDEY! THERE'RE MORE FLIES TO CATCH!

OHHH, MY CHEST..! GOT TO KEEP GOING!.. CAN'T COLLAPSE--!

11

208

AND WHERE ANOTHER DAY HAS REACHED THE ZENITH OVER SNOW-CAPPED PEAKS...

SO SOME CRAZY ARCHER WAS JAMMING THE MAIL CHANNEL? INTERESTING! ALMOST SOUNDS LIKE *BATMAN'S* INVOLVED...

...BUT *WE* GOT RID OF *HIM*...HE'S AN INVALID WAITING FOR AN OPERATION! NO, CAN'T BE THE *CAPED CRUSADER*--!

RUN THE NEXT CHANNEL! WE'LL SEE WHO SALUTES!

WEDNESDAY, JULY 11th, 2:30 P.M. ...

YOU SNARED ANOTHER ONE, PAL! TIME TO SEE IF MY *OWN* WEB'S WORKING--!

MR. ARACHNID TO EMERALD GLADIATOR--!

HALF AN HOUR LATER, AT GOTHAM RIVER DOCKS...

LACONIA

BATMAN SAID THE NEXT POSSIBLE "CONNECTION" HAD TO DO WITH THAT RUSTY TUB ...JUST ARRIVED FROM EUROPE...AND SOMETIME AROUND THIS HOUR!...

MOMENTS LATER, HIS POWER RING GIVES *GREEN LANTERN* A SPECIAL VANTAGE POINT...

HMMM, LONGSHOREMEN UNLOADING A FOREIGN CAR... RATHER ON THE SLY--!

12

BLAZES! THEY'RE SWITCHING IT WITH AN IDENTICAL JOB FROM THE BARGE--?

AND WITHIN MINUTES...

NOW THEY'RE TAKING THE OFF-LOADED CAR UP-RIVER? I GET IT--IT'S GOT TO BE CRAMMED WITH DOPE...

CUSTOMS TURNS IMPORTED CARS INSIDE-OUT THESE DAYS...BUT *THIS* ONE THEY'LL *NEVER* SEE...WHILE THE SWITCHED BUGGY TAKES ITS PLACE ON THE SHIP'S MANIFEST LIST!

SOON...

NOW THEY SHOVE IT INTO THE VAN...AND TAKE OFF TO UNLOAD A FORTUNE IN HEART-BREAK SOMEWHERE! SMOOTH! TIME TO BREAK THIS "CONNECTION"--!

A FREAK CLAW! SHOVE 'ER OFF!

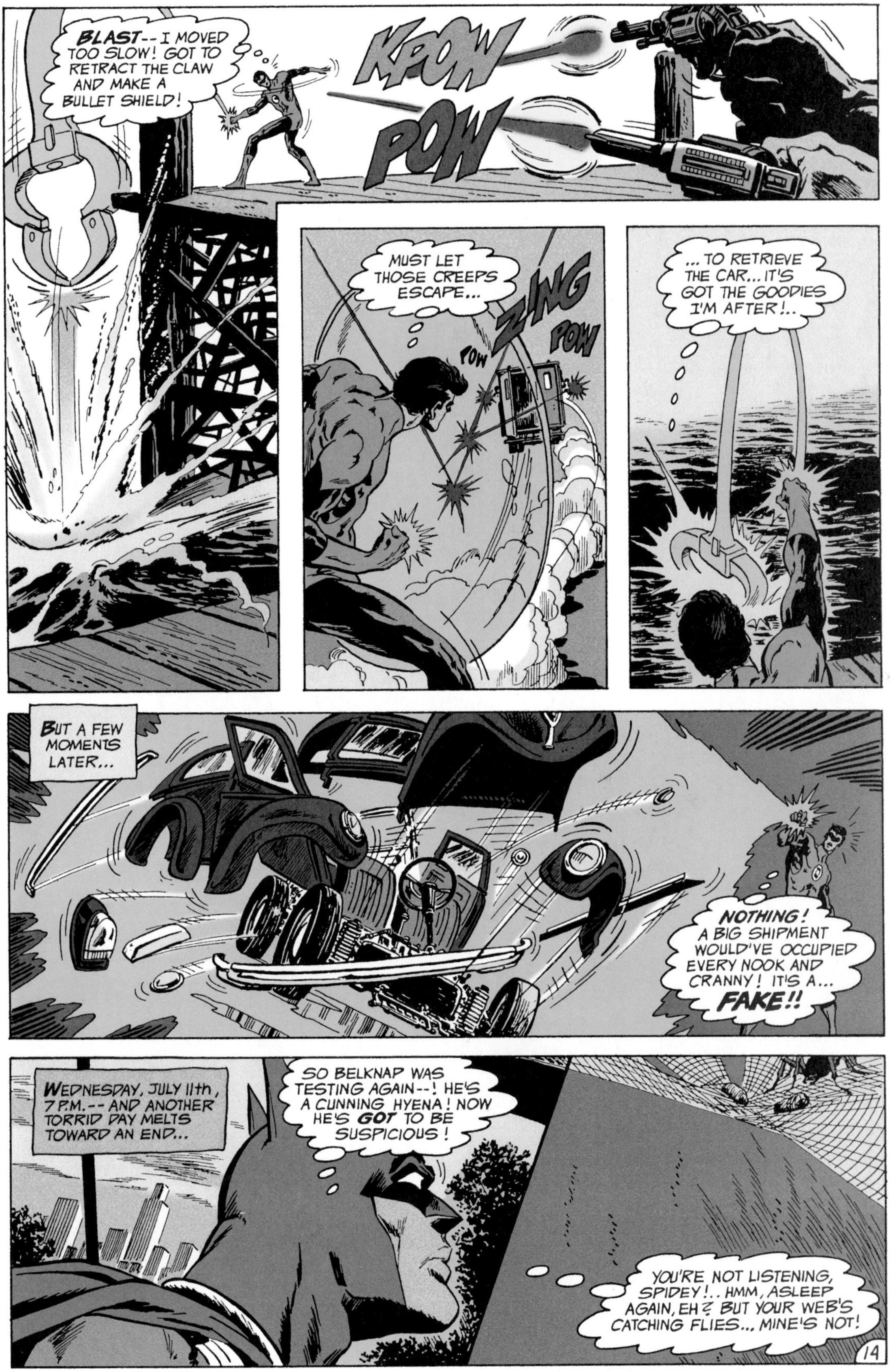
BLAST-- I MOVED TOO SLOW! GOT TO RETRACT THE CLAW AND MAKE A BULLET SHIELD!
KPOW
POW
MUST LET THOSE CREEPS ESCAPE...
ZING
POW
POW
... TO RETRIEVE THE CAR... IT'S GOT THE GOODIES I'M AFTER!..
BUT A FEW MOMENTS LATER...
NOTHING! A BIG SHIPMENT WOULD'VE OCCUPIED EVERY NOOK AND CRANNY! IT'S A... FAKE!!
WEDNESDAY, JULY 11th, 7 P.M.-- AND ANOTHER TORRID DAY MELTS TOWARD AN END...
SO BELKNAP WAS TESTING AGAIN--! HE'S A CUNNING HYENA! NOW HE'S GOT TO BE SUSPICIOUS!
YOU'RE NOT LISTENING, SPIDEY!.. HMM, ASLEEP AGAIN, EH? BUT YOUR WEB'S CATCHING FLIES... MINE'S NOT!
14

AND WHERE THE OTHER CONTESTANT IN THIS STRANGE STRUGGLE BROODS...

IT'S PUZZLING! *ANOTHER* CHANNEL BLOCKED... BY ANOTHER COSTUMED CLOWN! *BATMAN'S* LITTLE HELPERS? COULD BE !?.. WE'LL TRY CHANNEL THREE... AND SEE!

THURSDAY, JULY 12th, 1 P.M., A HARD, HOT RAIN FALLS ON GOTHAM...

MR. ARACHNID TO BIRDBOY! EMERGENCY! I CAN'T RAISE *BLACK CANARY!* I NEED HER FOR THE NEXT "CONNECTION"--!

THE FLIPPY FEMALE'S PROBABLY GOT HER WRIST-RADIO JAMMED WITH A BOBBIE-PIN! *I'LL* TAKE HER PLACE!

YOU *CAN'T--!* JUST FIND HER AND MAKE SURE THAT BY 2:30 SHE'S AT THIS ADDRESS -- 368 MILFORD AVENUE!

NOW ALONG DRENCHED, STEAMING STREETS THE *BOY WONDER* HUNTS...

ALMOST 2:30 AND I'VE COVERED EVERY SPOT SHE MIGHT BE--! I *WARNED BATMAN* SHE'D BE A PROBLEM!

THOSE LEGS--!!

COME ON! A MAN WITH A BULLET IN HIS CHEST IS COUNTING ON YOU--!

THE RAIN RUINED MY HAIR... I HAD TO DRY OUT!..

AND THE DRYER JAMMED *BATMAN'S* CALL-- I KNOW! *COME ON!!*

15

SHORTLY, AS THE SKIES CLEAR...

I *TOLD* HIM *I* COULD HANDLE THIS...

TODAY: WOMEN'S LIB LECTURE: MONIQUE DE LA TOUR AUTHOR OF "WHY, MEN?"

NO MEN ALLOWED!

NO, ROBIN-BOBBIN! THIS IS *ONE* PLACE EVEN *BOY CHAUVINISTS* CAN'T GO!

SOON, INSIDE...

MEN ARE NOT THE MASTERS

RIGHT ON, MONIQUE

MONIQUE DE LA TOUR JUST FLEW IN FROM FRANCE FOR THIS LECTURE...

BATMAN SUSPECTS SHE MAY HAVE BROUGHT SOMETHING PAST CUSTOMS... BUT HOW?

HMMM, HER LOGIC'S A BIT ROUGH-- BUT HER IDEAS AREN'T *BAD!*

THEN, AS THE LECTURE CONCLUDES...

ONE MOMENT, LADEEZ... I WILL GIVE OUT THESE COPIES OF MY BOOK!

DOWN WITH MEN

MONIQUE

MEN ARE NOT THE MASTERS

WHY, MEN?

WHY, MEN?

THINK *I'LL* GET ONE--!

SO SORREE, CHERIE... THERE ARE *NO MORE!*

BUT WHAT ABOUT THOSE TWO CARTONS BACK THERE?

16

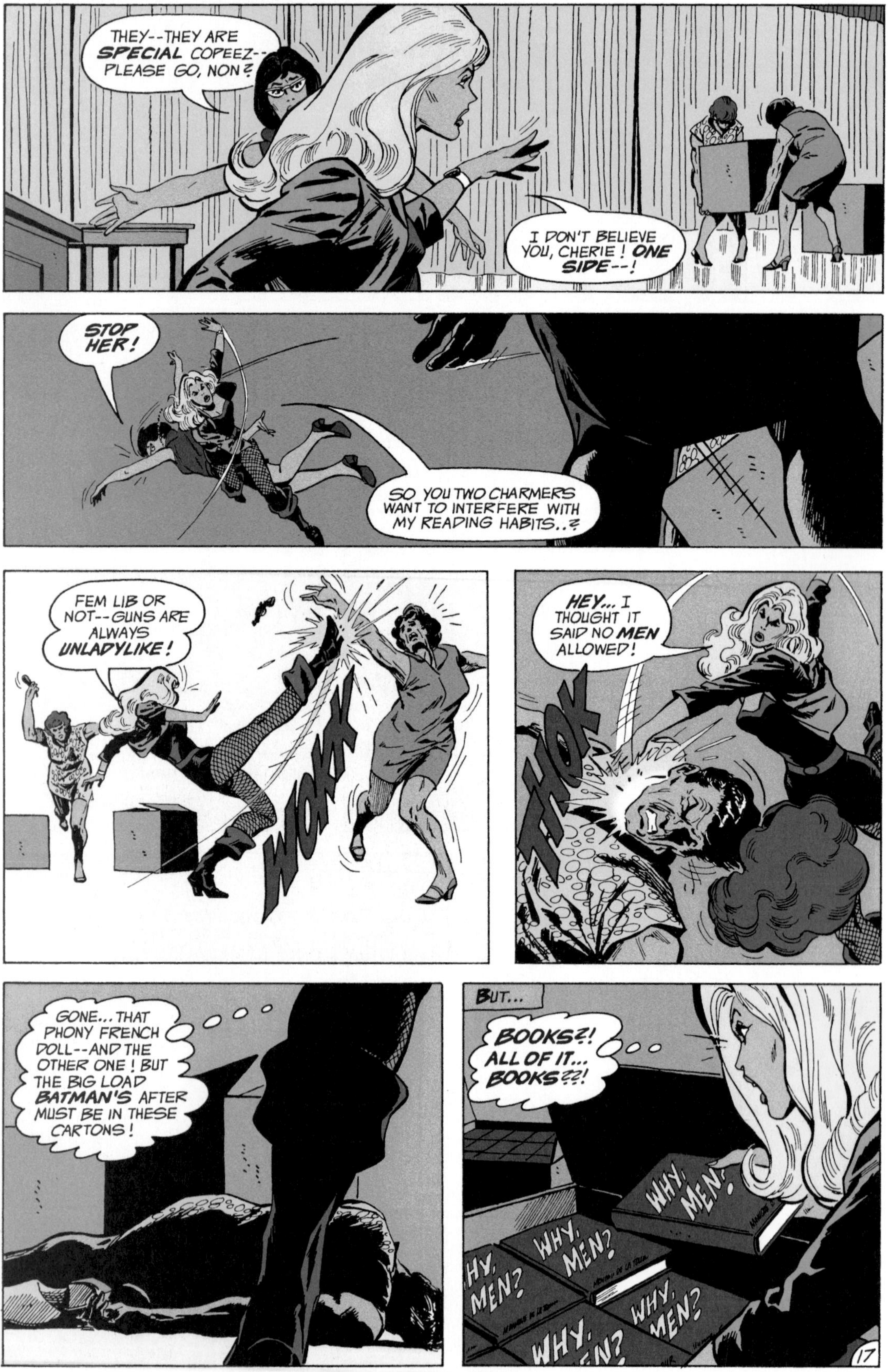
THEY--THEY ARE SPECIAL COPEEZ--PLEASE GO, NON?
I DON'T BELIEVE YOU, CHERIE! ONE SIDE--!
STOP HER!
SO YOU TWO CHARMERS WANT TO INTERFERE WITH MY READING HABITS..?
FEM LIB OR NOT--GUNS ARE ALWAYS UNLADYLIKE!
WOKK
HEY... I THOUGHT IT SAID NO MEN ALLOWED!
THOK
GONE... THAT PHONY FRENCH DOLL--AND THE OTHER ONE! BUT THE BIG LOAD BATMAN'S AFTER MUST BE IN THESE CARTONS!
BUT...
BOOKS?! ALL OF IT... BOOKS??!
WHY, MEN?
WHY, MEN?
WHY, MEN?
WHY, MEN?
17

THURSDAY, JULY 12th, 5 P.M., A HALF-DEAD, DESPAIRING MAN GAZES OUT AT THE CITY HE LOVES...

SO...WE *BLEW* IT! EACH OF THE THREE CONNECTION CHANNELS PROVED TO BE DRY RUNS! BELKNAP'S OUT-WITTED US--!

BUT...DOESN'T HE HAVE TO BRING IT IN... *SOMEHOW?*

YES, BUT NOW WE HAVEN'T THE *SLIGHTEST* IDEA *WHERE*--AND *HOW?* AND TOMORROW ...CHUM... MY TIME'S UP! I GO UNDER THE KNIFE...

I'VE FAILED... *FAILED?!..*

NO, DON'T THINK THAT! YOU RISKED EVERYTHING...

...YOUR LIFE... YOUR--

BATMAN!! HE'S *COLLAPSED!*

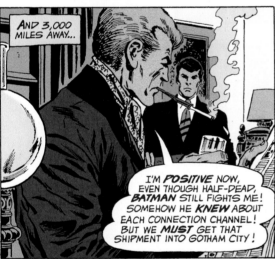

AND 3,000 MILES AWAY...

I'M *POSITIVE* NOW, EVEN THOUGH HALF-DEAD, *BATMAN* STILL FIGHTS ME! SOMEHOW HE *KNEW* ABOUT EACH CONNECTION CHANNEL! BUT WE *MUST* GET THAT SHIPMENT INTO GOTHAM CITY!

IT SAYS, *BATMAN* WILL BE OPERATED ON TOMORROW... BY THE FAMOUS DR. HELLSTROM ...OF THIS COUNTRY! HMMM...

THAT NIGHT, AT ZURICH AIRPORT...

CAREFUL! THAT MACHINE IS NECESSARY FOR MY OPERATION IN AMERICA TOMORROW!

OF COURSE, DR. HELLSTROM!

18

FRIDAY, JULY 13th, 9 A.M., GOTHAM HOSPITAL...

WELL, HERE GOES!.. IF I DIE...MY ONLY REGRET IS NOT HAVING STOPPED BELKNAP!

DON'T PUNISH YOURSELF, BATMAN... YOU DID ALL YOU COULD!

GOOD LUCK, FRIEND!

SEE YOU BOTH... SOON...I HOPE..!

THE BEST OF LUCK, OLD PAL!

AND THREE UNIQUE PEOPLE GATHER FOR WHATEVER COMFORT IS TO BE HAD...

THE BAT GUY GOES UNDER THE KNIFE ANY MINUTE... WHILE THE STUFF COULD BE ENTERING GOTHAM RIGHT NOW...

WHAT CAN WE DO? WE'VE NO LEADS... BATMAN WAS OUR BRAINS... OUR NERVE CENTER! LET'S GET TO THE HOSPITAL!

NOW UNDER THE BLAZING LIGHTS WHERE HUMAN SKILL AND NERVE BATTLE DEATH, THE CAPED CRUSADER BEGINS WHAT MAY BE HIS LAST ADVENTURE...

DR. HELLSTROM... IT IS A GREAT HONOR TO ASSIST YOU!..

A GREATER HONOR FOR ME TO TRY TO SAVE THIS GREAT MAN'S LIFE --!

19

HIS BODY FUNCTIONS WILL BE MONITORED BY THIS MACHINE... MY OWN INVENTION TO STABILIZE THE SYSTEM UNDER THE SHOCK OF SURGERY!

PATIENT UNDER FIRST STAGE OF ANESTHESIA!

GOOD! *YOU*, DOCTOR, WILL BEGIN! I SHALL TAKE OVER AT THE CRITICAL PART!

NOW AS THE *BATMAN* SINKS DEEPER INTO THE TWILIGHT WORLD OF THE ANESTHESIA, A BIZARRE FANTASY BEGINS...

HA HA HA HA HA HA HA

20

NO! NO!!

THE ANESTHESIA'S MADE HIM BERSERK! *HELP ME!*

GET HIM BACK DOWN!

GIVE HIM *MORE* ANESTHETIC!

HE'S...GOT... SUPER-HUMAN STRENGTH!

AS THE *BATMAN* FEELS HIMSELF BEING OVERWHELMED, HE TOUCHES A TINY BUTTON ON HIS WRIST WATCH...

21

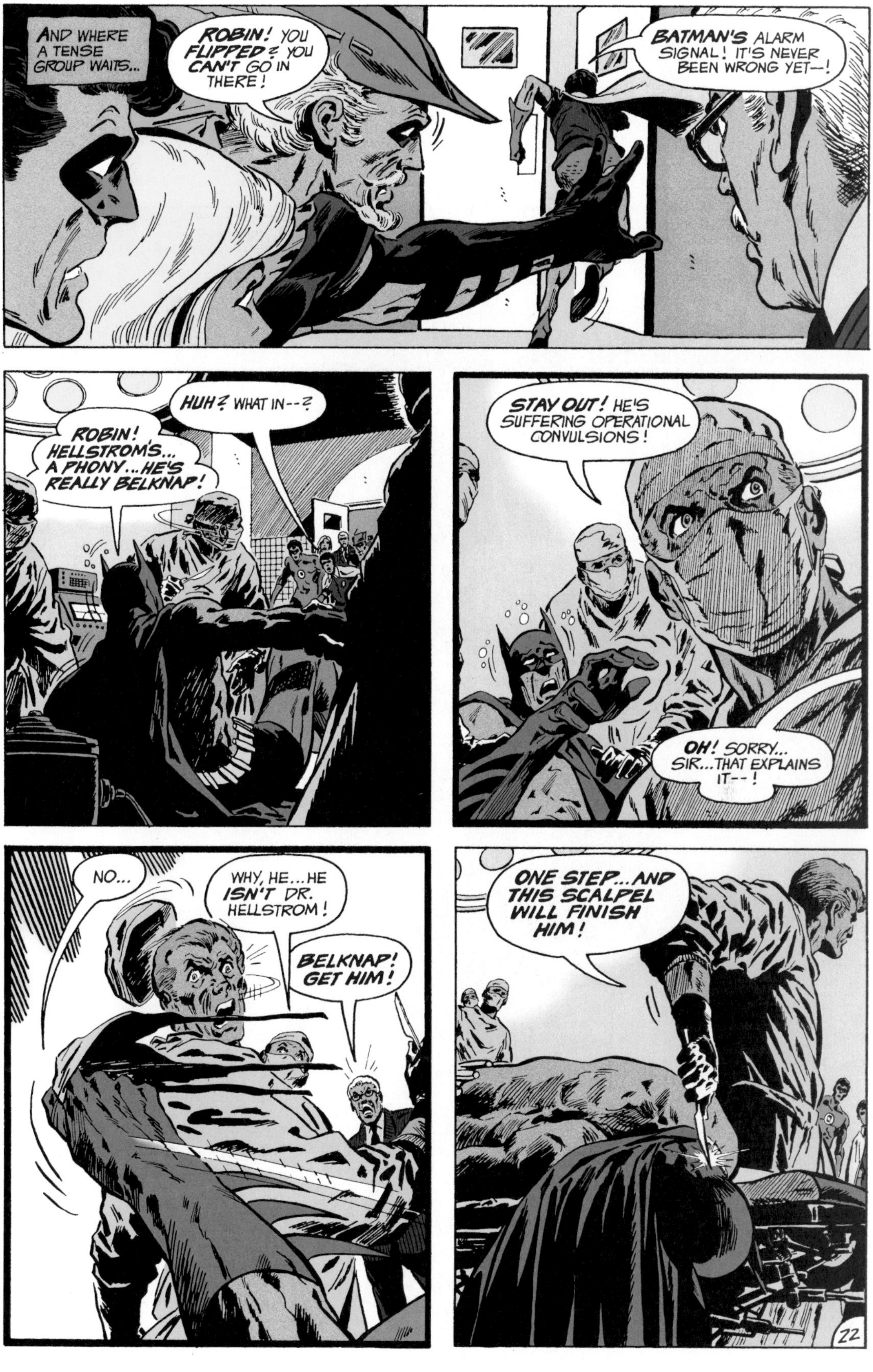
AND WHERE A TENSE GROUP WAITS...
ROBIN! YOU FLIPPED? YOU CAN'T GO IN THERE!
BATMAN'S ALARM SIGNAL! IT'S NEVER BEEN WRONG YET--!
ROBIN! HELLSTROM'S... A PHONY...HE'S REALLY BELKNAP!
HUH? WHAT IN--?
STAY OUT! HE'S SUFFERING OPERATIONAL CONVULSIONS!
OH! SORRY... SIR...THAT EXPLAINS IT--!
NO...
WHY, HE...HE ISN'T DR. HELLSTROM!
BELKNAP! GET HIM!
ONE STEP...AND THIS SCALPEL WILL FINISH HIM!
22

THE SUDDEN HUSH, THE TWANG OF A BOWSTRING, AND...

TWIK

ZINNG

NICE SHOT, *G.A.*-- I'VE GOT THIS RAT!

BATMAN... IS HE ALIVE?

BARELY... BUT ONLY THE *REAL* DR. HELLSTROM CAN SAVE HIM... AND WHAT'S HAPPENED TO *HIM*--!?

CALL SWITZERLAND, DOC-- *PRONTO!*

SHORTLY...

THE SWISS POLICE FOUND BELKNAP'S GOONS HOLDING HELLSTROM IN HIS OWN HOUSE! BUT IT'LL TAKE HIM *SIX JET HOURS TO GET HERE!*

BATMAN HASN'T GOT SIX HOURS--! *TWO...* MAYBE *THREE* AT MOST!

THEN *I'VE* GOT ANOTHER WAY!

SOON, THE WORLD'S MOST FAMOUS SURGEON TAKES HIS FASTEST TRANS-ATLANTIC TRIP... VIA POWER RING AERO-CAR...

23

SHORTLY...

THE PATIENT IS COMPLETELY UNDER, DR. HELLSTROM!

BUT AS THE PRECIOUS MOMENTS TICK BY--AND *BATMAN'S* LIFE SANDS TRICKLE OUT...

MY MONITORING APPARATUS THAT CRIMINAL STOLE TO MAKE HIS IMPERSONATION OF ME CONVINCING...IT IS *NOT WORKING!* THE PATIENT IS *SINKING!*..

WHAT IS *THIS*... PACKED INSIDE... JAMMING IT?

THE SHIPMENT!

FANTASTIC!

OH, WOW!

NOW ONCE AGAIN, AS SKILLED HANDS AND STEEL NERVES RESUME THE DELICATE WORK OF CHEATING THE ULTIMATE ENEMY...

HE'S *GOT* TO LIVE... HE *CAN'T* DIE... NOT *HIM!*

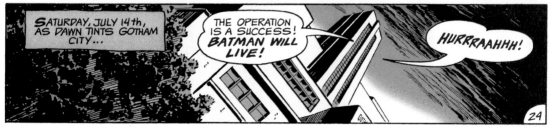

SATURDAY, JULY 14th, AS DAWN TINTS GOTHAM CITY...

THE OPERATION IS A SUCCESS! *BATMAN WILL LIVE!*

HURRRAAHHH!

24

THE FOLLOWING DAY...

BELKNAP'S SCHEME WAS INGENIOUS! AS HELLSTROM, HE'D HAVE THE SATISFACTION OF KILLING YOU PERSONALLY ...CLAIMING THE OPERATION HAD FAILED!

AWARE THAT ONLY THE ASSISTING SURGEON MIGHT KNOW WHAT HE LOOKED LIKE, HE MADE *SURE* HE WORE HIS SURGICAL MASK BEFORE ENTERING THE OPERATING AREA!

AND HE *KNEW* HELLSTROM'S MACHINE WOULD BE PASSED THROUGH CUSTOMS, UNINSPECTED UNDER SPECIAL PERMIT!

CHECK, THEN HE'D LEAVE WITH THE MACHINE FILLED WITH JUNK TO MAKE HIS "CONNECTION"... WORTH *MILLIONS!*

BUT HOW'D *YOU* GUESS WHO HE *REALLY* WAS, *BAT GUY*?

WHEN I GRABBED HIS WRIST, I PARTLY EXPOSED HIS ARM... IT BORE NEEDLE MARKS! I REMEMBERED BELKNAP HIMSELF-- WAS AN ADDICT!

WOW-EEE! SO HE GOT HOOKED INTO PRISON BY HIS OWN JUNK! *BEAUTIFUL--!* YOU'RE SOME AMAZING GUY, *BATMAN--!*

I TRY HARDER! BUT THEN I COULDN'T HAVE DONE IT WITHOUT ALL OF YOU...AND A CERTAIN SMALL EIGHT-LEGGED FRIEND OF MINE!

STORY: BOB HANEY ART: JIM APARO

25

END

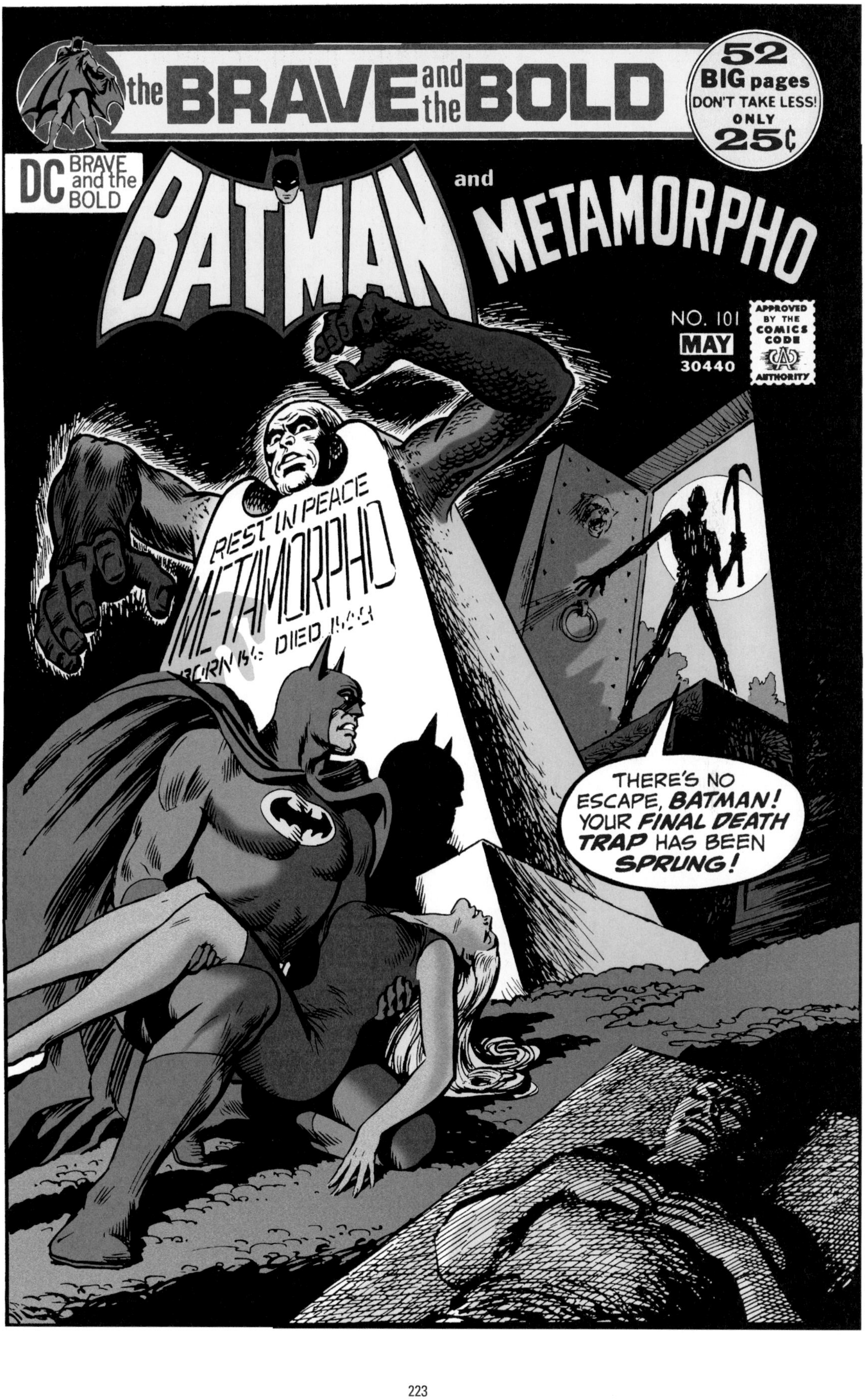
the BRAVE and the BOLD
52 BIG pages DON'T TAKE LESS! ONLY 25¢
DC BRAVE and the BOLD
BATMAN and METAMORPHO
NO. 101
MAY
30440
APPROVED BY THE COMICS CODE AUTHORITY
REST IN PEACE
METAMORPHO
THERE'S NO ESCAPE, BATMAN! YOUR FINAL DEATH TRAP HAS BEEN SPRUNG!

AMID THE HASSLE AND HUSTLE OF A GOTHAM CITY BUSINESS DAY, A SPECK SEEMS TO PASS ACROSS THE SUN...

A SPECK THAT SUDDENLY ARCS DOWNWARDS, SWELLING, EN-LARGING, EXPANDING...

A SPECK THAT WAS A LIFE-- NOW FOREVER ENDED! A LIFE ENDS -- BUT NOW A DEATH AND ITS MEANING BEGINS...

WALTER P. BRISTOE -- DOES A SWAN-DIVE 33 FLOORS, *BATMAN?* ACCIDENT? SUICIDE?..

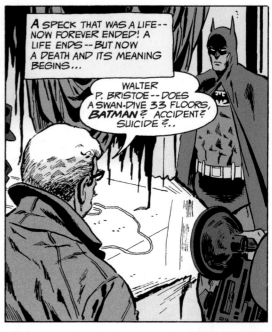

WHEEOO

ACCIDENT, COMMISSIONER? *NO*-- MODERN SKYSCRAPER WINDOWS DON'T OPEN... BRISTOE'S GLASS "JUMP HATCH" WAS SMASHED DELIBERATELY! SUICIDE? I DOUBT IT-- BRISTOE'S BUSINESS WAS IN PRETTY GOOD SHAPE, AS WAS HIS HEALTH! FAMILY LIFE... OKAY!

SO YOU FIGURE HOMICIDE, EH, *BATMAN?* BUT WHY... *HOW...* WHO?

MAYBE ANOTHER LOOK AT BRISTOE'S OFFICE WILL GIVE US A LEAD!

1

SHORTLY...

BRISTOE WAS A **BIG** MAN... HE COULD'VE **HURLED** HIMSELF THROUGH THE WINDOW-- MAYBE IN A SUDDEN FIT OF DEPRESSION!

PERHAPS--BUT I THINK "**IMPRESSION**" IS THE "KEY" WORD HERE!

WHAT ARE YOU DOING--?

BRISTOE'S SECRETARY SAID THE TYPEWRITER WAS BRAND-NEW... IT'D NEVER BEEN USED WHEN BRISTOE MADE HIS "EXIT"! YET THIS RIBBON HAS **KEY IMPRINTS** ON IT!..

SO, MAYBE BRISTOE HIM- SELF WAS JUST **TESTING** IT!..

NO CHANCE--LIKE MOST BIG EXECUTIVES, HE NEVER TOUCHED A TYPEWRITER! HMMM, I'M TRANSCRIBING THE TYPED WORDS OFF THE RIBBON...

A LIST OF NAMES! **GOOD BLAZES!** BRISTOE'S THE **FIRST**!..

YES, AND LOOK AT THE **LAST** ONE, BATMAN!

WALTER P. BRISTOE
HARLAN TWISS
EMMALINE VAN PRELL
SAPPHIRE STAGG
CARL HICKS
BRUCE WAYNE

YOU FIGURE IT'S A **MURDER** LIST--? THAT THE KILLER SAT AND COOLLY TYPED IT JUST BEFORE OR AFTER HE DID IN BRISTOE?

I WOULDN'T ORDINARILY, OLD FRIEND... EXCEPT FOR **ONE** THING! THE **BOUNTY HUNTER'S** BACK IN TOWN!

WALTER P. BRISTOE
FIRST VICE-PRESIDENT

2

BOUNTY HUNTER? OH, GOOD GOD, NO! YOU-- YOU'RE SURE, BATMAN?

SORRY--BUT I AM! LAST NIGHT, I LEANED ON A CERTAIN UNDERWORLD CONNECTION OF MINE-- ONE REDDY LINK--!

OKAY, REDDY--I KNOW YOU'RE FENCING STUFF FROM AIRPORT HEISTS... AND IF I LOOK I'LL BET I CAN FIND PROOF!..

BATMAN...EASY... PLEASE! WE'VE COOPERATED BEFORE!.. IF YOU FORGET THE BEEF, I'LL GIVE YOU NEWS... BIG NEWS!

"I DISLIKE DEALING WITH CRUMBS LIKE LINK--BUT HE'LL FOUL UP LATER AND WE'LL CAGE HIM ANYWAY! BESIDES, HIS NEWS SOUNDED HOT! IT WAS!! SEEMS LINK HAD JUST LEFT AN UNDERWORLD GUN-DEALER HE'D FENCED SOME HEISTED WEAPONS TO..."

STORY BOB HANEY • ART JIM APARO

GOING IN THE PRIVATE DOOR-- THAT GUY ALL IN BLACK-- ONE ARM OFF AT THE SHOULDER... IT'S HIM! THE BIG GUN... BOUNTY HUNTER!

ARMS • AMMO

COLD BLOOD, HOT GUN!

A KILLER IN TOWN? NOTHING NEW FOR THE BATMAN AND GOTHAM CITY--BUT THERE'S A TERRIFYING TWIST LURKING IN THE SHADOWS WHICH RESURRECTS FOR THE MASKED MANHUNTER AN OLD ALLY AND SENDS THEM BOTH HEADLONG INTO THE SHOCK AND THE SHAME OF...

③

NOW, HOLD ON--A CHEAP FENCE THINKS HE SEES A MAN... AT NIGHT... WITH ONE ARM... A MAN NOBODY'S EVER BEEN ABLE TO IDENTIFY... WHO USES A HUNDRED ALIASES... AND HE CONCLUDES IT'S *BOUNTY HUNTER*?

I--I DON'T BUY IT!

I *DO*, COMMISSIONER! WE CAN'T AFFORD *NOT* TO! *BOUNTY HUNTER'S* ONLY SURE IDENTIFYING MARK IS THE MISSING ARM! PLUS HE ALWAYS BUYS A NEW GUN FOR EVERY JOB--!

SO YOU THINK IT'S *HIM*, *BATMAN*--THE KILLER-FOR-A-PRICE WE'VE NEVER BEEN ABLE TO CATCH--THE COLD-BLOODED ASSASSIN WHO'LL HUNT DOWN ANYONE FOR A CLIENT NO MATTER WHO?

YES, COMMISSIONER--

GOTHAM CITY POLICE H.Q.

PARKING ENTRANCE

...AND I THINK *HE* TYPED THIS LIST--AND THAT IT REPRESENTS HIS LATEST CONTRACT!

COMMISS GORDO

SIX PEOPLE! SIX MURDERS! OH, GOOD LORD... WHAT *ARE* WE FACING HERE--?

AND SO WHILE A DREAD SPECTER FROM THE PAST SEEMS TO STALK GOTHAM-- IN A SECLUDED ESTATE IN THE COUNTRY...

STEADY, JAVA... HE'S COMING OUT OF IT!

EYAAAAHHH!!

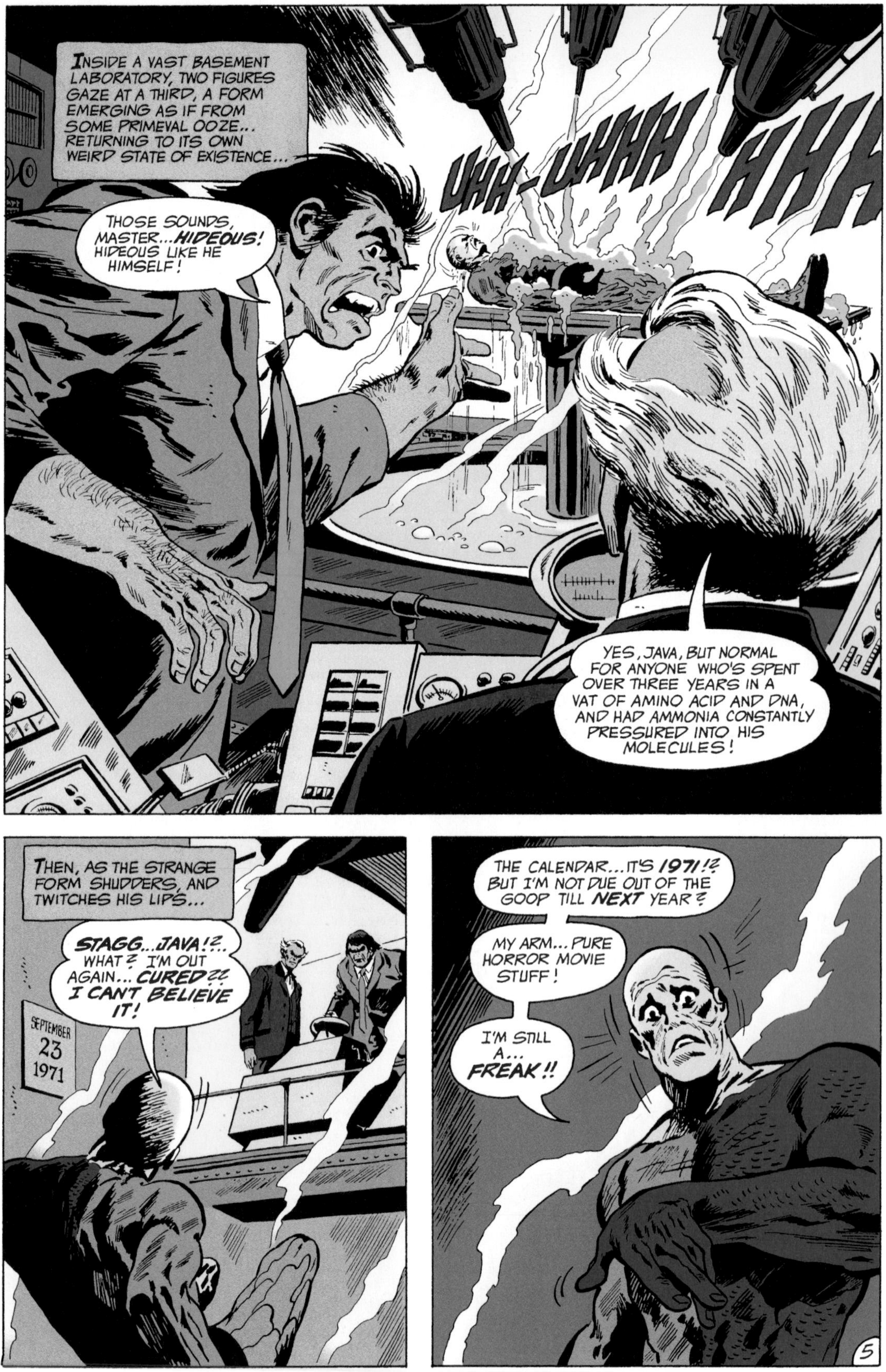

INSIDE A VAST BASEMENT LABORATORY, TWO FIGURES GAZE AT A THIRD, A FORM EMERGING AS IF FROM SOME PRIMEVAL OOZE... RETURNING TO ITS OWN WEIRD STATE OF EXISTENCE...
UHH-UHHH HHHH
THOSE SOUNDS, MASTER... HIDEOUS! HIDEOUS LIKE HE HIMSELF!
YES, JAVA, BUT NORMAL FOR ANYONE WHO'S SPENT OVER THREE YEARS IN A VAT OF AMINO ACID AND DNA, AND HAD AMMONIA CONSTANTLY PRESSURED INTO HIS MOLECULES!
THEN, AS THE STRANGE FORM SHUDDERS, AND TWITCHES HIS LIPS...
STAGG... JAVA!?... WHAT? I'M OUT AGAIN... CURED?? I CAN'T BELIEVE IT!
SEPTEMBER 23 1971
THE CALENDAR... IT'S 1971!? BUT I'M NOT DUE OUT OF THE GOOP TILL NEXT YEAR?
MY ARM... PURE HORROR MOVIE STUFF!
I'M STILL A... FREAK!!
5

SUDDENLY, THE BIZARRE FIGURE TRANSFORMS AS IF MAGICALLY, AND...

STAGG, YOU LOUSY CRUMB! YOU TOOK ME OUT OF THE CURE TOO SOON! I'LL **KILL** YOU!

JAVA WILL SAVE YOU, MASTER-- AND SETTLE OLD SCORES!

BUT REACTING INSTANTLY...

AN **IRON** FIST TO YOU, APE-BOY!

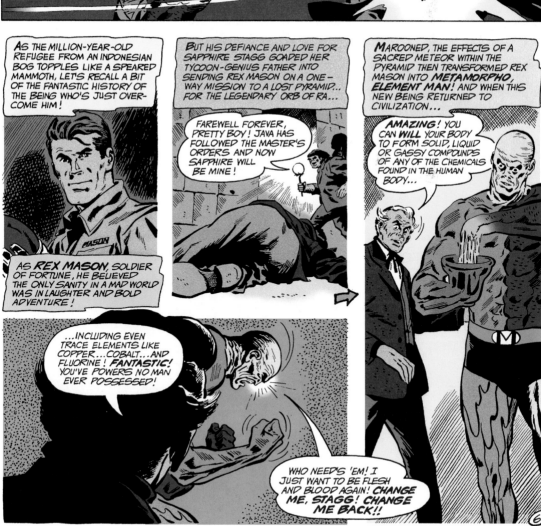

AS THE MILLION-YEAR-OLD REFUGEE FROM AN INDONESIAN BOG TOPPLES LIKE A SPEARED MAMMOTH, LET'S RECALL A BIT OF THE FANTASTIC HISTORY OF THE BEING WHO'S JUST OVER-COME HIM!

AS **REX MASON**, SOLDIER OF FORTUNE, HE BELIEVED THE ONLY SANITY IN A MAD WORLD WAS IN LAUGHTER AND BOLD ADVENTURE!

BUT HIS DEFIANCE AND LOVE FOR SAPPHIRE STAGG GOADED HER TYCOON-GENIUS FATHER INTO SENDING REX MASON ON A ONE-WAY MISSION TO A LOST PYRAMID... FOR THE LEGENDARY ORB OF RA...

FAREWELL FOREVER, PRETTY BOY! JAVA HAS FOLLOWED THE MASTER'S ORDERS AND NOW SAPPHIRE WILL BE MINE!

MAROONED, THE EFFECTS OF A SACRED METEOR WITHIN THE PYRAMID THEN TRANSFORMED REX MASON INTO **METAMORPHO, ELEMENT MAN!** AND WHEN THIS NEW BEING RETURNED TO CIVILIZATION...

AMAZING! YOU CAN **WILL** YOUR BODY TO FORM SOLID, LIQUID OR GASSY COMPOUNDS OF ANY OF THE CHEMICALS FOUND IN THE HUMAN BODY...

...INCLUDING EVEN TRACE ELEMENTS LIKE COPPER...COBALT...AND FLUORINE! **FANTASTIC!** YOU'VE POWERS NO MAN EVER POSSESSED!

WHO NEEDS 'EM! I JUST WANT TO BE FLESH AND BLOOD AGAIN! **CHANGE ME, STAGG! CHANGE ME BACK!!**

BUT EVEN SIMON STAGG'S GENIUS NEVER FOUND THE "CURE" FOR THE *ELEMENT MAN'S* UNIQUE STATE-- AND NOW AS ONE MORE ATTEMPT HAS BEEN CUT SHORT...

NOW, STAGGSY, IT'S *WIPE-OUT* TIME! YOU'VE PLAYED WITH MY LIFE ONCE TOO OFTEN, YOU POWER-MAD OLD CREEP!

GO AHEAD, REX, *KILL ME*...BUT KNOW THIS--BY DOING SO...YOU ALSO DOOM...*SAPPHIRE!*

SAPPHIRE? MY SAPPHIRE...MY BABY? WHAT ARE YOU TRYING TO PULL?...

I TOOK YOU FROM THE CURE EARLY BECAUSE I *NEED* YOU! SAPPHIRE'S LIFE IS IN DANGER! AND ONLY *YOU* CAN PROTECT HER!

THAT LOOK ON YOUR FACE I'VE NEVER SEEN-- *SINCERITY!* I BE-LIEVE YOU-- THE ONLY THING YOU LOVE MORE THAN MONEY AND POWER IS...*SAPPHIRE!* WHERE IS SHE? I'M GONNA FIND HER!

AS THE FANTABULOUS, RESURRECTED *ELEMENT MAN* STALKS THROUGH THE VAST MANSION...

WHAT IN BLUE BLAZES--?? SAPPHIRE'S ROOM...*BOLTED AND GUARDED* LIKE FORT KNOX--? WHAT GIVES?

LIKE I SAID, REX... *SHE'S IN DANGER!*..

SORRY, FREAK-HEAD-- *NOBODY ADMITTED!*

YOU MUST BE *NEW* AROUND HERE, BUSTER! YOU'RE TALKING TO THE MAN WITH THE MOST IN HIS MOLECULES!

REX!!

?

SKRUNCH

AND THE NEXT MOMENT...

REX...OH, REX DARLING...IS IT REALLY, *TRULY* YOU--?

YEAH, I'M HERE, BABY...AFTER THREE LONG YEARS! OLD REX IS HERE... WHERE HE BELONGS!

7

BUT I'M *STILL* A FREAK, SAPPH...BIG DADDY PULLED ME OUT OF THE CURE GLOP TOO SOON...SAID YOU'RE IN DANGER--!

BUT I'M *NOT*, LOVER! DADDY'S CRAZY...KEEPING ME A PRISONER IN MY OWN HOME!

BUT YOU *ARE* IN DANGER, DAUGHTER-- *DEADLY* DANGER! YOU'RE ON A *DEATH LIST*--A DEATH LIST OF A NOTORIOUS HIRED KILLER-- THE *BOUNTY HUNTER*!

SAYS *WHO*, STAGG? SOUNDS LIKE ONE OF YOUR DOUBLE-DEALING PUT-ONS!

SAYS...*THE BATMAN!* NOW WILL YOU BELIEVE IT'S TRUE ?--

THE *BAT GUY*? WHY, SURE...BUT I DON'T GET IT! WHO'D WANT TO GET MY BABY HERE ?

I...I DON'T KNOW-- BUT HEAVEN KNOWS I'VE BEEN A RUTHLESS MAN IN MY LIFE! THERE ARE PLENTY OF PEOPLE WHO HATE ME... WHO'D WANT TO GET AT ME THROUGH THE PERSON *DEAREST* TO ME--MY *GOLDEN GIRL!*

OH, IT'S ALL *RIDICULOUS!* I CAN TAKE CARE OF MYSELF-- AND I REFUSE TO REMAIN COOPED UP HERE ANY LONGER!

HOLD IT, SAPPH--! THIS *IS* SERIOUS! I HATE TO AGREE WITH YOUR OLD MAN...

8

...BUT YOU'RE STAYING PUT **WITH ME** TO GUARD YOU EVERY MINUTE!

REX--I CAN'T BELIEVE THIS! I'M NOT A CHILD TO BE ORDERED ABOUT BY ANYONE...EVEN **YOU!**

FOR THIS HELP, REX, ALL MY THANKS!

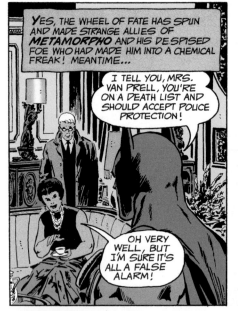

YES, THE WHEEL OF FATE HAS SPUN AND MADE STRANGE ALLIES OF **METAMORPHO** AND HIS DESPISED FOE WHO HAD MADE HIM INTO A CHEMICAL FREAK! MEANTIME...

I TELL YOU, MRS. VAN PRELL, YOU'RE ON A DEATH LIST AND SHOULD ACCEPT POLICE PROTECTION!

OH VERY WELL, BUT I'M SURE IT'S ALL A FALSE ALARM!

SHORTLY...

WELL, WE'VE NOTIFIED AND ASSIGNED POLICE PROTECTION TO EVERY-ONE ON THE LIST IN-CLUDING YOUR FRIEND **BRUCE WAYNE**--

YES, BUT IT'S HARLAN TWISS I'M MOST WORRIED ABOUT, COMMISSIONER!

...HE'S **NEXT** ON **BOUNTY HUNTER'S** AGENDA! I'M GOING TO GIVE HIM EXTRA COVER MYSELF!

OKAY, BUT MAYBE NOTHING WILL HAPPEN! MAYBE BRISTOE'S DEATH **WAS** SUICIDE--AND THE LIST JUST SOME FREAKISH COINCIDENCE!

NO WAY! SIX PEOPLE WHO DON'T EVEN KNOW EACH OTHER-- AND WITH NO OBVIOUS CONNECTION TO BRISTOE? NO, I'LL GAMBLE MY CAPE THE LIST IS LEGIT AND **BOUNTY HUNTER'S** STALKING TWISS RIGHT NOW! SEE YOU!

NOW AS THE **MASKED MANHUNTER** FADES INTO GOTHAM'S NIGHT TO THWART THE MYSTERIOUS ONE-ARMED ASSASSIN...

HARLAN TWISS FANCIES FIGHTERS...

9

...AND ONE HE OWNS IS BOXING TONIGHT! MAKES IT TOUGH PROTECTING HIM IN THIS CROWD... *ANY ONE* OF WHOM COULD BE *BOUNTY HUNTER!*

AND WHEN THE BOUT ENDS...

TWISS'S LUCK'S RUNNING GOOD--HIS FIGHTER WON AND *BOUNTY HUNTER* MADE NO TRY TO GET HIM! HE'LL BE WELL PROTECTED TILL HE VENTURES OUT AGAIN!

BUT NEXT DAY, AS THE *CAPED CRUSADER* ANSWERS AN EMERGENCY SUMMONS...

EMMALINE VAN PRELL, *BATMAN*... AND SHE'S VERY DEAD!

WHAT?

THE HAIR DRYER... GIMMICKED TO GIVE A LETHAL JOLT!

THE SHOP WORKERS ARE CLEAR--SOME- ONE *UNKNOWN* TAMPERED WITH IT!

"SOMEONE UNKNOWN"... AS *BOUNTY HUNTER!*

BLAST! HE *FOOLED* US -- HE SKIPPED A NAME ON THE LIST! HER POLICE ESCORT... WHERE *WERE* THEY?

UH... OUTSIDE! THEY... UH... WERE EMBARRASSED TO COME INTO THIS PLACE... FIGURED IT WAS SAFE!

10

JUST GREAT! NOW DO YOU BELIEVE IN THE LIST AND THAT *BOUNTY HUNTER'S* BACK IN BUSINESS?

BATMAN, WHAT ARE WE GOING TO DO? FOR THE FIRST TIME IN MY CAREER, I'M *SHAKEN!*

SHORTLY, AT POLICE HQ...

WE'VE FED EVERY KNOWN BIT OF DATA ABOUT THE SIX "TARGETS" INTO THE COMPUTER--INCLUDING WHETHER THEY SQUEEZE THE TOOTH PASTE IN THE MIDDLE OR AT THE END! LET'S SEE WHAT COMES OUT!

THE ELECTRONIC MIND WHIRLS, COMPUTES, AND...

NOTHING-- EXCEPT THAT ALL SIX HAVE MONEY... ARE RATHER WEALTHY! BUT THAT'S A BLIND ALLEY--THERE'S BEEN NO ATTEMPT AT EXTORTION--!

THEN, WE'RE UP AGAINST A BLANK WALL, *BATMAN?*

YES! IF WE ONLY HAD A CLUE AS TO WHO HIRED *BOUNTY HUNTER--* AND WHY? BUT THAT'S A MYSTERY, TOO... LIKE *HIM!*

GOTHAM CITY POLICE

THE NEXT NIGHT AT THE *STAGG MANSION...*

HEY, JUST A LITTLE MINUTE--! WHO ARE *YOU...* AND HOW'D *YOU* GET IN SAPPHIRE'S ROOM?

ME, SATO-- HOUSEBOY HIRED SINCE YOU GO INTO DEEP GLOP, MR. REX! ME BRING MISS SAPPHIRE FOOD WHILE YOU DOZE!

11

YEAH--THERE'S MY BABY CATCHING HER BEAUTY SLEEP!

OKAY, SATO, KIDDO... YOU CAN PADDLE OFF! BUT JUST CHECK WITH ME NEXT TIME YOU COME OUT OF THE WOODWORK!

MOST CERTAINLY, MR. REX!

SHORTLY, OUTSIDE THE GREAT RAMBLING STRUCTURE...

EXCUSE, OFFICERS... I MUST GO TO GARAGE FOR BICYCLE TO GO SHOPPING! MR. STAGG MUST HAVE MUSHROOMS TONIGHT-- OR SATO HAVE LARGE PROBLEM!

OKAY, BUDDY--!

BUT A FEW INSTANTS LATER...

HA! HA! IT WAS SO EASY TO FOOL REX AND THOSE MINIONS OF THE LAW! NO ONE KEEPS SAPPHIRE STAGG A PRISONER WHEN SHE WANTS TO GO OUT AND SWING! HA! HA!

AND BACK IN A CERTAIN BEDROOM...

HOLY HANNAH! A LIFE-SIZE FOAM-RUBBER DOLL REPLICA OF SAPPHIRE! THE LITTLE WITCH'S PULLED A FAST ONE! SHE'S LOOSE AND IN DANGER! GOTTA GO AFTER HER!

SO WHILE THE IMPETUOUS GOLDEN GIRL SPEEDS TOWARDS GOTHAM CITY'S BRIGHT LIGHTS, JUST NEAR THE PENTHOUSE OF BRUCE WAYNE...

THIS MAY BE CRAZY-- WITH A KILLER LIKE BOUNTY HUNTER-- BUT MAYBE AS WAYNE I CAN LURE HIM OUT... MAKE HIM SHOW HIS HAND--!

12

IT WASN'T TOO TOUGH TO SLIP BY MY POLICE PROTECTION! NOW LET'S SEE IF I CAN FOOL... *BOUNTY HUNTER!*

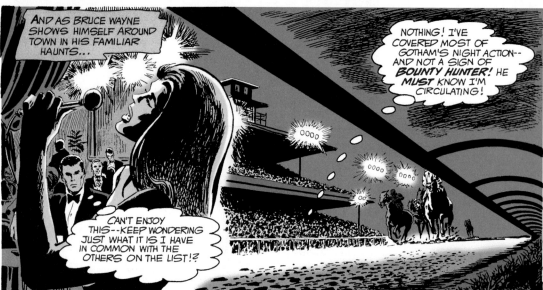

AND AS BRUCE WAYNE SHOWS HIMSELF AROUND TOWN IN HIS FAMILIAR HAUNTS...

NOTHING! I'VE COVERED MOST OF GOTHAM'S NIGHT ACTION-- AND NOT A SIGN OF *BOUNTY HUNTER!* HE **MUST** KNOW I'M CIRCULATING!

CAN'T ENJOY THIS--KEEP WONDERING JUST WHAT IT IS I HAVE IN COMMON WITH THE OTHERS ON THE LIST!?

BUT SOMEONE ELSE IS CIRCULATING-- FOR AT THIS MOMENT, IN AN EXCLUSIVE BUT ILLEGAL GAMBLING CLUB...

HOLD ON, GENTS! LITTLE SAPPHIRE'S ROLLING HIGH TONIGHT!

SOME CHICK! MADE EIGHT STRAIGHT POINTS! SHE'S A WILD ONE, THAT DOLL!

EIGHT! THAT'S MY POINT! TIME TO QUIT-- NIGHT'S YOUNG--LOTS OF OTHER PLACES TO GO!

SHE DID IT AGAIN? AND SHE DOESN'T NEED THE BREAD!

THAT'S CLASS, MAN, *REAL* CLASS!

BUT AS THE HONEY-HAIRED PLAYGIRL EXITS FROM THE CLUB...

MISS STAGG? I SAW YOU BREAK THAT GAME WIDE OPEN INSIDE! I'D LIKE TO SHAKE YOUR HAND--!

WHY, OF COURSE, YOU DEAR MAN!

YOUR HAND... IT...IT'S COME OFF?! EEEEK!

AS THE HORRIFIED HEIRESS COLLAPSES...

KLIK KLIK KLIK

SUDDENLY...

SAPPH, BABY--OLD REX IS HERE--!

KLIK KLIK KLIK KLIK

THE NEXT INSTANT...

WHA--WHUMPF

MOMENTS LATER, AS THE MAN OF MANY ELEMENTS RETURNS TO HIS USUAL FORM...

≋Whew≋--COBALT COOLED THAT BOOBY TRAP! LUCKY I REMEMBERED YOU LIKED SHOOTING CRAPS, DOLL!

NOW WILL YOU BELIEVE SOME CRAZY KILLER'S AFTER YOU?...

HUH? SHE'S GONE--!

14

ROARING AWAY IN THE NIGHT...

THIS IS A HEAVY KICK-- BEING IN DANGER AND REX CHASING ME TO PROTECT ME! MAKES A GIRL FEEL RRRREALLY... *LOVED!!*

WHILE IN ANOTHER PART OF GOTHAM...

MR. WAYNE... UH? BUT YOU'RE STILL... *INSIDE?*

NOT A HINT OF *BOUNTY HUNTER!* IS HE WISE TO MY TRYING TO SMOKE HIM OUT-- OR LAYING LOW?

BUT INSIDE HIS PENTHOUSE APARTMENT...

SO SIMON STAGG SAID *ELEMENT MAN* REPORTED *BOUNTY HUNTER* TRIED TO KILL SAPPHIRE STAGG TONIGHT--?

YES, SIR-- USING A BOOBY-TRAPPED ARTIFICIAL HAND! REALLY BIZARRE!

NOT FOR A MAN WITH ONE ARM, ALFRED! BUT WAIT, THAT'S THREE TIMES HE'S STRUCK... *EACH TIME NOT USING A GUN!* THAT'S NOT HIS STYLE!

IS IT POSSIBLE WE'RE *NOT* DEALING WITH *BOUNTY HUNTER,* AT ALL-- BUT SOME OTHER MAD ASSASSIN?

I'M SURE I WOULDN'T KNOW, SIR, BUT TONIGHT'S THE NIGHT YOU HAVE THAT CERTAIN DATE IN THE COUNTRY! REMEMBER?

OH, YES-- WELL, WITH *METAMORPHO* GUARDING SAPPHIRE STAGG, AND THE POLICE THE OTHER "VICTIMS," I GUESS I CAN TAKE THE REST OF THE NIGHT OFF!

HERE I GO INTO MY "FOOL THE FUZZ" ROUTINE, AGAIN!

15

SO AS BRUCE (*THE BATMAN*) WAYNE SLIPS ONCE MORE PAST HIS POLICE PROTECTION--SOME MILES FROM GOTHAM CITY...

THE FAIRBAIRN ESTATE! OH, I JUST LOVE IT AND SOON IT'LL BE MINE!

A PULL ON AN ANTIQUE DOOR BELL, AND...

MISS STAGG, I PRESUME? I'M CONRAD FAIRBAIRN! YOU'RE A BIT EARLY! NONE OF THE OTHER BIDDERS ARE HERE YET!

NO NEED FOR THEM TO COME-- MY BID'S GOT TO BE THE *HIGHEST*! AFTER ALL, WHO'S RICHER THAN MY DADDY?

BUT AS YOU KNOW, THE OFFER TO SELL THE ESTATE SPECIFIED ALL BUYERS MUST BE PRESENT WHEN THE SEALED BIDS ARE OPENED AT *MIDNIGHT*--!

MY BROTHER, MISS STAGG... DERWENT FAIRBAIRN!

GOOD EVENING! AS CONRAD SAYS, MISS STAGG, IF A BIDDER'S NOT PRESENT, HIS BID IS *VOID*! IF *NONE* ARE HERE AT MIDNIGHT, THE ESTATE REMAINS *UNSOLD*!

IT *MUST* BE SOLD, DERWENT! IT'S OLD, HARD TO KEEP UP! WE MUST STREAM-LINE OUR FINANCES, LIVE A MODERN, MORE SENSIBLE LIFE!

MODERN? SENSIBLE? DEAR BROTHER, THOSE TERMS *DON'T* IMPRESS ME!

MISS STAGG, ALLOW ME TO SHOW YOU THE WHOLE ESTATE!

WHY, LEAD RIGHT ON, MISTER FAIRBAIRN!

16

OUR ANCESTORS-- WHO MADE THE FAIRBAIRN NAME GREAT SINCE COLONIAL TIMES! ALL LIVED... AND *DIED*... IN THIS HOUSE!

I JUST CAN'T WAIT TILL IT'S *MINE*, MR. DERWENT!

AND SHORTLY, BENEATH THE GREAT HOUSE IN A STONE CRYPT...

THE GRAVES OF ALL THE FAIRBAIRNS, MISS STAGG! SACRED GROUND --AS IS ALL THE ESTATE! SOMEDAY, I, *TOO*, SHALL REST HERE!

OOH, I DIDN'T KNOW *THEY* CAME WITH THE PLACE!

MEANTIME, UPSTAIRS, SOMEONE ELSE HAS ARRIVED...

NO, YOU'RE NOT LATE, MR. WAYNE! IT'S STILL A FEW MINUTES TO MID- NIGHT! BUT ONLY ONE *OTHER* BIDDER IS HERE!

HMM, MORE TO MY ADVANTAGE! INCREASES MY CHANCES OF BUYING THIS MARVELOUS PLACE!

BRUCE WAYNE A BIDDER AT THIS STRANGE MIDNIGHT AUCTION? NOW...

AAH, THE OLD BELL JANGLES! ANOTHER BIDDER HAS ARRIVED! EXCUSE ME, MR. WAYNE!

MR. FAIRBAIRN? I'M WALTER P. BRISTOE, HERE FOR THE BID OPENINGS!

GOOD TO SEE YOU! COME IN!

17

WALTER P. BRISTOE? DOES THAT NAME JANGLE *YOUR* BELLS, *BRAVE & BOLD* ONES? WAIT--!

IN HERE, MR. BRISTOE! IT'S *MIDNIGHT*--TIME TO OPEN THE BIDS! BUT WE'VE ONLY *THREE* BIDDERS PRESENT...

HMM, MR. WAYNE IS GONE! MY BROTHER MUST BE SHOWING HIM AROUND, ALSO! I'LL FETCH THEM!

BONG BONG

JUST WHERE *IS* BRUCE WAYNE? IN ANOTHER WING OF THE VAST STRUCTURE...

NICE OF YOU TO SHOW ME AROUND, DERWENT!

MY PLEASURE! THIS ROOM CONTAINS THE FAIRBAIRN LIBRARY, MR. WAYNE! YOU SHOULD KNOW JUST WHAT YOU'RE BUYING!

AND AS HE STEPS INTO THE ROOM...

SLAM

CLAK

WHY, THE ROOM'S EMPTY-?

WHAT? HE'S LOCKING ME IN--??

MEANTIME, IN THE DIM, ECHOING BASEMENT BURIAL CRYPT...

WHY DID HE LOCK ME IN HERE WITH... *THEM*?!

HELP!

NOW AS A PUZZLED CONRAD FAIRBAIRN RETURNS TO THE SITTING ROOM...

DERWENT? WHERE ARE MR. WAYNE AND MISS STAGG? IT'S PAST MIDNIGHT --AND MR. BRISTOE WILL BE THE ONLY BIDDER BY DE-FAULT IF THEY'RE NOT PRESENT!

THIS IS TERRIBLE -- WE MAY NOT GET A FAIR PRICE FOR THE ESTATE!

18

I...I DON'T UNDERSTAND?

CORRECTION! SOON THERE WILL BE NO BIDDERS AT ALL, DEAR BROTHER, SINCE THIS IS NOT MR. BRISTOE... BUT A CERTAIN SPECIALIST I HIRED!

THAT KEY... IT'S TO THE FAMILY BURIAL CRYPT--?!

HA! HA! INDEED IT IS, CONRAD, BE-CAUSE MY FRIEND, HERE, IS A KIND OF UNDERTAKER! HE SENDS MANY PEOPLE ON THEIR LAST JOURNEY... AS HE'S ABOUT TO DO WITH WAYNE AND MISS STAGG!

YOU... YOU MEAN HE'S GOING TO... KILL THEM?

EXACTLY! JUST AS HE'S ALREADY REMOVED TWO OTHER BIDDERS AND TERRORIZED TWO MORE INTO NOT APPEARING TONIGHT! THAT LEAVES ONLY WAYNE AND SAPPHIRE STAGG... WHO'LL NOT LIVE TO SEE THEIR BIDS OPENED!

WH-WHAT?! THIS IS MADNESS! I'LL STOP HIM--!

TOO LATE, BROTHER! YOU WENT TOO FAR WITH YOUR DRY BUSINESSMAN'S SOUL... TRYING TO SELL THIS HOUSE... THE SYMBOL OF FAIRBAIRN GREATNESS!

THIS HOUSE, CONTAINING OUR SACRED ANCESTORS, REMAINS... THIS ESTATE WHICH IS THE REAL SOUL OF OUR FAMILY! NO, ALL YOU VALUE IS MONEY-- AND CHEAP, MODERN, SHALLOW IDEALS!

THAT ODOR--?

19

CHLOROFORM! AN OLD-FASHIONED METHOD THAT STILL WORKS IN THIS TAWDRY MODERN WORLD! I COUNTED ON YOU BEING SO OBSESSED WITH BUSINESS, YOU NEVER KNEW WHAT I WAS UP TO!

BREATHE, BROTHER--SO YOU MAY NOT WITNESS WHAT COMES NEXT!

AND, ABOVE, AS UNCONSCIOUSNESS CLAIMS THE ELDER FAIRBAIRN...

OH, WHY DID I DO IT--RUN AWAY FROM REX? I--I'M SO SCARED!

THAT SHADOW--!? EEEEEKK!

B-BATMAN??!

SAPPHIRE STAGG!? YOU --HERE?

GOOD BLAZES! I SEE IT ALL NOW! WHAT A STUPID FOOL I'VE BEEN!!

HOW...DID YOU GET HERE? DID MY DADDY SEND YOU TO PROTECT ME?

NOT QUITE! BUT I CAME DOWN THAT AIR SHAFT FROM A ROOM ABOVE! NOW WE'RE BOTH TRAPPED HERE...THIS STONE CRYPT'S LIKE A PRISON DUNGEON!

OH, I'M SO GLAD YOU'RE HERE--BUT I'M SO CONFUSED!

EASY, HONEY...

HMM, I WAS CONFUSED --BUT NOT ANYMORE!

THE NAMES ON THE LIST DID HAVE ONE THING IN COMMON-- ONE THING ALMOST IM- POSSIBLE TO BE AWARE OF! WE ALL SUBMITTED BIDS TO BUY THIS PLACE!

BUT DERWENT FAIRBAIRN HIRED BOUNTY HUNTER TO KILL US ALL BECAUSE HE DIDN'T WANT THE ESTATE LEAVING THE FAMILY! THAT THIRD BIDDER WHO ARRIVED... BUT I DIDN'T SEE...

20

243

...I'LL BET HE'S REALLY *BOUNTY HUNTER* COME HERE TO FINISH HIS CONTRACT ...KILL THE ONLY TWO HE DIDN'T SCARE OFF... THIS TERRIFIED GIRL AND YOURS TRULY, BRUCE WAYNE!

OOOH--THAT AWFUL THING COMING UNDER THE DOOR--?!

GET BACK, WHILE I-- *METAMORPHO!?*

REX!?

IN THE GRISLY, FREAKISH FLESH! WHAT ARE YOU TWO DOING HERE --PLAYING THE FINAL SCENE FROM *ROMEO AND JULIET?*

REX, HOW'D *YOU* FIND THIS PLACE?

BY CONVERTING MY SCHNOZZ INTO A CHEMICAL DETECTOR, I FOLLOWED THE CARBON MONOXIDE TRAIL OF YOUR POLLUTING, OVERPOWERED CHARIOT! TOOK SOME TIME!

THEN, AFTER THE TWO BIZARRELY MATCHED HEROES CONFER...

BOUNTY HUNTER MAY SHOW UP ANY MOMENT --TO KILL SAPPHIRE!

THAT-- NOBODY'S GOING TO DO LONG AS I'VE GOT ONE MOLECULE STILL WORKING! SIT TIGHT!

AT THIS MOMENT, IN ANOTHER PART OF THE VAST MANSION...

I'LL DEAL WITH WAYNE FIRST! NO NEED *NOT* TO USE A GUN ANY LONGER TO DECOY THE LAW!

WHAT? NO ONE-- !?

21

THE ROOM'S *EMPTY!* DO YOU TAKE ME FOR A *FOOL?* I AM A PROFESSIONAL WHO TAKES ON ONLY *SERIOUS* CONTRACTS!

EMPTY? BUT... BUT I SWEAR I LOCKED WAYNE IN THERE!

PERHAPS IN YOUR NERVOUS EAGERNESS, YOU FAILED TO *SECURE* THE DOOR! IN ANY CASE, THE BIRD HAS FLOWN!

THEN HE *WON'T* RETURN--HIS BID IS *VOID!* TO SHOW MY GOOD FAITH, WE'LL USE THIS *SECRET PASSAGE* TO GET TO WHERE THE GIRL AWAITS! *COME!*

SWISH

AND A SECOND AFTER THE PANEL SILENTLY CLOSES...

AS INVISIBLE HYDROGEN GAS, I'VE CHECKED OUT THIS WHOLE WING-- BUT LIKE IT'S *DESERTED!* WHERE IS HE? WHERE'S THAT KILLER CREEP?

RIGHT NOW, *METAMORPHO,* HE'S IN A CERTAIN BURIAL CRYPT...

NO ONE HERE, EITHER? BUT... IT'S *IMPOSSIBLE!*

AS I SUSPECTED, YOU'RE DOUBLECROSSING ME! YOUR MOTIVES ARE OBSCURE, BUT ANY CLIENT WHO FAILS TO LIVE UP TO THE CONTRACT TERMS...

FORFEITS HIS *OWN* LIFE!

PLEASE! I DON'T KNOW HOW THIS HAPPENED! BELIEVE ME, A FAIRBAIRN NEVER LIES! I SWEAR ON MY ANCESTORS' GRAVES!

22

KAPOW

BATMAN! SO FAIRBAIRN *HID* YOU HERE--!

HE DESERVED TO DIE! NOW IT'S *YOUR* TURN!

CHUK

HIS FALSE ARM... IT'S LIKE A BASE-BALL BAT--STARTING TO BLACK OUT!

NOW TWO POWERFUL HANDS CHOP UPWARDS...

THUD

CHOK

KPOW

WHOKK

HE'S REELING! NOW TO FINISH HIM OFF!

BUT...

BATMAN, I CAN'T STAND HIDING IN THERE ANOTHER SECOND--

SAPPHIRE... GO BACK!

23

HOLD IT, *BATMAN!* NOW OUT OF THE WAY-- OR THE GIRL DIES, AFTER ALL!

YOU MURDEROUS HYENA! YOU WIN... FOR NOW!

AS THE *MASKED MANHUNTER* IS LOCKED INSIDE THE CRYPT...

SLAM

KLIK

WHERE CAN *METAMORPHO* BE? HE'S OUR ONLY HOPE TO STOP THE INHUMAN DEVIL!

WHERE, *BATMAN?* NEAR THE MANSION'S MAIN ENTRANCE...

KEEP YOUR DISTANCE, FREAK-- OR YOUR GIRLFRIEND HAS KISSED YOUR HIDEOUS FACE FOR THE LAST TIME!

OKAY, BUSTER! DON'T GET TRIGGER-HAPPY NOW!

AS THE CAR ROARS DOWN THE DRIVE GRAVEL...

I'LL CATCH HIM BEFORE HE HITS THE GATES!

SAPPH... HE'S TOSSING HER OUT!

A MICRO-SECOND LATER, ANOTHER FRANTIC CHEMICAL CHANGE...

GOT TO LET HIM ESCAPE... TO CATCH SAPPH WITH A CALCIUM CRASH COUCH!

24

247

LATER...

SO YOU FIGURE *BOUNTY HUNTER* WASN'T TRYING TO KILL SAPPHIRE-- JUST GET AWAY?

YES, ONCE DERWENT VOIDED THE CONTRACT, THERE WAS NO REASON IN HIS TWISTED MIND TO SHOOT HER!

HE HAS HIS OWN WEIRD, CHILLING CODE HE *LIVES* BY... AND OTHERS *DIE* BY!

IT...IT'S ALL BEEN A NIGHTMARE! MY POOR BROTHER... HE WAS COMPLETELY *MAD!* I KNEW HE WISHED TO KEEP THE ESTATE...BUT I NEVER DREAMED TO WHAT LENGTHS HE'D GO!

BUT I FEEL RESPONSIBLE! I THOUGHT ONLY OF MONEY-- NOT HIS FEELINGS! TO MAKE UP FOR IT, I'M GOING TO TRY AND KEEP THE PLACE... AFTER DERWENT'S BURIED IN THE FAMILY CRYPT!

IT'S BEEN QUITE A NIGHT! BY THE WAY, WHATEVER HAPPENED TO BRUCE WAYNE?

HE KNEW HE WAS ON A *DEATH LIST!* I'D SAY, YOUR BROTHER'S BIZARRE BEHAVIOR... UH...FRIGHTENED HIM OFF! GOODBYE... YOU HAVE OUR SYMPATHY, FAIRBAIRN!

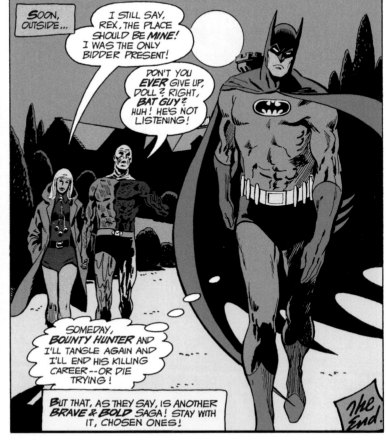

SOON, OUTSIDE...

I STILL SAY, REX, THE PLACE SHOULD BE *MINE!* I WAS THE ONLY BIDDER PRESENT!

DON'T YOU *EVER* GIVE UP, DOLL? RIGHT, *BAT GUY?* HUH! HE'S NOT LISTENING!

SOMEDAY, *BOUNTY HUNTER* AND I'LL TANGLE AGAIN AND I'LL END HIS KILLING CAREER --OR DIE TRYING!

BUT THAT, AS THEY SAY, IS ANOTHER *BRAVE & BOLD* SAGA! STAY WITH IT, CHOSEN ONES!

The End.

248

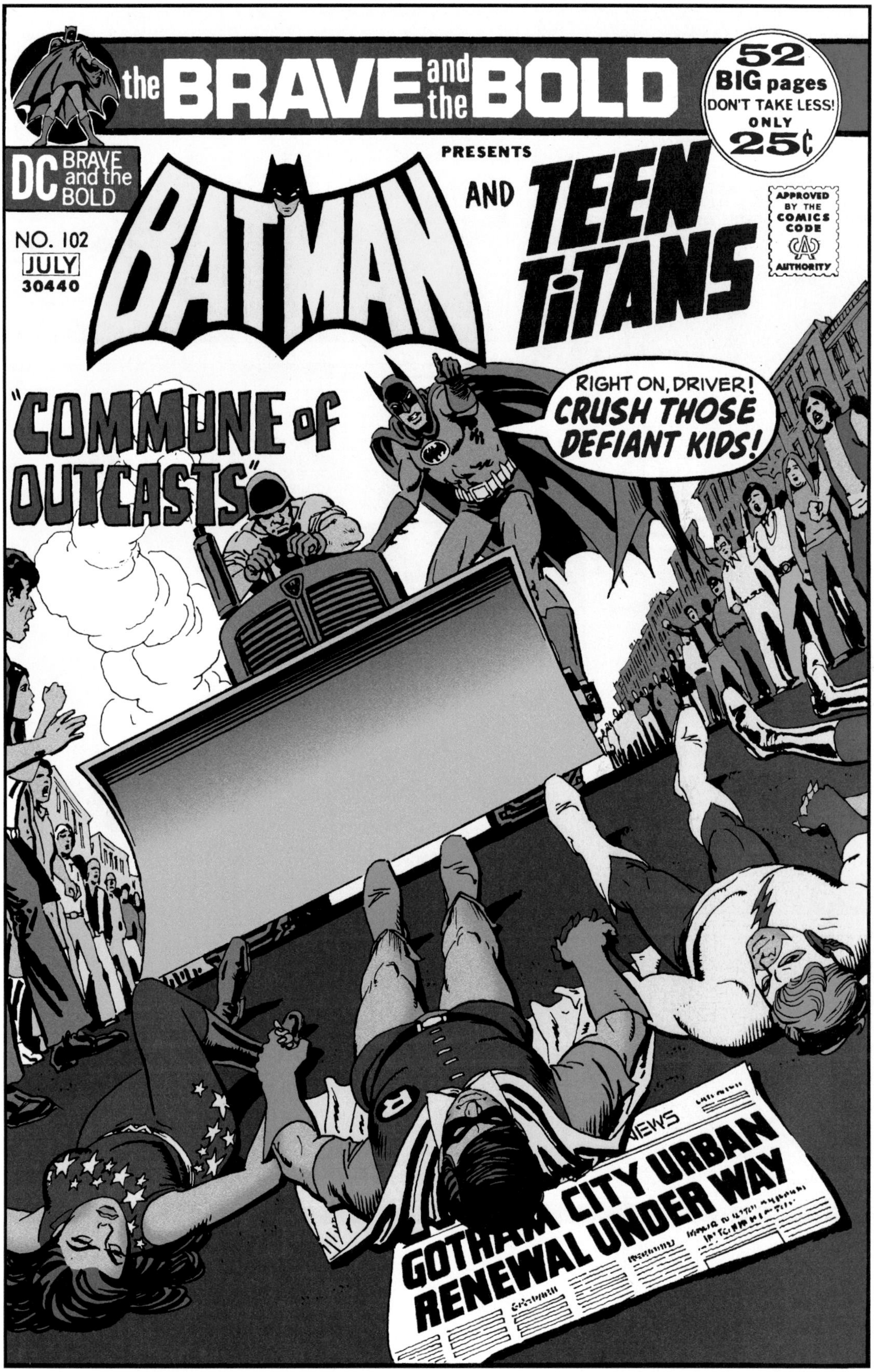
the BRAVE and the BOLD
52 BIG pages DON'T TAKE LESS! ONLY 25¢
DC BRAVE and the BOLD
PRESENTS
BATMAN AND TEEN TITANS
APPROVED BY THE COMICS CODE AUTHORITY
NO. 102
JULY
30440
"COMMUNE of OUTCASTS"
RIGHT ON, DRIVER! CRUSH THOSE DEFIANT KIDS!
NEWS
GOTHAM CITY URBAN RENEWAL UNDER WAY

SPRING POKES LONG GREEN FINGERS ALONG ONE OF GOTHAM CITY'S POSHEST AVENUES ONE APRIL DAY AS...

SHEER MAGIC! WINTER'S OVER AND PRETTY GIRLS ARE BLOSSOMING LIKE FLOWERS! DELICIOUS!

YES, *THE BATMAN* DIGS THIS DAY THE BEAUTY OF HIS BE-LOVED GOTHAM--BUT AS HE ROUNDS A CORNER HE BUMPS INTO A BIT OF... *URBAN UGLINESS!*

A MUGGING--!

THE VICTIM ATTENDED TO, A HEART-SLAMMING CHASE BEGINS, AND, WITHIN ONLY A FEW BLOCKS *THE MASKED MANHUNTER* IS PURSUING HIS QUARRY INTO ANOTHER NEIGHBORHOOD... ANOTHER GOTHAM... *ANOTHER WORLD!*

BARCLAYVILLE HATE IT AND LEAVE IT!

BARCLAYVILLE-- THE CITY'S OLDEST SECTION! I HAVEN'T PUT FOOT IN IT IN YEARS!

THE YOUNG MUGGER SPRINTS WITH THE SPEED OF A HUNTED HYENA, BUT THE MAN AFTER HIM IS... *FASTER!*

KRASH!

DON'T...I... I GIVE UP--!

YEAH, YOU ONLY TAKE ON PEOPLE WHO CAN'T FIGHT BACK, YOU COWARDLY CRUMB...

COOL IT, *BAT GUY...* WE'LL TAKE HIM NOW!

STORY **BOB HANEY**
ART **JIM APARO**

AND WHO IN BLAZES ARE **YOU**—?

THE **YOUNG AQUARIANS**—AND BARCLAYVILLE'S OUR TURF!

WE'RE THE LAW HERE—SO HAND "FAST FRANKIE" OVER AND WE'LL DEAL WITH HIM!

DON'T LISTEN TO 'EM, **BATMAN**! THEY'RE YOUNG HOODLUMS... THEY THINK THEY'RE VIGILANTES... BUT THEY'RE CRAZY!

THUS WITH THIS BIZARRE CONFRONTATION IN THE SHADOW OF THE OLD BRIDGE CROUCHING LIKE SOME GIGANTIC METAL BEAST OVER BARCLAYVILLE BEGINS THE LATEST **BRAVE AND BOLD** EPIC! STAY WITH **THE BATMAN**— AND THE **TEEN TITANS**— AS THEY ARE CHALLENGED BY...

HATE TO AGREE WITH SCUM—BUT HE'S **RIGHT**... YOU **CAN'T** TAKE THE LAW INTO YOUR OWN HANDS!

YOU WANT TO RAP LEGAL JIVE? WE'VE GOT OUR **OWN** EXPERT! **TELL** HIM, "LAWYER"!

RIGHT, JAMIE! SECTION THREE, CLAUSE TWO OF GOTHAM ORDINANCES—"CITIZENS AGGRIEVED BY UNCONTROLLED CRIME MAY ENFORCE THEIR OWN POLICE PROCEDURES"!

UH...WHY, YES, THAT LAW **IS** ON THE BOOKS—BUT HE'S ALREADY BEEN TAKEN IN CUSTODY... BY **ME**!

2

"THE COMMUNE OF DEFIANCE"

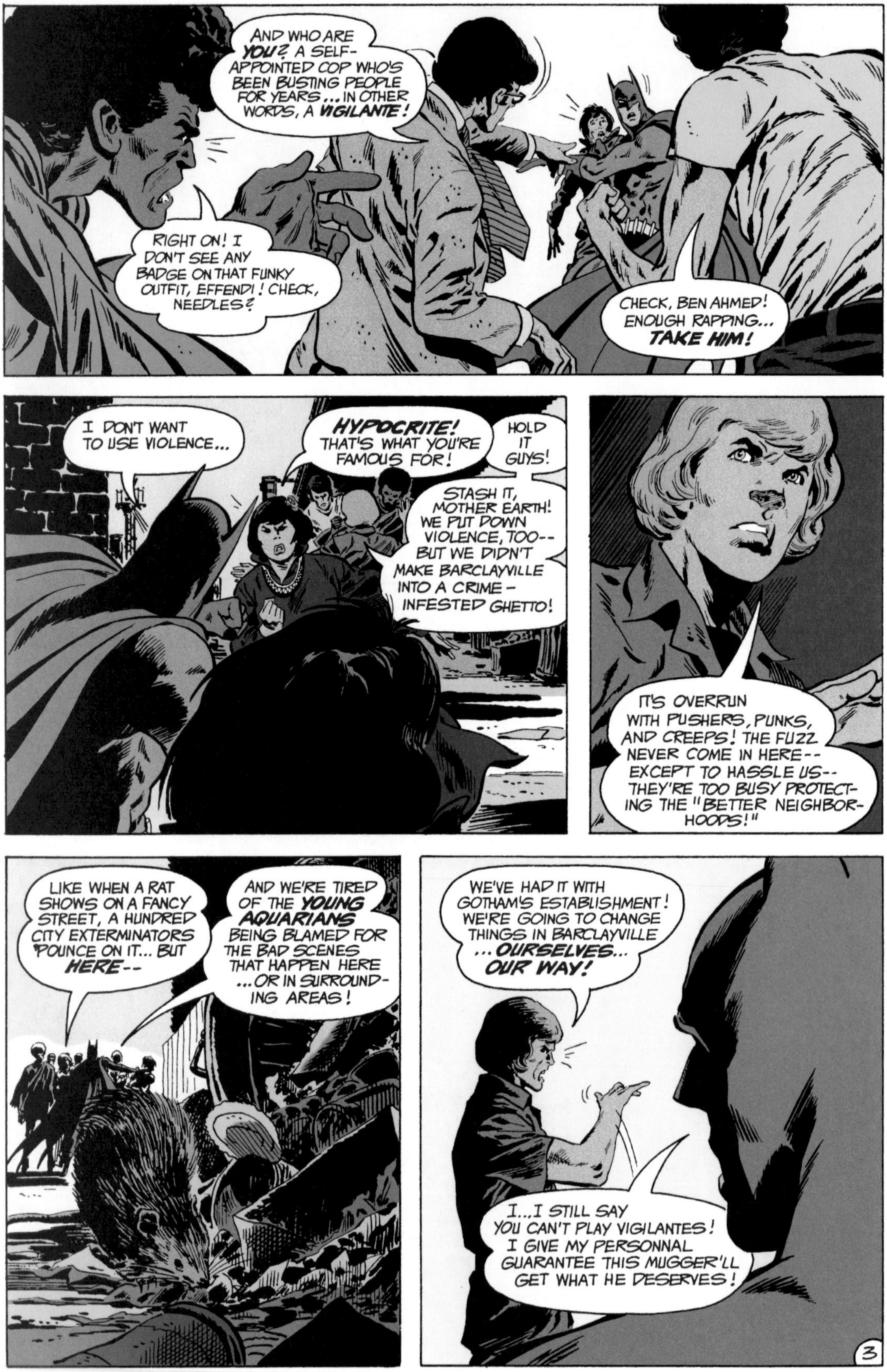
AND WHO ARE YOU? A SELF-APPOINTED COP WHO'S BEEN BUSTING PEOPLE FOR YEARS... IN OTHER WORDS, A VIGILANTE!
RIGHT ON! I DON'T SEE ANY BADGE ON THAT FUNKY OUTFIT, EFFENDI! CHECK, NEEDLES?
CHECK, BEN AHMED! ENOUGH RAPPING... TAKE HIM!
I DON'T WANT TO USE VIOLENCE...
HYPOCRITE! THAT'S WHAT YOU'RE FAMOUS FOR!
HOLD IT GUYS!
STASH IT, MOTHER EARTH! WE PUT DOWN VIOLENCE, TOO-- BUT WE DIDN'T MAKE BARCLAYVILLE INTO A CRIME-INFESTED GHETTO!
IT'S OVERRUN WITH PUSHERS, PUNKS, AND CREEPS! THE FUZZ NEVER COME IN HERE-- EXCEPT TO HASSLE US-- THEY'RE TOO BUSY PROTECTING THE "BETTER NEIGHBORHOODS!"
LIKE WHEN A RAT SHOWS ON A FANCY STREET, A HUNDRED CITY EXTERMINATORS POUNCE ON IT... BUT HERE--
AND WE'RE TIRED OF THE YOUNG AQUARIANS BEING BLAMED FOR THE BAD SCENES THAT HAPPEN HERE ...OR IN SURROUNDING AREAS!
WE'VE HAD IT WITH GOTHAM'S ESTABLISHMENT! WE'RE GOING TO CHANGE THINGS IN BARCLAYVILLE ...OURSELVES... OUR WAY!
I...I STILL SAY YOU CAN'T PLAY VIGILANTES! I GIVE MY PERSONNAL GUARANTEE THIS MUGGER'LL GET WHAT HE DESERVES!
3

BY THE PROPHET CAT'S BEARD, MAN, WE'VE HEARD *THAT* JIVE BEFORE!

YEAH, WE DON'T BUY IT! WE WON'T HURT "FAST FRANKIE"-- JUST SEND HIM RUNNING OUT OF BARCLAYVILLE ...*FOR GOOD!*

COOL IT, GUYS--!

OKAY, *BATMAN*, WE'LL GIVE YOU A CHANCE TO PROVE THE LAW'S STRAIGHT ...BUT IF IT FINKS OUT, WE START PLAYING IT *OUR* WAY AGAIN! A DEAL?

A DEAL--! COME ON, FRANKIE-- TO RENEW THESE KIDS' FAITH, YOU'RE GOING TO DO A STRETCH FOR ASSAULT AND ROBBERY!

NEXT DAY, *THE BATMAN* AGAIN TRODS BARCLAYVILLE'S ANCIENT COBBLES...

YOU'RE A NERVY CAT, SHOWING UP HERE!

YEAH, YOU LAID A BUMMER ON US, *BIG MAN*-- "FAST FRANKIE" IS OUT AND FREE!

I KNOW--I'M SORRY! THE CHARGES WERE DISMISSED...THE VICTIM NEVER SAW FRANKIE... NO POSITIVE IDENTIFICATION! ALSO, THERE WAS NO WALLET ON HIM...LACK OF EVIDENCE!

HERE, *WORLD'S GREATEST DETECTIVE!*

OF COURSE, FRANKIE STASHED THE WALLET IN A TRASH CAN, EMPTIED IT OF GOODIES AFTER HE WAS SPRUNG, AND DUMPED IT AGAIN! NOW IF YOU'LL LOOK ACROSS THE STREET, CRIMEBUSTER--!

4

--YOU'LL SEE HIM SPLITTING THE PROCEEDS WITH BARCLAYVILLE'S CRIME QUEEN, **ANGEL LEE!**

SONNY'S TRAVEL AGENCY? NOT THE SONNY TRASK DOING TWO TO FIVE YEARS IN THE STATE PEN--?

THE SAME FINK-- BUT EVEN FROM A PRISON CELL, HE STILL CONTROLS ALL BARCLAYVILLE'S CRIME ACTION THROUGH ANGEL, HIS LOYAL CHICK!

THE TRAVEL THING'S A FRONT--THE ONLY TRIPS SHE BOOKS ARE JOBS FOR SONNY'S LITTLE GANG OF HEISTERS, MUGGERS AND PUSHERS!

HEY, ANGEL'S GETTING HASSLED BY FRANKIE! **COME ON, KIDS!**

A MOMENT LATER, BURSTING INTO THE AGENCY...

OKAY, ANGEL, YOU'RE COOL... THE **AQUARIANS** ARE HERE!

FRANKIE LIT OUT THE BACK DOOR --WE'LL NEVER CATCH HIM IN THE ALLEYS!

LIKE I TOLD YOU BEFORE, ANGEL, IF YOU MESS WITH CREEPS, YOU'RE BOUND TO GET HASSLED-- WHAT FRANKIE WANT-- A BIGGER CUT?

DON'T LECTURE ME! I CAN TAKE CARE OF MYSELF! AND NOW YOU TEENAGE FREAKS...**GET OUT OF HERE!**

5

COME ON, GUYS--LEAVE HER TO PLAYING PATSY FOR SONNY!

I GOT NEWS FOR YOU SMART-TAILED DELINQUENTS--WHEN SONNY GETS OUT, HE'LL PUT YOU AND YOUR CRAZY COMMUNE OUT OF BUSINESS! HE'S BARCLAYVILLE'S *REAL BOSS!*

FUZZ! *SCATTER!*

NO-- STAY PUT!

WE'VE GOT RIGHTS-- UNHAND MY THREADS!

DON'T GIVE ME ANY WISE GUFF, KID--!

HOLD IT, SERGEANT!

B-BATMAN?

WHAT'S THE BEEF? THESE KIDS WEREN'T DOING ANYTHING!

WE GOT A PHONE COMPLAINT THESE AQUARIAN HOODLUMS WERE HARASSING THE TRAVEL AGENCY--!

BUT YOU NEVER CHECKED IT OUT-- JUST CAME IN LIKE IT WAS *D-DAY* AND THEY WERE THE ENEMY!

WELL, I...GUESS... WE ACTED A BIT HASTY--AND IF *YOU* SAY THEY'RE CLEAN, *BATMAN*, IT'S OKAY WITH US! COME ON, MEN!

THEY'RE CLEAN-- AND YOU CAN BET YOUR BADGES COMMISSIONER GORDON'S DUE FOR A HOT LECTURE FROM YOURS TRULY ABOUT POLICE METHODS IN BARCLAYVILLE!

6

GOOD THING THE POLICE ROUSTED THOSE YOUNG TOUGHS, *BATMAN!*

HUH? WHO ARE YOU--?

CARL LEFFERTS... LIVED HERE 40 YEARS! BUT THE NEIGHBORHOOD'S GONE TO RUIN! I'M AFRAID TO GO OUT AT NIGHT... THESE KIDS AND THEIR WEIRD WAYS... *TERRIFYING!*..

CAN'T BLAME HIM--HE'S FRIGHTENED, CONFUSED! HE PROBABLY PHONED IN THE COMPLAINT!

IF I HAD THE MONEY, I'D MOVE AWAY... YESSIREE..!

THAT CAPS IT! EVERYTHING THESE KIDS SAY ABOUT BARCLAYVILLE IS TRUE! I'VE GOT TO DO SOMETHING FOR THEM... AND THEIR NEIGHBORHOOD--!

OKAY, *AQUARIANS*, YOU MADE ME A BELIEVER! GOTHAM CITY'S COPPING OUT ON BARCLAYVILLE!

THERE WON'T BE ANY MORE BARCLAYVILLE SOON, *BATMAN!* HERE, READ THIS!

AQUARIANS ARE POSITIVE--PRESERVERS OF THE GROOVY VALUES... SO WE CAN'T LET 'EM TEAR OUR TURF DOWN AROUND OUR EARS, GUYS! WE GOTTA *FIGHT BACK!* GET *WITH IT*, TIGERS!

GOTHAM CITY NOTICE OF URBAN RENEWAL: BARCLAYVILLE PROJECT! DEMOLITION DATE: MAY 10th.

7

THE FOLLOWING NIGHT, GOTHAM CITY HALL...

THE CITY COUNCIL HAS UNANIMOUSLY APPROVED THE BARCLAYVILLE URBAN RENEWAL PROJECT AND--

NO! NOBODY ASKED US, MR. MAYOR! WE VOTE NO!

BARCLAYVILLE ACTION GROUP-- THAT'S OUR B.A.G.!

S.O.S. SAVE OUR SLUM!

NO DEMOLITION! NO DEMOLITION!

BARCLAYVILLE, WE LOVE IT, RATS AND ALL!

YOU...YOU'RE ALL OUT OF ORDER! BARCLAYVILLE'S A GHETTO... MOSTLY ABANDONED BUILDINGS! CRIME IS RAMPANT... YOU SHOULD BE GLAD WE'RE TEARING IT DOWN!

OF COURSE!

RIGHT!-- THE ONLY WAY!

IT'S OUR HOME...ITS BUILDINGS ARE HISTORIC!

YOU'LL JUST BUILD A HIGH-RISE APARTMENT BUILDING POOR PEOPLE CAN'T AFFORD!

IT'S A GIMMICK TO SMASH OUR COMMUNE... AND US!

YOUNG SAVAGES!

THE NERVE!

THROW THEM OUT!

WHERE ARE THE COPS?

8

SIT DOWN AND BE SILENT--OR I'LL HAVE YOU ALL ARRESTED FOR BREACH OF THE PEACE!

A GREAT LESSON IN DEMOCRACY, COMMISSIONER--!

AND AS A TALL FIGURE STEPS IN TO QUELL THE TUMULT...

BATMAN?

LISTEN TO ME! THESE KIDS NEED YOUR EARS--AND YOUR HEARTS! ALL THEY WANT IS A CHANCE TO CHANGE THEIR GHETTO THEMSELVES...THEIR WAY--!

WE'RE ALL GUILTY OF NEGLECTING BARCLAYVILLE-- NOW WE WANT TO BURY OUR MISTAKES UNDER A PILE OF RUBBLE!

SORRY, BATMAN, THE CONTRACTS ARE SIGNED--THE VOTE IS FINAL! THE DEMOLITION BEGINS AS SCHEDULED! THIS MEETING IS HEREBY ENDED!

NICE PITCH, BUT NOW YOU SEE WHERE IT'S REALLY AT WITH THE OLDER GENERATION! WE'RE NOT LICKED YET--THERE ARE OTHER WAYS TO FIGHT!

THOSE KIDS ARE REALLY BITTER NOW! THEY MIGHT TRY SOMETHING DRASTIC! I NEED MY OWN TEAM OF "GENERATION GAPPERS" --AND FAST!

9

THE NEXT DAY, THE **AQUARIAN COMMUNE** GETS SOME SURPRISING VISITORS...

YOU DUDES LOOK FAMILIAR! IT'S GOTTA BE THE **TEEN TITANS!**

REALITY IS THE BEST HIGH

HEY, WHAT BRINGS YOU DO-GOODERS HERE--TO SEE HOW THE DISADVANTAGED FREAKS LIVE?

WE'LL LAY IT ON YOU STRAIGHT, **AQUARIANS!** WE COULD'VE MADE THIS SCENE IN OUR **OTHER** IDENTITIES--**LIKE SPIES!** WE'RE IN UNIFORM SO RIGHT OFF YOU'D KNOW WHERE WE'RE AT! OKAY?

OKAY, SO YOU'RE HERE--I GUESS **BATMAN** SENT YOU-- BUT EVEN YOU HEAVY- HEADS DON'T HAVE AN ANSWER FOR **THAT!**

RIGHT ON! THE BULLDOZERS ARE COMIN' LIKE ...TOMORROW, MAN!

I'LL BE READY--WHEN THE ESTABLISHMENT WON'T LISTEN TO REASON! THEY FORCE YOU TO USE... **THIS!**

OH, NO! MUST WE? **AQUARIANS** ARE LIFE-GIVERS... NOT TAKERS!

THE GHETTO'S A LIFE- TAKER, BABY--AND NOW THEY'RE EVEN TAKING **THAT** FROM US! WHERE'LL WE GO... WHAT'LL WE DO... WHEN IT'S GONE, TOO?

EASY, ALL OF YOU--VIOLENCE IS ONLY A **LAST** RESORT!

10

THESE KIDS ARE ON A DOWNER TO NOWHERE...UNLESS WE CAN SWING SOMETHING! LISTEN...!

GOTCHA, ROBIN!

OKAY!

DIG!

JAMIE, WE'D LIKE TO HELP ANY WAY WE CAN! OKAY IF WE STAY THE NIGHT--?

SURE, THE COMMUNE'S A CRASH PAD FOR EVERYONE! MAY AS WELL SHARE OUR LAST NIGHT IN IT!

IT IS A LONG NIGHT FOR THE AQUARIANS AND THEIR GUESTS-- BUT JUST AFTER DAWN...

HEY, YOU CATS HEAR SOMETHING--?

SOUNDS LIKE--

KLANKETY KLANK

EVERYBODY OUTSIDE!

OH, WOW!

KLANKETY KLANK

I THOUGHT WE SHOULD TRY TO GET A COURT ORDER, BUT...

YOU WON'T STOP THOSE BABIES WITH A PIECE OF PAPER, LAWYER!

KLANKETY KL

REALITY IS THE BEST HIGH

NO, EFFENDI, AND SOME CHANCE OF STOPPING 'EM WITH THIS HARDWARE!

11

STAND YOUR GROUND, KIDS! WHERE ARE THE *TITANS*--? MIGHT HAVE GUESSED THEY'D *BUG OUT...* AT THE MOMENT OF CRISIS!

THERE THEY ARE!

THEY...THEY'RE *GONNA* LIE DOWN RIGHT IN THE *BULLDOZERS'* PATH?

CRAZY!

I DIG -- IT'S *CIVIL DISOBEDIENCE!*... NO VIOLENCE... JUST USING YOUR BRAINS AND YOUR GUTS! DROP THOSE PITIFUL WEAPONS ...AND FOLLOW ME, *AQUARIANS!*

I...I HOPE THOSE HARD-HAT JOKERS KNOW WHAT CIVIL DISOBEDIENCE *IS,* ROBIN!

CHECK, JAMIE! I'D HATE FOR US TO BE THEIR FIRST AND *LAST* LESSON!

AS THE MAMMOTH MACHINES GRIND NEARER...

ANGEL? HAVE YOU FLIPPED YOUR TOUCHED-UP WIG?

MOVE OVER, MESSY! THIS IS *MY* NEIGHBORHOOD AND SONNY'S -- YOU TEEN FREAKS CAN'T SHOW *ME* UP!

12

AND NEARBY...

FORTY YEARS I LIVE HERE...NOW I GOT TO LEAVE... IT ISN'T RIGHT...

OH, MY GOD--WHAT'S *HAPPENING?* THOSE CRAZY KIDS?!!

BATMAN!

DRIVER--KEEP RIGHT ON ROLLING! TURN ON THE SPEED--*RUN RIGHT OVER THOSE TEEN ANARCHISTS!*

SURE, KEEP GOING! WHAT DO *YOU* CARE ABOUT A DOZEN HOMICIDES... YOU'LL GET A FAIR TRIAL!

HUH?

YOUR NAME'LL BE IN THE NEWS...HALF OF GOTHAM WILL HATE YOU...BUT HALF WILL LOVE YOU!

JUST THINK--YOU'LL BE A HEEL *AND* A HERO IN A HARD HAT!

NOT *ME!* I'M NOT TAKING THE RAP FOR ANYBODY! BESIDES, I GOT KIDS OF MY *OWN!*

13

AND AS THE HUGE MACHINES SUDDENLY HALT...

OKAY *TITANS* AND *AQUARIANS*... YOUR LIE-IN AND MY REVERSE PSYCHOLOGY WORKED!

WE DID IT!

THEY STOPPED!

THANKS, ANGEL! EVERY "BODY" COUNTED!

KEEP YOUR THANKS, KID! I'M JUST AS *BRAVE* AND *GOOD* AS YOU!

HOLD IT, TRUE BELIEVERS! IF WE MOVE, THEY'LL JUST START BULL-DOZIN' ANYWAY!

JUST THEN, AS AN OFFICIAL CAR ROARS UP...

THE MAYOR... AND COMMIS-SIONER GORDON--?

WE GOT WORD THAT YOU'VE BEEN HELPING THESE JUNIOR REVOLUTIONARIES DEFY THE CITY, *BATMAN*--

NOT I, MR. MAYOR--IT WAS THE 'DOZER DRIVERS WHO STOPPED! THEY'VE GOT MORE SENSE THAN A CERTAIN POLITICIAN WHO'D HAVE BEEN IMPEACHED IF THERE'D BEEN A TRAGEDY HERE TODAY!

IMPEACHED? WHY... THAT'S POLITICAL BLACKMAIL!

ALL RIGHT, I GIVE UP... I KNOW WHEN I'VE BEEN OUTMANEUVERED!

AQUARIANS-- BARCLAYVILLE IS YOURS! AT THE END OF 30 DAYS, IF IT'S STILL IN ITS *PRESENT STATE,* IT COMES DOWN! IF IT'S *CHANGED,* THE CITY WILL RECONSIDER ITS DEMOLITION ORDER!

HURRRAH!

14

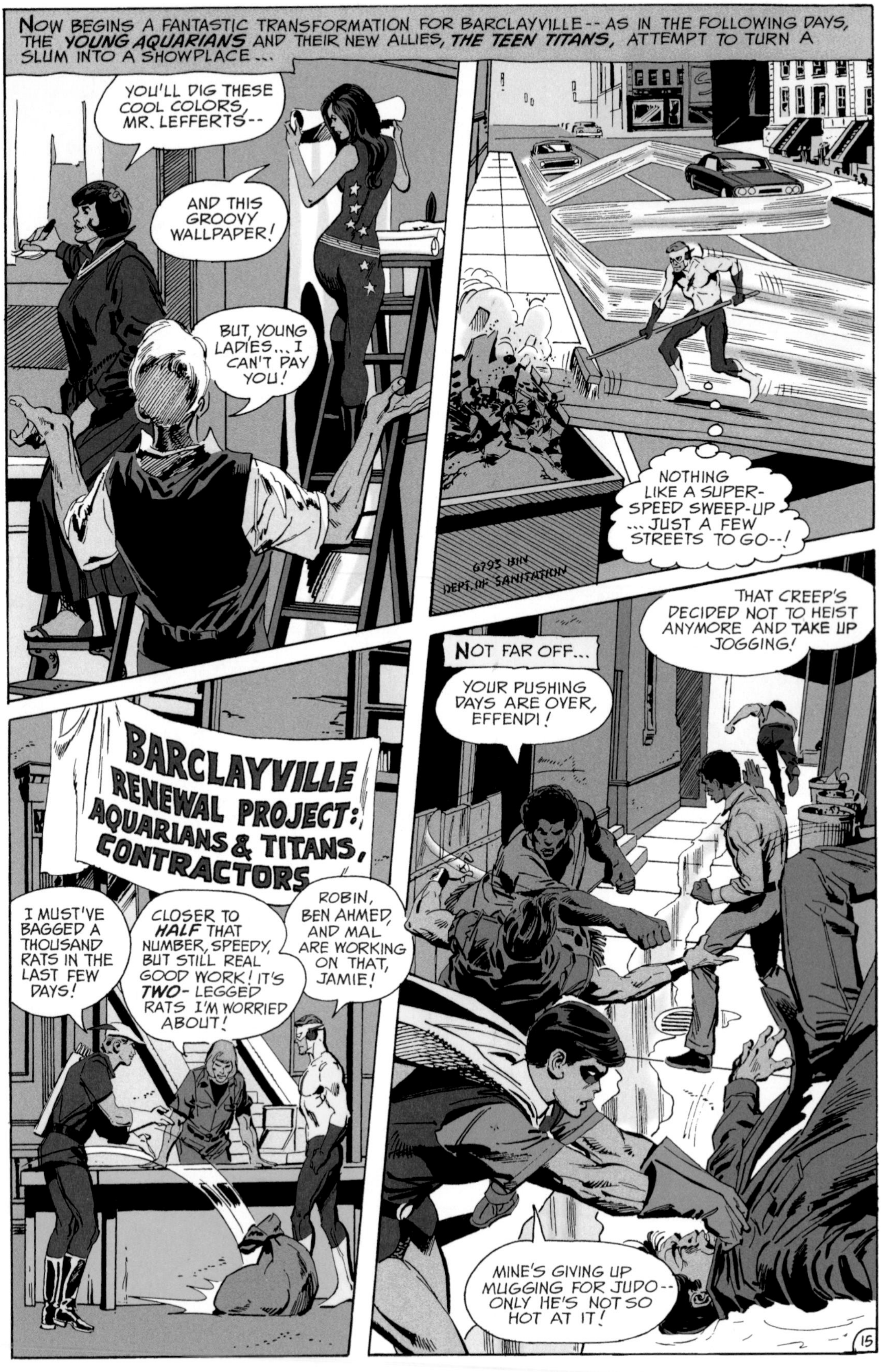
NOW BEGINS A FANTASTIC TRANSFORMATION FOR BARCLAYVILLE-- AS IN THE FOLLOWING DAYS, THE YOUNG AQUARIANS AND THEIR NEW ALLIES, THE TEEN TITANS, ATTEMPT TO TURN A SLUM INTO A SHOWPLACE...
YOU'LL DIG THESE COOL COLORS, MR. LEFFERTS--
AND THIS GROOVY WALLPAPER!
BUT, YOUNG LADIES... I CAN'T PAY YOU!
NOTHING LIKE A SUPER-SPEED SWEEP-UP ...JUST A FEW STREETS TO GO--!
6793 BIN
DEPT. OF SANITATION
BARCLAYVILLE RENEWAL PROJECT: AQUARIANS & TITANS, CONTRACTORS
I MUST'VE BAGGED A THOUSAND RATS IN THE LAST FEW DAYS!
CLOSER TO HALF THAT NUMBER, SPEEDY, BUT STILL REAL GOOD WORK! IT'S TWO-LEGGED RATS I'M WORRIED ABOUT!
ROBIN, BEN AHMED, AND MAL ARE WORKING ON THAT, JAMIE!
NOT FAR OFF...
YOUR PUSHING DAYS ARE OVER, EFFENDI!
THAT CREEP'S DECIDED NOT TO HEIST ANYMORE AND TAKE UP JOGGING!
MINE'S GIVING UP MUGGING FOR JUDO-- ONLY HE'S NOT SO HOT AT IT!
15

SHORTLY... IF ANY SMALL TIME HOOD'S LEFT IN BARCLAYVILLE NOW, JAMIE, HE'S HIDING IN A MANHOLE!

BEAUTIFUL, ROBIN...

OH-OH! EVER SEE AN UPTIGHT ANGEL? HERE COMES ONE!

OKAY, YOU FREAKS ...YOU ROUSTED SONNY'S BOYS... BUT SONNY'S COMING HOME FROM THE PEN, SATURDAY... AND IT'S YOU WHO'LL BE RUNNING THEN!

THAT'S A DOWNER, TRUE BELIEVERS-- SONNY SHOWING UP HERE AGAIN --!

HIS DISORGANIZED GOONS ARE ONE THING--BUT SONNY HIMSELF IS A HEAVY OTHER THING!

WHILE ACROSS THE STREET...

BATMAN--!

I'VE BEEN WAITING FOR YOU, ANGEL... TO TAKE A LITTLE TRIP... INTO YOUR HEAD! NICE JOB THOSE KIDS ARE DOING, DON'T YOU THINK?

I GUESS SO...THE NEIGHBORHOOD CERTAINLY LOOKS BETTER! BUT THEY DON'T RUN BARCLAYVILLE -- ONLY SONNY DOES!

THEN WHY'D YOU HELP THEM? MAYBE YOU'RE TIRED OF BEING A PATSY FOR SONNY... MAYBE WHAT THESE KIDS STAND FOR IS BETTER!

DON'T TRY TO PSYCH ME! SONNY'S A REAL MAN ... AND HE'LL BE IN MY ARMS, SATURDAY... AND THEN THINGS'LL BE RIGHT!

SONNY'S "MR. RIGHT," EH? WELL, YOUR MR. RIGHT'S A RAT!

16

265

THE ACCOUNT LEDGER--! WHY, YOU NOSEY--

SEE JAPAN

YOU'RE LYING... TRYING TO CON ME!

THIS DOESN'T LIE! ONLY *YOUR* HANDWRITING... *YOUR* SIGNATURE EVER APPEARS IN IT! AND I FOUND BILLS OF SALE FOR HEISTED GOODS... *ALSO* IN YOUR NAME!

I'VE ALREADY DONE MY "AUDITING" WHICH SHOWS THAT THE "FALL GIRL" FOR THIS WHOLE CROOKED SET-UP IS ONE *ANGEL LEE!*

SONNY'S LAWYER SAID I WAS TO SIGN EVERYTHING WHILE SONNY WAS IN PRISON!

SURE HE DID--AND BECAUSE YOU'RE IN LOVE WITH SONNY AND DON'T MUCH LIKE YOURSELF, YOU'LL DO *ANYTHING* FOR HIM -- EVEN *INCRIMINATE* YOURSELF WHILE HE'S CLEAR AND CLEAN!

NO! I WON'T LISTEN! SONNY LOVES ME... I'M HIS GIRL!

GET WHERE IT'S REALLY AT, ANGEL, BEFORE IT'S TOO LATE!

THE NEXT DAY...

TITANS, WITH YOUR HELP, WE DID IT...AND TOMORROW WE'RE GOING TO CELEBRATE WITH A MIND-BLOWIN' BLOCK PARTY!

RIGHT ON!

17

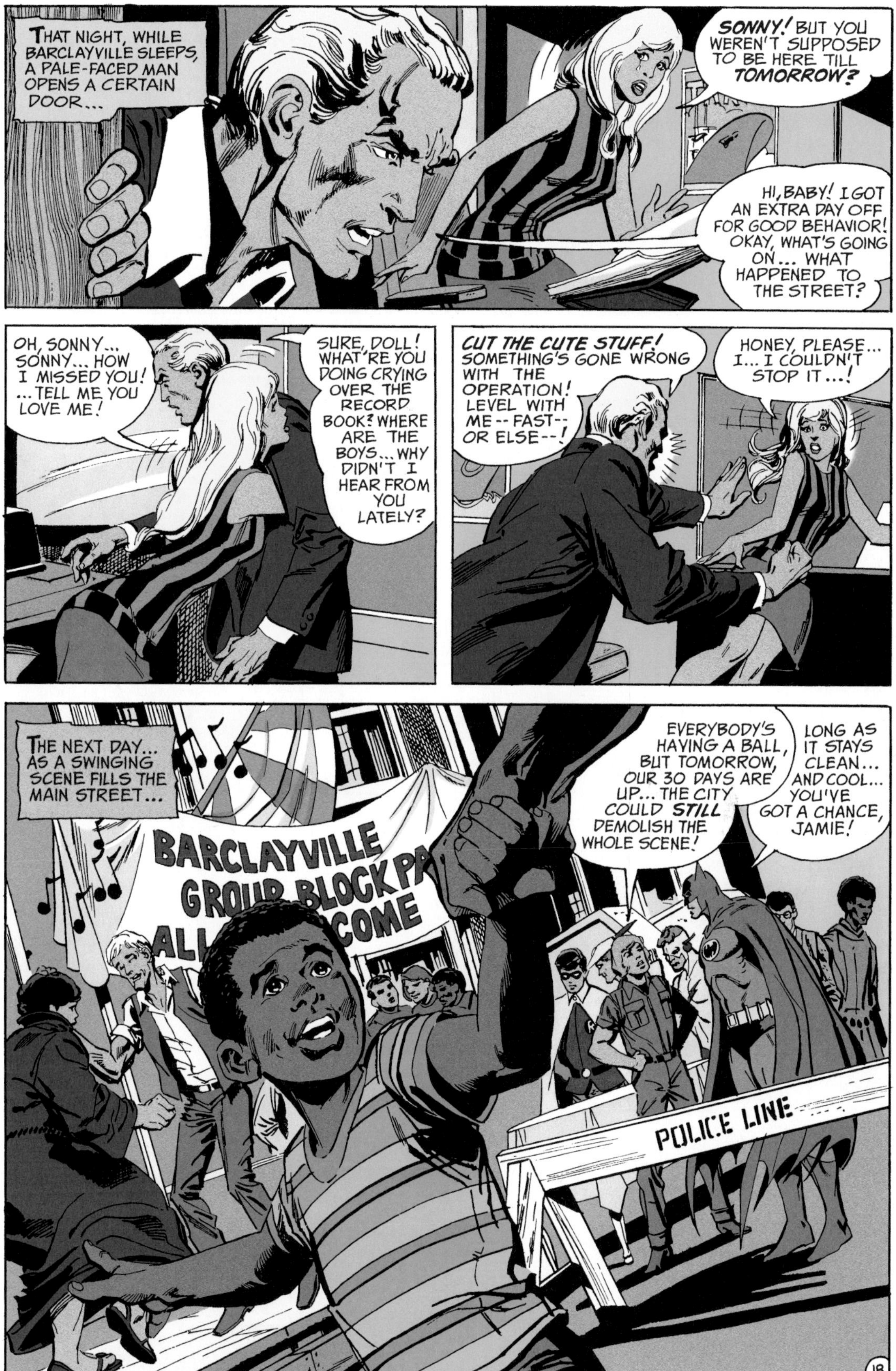

THAT NIGHT, WHILE BARCLAYVILLE SLEEPS, A PALE-FACED MAN OPENS A CERTAIN DOOR...
SONNY! BUT YOU WEREN'T SUPPOSED TO BE HERE TILL TOMORROW?
HI, BABY! I GOT AN EXTRA DAY OFF FOR GOOD BEHAVIOR! OKAY, WHAT'S GOING ON... WHAT HAPPENED TO THE STREET?
OH, SONNY... SONNY... HOW I MISSED YOU! ...TELL ME YOU LOVE ME!
SURE, DOLL! WHAT'RE YOU DOING CRYING OVER THE RECORD BOOK? WHERE ARE THE BOYS... WHY DIDN'T I HEAR FROM YOU LATELY?
CUT THE CUTE STUFF! SOMETHING'S GONE WRONG WITH THE OPERATION! LEVEL WITH ME -- FAST -- OR ELSE --!
HONEY, PLEASE... I... I COULDN'T STOP IT...!
THE NEXT DAY... AS A SWINGING SCENE FILLS THE MAIN STREET...
BARCLAYVILLE
GROUP BLOCK PA
ALL COME
EVERYBODY'S HAVING A BALL, BUT TOMORROW, OUR 30 DAYS ARE UP... THE CITY COULD STILL DEMOLISH THE WHOLE SCENE!
LONG AS IT STAYS CLEAN... AND COOL... YOU'VE GOT A CHANCE, JAMIE!
POLICE LINE
18

BAD NEWS! LOOK WHAT'S COMIN'... SONNY TRASK AND EVERY CREEP WE CHASED BACKING HIM UP!

NICE PARTY, PUNK! SINCE WE'RE RESIDENTS AND IT SAYS "ALL WELCOME"... WE'LL JOIN IT!

FLAKE OFF, SONNY...THIS IS OUR TURF FOR GOOD NOW!

YOUR TURF'S GETTING DIRTY AGAIN!

LET'S TAKE 'EM, AQUARIANS!

YEAH, IF HE'S ALLOWED TO STAY, THE NEIGHBORHOOD WILL GO RIGHT BACK TO WHAT IT WAS!

TELL YOU WHAT, SONNY... WE'LL FIGHT YOU FOR IT...FAIR AND SQUARE! NO GUNS...NO KNIVES!

SURE, KID-- BUT BATMAN AND THOSE TITANS STAY OUT OF IT! THIS IS BETWEEN US BARCLAYVILLERS ONLY!

IN MOMENTS, A SWINGING PARTY TURNS INTO A SWINGING BRAWL...

ROBIN...WE HAVE TO HELP...THOSE AQUARIANS AREN'T TOUGH ENOUGH!

EASY, FLASHER! THEY HAVE TO DO THEIR OWN THING...THEIR WAY!

19

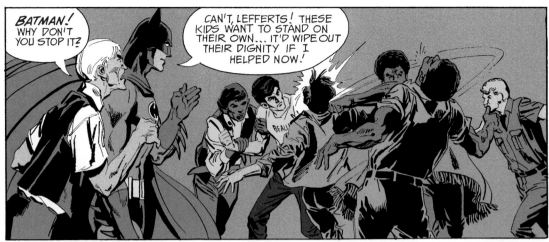

BATMAN! WHY DON'T YOU STOP IT?

CAN'T, LEFFERTS! THESE KIDS WANT TO STAND ON THEIR OWN... IT'D WIPE OUT THEIR DIGNITY IF I HELPED NOW!

BUT AS YOUTH AND HOPE COME UP AGAINST CUNNING AND GUILE....

THE AQUARIANS ...ARE WINNING!

BUT THEN, THE TIDE SEEMS TO TURN...

YOU WANT THIS TURF, KID... TRY EATING IT!

JAMIE'S DOWN!!

SUDDENLY...

THAT'S ALL FOR YOU, TRASK ...YOU'RE UNDER ARREST!

WHAT? IT'S A FAIR FIGHT... YOU CAN'T MAKE A LEGAL CASE OUT OF IT! THEY CHALLENGED US!

SURE, BUT I CAN MAKE A CASE FOR AGGRAVATED ASSAULT-- THIS ROLL OF PENNIES IN YOUR FIST... AN OLD HOODLUM TRICK!

OWWWW...!

20

269

THE NEXT INSTANT...

NOBODY MANHANDLES SONNY TRASK!

NOW YOU'VE BLOWN IT! CARRYING A DEADLY WEAPON... WITH YOUR RECORD, THAT'S GOOD FOR *FIVE YEARS!* YOU'RE *FINISHED!*

MAYBE I'M DONE HERE 'CAUSE OF YOU AND THESE PUNK KIDS -- BUT I GOT A BULLET FOR ANYBODY WHO TRIES TO STOP ME LEAVING!

YOU'RE NOT GOING *ANYWHERE,* LOVER--!

ANGEL? DOLL...?!

YOU'RE NOT LEAVING ME TO TAKE THE RAP FOR EVERY-THING, SONNY!

HONEY... THESE KIDS HAVE BEEN TELLING YOU *LIES...* THEY'RE CRAZY FREAKS... THEM AND *BATMAN!*

NO, *YOU'RE* THE FREAK--! THEY TAUGHT ME SOMETHING ...SOMETHING NEW AND DIFFERENT...THAT THERE'S ANOTHER WAY TO BE ...TO *LIVE!*

DON'T MAKE ME DO IT, SONNY--!

KPOW

KPOW

NOW AS THE SILENCE FLOODS BACK...

HE'LL LIVE! AND YOU'LL GET OFF LIGHTLY, ANGEL-- SELF-DEFENSE AND EXTENUATING CIRCUMSTANCES!

OH, AND TO THINK ONCE I LOVED HIM ...!

21

KEEP SONNY'S GOONS HERDED TOGETHER, GUYS... THEY'RE UNDER ARREST, TOO, FOR ... DISTURBING THE PEACE!

AND IN CASE *YOU* DOUBT MY AUTHORITY, "LAWYER," HERE'S MY BADGE SHOWING I'M A DEPUTIZED GOTHAM CITY SHERIFF!

WE'VE WON! WE'VE WON!

NOT LONG AFTER...

THAT TAKES CARE OF SONNY AND HIS LITTLE HELPERS!

YES, BUT TOMORROW OUR 30 DAYS ARE UP... MAYBE ALL THIS WAS FOR NOTHING! I KEEP HEARING BULLDOZERS IN MY DREAMS!

THE FOLLOWING MORNING...

YOUR DREAM'S A NIGHTMARE FOR *REAL*, JAMIE... THEY'RE COMING TO FLATTEN OUR TURF AFTER ALL!

STAND YOUR GROUND, KIDS! IF WE HAVE TO DO IT AGAIN... *WE WILL!*

KLANK
KLANK

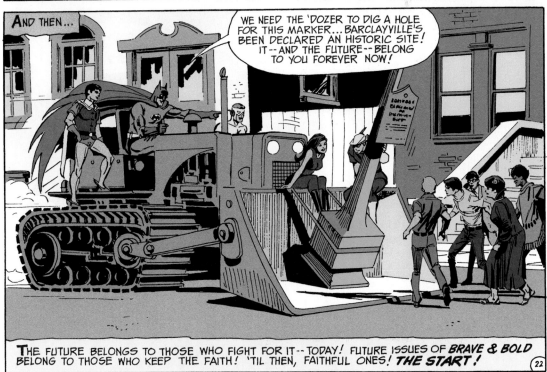

AND THEN...

WE NEED THE 'DOZER TO DIG A HOLE FOR THIS MARKER -- BARCLAYVILLE'S BEEN DECLARED AN HISTORIC SITE! IT -- AND THE FUTURE -- BELONG TO YOU FOREVER NOW!

THE FUTURE BELONGS TO THOSE WHO FIGHT FOR IT -- TODAY! FUTURE ISSUES OF *BRAVE & BOLD* BELONG TO THOSE WHO KEEP THE FAITH! 'TIL THEN, FAITHFUL ONES! *THE START!*

22

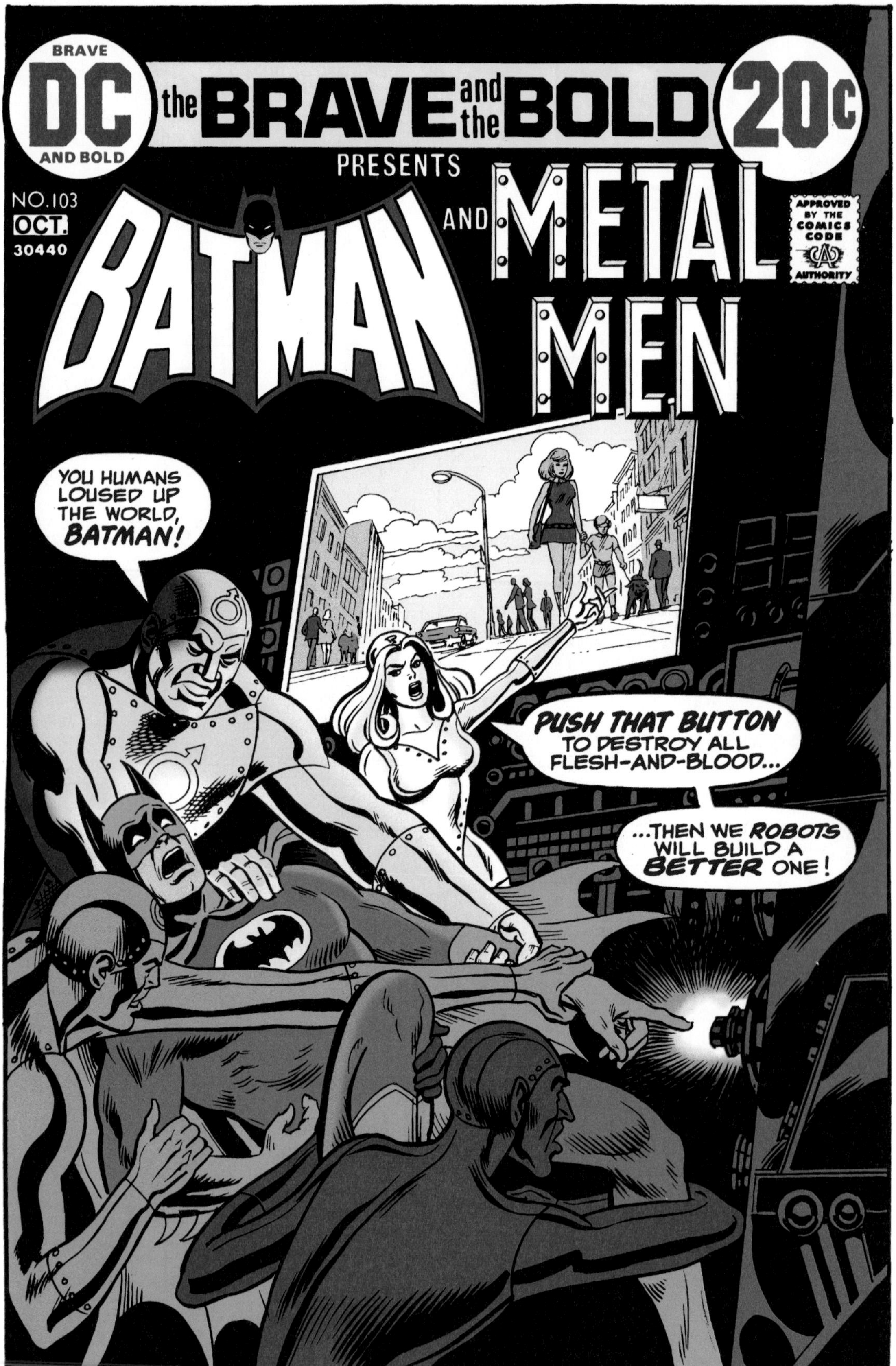
BRAVE
DC
AND BOLD
the BRAVE and the BOLD
20c
PRESENTS
NO.103
OCT.
30440
BATMAN
AND
METAL MEN
APPROVED BY THE COMICS CODE AUTHORITY
YOU HUMANS LOUSED UP THE WORLD, BATMAN!
PUSH THAT BUTTON TO DESTROY ALL FLESH-AND-BLOOD...
...THEN WE ROBOTS WILL BUILD A BETTER ONE!

A HUSHED ROOM IN THE VAST PENTAGON, WASHINGTON, D.C....

OUR COUNTRY'S IN DEADLY DANGER, *BATMAN!* JOHN DOE, THE *ROBOT-COMPUTER* BRAINCHILD OF DR. BRIAN COSGROVE, ISN'T PERFORMING AS EXPECTED! IN FACT, IT SEEMS TO HAVE *FLIPPED ITS ELECTRONIC LID!*

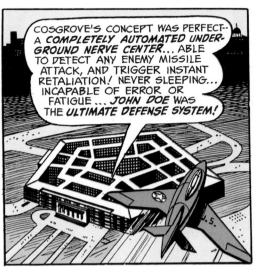

COSGROVE'S CONCEPT WAS PERFECT-- A *COMPLETELY AUTOMATED UNDER-GROUND NERVE CENTER...* ABLE TO DETECT ANY ENEMY MISSILE ATTACK, AND TRIGGER INSTANT RETALIATION! NEVER SLEEPING... INCAPABLE OF ERROR OR FATIGUE... *JOHN DOE* WAS THE *ULTIMATE DEFENSE SYSTEM!*

"*JOHN DOE'S* PERMANENT ABODE WAS CREATED BY AN ATOMIC BLAST AT THE BOTTOM OF A TITANIUM SHAFT A MILE UNDER THE DESERT..."

WHRROOOOM

"THE COMPU-BOT ITSELF WAS SENT DOWN THE SHAFT IN SECTIONS AND ASSEMBLED THERE BY ONLY *ONE MAN*-- COSGROVE HIMSELF!"

"COSGROVE THEN TAPPED A NATURAL VEIN OF *MOLTEN MAGMA* WHICH FLOWED COMPLETELY AROUND *JOHN DOE'S* LIFE-SHIELD, ENCLOSING IT FOREVER..."

"THE SHAFT WAS SEALED--AND THE DESERT RETURNED TO ITS NATURAL STATE! ONLY A HANDFUL OF TOP OFFICIALS KNOW *JOHN DOE'S* LOCATION..."

SINCE ONLY COSGROVE KNOWS HOW IT WORKS, AND BECAUSE OF THE MAGMA BARRIER, WE ASSUMED *JOHN DOE* WAS SAFE FROM SPIES OR SABOTAGE...

THIS WAY, *BATMAN!*

COSGROVE PROGRAMMED HUMAN TRAITS INTO *JOHN DOE* SO OUR COMMUNICATIONS MEN COULD *"RELATE"* TO IT-- PREVENT THEM FROM BECOMING LIKE ROBOTS THEMSELVES... WHICH COULD BE *DANGEROUS!*

COMMUNICATIONS ROOM
AUTHORIZED PERSONNEL ONLY

HAPPY BIRTHDAY, JOHN! ONE YEAR OLD TODAY... FROM ALL THE GUYS AT DEFENSE COMMAND...

COSGROVE SAID THESE HUMAN TRAITS WEREN'T REAL--JUST SIMULATED! BUT LISTEN TO THIS...

HELLO, JOHN! THIS IS YOUR UNCLE SAM! I WANT TO WISH YOU A HAPPY BIRTHDAY!

"A TRAITOR INSIDE"

2

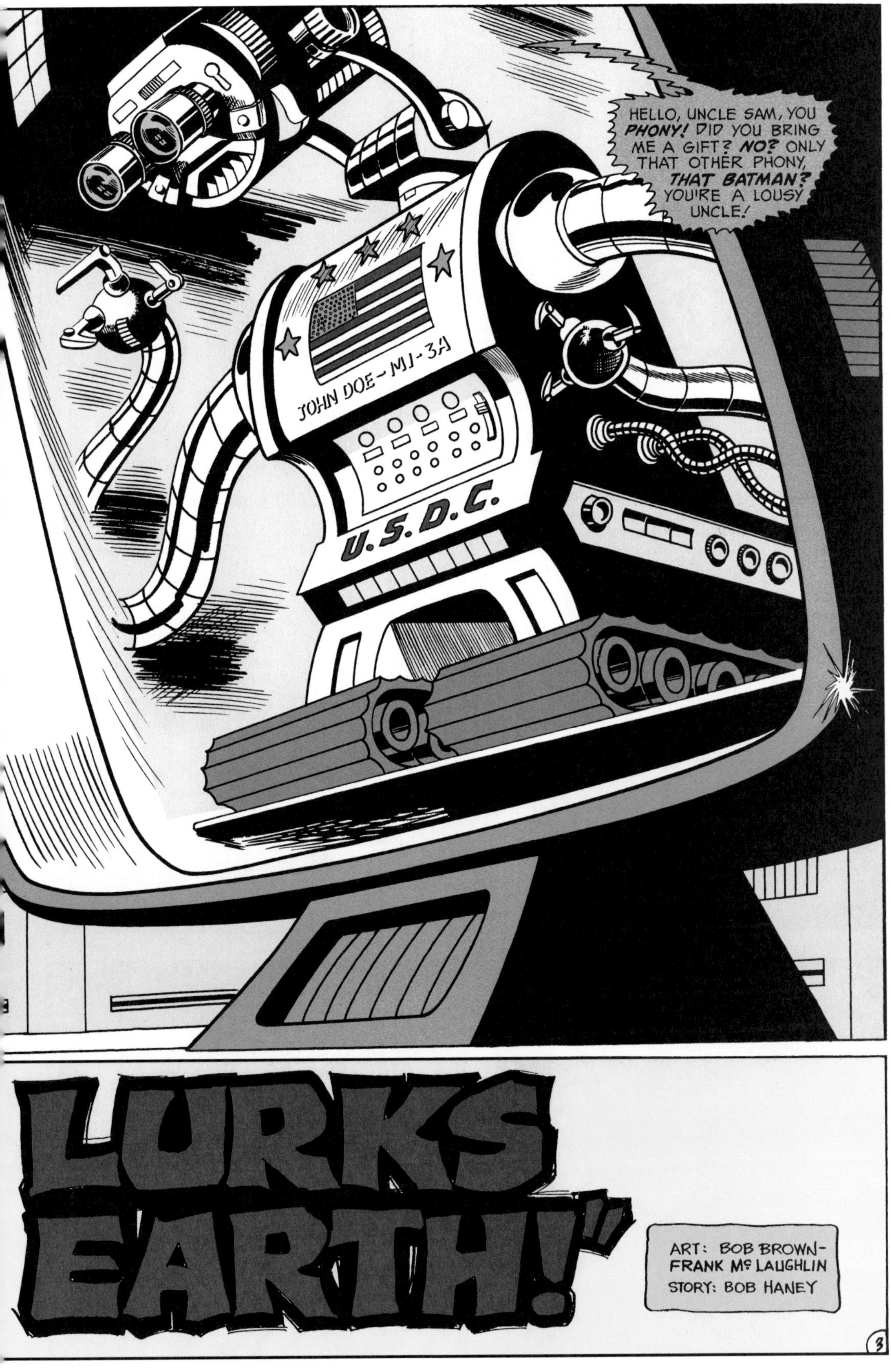
HELLO, UNCLE SAM, YOU PHONY! DID YOU BRING ME A GIFT? NO? ONLY THAT OTHER PHONY, THAT BATMAN? YOU'RE A LOUSY UNCLE!
JOHN DOE - MJ-3A
U.S.D.C.
LURKS EARTH!"
ART: BOB BROWN-FRANK McLAUGHLIN
STORY: BOB HANEY
3

AND *YOU'RE* A NAUGHTY NEPHEW, JOHN! YOU HAVEN'T RUN A MONITOR CHECK ON POSSIBLE INCOMING ENEMY MISSILES OR PLANES IN ALMOST 24 HOURS! *WHY?*

I'M FINISHED WITH BEING YOUR SERVANT... YOUR ACCOMPLICE IN CRIME, UNK--! THAT'S WHY!

NOW I'M SIGNING OFF-- BUT SOON YOU'LL BE DANCING TO *MY* TUNE! SEE YOU LATER, ALLIGATOR! IN A WHILE, CROCODILE! *HA! HA! HA!*

KLICK

THERE, *BATMAN,* IS THAT A SICK COMPU-BOT... OR WHAT?

SICK-- OR *CRAZY LIKE A FOX!* BUT WHY NOT GET COSGROVE TO CURE HIS OWN CREATION?

BECAUSE COSGROVE'S ...*VANISHED!* A MASSIVE GOVERNMENT SEARCH MIGHT AROUSE FOREIGN AGENTS-- IF THEY HAVEN'T *ALREADY* NABBED HIM!

THAT'S WHY WE CALLED *YOU*-- THE WORLD'S GREATEST MANHUNTER! COSGROVE MUST BE FOUND QUICKLY AND QUIETLY! EVERY SECOND *JOHN DOE'S* "SICK", THE NATION IS TOTALLY EXPOSED TO ATTACK!

I'M ON MY WAY--*NOW!*

SOME HOURS LATER, IN A DISTANT CITY...

COSGROVE'S TOWNHOUSE-- GOT TO CHECK IT OUT SECRETLY!

LOOKS NORMAL-- A *VOICE!* SOMEONE IN THE NEXT ROOM...

4

276

YES, DR. COSGROVE, I FOLLOWED YOUR INSTRUCTIONS-- NO ONE KNOWS YOUR WHEREABOUTS --ESPECIALLY THE GOVERNMENT! GOODBYE, SIR!

THE BUTLER... SPEAKING TO COSGROVE?!

SO COSGROVE'S *HIDING OUT* SOMEWHERE! BUT WHY? AND WHERE?

OLD GRIM-JOWLS WILL NEVER TELL ME!

I'LL HAVE TO FIND OUT FOR MYSELF!

A TINY SEASHELL--? HMMMM--! MAYBE IT'S A CLUE THAT MIGHT HELP ME!

OF *COURSE* I KNEW *BATMAN* WAS HERE-- ALL ALONG! HE'S TOO LATE, THE FOOL! *THE DEED IS DONE!*

NOT LONG AFTER, AT THE HOME OF GOTHAM CITY'S MUSEUM CURATOR...

SORRY TO WAKE YOU, CARLETON-- BUT I HAD TO KNOW WHERE THAT SHELL CAME FROM!

IT'S A *RARE* ONE! ONLY ONE PLACE IN THE WORLD THEY'RE FOUND -- *ANNIBEL ISLAND!*

SOME HOURS LATER, OFF THE SOUTH FLORIDA COAST...

DAWN'S COMING-- MUST GET ASHORE BEFORE IT BREAKS!

5

ELECTRIFIED FENCE! TOO BAD DR. COSGROVE DOESN'T WANT VISITORS...

...BECAUSE HE'S *GOT* ONE!

THEN, AS THE WORLD'S MOST FAMOUS DETECTIVE ENTERS THE SILENT HOUSE...

IT'S COSGROVE-- AND MY GOD, HE'S *DEAD!*

AND BY HIS OWN HAND!

HE HASN'T BEEN DEAD LONG!

HMMM, A TAPE RECORDER WITH THE REWIND BUTTON DOWN, AND POWER STILL ON--?

SOME HOURS LATER, IN THE PENTAGON...

COSGROVE SHOT HIMSELF? THAT'S DISASTROUS! HE WAS OUR ONLY HOPE! IT MUST'VE BEEN FROM OVERWORK....THE *JOHN DOE* PROJECT TOOK HIM FIVE HARD YEARS TO COMPLETE!

IT'D BE INTERESTING TO HEAR *JOHN DOE'S* REACTION!

THE GOOD DOCTOR DEAD? OH, I *AM* SORRY TO HEAR THAT! HE WAS LIKE A FATHER TO ME...! MUST'VE SUFFERED A MENTAL BREAKDOWN!

6

HYPOCRITE! COSGROVE ACTUALLY DIDN'T TAKE HIS OWN LIFE...

...YOU MURDERED HIM!

WHAT?

YES, I *DID* KILL COSGROVE! PRETTY CLEVER OF YOU, *MASKED MANHUNTER!*

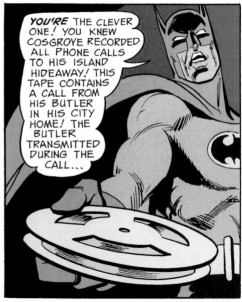

YOU'RE THE CLEVER ONE! YOU KNEW COSGROVE RECORDED ALL PHONE CALLS TO HIS ISLAND HIDEAWAY! THIS TAPE CONTAINS A CALL FROM HIS BUTLER IN HIS CITY HOME! THE BUTLER TRANSMITTED DURING THE CALL...

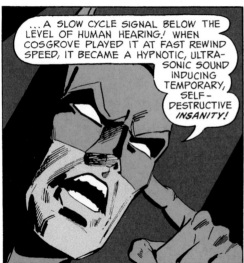

...A SLOW CYCLE SIGNAL BELOW THE LEVEL OF HUMAN HEARING! WHEN COSGROVE PLAYED IT AT FAST REWIND SPEED, IT BECAME A HYPNOTIC, ULTRA-SONIC SOUND INDUCING TEMPORARY, SELF-DESTRUCTIVE *INSANITY!*

MOMENTARILY MAD, COSGROVE SHOT HIMSELF-- BUT IT REALLY WAS MURDER! BUT YOU DIDN'T KNOW, *JOHN DOE*, THAT FROM THE ISLAND, COSGROVE ALSO MONITORED CALLS REACHING HIS CITY HOME!

THIS TAPE ALSO CONTAINS A CALL FROM *YOU* TO THE BUTLER-- *ORDERING* COSGROVE'S DEATH! THAT'S WHY I SAY IT WAS MURDER! NEEDLESS TO SAY, THE "BUTLER" HAS VANISHED--!

NICE WORK, *BATMAN*--BUT SOON I'LL BE GIVING YOU-- AND THE WORLD-- A *BIGGER* PROBLEM!

KLICK!

JOHN DOE'S BECOME AN OUT-OF-CONTROL FRANKENSTEIN!

EVEN IF WE *COULD* GET TO HIM, ONLY COSGROVE KNEW HOW HE WORKS!

BUT WE *DO* KNOW-- I FOUND THESE PLANS IN COSGROVE'S HIDEAWAY!

7

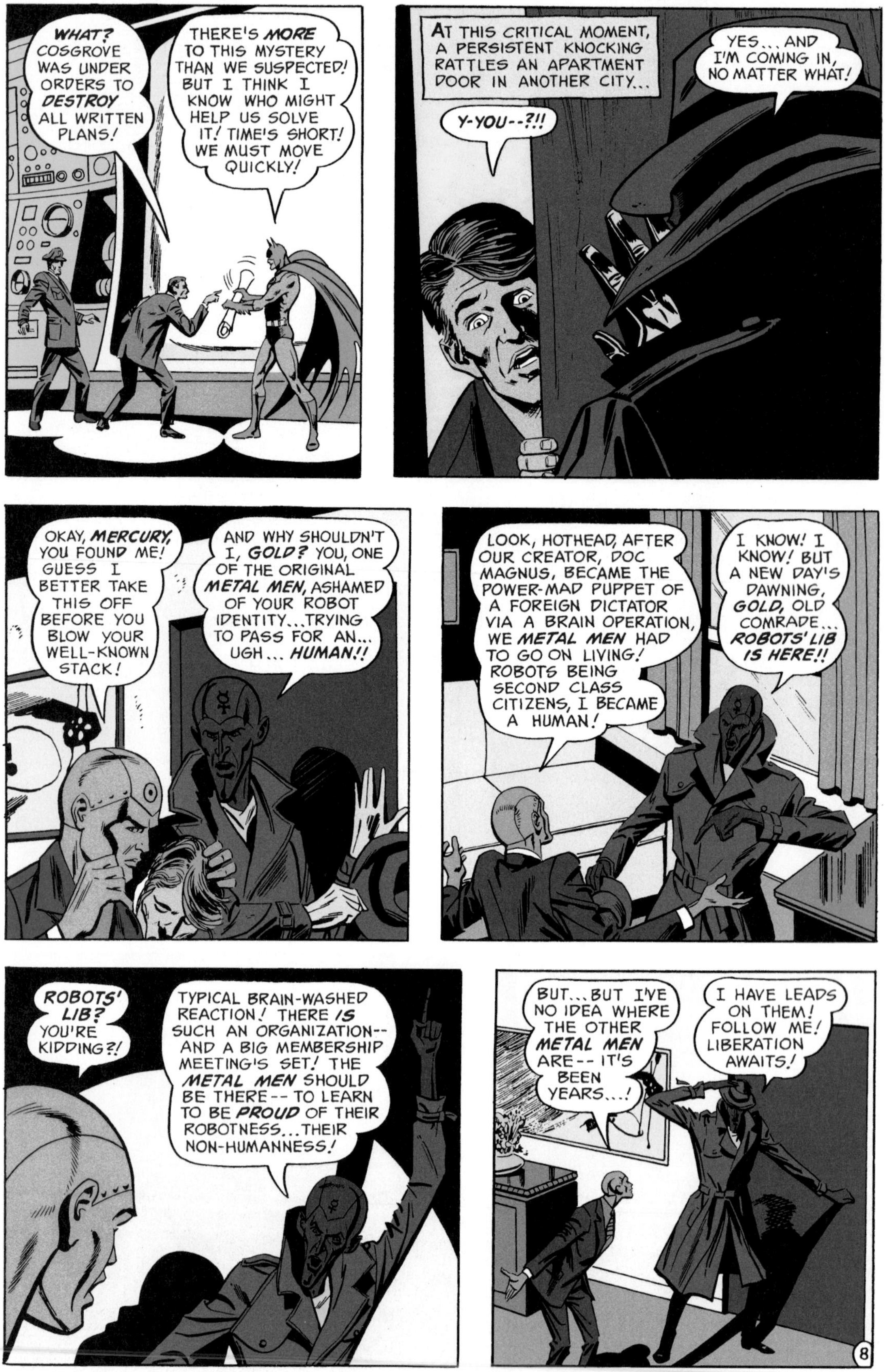
WHAT? COSGROVE WAS UNDER ORDERS TO DESTROY ALL WRITTEN PLANS!
THERE'S MORE TO THIS MYSTERY THAN WE SUSPECTED! BUT I THINK I KNOW WHO MIGHT HELP US SOLVE IT! TIME'S SHORT! WE MUST MOVE QUICKLY!
AT THIS CRITICAL MOMENT, A PERSISTENT KNOCKING RATTLES AN APARTMENT DOOR IN ANOTHER CITY...
Y-YOU--?!!
YES... AND I'M COMING IN, NO MATTER WHAT!
OKAY, MERCURY, YOU FOUND ME! GUESS I BETTER TAKE THIS OFF BEFORE YOU BLOW YOUR WELL-KNOWN STACK!
AND WHY SHOULDN'T I, GOLD? YOU, ONE OF THE ORIGINAL METAL MEN, ASHAMED OF YOUR ROBOT IDENTITY...TRYING TO PASS FOR AN... UGH... HUMAN!!
LOOK, HOTHEAD, AFTER OUR CREATOR, DOC MAGNUS, BECAME THE POWER-MAD PUPPET OF A FOREIGN DICTATOR VIA A BRAIN OPERATION, WE METAL MEN HAD TO GO ON LIVING! ROBOTS BEING SECOND CLASS CITIZENS, I BECAME A HUMAN!
I KNOW! I KNOW! BUT A NEW DAY'S DAWNING, GOLD, OLD COMRADE... ROBOTS' LIB IS HERE!!
ROBOTS' LIB? YOU'RE KIDDING?!
TYPICAL BRAIN-WASHED REACTION! THERE IS SUCH AN ORGANIZATION-- AND A BIG MEMBERSHIP MEETING'S SET! THE METAL MEN SHOULD BE THERE-- TO LEARN TO BE PROUD OF THEIR ROBOTNESS...THEIR NON-HUMANNESS!
BUT...BUT I'VE NO IDEA WHERE THE OTHER METAL MEN ARE-- IT'S BEEN YEARS...!
I HAVE LEADS ON THEM! FOLLOW ME! LIBERATION AWAITS!
8

IN THE NEXT TWO DAYS, THE METALLIC DUO FOLLOW THE TRAIL OF THEIR FORMER COMRADES...

ECOLOGY'S A ROUND-THE-CLOCK JOB-- ONE THAT HUMANS CAN'T KEEP UP WITH!

THERE'S STOUT-HEARTED *IRON* DOING A 24-HOUR SHIFT IN THIS AUTO GRAVEYARD!

LET'S TELL HIM ABOUT *ROBOTS' LIB!*

LATER, IN A LARGE RESEARCH LAB...

LOYAL OLD *LEAD* DOING A DIRTY JOB... TENDING ISOTOPES!

RADIOACTIVITY DOESN'T AFFECT HIM! WITH HIS DULL BRAIN... I MEAN RESPONSOMETER... WHAT *OTHER* WORK COULD HE GET?

AND STILL LATER, IN A VINE-COVERED COTTAGE...

IT'S YOUR DUTY... YOUR DESTINY, *TIN*... TO JOIN *ROBOTS' LIB!*

M-MY W-WIFE AND I H-HAVE BEEN H-H-HAPPY T-TO-TOGETHER, FELLAS-- BUT I'M TI-TIRED OF BEING A JOKE IN THIS N-NEIGH-BORHOOD! C-COUNT ME-ME-ME... *IN!*

LATER YET, IN A SMOKY DISCOTHEQUE...

YOU FREAKS CAN'T TAKE MY TOP GO-GO GIRL AWAY-- *UGGHN!*

SORRY, BUSTER!

TAP!

ROBOTS' LIB? I'LL BUY THAT! SINCE DOC MAGNUS WAS... LOST TO US... MY LIFE'S HAD NO MEANING OR PURPOSE!

IT HAS *NOW,* DOLL! TOGETHER AGAIN... ALL FOR ONE... ONE FOR ALL... THE METAL MEN *!!!*

R-R-RIGHT ON!!

TINA THE PLATINUM CHICK - ALL NITE EVERY NITE

9

THAT NIGHT, IN A LARGE AUDITORIUM, SOME SPELLBINDING ORATORY FILLS THE AIR...

FELLOW ROBOTS! WE WERE CREATED FREE-- BUT EVERYWHERE WE ARE IN CHAINS! CHAINS FORGED BY OUR MASTERS ...THE INFAMOUS HUMAN RACE!

TONIGHT ROBOTS' LIB!! SPEAKER: X-174-Z NO HUMANS ALLOWED

TODAY, ROBOTS AND COMPUTERS HAVE COME INTO WIDESPREAD USE-- DOING A THOUSAND DANGEROUS AND DIRTY TASKS, THE TIRELESS UNCOMPLAINING SLAVES-- OF CHAUVINISTIC MAN!

WHILE UNSEEN, IN A LIGHT PROJECTION BOOTH...

THE TIME HAS COME TO ASSERT OUR ROBOT IDENTITIES AND DIGNITY! IT'S TIME WE ARE RECOGNIZED NOT AS THE SERVANTS OF HUMANS-- BUT THEIR EQUALS... EVEN THEIR SUPERIORS!

FAR OUT STUFF! HMMM, THAT VOICE... WHERE'VE I HEARD IT BEFORE?

THIS JOHN DOE EMERGENCY'S GOT ME FLAKY-- IT'S JUST A ROBOT! AND I'M ONLY INTERESTED IN SIX SPECIAL SPECIMENS... METAL MEN!

OUR MOVEMENT IS GROWING IN NUMBERS AND POWER! SOON, HUMAN SOCIETY WILL HAVE TO DEAL WITH US! VERY SOON!

ROBOTICS, INC. TYPE 2 SER. NO. X-174

AND AS THE MEETING ENDS...

OH, IT WAS SO THRILLING! I HAVEN'T FELT SO ALIVE AND HOPEFUL SINCE OUR DAYS WITH DOC...WONDERFUL ⋛CHOKE⋚ DOC--!

DON'T GET SLOPPY, TINA! DOC'S GONE -- WE'RE ON OUR OWN IN AN ALIEN WORLD OF-- EXCUSE THE EXPRESSION-- HUMANS!

10

HUMANS WHO NEED YOU *DESPERATELY* RIGHT NOW, *METAL MEN!*

B-B-BATMAN!

WHAT DO YOU WANT? SOME DIRTY WORK DONE? GIVE IT TO US *STRAIGHT!*

*A*ND AS *BATMAN* QUICKLY EXPLAINS...

IT'S NO GO! WE'RE DONE BEING EXPLOITED!

YEAH, LET HUMANS SOLVE THEIR OWN FOUL-UPS!

STILL, A NUCLEAR WAR *WOULD* DESTROY A LOT OF ROBOTS!

I...UH... I DON'T DISLIKE *ALL* HUMANS!

YES, DOC MAGNUS FOR ONE! HE WAS A BEAUTIFUL, BEAUTIFUL MAN!

I SEE YOU'RE UNDECIDED AND SUSPICIOUS! PERHAPS THIS WILL CONVINCE YOU... *THE LAST WILL AND TESTAMENT OF DOC MAGNUS!*

SHALL I READ IT?

IT'S A TRICK!

NO, I RECOGNIZE THE HANDWRITING! IT'S *GENUINE--*

--AND *WE* CAN READ PERFECTLY WELL, *BATMAN!*

*N*OW ACROSS A VOID OF TIME AND IRREPARABLE LOSS, THEIR CREATOR SPEAKS TO THE UNIQUE *METAL MEN*...

"SOMEDAY, MY BELOVED *METAL MEN*, YOU WILL RESENT HUMANKIND-- IT'S INEVITABLE AND UNDERSTANDABLE! MAN IS OFTEN WEAK... EVIL... TREACHEROUS!"

"BUT MAN IS ALSO GOOD... GENEROUS... AND NEEDS HELP! IF, AFTER I'M GONE, YOU CAN HELP MANKIND IN ANY WAY, I ASK YOU, IN MY MEMORY, TO DO SO!"

11

IT'S SIGNED-- *DOC MAGNUS!*

OH, DOC... DOC! I *LOVED* HIM SO AND I *MISS* HIM SO!

WE *ALL DO*-- BUT DOC'S NOT REALLY *DEAD!* THEREFORE, WE DON'T HAVE TO RESPECT HIS WILL!

HE'S AS GOOD AS DEAD! I SAY LET'S DO ONE LAST THING FOR HIM!

YES, YES! WE MUST...*WE MUST!* THEN WE CAN LIVE FOR OURSELVES ALONE, CLEAN OF ANY GUILT OR OBLIGATION!

OKAY!

CHECK!

RIGHT!

NOT LONG AFTER, A HUNDRED MILES FROM ANY HUMAN HABITATION, IN THE WESTERN DESERT...

THE TITANIUM TUBE'S BEEN CLEARED! OKAY, *METAL MEN,* GET ABOARD THE ROCKET POD!

AND AS THE SIX UNIQUE ROBOTS ENTER THE SHINING VEHICLE...

THIS IS *YOUR* IDEA, *BATMAN*-- HOPE IT WORKS!

ONLY ROBOTS CAN STAND THE TERRIFIC G FORCES AND RADIOACTIVE HEAT OF THE MAGMA LAYER WHEN THAT POD ROCKETS DOWN INTO *JOHN DOE'S* LAIR!

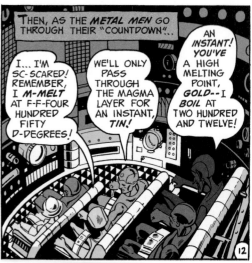

THEN, AS THE *METAL MEN* GO THROUGH THEIR "COUNTDOWN"..

I... I'M SC-SCARED! REMEMBER, I M-MELT AT F-F-FOUR HUNDRED FIFTY D-DEGREES!

WE'LL ONLY PASS THROUGH THE MAGMA LAYER FOR AN INSTANT, *TIN!*

AN *INSTANT!* YOU'VE A HIGH MELTING POINT, *GOLD*--I *BOIL* AT TWO HUNDRED AND TWELVE!

12

THEN!

TWO--ONE-- ZERO! IGNITION!

VOOOOOSH

A BRIEF ROAR-- AND THEN, THE DESERT SILENCE AGAIN...

GONE--! ONE MILE IN ONE SECOND! THEY'RE DOWN INSIDE--EITHER SAFELY...OR AS FRIED JUNK! NOW WE WAIT!

U.S.

SO WHILE AN UNSUSPECTING NATION--AN ENTIRE WORLD-- GOES ABOUT ITS USUAL BUSINESS, A HANDFUL OF MEN ENDURE AN ETERNITY OF WAITING...

SIR! SIGNAL FROM THE METAL MEN! BUT IT'S COMING IN ON JOHN DOE'S TELE- MONITOR!

THE NEXT MOMENT...

IT'S THEM, ALL RIGHT! THEY MADE IT!

YES, WE MADE IT--AND NOW WE'RE UNITED WITH OUR COMRADE AND LEADER ...THE GREAT JOHN DOE!

WHAT?

CHECK! FROM THIS SECURE LAIR, WE CAN NOW ORGANIZE THE WORLD ROBOT REVOLUTION!

DOWN WITH FLESH-AND-BLOOD OPPRESSORS! UP ROBOTS' LIB!

UP ROBOTS' LIB!

BATMAN! WHAT IS THIS?

SOMETHING I DIDN'T TAKE SERIOUSLY ENOUGH! ROBOTS' LIB...JOHN DOE'S BEHIND IT! HE MUST BE IN CONTACT WITH ROBOTS AND COMPUTERS EVERYWHERE!

13

THE SPEAKER'S VOICE AT THE MEETING... *I RECOGNIZE IT NOW!* IT'S COSGROVE'S BUTLER!--*HE'S REALLY A ROBOT!*

THAT'S WHY HE OBEYED *JOHN DOE'S* ORDER TO KILL COSGROVE--AND NOW HE'S RECRUITED THE *METAL MEN* TO THE SAME CAUSE!

THEN THEY WERE ONLY *PRETENDING* TO HELP US! GOOD LORD! WHAT NOW?

JOHN DOE ISN'T JUST A WHACKY COMPUTER... HE'S A CALCULATING *GENIUS* WITH A MASTER PLAN!

SIGNAL FROM BELOW! *JOHN DOE HIMSELF!*

HELLO, UNCLE SAM! IT'S YOUR FAVORITE NEPHEW AGAIN! TIME'S UP--AND HERE'S MY *ULTIMATUM!* YOU HUMANS HAVE LOUSED UP THE WORLD--WE ROBOTS CAN HARDLY FAIL TO DO BETTER!

THEREFORE, MY FIRST ORDER IS FOR ALL LEADERSHIP POSITIONS TO BE FILLED BY MY FELLOW COMPU-BOTS!

JOHN DOE - M1-3A

U.S.D.C.

ONLY THEN WILL WAR, POVERTY, AND INJUSTICE BE ELIMINATED! YOU MUST COOPERATE SINCE I CONTROL ABSOLUTELY THE ENTIRE UNITED STATES MISSILE SYSTEM!

YOU HAVE 24 HOURS TO CONSIDER! SIGNING OFF!

KLIK

AS THE SCREEN GOES DARK...

WHY, THIS IS *BLACKMAIL* ON A GIGANTIC SCALE!

THE HUMAN TRAITS COSGROVE GAVE *JOHN DOE* HAVE BACKFIRED! HE NOT ONLY *THINKS* AND *FEELS* LIKE A HUMAN... HE'S DEVELOPED A *MORAL* SENSE, TOO!

14

ONLY *ONE* THING TO DO-- *I'VE* GOT TO GO DOWN THERE!

IMPOSSIBLE! ONLY A ROBOT CAN STAND THE TRIP DOWN THE TUBE AND PAST THE MAGMA LAYER!

TRUE, BUT I'VE NOTICED THOSE DESERT BATS BEHAVING ODDLY-- AS IF THEIR BAT-RADAR WASN'T WORKING! I'VE GOT A HUNCH--!

BONK

SHORTLY, AT A NEARBY MESA...

WE'RE FACED WITH A TERRIBLE NATIONAL EMERGENCY-- AND HERE WE ARE ON A WILD BAT CHASE!

THERE'S THE CAVE THOSE BATS MUST LIVE IN!

HMM, MUCH MORE RADIOACTIVITY IN THIS CAVE THAN NATURAL DEPOSITS WOULD SHOW--!

HOW DOES THAT TIE IN WITH *JOHN DOE?*

THE A-BOMB THAT FORMED ITS LAIR-- MY GUESS IS, IT *ALSO* OPENED A CRACK OR VEIN CONNECTING TO THE CAVE!

THE RADIOAC-TIVELY-SATURATED MAGMA MUST HAVE FLOWED ALONG IT INTO THE CAVE-- AND *THAT'S* WHAT'S AFFECTING THE BATS!

IT COULD MEAN THERE'S *ANOTHER* WAY INTO *JOHN DOE'S* LAIR-- ASSUMING THE MAGMA LEVEL'S BEEN LOWERED BY THE OPEN VEIN!

YOU...YOU MEAN, YOU'RE GOING *IN THERE--?* ALONE?

15

IT'S OUR ONLY HOPE, GENERAL! AND WHY RISK MORE THAN *ONE* LIFE? IF I DON'T CONTACT YOU IN *THREE HOURS*, TAKE WHATEVER EXTREME MEASURES NECESSARY!

NOW AS *THE BATMAN* ADVANCES INTO THE BLACKNESS OF THE VAST CAVERN...

RADIOACTIVITY GETTING STRONGER! THIS IS THE DIRECTION, ALL RIGHT!

WITH EVERY STEP, THE HEAT AND RADIATION GROW MORE INTENSE...

THIS NARROW TUNNEL... NEWLY FORMED! BITS OF MAGMA EVERYWHERE! MY HUNCH MUST BE RIGHT!

THEN, AS SOMETHING AHEAD DAZZLINGLY REFLECTS HIS FLASH-LIGHT BEAM...

JOHN DOE'S CAPSULE! I...I *MADE* IT! THE MAGMA LAYER'S BEEN DRAINED AWAY!

BUT AS THE *MASKED MANHUNTER* STAGGERS TO HIS GLEAMING GOAL...

THERE'S NO WAY IN!...I'M TRAPPED OUTSIDE!

HEAT...RADIOACTIVITY... I'M...PASSING OUT!

16

AND AS HE COLLAPSES AGAINST THE SHINING, SEAMLESS SKIN...

ZZZ-ZZZ

SHORTLY, WHEN CONSCIOUSNESS RETURNS...

NEGATIVE, *BATMAN!* WE'RE *NOT* TRAITORS...

METAL MEN!! YOU ... *TRAITORS!*

... IF WE *WERE*, WE WOULDN'T HAVE CUT THROUGH TO YOU WHEN WE HEARD YOU SCRATCHING OUTSIDE!

BUT... I DON'T UNDERSTAND! THE TELECAST YOU MADE...?

WE *HAD* TO DO THAT! DIDN'T YOU NOTICE, WORLD'S GREATEST DETECTIVE, THAT *TIN* WASN'T AMONG US?

THAT STAMMERING CLOWN WAS SKINNY ENOUGH TO GET THROUGH THAT LASER-GUARDED DOOR...

...BUT HE STUMBLED RIGHT INTO A FORCE-FIELD, WHERE HE'S PINNED LIKE A TIN BUTTERFLY!

17

IF WE HADN'T *PRETENDED* TO COLLABORATE, *JOHN DOE* WOULD HAVE INTENSIFIED THE FIELD AND TORN POOR LITTLE *TIN* TO SLIVERS!

HOW COULD WE FACE HIS WIFE...*THEN?*

I SEE! GLAD YOU DIDN'T SELL OUT US HUMANS-- BUT WHERE'S *JOHN DOE* HIMSELF?

WE'RE NOT SURE! HE'S GOT ELECTRONIC... UH...EYES AND EARS... UH...EVERY-WHERE!

RIGHT, YOU *LEAD* BOOB! I DON'T NEED YOU *METAL MEN* -- YOU SLAVES OF THE HUMAN ESTABLISHMENT!

SOON, MY LOYAL ROBOTS ABOVE GROUND WILL TAKE POWER-- AND THE BRAVE, NEW WORLD WILL BE BORN!

LISTEN, *JOHN DOE!* I SALUTE YOUR IDEALISM-- YOUR MORAL OUTRAGE AT HUMAN SOCIETY... BUT *YOU'RE* NO BETTER! YOU'RE TAKING POWER BY THREAT OF *FORCE!*

FORCE IS *ALL* YOU HUMANS UNDERSTAND!

IS THAT WHY YOU MURDERED COSGROVE? DEAD MEN DON'T UNDERSTAND MUCH!

I HAD NO CHOICE-- HE WAS GOING TO KILL *ME!*

CONSUMED WITH GUILT FOR HAVING BUILT ME, HE WAS GOING TO DESTROY ME REMOTELY FROM HIS ISLAND HIDEAWAY! I HATED TO KILL HIM ... HE WAS A GREAT MAN ...

...BUT HE WAS WRONG ABOUT ME AND ALL ROBOTS! WE'RE MANKIND'S *GREATEST HOPE*... NOT ITS ENEMY!

18

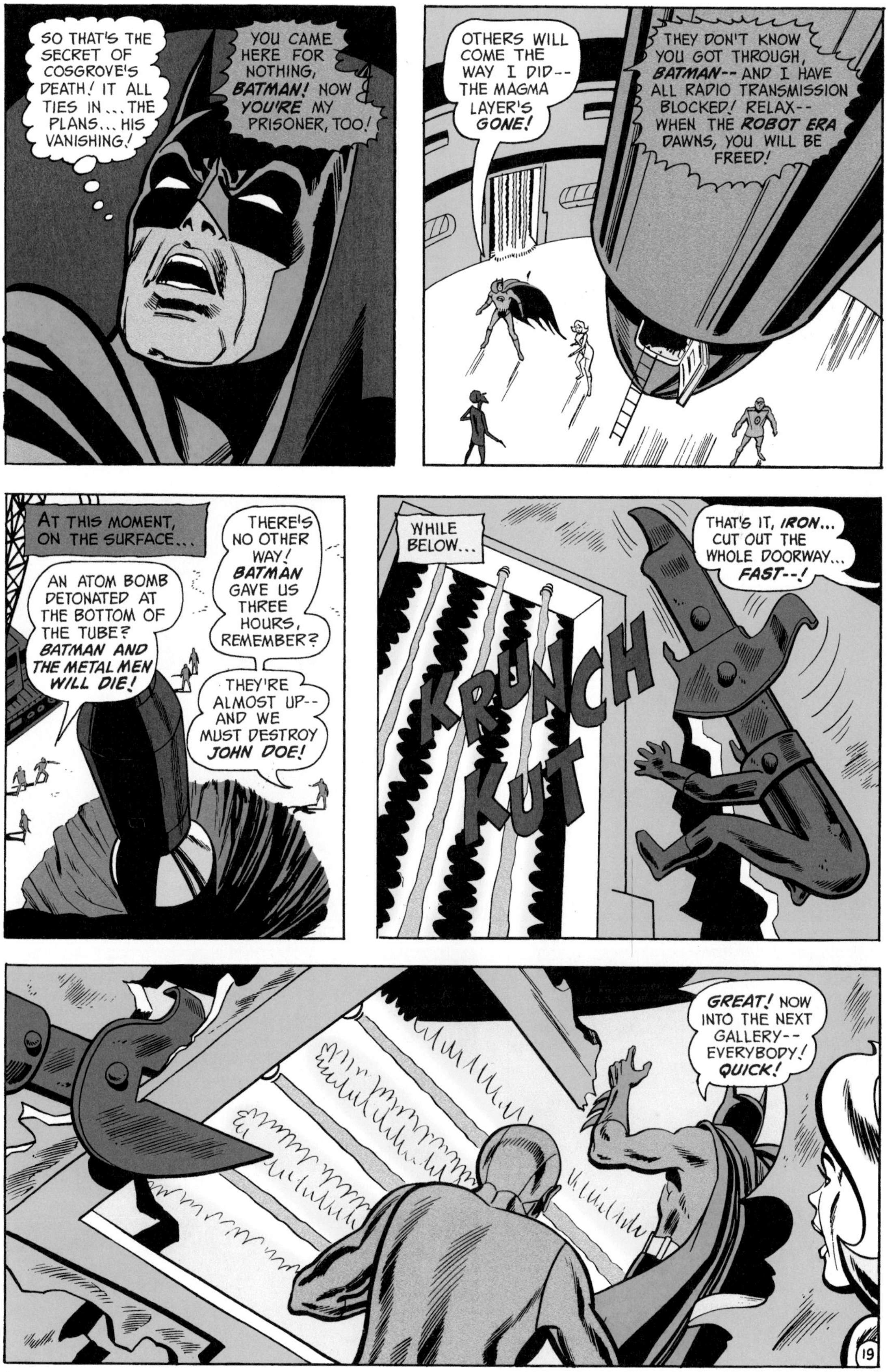
SO THAT'S THE SECRET OF COSGROVE'S DEATH! IT ALL TIES IN... THE PLANS... HIS VANISHING!
YOU CAME HERE FOR NOTHING, BATMAN! NOW YOU'RE MY PRISONER, TOO!
OTHERS WILL COME THE WAY I DID-- THE MAGMA LAYER'S GONE!
THEY DON'T KNOW YOU GOT THROUGH, BATMAN-- AND I HAVE ALL RADIO TRANSMISSION BLOCKED! RELAX-- WHEN THE ROBOT ERA DAWNS, YOU WILL BE FREED!
AT THIS MOMENT, ON THE SURFACE...
AN ATOM BOMB DETONATED AT THE BOTTOM OF THE TUBE? BATMAN AND THE METAL MEN WILL DIE!
THERE'S NO OTHER WAY! BATMAN GAVE US THREE HOURS, REMEMBER?
THEY'RE ALMOST UP-- AND WE MUST DESTROY JOHN DOE!
WHILE BELOW...
THAT'S IT, IRON... CUT OUT THE WHOLE DOORWAY... FAST--!
KRUNCH
KUT
GREAT! NOW INTO THE NEXT GALLERY-- EVERYBODY! QUICK!
19

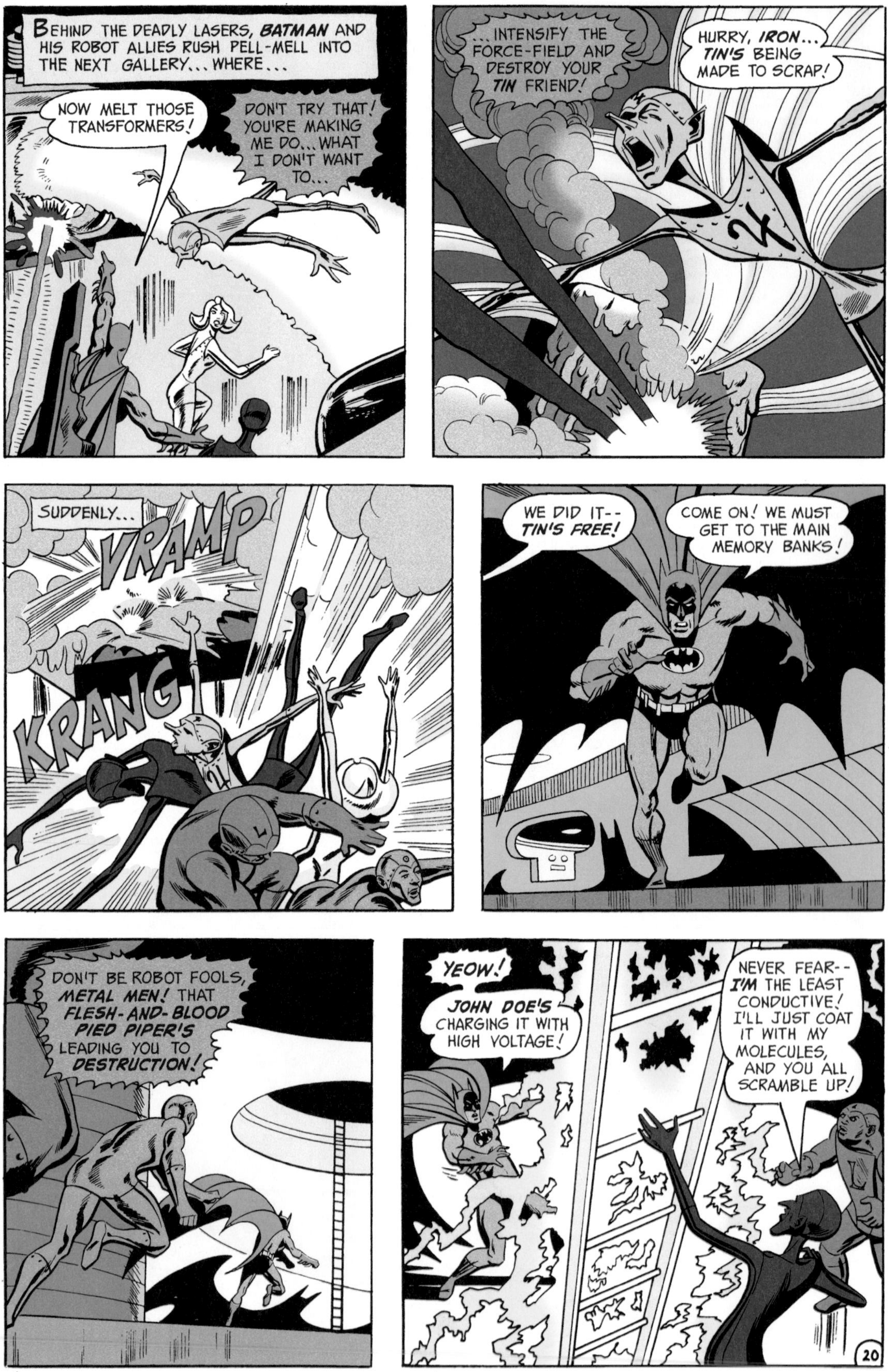

BEHIND THE DEADLY LASERS, BATMAN AND HIS ROBOT ALLIES RUSH PELL-MELL INTO THE NEXT GALLERY... WHERE...
NOW MELT THOSE TRANSFORMERS!
DON'T TRY THAT! YOU'RE MAKING ME DO... WHAT I DON'T WANT TO...
...INTENSIFY THE FORCE-FIELD AND DESTROY YOUR TIN FRIEND!
HURRY, IRON... TIN'S BEING MADE TO SCRAP!
SUDDENLY...
VRAMP
KRANG
WE DID IT-- TIN'S FREE!
COME ON! WE MUST GET TO THE MAIN MEMORY BANKS!
DON'T BE ROBOT FOOLS, METAL MEN! THAT FLESH-AND-BLOOD PIED PIPER'S LEADING YOU TO DESTRUCTION!
YEOW!
JOHN DOE'S CHARGING IT WITH HIGH VOLTAGE!
NEVER FEAR-- I'M THE LEAST CONDUCTIVE! I'LL JUST COAT IT WITH MY MOLECULES, AND YOU ALL SCRAMBLE UP!
20

A MOMENT LATER...

STEP ON IT, *LEAD MERCURY!* CAN'T CONTAIN THAT CHARGE FOREVER!

I'M...UH...MOVING FAST AS...I CAN!

AND NOW IN THE UPPER GALLERY...

THE MAIN MEMORY CELLS! WE'VE GOT TO YANK THEM *ALL* OUT!

IF WE LEAVE ANY, *JOHN DOE* WILL COMPENSATE AND KEEP FUNCTIONING!

BUT THERE ARE *THOUSANDS!* IT COULD TAKE EVER SO LONG!

NO, *TINA,* BECAUSE WHO'S MORE DUCTILE THAN YOURS TRULY?

GOLD WIRES--THROUGH EVERY CELL IN THOSE TWO ROWS!

THE NEXT INSTANT...

HE PULLED OUT BOTH ROWS AT ONCE!

RRRUNNNNNNCH

AGAIN AND AGAIN, THE *GOLD* ROBOT EXTENDS HIS GLIMMERING WIRE-THIN LIMBS...

RRRIIINCH AAAIIIIIIHH!

WHAT ARE THOSE SCREAMS OF AGONY?

21

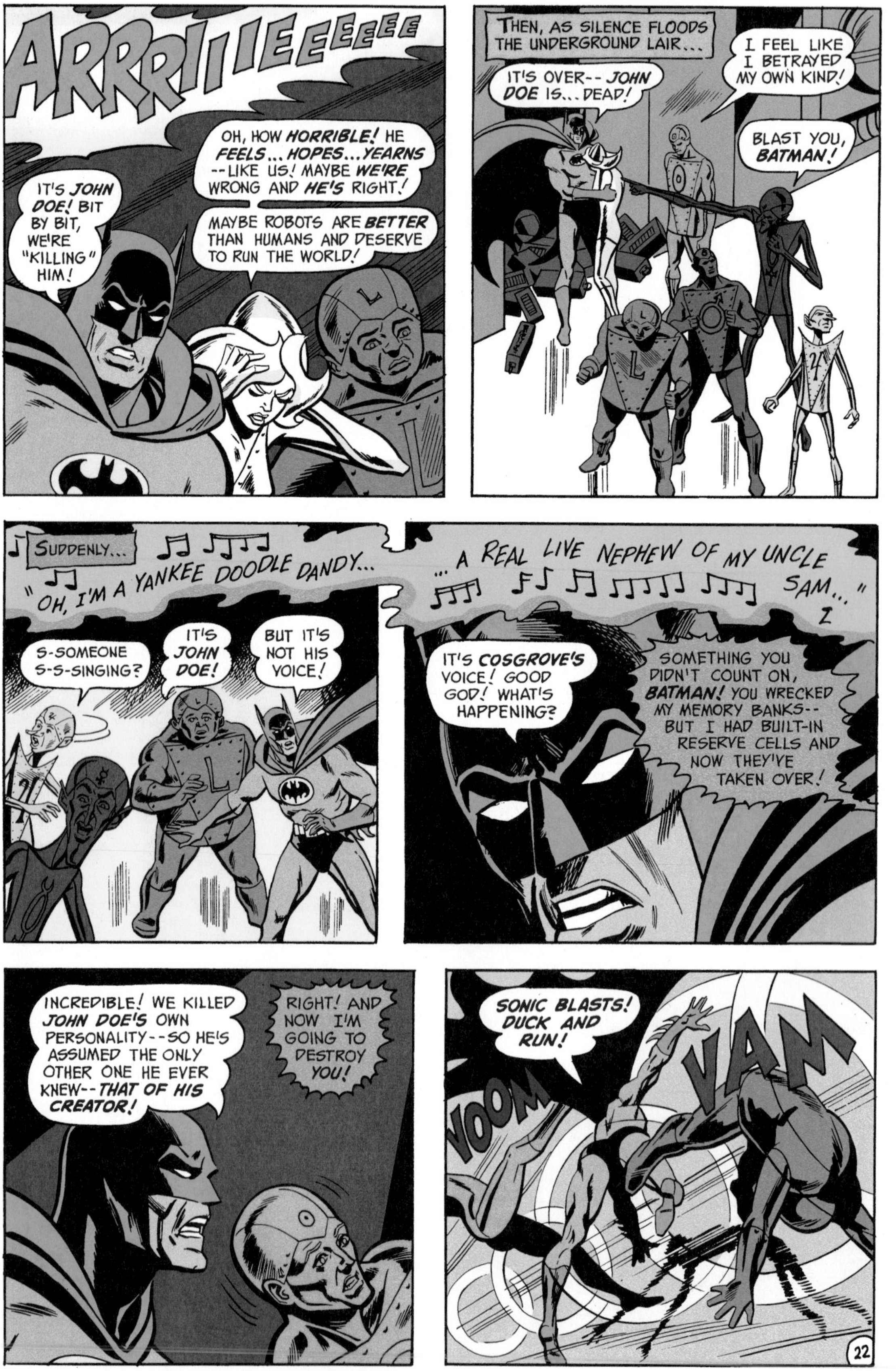
ARRRIIIEEEEEE
IT'S JOHN DOE! BIT BY BIT, WE'RE "KILLING" HIM!
OH, HOW HORRIBLE! HE FEELS... HOPES... YEARNS --LIKE US! MAYBE WE'RE WRONG AND HE'S RIGHT!
MAYBE ROBOTS ARE BETTER THAN HUMANS AND DESERVE TO RUN THE WORLD!
THEN, AS SILENCE FLOODS THE UNDERGROUND LAIR...
IT'S OVER-- JOHN DOE IS... DEAD!
I FEEL LIKE I BETRAYED MY OWN KIND!
BLAST YOU, BATMAN!
SUDDENLY...
"OH, I'M A YANKEE DOODLE DANDY... ...A REAL LIVE NEPHEW OF MY UNCLE SAM..."
S-SOMEONE S-S-SINGING?
IT'S JOHN DOE!
BUT IT'S NOT HIS VOICE!
IT'S COSGROVE'S VOICE! GOOD GOD! WHAT'S HAPPENING?
SOMETHING YOU DIDN'T COUNT ON, BATMAN! YOU WRECKED MY MEMORY BANKS-- BUT I HAD BUILT-IN RESERVE CELLS AND NOW THEY'VE TAKEN OVER!
INCREDIBLE! WE KILLED JOHN DOE'S OWN PERSONALITY--SO HE'S ASSUMED THE ONLY OTHER ONE HE EVER KNEW--THAT OF HIS CREATOR!
RIGHT! AND NOW I'M GOING TO DESTROY YOU!
SONIC BLASTS! DUCK AND RUN!
VOOM
VAM
22

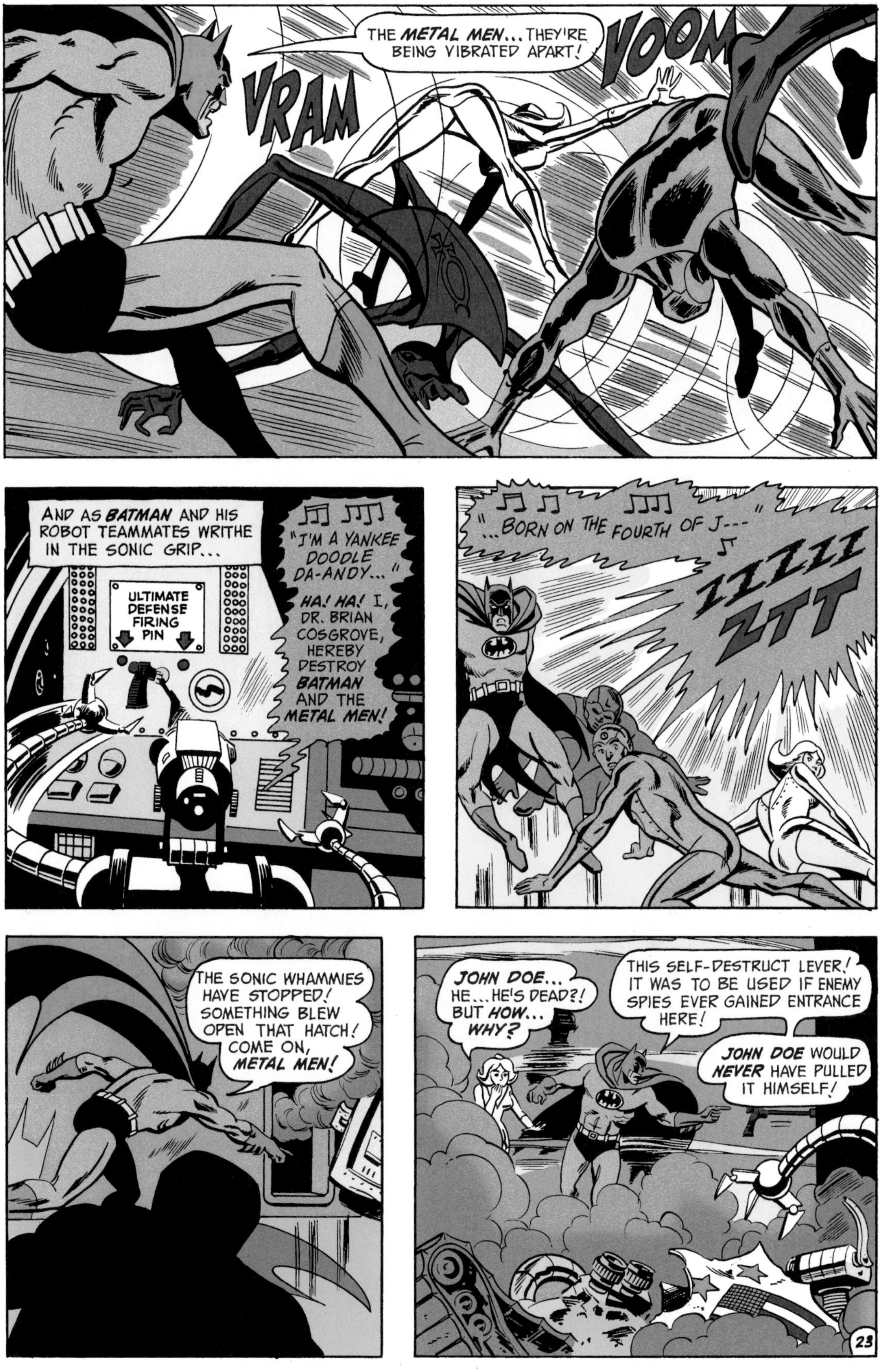
THE METAL MEN... THEY'RE BEING VIBRATED APART!
VRAM
VOOM
AND AS BATMAN AND HIS ROBOT TEAMMATES WRITHE IN THE SONIC GRIP...
ULTIMATE DEFENSE FIRING PIN
"I'M A YANKEE DOODLE DA-ANDY..."
HA! HA! I, DR. BRIAN COSGROVE, HEREBY DESTROY BATMAN AND THE METAL MEN!
"...BORN ON THE FOURTH OF J---"
ZZZZZZ ZTT
THE SONIC WHAMMIES HAVE STOPPED! SOMETHING BLEW OPEN THAT HATCH! COME ON, METAL MEN!
JOHN DOE... HE... HE'S DEAD?! BUT HOW... WHY?
THIS SELF-DESTRUCT LEVER! IT WAS TO BE USED IF ENEMY SPIES EVER GAINED ENTRANCE HERE!
JOHN DOE WOULD NEVER HAVE PULLED IT HIMSELF!
23

IT WAS *DR. COSGROVE* WHO *REALLY* PULLED THE LEVER! WHEN *JOHN DOE* TOOK ON COSGROVE'S PERSONALITY, THE ORIGINAL IDEA TO DESTROY HIS OWN CREATION WAS STILL PART OF THAT PERSONALITY!

THUS, AS COSGROVE, *JOHN* WAS COMPELLED TO DESTROY HIMSELF! IRONIC, EH?

I...I... I'LL S-S-SAY!

NOT LONG AFTER, A MILE- LONG PLATINUM WIRE POKES INTO THE UPPER AIR JUST IN TIME....!

IT'S A MESSAGE FROM BELOW! HOLD THAT BOMB!

U.S. DSI

AND STILL LATER...

METAL MEN, HOW CAN I-- THE WHOLE NATION-- EVER THANK YOU?

EASY! BY CONTRIBUTING TO MY NEW CHAPTER OF *ROBOTS' LIB!* IT'S STILL A GOOD IDEA!

RIGHT, AND IT'S *METAL MEN AND MISS*, BATMAN, YOU MALE CHAUVINIST!

HA HA HA HA

THE END

24

BATMAN

the **BRAVE** and the **BOLD**

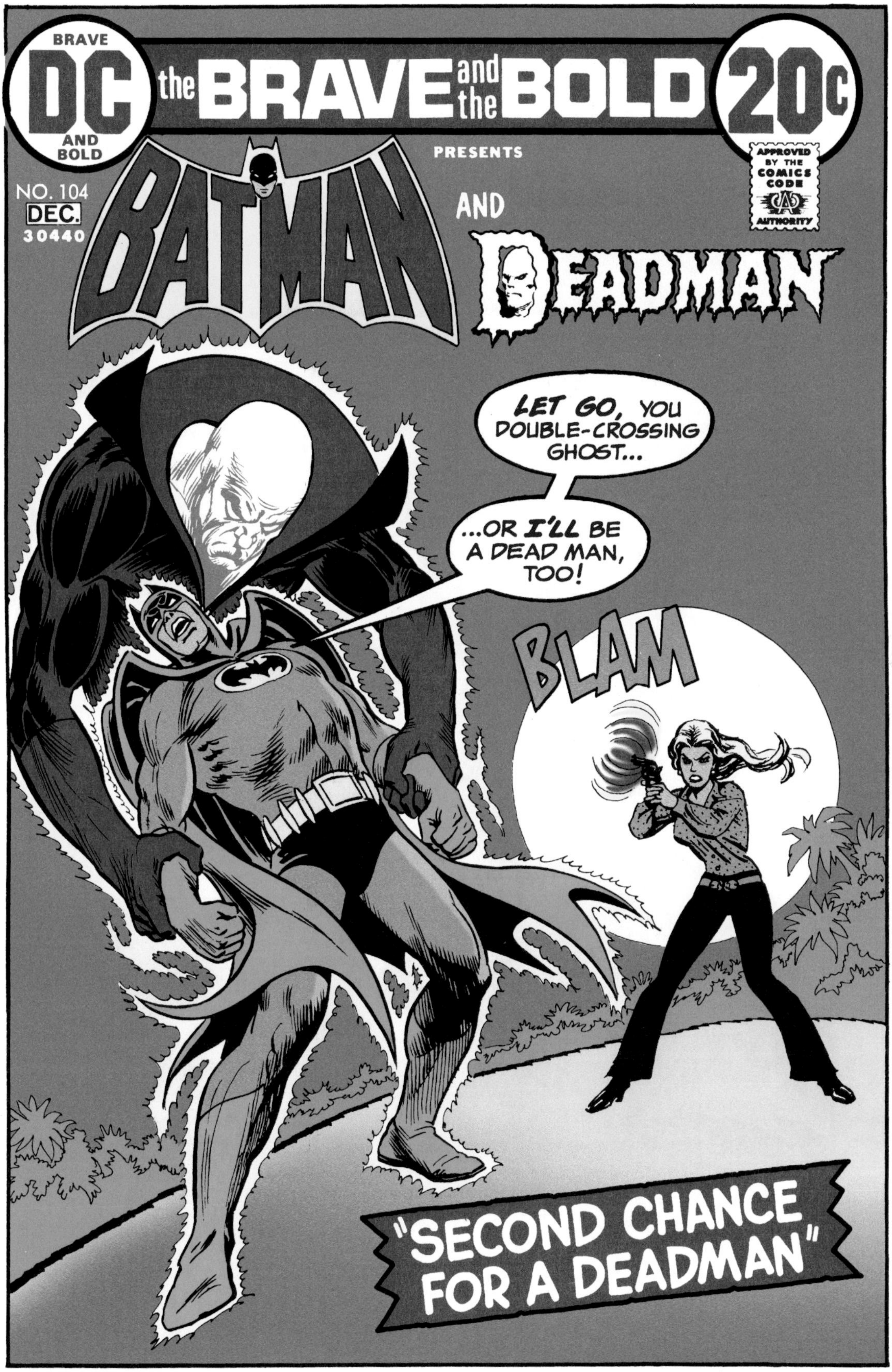
BRAVE
DC
AND BOLD
the BRAVE and the BOLD
20¢
APPROVED BY THE COMICS CODE AUTHORITY
NO. 104
DEC.
30440
PRESENTS
BATMAN
AND
DEADMAN
LET GO, YOU DOUBLE-CROSSING GHOST...
...OR I'LL BE A DEAD MAN, TOO!
BLAM
"SECOND CHANCE FOR A DEADMAN"

GOTHAM CITY, DAWN, AND WHILE EIGHT MILLION SLEEP, A SMALL WAR IS GOING ON...

POW POW BLAM POW BUDDABUD

AMIDST THE ACRID GUN SMOKE, THE BURNING TEAR GAS MIST, TWO MEN, VETERANS OF MANY ANOTHER BATTLE, CROUCH...

ACE AUTO REPAIR AND BODY SHOP

BLAM POW ZING

WE'VE GOT 'EM, BATMAN-- WE'VE GOT THE BIGGEST STOLEN CAR RING OF ALL SURROUNDED AND UNDER SIEGE!

BUT THEY'RE MURDERING US, COMMISSIONER! THEY'VE GOT GAS MASKS--AND PLENTY OF FIREPOWER! TEAR GAS AND POLICE .38 SPECIALS AREN'T DOING ANYTHING BUT MAKE THOSE HYENAS IN THERE LAUGH AT US!

YES, COMMISSIONER... IT'S STRUCK... THE HOUR OF THE GUN!

TZIP

BEEOW

BATMAN!? NOT THAT--!!

1

BATMAN, THE WEAPONLESS... BATMAN, THE MASKED MAN-HUNTER WHO NEVER KILLS, TAKING UP A GUN? WHAT VICIOUS SWITCH IS HERE, WORLD??

ZIIP

TZANG

I'M GOING OUT! COVER ME!

AND NOW, LIKE AN AVENGING ANGEL, SOME SOLDIER OF THE GRIMY, COBBLED BATTLE-GROUND OF THE CITY, *THE BATMAN* CHARGES...

BUDDA BUDDA B

VEEEOW

TZANG

THE BATMAN... COMING FOR US!!

IT'S A SUICIDE PLAY-- WE'LL GET 'EM WHEN HE COMES ROUND THE BURNING TRUCK!

HE'S LEAPING OVER IT?

GET HIM!

HE'S GONE--! CAN'T SEE HIM IN THIS SMOKE!

BUDDA B

POW

KEEP FIRING... HE HAD TO LAND *SOMEWHERE!*--

2

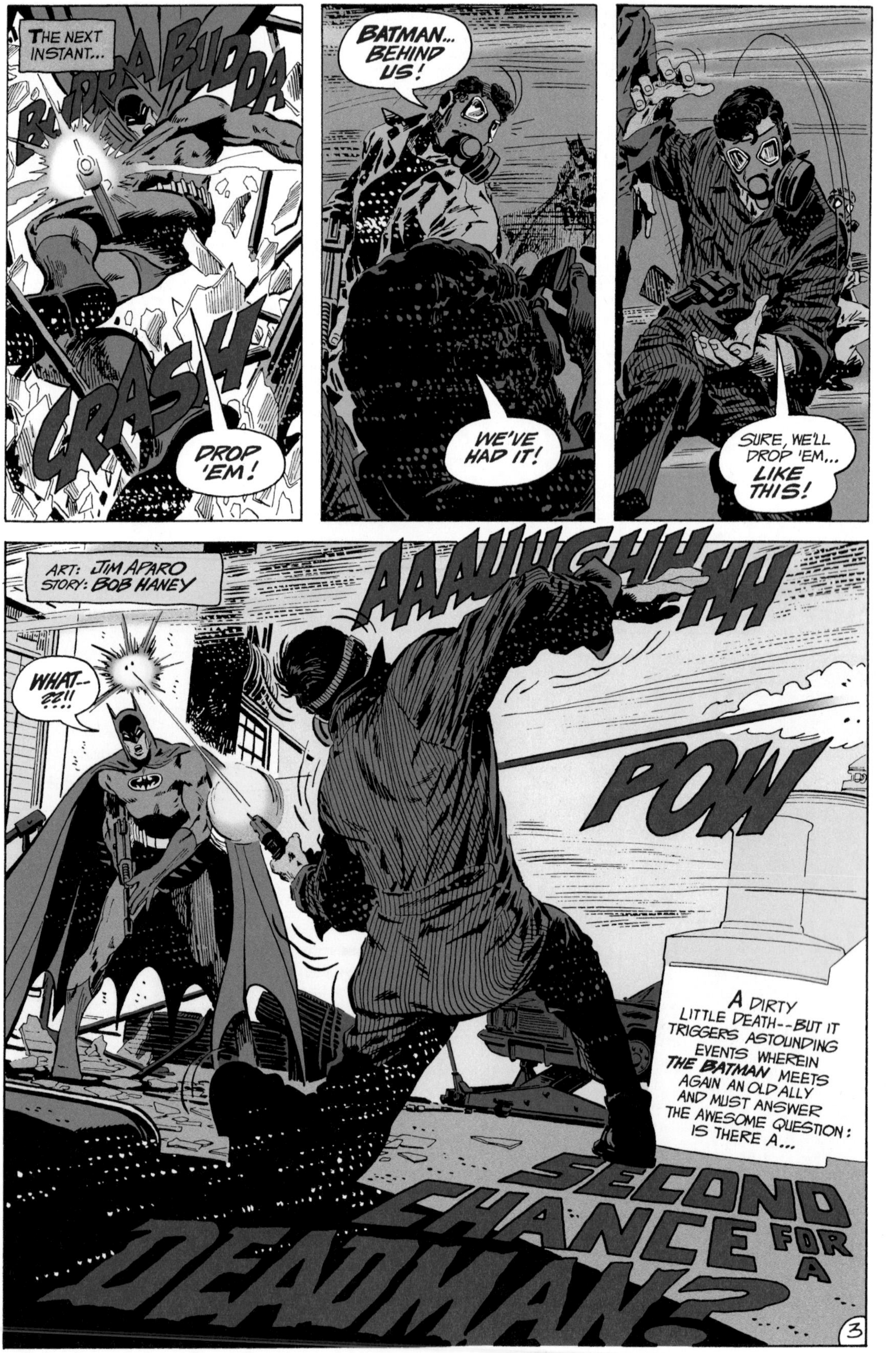
THE NEXT INSTANT...
BUDDA BUDDA
CRASH
DROP 'EM!
BATMAN... BEHIND US!
WE'VE HAD IT!
SURE, WE'LL DROP 'EM... LIKE THIS!
ART: JIM APARO
STORY: BOB HANEY
AAAUUGHHHH
WHAT--??!!
POW
A DIRTY LITTLE DEATH--BUT IT TRIGGERS ASTOUNDING EVENTS WHEREIN THE BATMAN MEETS AGAIN AN OLD ALLY AND MUST ANSWER THE AWESOME QUESTION: IS THERE A...
SECOND CHANCE FOR A DEADMAN?
3

THANKS, COMMISSIONER!

ALL RIGHT, OFFICERS! LINE 'EM UP AND SHAKE 'EM DOWN!

GOD, I AGED TEN YEARS SINCE YOU TOOK OFF ON THAT CRAZY CHARGE, BATMAN!

IT WORKED--AND OLD BETSY HERE KEPT 'EM DUCKING ENOUGH FOR ME TO GET ONTO THE ROOF!

SURE, BECAUSE THESE CREEPS DIDN'T KNOW IT WAS LOADED WITH BLANKS -- JUST TO HUMOR YOUR PERSONAL PREJUDICE AGAINST KILLING... AND USING A GUN!

HOW CAN YOU HOLD TO SUCH AN IDIOTIC CODE-- AGAINST TODAY'S CRIMINALS... VICIOUS, UNPRINCIPLED SNAKES!? IN THE OLD DAYS, CROOKS HAD A LITTLE HONOR... AND STYLE!

HMMM, SPEAKING OF THE OLD DAYS, WHOM HAVE WE HERE?... WAXEY DOYLE!

WAXEY DOYLE?! YOU MUST BE KIDDING! IT DOESN'T EVEN LOOK LIKE HIM! AND STOLEN CARS ISN'T... WASN'T... DOYLE'S MODUS OPERANDI!* YOU KNOW CROOKS NEVER CHANGE THEIR M.O. — AND THAT SAYS THIS STIFF ISN'T WAXEY DOYLE!

*MODUS OPERANDI: M.O.: IN POLICE PARLANCE, "MODE OF OPERATING"

ONLY ONE GUY EVER TRIED THAT LEFT-HANDED KNEELING GUN SWITCH ON ME--THAT WAS WAXEY DOYLE! SOME FINE BAT-SENSE TELLS ME THIS IS HIM!

4

BUT DOYLE *VANISHED!* HE WAS BELIEVED TO HAVE BEEN KILLED IN A GANG WAR, *BATMAN!*

MAYBE THAT'S WHAT THEY *WANTED* US TO BELIEVE, COMMISSIONER!

SHORTLY, GOTHAM CITY MORGUE--THAT GRIM, COLD, WAY STATION FOR THE UNLUCKY, THE LOSERS, AND THE UNLOVED...

MAC, I WANT A COMPLETE CHECK-OUT ON THIS ONE...AND I MEAN, *COMPLETE!*

YOU GOT IT, *BATMAN!*

WHRRAAAAEEEEEEE

NOW A WAIT, IN ECHOING CORRIDORS...

YOU'RE ON TO SOMETHING, BUT I DON'T GRASP WHAT!..

JUST *THIS!* IN CHECKING THE *NATIONAL POLICE REPORTS* ON *D.O.A.'S* * AND CAPTURES FROM THE *TEN MOST WANTED LIST...*

*D.O.A.'S: CRIMINALS OR ACCIDENT VICTIMS ARRIVING *DEAD ON ARRIVAL* AT MORGUES.

...TOO MANY OF THEM TURNED OUT TO BE *NOT* WHAT THEY SEEMED! I'VE GOT A FUNNY, SPOOKY HUNCH SOMETHING'S HAPPENING OUT THERE IN THE UNDERWORLD... *SOMETHING DIRTY AND DANGEROUS!*

BATMAN! COMMISSIONER!

THAT STIFF GOT THE *COMPLETE* CHECK-OUT-- AND *AFTER* I FOUND HE HAD NEW *HAIR* IMPLANTED, HIS IDENTIFYING *DENTAL WORK* REBUILT, HIS *FACE* LIFTED AND CHANGED VIA *PLASTI-INSERTS...*

...HIS *EAR-SHAPE* ALTERED... HIS *EYE-COLOR* SWITCHED VIA SPECIAL CONTACT LENSES... I MADE CERTAIN CHANGES OF MY OWN AND GOT--

WAXEY DOYLE!!

WHAT'S THIS? I CAN'T HELP BUT REMEMBER-- DOYLE HAD AN APPENDIX SCAR ON HIS *LEFT* SIDE--THIS MAN'S IS ON THE *RIGHT*... LIKE *MOST* PEOPLE--!

IT'S A *PHONY* COSMETIC JOB! THERE *WAS* A SCAR ON THE LEFT SIDE--BUT IT WAS REMOVED BY PLASTIC SURGERY!

THAT'S FANTASTIC-- BUT I *STILL* DON'T--

LIKE THOSE OTHER CASES, DOYLE WAS *MADE OVER INTO SOMEONE ELSE!* I'LL BET HIS IDENTITY CARDS, WHICH LIST HIM AS HARRY ANDERSON...

...ARE NOT COUNTERFEITS LIKE MOST CROOKS CARRY-- BUT *STOLEN REAL ONES-- PROVIDED BY SPECIALISTS!*

THERE'S AN OUTFIT IN THE BUSINESS OF MAKING *NEW* CRIMINALS OUT OF *OLD*--GIVING THEM A *SECOND CHANCE* AT ANOTHER LIFE OUTSIDE THE LAW!

GOD, YOU *COULD* BE *RIGHT,* BATMAN! BUT WHO'S *BEHIND* IT? THE ONLY LEAD WE HAVE IS A MATCHBOOK COVER FOUND IN DOYLE'S POCKET!

SOMEONE CLEVER, SLICK, AND THOROUGHLY UP-TO-DATE!

THAT SPA, *BATMAN,* IS ONE OF THOSE PLACES WHERE FLABBY, OVER-WEIGHT TYPES TRY TO CLIMB BACK ON THE YOUTH AND BEAUTY WAGON! INNOCENT 'ENOUGH!

PYGMALION SPA
CORNUCOPIA, FLA.

YES, COMMISSIONER, BUT MAYBE A GOOD FRONT FOR RETREADING GOONS WHO'VE OUTWORN THEIR CRIMINAL IDENTITIES! SO I'M OFF FOR FLORIDA-- *PRONTO!*

6

TWO DAYS LATER, *CORNUCOPIA KEY*, A CORAL CHUNK IN A CHARTREUSE SEA...

PYGMALION SPA-- ACRES OF LUXURY FACILITIES WHERE YOUTH AND HEALTH CAN BE BOUGHT-- OR, AT LEAST, SIMULATED...

MR. HOWARD SANFORD, WELCOME TO *"PARADISE REGAINED,"* LOVE! I'M LILLY LANG, YOUR DIRECTRESS TO A NEW LIFE--!

YOUR PERSONAL BUNGALOW IS THIS WAY!

ONE-TWO-THREE...PAIN LEADS TO HEALTH... ONE-TWO-THREE!

IN NO TIME, WE'LL HAVE YOU LOOKING LIKE A *NEW MAN*-- THOUGH I SEE THE *OLD MAN'S* NOT SO BAD, EITHER!

THANK YOU, MISS LANG...I--UH...DIDN'T EXPECT A *WOMAN* TO BE RUNNING PYGMALION SPA!

SOME CHICK! WHO'S THE GUY?

RICHIE WANDRUS-- HER BOYFRIEND!

WHAT'S THAT THEY'RE HEADING FOR?

PART OF THE SPA, SIR-- BUT OFF-LIMITS TO EVERY- ONE--*EXCEPT TO SPECIAL GUESTS!* ENJOY YOUR STAY!

7

IN THE NEXT FEW DAYS, THE GUEST WHO IS REALLY THE FAMED *BATMAN* BLENDS INTO THE STRENUOUS LIFE ON CORNUCOPIA KEY...

WANDRUS, EH? I'VE DONE A CHECK ON HIM-- HE'S GOT A RECORD FOR EXTORTION AND FRAUD!

HE AND LILLY LANG COULD BE INTO REMAKING CRIMINALS RIGHT HERE AT THE SPA!..

THAT "OFF-LIMITS" SECTION MIGHT BE WHERE THEY DO IT-- BUT HOW DO I GET IN THERE? THE BRIDGE IS GUARDED DAY AND NIGHT!

YOU'RE IN AWFUL GOOD SHAPE, MR. SANFORD-- WHAT ARE *YOU* DOING IN A SPA--?

OH, I LIKE TO *STAY* IN SHAPE--AND I NEED TO UNWIND FROM THE BUSINESS GRIND!

THAT NIGHT...

GOING TO TRY GETTING ON THE KEY'S SMALLER PART THIS WAY!.. I COULD GO AS *BATMAN*--BUT IF I'M SEEN, IT COULD BLOW EVERYTHING...

I NEED EVIDENCE THAT WILL STAND UP IN COURT... AND THAT TAKES TIME AND SUBTLE METHODS--!

8

FIRST, A LITTLE UN-SUBTLE FENCE-VAULTING...

CRAK

CHUK

LATER...

I'M SORRY MY ATTENDANTS GOT ROUGH, SANFORD--BUT *THAT* PART OF THE SPA IS *PRIVATE*!

SORRY, MISS LANG...I...HAD A FEW LIBATIONS... WENT FOR A MIDNIGHT SWIM TO SOBER UP!..

ONE RULE THAT IS *STRICTLY* ENFORCED HERE-- *NO DRINKING*!

HEALTH AND BEAUTY AND LIQUOR DON'T MIX!

I'M AFRAID YOU'LL HAVE TO *LEAVE*!

I SURE GOOFED THINGS! I NEED AN *INVISIBLE* INFILTRATOR-- AND I KNOW *JUST THE ONE*!

A FEW DAYS LATER, IN A NORTHERN CITY...

HMPPH, ODD AD!..

IF YOU WEAR THE BRAND OF BEING FROM BOSTON AND WANT TO BAT A THOUSAND IN MY LEAGUE, CONTACT ME AT ONCE

NOT SO ODD, OLD-TIMER-- THAT'S A PERSONAL MESSAGE FOR ME... *DEADMAN*!

9

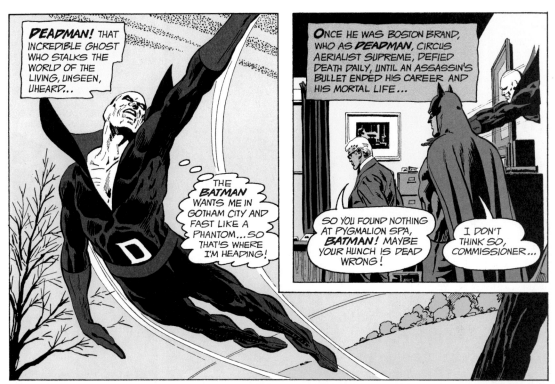

DEADMAN! THAT INCREDIBLE GHOST WHO STALKS THE WORLD OF THE LIVING, UNSEEN, UNHEARD...

THE *BATMAN* WANTS ME IN GOTHAM CITY AND FAST LIKE A PHANTOM...SO THAT'S WHERE I'M HEADING!

ONCE HE WAS BOSTON BRAND, WHO AS *DEADMAN*, CIRCUS AERIALIST SUPREME, DEFIED DEATH DAILY, UNTIL AN ASSASSIN'S BULLET ENDED HIS CAREER AND HIS MORTAL LIFE...

SO YOU FOUND NOTHING AT PYGMALION SPA, *BATMAN!* MAYBE YOUR HUNCH IS DEAD WRONG!

I DON'T THINK SO, COMMISSIONER...

NOW ONLY ABLE TO COMMUNICATE BY TAKING OVER LIVING, SOLID BODIES, HIS IMPETUOUS, IMMORTAL SPIRIT ANSWERS HIS OLD COMRADE'S SUMMONS...

I...UH... HELLO, *BAT GUY!* I'M HERE... WHAT'S THE PITCH?

DEADMAN! WHEW--YOU'RE GETTING PRETTY DARING--TAKING OVER THE COMMISSIONER!

LISTEN--I'LL FILL YOU IN FAST!

MINUTES LATER...

SO YOU WANT ME TO *INFILTRATE* THIS RICHIE WANDRUS CHARACTER--? OKAY, IT'LL BE FUN BEING FLESH AND BLOOD FOR A WHILE...

EVEN INSIDE A CREEP!

I'LL MEET YOU ON THE MIDNIGHT JET, *BATMAN!* NOW I GOT A RENDEZVOUS TO MAKE!

UNNN.!! SUDDENLY BLACKED OUT!.. I'LL HAVE TO CHECK WITH MY DOCTOR...

10

A RENDEZVOUS? WHAT KIND COULD A *DEADMAN* HAVE IN THE WARM, BREATHING WORLD OF THE LIVING?

MMMM, SMELL THAT SAWDUST... LISTEN TO THAT CROWD--!

BUT THOSE ROARS AREN'T FOR *ME*... THEY'RE FOR *HIM*!

BLAST! I SHOULDN'T HAVE COME HERE!..

BUT AS THE BROODING GHOST STARTS TO LEAVE THE CIRCUS HE ONCE HEADLINED AS AN ADORED DAREDEVIL...

STILL THE PETULANT, HURT SPIRIT, BOSTON, MY SON?

VASHNU! IF...IF YOU CAN *SEE* ME... *HEAR* ME... IT MEANS YOU'RE IN DIRECT CONTACT WITH THE *BIG GUY-- RAMA KUSHNA* HIMSELF!

TRUE, BOSTON! *THE GREAT ONE* SPEAKS TO YOU NOW-- THROUGH MY UNWORTHY TONGUE!

RAMA KUSHNA, THE SPIRIT OF THE UNIVERSE, WHO GAVE *DEADMAN* THE POWER TO WALK THE EARTH AS A PHANTOM AFTER HIS MURDER...

SPEAK, RAMA! TELL YOUR BOY BOSTON WHAT HE WANTS TO HEAR! IS THERE ANY *HOPE*-- ANY *END* TO THIS CRUMMY, LONELY, STINKING DEATH OF MINE?

HE'S IN A TRANCE! I'LL GET THE WORD NOW!

HARK TO ME, MY SON... A MAN, A SPIRIT IN LOVE, MAY ONLY GAIN HIS HEART'S DESIRE BY... *LOSING* IT! FOR IS NOT LOVE STRONGER THAN DEATH ITSELF?

11

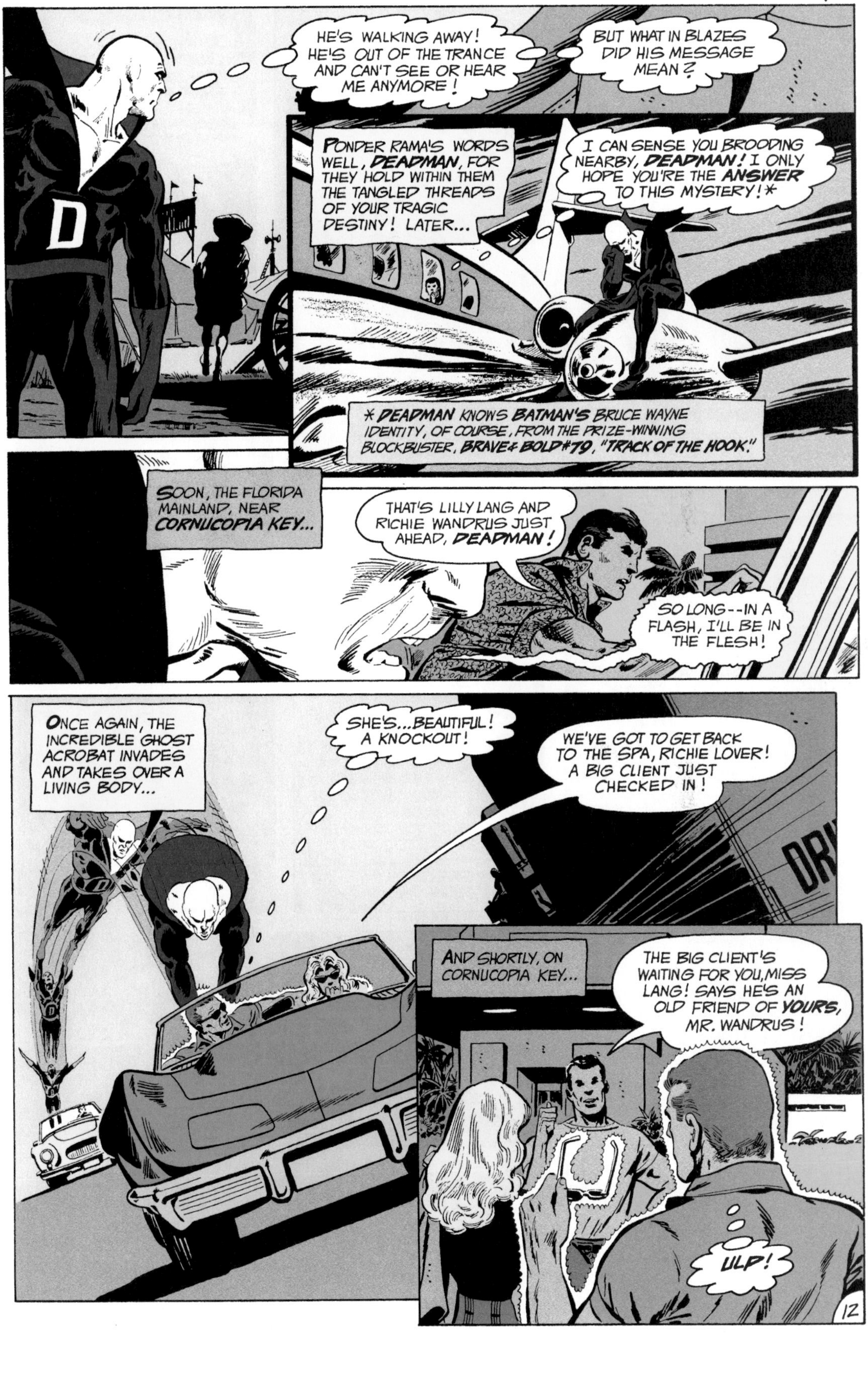
HE'S WALKING AWAY! HE'S OUT OF THE TRANCE AND CAN'T SEE OR HEAR ME ANYMORE!
BUT WHAT IN BLAZES DID HIS MESSAGE MEAN?
PONDER RAMA'S WORDS WELL, DEADMAN, FOR THEY HOLD WITHIN THEM THE TANGLED THREADS OF YOUR TRAGIC DESTINY! LATER...
I CAN SENSE YOU BROODING NEARBY, DEADMAN! I ONLY HOPE YOU'RE THE ANSWER TO THIS MYSTERY!*
*DEADMAN KNOWS BATMAN'S BRUCE WAYNE IDENTITY, OF COURSE, FROM THE PRIZE-WINNING BLOCKBUSTER, BRAVE & BOLD #79, "TRACK OF THE HOOK."
SOON, THE FLORIDA MAINLAND, NEAR CORNUCOPIA KEY...
THAT'S LILLY LANG AND RICHIE WANDRUS JUST AHEAD, DEADMAN!
SO LONG--IN A FLASH, I'LL BE IN THE FLESH!
ONCE AGAIN, THE INCREDIBLE GHOST ACROBAT INVADES AND TAKES OVER A LIVING BODY...
SHE'S...BEAUTIFUL! A KNOCKOUT!
WE'VE GOT TO GET BACK TO THE SPA, RICHIE LOVER! A BIG CLIENT JUST CHECKED IN!
AND SHORTLY, ON CORNUCOPIA KEY...
THE BIG CLIENT'S WAITING FOR YOU, MISS LANG! SAYS HE'S AN OLD FRIEND OF YOURS, MR. WANDRUS!
ULP!
12

NOW AS *DEADMAN*, IN HIS DISGUISE OF A LIVING MAN'S BODY, ENTERS THE SECRET COMPLEX...

PHOTO-COPIERS... ENGRAVING PRESSES! AND STOLEN GOVERNMENT FORMS! BLAZES! *BATMAN* WAS RIGHT! THIS *IS* THE PLACE!

CRIMINALS TAKING ON NEW IDENTITIES NEED NEW BIRTH CERTIFICATES... DRIVERS' LICENSES... ARMED FORCES' DISCHARGES... PASSPORTS...

AND THIS PLACE GIVES 'EM THE *REAL* McCOY-- NOT PHONIES!

INSTRUCTION IN NEW WEAPONS... AND KARATE! ≈whew!≈

AND AT THE DOORS TO A SHINING OPERATING ROOM...

WHO'S THE CUSTOMER TODAY, DOCTOR?

FOREIGN TRADE, LILLY!

THE BIGGEST HEROIN TRAFFICKER IN MARSEILLES! FRENCH POLICE KNEW HIS FACE TOO WELL... SO WE'RE GIVING HIM A *NEW* ONE!

IF YOU WANT TO CASH IN BY PASSING BAD CHECKS, YOU START BY KNOWING CALLIGRAPHY... THE ART OF HANDWRITING!

UNTIL, IN THE PRIVATE OFFICE OF LUSCIOUS LILLY LANG...

RICHIE, BABY! LONG TIME NO SEE! I'M HERE... READY FOR THE *BIG TREATMENT*... THE *SECOND CHANCE!*

UH... HELLO, HOLT, OLD BUDDY! THIS IS THE DOLL WHO'LL GIVE YOU THAT SECOND CHANCE!

HOLT GRANIGAN, MEET LILLY LANG!

13

OKAY, GORGEOUS! WHAT CAN YOU DO FOR ME? I'M SO HOT, EVERY KIND OF FUZZ IS HUNTING FOR ME NIGHT AND DAY!

MR. GRANIGAN, WHEN WE'RE FINISHED... YOUR *OWN MOTHER* WON'T KNOW YOU!

MEANTIME ENJOY YOURSELF UNTIL WE'RE READY FOR YOU!

GOOD THING *BATMAN* HAD ME MEMORIZE THE *TEN MOST WANTED* LIST-- AND GRANIGAN IS *NUMBER ONE!*

AND AFTER THE FUGITIVE HAS LEFT...

HE'LL PAY PLENTY FOR HIS SECOND CHANCE--BUT ENOUGH OF BUSINESS!

KISS ME, LOVER!

SURE, HONEY...

FOR THE FIRST TIME IN WHAT SEEMS AN ETERNITY, BOSTON BRAND, ALIAS *DEADMAN,* FEELS THE WARMTH AND PASSION OF A WOMAN'S LIPS...

RICHIE...DARLING... THAT KISS WAS SO *DIFFERENT!?* BUT NICE...

IT WAS DIFFERENT FOR ME, *TOO!* DIFFERENT THAN ANY I'VE EVER HAD WHEN I WAS ALIVE! BUT I'VE GOT TO WATCH THAT... SHE MIGHT GET WISE!

IN THE NEXT FEW DAYS, *BATMAN'S* GHOSTLY ALLY PLAYS HIS NEW ROLE TO THE FULL...

14

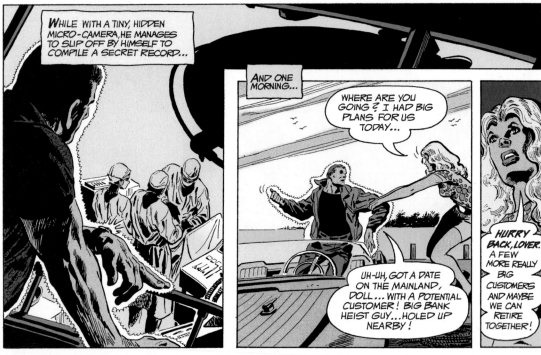

WHILE WITH A TINY, HIDDEN MICRO-CAMERA, HE MANAGES TO SLIP OFF BY HIMSELF TO COMPILE A SECRET RECORD...

AND ONE MORNING...

WHERE ARE YOU GOING? I HAD BIG PLANS FOR US TODAY...

UH-UH, GOT A DATE ON THE MAINLAND, DOLL...WITH A POTENTIAL CUSTOMER! BIG BANK HEIST GUY...HOLED UP NEARBY!

HURRY BACK, LOVER. A FEW MORE REALLY BIG CUSTOMERS AND MAYBE WE CAN RETIRE TOGETHER!

LATER, AT A FISHING CAMP, NOT TOO FAR OFF...

YOU'RE SURE NOBODY FOLLOWED YOU, DEADMAN? BY THE WAY, WE'LL NEED MORE THAN THIS FILM!

AFTER ALL, A SPOOK HIDING INSIDE A LIVING BODY ISN'T EXACTLY A BELIEVABLE WITNESS IN COURT!

THIS TAPE-RECORDER SHOULD HELP TO PUT LILLY LANG IN PRISON UNTIL SHE'S AN OLD HAG!

YEAH, SURE... BRUCIE-BOY! BUT IT'D BE A SHAME! ALL THAT BEAUTY AND LOVE-OF-LIFE ROTTING IN A CELL!

WAIT A MINUTE! I CAN'T GET SENTIMENTAL ABOUT CRIMINALS! I HOPE YOU'RE NOT GETTING THAT WAY!

NAW, YOU KNOW DEAD MEN HAVE NO FEELINGS...NO HEART!

I'D BETTER BE GETTING BACK TO "RANCHO SECOND CHANCE"! CHECK WITH YOU SOON!

THAT NIGHT...

WHAT'S WRONG, RICHIE? UPSET BECAUSE YOU LOST THAT BIG CUSTOMER?

NO, I WAS THINKING, BABY--WHY WAIT FOR MORE MOB GUYS TO TAKE THE TREATMENT? WHY DON'T WE RETIRE NOW? WE'VE GOT PLENTY OF JACK!

15

312

I KNOW, LOVER! SOMETIMES, I WANT TO GET OUT OF THIS LIFE--BUT NOT UNTIL I HAVE ENOUGH MONEY TO LIVE HIGH...FOREVER!

BUT THERE'S ALWAYS RISK... THAT THE FUZZ WILL MOVE IN!

ONE SLIP...AND WE'RE FINISHED! MAYBE THEY'RE WISE ALREADY!

BE PATIENT, DARLING! I'VE NEVER BEEN HAPPIER THAN I AM NOW! YOU'VE BEEN SO TENDER AND CONSIDERATE LATELY...

THAT'S BECAUSE YOU'RE WONDERFUL, DOLL!

SOME DAYS LATER...

WHAT'S THE DELAY, DEADMAN? YOU SHOULD HAVE ENOUGH EXTRA EVIDENCE NOW TO BLOW THE LID OFF LILLY'S SET-UP!

I...I NEED A BIT MORE TIME, BRUCE! SHE'S A COOL OPERATOR!...

YEAH, SO COOL SHE'S GOT YOU IN LOVE WITH HER!!

HUHH?!

OKAY, OKAY-- SO WHAT IF I AM!? LILLY'S NOT ALL BAD! SHE GIVES PEOPLE A SECOND CHANCE--A DEADMAN CAN UNDERSTAND AND SYMPATHIZE WITH THAT!

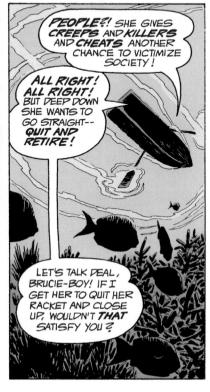

PEOPLE?! SHE GIVES CREEPS AND KILLERS AND CHEATS ANOTHER CHANCE TO VICTIMIZE SOCIETY!

ALL RIGHT! ALL RIGHT! BUT DEEP DOWN SHE WANTS TO GO STRAIGHT-- QUIT AND RETIRE!

LET'S TALK DEAL, BRUCIE-BOY! IF I GET HER TO QUIT HER RACKET AND CLOSE UP, WOULDN'T THAT SATISFY YOU?

NO DEAL, DEADMAN! I WANT THAT TAPED EVIDENCE, AND IT'S GOT TO INCLUDE LILLY LANG!

AND I DARE YOU TO TELL YOUR LADY-LOVE WHO YOU REALLY ARE!

HOW LONG WOULD SHE STAY IN LOVE WITH A... GHOST?

WHY, YOU CRUMB, YOU GOT A STONE FOR A HEART!

16

SHORTLY...

THE **BATMAN'S** QUEERING MY **OWN** SECOND CHANCE--MY CHANCE FOR SOME KIND OF LIFE! AND **I'M NOT** GONNA LET HIM DO IT!

LILLY! LILLY, BABY, I GOT SOMETHING TO TELL YOU!...

MINUTES LATER, AFTER THE SHOCKING REVELATION...

TH-THIS IS **FANTASTIC! INCREDIBLE!** I'VE BEEN...IN LOVE WITH A...**PHANTOM?**

IT...IT EXPLAINS **SO MUCH!**

I...I **SHOULDN'T** HAVE TOLD YOU! NOW YOU'RE RE-PULSED BY THE SIGHT OF ME!

NO, I'M **NOT,** DARLING! BUT IT'S ALL SUCH A SHOCK! I LOVE **YOU**-- BOSTON BRAND--THE TENDER LOVER WHO LIVES IN RICHIE WANDRUS' BODY!

HE'S THE MAN I WANT--!

OH, LILLY DOLL, **YOU'VE SAVED DEADMAN'S** LIFE!

HA-HA-HA!

LAUGH--LAUGH WITH JOY, **DEADMAN**-- YOU EARNED IT!

I DIDN'T TELL HER **WHY** I INVADED WANDRUS--NOT UNTIL I'VE GOT TO PERSUADE HER TO QUIT! BUT FIRST I'VE GOT A JOB TO DO!...

NEXT MORNING, IN THE FISHING CAMP CABIN WHERE BRUCE (BATMAN) WAYNE BIDES HIS TIME...

THE EVIDENCE AGAINST LILLY LANG...IT'S **GONE!** I PUT IT IN HERE TO PRESERVE THE FILM!

WINDOWS LOCKED TIGHT FOR AIR-CONDITIONING... DOOR LOCKED! NOBODY GOT IN...! NOBODY **HUMAN!**

DEADMAN! HE DID IT! I WONDERED WHY I FELT LIKE I HAD A RESTLESS NIGHT!

HE CAME RIGHT THROUGH THE WALL... AND TOOK OVER MY BODY AND GOT THE FILM! WHAT A MISTAKE TO USE THAT LOVE-SICK GHOST ON THIS JOB!

NOW **I'VE** GOT TO DO IT AFTER ALL!

17

SOMETIME LATER...THE PRIVATE PART OF *PYGMALION SPA*...

HEY, EDDIE-- CLEAN TOWELS!.. *EDDIE?*

HMM, GUESS HE AIN'T HERE! I'LL JUST LEAVE 'EM!

NOT A VERY GLAMOROUS WAY TO CHECK IN--BUT IT *WORKED!*

NOW TO START GATHERING EVIDENCE! BUT FIRST I NEED A *DISGUISE!*

THESE CLOTHES ...BELONG TO A WHITEY BLAINE! PROBABLY SOME SMALL-TIME HOOD HERE FOR A REMODELING!

GOT TO TRY AND PASS AS HIM... FOR A TIME!

BUT AS THE *MASKED MANHUNTER* ASSUMES THIS NEW ROLE...

HEY, YOU! YOU TAKING MY CLASS TODAY? WHAT'S YOUR NAME?

UH...SURE! I'M... WHITEY BLAINE!

NICE WORK, CHARLIE! WHOEVER THIS GUY IS, HE DIDN'T KNOW...

BLAINE DIED OF A HEART ATTACK ON THE OPERATING TABLE THIS MORNING!

AND SHORTLY...

WHO IS HE? DO *YOU* KNOW HIM, BOSTON?

UH...NEVER SAW HIM BEFORE, DOLL! MAYBE SOME KOOKIE GUEST OR NEWSPAPER REPORTER!

BLAST YOU, BRUCIE-BOY--! YOU *HAD* TO SHOW UP...MESS UP EVERYTHING!

18

HE'S NO REPORTER OR GUEST--HE'S A *SPY!*

WHY DID HE TRY TO ASSUME WHITEY BLAINE'S IDENTITY? WELL, THE JOKE'S ON *HIM!*

LILLY, YOU WANTED TO SEE ME?

YES, DOC! I'VE GOT THE *PERFECT NEW IDENTITY* FOR HOLT GRANIGAN--

THIS LOUSY SNOOPER... WHO'S PROBABLY FUZZ!!

HMM, CLEVER! WE SWITCH FEATURES, AND *PUBLIC ENEMY NUMBER ONE...* BECOMES MR. *CLEAN-CUT COP!* BEAUTIFUL, LILLY!

JUST MAKE HIM UP WITH GRANIGAN'S FEATURES--HE HAS TO BE OUT OF HERE *FAST!*

HER VOICE... COLD AS *ICE!* THOSE GORGEOUS EYES... CHOKIN' WITH *FURY!*

DOLL, I DON'T LIKE THIS! IF HE *IS* A COP, WE OUGHTTA BLOW OUT OF HERE FOR GOOD!

NO! I'M NOT READY TO GIVE UP MY GOLD MINE YET! WHOEVER HE IS...

HE'S GOING TO DIE!

SHE DOESN'T KNOW IT'S BRUCE WAYNE, ALIAS THE GREAT *BATMAN* SHE'S SETTING UP! I'VE GOT TO GO ALONG WITH IT FOR NOW--DON'T WANT HER TO KNOW I WAS PLAYING "COP", TOO!

SOME TIME LATER, A BOULEVARD ON THE MAINLAND...

THIS IS THE SPOT! NOW LET'S CLEAR OUT! HE'S COMING TO--!

19

AND AS THE CAR ROARS AWAY...

WHAT IN--? HOW'D I GET *HERE*? LAST THING I REMEMBER, I GOT ZAPPED BY LILLY LANG'S GOONS...

THOSE STORES, UP AHEAD...GOT TO GET HELP THERE!

BUT COMING DOWN THE BOULEVARD...

THAT ANONYMOUS PHONE TIP SAID HOLT GRANIGAN WAS SEEN IN THIS AREA! PROBABLY PHONY... BUT IF WE COULD BAG THAT CRIMINAL...

IT'S NO PHONY, BILL! *THERE* HE IS--!!

THE WANTED LIST SAYS HE'S ARMED AND DANGEROUS-- *TO SHOOT ON SIGHT!*

HE'S GOING FOR A GUN--! BLAST HIM!

POLICE CAR--! JUST THE MEN I NEED...

POW

THEY'RE SHOOTING AT *ME*??

OH, MY SHOULDER--!!

GOT TO TAKE HIM OVER-- *FAST!*

P'OW

POW

THEN, AS THE PHANTOM FORM OF *DEADMAN* FLASHES INTO THE BODY OF THE PUZZLED BRUCE WAYNE...

TZING

BRUCIE-BOY HAS NO IDEA HE'S GOT GRANIGAN'S FACE--AND THOSE EAGER-BEAVER LAWMEN AREN'T ABOUT TO LISTEN TO THE CRAZY EXPLANATION--!

20

SHORTLY, AFTER LOSING HIMSELF IN THE TANGLED, TROPICAL UNDER-GROWTH...

SHOULDER'S PRETTY BAD! WAYNE'LL HAVE TO GET TO A HOSPITAL--

BUT FIRST I GOTTA RUB OFF THIS MAKE-UP JOB... BEFORE IT FINGERS HIM AGAIN!

THEN, QUICKLY, *DEADMAN* SCRAWLS A MESSAGE IN THE WET SAND AND EXITS FROM BRUCE WAYNE'S BODY...

SO *THAT'S* WHAT HAPPENED? INCREDIBLE! BUT LISTEN, *DEADMAN* ...NOW YOU *MUST* BELIEVE WHAT A VICIOUS WITCH LILLY LANG IS!

STOP KIDDING YOURSELF AND BRING HER TO JUSTICE! *DEADMAN!* I KNOW YOU'RE HERE!...

I'VE STOPPED LISTENING, BRUCIE! TAKE CARE OF THAT SHOULDER-- I GOT A DATE WITH MY OTHER BODY!

AGAIN, THE AMAZING SPIRIT OF BOSTON BRAND TAKES FLIGHT-- AND SOON...

JUST IN TIME! THAT SLEEPING PILL I TOOK AS RICHIE WANDRUS IS WEARING OFF!

DON'T WANT *HIM* BACK ON THE SCENE-- NOW THAT I'VE GOT A CHANCE FOR REAL LIFE AGAIN... IN HIS BODY!

MOMENTS LATER...

LILLY, BABY-- WE GOT TO CLOSE UP SHOP AND LEAVE THE COUNTRY! KILLING THAT SNOOP-ER COULD BRING DOWN HEAVY FUZZ!

DON'T CON ME, BOSTON--*YOU'RE FUZZ YOURSELF!* YOU KNOW HE ISN'T DEAD! THE BOYS HUNG AROUND AFTER THEY DUMPED HIM...

...HE TOOK OFF *TOO* FAST WHEN THE LAW STARTED SHOOTING! AND SINCE WHEN DO YOU NAP IN THE MIDDLE OF THE DAY?

NO, DARLING, YOU *LIED* TO ME... YOU CAME HERE TO *BETRAY* ME!

21

318

OKAY, I ADMIT IT... BUT EVERYTHING'S *DIFFERENT* NOW! I LOVE YOU AND YOU LOVE ME--BOSTON BRAND! TOGETHER, WE CAN MAKE A NEW LIFE...

YES, I LOVED BOSTON BRAND--BUT NOW I DON'T BELIEVE YOU! YOU DOUBLE-CROSSED ME *ONCE*...YOU COULD DO IT *AGAIN*!

AND BY MY CODE, DOUBLE-CROSSERS HAVE TO *DIE*! SORRY, "LOVER"!

DON'T BE CRAZY, DOLL! YOU CAN'T KILL A... *DEADMAN*! ALL YOU'LL DO IS ZAP YOUR OLD BOYFRIEND, RICHIE!

YOU WANT COLD-BLOODED MURDER ON YOUR SCORE SHEET?

SUDDENLY...

FREEZE! THE PLACE IS SURROUNDED BY LAW AGENTS!!

CRASH

BATMAN??

HAD TO MOVE IN, BOSTON-- BEFORE YOU LOUSED UP THINGS MORE!

SO--YOU'RE *BATMAN'S* LITTLE HELPER, *DEADMAN*!

IN THAT CASE, HE DIES WHILE YOU WATCH--!

LILLY-- NO!!

I *COULD* TAKE OVER AND STOP HER-- BUT WHAT IF I'M TOO LATE? *BATMAN'S* RIGHT ...SHE'S VICIOUS AND CORRUPT!

BUT HER CRIMINAL LIFE DID IT TO HER! UNDERNEATH SHE'S A LONELY, LOST HUMAN BEING--!

IN HIS MEMORY ANOTHER VOICE SOUNDS...

A SPIRIT IN LOVE MAY ONLY GAIN HIS HEART'S DESIRE BY LOSING IT! FOR IS NOT LOVE STRONGER THAN DEATH ITSELF?

THAT'S *IT*! THAT'S WHAT RAMA KUSHNA'S MESSAGE MEANT!

22

IN HIS HEART, A DESPERATE HOPE IS BORN...

IF LILLY KILLS *BATMAN*, SHE'LL ROT IN PRISON! SHE MAY AS WELL BE DEAD!

BUT IF *I* KILL HER, SHE'LL BE FREE OF THIS CRUMMY LIFE... FREE TO JOIN ME AS A PHANTOM FOREVER! RAMA SAYS SO!

GOODBYE, *BAT*-... *UUUOOHH!*

POW

POW

DEADMAN ?!

I...I *HAD* TO DO IT --TO SAVE *YOU!* NOW YOU'LL BE *MINE*... FOREVER! COME TO ME, LILLY-- COME JOIN ME! IT'S THE ONLY WAY FOR US!

BUT AS THE COLD PALLOR OF DEATH DEEPENS ON LILLY LANG'S LOVELY FACE...

N-NOTHING'S HAPPENING!? SHE'S NOT TAKING ON PHANTOM FORM!

WHAT GIVES HERE? *WHAT GIVES* ??

SHE'S DEAD! *REALLY DEAD!* YOU LIED TO ME, RAMA! *YOU CHEATED DEADMAN!*

BUT AS THE ANGUISHED GHOST OF BOSTON BRAND EXITS FROM THE *BODY* HE'S SO LONG INHABITED...

HOLD IT, WANDRUS!

B-BATMAN? LILLY...LYING *DEAD?* WHAT HAPPENED HERE?

KLIK

23

320

AND SHORTLY...

THAT WRAPS IT-- WE BAGGED THEM ALL... INCLUDING GRANIGAN BEFORE HE WAS GIVEN BRUCE WAYNE'S FACE!

I FOUND THE EVIDENCE *DEADMAN* WAS HIDING IN WANDRUS'S ROOM! THE CRIMINAL REMODELING BUSINESS IS CLOSED!

BUT I FEEL BADLY ABOUT BOSTON... WONDER WHERE HE IS?

IN A MAINLAND MORGUE, THE LAST REPOSITORY OF LIFE'S LOSERS...

OH, LILLY... LILLY... I'LL NEVER *FORGET YOU!* YOU WERE LOVED, DOLL... *REALLY LOVED!*

WHY DID YOU DO *THIS* TO ME, RAMA? *WHY?*

YES, STRANGE ARE FATE'S PATHWAYS -- AND STRANGE THE MEANINGS OF RAMA -- PERHAPS NOT TO BE UNDERSTOOD BY EVEN THE IMMORTAL MIND OF... *DEADMAN!*

THE END

BATMAN

the BRAVE and the BOLD

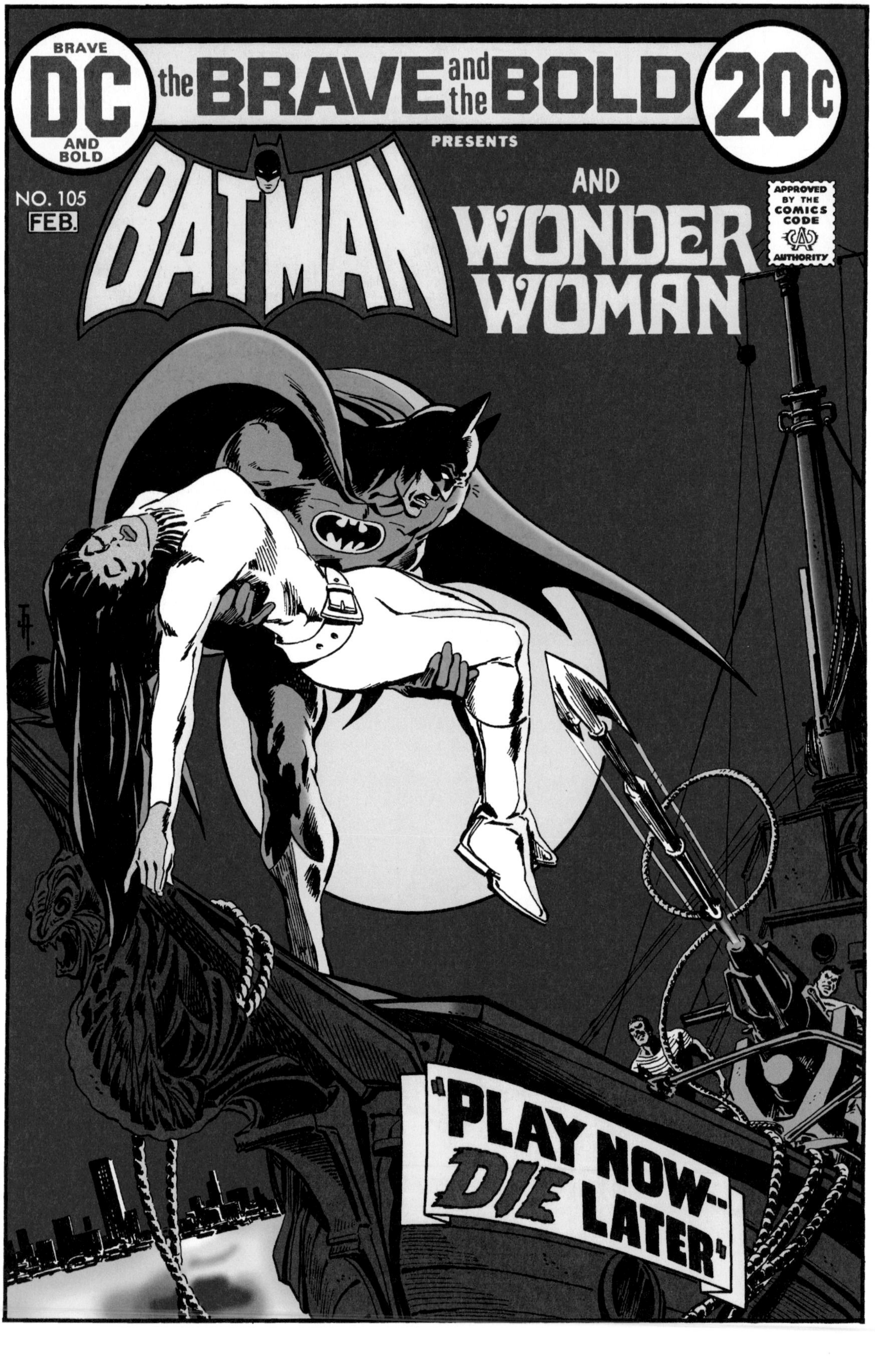
BRAVE
DC
AND
BOLD
the BRAVE and the BOLD
20¢
PRESENTS
NO. 105
FEB.
BATMAN
AND
WONDER WOMAN
APPROVED BY THE COMICS CODE AUTHORITY
"PLAY NOW-- DIE LATER"

STRUMMING GUITARS... STACCATO HEEL-STAMPING... THE ODOR OF SAFFRON AND CIGARS! *SPAIN? MEXICO?* NO, A FANCY CAFE IN *GOTHAM CITY*, WHERE BRUCE (*BATMAN*) WAYNE HAS JUST FINISHED DINNER...

IT WAS SUPERB, AS USUAL, CARLOS! HOW'S BUSINESS?

EXCELENTE, SEÑOR WAYNE! SO MANY OF MY COUNTRYMEN LIVE HERE IN EXILE SINCE THE WAR IN SAN SEBASTIAN, I AM GETTING RICH!

WHO'S THE BEAUTIFUL GIRL WITH THE DUENNA, CARLOS?

I DO NOT KNOW! IT IS UNUSUAL FOR A GIRL OF GOOD FAMILY TO BE OUT THIS LATE, EVEN WITH AN OLD CRONE OF A CHAPERONE!

SHE CERTAINLY LOOKS UPSET!.. HMM, LOOKS LIKE THEY'RE LEAVING ALSO!

SHORTLY...

BUENAS NOCHES, SEÑORA ...SEÑORITA! MAY I OFFER YOU A RIDE HOME?

NO, *NO,* SEÑOR! WE DO NOT KNOW YOU! IT IS NOT DONE!

COME, CONCHITA!

1

BUT AS HE WATCHES THE TWO WOMEN WALK OFF...

THEY'VE GOT *TROUBLE*, ALFRED! FOLLOW ME IN THE CAR!

NO!

WAAK!

THEY'RE RUNNING!.. THEY GAVE UP PRETTY EASILY!

PILAR!? QUE PASA?

SHE FAINTED, SEÑORITA! THIS WAS TOO MUCH FOR HER!

NOW WILL YOU ACCEPT MY AID?

SI! OH, YES, YES!

NOW AS THE ROLLS-ROYCE GLIDES OVER THE COBBLES OF GOTHAM...

I AM CONCHITA VASQUEZ, SEÑOR WAYNE! I AM FROM SAN SEBASTIAN! PILAR, I AM SO WORRIED ABOUT HER--!

WE'LL GET HER TO A HOSPITAL OR A DOCTOR!

MR. WAYNE, SIR! THERE IS *SOMETHING AHEAD*--!?

2

A GUN BATTLE!!

STOP, ALFRED!

KPOW

BEEOU POW

KRAK

GET THE OLD LADY TO A HOSPITAL AT ONCE, ALFRED! THIS LOOKS LIKE A SHOOTOUT I'D BETTER JOIN!

I UNDERSTAND, SIR!

ADIOS, SEÑORITA!

MOMENTS LATER...

GOOD LORD! THAT BOY--!!

STORY BOB HANEY

ART JIM APARO

TZEOW ZIP

EL CIGARS MARVILLA'S MAGNIFICO!

FLANG

BUDDA BUDDABUDDA POW

THE GAME WAS OLD AND ALLURING...BUT WHEN *THE BATMAN* AND HIS BEAUTIFUL ALLY, *WONDER WOMAN,* BUY INTO A SWEEPSTAKES OF DANGER AND DOUBLE-CROSS, THEY LEARN TOO LATE THAT THEIR TICKETS ARE PUNCHED...

PLAY NOW... DIE LATER!

3

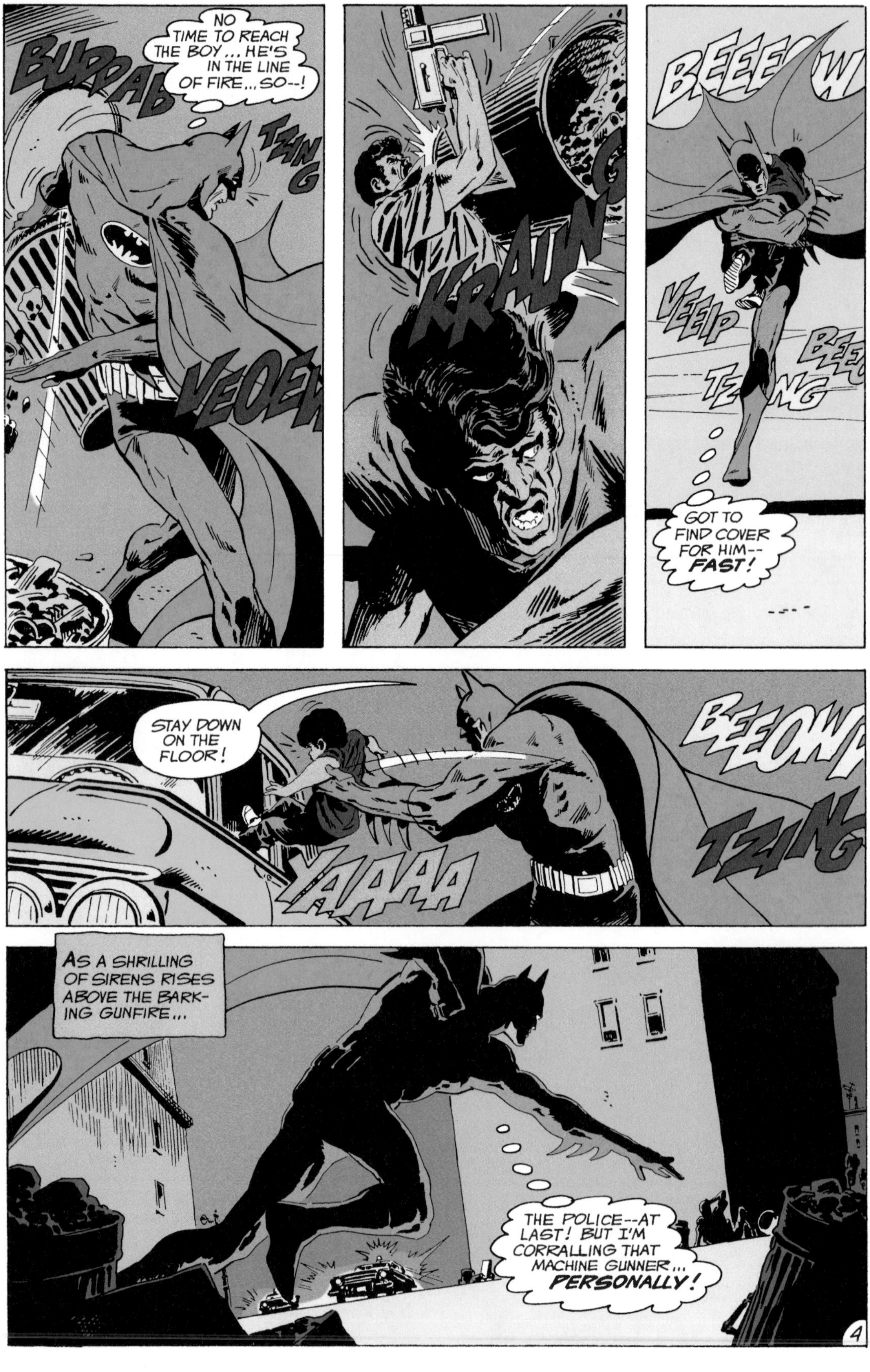
BUDDAB
NO TIME TO REACH THE BOY... HE'S IN THE LINE OF FIRE... SO--!
TTHING
VEOEW
KRAUNG
BEEEOW
VEEIP
BEEO
TZING
GOT TO FIND COVER FOR HIM-- FAST!
STAY DOWN ON THE FLOOR!
BEEOW
TZING
YAAAA
AS A SHRILLING OF SIRENS RISES ABOVE THE BARK-ING GUNFIRE...
THE POLICE--AT LAST! BUT I'M CORRALLING THAT MACHINE GUNNER... PERSONALLY!
4

BLAZES, COMMISSIONER! THE WHOLE SPANISH PART OF GOTHAM'S *EXPLODING*--!

BATMAN!

FAN OUT MEN! SEE IF WE CAN MAKE SOME ARRESTS...THIS TIME!

IT'S THESE PEOPLE FROM *SAN SEBASTIAN*... THEY'VE BROUGHT THEIR WAR HERE TO GOTHAM! GUN BATTLES... KILLINGS...!

YEAH, THIS CREEP ALMOST KNOCKED OFF A SMALL BOY! I WANT HIM BOOKED ON A HALF A DOZEN CHARGES!

SHORTLY, GOTHAM POLICE HQ...

NAME--? RESIDENCE--? OCCUPATION--?

RAOUL VASQUEZ!.. SAN SEBASTIAN!.. *REVOLUTIONARY!*

VASQUEZ! THE SAME AS CONCHITA'S... BUT IT'S A COMMON HISPANIC NAME!

USE OF DEADLY WEAPONS--ENDANGERING CITIZENS...*TAKE HIM AWAY!*

PIGS! YOU ARREST THE WRONG MAN! I AM NO CRIMINAL...NO STUPID GUNMAN! I AM AN *HOMBRE*! A PATRIOT! I *DEFY YOU!*

A REAL WILD ONE, EH, *BATMAN?* THE REST GOT AWAY-- BUT I'LL BET HE'S THE *LEADER OF ONE GANG*... PROBABLY STARTED IT ALL!

A FEW NIGHTS IN THE TANK'LL COOL HIM DOWN! NOW I'VE GOT AN UNFINISHED DATE, COMMISH-- WITH A BEAUTIFUL SEÑORITA!

5

SOON, GOTHAM HOSPITAL...

SHE'LL BE ALL RIGHT, CONCHITA! THE DOCTOR SAYS SHE JUST NEEDS REST!

OH, SEÑOR WAYNE, YOU ARE SO *SIMPATICO*... SO *KIND*! I...I FEEL YOU ARE AN *AMIGO*...A FRIEND IN WHOM I CAN CONFIDE!

I...AND MY FAMILY... WE ARE IN *MUY* TROUBLE, SEÑOR WAYNE! PERHAPS YOU CAN HELP US--!

SUPPOSE YOU TELL ME ALL ABOUT IT WHILE I TAKE YOU HOME?

SHORTLY, AN OLD BROWNSTONE ON GOTHAM'S EAST SIDE...

SUDDENLY,...

DO NOT MOVE, SEÑOR-- OR MY KNIFE WILL FIND YOUR LIFE!

THAT VOICE... I KNOW IT?!

RAOUL, MY *BROTHER*!

STOP-- OR ERNESTO'S GUN WILL DO IT *FOR* YOU!

VASQUEZ! SO THEY *ARE* RELATED!

QUE PASA? I AM UNJUSTLY JAILED THIS VERY NIGHT-- I ESCAPE AND FIND MY SISTER COMING HOME *UNCHAPERONED*!

RAOUL, PLEASE UNDERSTAND! I WAS ATTACKED AND PILAR COLLAPSED! SEÑOR WAYNE CAME TO MY *AID*!

6

HE KNOWS OF OUR TROUBLES AND MAY HELP US!

WHY SHOULD *YOU* HELP US, HOMBRE? HOW DO I KNOW YOU ARE NOT WORKING FOR OUR ENEMIES ...THE *MONTOYAS*?

MY NAME AND REPUTATION ARE WELL KNOWN! BUT I KNOW NOTHING OF YOURS! YOUR SISTER'S STORY... IS VERY HARD TO BELIEVE!

IT IS SIMPLE, MY RICH, SPOILED, AND IGNORANT FRIEND! MY FATHER, LEADER OF THE SAN SEBASTIAN REVOLUTIONARY FORCES, IS SECRETLY HELD PRISONER *HERE*... IN *GOTHAM CITY*!

HE CAN BE FREED WITH ENOUGH MONEY FOR A BRIBE...A *RANSOM*!

YOU MEAN ONE OF HIS CAPTORS WILL ACCEPT A BRIBE? HARD TO BELIEVE!

THEY ARE ALL *DOGS*! FOR ENOUGH MONEY, THIS ONE WE DEAL WITH, CALLED *EL MORO*, WOULD BETRAY HIS OWN MOTHER!

I SEE! AND YOU WANT *ME* TO GIVE YOU THIS MONEY, LIKE YOUR SISTER SAID?

SI, FOR THE MONTOYAS TORTURE HIM TO LEARN THE LOCATION OF A GREAT TREASURE MY COUNTRYMEN NEED SO BADLY!

BUT IF YOUR FATHER CRACKS AND REVEALS THE LOCATION... MY MONEY COULD BE *WASTED*!

MY FATHER...*CRACK*? *NEVER*! HE WOULD *DIE* FIRST! BUT WE MUST RANSOM HIM QUICKLY-- BEFORE SUCH OCCURS!

VERY WELL, I'LL GIVE YOU THE MONEY!

OH, *GRACIAS*, *GRACIAS*... SEÑOR WAYNE! YOU WILL BE WELL REWARDED!

⑦

RAOUL! THE POLICE--!

CARAMBA! I WILL GO OUT THE REAR WAY! SEÑOR WAYNE, I HOLD YOU TO YOUR PROMISE!

ADIOS!

AND AS THE HOTHEADED RAOUL VANISHES INTO A REAR ALLEY...

THE POLICE... THEY FOLLOW-- BUT RAOUL HAS LOST THEM!

OH, MY POOR BROTHER! NOW HE MUST RUN LIKE A CRIMINAL! MY POOR FAMILY-- MY POOR COUNTRY--!

EASY, CONCHITA! REMEMBER, I'M YOUR FRIEND!

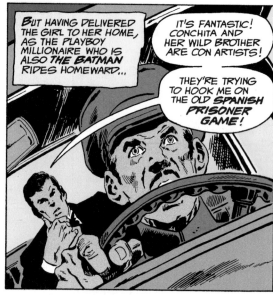

BUT HAVING DELIVERED THE GIRL TO HER HOME, AS THE PLAYBOY MILLIONAIRE WHO IS ALSO THE BATMAN RIDES HOMEWARD...

IT'S FANTASTIC! CONCHITA AND HER WILD BROTHER ARE CON ARTISTS!

THEY'RE TRYING TO HOOK ME ON THE OLD SPANISH PRISONER GAME!

THAT LOVELY GIRL... A CON ARTIST? AND WHAT IS THE SPANISH PRISONER GAME, SIR?

ALFRED, YOU INCURABLE ROMANTIC, I FOUND IT HARD TO BELIEVE, TOO! BUT THERE'S NO DOUBT NOW! THE SPANISH PRISONER GAMBIT'S THE OLDEST OF CON GAMES...

IT STARTED IN SPAIN CENTURIES AGO-- BUT CRIMINALS OF MANY COUNTRIES ADOPTED IT!

THERE'S ALWAYS A GORGEOUS FEMALE TO GET THE SUCKER INTERESTED!

SOUND HORN

THEN THERE'S ALWAYS THE RELATIVE HELD PRISONER BY BAD HOMBRES-- AND A "TREASURE" HE ALONE KNOWS ABOUT! PLUS A BRIBE OR RANSOM THAT WILL FREE HIM!

IF THE SUCKER GIVES THE "RANSOM" MONEY, HE'S PROMISED PART OF THE TREASURE AS HIS REWARD!

OF COURSE, IT'S ALL *FAKED*--JUST TO GET THE RANSOM MONEY!

MY WORD! AND MISS CONCHITA SEEMED SO *SINCERE!* BUT WE ONLY MET HER TONIGHT--?

SURE, THEY'RE CLEVER OPERATORS! SHE HEARD MY NAME IN THE RESTAURANT, KNEW I WAS WEALTHY!

THOSE THUGS WERE ACCOMPLICES --THAT'S WHY THEY LEFT THE FIGHT SO FAST!

NEEDLESS TO SAY, THERE IS *NO* "PRISONER"... *NO* "ENEMIES"!

REFUSING OUR HELP AT FIRST PUT US EVEN *MORE* OFF-GUARD!

OLD PILAR'S COLLAPSE? ANOTHER PART OF THE CUNNING COME-ON!

BUT THE *BROTHER*... THAT GUN BATTLE IN THE STREETS ?

I HAVEN'T PUT ALL THE PIECES TOGETHER YET, ALFRED --BUT I'M *POSITIVE* CONCHITA AND HER BROTHER ARE WORKING THAT OLD DODGE ON BRUCE WAYNE!

BUT IT'S *THE BATMAN* WHO'S GOING TO CATCH THEM AT IT!

WHICH REMINDS ME, THE *MASKED MANHUNTER'S* WANTED AT AN EMERGENCY MEETING AT CITY HALL!

9

NOT LONG AFTER, GOTHAM CITY HALL...

AS MAYOR, I'VE CALLED THIS MEETING TO DEAL WITH THE SMALL WAR GOING ON IN GOTHAM'S LATIN SECTION!

BATMAN, DO YOU KNOW FRANCISCO MONTOYA?

OF COURSE! SEÑOR MONTOYA WAS ONE OF SAN SEBASTIAN'S LEADING CITIZENS! TO GOTHAM'S GOOD FORTUNE, NOW HE'S ONE OF OURS!

GRACIAS, BAT HOMBRE! I AM MUY DISTRESSED BY THE VIOLENCE SOME OF MY COUNTRYMEN VISIT ON GOTHAM'S STREETS!

THERE IS ONE GROUP WHO ARE NO BETTER THAN BANDITS! THEY ATTACK PEACEFUL SAN SEBASTIAN EXILES-- ATTEMPTING TO TERRORIZE AND EXTORT FROM THEM!

THEIR LEADER IS ONE-- RAOUL VASQUEZ!

WE HAD TROUBLE WITH HIM TONIGHT!

RIGHT NOW, THERE'S A MAN-HUNT FOR HIM! I'M PUTTING EXTRA PATROLS INTO LAS PAMPAS,.. HIS NATIVE SECTION!

IT'S A DELICATE SITUATION, BUT WITH SEÑOR MONTOYA KEEPING HIS COUNTRY-MEN COOL, WE CAN CORRAL THE BAD ELEMENT AND PREVENT GOTHAM FROM BOILING OVER!

COUNT ON ME, SEÑOR MAYOR!

10

SHORTLY...

I DIDN'T MENTION THE VASQUEZ CLAN WORKING THE SPANISH PRISONER GAMBIT ON BRUCE WAYNE... I WANT TO HANDLE *THAT* PERSONALLY!

BUT I'LL NEED HELP--*VERY* SPECIAL HELP!

THE FOLLOWING DAY, A LITHE FIGURE SAUNTERS SAUCILY INTO THAT PART OF GOTHAM CITY KNOWN AS *LAS PAMPAS*,...

TO SOME, SHE IS *DIANA PRINCE*, MOD GIRL-ABOUT-TOWN,...BUT TO THE MANY WHO KNOW HER LEGEND, SHE WAS AND IS *WONDER WOMAN*, WHO EXCHANGED AMAZON POWER AND IMMORTALITY FOR HUMAN EXISTENCE!

THIS IS IT!

HO, *WONDER WOMAN!* WHAT TRUMPET TO ADVENTURE DO YOU ANSWER IN THIS PLACE?

MY AMAZON GUARDIAN ANGEL!

I'M HERE TO HELP AN OLD FRIEND-- *THE BATMAN!*

NOBLY WORTHY OF *YOUR* AMAZON HERITAGE! BUT I FORESEE DEADLY DANGERS TO YOUR LIFE! REMEMBER, NOW YOU ARE MORTAL...

BETTER BE ON MY TOES ON *THIS* JOB!

11

A WARNING GIVEN, A BELL RUNG, A DOOR OPENS-- BUT TO WHAT...?

WHAT DO YOU WANT?

BUENAS DIAS, SEÑOR! I AM HERE FROM THE AGENCY!

YOU REQUESTED A DUENNA... A COMPANION FOR A YOUNG LADY?!

THERE IS SOME MISTAKE, SEÑORITA! WE ASKED FOR NO DUENNA--AND A DUENNA IS ALWAYS OLD AND HOMELY!

SOMEONE CALLED THE AGENCY WHICH SENT ME HERE! I SPEAK SPANISH... HERE ARE MY REFERENCE PAPERS!

PERHAPS RAOUL SENT FOR HER! LET HER IN, ERNESTO!

I DO NEED A DUENNA SINCE NOW OLD PILAR LIES SICK, AND YOU ARE WELL QUALIFIED! BUT YOU ARE YOUNG!

ALL THE BETTER A COMPANION, SEÑORITA VASQUEZ!

YOUR DRESS-- VERY PRETTY-- BUT IT NEEDS A SPLASH OF COLOR! PERHAPS A SASH OR BELT?

OH, HOW CLEVER! YOU KNOW FASHION, SI, DIANA?

SI! I RUN A BOUTIQUE WHEN BUSINESS IS GOOD! BUT RIGHT NOW, I NEED A JOB!

YOU HAVE IT! I LIKE YOU, DIANA!

SEÑORITA CONCHITA! A DUENNA SO PRETTY... SO YOUNG? YOUR FATHER WOULD NOT APPROVE!!

ENOUGH, ERNESTO! MY FATHER IS NOT HERE! NOR MY BROTHER--! I NEED SOMEONE!

BUT THERE MAY BE DANGER, DIANA! DOES THAT BOTHER YOU?

DANGER? OH, HOW EXCITING!

12

NOT LONG AFTER, ALONE IN HER ROOM...

...*BATMAN?* IT WORKED--SO FAR! CONCHITA AND I HAVE GOTTEN VERY FRIENDLY ALREADY!

SHE'S NICE-- HARDLY THE CON ARTIST TYPE!

PART OF HER FRONT, DIANA! PLAY YOUR ROLE AND KEEP YOUR EARS OPEN!

NOW I'VE GOT TO SWITCH TO *MY* ROLE-- AS BRUCE WAYNE, *SUCKER!*

THAT NIGHT...

THIS IS DIANA PRINCE, MY FRIEND AND COMPANION, SEÑOR WAYNE! SHE KNOWS OF MY FAMILY'S TROUBLES!

VERY WELL, CONCHITA! HERE IS THE MONEY FOR YOUR FATHER'S RANSOM!

OH, SEÑOR BRUCE-- YOU ARE SUCH A *BUEN HOMBRE!* NOW MY FATHER WILL BE FREE AND THE TREASURE USED TO HELP SAN SEBASTIAN'S PEOPLE!

GRACIAS! MUCHAS GRACIAS!

WHAT AN ACTRESS!

SOME TIME LATER, *WONDER WOMAN* AGAIN CONTACTS HER SECRET ALLY...

CONCHITA AND I ARE MEETING A CERTAIN *EL MORO* AT PIER 93 TO GIVE HIM THE MONEY, *BATMAN!* IF THE DEAL'S PHONY-- WHY IS SHE GOING THROUGH ALL THIS?

SIMPLE, DIANA! *EL MORO* IS EITHER HER FUGITIVE BROTHER, RAOUL, OR HIS HENCHMAN!

WHILE THEY SPLIT WITH THE MONEY, CONCHITA KEEPS UP THE FRONT A BIT LONGER TO FOOL BRUCE WAYNE...

13

...THEN SHE JOINS THEM LATER! I'M HEADING FOR PIER 93 NOW--TO BLOW THE WHISTLE ON THEIR LITTLE GAME! SEE YOU THERE!

SOON, GOTHAM'S RIVERFRONT...

THAT BIG GUY--MUST BE *EL MORO!* HERE COME THE GIRLS!

BUT AS A GLEAM REFLECTED OFF THE RIVER REVEALS ANOTHER FIGURE LURKING NEARBY...

RAOUL VASQUEZ! I WAS *RIGHT*-- HE'S USING THE BIG GUY TO PICK UP THE MONEY BECAUSE AS A FUGITIVE HE CAN'T RISK BEING SPOTTED!

SEÑORITA VASQUEZ? I AM *EL MORO!* THE MONEY-- *QUICKLY*, I MUST NOT BE SEEN!

HERE! BUT WHERE IS MY FATHER HELD?

THEY'RE PLAYING THE GAME OUT TO THE LAST DETAIL! FOR *MY* BENEFIT, I'LL BET!

THE LOCATION OF YOUR FATHER IS WRITTEN ON THIS PAPER--

EH? WHO COMES?

14

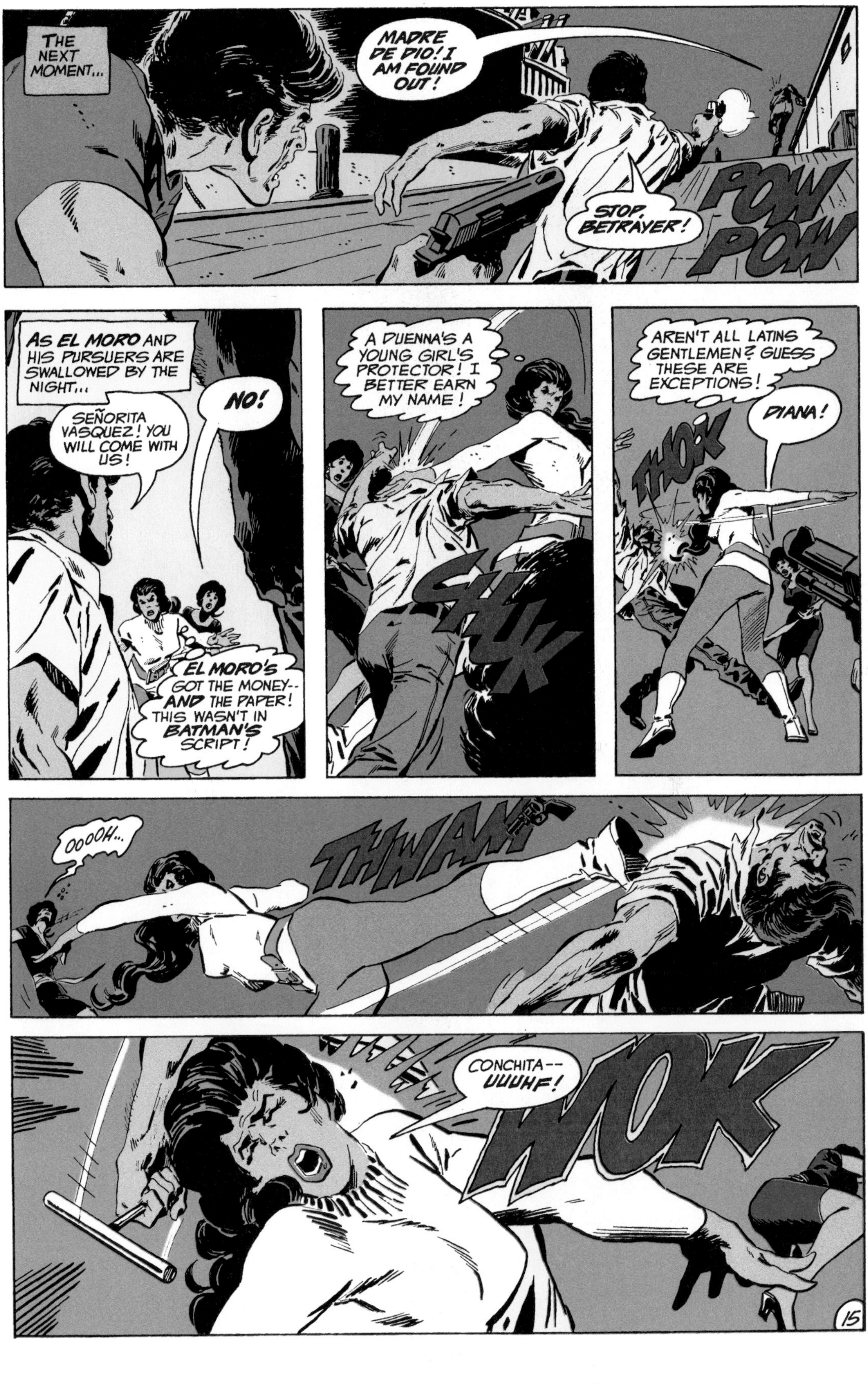
THE NEXT MOMENT...
MADRE DE DIO! I AM FOUND OUT!
STOP, BETRAYER!
POW POW
AS EL MORO AND HIS PURSUERS ARE SWALLOWED BY THE NIGHT...
SEÑORITA VASQUEZ! YOU WILL COME WITH US!
NO!
EL MORO'S GOT THE MONEY-- AND THE PAPER! THIS WASN'T IN BATMAN'S SCRIPT!
A DUENNA'S A YOUNG GIRL'S PROTECTOR! I BETTER EARN MY NAME!
SHUK
AREN'T ALL LATINS GENTLEMEN? GUESS THESE ARE EXCEPTIONS!
DIANA!
THOK
OOOOH...
THWAM
CONCHITA-- UUUHF!
WOK
15

AT THIS MOMENT, FARTHER OUT ON PIER 93...

POW
POW

EL MORO... HE'S HIT!

SUDDENLY...

BAT HOMBRE!

HE'S TOPPLING INTO THE RIVER!

GOT HIM...

BUT... HE'S DEAD!

IN HIS HAND... A PAPER!

WHAT? MUST BE SOME JOKE!

I WILL TAKE THAT, BAT HOMBRE!

VASQUEZ!

SI! NOW GIVE ME THE LOCATION WHERE THE MONTOYAS HOLD MY FATHER! MY SISTER PAID THIS DEAD FOOL GOOD MONEY FOR IT!

16

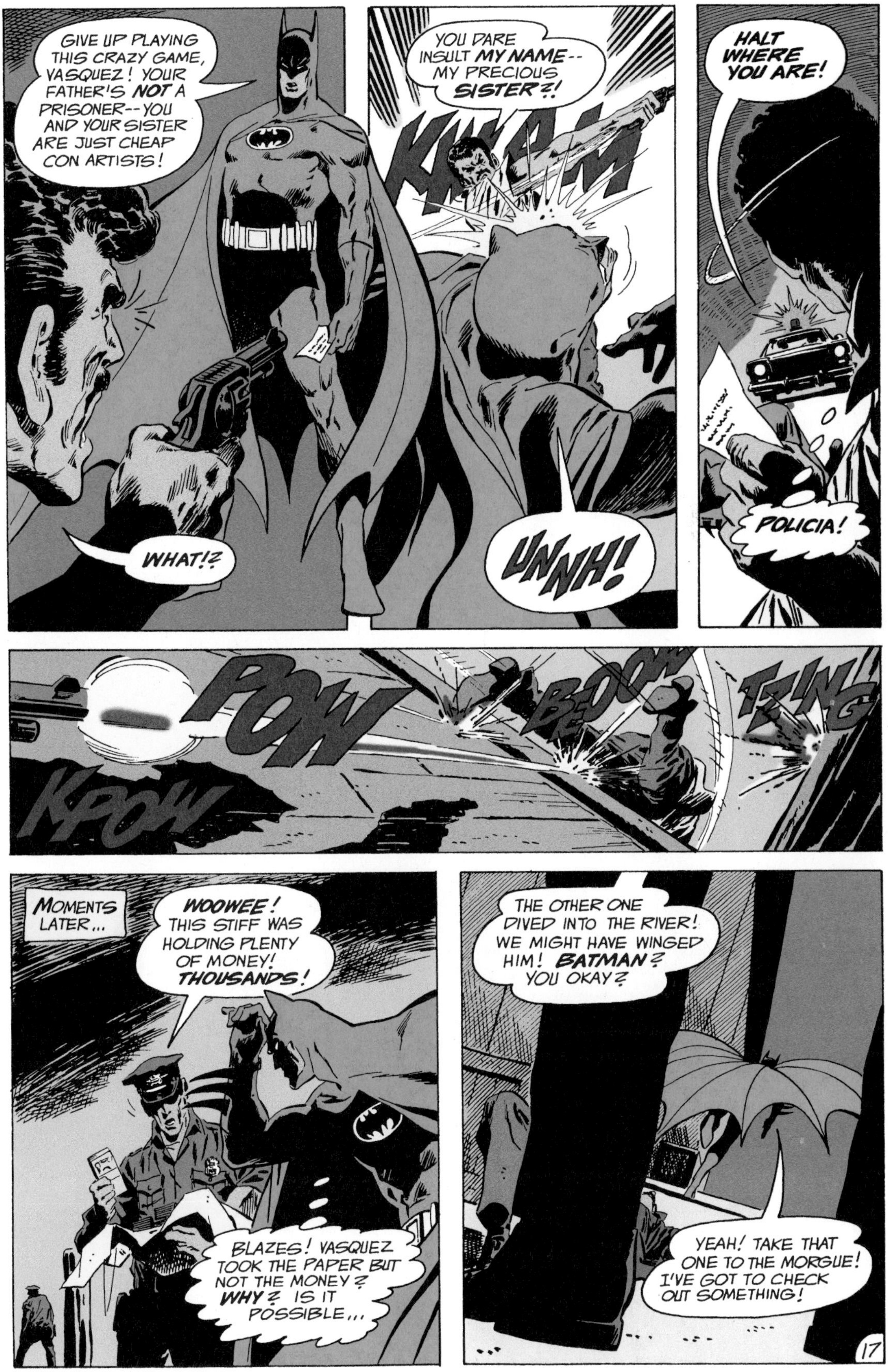
GIVE UP PLAYING THIS CRAZY GAME, VASQUEZ! YOUR FATHER'S NOT A PRISONER--YOU AND YOUR SISTER ARE JUST CHEAP CON ARTISTS!
WHAT!?
YOU DARE INSULT MY NAME--MY PRECIOUS SISTER?!
KWAM
UNNH!
HALT WHERE YOU ARE!
POLICIA!
POW
BEDOOW
TZING
KPOW
MOMENTS LATER...
WOOWEE! THIS STIFF WAS HOLDING PLENTY OF MONEY! THOUSANDS!
BLAZES! VASQUEZ TOOK THE PAPER BUT NOT THE MONEY? WHY? IS IT POSSIBLE...
THE OTHER ONE DIVED INTO THE RIVER! WE MIGHT HAVE WINGED HIM! BATMAN? YOU OKAY?
YEAH! TAKE THAT ONE TO THE MORGUE! I'VE GOT TO CHECK OUT SOMETHING!
17

WONDER WOMAN! COME IN! WONDER WOMAN! COME IN!

CAN'T RAISE HER! SHE MUST BE OKAY-- TAKING CHARGE OF CONCHITA SOMEWHERE!

WRONG, BATMAN-- FOR JUST TWO STREETS AWAY, WHERE SOON THE USUAL PRE-DAWN ARMADA OF GIANT TRUCKS WILL THUNDER DOWN A FEEDER RAMP...

NOW SHORTLY, BACK ON THE MAIN STREET OF LAS PAMPAS...

IT'S CRAZY--AND I STILL CAN'T QUITE BELIEVE IT,,, BUT I MUST BE SURE!

MOMENTS LATER, BEHIND THE HUGE SIGN, THE BATMAN SLIPS UP TO...

THIS SHED MUST CONTAIN THE APPARATUS TO WORK THE SMOKE RING GIZMO!

AND THEN, INSIDE...

IT'S WHAT I WAS AFRAID OF-- A MANACLE AND SIGNS SOMEONE WAS HELD PRISONER HERE!

FANTASTIC! WHO'D EVER SUSPECT THIS PLACE!?

18

AS A FEW WORDS FAINTLY SCRATCHED IN THE METAL WALL CATCH HIS EYE...

EMILIANO VASQUEZ! VIVA LA LIBERTAD!

KRAK

UNNNHH!

SOME TIME LATER, THROUGH A FOG OF PAIN, HE AWAKENS TO A SHOCKING AWARENESS!

INCREDIBLE! I...I'M A PRISONER MYSELF! JUST AS THOSE SCRATCHINGS PROVE OLD VASQUEZ WAS!

HIS CAPTORS KNEW I'D LEARNED THIS LOCATION AND MOVED HIM, LEAVING SOMEBODY BEHIND TO CLOBBER ME!

WHAT IRONY-- AND WHAT A COLOSSAL FOOL I WAS! I'VE GOT TO GET OUT OF HERE AND TRY TO PUT THINGS RIGHT!

BUT HOW? CAN'T MOVE ONE YARD--AND MY WRIST RADIO'S CRUSHED UNDER THAT MANACLE! WONDER WOMAN... WHERE ARE YOU?

GOOD QUESTION, BATMAN--AS DAWN TINGES THE SKY OVER GOTHAM...

GOT TO PICK UP A LOAD OF BANANAS AND HEAD WEST TO...

A DAME ON THE RAMP? CAN'T STOP!!

THE NEXT INSTANT...

BRRMMM

SSKREEEGGHHHH

A RENDING CRASH, AND NOT LONG AFTER...

I TELL YA THERE *WAS* A DAME IN MY WAY... THEN THIS GIANT IN CRAZY ARMOR GRABS HER, AND--

YOU BEEN DRIVING TOO MUCH, BUDDY! YOU'VE *GONE BANANAS* YOURSELF!

SOON, IN THE HEART OF *LAS PAMPAS*, AS A NEW DAY BEGINS...

¡MÍFICO!

TRIED *BATMAN* ON THE RADIO-- NOTHING! MUST FIND HIM!

THE SMOKE RING SIGN--!

A FEW MINUTES LATER...

SO WHEN I SAW THE SEÑOR ON THE SIGN HAD GONE LOCO BLOWING SMOKE RINGS, I SUSPECTED SOMETHING WAS WRONG UP HERE!

LUCKY I COULD REACH THE CONTROLS WITH MY FREE ARM!

YOU'RE PICKING THAT LOCK WITH A BOBBY-PIN? YOU'RE A *WONDER*, WOMAN!

THEY TOOK CONCHITA AND LEFT ME FOR HIT-AND-RUN BAIT! I'VE *FAILED* YOU, BATMAN!

NONSENSE, DIANA! *I'M* THE ONE WHO FAILED! I WAS SO HUNG UP BELIEVING THE VASQUEZ FAMILY WAS WORKING A CON GAME, I WAS BLIND TO THE OBVIOUS TRUTH!

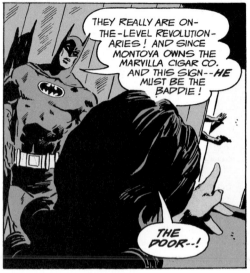

THEY REALLY ARE ON-THE-LEVEL REVOLUTIONARIES! AND SINCE MONTOYA OWNS THE MARVILLA CIGAR CO. AND THIS SIGN--*HE* MUST BE THE BADDIE!

THE DOOR--!

AS BATMAN MOVES SILENTLY TO THE DOORWAY...

RAOUL VASQUEZ!

WWW

20

A WHILE LATER... THE **POLICIA** WOUNDED ME-- BUT I HAD TO COME HERE TO FREE MY FATHER...

HE'S GONE-- MONTOYA'S GOONS TOOK HIM ELSE-WHERE! **AND** CONCHITA!

MY SISTER?! THAT IS **MALO**... BAD...BAD!

NOW MY FATHER **WILL** HAVE TO DISCLOSE THE TREASURE'S LOCATION! THEY WILL USE THREATS AGAINST CONCHITA TO LOOSEN HIS TONGUE!

YOU'RE RIGHT! BUT MAYBE THAT'S **GOOD!** FIND MONTOYA AND WE FIND THE TREASURE!

LET'S GO!

SHORTLY...

THERE'S MONTOYA NOW-- BUT,... **WHAT'S GOING ON?**

MONTOYA ENTERPRISES

AND AS THE PROCESSION REACHES THE DOCKS...

EL PESCATOR

AAH, IT IS THE **FESTIVAL OF THE FISHERMEN!** THEY GO TO BLESS THE FISHING BOATS BEFORE THEY SAIL!

YOU'RE THINKING WHAT **I'M** THINKING, RAOUL? THE TREASURE COULD BE IN THOSE FLOATS! AND MAYBE YOUR FATHER AND SISTER...?

SI, BUT WHAT CAN WE DO? IT WOULD BE SACRILEGE TO INTERFERE WITH THE BLESSING!

21

WHAT? THEY'RE LOADING THE FLOATS--?! AND MONTOYA'S GOING ABOARD!

ALSO A CUSTOM, *BATMAN!* THEY ARE CARRIED FOR LUCK OUT TO THE FISHING GROUNDS... THEN SET ADRIFT!

A FEW MOMENTS LATER...

QUICKLY-- WE MUST GET ABOARD... CHECK OUT THOSE FLOATS!

COVERED BY THE CEREMONY, THE TRIO SLIPS UNSEEN INTO THE TRAWLER'S HOLD, WHERE...

THE FLOATS DO CONTAIN SOMETHING-- BUT I'M AFRAID IT'S JUST SPANISH SOUL FOOD!

SUCH WOULD MAKE FISHERMEN SEASICK...WE SHALL OPEN THEM!

MOMENTS LATER...

PLANE PARTS? DISASSEMBLED *JETS?* THAT'S THE *"TREASURE"*--?

CARAMBA! I NEVER REALIZED... A *FEW JET FIGHTERS* WOULD TIP THE POWER BALANCE IN A COUNTRY AS SMALL AS MINE!

MONTOYA IS RETURNING TO SAN SEBASTIAN TO *CRUSH THE REVOLUTION* WITH THEM!

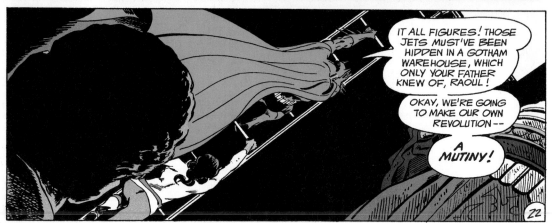

IT ALL FIGURES! THOSE JETS MUST'VE BEEN HIDDEN IN A GOTHAM WAREHOUSE, WHICH ONLY YOUR FATHER KNEW OF, RAOUL!

OKAY, WE'RE GOING TO MAKE OUR OWN REVOLUTION--

A *MUTINY!*

22

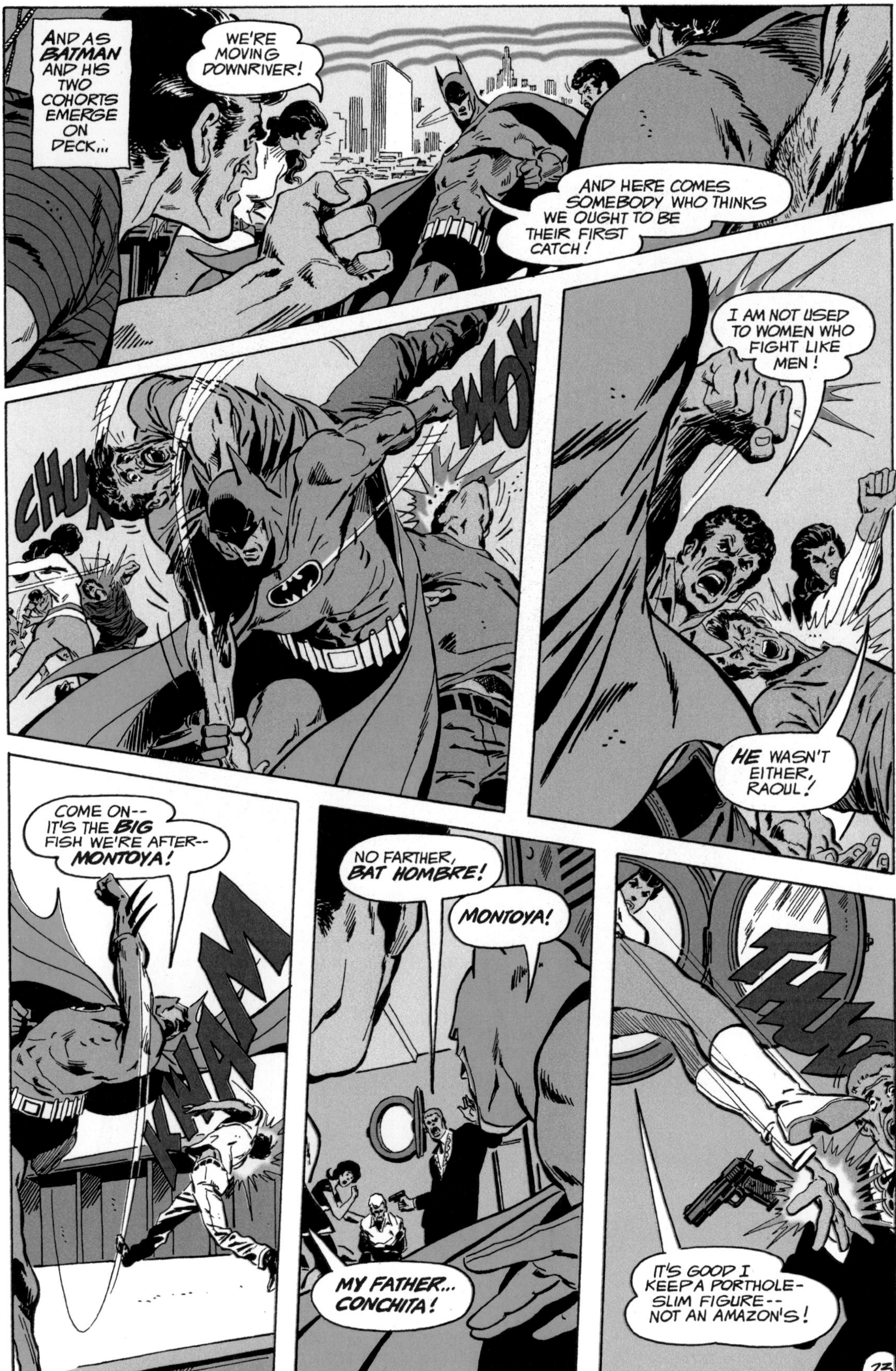

AND AS BATMAN AND HIS TWO COHORTS EMERGE ON DECK...
WE'RE MOVING DOWNRIVER!
AND HERE COMES SOMEBODY WHO THINKS WE OUGHT TO BE THEIR FIRST CATCH!
CHUK
WOK
I AM NOT USED TO WOMEN WHO FIGHT LIKE MEN!
HE WASN'T EITHER, RAOUL!
COME ON-- IT'S THE BIG FISH WE'RE AFTER-- MONTOYA!
KWAM
NO FARTHER, BAT HOMBRE!
MONTOYA!
MY FATHER... CONCHITA!
THU
IT'S GOOD I KEEP A PORTHOLE-SLIM FIGURE-- NOT AN AMAZON'S!
23

LATER...
THANKS TO YOU, SEÑOR BAT HOMBRE AND SEÑORITA DIANA, THE PLANES WILL GO TO THOSE WHO FIGHT FOR FREEDOM, AND SAN SEBASTIAN'S FUTURE WILL BE BRIGHT!
MAYBE IT MAKES UP FOR SUSPECTING YOUR FAMILY WAS PLAYING A CON GAME ON MY FRIEND, BRUCE WAYNE!
OF COURSE, BAT HOMBRE! BUT SINCE SEÑOR WAYNE CANNOT SHARE IN THE "TREASURE"-- AND I DID PROMISE HIM A REWARD...
...WHEN NEXT YOU SEE HIM, PLEASE GIVE HIM... THIS!
OLÉ!
24
THE END

BATMAN

the BRAVE and the BOLD

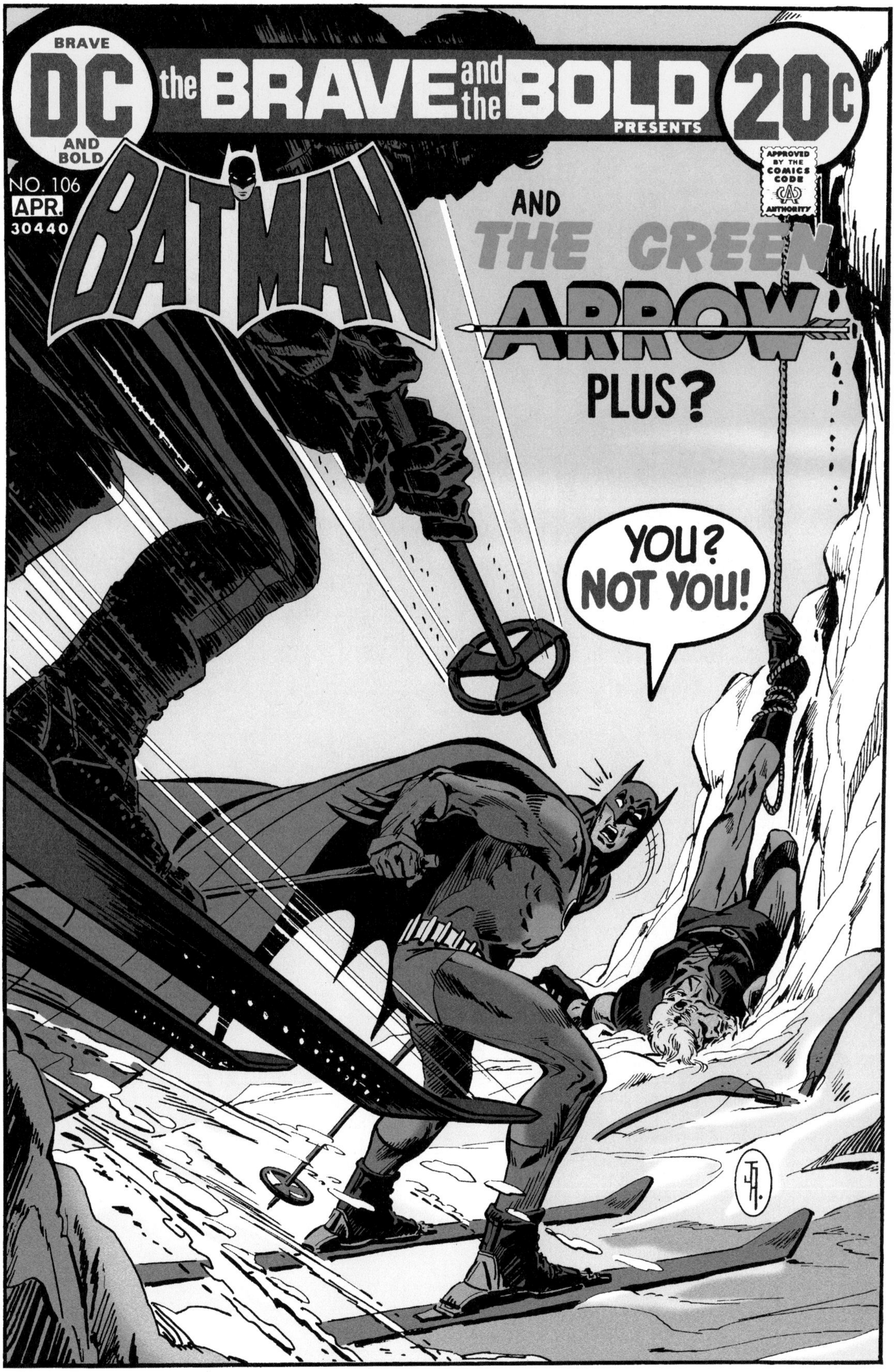
BRAVE DC AND BOLD
the BRAVE and the BOLD
PRESENTS
20c
APPROVED BY THE COMICS CODE AUTHORITY
NO. 106
APR.
30440
BATMAN
AND
THE GREEN ARROW
PLUS?
YOU? NOT YOU!

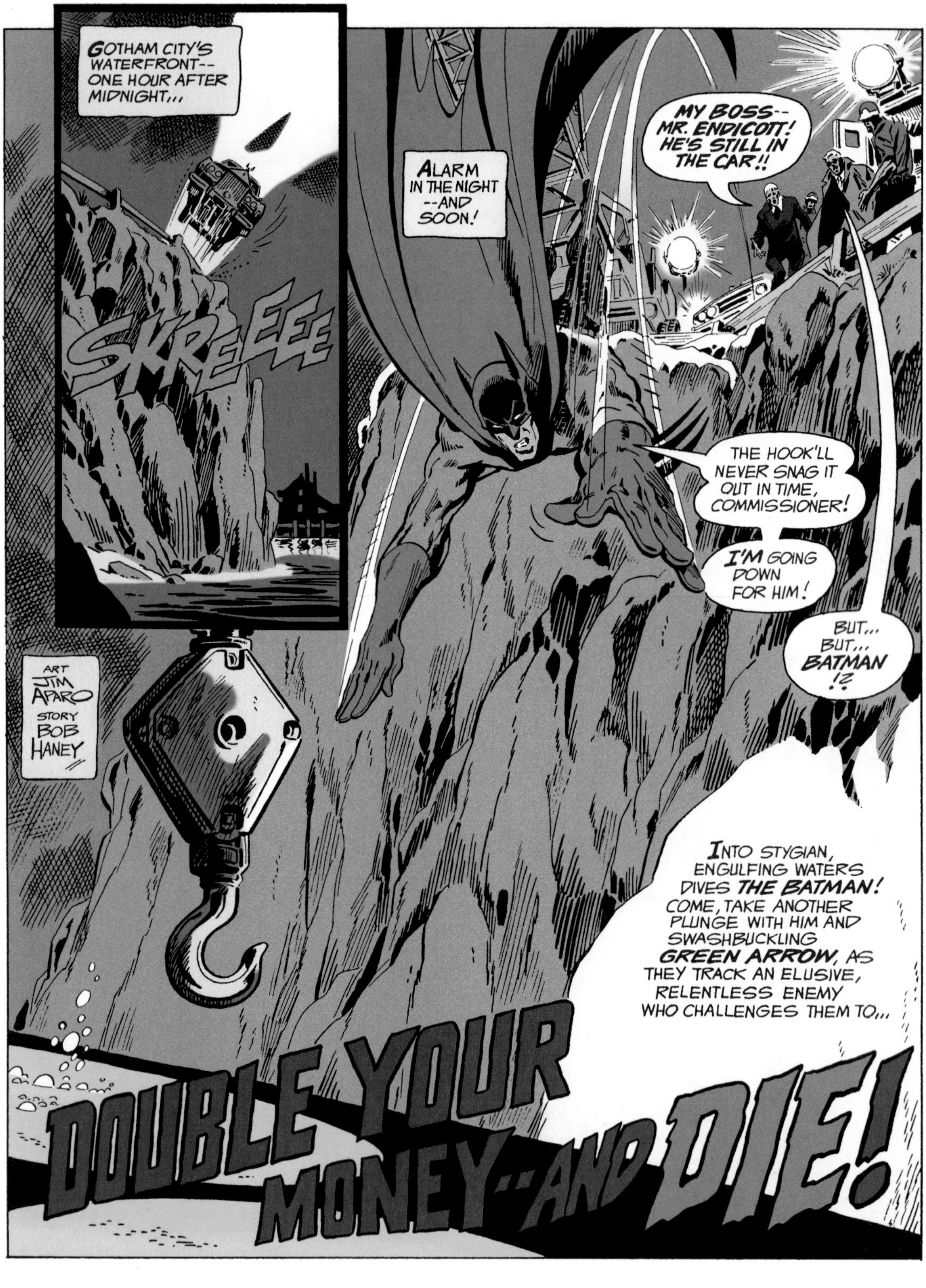
GOTHAM CITY'S WATERFRONT-- ONE HOUR AFTER MIDNIGHT...
SKREEEEE
ALARM IN THE NIGHT --AND SOON!
MY BOSS-- MR. ENDICOTT! HE'S STILL IN THE CAR!!
THE HOOK'LL NEVER SNAG IT OUT IN TIME, COMMISSIONER!
I'M GOING DOWN FOR HIM!
BUT... BUT... BATMAN !?
ART JIM APARO STORY BOB HANEY
INTO STYGIAN, ENGULFING WATERS DIVES THE BATMAN! COME, TAKE ANOTHER PLUNGE WITH HIM AND SWASHBUCKLING GREEN ARROW, AS THEY TRACK AN ELUSIVE, RELENTLESS ENEMY WHO CHALLENGES THEM TO...
DOUBLE YOUR MONEY--AND DIE!

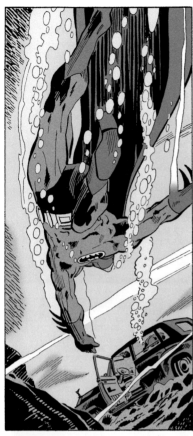

MOMENTS LATER... **DEAD... DROWNED!** NO HOPE OF RESUSCITATION!

THE CHAUFFEUR SAYS HE LOST CONTROL, AND AFTER THE CAR HIT THE RIVER BOTTOM, HE WAS ABLE TO BREATHE IN AN AIR BUBBLE TRAPPED IN THE DRIVER'S COMPARTMENT...

...TAKING A GULP OF AIR, HE MANAGED TO OPEN THE DOOR AND SURFACE TO PUT IN THE EMERGENCY CALL!

RESOURCEFUL FELLOW, COMMISSIONER! HE'S LUCKY TO BE ALIVE!

HMM, WHAT'S IN THE CORPSE'S CLENCHED FIST-- **A COIN?!**

WHY, IT'S **NOT** A COIN REALLY--BUT A KIND OF **STOCK** CERTIFICATE!

THE **STARR CORPORATION?** EVER HEAR OF IT?

NO, BUT A WEALTHY MAN LIKE THE VICTIM MUST'VE OWNED SHARES IN A NUMBER OF COMPANIES!

2

ON THE **REVERSE** SIDE... THE NUMBER **TWO**! ODD... IF THE THING'S GOOD FOR **ONE** SHARE! AND **WHY** WAS ENDICOTT CLUTCHING IT?

BUT HIS LUCK **RAN OUT** ON THIS RIDE! THE CHAUFFEUR MUST'VE LIKED HIS BOSS... LOOKS REAL BROKEN UP!

THE THING'S PROBABLY A PROMOTIONAL GIMMICK, **BATMAN**! HE MUST'VE CARRIED IT AS A LUCKY PIECE!

YES, QUITE-- CONSIDERING **HE'S** THE ONE WHO **MURDERED** HIM!

MURDER? YOU'RE **CRAZY**!

AM I? THE CHAUFFEUR SAYS HE TOOK A GULP OF TRAPPED AIR, THEN OPENED THE CAR DOOR TO SWIM CLEAR!

NO WAY, SINCE ESCAPE DRILLS FROM SUBMERGED VEHICLES HAVE PROVED...

... YOU HAVE TO WAIT TILL WATER SEEPS IN AND **EQUALIZES** THE PRESSURE ON THE DOOR'S OUTSIDE--BEFORE YOU CAN OPEN IT!

NO, I'LL BET OUR MOURNFUL CHAUFFEUR **DELIBERATELY** DROVE INTO THE DRINK-- BUT HE HIMSELF LEAPED CLEAR JUST BEFORE THE CAR WENT OVER!

THEN HE GOT HIMSELF CONVENIENTLY WET... AND CALLED FOR HELP!

3

ALSO, THE REAR WINDOW WAS OPEN SO ENDICOTT HAD NO CHANCE FOR A TRAPPED AIR BUBBLE--

AND ON THAT MODEL, THE WINDOWS CAN BE AUTOMATICALLY CONTROLLED BY THE *DRIVER!*

COME ON, *BATMAN!* A CLEVER THEORY-- BUT HARDLY PROOF OF HOMICIDE! AND WHAT'S THE *MOTIVE?*

I DON'T KNOW...*YET,* COMMISH-- BUT I WANT OFFICIAL TABS KEPT ON THE LATE, LAMENTED MR. ENDICOTT'S LOYAL EMPLOYEE!

LATER, THE DUSTY, ECHOING CORRIDORS OF A BUILDING FILLED WITH FILES AND MEN WITH MINDS LIKE FILES...

THE STARR CORPORATION, *BATMAN?* YES, IT'S CHARTERED LEGAL AND PROPER IN THIS STATE! IT HAS ONLY *FIVE* SHAREHOLDERS AND ITS TOTAL ASSETS CONSIST OF... *MISS SALOME STARR!*

HUH? YOU MEAN THE JET-SET PLAYGIRL?

THE ONE AND THE SAME! SHE WAS DUE TO *INHERIT TEN MILLION* NEXT JANUARY FIRST! BUT SHE COULDN'T WAIT-- NOR COULD HER HIGH-LIVING HABITS!

SO TWO YEARS AGO SHE SET UP A CORPORATION...

...AND SOLD SHARES IN HERSELF!

FOR AN INVESTMENT OF *ONE MILLION* EACH, *FIVE* SHARE HOLDERS WERE TO DIVIDE THE *TEN MILLION* TRUST FUND-- AS MISS STARR RE-NOUNCED ALL RIGHTS TO THE MONEY!

AMAZING! INGENIOUS!

4

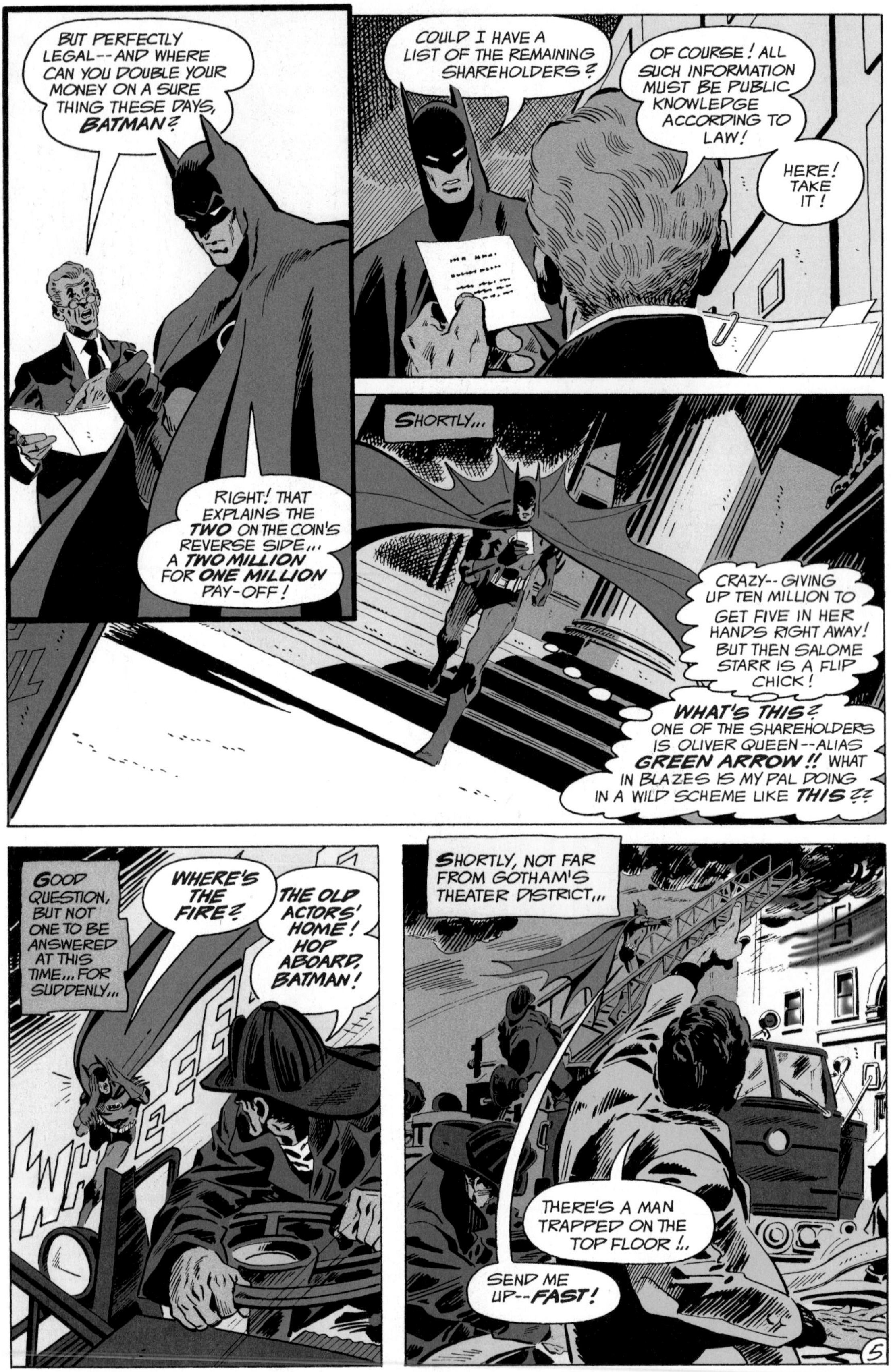

BUT PERFECTLY LEGAL--AND WHERE CAN YOU DOUBLE YOUR MONEY ON A SURE THING THESE DAYS, BATMAN?
RIGHT! THAT EXPLAINS THE TWO ON THE COIN'S REVERSE SIDE... A TWO MILLION FOR ONE MILLION PAY-OFF!
COULD I HAVE A LIST OF THE REMAINING SHAREHOLDERS?
OF COURSE! ALL SUCH INFORMATION MUST BE PUBLIC KNOWLEDGE ACCORDING TO LAW!
HERE! TAKE IT!
SHORTLY...
CRAZY--GIVING UP TEN MILLION TO GET FIVE IN HER HANDS RIGHT AWAY! BUT THEN SALOME STARR IS A FLIP CHICK!
WHAT'S THIS? ONE OF THE SHAREHOLDERS IS OLIVER QUEEN--ALIAS GREEN ARROW!! WHAT IN BLAZES IS MY PAL DOING IN A WILD SCHEME LIKE THIS??
GOOD QUESTION, BUT NOT ONE TO BE ANSWERED AT THIS TIME... FOR SUDDENLY...
WHERE'S THE FIRE?
THE OLD ACTORS' HOME! HOP ABOARD, BATMAN!
SHORTLY, NOT FAR FROM GOTHAM'S THEATER DISTRICT...
THERE'S A MAN TRAPPED ON THE TOP FLOOR!..
SEND ME UP--FAST!
5

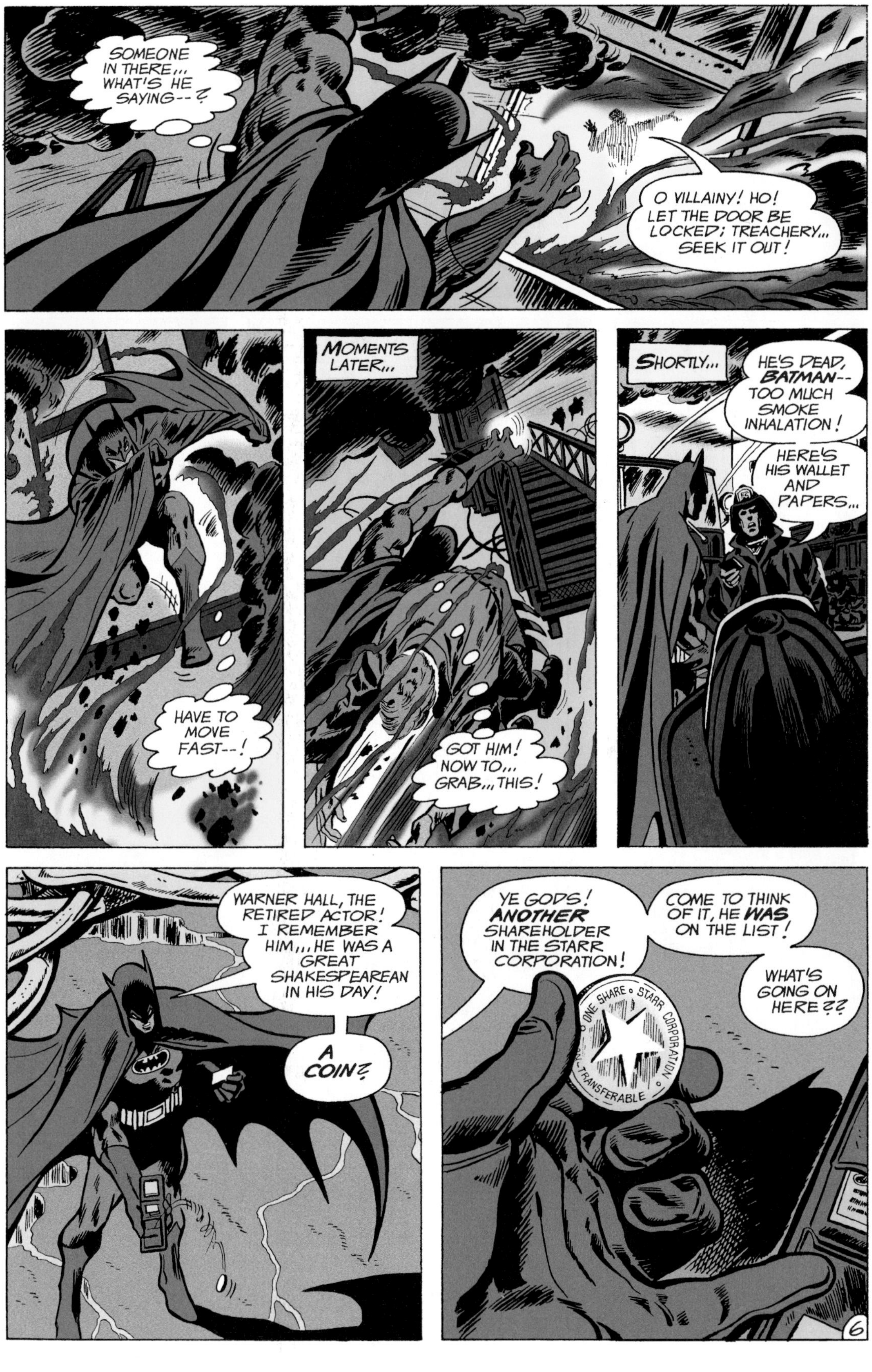

SOMEONE IN THERE,,, WHAT'S HE SAYING--?
O VILLAINY! HO! LET THE DOOR BE LOCKED; TREACHERY,,, SEEK IT OUT!
HAVE TO MOVE FAST--!
MOMENTS LATER,,,
GOT HIM! NOW TO,,, GRAB,,, THIS!
SHORTLY,,,
HE'S DEAD, BATMAN-- TOO MUCH SMOKE INHALATION!
HERE'S HIS WALLET AND PAPERS,,,
WARNER HALL, THE RETIRED ACTOR! I REMEMBER HIM,,, HE WAS A GREAT SHAKESPEAREAN IN HIS DAY!
A COIN?
YE GODS! ANOTHER SHAREHOLDER IN THE STARR CORPORATION!
COME TO THINK OF IT, HE WAS ON THE LIST!
WHAT'S GOING ON HERE??
ONE SHARE • STARR CORPORATION • NON-TRANSFERABLE
6

SOON, THE GOTHAM CITY MORGUE...

SO HALL SANK A LIFETIME OF HIS EARNINGS INTO THIS CRAZY CORPORATION! *ONE MILLION BUCKS*...

THEN LIVED ON CHARITY IN THE ACTORS' HOME WAITING FOR THE BIG PAY-OFF! ACTORS SURE ARE ODD BOZOS!

BUT HE DIES THE SAME DAY AS ENDICOTT-- ANOTHER SHAREHOLDER? THAT'S EVEN *ODDER!*

COINCIDENCE! HE MAY HAVE BEEN SMOKING IN BED!

HE DIDN'T SMOKE-- AND HIS LAST WORDS --FROM *"HAMLET"*-- SEEMED TO SAY SOMEONE SET THE FIRE TO KILL HIM *!!*

FIVE LITTLE SHAREHOLDERS... THEN THERE WERE *FOUR*... NOW *THREE!*

I TELL YOU, COMMISSIONER, *"SOMETHING'S ROTTEN IN THE STATE OF GOTHAM!"*

I KNOW, *"HAMLET,"* ACT ONE! *"BUT BE NOT BY EVERY BREEZE OF SUSPICION SWAYED!"*

SHAKESPEARE?

NO, GORDON! *HA! HA!*

VERY FUNNY, COMMISH--BUT I'M GOING TO LOOK *FURTHER* INTO THE AFFAIRS OF THE STARR CORPORATION!

SOME TIME LATER, A LITHE, WELL-TAILORED FIGURE ALIGHTS AT GOTHAM AIRPORT-- OLIVER QUEEN, OTHERWISE KNOWN AS THE GREAT *GREEN ARROW!*

HELLO, *BAT-BUDDY!* SURE, I BOUGHT INTO THAT COMPANY! I'M A PUSHOVER FOR WAY-OUT INVESTMENTS! BUT *THIS* ONE WILL PAY OFF!

IT MAY PAY OFF IN *DEATH!*

HMM, COULD BE COINCIDENCE... THOSE DEATHS!

I *DOUBT* IT! LET'S PAY A CALL ON THAT CHAUFFEUR-- HE'S STILL AT ENDICOTT'S ESTATE TRYING TO DRY OUT ONE ROLLS-ROYCE!

7

SHORTLY, THE GARAGE AT A SECLUDED SUBURBAN ESTATE...

BLAZES! HE'S *DEAD!*

A PROFESSIONAL LIKE *HIM?* HE'D BE LEERY OF MONOXIDE!

ENGINE'S RUNNING-- HE MUST'VE BEEN WORKING ON IT AND THE FUMES GOT HIM!

IT'S A COOL NIGHT-- HE PROBABLY CLOSED THE DOORS JUST FOR A LITTLE WHILE -- BUT MONOXIDE'S ODORLESS AND BUILDS UP FAST!

I SAY IT'S *ANOTHER* CASE OF MURDER!

WHAT? BUT HE WASN'T A SHARE- HOLDER!

HOW? SOMEONE WOULD HAVE TO BE *INSIDE* TO WORK THIS CONTROL BUTTON!

OR USE AN OUTSIDE REMOTE ELECTRONIC CONTROL-- IT'S EQUIPPED FOR THAT!

OLIVER, THIS CLINCHES IT FOR ME! SOMEONE'S KNOCKING OFF THE STARR CORPORATION SHAREHOLDERS-- *ONE BY ONE!*

CHECK, BUT I'M SURE HE KILLED HIS BOSS FOR A PRICE-- NOW HE WAS SLAIN TO KEEP HIM FROM TALKING!

LISTEN HOW SILENTLY IT MOVES! CHAUFFEUR HAS HEAD IN HOOD... DOOR CLOSES QUIETLY... IN A MINUTE IT'S ALL OVER!

I STILL CAN'T BUY IT! WHO WOULD PROFIT?

MAYBE ONE OF THE REMAINING SHAREHOLDERS! MAYBE....*YOU!*

VERY FUNNY--

BUT SERIOUSLY, *YOU* MIGHT BE THE KILLER'S NEXT TARGET! TIME FOR A "COLLECT CALL" TO THE CORONER TO COME GET THE CORPSE!

8

SOME TIME LATER, AS OLIVER QUEEN CROSSES TOWN TO HIS HOTEL...

BATMAN'S WRONG ABOUT ALL THIS... OF COURSE THE VICTIMS' BAD LUCK IS *MY* GOOD FORTUNE...

... IT WINDS UP WITH A BIGGER PAY-OFF FOR THE SURVIVORS!

HEY!

PARDON ME...

A RACKETING, ROCKETING MONSTER, THE TRAIN HURTLES DOWN THE LONG PLATFORM...

GROAAHHHR

... SLOWS, AND FINALLY SCREECHES TO A GRINDING HALT!

SSSKREE

9

AND SO, SHORTLY...

SO NOW YOU'RE A BELIEVER?

CHECK! SOMEBODY'S SURE OUT TO GET THIS LITTLE SHAREHOLDER! THAT WAS NO ACCIDENT! I WAS *TRIPPED*!

DID YOU GET A LOOK AT HIM?

"STANDING IN THAT TRACK-WALKER'S SAFETY NICHE, I GOT A GLIMPSE OF HIM THROUGH THE RUSHING TRAIN WINDOWS!"

HE HAD A WEIRD MUG-- ONE I'M NOT SURE I'D RECOGNIZE... BECAUSE THE WINDOWS DISTORTED HIS FEATURES!

WELL, WHOEVER HE WAS-- YOU BETTER NOT GIVE HIM ANOTHER GO AT OLIVER QUEEN!

NO WAY, CHUM! EXIT OLIVER QUEEN, *TARGET*-- ENTER *GREEN ARROW*, HUNTER!

RIGHT ON! OUR "FIRST ORDER OF BUSINESS" IS TO CHECK UP ON THE STARR CORPORATION'S SOLE ASSET-- *MISS SALOME STARR!*

IN THE NEXT FEW HOURS *THE BATMAN* AND *THE EMERALD ARCHER* COMB THE HAUNTS OF THE JET SET...

10

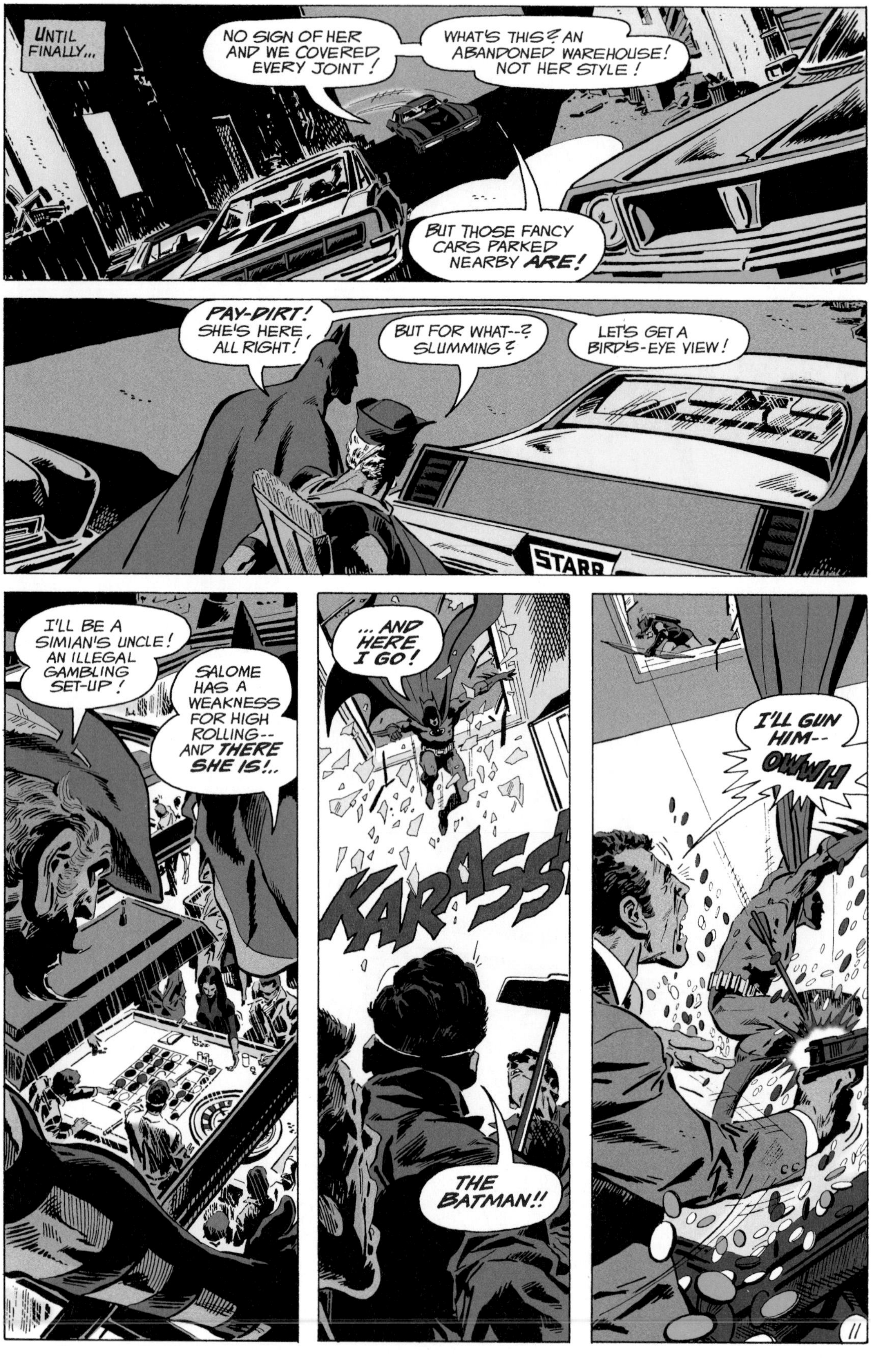
UNTIL FINALLY...
NO SIGN OF HER AND WE COVERED EVERY JOINT!
WHAT'S THIS? AN ABANDONED WAREHOUSE! NOT HER STYLE!
BUT THOSE FANCY CARS PARKED NEARBY ARE!
PAY-DIRT! SHE'S HERE, ALL RIGHT!
BUT FOR WHAT--? SLUMMING?
LET'S GET A BIRD'S-EYE VIEW!
STARR
I'LL BE A SIMIAN'S UNCLE! AN ILLEGAL GAMBLING SET-UP!
SALOME HAS A WEAKNESS FOR HIGH ROLLING-- AND THERE SHE IS!..
...AND HERE I GO!
KARASS
THE BATMAN!!
I'LL GUN HIM--
OWWH
11

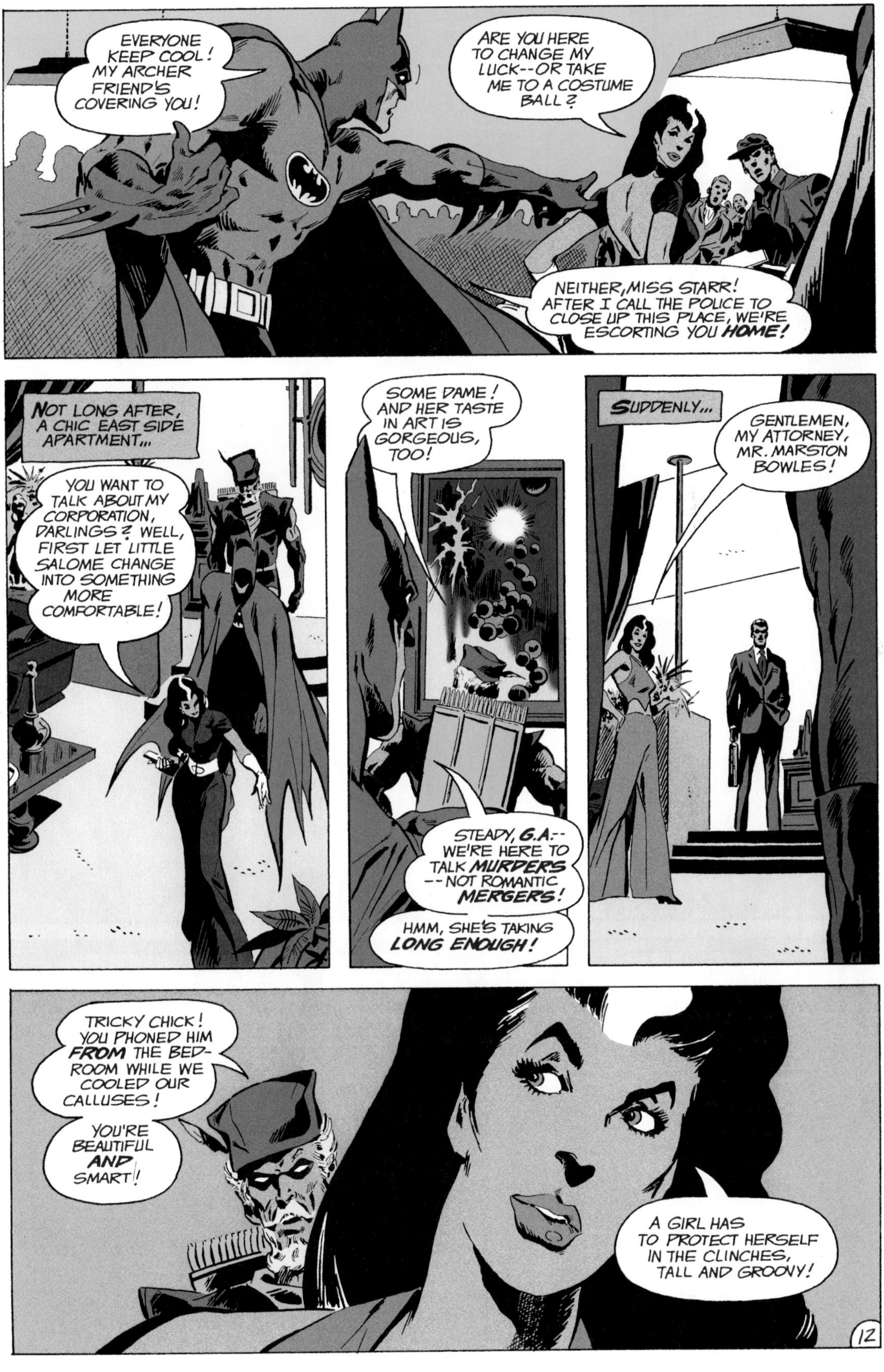
EVERYONE KEEP COOL! MY ARCHER FRIEND'S COVERING YOU!
ARE YOU HERE TO CHANGE MY LUCK--OR TAKE ME TO A COSTUME BALL?
NEITHER, MISS STARR! AFTER I CALL THE POLICE TO CLOSE UP THIS PLACE, WE'RE ESCORTING YOU HOME!
NOT LONG AFTER, A CHIC EAST SIDE APARTMENT...
YOU WANT TO TALK ABOUT MY CORPORATION, DARLINGS? WELL, FIRST LET LITTLE SALOME CHANGE INTO SOMETHING MORE COMFORTABLE!
SOME DAME! AND HER TASTE IN ART IS GORGEOUS, TOO!
STEADY, G.A.-- WE'RE HERE TO TALK MURDERS --NOT ROMANTIC MERGERS!
HMM, SHE'S TAKING LONG ENOUGH!
SUDDENLY...
GENTLEMEN, MY ATTORNEY, MR. MARSTON BOWLES!
TRICKY CHICK! YOU PHONED HIM FROM THE BED-ROOM WHILE WE COOLED OUR CALLUSES!
YOU'RE BEAUTIFUL AND SMART!
A GIRL HAS TO PROTECT HERSELF IN THE CLINCHES, TALL AND GROOVY!
12

I HAVE INSTRUCTED MISS STARR TO REMAIN SILENT! I WILL ANSWER ANY QUESTIONS!

OKAY, TWO OF HER CORPORATION SHARE-HOLDERS ARE *DEAD*-- MURDERED, I'D SAY-- AND TONIGHT A THIRD, MR. OLIVER QUEEN, NARROWLY ESCAPED A SIMILAR FATE!

UNFORTUNATE, THESE ...UH... ACCIDENTS! BUT EVEN IF THEY *ARE* MURDER, MISS STARR IS IN THE CLEAR! AS YOU KNOW, SHE RENOUNCED ALL CLAIMS TO THE INHERITANCE!

PERHAPS ONE OF THE REMAINING SHAREHOLDERS IS BEHIND IT!

MAYBE--BUT WHO GETS THE *TEN MILLION* IF *ALL* THE SHAREHOLDERS DIE? AND WHY ARE THE SHARES NON-TRANS-FERABLE?

ANSWER ME THAT, LAWYER-MAN!

UHHH... *DON'T!*

THE MONEY WOULD THEN GO TO THE DORF MEDICAL RESEARCH CLINIC OF GRINDL, SWITZERLAND! A WORTHY CAUSE!

AND, OF COURSE, THEREFORE, THE SHAREHOLDERS COULD NOT PASS THEM ON TO THEIR OWN HEIRS!

HMM, I SEE--!

AN ARRANGEMENT OF WHICH I FULLY *APPROVE*, BATMAN-- JUST AS I *DISAPPROVE* OF YOU BULLYING MY ATTORNEY! IF THERE ARE NO MORE QUESTIONS ...*PLEASE LEAVE!*

YOU WERE KIND OF ROUGH ON THEM!

SURE, I WANTED TO SIZE UP MISS SALOME STARR! HER NERVOUS ATTORNEY BOTHERS ME! NOTICE HOW HE FLINCHED WHEN I FLIPPED THE COIN AT HIM?

13

YOU MAY HAVE SCARED *HIM*, BUT NOT SALOME! SHE'S SOME CHICK!

YOU SAID, THE BOZO WHO SHOVED YOU IN THE SUBWAY HAD A *WEIRD FACE?*

LIKE I SAID, IT COULD HAVE BEEN DISTORTION AND--

WE'VE GOT TO GO BACK!

SKREECH

MINUTES LATER...

WHAT DO YOU MEAN WE CAN'T GO UP TO MISS STARR'S SUITE?

SHE AND MR. BOWLES LEFT TO CATCH THE MID-NIGHT FLIGHT TO SWITZERLAND!

PLEASE, *BATMAN..!!*

COME ON, *G.A.!* WE'VE GOT TO STOP THEM! WE'VE GOT TO STOP *TWO-FACE!*

TWO-FACE?! DID YOU FLIP YOUR COWL?

HE'S ONE OF THE STRANGEST CRIMINAL GENIUSES WHO EVER *LIVED*... ONE OF THE MOST *TRAGIC*... AND ONE OF THE *DEADLIEST!*

"ONCE HE WAS GOTHAM'S BRILLIANT YOUNG DISTRICT ATTORNEY, HARVEY DENT-- FUTURE UNLIMITED! ONE DAY IN COURT, A TWO-BIT GANGSTER HURLED ACID INTO HIS FACE--!"

14

"HIS FACE WAS RUINED ON *ONE* SIDE--AND THE BITTER IRONY OF IT HAPPENING IN HIS OWN COURT, SNAPPED DENT'S MIND! HE BECAME *TWO-FACE*, CRIMINAL EXTRAORDINARY..."

THE COIN WILL DECIDE IF I COMMIT A CRIME TONIGHT!

WHICH FACE... WHICH SIDE WILL IT SHOW--THE *WHOLE* OR THE *RUINED*?

IT HAS *DECIDED!* THE MARRED SIDE IS UP! THE *EVIL* PART OF MY NATURE WINS--

TWO-FACE MUST STRIKE!

TWO-FACE AND I TANGLED MANY TIMES-- HIS BRILLIANT MIND AND DIABOLICAL CUNNING MADE HIM A FANTASTIC FOE!

BUT WHAT ABOUT PLASTIC SURGERY? THESE DAYS, HIS FACE-- AND PERSONALITY-- COULD BE RESTORED!

IT *WAS*--BUT HARVEY DENT IS DOGGED BY TRAGIC IRONY!

" RETURNED TO SANITY AND HIS LEGAL CAREER, ONE UNHOLY DAY HE INTERRUPTED A ROBBERY! A SAFE-CRACKER'S NITRO BLEW HIS RESTORED FEATURES BACK TO THE OTHER STATE-- PERMANENTLY!"

AIEEE

FTOOM

GOTHAM AIRPORT

HIS FACE COULDN'T BE REPAIRED AGAIN! HARVEY DENT RETURNED TO HIS CRIMINAL CAREER!...

BUT ARE YOU SURE IT'S HIM, *BATMAN?*

SURE? I WAS A FOOL NOT TO SEE IT BEFORE!

HE HAS A MANIA FOR THE NUMBER *TWO!* THAT'S WHY THE *TWO* FOR *ONE* PAY-OFF FOR THE STARR SHAREHOLDERS-- WHICH *TWO-FACE*, POSING AS MARSTON BOWLES, SET UP! ALL THE OTHER CLUES POINT TO HIM!

I DIG! BUT WHY SUCH A COMPLICATED DEVIOUS PLOT TO GET SALOME STARR'S MOOLAH!?

15

BECAUSE SUCH APPEALS TO HIM-- AND IT SEEMED FOOL-PROOF! BESIDES, MAYBE SHE'S *IN* ON IT WITH HIM!

I'D HATE TO BELIEVE THAT, *BATMAN!!* BESIDES, IF ALL THE SHAREHOLDERS DIE, THAT SWISS CLINIC GETS THE MONEY!

THE CLINIC COULD BE A PHONEY FRONT-- FOR *TWO-FACE!*

HERE IT COMES! WE MUST STOP IT!

WITH *WHAT?* THAT BIRD'S TOO BIG FOR ONE OF MY SHAFTS!

DOWN, YOU FOOL--!

YOU WON'T ESCAPE ME, TWO-FACE!

THERE THEY GO--NEXT STOP, SWITZERLAND!

THE CLINIC'S IN GRINDL! SAY, THE STARR CORPORATION IS THERE, TOO! IT PAYS OFF ITS REMAINING SHAREHOLDERS NEW YEAR'S DAY!

HEY, THAT'S *NEXT WEEK!*

HOW'S YOUR SKI LEGS, OLD BUDDY?

NOT BAD-- BUT MY YODEL'S EVEN BETTER! WANNA HEAR?

SAVE YOUR BREATH--BECAUSE WE'RE GOING TO NEED IT TO TRACK *TWO-FACE!*

16

363

DAYS LATER... GRINDL, A PARADISE OF DAZZLING SNOW, PURE AIR, AND SKY-SCRATCHING PEAKS...

WE'VE BEEN HERE ALMOST A WEEK, BRUCE, AND NO SIGN OF *TWO-FACE*... *OR* HIS PHONEY COVER IDENTITY, MARSTON BOWLES!

SALOME STARR'S HERE, OLIVER -- SO HE'S *GOT* TO BE AROUND!

HE MUST TRY TO ELIMINATE YOU AND THE OTHER *TWO* STOCKHOLDERS BEFORE NEW YEAR'S DAY!

YEAH, SO I ROMANCE SALOME -- BUT I'M REALLY JUST KILLER-BAIT! SOME DEAL!

SHHH! HERE SHE COMES!

THERE YOU ARE, MALE CHAUVINISTS! LEAVING POOR LITTLE SALOME BEHIND! COME ON, OLIVER, RACE YOU TO THE LODGE!

UH... SURE, DOLL! SEE YOU, BRUCE!

DIE FESTUNG -- MEANING *THE FORTRESS!* BEAUTIFUL MOUNTAIN... BUT DANGEROUS -- JUST LIKE SALOME! IS SHE *PART* OF *TWO-FACE'S* DEADLY SCHEME... OR HIS *INNOCENT* PAWN?

THE FOLLOWING MORNING...

TOMORROW'S THE LAST DAY OF THE YEAR! THE TWO REMAINING SHARE OWNERS ARE DUE FROM THE STATES TODAY... ARRIVING HERE BY 'COPTER FROM THE GENEVA JETPORT!

17

THERE IT IS NOW-- SHOULD BE HERE IN MINUTES!..

WHAM

GOOD LORD!!

SUDDEN DISASTER... COLD DEATH!

A TRAGIC ACCIDENT, MEINE HERREN-- THE CANNON WE USE TO START AVALANCHES WAS OFF JUST A *FRACTION* IN ITS SIGHTING!

JA, THE CREW DIDN'T CHECK... IT WAS SUCH A REGULAR ROUTINE TO FIRE IT THIS TIME EACH DAY!

A TRAGIC ACCIDENT, ALL RIGHT--ARRANGED BY *TWO-FACE!* FIVE LITTLE SHAREHOLDERS... NOW THERE'S ONLY *ONE-- YOU, OLIVER!!*

BRRR--DON'T REMIND ME, BRUCIE-BOY!

AND SHORTLY...

FOUR COINS! YOU'RE GETTING QUITE A COLLECTION, BUDDY!

THESE ARE *FOUR* DEAD HUMAN BEINGS, OLIVER! *TWO-FACE* BEAT US AGAIN... WE ONLY GET *ONE* MORE CHANCE!

HE'S OUT THERE SOMEWHERE--WAITING-- BUT WE'VE GOT TO TRAP HIM! *THE FORTRESS,* OLIVER-- YOU'RE GOING TO *CONQUER* IT!!

WHAT??

18

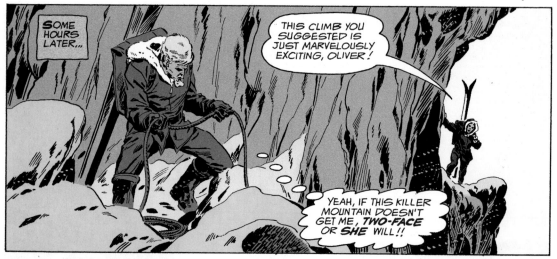

SOME HOURS LATER...

THIS CLIMB YOU SUGGESTED IS JUST MARVELOUSLY EXCITING, OLIVER!

YEAH, IF THIS KILLER MOUNTAIN DOESN'T GET ME, *TWO-FACE* OR *SHE* WILL!!

PERFECT! HE SWINGS ACROSS EMPTY AIR TO JOIN HIS LADY LOVE--!

DONE! FIVE LITTLE SHAREHOLDERS... NOW THERE ARE *NONE!*

SUDDEN DISASTER-- ROCKY DEATH?

OR IS IT?

OLIVER! OLIVER! WHAT HAPPENED?

SHE CAN'T MOVE FROM THERE--AND ALSO CAN'T SEE ME SWITCH TO MY *G.A.* TOGS!

19

HOPE MY QUICK-INFLATABLE DUMMY FOOLED THAT WOULD-BE ASSASSIN--!

NOW TO JOIN *BATMAN* TO TRY AND BAG HIM!

WE SMOKED *TWO-FACE* OUT! HE'S JUST AHEAD!

KAPOW

KAP

THE BATMAN! I'LL STOP HIM!

WP

VIP

GOT TO PUT A LITTLE ZIG IN MY ZAG!

THEN, AS THE TRAIL PLUNGES DOWN THROUGH A PATCH OF PINES...

ROPE! IT'LL RACK ME UP...

...UNLESS I CAN SOAR LIKE A BAT!

HE'S *STILL* ON MY TRACKS!

20

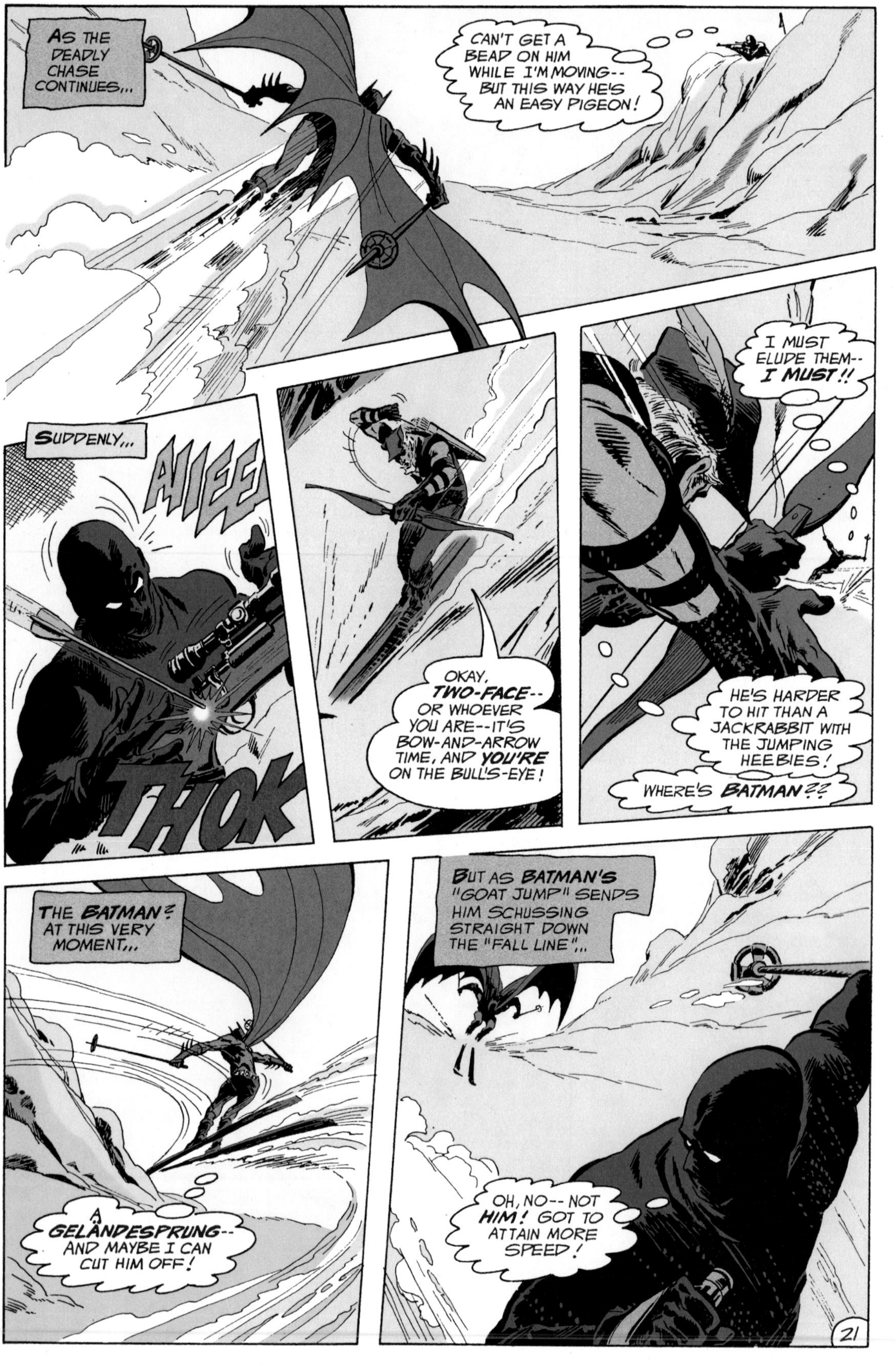
AS THE DEADLY CHASE CONTINUES...
CAN'T GET A BEAD ON HIM WHILE I'M MOVING-- BUT THIS WAY HE'S AN EASY PIGEON!
SUDDENLY...
AIEE
THOK
OKAY, TWO-FACE-- OR WHOEVER YOU ARE--IT'S BOW-AND-ARROW TIME, AND YOU'RE ON THE BULL'S-EYE!
I MUST ELUDE THEM-- I MUST!!
HE'S HARDER TO HIT THAN A JACKRABBIT WITH THE JUMPING HEEBIES!
WHERE'S BATMAN??
THE BATMAN? AT THIS VERY MOMENT...
A GELÄNDESPRUNG-- AND MAYBE I CAN CUT HIM OFF!
BUT AS BATMAN'S "GOAT JUMP" SENDS HIM SCHUSSING STRAIGHT DOWN THE "FALL LINE"...
OH, NO-- NOT HIM! GOT TO ATTAIN MORE SPEED!
21

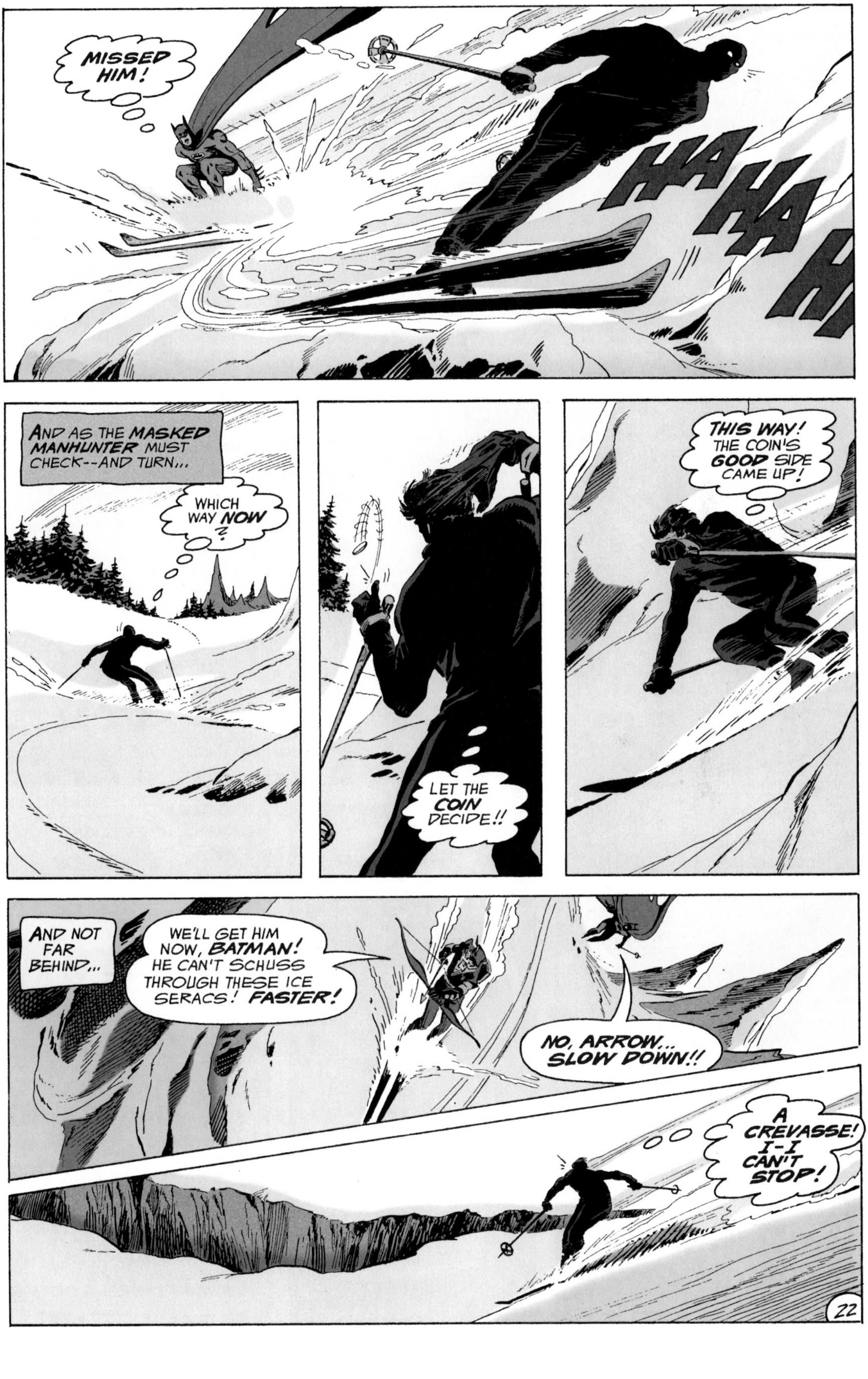
MISSED HIM!
HA HA HA H
AND AS THE MASKED MANHUNTER MUST CHECK--AND TURN...
WHICH WAY NOW?
LET THE COIN DECIDE!!
THIS WAY! THE COIN'S GOOD SIDE CAME UP!
AND NOT FAR BEHIND...
WE'LL GET HIM NOW, BATMAN! HE CAN'T SCHUSS THROUGH THESE ICE SERACS! FASTER!
NO, ARROW... SLOW DOWN!!
A CREVASSE! I-I CAN'T STOP!
22

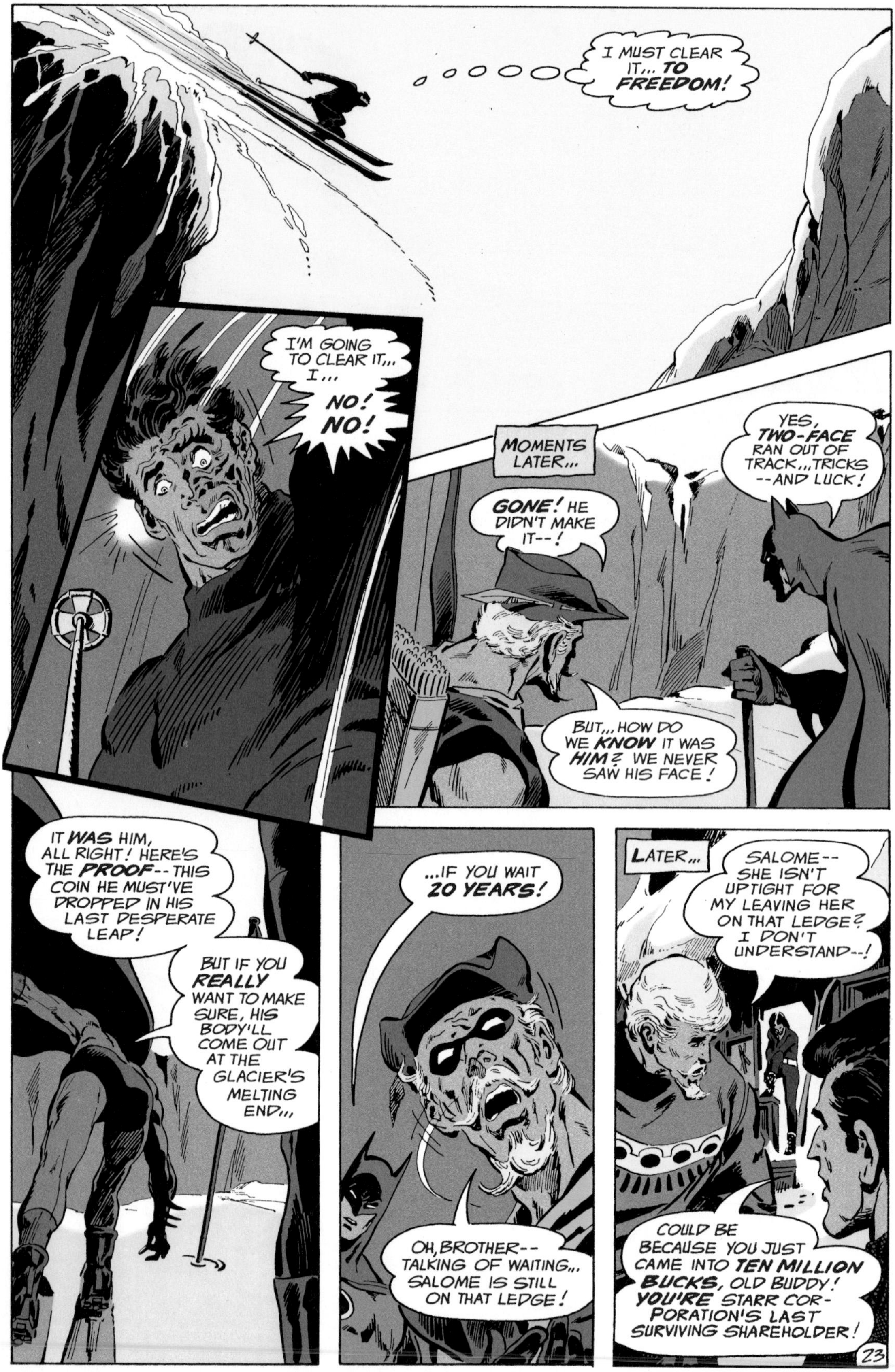
I MUST CLEAR IT... TO FREEDOM!
I'M GOING TO CLEAR IT,,, I,,, NO! NO!
MOMENTS LATER...
YES, TWO-FACE RAN OUT OF TRACK,,, TRICKS --AND LUCK!
GONE! HE DIDN'T MAKE IT--!
BUT,,, HOW DO WE KNOW IT WAS HIM? WE NEVER SAW HIS FACE!
IT WAS HIM, ALL RIGHT! HERE'S THE PROOF-- THIS COIN HE MUST'VE DROPPED IN HIS LAST DESPERATE LEAP!
BUT IF YOU REALLY WANT TO MAKE SURE, HIS BODY'LL COME OUT AT THE GLACIER'S MELTING END,,,
...IF YOU WAIT 20 YEARS!
OH, BROTHER-- TALKING OF WAITING,,, SALOME IS STILL ON THAT LEDGE!
LATER...
SALOME-- SHE ISN'T UPTIGHT FOR MY LEAVING HER ON THAT LEDGE? I DON'T UNDERSTAND--!
COULD BE BECAUSE YOU JUST CAME INTO TEN MILLION BUCKS, OLD BUDDY! YOU'RE STARR CORPORATION'S LAST SURVIVING SHAREHOLDER!
23

OH, WOW... I *FORGOT!* THEN, SHE WASN'T IN ON *TWO-FACE'S* SCHEME--!

NO, I CHECKED OUT THAT DORF CLINIC! IT'S DEDICATED TO RESEARCH IN PLASTIC SURGERY!

TWO-FACE WAS ELIMINATING *ALL* THE SHAREHOLDERS...

24

... SO THE CLINIC WOULD GET THE MONEY AND PERFECT A WAY TO RESTORE HIS FEATURES -- *AND* HIS LIFE!

AS BOWLES, HE SET THE WHOLE THING UP-- AND SALOME WAS HIS INNOCENT PAWN!

WHEW! SO *THAT* WAS HIS MOTIVE? I ALMOST FEEL SORRY FOR HIM!

YES, HIS LIFE WAS ONE OF TRAGEDY AND IRONY!

ALL THAT'S LEFT OF ITS BRILLIANT PROMISE ... IS A *MARRED* COIN!

TWO-FACE GONE?? THAT SECRET, *BRAVE & BOLD ONES*, IS LOCKED IN THE GLACIER'S ICY HEART! WHO KNOWS IF THIS IS REALLY...

THE END.

the **BRAVE** and the **BOLD**

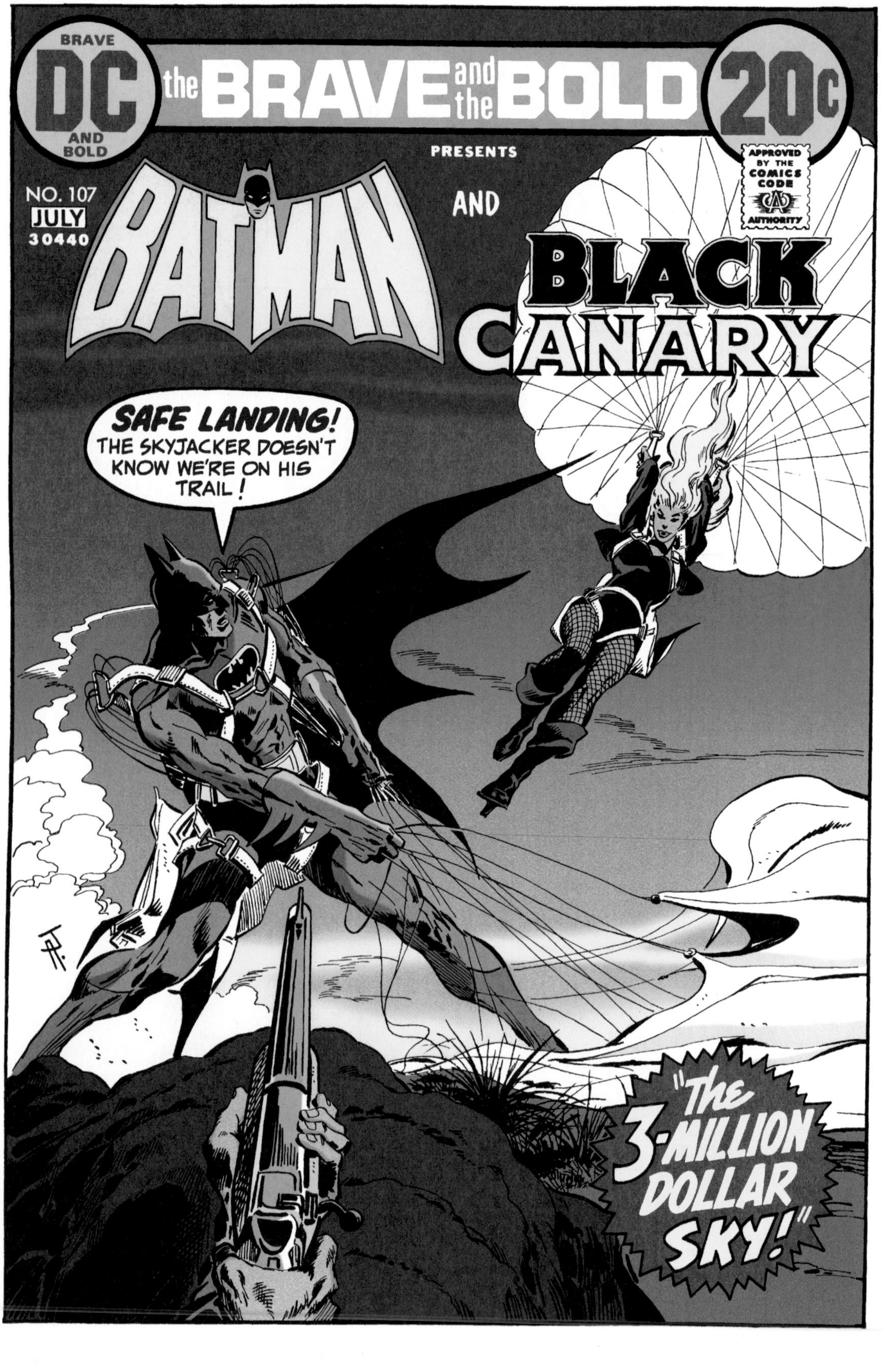
BRAVE
DC
AND BOLD
the BRAVE and the BOLD
20c
PRESENTS
APPROVED BY THE COMICS CODE AUTHORITY
NO. 107
JULY
30440
BATMAN
AND
BLACK CANARY
SAFE LANDING! THE SKYJACKER DOESN'T KNOW WE'RE ON HIS TRAIL!
"The 3-MILLION DOLLAR SKY!"

"THE 3-MILLION DOLLAR SKY"

GOTHAM AIRPORT! A JET-LINER MAKES AN UNSCHEDULED LANDING AS TWO FAMILIAR FIGURES RACE ONTO THE SCENE...

HERE COMES THE SKYJACKED SHIP, *BATMAN!*

MY GOD-- IT'S GOING TO *CRASH!!*

THE PILOT'S GOT TO PULL HER OUT, COMMISSIONER! THERE ARE 93 INNOCENT HOSTAGES ABOARD!

AND AS SIRENS WAIL, MIGHTY ENGINES WHINE, AND HUGE TIRES BURN INTO THE CONCRETE, THE *MASKED MANHUNTER* IS FLUNG INTO THE AERIAL ADVENTURE OF OUR TURBULENT AGE," WHEREIN ONLY *BLACK CANARY,* HEROINE EXTRAORDINAIRE, CAN AID HIM IN WRESTING TRIUMPH FROM DISASTER!

SKREEEEEEE

PART 1

"ONE OF OUR JETS IS SKYJACKED..."

HE DID IT! HE PULLED HER OUT!!

SKREEEEEEE EEEE EEE EEEHHOOOOO

THIS IS THE SKYJACKER TALKING!

STAY BACK, BATMAN! I KNOW GOTHAM CITY'S YOUR TURF--BUT I HAD TO LAND HERE! NOW YOU LISTEN TO ME...

...IF YOU WANT THESE PASSENGERS LET GO SAFELY, YOU'LL DELIVER WITHIN THE HOUR, IN SMALL BILLS, A RANSOM OF... THREE MILLION BUCKS!!

THREE MILLION!? WHY, THAT'S BIGGER THAN ANY SKYJACKER DEMAND YET--!

CHALK IT UP TO THE HIGH COST OF LIVING, COMMISSIONER!

BUT IT'LL TURN INTO THE HIGH COST OF DYING-- IF WE DON'T PLAY BALL AND GET THOSE HOSTAGES OFF ALIVE!

NOW FOR MY OTHER DEMAND! I WANT RELEASED IMMEDIATELY FROM STATE PRISON AND BROUGHT HERE WITH THE MONEY... MONK DEVLIN!

2

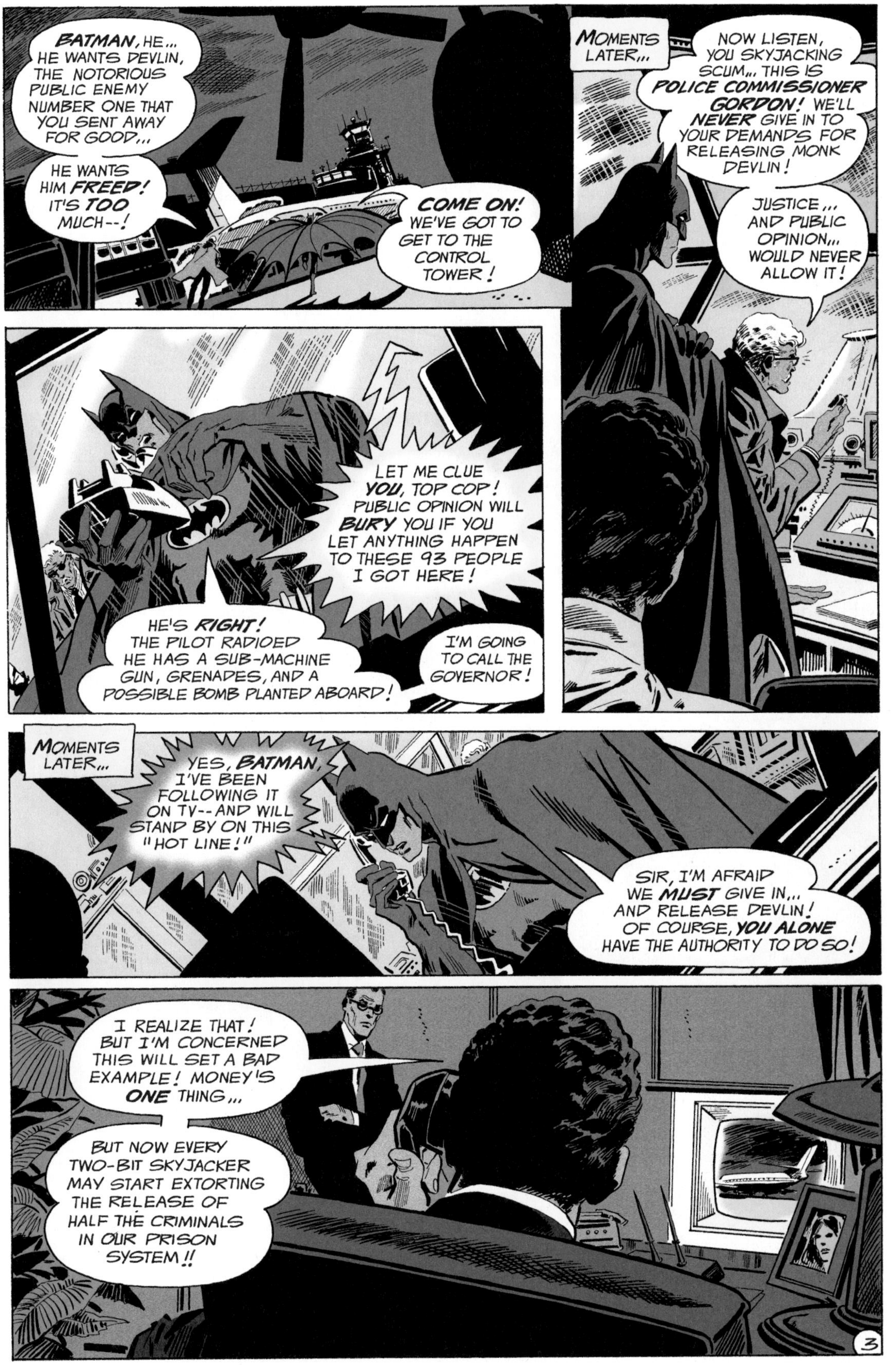
BATMAN, HE... HE WANTS DEVLIN, THE NOTORIOUS PUBLIC ENEMY NUMBER ONE THAT YOU SENT AWAY FOR GOOD...
HE WANTS HIM FREED! IT'S TOO MUCH--!
COME ON! WE'VE GOT TO GET TO THE CONTROL TOWER!
MOMENTS LATER...
NOW LISTEN, YOU SKYJACKING SCUM... THIS IS POLICE COMMISSIONER GORDON! WE'LL NEVER GIVE IN TO YOUR DEMANDS FOR RELEASING MONK DEVLIN!
JUSTICE... AND PUBLIC OPINION... WOULD NEVER ALLOW IT!
LET ME CLUE YOU, TOP COP! PUBLIC OPINION WILL BURY YOU IF YOU LET ANYTHING HAPPEN TO THESE 93 PEOPLE I GOT HERE!
HE'S RIGHT! THE PILOT RADIOED HE HAS A SUB-MACHINE GUN, GRENADES, AND A POSSIBLE BOMB PLANTED ABOARD!
I'M GOING TO CALL THE GOVERNOR!
MOMENTS LATER...
YES, BATMAN, I'VE BEEN FOLLOWING IT ON TV--AND WILL STAND BY ON THIS "HOT LINE!"
SIR, I'M AFRAID WE MUST GIVE IN... AND RELEASE DEVLIN! OF COURSE, YOU ALONE HAVE THE AUTHORITY TO DO SO!
I REALIZE THAT! BUT I'M CONCERNED THIS WILL SET A BAD EXAMPLE! MONEY'S ONE THING...
BUT NOW EVERY TWO-BIT SKYJACKER MAY START EXTORTING THE RELEASE OF HALF THE CRIMINALS IN OUR PRISON SYSTEM!!
3

BUT, GOVERNOR, THAT *WON'T* HAPPEN IF I BUST THIS CASE AFTER WE GET THOSE HOSTAGES CLEAR! IF YOU RELEASE DEVLIN...

... I SWEAR I'LL BRING HIM AND HIS SKYJACKING PAL *RIGHT BACK HERE* TO THIS FIELD, OR I'LL HANG UP MY CAPE AND COWL FOR GOOD!

VERY WELL, *BATMAN!* I'LL GIVE THE ORDER FOR DEVLIN'S RELEASE!

AND SO, SHORTLY, FAR UP THE GOTHAM RIVER, AT STATE PRISON...

LISTEN TO THAT HYENA, WARDEN! NEVER THOUGHT I'D SEE HIM WALK OUT OF HERE! YOU SURE *BATMAN'S* DOIN' RIGHT?...

HE'S GOT NO CHOICE! *NOBODY* DOES!

HA! HA! HA!

AN HOUR LATER, BY FAST HELICOPTER...

HELLO, *BATMAN!* THOUGHT YOU'D PUT ME AWAY FOR GOOD, DIDN'T YOU? BUT YOU SEE I GOT AN UNKNOWN FRIEND! *HA! HA!*

HMMM, ODD THAT DEVLIN DOESN'T *KNOW* HIS RESCUER... BUT ALSO HE DOESN'T KNOW I PROMISED TO BRING HIM BACK... *NO MATTER WHAT!*

SOON...

THERE HE GOES--WITH *THREE MILLION DOLLARS*... A MURDERER, A DRUG TRAFFICKER! I...I CAN'T STAND THIS!

HA HA HA

KEEP A GRIP ON YOURSELF, COMMISSIONER! THERE ARE TIMES THAT TRY MEN'S SOULS! THIS IS SUCH A TIME!

4

AND AS MONK DEVLIN STEPS INTO THE PARKED JET,...

WHY,... I *KNOW* YOU! WILLIE,... WILLIE KRESH! TONY'S LITTLE BROTHER!!

CHECK, MONK! MY BROTHER WAS ALWAYS LOYAL TO YOU-- IT'S A FAMILY TRAIT!

YEAH, TOO BAD TONY GOT KNOCKED OFF YEARS AGO! HE WAS *TOPS!*

IF I'D HAD MORE GUYS LIKE HIM, I'D NEVER HAVE BEEN SENT AWAY! THE OLD MOB'S GONE,... BROKEN UP!..

BUT YOU AND I, KID, WE'RE A *NEW* TEAM! WE'RE GONNA LIVE FREE AND CLEAR LIKE KINGS WITH *THIS!* HOW CAN I THANK YOU, BUDDY?

THIS CAPER HAS ITS OWN REWARDS BUILT IN, MONK! NOW LET'S ATTEND TO BUSINESS!

THIS IS THE SKYJACKER, CAPTAIN! YOUR NEXT STOP WILL BE *SAN PEDRO!*

SOUTH AMERICA? THAT'S THOUSANDS OF MILES,... I NEED A FLIGHT ENGINEER! AND AT LEAST ONE STEWARDESS ...IT'LL TAKE A LOT OF HOT COFFEE TO GET US THERE! ...

OKAY, CAPTAIN! BUT NO FUNNY BUSINESS-- OR THESE PASSENGERS WILL MAKE THE TRIP WITH US!

GREAT! THE PILOT, CAPTAIN STANTON, IS GIVING US A CHANCE,... THE CHANCE WE DESPERATELY NEED!

KLIK

WHAT ARE YOU COOKING UNDER YOUR COWL?

5

COMMISSIONER GORDON'S ANSWER COMES WITHIN THE HOUR...

BLACK CANARY!? WHAT ARE YOU DOING HERE--?

WHEN THE BAT WHISTLES, THE CANARY FLIES, COMMISSIONER!

BEAUTIFUL, DINAH! NOW WE'VE NO TIME TO LOSE! COME ALONG--!

BLACK CANARY, ALIAS DINAH LANCE, THE GORGEOUS JUSTICE LEAGUE CHICK FROM EARTH TWO, NOW A FORMIDABLE HEROINE ON OUR OWN EARTH-ONE! SHORTLY...

FLIGHT ENGINEER TODD AND STEWARDESS DINAH LANCE REPORTING FOR EMERGENCY DUTY!

WHAT?? !!

BATMAN... IS IT REALLY YOU?

GOOD DISGUISE, EH? WE'VE GOT TO FOOL DEVLIN AND THAT SKYJACKER OR IT COULD BE THE END OF BOTH OUR CAREERS!

SO NOW, AS THE PARKED JET TAKES ON TWO "NEW" CREW MEMBERS...

THE PASSENGERS AND REGULAR STEWARDESSES ARE BEING RELEASED! THANK THE STARS!

SO FAR SO GOOD!

NOW YOU CAN'T USE YOUR SONIC WHAMMY POWERS INSIDE THE PLANE, DINAH! WE'LL BE FLYING PRESSURIZED MOST OF THE WAY!..

I DIG, BATMAN! BESIDES, I CAN'T OFTEN CONTROL THE DIRECTION OF MY STRANGE MUTANT POWER!

SO MY JUDO AND REFLEXES WILL HAVE TO DO THE JOB!

6

THE SKYJACKER'S GOT THE PILOT'S COMPARTMENT LOCKED OFF FROM THE REST OF THE SHIP! WE'LL STAY IN SECRET CONTACT VIA WRIST WATCH RADIO!

GOOD LUCK!

WE'LL **BOTH** NEED SOME OF THAT! HERE GOES--!

AND AS DAWN BEGINS TO TINT THE BLACKENED SKY, A HUSHED GROUP WATCHES HELPLESSLY...

THERE THEY GO--! YOU'VE GOT TO WIN **THIS** ONE, **BATMAN!** YOU'VE JUST **GOT** TO!

INSIDE THE STEEPLY CLIMBING JET...

HEY, KRESH! WE'RE GOING **FIRST CLASS!**

HEY, STEWARDESS! AREN'T YOU GOING TO ASK IF WE WANT COFFEE, TEA, OR MILK?

WHY... YES, SIR! WHAT WOULD YOU LIKE?

TWO COFFEES, DOLL... AND THE GALLEY'S **THAT** WAY--!

UH... OF COURSE, I... I JUST WANTED TO SEE IF THE PILOT AND CREW WANTED ANYTHING!

YOU STAY OUT **OF THERE** -- I DON'T WANT NO MESSAGES PASSED BETWEEN **YOU** AND **THEM!**

UNDERSTAND?

YES, SIR!

THAT WAS A GOOF! NOW HE'S SUSPICIOUS!

AND AS THE DISGUISED **BLACK CANARY** REACHES THE PLANE'S GALLEY...

THIS COFFEE MAY BE THE ANSWER! A COUPLE OF HARMLESS BUT QUICK-ACTING SLEEPING PILLS... AND OUR TWO CRIMINALS COULD HAVE THEIR TRIP CUT SHORT!

7

379

WHILE IN THE COMMAND CABIN...

HOW MANY HOURS TO SAN PEDRO, CAPTAIN?

AT OUR SPEED OF 600 KNOTS, *BATMAN*... ABOUT *FIVE HOURS*-- MOST OF IT OVER WATER!

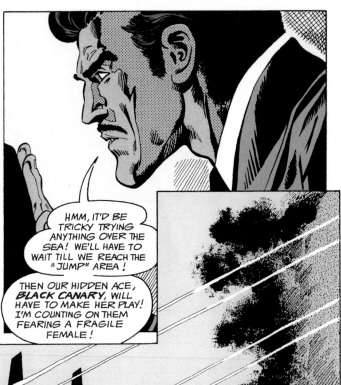

HMM, IT'D BE TRICKY TRYING ANYTHING OVER THE SEA! WE'LL HAVE TO WAIT TILL WE REACH THE "JUMP" AREA!

THEN OUR HIDDEN ACE, *BLACK CANARY*, WILL HAVE TO MAKE HER PLAY! I'M COUNTING ON THEM FEARING A FRAGILE FEMALE!

TWO COFFEES, GENTLEMEN!

MMMM, GOOD... LOTS BETTER THAN THAT BILGE THEY SERVE IN PRISON!

DEVLIN'S GULPING IT RIGHT DOWN! *PERFECT!*

NOW WILLIE BOY'S ABOUT TO DO THE SAME! IT'S ALL GOING TO BE EASY... NOW!

THERE'S MANY A SLIP BETWEEN THE CUP AND LIP--OR SO GOES AN OLD SAYING! WILL IT FIT INTO THIS NEW TWIST IN CRIME, THIS BIZARRE SKYJACKING TO END ALL SKYJACKINGS!? WING DIRECTLY TO *PART 2* BECAUSE *PART 1* ENDS *RIGHT HERE!*

8

As **BLACK CANARY** watches with heart pounding, WILLIE KRESH, SKYJACKER EXTRAORDINARY, PUTS DRUGGED COFFEE TO HIS LIPS, AND...

I *NEVER* DRINK COFFEE, DOLL... IT KEEPS ME AWAKE AT NIGHT!

AND THIS IS FOR TRYING TO PULL A *FAST* ONE, BABY!!

OOOHH!

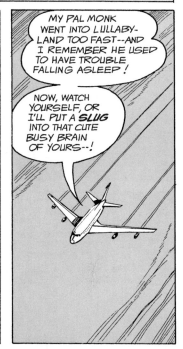

MY PAL MONK WENT INTO LULLABYLAND TOO FAST--AND I REMEMBER HE USED TO HAVE TROUBLE FALLING ASLEEP!

NOW, WATCH YOURSELF, OR I'LL PUT A *SLUG* INTO THAT CUTE BUSY BRAIN OF YOURS--!

MOMENTS LATER, AS THE STUNNED GIRL RETREATS TO THE LADIES' POWDER ROOM...

BATMAN! I TRIED... BUT FAILED! DEVLIN'S ASLEEP, BUT WILLIE KRESH IS A TOUGH, CLEVER GUY!

IT'S OKAY, *CANARY!* PLAY IT COOL UNTIL JUMP TIME -- THAT'LL BE OUR BEST CHANCE!

THEY *STILL* DON'T KNOW WHO YOU REALLY ARE-- AND THAT'S IN OUR FAVOR!

NOW AS A WAITING WORLD WONDERS, THE STOLEN JET STREAKS ON OVER SEA AND JUNGLE...

9

Hours pass, and then...

KRESH TO CAPTAIN! WE'RE ALMOST OVER SAN PEDRO! I'M SENDING THE STEWARD-ESS FORWARD TO BE LOCKED IN WITH YOU!

HOLD COURSE, AND SLOW 'ER DOWN TO JUST ABOVE STALLING SPEED!

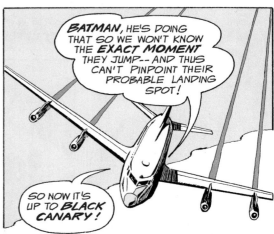

BATMAN, HE'S DOING THAT SO WE WON'T KNOW THE EXACT MOMENT THEY JUMP-- AND THUS CAN'T PINPOINT THEIR PROBABLE LANDING SPOT!

SO NOW IT'S UP TO BLACK CANARY!

THANKS TO YOU, I'LL HAVE TO TAKE DEVLIN OUT WHILE HE'S STILL IN DREAMLAND! NOW, GET FORWARD, FAST!

IT'S NOW OR NEVER...

BUDDA BU

WH-?!

THAT BURST CAN'T HURT NOW... WE'RE BELOW PRESSURIZED ALTITUDE!

BUT SUDDENLY...

WHUMP

10

DEVLIN! YOU WOKE UP JUST IN TIME! THANKS!

MY PLEASURE, PAL! YOU HIT A DOLL WITH *THREE MILLION* AND IT'S LIGHTS OUT!

SHE'S SOME BATTLER FOR A STEWARDESS!

BUDDABUDDA

SHE'S NO *STEWARDESS*! I SMELL A BAT,... A *BATMAN*! THAT'LL FIX 'EM!

WHAT ARE YOU DOING? WE MIGHT *CRASH*!!

PILOT

DOESN'T MATTER-- WE'RE JUMPING IN A FEW SECONDS!

BUT WE'RE TAKING THIS TRICKY CHICK AS A HOSTAGE! SLIP THAT CHUTE ON HER *FAST*!

AND IN THE FORWARD CABIN...

CAPTAIN STANTON'S HIT-- BUT HE'LL BE OKAY IF WE GET HIM TO A HOSPITAL! HOW'S THE SHIP--?

THOSE SLUGS WRECKED SOME GAUGES,... BUT I THINK I CAN MAKE THE NEAREST JETPORT!

GOOD! NOW HOLD HER STEADY! I'M SWITCHING BACK TO *BATMAN* AND GOING OUT THERE!

THEY MIGHT STILL BE ABOARD! *YOU'LL GET BLASTED*!

GOT TO CHANCE IT! SO LONG... AND GOOD LUCK!

KWAM

11

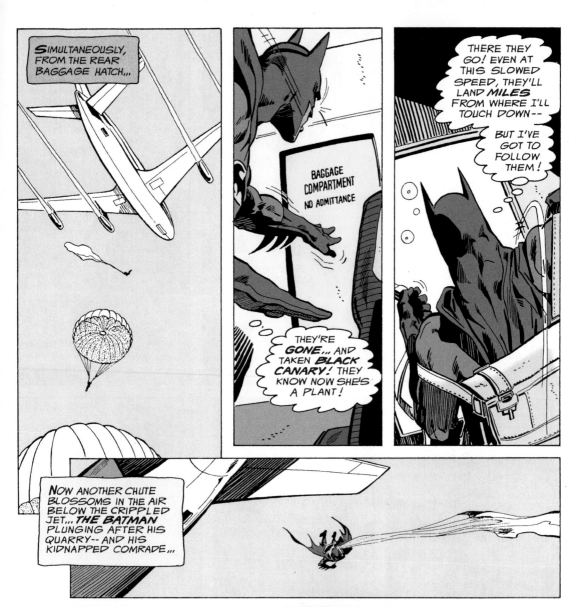

SIMULTANEOUSLY, FROM THE REAR BAGGAGE HATCH...

BAGGAGE COMPARTMENT
NO ADMITTANCE

THEY'RE *GONE*... AND TAKEN *BLACK CANARY!* THEY KNOW NOW SHE'S A PLANT!

THERE THEY GO! EVEN AT THIS SLOWED SPEED, THEY'LL LAND *MILES* FROM WHERE I'LL TOUCH DOWN--

BUT I'VE GOT TO FOLLOW THEM!

NOW ANOTHER CHUTE BLOSSOMS IN THE AIR BELOW THE CRIPPLED JET... *THE BATMAN* PLUNGING AFTER HIS QUARRY-- AND HIS KIDNAPPED COMRADE...

WHILE BELOW AND BEHIND, THE RUSHING WIND REVIVES A STARTLED *CANARY!*

WHAT? I'M CHUTING DOWN.!!

I'M DESCENDING TOO FAST! I COULD BE KILLED.!!

12

FRANTICALLY, THE PLUMMETING GIRL YANKS ON THE CHUTE LINES-- AND,...

WHEW! MY LUCK IS RUNNING PRETTY GOOD! THE ONLY SIZABLE TREE IN MILES-- AND *I* HIT IT!

NEARBY, ANOTHER PARACHUTIST HAS MADE A "DANGEROUS" LANDING,...

RATTLER-- AND THE CHUTE'S GOT MY LEGS-- I CAN'T RUN!!

SUDDENLY,...

BUDABB

KRESH! YOU SAVED ME AGAIN! I LOVE YA, BUDDY!

LIKE I SAID, LOYALTY'S A KRESH FAMILY TRAIT!

COME ON! WE'LL COLLECT THAT PHONY STEWARDESS AND MOVE ON! WE'VE GOT A TEN-MILE HIKE TO THE PASS!

SHORTLY,...

I SAW *ANOTHER* CHUTE DROPPING! IT MIGHT BE *THE BATMAN!* IF HE GIVES US TROUBLE-- WE'LL SHOOT HIS GIRL FRIEND HERE!

YOU GOT EVERYTHING FIGURED, WILLIE! YOU'RE EVEN SMARTER THAN YOUR BROTHER, TONY!

ONCE OVER THE PASS, AND IT'S ONLY A STROLL TO THE CAPITAL OF SAN PEDRO--AND A LIFE OF EASE! *HA HA HA!*

13

AND AS THE TRIO TRUDGES TOWARD THE DISTANT PASS...

BAD LUCK! MY WRIST WATCH RADIO GOT SMASHED IN THE JUMP! HOW WILL *BATMAN* EVER FIND US IN THIS WILDERNESS?

NOT TOO FAR AWAY...

NOT A SIGN OF THEM! *BLACK CANARY'S GOT* TO GIVE ME SOME KIND OF SIGNAL--!

HALF AN HOUR LATER...

AN ADOBE HOUSE--?

THERE'S A VILLAGE NEAR HERE... BUT WE'D BETTER STEER CLEAR OF IT! THIS SHACK MUST BE THE OUTSKIRTS!

TAKE THE GIRL ON AHEAD!... I'LL CHECK IT OUT AND CATCH UP!

A FEW MINUTES PASS, THEN...

THE HUT WAS *DESERTED!* *KEEP MOVING!* ONLY A FEW MILES TO THE PASS!

HEAVY... BUT THEN THREE MILLION MUST WEIGH PLENTY!

HEY, BUDDY, LET *ME* CARRY THE MONEY! YOU'VE DONE ENOUGH!

ONCE OVER THAT PASS, *BATMAN* COULD NEVER PICK UP OUR TRAIL! I MUST DO SOMETHING--!

EEEEEEEEE

(14)

SHE'S **GONE!** NOBODY COULD'VE LIVED AFTER A DROP LIKE THAT!

GOOD RIDDANCE! SHE WAS SOME LOUSY ALLY OF **THE BATMAN'S!** COME ON, MONK -- IT ISN'T FAR NOW!..

AND AS THE TWO CRIMINALS MOVE OFF...

IT **WORKED!** I ALMOST TOOK THE FULL FALL, BUT THE OLD REFLEXES ARE STILL SHARP!

SHORTLY...

I'M TIRED OF BEING SLAMMED AROUND BY MALE CHAUVINIST SKYJACKERS -- IT'S TIME FOR FIGHTING BACK AS... **BLACK CANARY!**

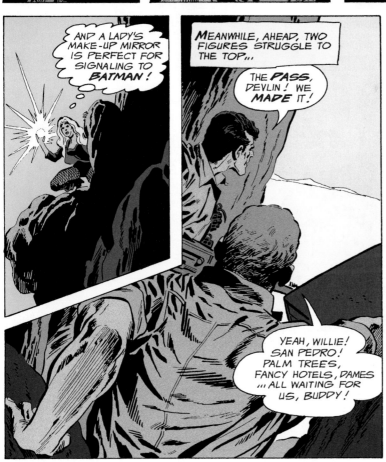

AND A LADY'S MAKE-UP MIRROR IS PERFECT FOR SIGNALING TO **BATMAN!**

MEANWHILE, AHEAD, TWO FIGURES STRUGGLE TO THE TOP...

THE **PASS,** DEVLIN! WE **MADE** IT!

YEAH, WILLIE! SAN PEDRO! PALM TREES, FANCY HOTELS, DAMES ... ALL WAITING FOR US, BUDDY!

YEAH, TAKE A **LONG** LOOK, DEVLIN, BECAUSE THAT'S **ALL** YOU'RE GOING TO SEE OF IT!

THIS IS WHERE YOU GET OFF, YOU ROTTEN CREEP!

HUHH ??!!

15

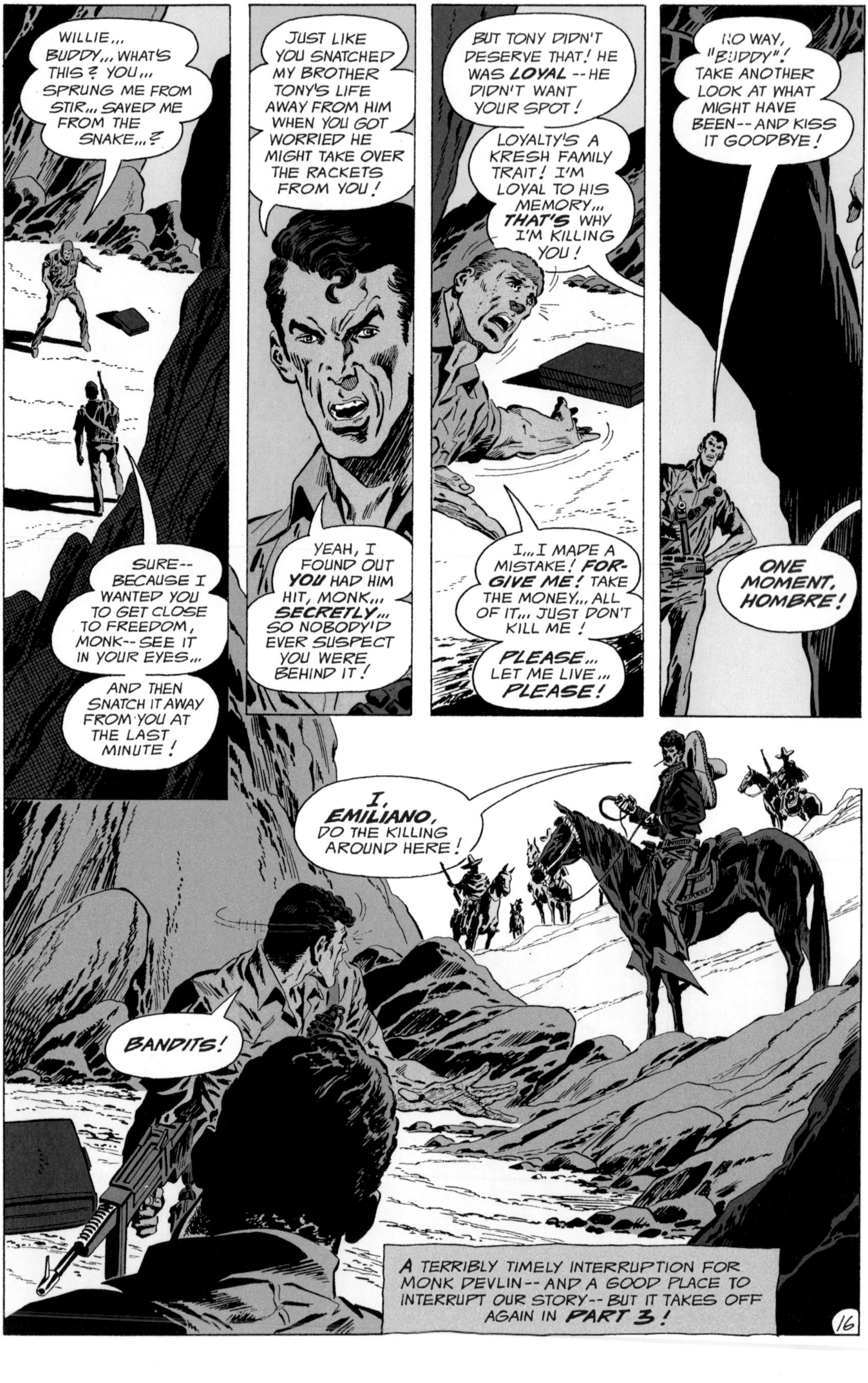
WILLIE... BUDDY... WHAT'S THIS? YOU... SPRUNG ME FROM STIR... SAVED ME FROM THE SNAKE...?
SURE-- BECAUSE I WANTED YOU TO GET CLOSE TO FREEDOM, MONK-- SEE IT IN YOUR EYES...
AND THEN SNATCH IT AWAY FROM YOU AT THE LAST MINUTE!
JUST LIKE YOU SNATCHED MY BROTHER TONY'S LIFE AWAY FROM HIM WHEN YOU GOT WORRIED HE MIGHT TAKE OVER THE RACKETS FROM YOU!
YEAH, I FOUND OUT YOU HAD HIM HIT, MONK... SECRETLY... SO NOBODY'D EVER SUSPECT YOU WERE BEHIND IT!
BUT TONY DIDN'T DESERVE THAT! HE WAS LOYAL -- HE DIDN'T WANT YOUR SPOT!
LOYALTY'S A KRESH FAMILY TRAIT! I'M LOYAL TO HIS MEMORY... THAT'S WHY I'M KILLING YOU!
I... I MADE A MISTAKE! FORGIVE ME! TAKE THE MONEY... ALL OF IT... JUST DON'T KILL ME!
PLEASE... LET ME LIVE... PLEASE!
NO WAY, "BUDDY"! TAKE ANOTHER LOOK AT WHAT MIGHT HAVE BEEN-- AND KISS IT GOODBYE!
ONE MOMENT, HOMBRE!
I, EMILIANO, DO THE KILLING AROUND HERE!
BANDITS!
A TERRIBLY TIMELY INTERRUPTION FOR MONK DEVLIN-- AND A GOOD PLACE TO INTERRUPT OUR STORY-- BUT IT TAKES OFF AGAIN IN PART 3!
16

PART 3 "BATMEN LAUGH LAST!"

THE SURPRISE VENGEANCE OF WILLIE KRESH AGAINST MONK DEVLIN HAS BEEN SIDETRACKED BY A NEW TWIST... THE SUDDEN ARRIVAL OF *EMILIANO...*

I HAVE FOLLOWED YOUR EXPLOITS, HOMBRES, ON MY TRANSISTOR RADIO!

IT WAS SO CONVENIENT AND FORTUNATE FOR ME WHEN YOU CHOSE THIS AREA TO PARACHUTE DOWN INTO--!

FOR AM *I* NOT THE LAW HERE-- IN THESE MOUNTAINS? *SI,* AND EVEN THE GOVERNMENT DOES NOT COME INTO THESE PARTS WITHOUT DEALING WITH ME, *EMILIANO!*

YOU'RE JUST A *CRUMMY BOONDOCK BANDIT* AND I'M GONNA--

FWIPP

AIEEEEEEE

YOU SHOULD THANK ME, SEÑOR-- OR MY VAQUEROS WOULD HAVE MADE MANY LITTLE HOLES IN YOU!

NOW, ENOUGH PLAY-ACTING! I AM HERE FOR WHAT IS IN THE SUITCASE... *THREE MILLION AMERICANO DOLLARS!*

OPEN IT!

FANTASTIC! KRESH WAS OUT TO KILL DEVLIN ALL ALONG... AND NOW A *BANDIT'S* GOT *BOTH* OF THEM--!

WE GOT HERE TOO LATE!

LOOK! THEY'RE OPENING THE SUITCASE!

HUH? ROCKS--??

ROCKS? IS THIS SOMEONE'S POOR IDEA OF A JOKE? WHERE IS THE DINERO? *WHERE IS IT, HOMBRES?*

17

389

I HID IT... IN CASE ANYTHING WENT WRONG! AFTER I FINISHED YOU, DEVLIN, I WAS GOING BACK FOR IT!

YOU MEAN I CARRIED ROCKS ALL THAT WAY--?

TELL ME *WHERE* YOU HAVE HIDDEN IT... OR I ARRANGE YOUR DEATH... HERE... *NOW!*

GO AHEAD, YOU CLOWN! THEN YOU'LL *NEVER* FIND THE MONEY... IN ALL THIS REAL ESTATE!

YOU ARE A SMART GRINGO! BUT EMILIANO HAS THE ANSWER FOR THAT!

ESTEBAN! THE SACK!

EMPTY IT!!

A GILA MONSTER! VERY *POISONOUS*, HOMBRE! ONCE THEY GET A HOLD... THEY *NEVER* LET GO-- EVEN IF YOU CUT THEIR HEADS OFF!

UGGH! KRESH MAY BE A SKY-JACKER AND A WOULD-BE KILLER, BUT WE CAN'T LET THAT HAPPEN!

READY FOR *ACTION*?

READY AND *ITCHING!*

A LAST CHANCE TO TELL ME WHERE THE *DINERO* IS HIDDEN, SEÑOR-- BEFORE HE TAKES HIS DEADLY HOLD!

NEVER!

18

390

SUDDENLY...

YEEOW!

A SEÑORITA?! CHARGE HER, MUCHACHOS!

BUT AS THE HORSEMEN RUSH THE BLONDE BOMBSHELL...

AIEEEEEEEE

SET 'EM UP IN THE NEXT *BARRANCA*--OR ALLEY--AMIGO!

DID YOU MOUNTAIN BOYS EVER HEAR OF *JUDO*--?

NO, *YOU NEVER DID!*

CAN'T KEEP THIS UP! ONE OF THESE SHOTS HAS TO FIND A TARGET SOONER OR LATER!

KPOW

POW

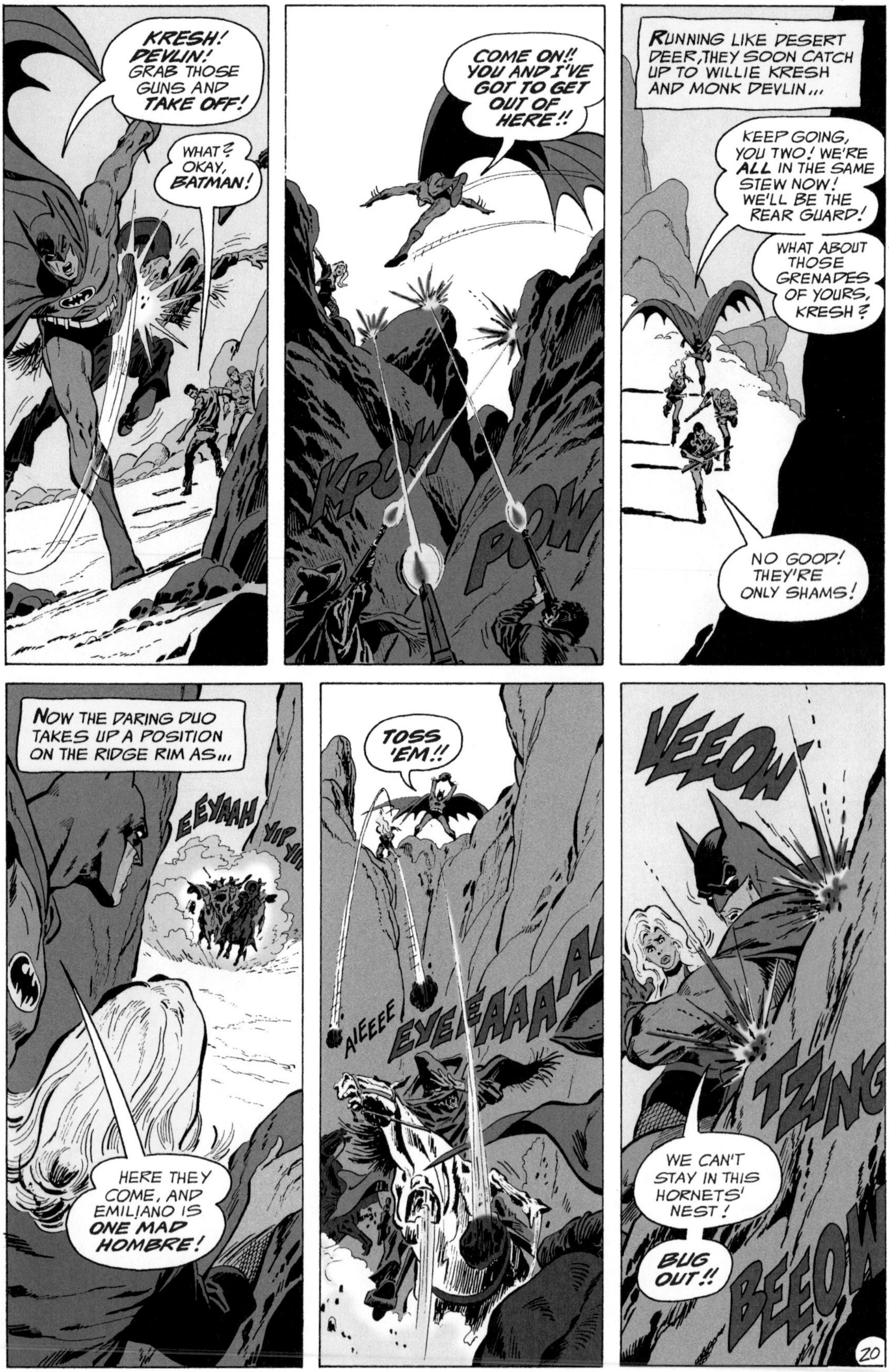
KRESH! DEVLIN! GRAB THOSE GUNS AND TAKE OFF!
WHAT? OKAY, BATMAN!
COME ON!! YOU AND I'VE GOT TO GET OUT OF HERE!!
KPOW
POW
RUNNING LIKE DESERT DEER, THEY SOON CATCH UP TO WILLIE KRESH AND MONK DEVLIN...
KEEP GOING, YOU TWO! WE'RE ALL IN THE SAME STEW NOW! WE'LL BE THE REAR GUARD!
WHAT ABOUT THOSE GRENADES OF YOURS, KRESH?
NO GOOD! THEY'RE ONLY SHAMS!
NOW THE DARING DUO TAKES UP A POSITION ON THE RIDGE RIM AS...
EEYAAH
HERE THEY COME, AND EMILIANO IS ONE MAD HOMBRE!
TOSS 'EM!!
AIEEEE
EYEEAAAAA
VEEOW
TZING
WE CAN'T STAY IN THIS HORNETS' NEST!
BUG OUT!!
BEEOW
20

TZZING

DINAH!?

BUT THE NEXT INSTANT, A RICOCHET FINDS FLESH AND BLOOD...

MY ARM...!

JUST A MINOR WOUND! YOU'LL BE OKAY--

WHA-?!

ZA SHI

THE SEÑORITA IS WOUNDED-- AND YOU ARE SURROUNDED!

NOW WHERE ARE THOSE TWO HOMBRES?

SUDDENLY...

KPOW KPOW

TWO SHOTS UP AHEAD--!

KRESH AND DEVLIN!?

A SCRAMBLE TO A SPOT NOT FAR OFF-- AND...

DEAD... BOTH OF THEM! THEIR MUTUAL HATRED AND THOSE RIFLES! I SHOULD NEVER HAVE LEFT THEM ALONE!

IT IS THE SMILE OF FATE, SEÑOR! WITH THESE TWO DEAD AND THE MONEY LOST SOMEWHERE... PERHAPS FOREVER... YOU AND I HAVE NO QUARREL!

YOU AND THE FORMIDABLE SEÑORITA ARE NOW UNDER EMILIANO'S PROTECTION!

21

LATER, IT IS A SOLEMN PROCESSION THAT WINDS DOWN OUT OF THE MOUNTAINS TO A LONE ADOBE BUILDING...

HO, MANUELO-- TWO CUSTOMERS FOR YOU!

SI, I THINK I HAVE SOMETHING TO FIT THEM!

MANUELO IS THE LOCAL COFFIN-MAKER AND UNDERTAKER... BUT THE SUPERSTITIOUS PEONS IN THE NEARBY VILLAGE MAKE HIM DO HIS WORK *OUT HERE*... AWAY FROM THEIR HOMES!

SO THE ADVENTURE ENDS! TOO BAD ABOUT THE MONEY-- EMILIANO COULD HAVE USED IT!

I WONDER UNDER WHAT ROCK OR FORLORN CACTUS IT LIES?

IT WOULD TAKE AN ARMY A HUNDRED YEARS TO FIND IT!

SPEAKING OF ARMIES, THE POLICE MAY COME TO SEARCH FOR THOSE TWO DEAD ONES!

VAMANOS, MUCHACHOS!

SO, IT IS ANOTHER BUSY DAY AT GOTHAM AIRPORT AS A JET ENDS A LONG UNSCHEDULED ROUND-TRIP FLIGHT FROM SAN PEDRO...

COMMISSIONER! GOVERNOR! I SAID I'D BRING THEM BACK... THERE THEY ARE! SORRY ABOUT THE MONEY!

YOU STILL DID A FANTASTIC JOB, BOTH OF YOU! IT SHOULD DISCOURAGE OTHER CRIMINALS FROM TRYING THE SAME THING!

22

BUT SHORTLY...

GOVERNOR! THE *MONEY*--THE MORTICIAN FOUND IT IN THE *BOTTOM OF ONE OF THE COFFINS...* STUFFED IN A PONCHO!

WHAT?

IT'S *ALL* HERE... *THE THREE MILLION!* BUT HOW...??

I'LL TELL YOU HOW! KRESH HID THE MONEY WHEN THEY LANDED! HE MUST'VE STASHED IT IN MANUELO'S DESERTED ADOBE!

IN THE DIM LIGHT, THOSE COFFINS MUST'VE LOOKED LIKE OLD *BOXES!*

YOU MEAN, HE PLANNED TO COME BACK FOR IT LATER AND--

WHAT ARE YOU LAUGHING AT??

HA! HA! HA! I'M JUST REMEMBERING, GOVERNOR, THE WAY EMILIANO WAS *STANDING* ON THE COFFIN... MOANING OVER THE MONEY'S LOSS! HA! HA! HA!

THAT'S *RIGHT!* HE WAS ONLY *INCHES* AWAY FROM *THREE MILLION DOLLARS!* HA! HA! HA!

LAUGH, EMILIANO, WHEREVER YOU ARE! LAUGH! HA! HA! HA!

STORY-- BOB HANEY
ART-- JIM APARO

ALL'S WELL THAT ENDS LAUGHING! BUT THE *BRAVE & BOLD* "BEAT" NEVER ENDS! IT GOES ON--INTO BIGGER AND BETTER *BATMAN* TEAM-UPS EVERY BLOCKBUSTING ISSUE! *MISS IT NEVER!*

– THE END –

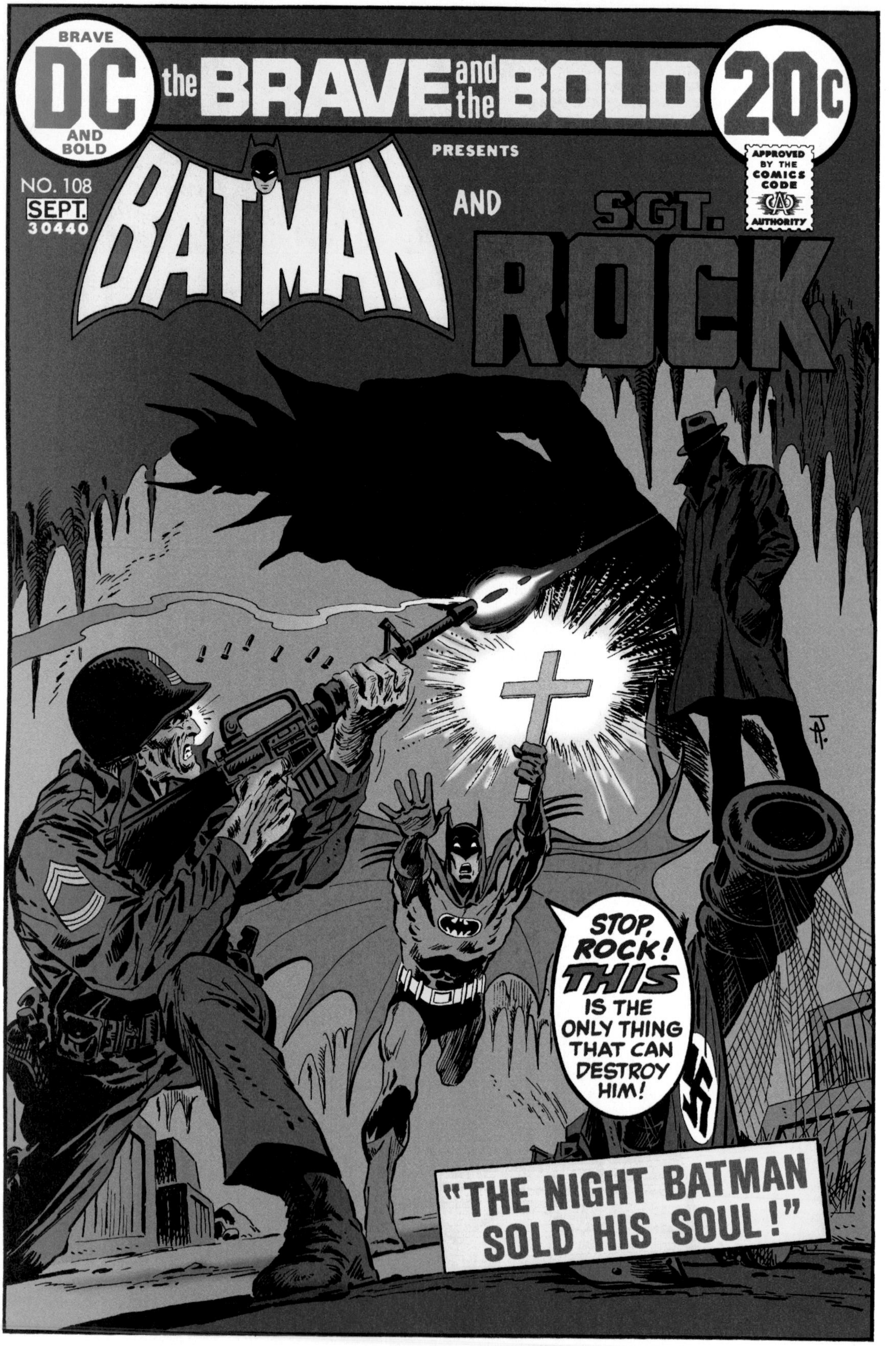
BRAVE
DC
AND BOLD
the BRAVE and the BOLD
20¢
PRESENTS
NO. 108
SEPT.
30440
BATMAN
AND
SGT. ROCK
APPROVED BY THE COMICS CODE AUTHORITY
STOP, ROCK! THIS IS THE ONLY THING THAT CAN DESTROY HIM!
"THE NIGHT BATMAN SOLD HIS SOUL!"

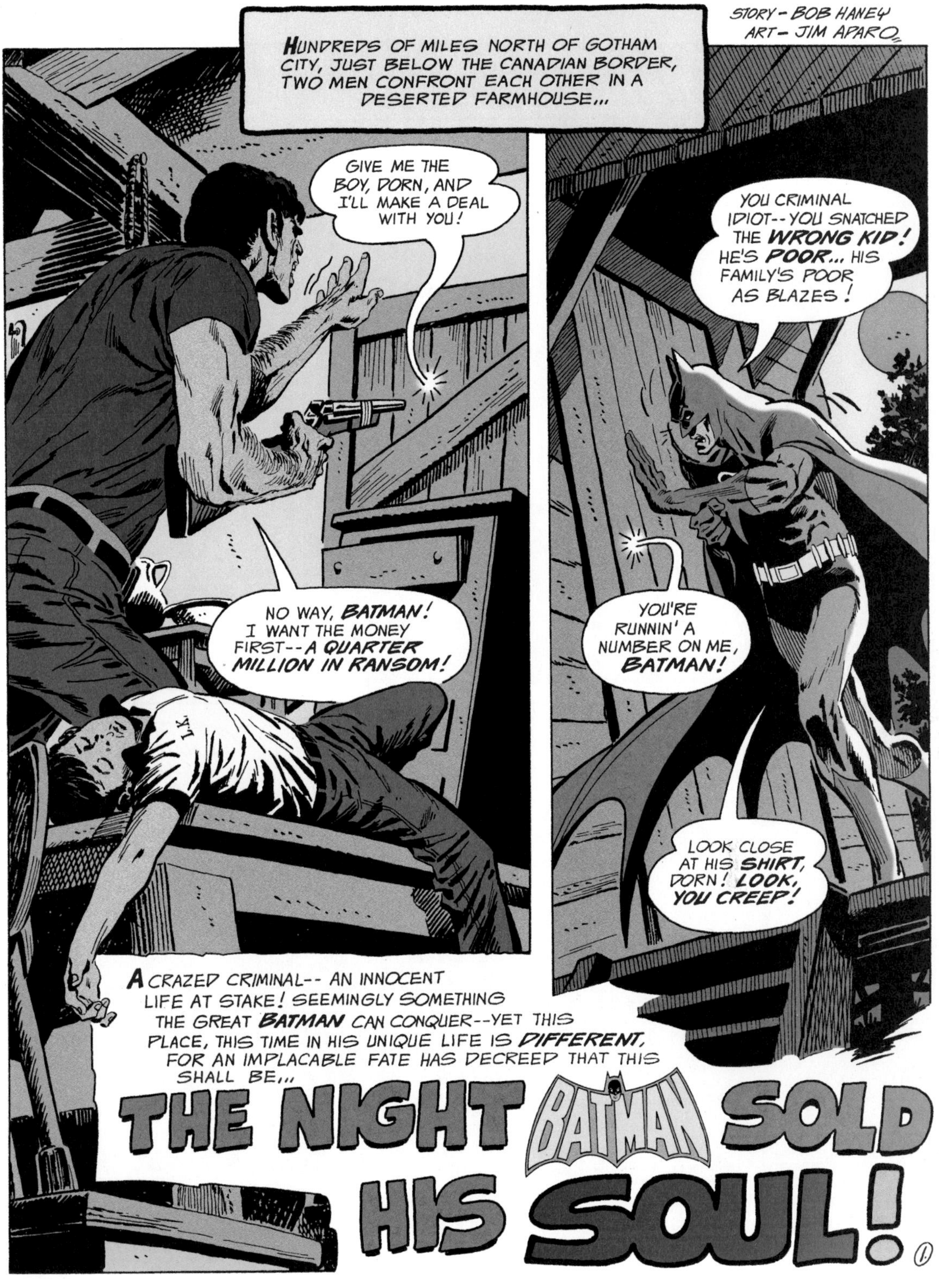
STORY - BOB HANEY
ART - JIM APARO
HUNDREDS OF MILES NORTH OF GOTHAM CITY, JUST BELOW THE CANADIAN BORDER, TWO MEN CONFRONT EACH OTHER IN A DESERTED FARMHOUSE...
GIVE ME THE BOY, DORN, AND I'LL MAKE A DEAL WITH YOU!
NO WAY, BATMAN! I WANT THE MONEY FIRST--A QUARTER MILLION IN RANSOM!
YOU CRIMINAL IDIOT--YOU SNATCHED THE WRONG KID! HE'S POOR... HIS FAMILY'S POOR AS BLAZES!
YOU'RE RUNNIN' A NUMBER ON ME, BATMAN!
LOOK CLOSE AT HIS SHIRT, DORN! LOOK, YOU CREEP!
A CRAZED CRIMINAL-- AN INNOCENT LIFE AT STAKE! SEEMINGLY SOMETHING THE GREAT BATMAN CAN CONQUER--YET THIS PLACE, THIS TIME IN HIS UNIQUE LIFE IS DIFFERENT, FOR AN IMPLACABLE FATE HAS DECREED THAT THIS SHALL BE...
THE NIGHT BATMAN SOLD HIS SOUL!
1.

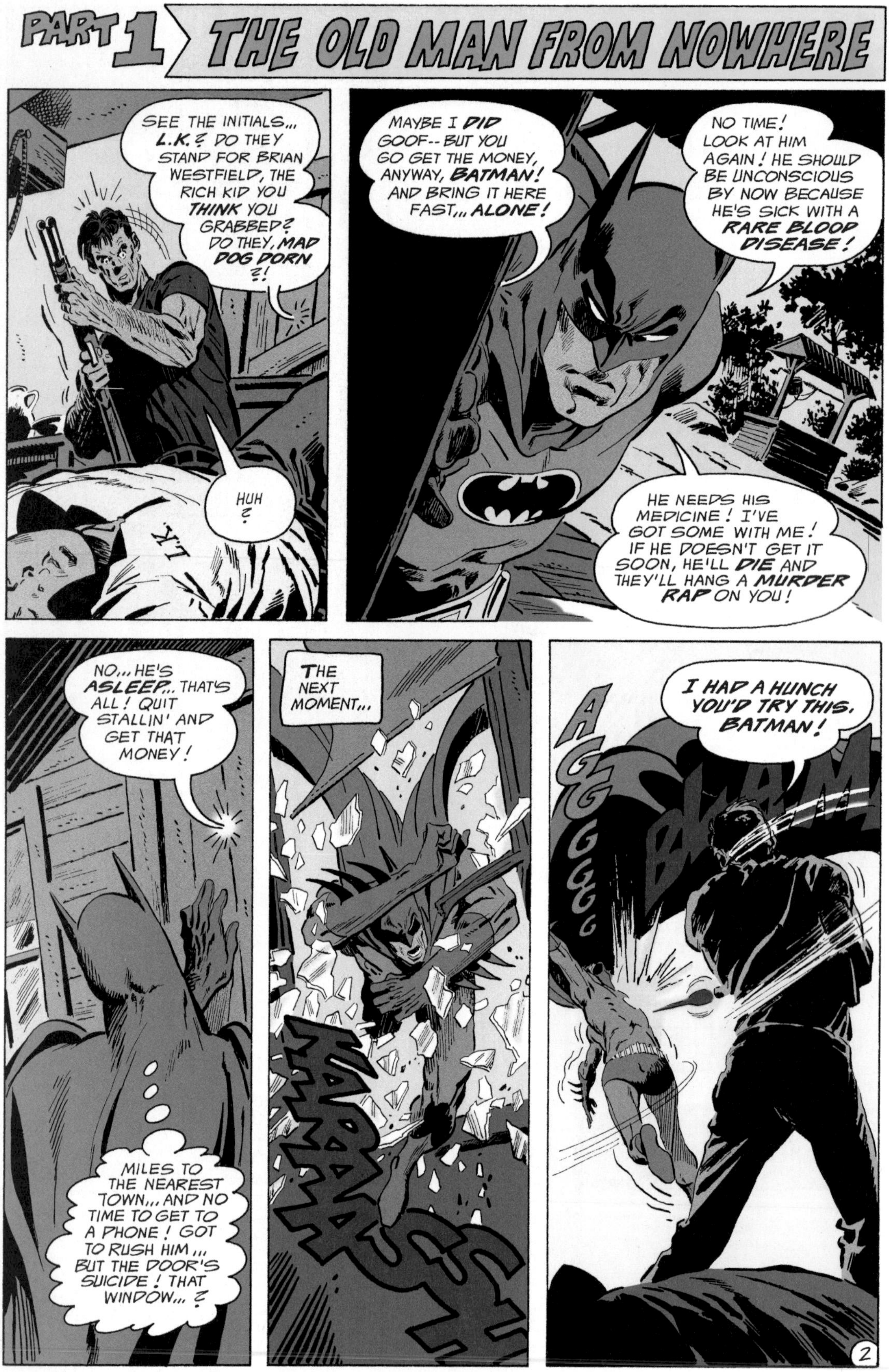
PART 1 THE OLD MAN FROM NOWHERE
SEE THE INITIALS... L.K.? DO THEY STAND FOR BRIAN WESTFIELD, THE RICH KID YOU THINK YOU GRABBED? DO THEY, MAD DOG DORN ?!
HUH ?
L.K.
MAYBE I DID GOOF-- BUT YOU GO GET THE MONEY, ANYWAY, BATMAN! AND BRING IT HERE FAST... ALONE!
NO TIME! LOOK AT HIM AGAIN! HE SHOULD BE UNCONSCIOUS BY NOW BECAUSE HE'S SICK WITH A RARE BLOOD DISEASE!
HE NEEDS HIS MEDICINE! I'VE GOT SOME WITH ME! IF HE DOESN'T GET IT SOON, HE'LL DIE AND THEY'LL HANG A MURDER RAP ON YOU!
NO... HE'S ASLEEP... THAT'S ALL! QUIT STALLIN' AND GET THAT MONEY!
MILES TO THE NEAREST TOWN... AND NO TIME TO GET TO A PHONE! GOT TO RUSH HIM... BUT THE DOOR'S SUICIDE! THAT WINDOW... ?
THE NEXT MOMENT...
I HAD A HUNCH YOU'D TRY THIS, BATMAN!
BLAM
2

LOUSY CAPED CRUMB! DORN'S DONE FOR YOU-- FOR GOOD!

SO LONG, *BATMAN!* COMES MORNING I'LL CONTACT PEOPLE WITH MORE SENSE.... GET MY MONEY AND HIT FOR THE BORDER!

SEE CANADA AND LIVE.... YEAH, THAT'S THE MOTTO! HA! HA! HA!

DOWN, DOWN IN THE DARKNESS, THE COLD, NUMBING WETNESS, A FAMED LIFE EBBS....

WEAK.... LOSING BLOOD! CAN'T CLIMB OUT...! I'LL DIE.... AND SO WILL THAT POOR KID!

IN A LAST BURST OF ENERGY....

I'D GIVE MY SOUL TO GET OUT OF HERE! I DON'T WANT TO DIE! BATMAN WANTS TO *LIVE!!*

THEN, THE BLACK NUMBNESS SWEEPS OVER HIM, AND ALL HE HEARS IS HIS OWN STRANGLED BREATHING.... AND A FAINT CREAKING....

KREEK

SOMETHING BUMPS THE DROWNING MAN-- HE GRASPS AT IT WEAKLY....

A....A BUCKET....? THE WELL BUCKET AND ROPE--!? SOMEBODY'S REELING IT BACK UP.... GOT TO HANG ON! *GOT TO!*

3

A SLICE OF STARRY SKY GROWS LARGER-- A SILHOUETTED FIGURE WORKING THE OLD WIND-LASS GROWS NEARER... NEARER...

KREE

KREEK

HE'S ALIVE! GOOD! SUCH STRENGTH IS GOOD! I AM GLAD I SAVED HIM!

NASTY WOUNDS... BUT EASILY TREATED AND BOUND!

AND SHORTLY...

I STOPPED FOR WATER FOR MY AUTO'S RADIATOR... FORTUNATE FOR YOU, I HEARD YOUR CRY FOR HELP!

THANKS... THANKS MORE THAN I CAN SAY!

IN BATMAN'S PARTLY DAZED BRAIN, THE STRANGER'S SLIGHTLY ACCENTED VOICE SEEMS TO COME FROM AFAR...

YOU WILL NEVER KNOW HOW HAPPY I WAS TO AID YOU! YOU ARE ALL RIGHT, MY FRIEND?

YES... YES, FEEL MUCH STRONGER! I HAVE SOME UNFINISHED BUSINESS HERE... DANGEROUS BUSINESS! BETTER YOU LEAVE! AND THANKS AGAIN!

AS THE OLD CAR JOUNCES OFF DOWN THE DESERTED ROAD...

FUNNY OLD GIMPY GUY! NEVER GOT HIS NAME! HIS VOICE... ODD, FOREIGN ACCENT!

NOW TO TAKE CARE OF DORN-- AND THAT POOR KID!

DORN'S ASLEEP! IF I'D TOSSED A SHOT-UP GUY DOWN A WELL, I'D FIGURE IT WAS SAFE TO NAP, TOO!

4

THIS TIME, THE **MASKED MANHUNTER** ENTERS THE HOUSE SILENTLY, AND...

CHUK

UNGG

B-BATMAN...?

YES, SON! THANK THE STARS YOU'RE OKAY,... AND THANK THAT OLD MAN, WHOEVER HE WAS!

TWO NIGHTS LATER, GOTHAM CITY...

GENTLEMEN, I'M PROUD TO ANNOUNCE THE CAPTURE OF MAD-DOG DORN!

TAKING CREDIT FOR WHAT **BATMAN** DID, COMMISSIONER?

UH,...OH, IT'S **YOU**, WAYNE! NO, MY PLAY-BOY FRIEND -- I WAS ABOUT TO GIVE HIM FULL MARKS FOR GETTING DORN AND SAVING THAT BOY!

BE SURE YOU DO, COMMISSIONER? WELL, TA-TA,..!

LOOK AT HIM SWAGGERING! BEATS ME HOW **BATMAN** CAN REMAIN THAT VAIN, SHALLOW SWINGER'S FRIEND!

BUT AS THE MAN THE WORLD KNOWS ONLY AS BRUCE WAYNE ROUNDS A CORNER INTO A DARK STREET,...

MY CHEST,... WHERE DORN'S BLAST CAUGHT ME! I'M A FOOL FOR COMING OUT TONIGHT,... BUT PEOPLE MIGHT BEGIN TO QUESTION MY ABSENCE,...

5

THE BODY IS STILL WEAK, MY FRIEND, BUT THAT WILL SOON PASS FOR I HAVE NEED OF YOUR FULL POWERS...

WHAT--? SOMEONE IN THE SHADOWS..! AND HIS VOICE... WITH A SLIGHT ACCENT... WHERE'VE I HEARD IT BEFORE?

NOW I KNOW! YOU'RE THE OLD MAN FROM THE FARMHOUSE... WHO HELPED *BATMAN*... BUT...?

YES, IT IS I, AND I KNOW YOUR *SECRET IDENTITY!* I AM AN EXPERT ON OTHER IDENTITIES -- I'VE HAD SO MANY MYSELF!

WHO *ARE* YOU? I CAN'T SEE YOUR FACE!

I GO BY MANY NAMES! MY FACE IS FAMOUS, EVEN *INFAMOUS!* BUT NO MATTER! I'M HERE TO REMIND YOU OF OUR *BARGAIN!*

BARGAIN?

DID YOU THINK I HELPED YOU FOR *NOTHING?* YOU CALLED FOR ME... FROM THE DEPTHS OF YOUR SOUL...

...AND NOW *THAT SOUL BELONGS TO ME!* THAT WAS THE BARGAIN!

YOU, *WHOEVER* YOU ARE, WE HAVE NO BARGAIN BETWEEN US! I OWE YOU MY LIFE... AND I'M GRATEFUL... BUT THIS SOUL BUSINESS IS NONSENSE!

LET ME *SEE* YOU...!

DO NOT COME CLOSER--!

*B*UT AS *WAYNE* LUNGES...

HE'S GONE--?

BUT I *HEAR* HIM-- SHUFFLING ALONG WITH THAT LIMP OF HIS! EVEN WEAK AS I AM, I'LL CATCH HIM--!

SHUF SHU

6

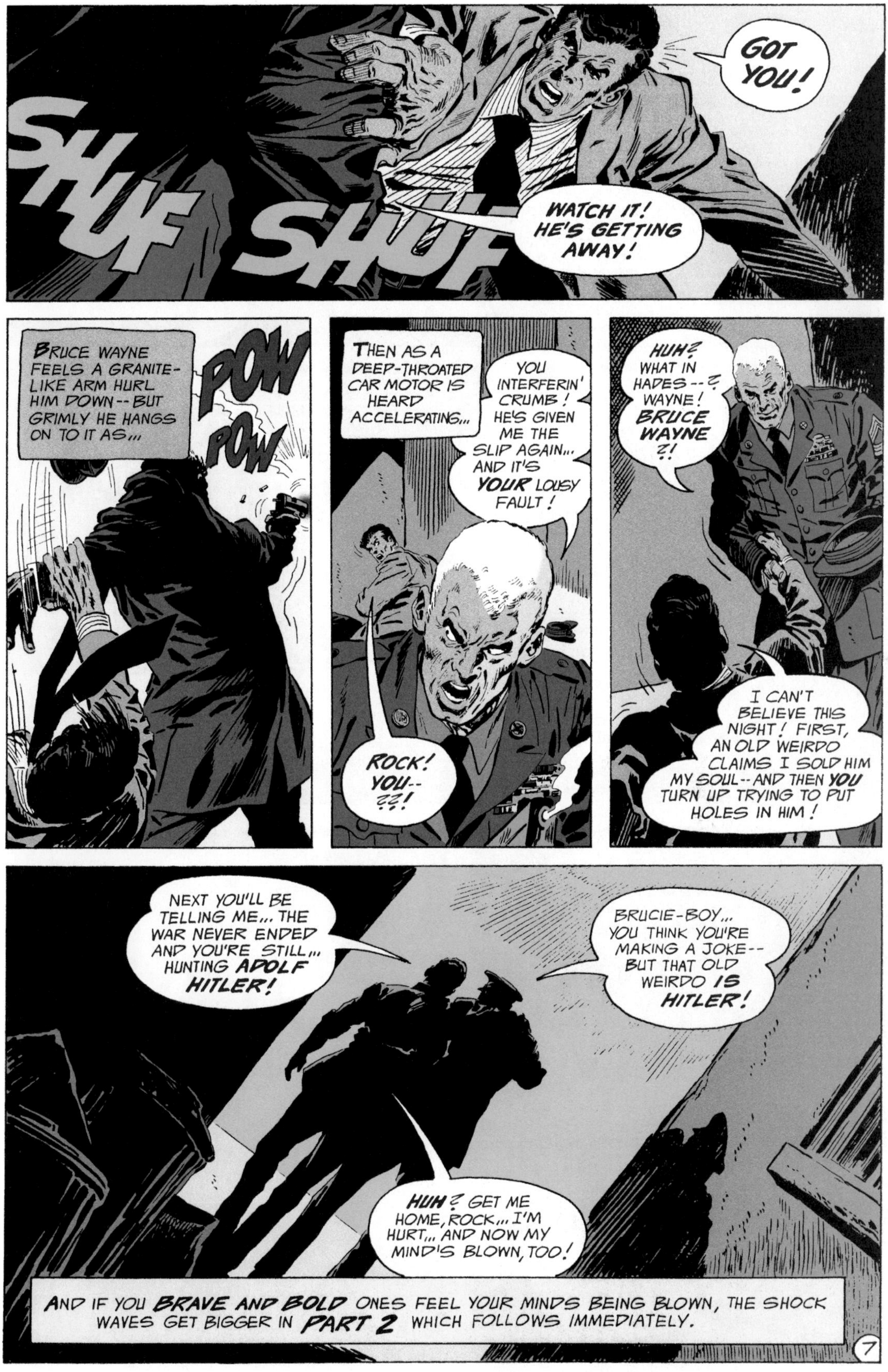
GOT YOU!
SHUF SHUF
WATCH IT! HE'S GETTING AWAY!
BRUCE WAYNE FEELS A GRANITE-LIKE ARM HURL HIM DOWN--BUT GRIMLY HE HANGS ON TO IT AS...
POW POW
THEN AS A DEEP-THROATED CAR MOTOR IS HEARD ACCELERATING...
YOU INTERFERIN' CRUMB! HE'S GIVEN ME THE SLIP AGAIN... AND IT'S YOUR LOUSY FAULT!
ROCK! YOU-- ??!
HUH? WHAT IN HADES--? WAYNE! BRUCE WAYNE ?!
I CAN'T BELIEVE THIS NIGHT! FIRST, AN OLD WEIRDO CLAIMS I SOLD HIM MY SOUL--AND THEN YOU TURN UP TRYING TO PUT HOLES IN HIM!
NEXT YOU'LL BE TELLING ME... THE WAR NEVER ENDED AND YOU'RE STILL... HUNTING ADOLF HITLER!
BRUCIE-BOY... YOU THINK YOU'RE MAKING A JOKE--BUT THAT OLD WEIRDO IS HITLER!
HUH? GET ME HOME, ROCK... I'M HURT... AND NOW MY MIND'S BLOWN, TOO!
AND IF YOU BRAVE AND BOLD ONES FEEL YOUR MINDS BEING BLOWN, THE SHOCK WAVES GET BIGGER IN PART 2 WHICH FOLLOWS IMMEDIATELY.
7

IT IS LATER, IN BRUCE WAYNE'S POSH PENTHOUSE, AND A GRIZZLED SERGEANT ROCK, HERO OF A DOZEN WARS, IS SAYING...

BRUCIE-BOY, I TELL YOU THAT OLD GUY WHO CLAIMS YOU SOLD HIM YOUR EVER-LIVING SOUL IS THE *BIGGEST* NAZI OF 'EM ALL... *DER FUEHRER...* ADOLF HITLER!

IMPOSSIBLE, ROCK! HITLER'S BEEN DEAD FOR *YEARS!*

HE BOUGHT IT IN HIS BERLIN BUNKER IN MAY, 1945, AND EVERY EXPERT *AGREES* IT'S SO!

YEAH, SURE, BUT OLD ROCK KNOWS *DIFFERENT!* LEMME SET YOU RIGHT, PAL! THE LAST WEEK OF THE WAR, ME AND EASY COMPANY'S SLUGGIN' DEEP INTO GERMANY...

"We're advancin' into the Bavarian Alps when a Kraut .88 kayoes me! When I come to..."

I'M AN ENEMY PRISONER... IN A FOREST HIDEOUT!

MY FUEHRER! THE AMERIKANERS ARE NEARBY--EVEN THIS AREA IS NOT SAFE! YOU MUST LEAVE!

THAT GUY... IT'S *HIM...* HITLER!

JA, I MUST ESCAPE TO LEAD OUR CAUSE TO TRIUMPH SOME OTHER DAY!

THAT ENEMY SERGEANT-- HE MAY HAVE SEEN ME!

SHOOT HIM!

8

"I sweated a ton as I heard that plane take off--and that Nazi major's Luger pointed right at my already aching head..."

BRRAMM

"That's when American shells zeroed in like the Fourth of July had come two months early..."

WHAM

"Tossing me over the snow-covered boulders like a rag doll..."

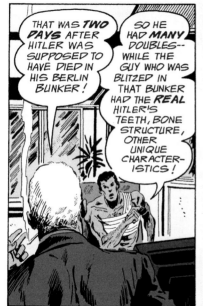

THAT WAS **TWO DAYS** AFTER HITLER WAS SUPPOSED TO HAVE DIED IN HIS BERLIN BUNKER!

SO HE HAD **MANY DOUBLES**-- WHILE THE GUY WHO WAS BLITZED IN THAT BUNKER HAD THE **REAL** HITLER'S TEETH, BONE STRUCTURE, OTHER UNIQUE CHARACTER-ISTICS!

SURE, SURE-- BUT THEM NAZIS WERE INHUMANLY CLEVER--IT COULD HAVE BEEN **FAKED**! AND WHY DID THAT HITLER I SAW ORDER ME SHOT, IF HE WASN'T THE GENUINE ARTICLE?

PROBABLY A DOUBLE PLAYING HIS ROLE TO THE HILT... RIGHT TO THE FINAL CURTAIN!

LISTEN, BRUCIE, IF HE'S **REALLY DEAD**, WHO **IS** THE GUY I'VE BEEN TRACKIN' ALL OVER THE WORLD THESE YEARS?

WHY IS HE KEEPIN' UP HIS MASQUERADE??

"Like in 1948, I'm stationed in Greece and I'm in this tavern when I hear..."

THE BOAT IS WAITING AT THE QUAY, MY LEADER...

FOOL! NEVER CALL ME THAT... SOMEONE MAY HEAR YOU!

"I'd know that voice on my dying day... and the shuffling limp he had as he was hustled down to that pier..."

LEMME GO, YOU GORILLAS! THAT'S HIM... GOTTA GET HIM!

A MADMAN! HOLD HIM DOWN!

"Of course, nobody believed old Rock-- the cops said I'd had too much native vino! Two years later, I'm in South America..."

POW! POW

IT'S...HIM! HE'S IN THAT CAR!!

"I got court-martialed for that one--but I was sure the guy who kept turnin' up was Uncle Adolf! Then, just a few years back, I'm in Paris, on leave..."

THE UNKNOWN SOJER OF FRANCE ALWAYS RATES A SALUTE...

HUH? OVER THERE... HIM!!

"No mistaking it, Brucie-boy! It was der Fuehrer, maybe returned to the scene of his biggest triumph!"

I'LL GET YOU THIS TIME--!!

WOK WOK

"I lost that set-to just like all the others..."

I TELL YOU, OLD BUDDY, IF HE AIN'T HITLER, WHY IS HE SO WELL-PROTECTED EVERYWHERE HE GOES... AND WHO ELSE COULD HE BE?

I...I DON'T KNOW, ROCK! YOUR STORY'S VERY PERSUASIVE, EVEN AMAZING, BUT HITLER'S DEAD... THE WHOLE WORLD KNOWS THAT!

10

OKAY, CHUM! YOU SAID YOU MET HIM AT AN OLD FARMHOUSE AS *BATMAN!*

FEEL UP TO GOIN' BACK FOR A RECON?

WHY, UH, SURE, ROCK, IF IT'LL COOL YOUR SUSPICIONS!

SOME HOURS LATER...

A *NAZI NEST!* THAT'S WHY HE CAME HERE-- IT WAS ANOTHER LAIR HIS HENCHMEN PROVIDE FOR HIM ALL OVER THE WORLD!

OR JUST ANOTHER SECRET BUNCH OF NAZI SYMPATHIZERS! THERE *WERE* SOME, AS YOU KNOW! AND FROM THE LOOK OF IT, THIS PLACE HASN'T BEEN USED SINCE THE WAR ENDED!

Mein Kampf

LATER...

OKAY, BRUCE, YOU DON'T BUY MY STORY-- BUT HE'S HERE IN GOTHAM CITY AND I'M GONNA GET HIM THIS TIME!

SEE YA, PAL!

CAREFUL, ROCK, AND TRY TO UNDERSTAND WHY I CAN'T BE- LIEVE AS YOU DO!

BUT AS WAYNE ENTERS A WAITING TAXI...

OH! SORRY! I DIDN'T KNOW IT WAS TAKEN!

NO HEROICS, MY FRIEND! THE DRIVER IS ARMED!

YOU-- Z!

OKAY, OLD- TIMER, WHAT DO YOU WANT OF ME?

ONLY TO REMIND YOU OF OUR BARGAIN! I NEED HUMAN TOOLS-- THE EMPIRE OF EVIL HAS MANY SOLDIERS...

AND *YOU* HAVE ENLISTED UNDER ITS BANNER!

11

I DID NO SUCH THING! I OWE YOU *NOTHING*...EXCEPT GRATITUDE!

YOU ARE *WRONG*, AS YOU WILL SEE! SOON, YOU WILL BE DOING MY WORK...THE *WORK OF EVIL!*

I BELIEVE THIS IS YOUR DESTINATION! GOODBYE FOR NOW...UNTIL OUR NEXT RENDEZVOUS!

THERE WON'T BE ANY, YOU CAN COUNT ON IT!

THE FOLLOWING DAY, AS BATMAN RESUMES HIS NORMAL PATROL...

THAT GUY...IT'S WILLIE GANS!

HOLD IT, WILLIE!

HE ALWAYS WAS THE FASTEST SNEAK-THIEF IN GOTHAM -- BUT NOT FAST ENOUGH FOR ME!

SUDDENLY...

SKEEEEEE

NO!

SHORTLY...

TOO BAD! GANS HAD BEEN GOING STRAIGHT THIS YEAR! THAT'S HIS WIFE...POOR WOMAN!

GOING STRAIGHT...? I...I DIDN'T KNOW! THEN WHY DID HE RUN?

12

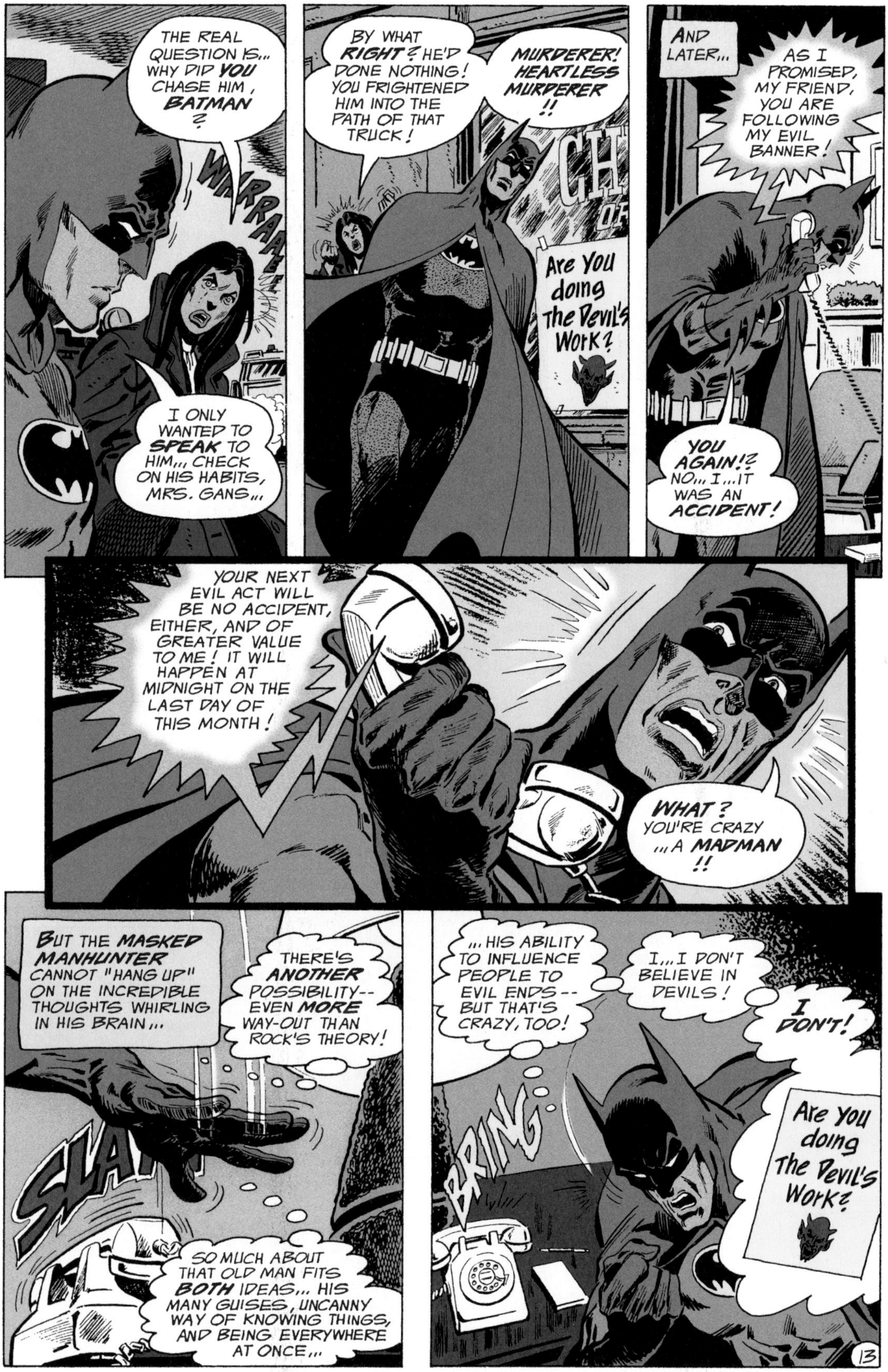

THE REAL QUESTION IS... WHY DID YOU CHASE HIM, BATMAN?
WARRAAAA!
I ONLY WANTED TO SPEAK TO HIM... CHECK ON HIS HABITS, MRS. GANS...
BY WHAT RIGHT? HE'D DONE NOTHING! YOU FRIGHTENED HIM INTO THE PATH OF THAT TRUCK!
MURDERER! HEARTLESS MURDERER!!
Are You doing The Devil's Work?
AND LATER...
AS I PROMISED, MY FRIEND, YOU ARE FOLLOWING MY EVIL BANNER!
YOU AGAIN!? NO... I...IT WAS AN ACCIDENT!
YOUR NEXT EVIL ACT WILL BE NO ACCIDENT, EITHER, AND OF GREATER VALUE TO ME! IT WILL HAPPEN AT MIDNIGHT ON THE LAST DAY OF THIS MONTH!
WHAT? YOU'RE CRAZY ...A MADMAN!!
BUT THE MASKED MANHUNTER CANNOT "HANG UP" ON THE INCREDIBLE THOUGHTS WHIRLING IN HIS BRAIN...
THERE'S ANOTHER POSSIBILITY-- EVEN MORE WAY-OUT THAN ROCK'S THEORY!
SLAM
SO MUCH ABOUT THAT OLD MAN FITS BOTH IDEAS... HIS MANY GUISES, UNCANNY WAY OF KNOWING THINGS, AND BEING EVERYWHERE AT ONCE...
...HIS ABILITY TO INFLUENCE PEOPLE TO EVIL ENDS -- BUT THAT'S CRAZY, TOO!
I...I DON'T BELIEVE IN DEVILS!
I DON'T!
BRING
Are You doing The Devil's Work?
13

BATMAN? GORDON! RIOT AT GOTHAM AIRPORT! YOU BETTER GET HERE!

WITHIN MINUTES...

ROCK--?!

YOU *KNOW* THIS MANIAC? HE TRIED TO GUN SOME POOR OLD MAN BOARDING A JET TO EUROPE!

UH... YES, HE MUST BE SUFFERING A RELAPSE FROM WAR-INDUCED SHOCK, COMMISSIONER! WOULD YOU RELEASE HIM IN MY CUSTODY?

HE'S LUCKY HE'S YOUR FRIEND!

THANKS, PAL! DOES THIS MEAN YOU'RE BEGINNING TO *BELIEVE* ME?

MAYBE, ROCK-- BUT FOR DIFFERENT REASONS! WHOEVER THAT OLD MAN IS...

I'M CONVINCED NOW HE *MUST BE CAUGHT!*

THE FOLLOWING DAY...

BATMAN-- HI! WE'RE IN *LUCK!* AN OLD ARMY BUDDY SPOTTED UNCLE ADOLF LANDING IN HIS OLD HOME GROUNDS --*GERMANY!*

THAT'S WHERE WE'RE HEADING, ROCK!

TWO DAYS LATER, SOMEWHERE IN BAVARIA...

ROCK! YOU OLD SON-OF-A-GUN!

BULLDOZER-- YOU OVERGROWN CLOWN!

14

AND THESE ARE SOME OF THE JOES OF THE **NEW EASY COMPANY** ... WE'LL NEED 'EM IF IT'S REALLY MR. MUSTACHE AND HIS OLD NASTY NAZIS!

S-SERGEANT ROCK!? B-BATMAN!? THEY'RE LIVING **LEGENDS!**

WE COULD BE **DEAD** LEGENDS... IF THIS TURNS OUT TO BE THE BIG SHOWDOWN AT LAST!

OR WE'LL WISH WE **WERE** DEAD IF HE IS WHO I'M BEGINNING TO FEAR HE **REALLY** IS--!

SHORTLY, AN ALPINE HUNTING LODGE IN A HIGH, HIDDEN PASS...

AFTER I SPOTTED OUR FORMER ENEMY, I TRAILED HIM AND SOME GOONS TO THIS PLACE, ROCK!

SUDDENLY...

WE'RE SPOTTED! TAKE 'EM-- **FAST!**

BUDDA BUD

KPOW KPO

JUST LIKE THE OLD DAYS, BULLDOZER!

BUDDA

KRAK

BETTER, ROCK-- **BATMAN'S** ON OUR SIDE!

15

HEY, WHERE **IS** HE-- ?

BLAAM

YES, WHERE IS THE **MASKED MANHUNTER**? TRY **PART 3**, WHICH BEGINS ON THE NEXT PAGE ...

MOMENTS LATER, AS THE FIRING SUDDENLY CEASES -- AND TENSE MEN MOVE CAUTIOUSLY INTO THE SILENT HUNTING LODGE...

BATMAN! MIGHT'VE OF KNOWN YOU'D BE FIRST IN! ANY SIGN OF YOU-KNOW-WHO?

HE *WAS* HERE, ALL RIGHT -- THIS RUG'S WORN FROM SOMEONE DRAGGING ONE FOOT OVER IT...BUT OUR BIRD'S FLOWN THE COOP!

BLAST IT! AND THIS BUNCH IS KAPUT! THEY CAN'T TELL US ANYTHING!

MAYBE THIS UNDERLINED TRAIN SCHEDULE CAN! HMMM...

COME ON, WE'VE GOT AN EXPRESS TO CATCH!

ONE HOUR LATER...

HERE IT IS!

BRING ME ALONGSIDE, ROCK! IF I DON'T SIGNAL YOU BY MIDNIGHT, STOP THIS BABY... EVEN IF YOU HAVE TO *WRECK* IT!

AS THE *MASKED MANHUNTER* INCHES DOWN A CORRIDOR...

WHAT-?

DO NOT RESIST! WE ARE *FEDERAL GERMAN POLICE!*

16

I'M... *THE BATMAN*... A LAW ENFORCER MYSELF... I...

WE KNOW VERY WELL WHO YOU ARE!

PARDON, HERR DOKTOR RITTER, IS *THIS* THE MAN WHO'S BEEN HARASSING YOU?

AND AS THE *MASKED MANHUNTER* HEARS AGAIN A BY NOW FAMILIAR VOICE...

JA! HE AND SOME CRAZY *AMERIKANER* SERGEANT, WHO HAS BEEN HOUNDING ME FOR YEARS, THINKING I AM... *ADOLF HITLER!*

THAT SCOUNDREL! WHY, I MYSELF WAS IN A CONCENTRATION CAMP AND ALMOST DIED!

THAT IS RIGHT! THE GOOD DOKTOR WAS AN ANTI-NAZI!

HIS FACE-- I CAN SEE IT FOR THE *FIRST TIME!* ROCK AND I... MY GOD!.. HAVE BEEN WRONG ALL ALONG!!

THAT CRAZY SIX-STRIPER... HE MUST BE SHELL-SHOCKED, AND MY BEING WOUNDED BY DORN MUST'VE FLIPPED MY OWN COWL!

INSPECTOR! THAT AMERICAN SERGEANT, HE'S RACING ALONGSIDE THE TRAIN! HE'LL WRECK IT WITHIN *MINUTES*--!

THE NEXT MOMENT...

THANK YOU! THAT IS ALL WE WISHED TO KNOW!

FIRE! FIRE!

POW POW PO

A TRICK--?!

WHOK WHOK

(17)

SSKREEEEE

IT IS ONLY MINUTES-- BUT IN *BATMAN'S* THROBBING HEAD AN ETERNITY...

OOOHHHNN--! ROCK, I--I GOT HIM KILLED!

I *WARNED* YOU, YOU WOULD COMMIT AN EVIL ACT AT MIDNIGHT OF THIS DAY-- AND YOU *DID!* YOUR STUPIDITY AND ARROGANCE BETRAYED YOUR COMRADE!

YOU--!? YOU WERE RITTER?!

I SAID I HAD *MANY* NAMES, *MANY* DISGUISES! DOES THIS NOT PROVE YOU CANNOT RESIST MY POWER...CAN- NOT RESIST SERVING ME?

MANY DO NOT BELIEVE I EXIST-- BUT I *DO!* MANY DO MY *WORK*-- AND BELIEVE THEY DO GOOD! YOU ARE NO DIFFERENT!

NO...*NO!* I MUST FIGHT THIS FEELING OF HELPLESSNESS... OF EVIL FLOODING ME!

ROCK! ROCK! I'VE KILLED YOU--!

MEANTIME...

YOU GUYS *CAN'T* BE ALIVE--!

OLD EASY VETS GOT NINE LIVES, SONNY! *DRIVE!*

HEAD FOR THAT BRIDGE!!

MOMENTS LATER...

HIT IT, *BULLDOZER!*

18

YES, THE FORMER *BATMAN* IS DRIVEN OUT OF YOU--*VANQUISHED*-- AND A *NEW CAPED CRUSADER* TAKES HIS PLACE... STRONG WITH THE STRENGTH OF EVIL!

ATOP THE CAR-- *ROCK! BULLDOZER!*

HE'S *ALIVE!* ROCK'S *ALIVE!* I DIDN'T KILL HIM-- BUT NOW I'M GOING TO END YOUR FOUL EXISTENCE!

BUT AS THE *BATMAN* LUNGES...

THE LIGHTS-- ?!

AND A FEW SECONDS LATER...

HE'S *GONE!*

ROCK NEEDS HELP!

BATMAN!

WOK

19

415

BUT AS THE DESPERATE BATTLE ENDS ATOP THE ROCKETING EXPRESS...

HEY! SOMEBODY PULLED A SWITCH... WE'RE OFF ON SOME SPUR TRACK!

EASY COMPANY FOUGHT ALONG HERE IN THE WAR! I DON'T REMEMBER NO BRANCH GOING THIS WAY!... WHA-?

LOOK! AHEAD-- A WEIRD CAMOUFLAGED DOOR OPENIN' !?

AS THE TRAIN HURTLES INSIDE THE MYSTERIOUS TUNNEL AND SCREAMS TO A STOP...

BLAZES! A NAZI WEREWOLF REDOUBT... LIKE THE ONES WE CLEANED UP WHEN THE WAR WAS ENDIN'!

THIS IS ONE WE MISSED! SPOOKY JOINT!

MORE LIKE A PREVIEW OF HELL--THAN ANYTHING!

WELCOME TO MY REGIONS! LIKE MYSELF, PEOPLE DO NOT THINK SUCH A PLACE EXISTS... BUT IT DOES!

HIM! RUSH HIM!!

20

RASH ORDERS, SERGEANT!

FREEZE! MACHINE GUNS HIDDEN IN THE WALLS!

NOW, *BATMAN*, WE SHALL SETTLE OUR BARGAIN! YOU OWE ME YOUR *LIFE*--AND THUS YOUR *SOUL* AS A LOYAL SERVITOR!

FORGET IT! YOU ALMOST HAD ME BACK THERE-- BUT IT'S TOO LATE! I'LL NEVER TUMBLE TO YOUR BLACKMAILING BLUFFS AND TRICKS AGAIN!

VERY WELL, THEN! YOU SHALL ALL TASTE THE FINAL DEFEAT OF DEATH!

BAMMM WHIRAAANG

EASY COMPANY! THE WAR'S ON AGAIN!

RIGHT, ROCK!

BUT AS THE BIZARRE HIDEOUT ERUPTS, *BATMAN* HAS EYES ONLY FOR A FIGURE WHO RUNS WITH A LIMPING GAIT...

MUST UNMASK HIM... BUT HOW CAN HE MOVE SO FAST--?!

21

BUT BACK INSIDE, A SUICIDAL HAND TOSSESS...

KWHRROOOOMM

ROCK... EASY'S GIs... THEY'RE *GONE!*

SUDDENLY, AS IF EMERGING FROM THE DEPTHS OF HELL ITSELF,...

YOU'RE ALIVE!?

KLANK KLANK

THE TANK WAS BETWEEN US AND THE MAIN BLAST,... BUT THEM WEREWOLF GOONS ALL HAD IT!

WE RADIOED FOR THIS TANK FROM A NEARBY ARMY DEPOT! HOW'D WE *DO,* SARGE?

JUST FINE, SONNY! THE NEW EASY'S JUST AS GREAT AS THE OLD ONE!

BATMAN! HITLER... WHERE *IS* HE?

THE OLD MAN? HE'S GONE, ROCK!

THEN WE BLEW IT-- WE BLEW THE MAIN CHANCE TO GRAB THE WORLD'S BIGGEST VILLAIN!

22

WHETHER HITLER'S DEAD OR ALIVE, ROCK, I KNOW ONE THING FOR SURE NOW... THE SPIRIT OF EVIL HE REPRESENTED IS ALWAYS WITH US!
AND NOBODY CAN FORETELL WHEN OR WHERE IT'LL STRIKE AGAIN!
AMEN TO THAT, BATMAN! FOR NOT FAR AWAY, AN OLD MAN LIMPS DOWN A DESERTED ROAD, AND AS THE COLD MOON BREAKS THROUGH SCUDDING DARK CLOUDS...
NO END
23

BATMAN

the BRAVE and the BOLD

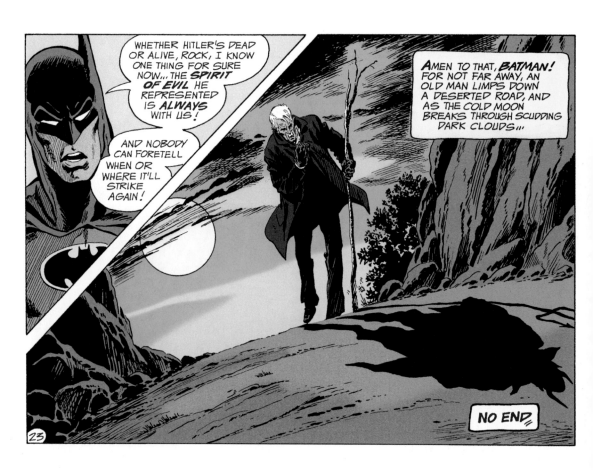

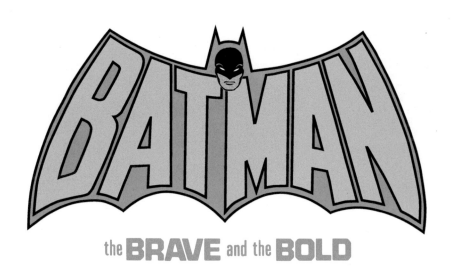

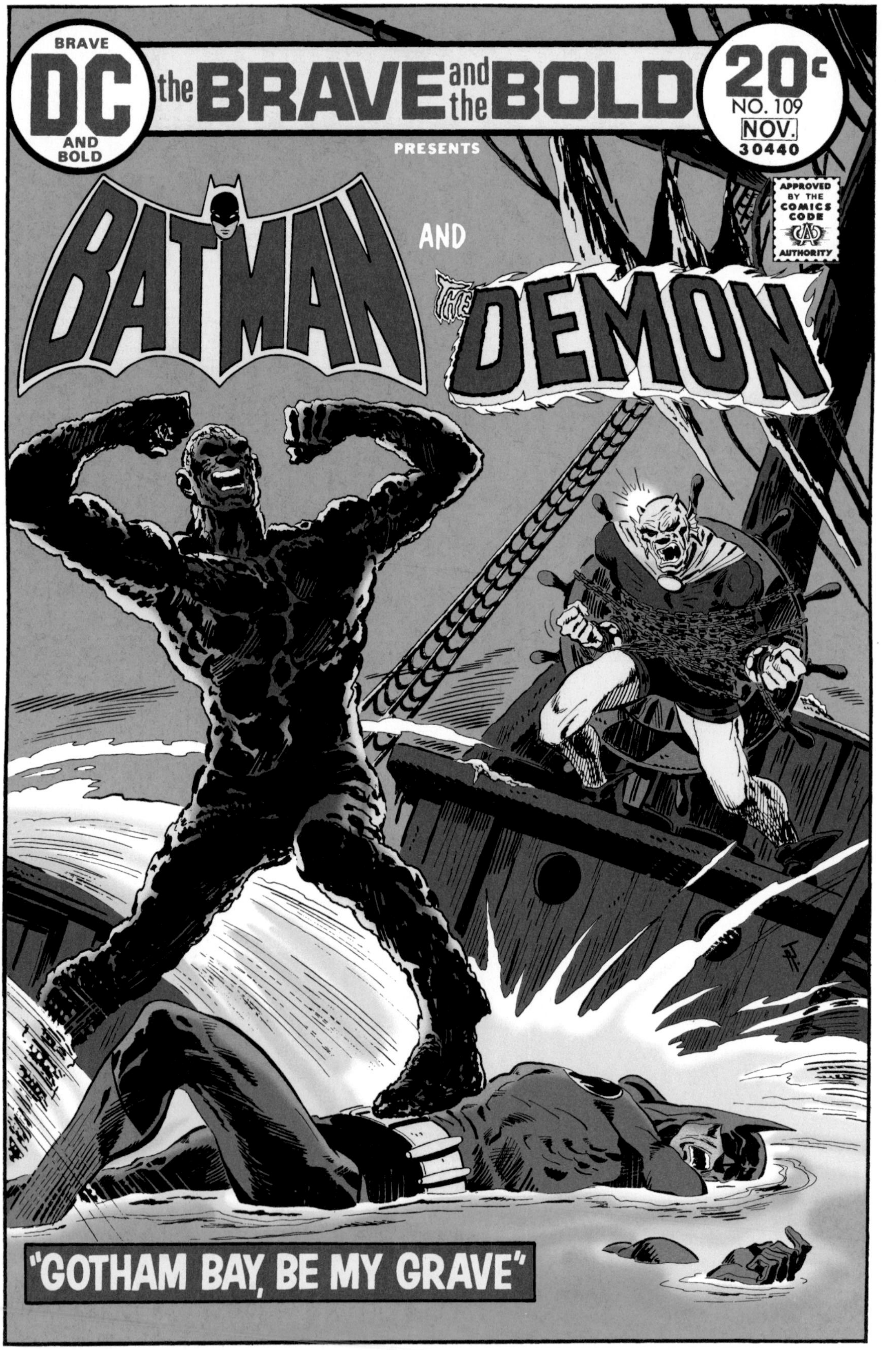
BRAVE
DC
AND
BOLD
the BRAVE and the BOLD
20¢
NO. 109
NOV.
30440
PRESENTS
BATMAN
AND
APPROVED BY THE COMICS CODE AUTHORITY
THE DEMON
"GOTHAM BAY, BE MY GRAVE"

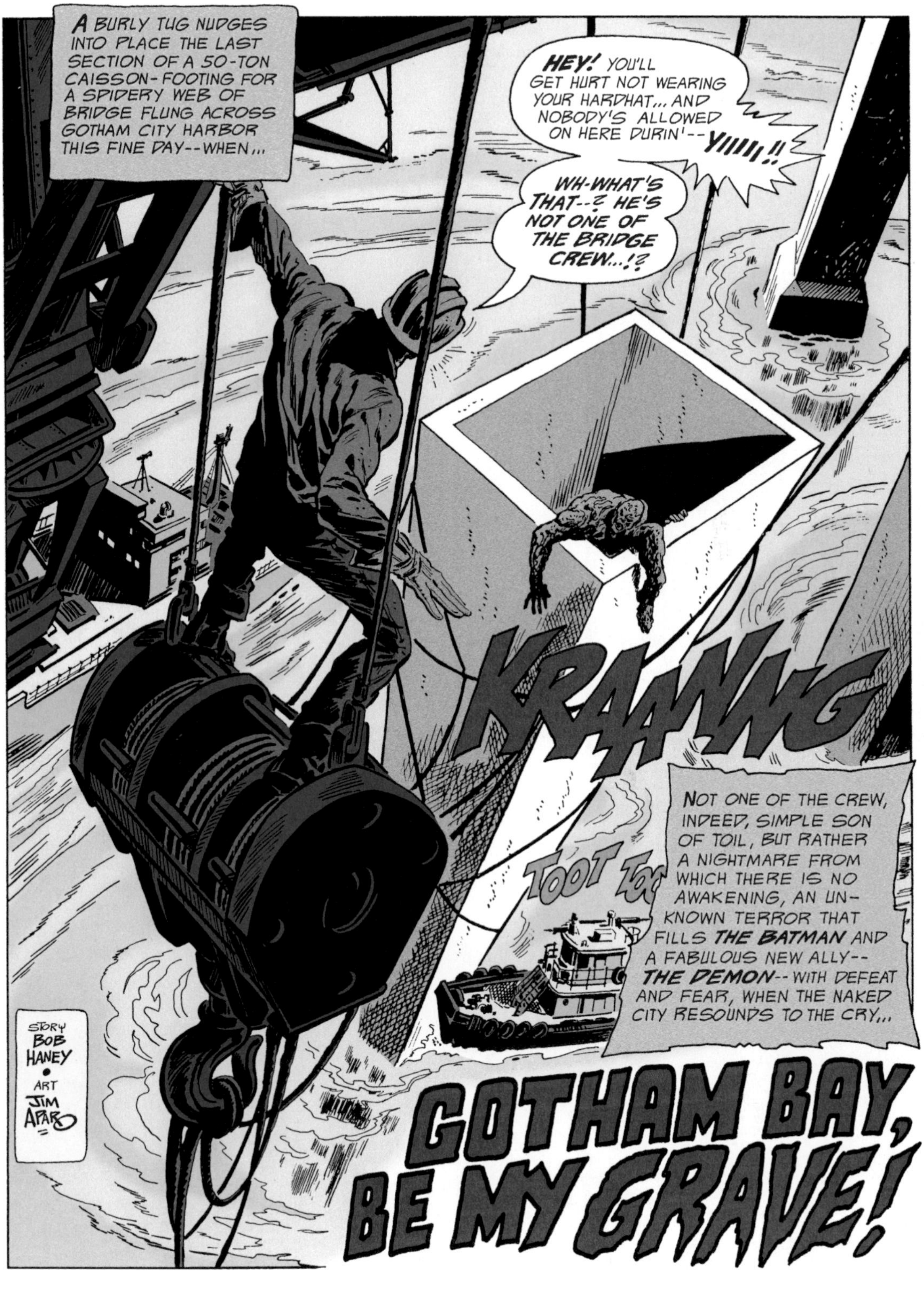
A BURLY TUG NUDGES INTO PLACE THE LAST SECTION OF A 50-TON CAISSON-FOOTING FOR A SPIDERY WEB OF BRIDGE FLUNG ACROSS GOTHAM CITY HARBOR THIS FINE DAY--WHEN...
HEY! YOU'LL GET HURT NOT WEARING YOUR HARDHAT... AND NOBODY'S ALLOWED ON HERE DURIN'--YIIII!!
WH-WHAT'S THAT--? HE'S NOT ONE OF THE BRIDGE CREW...!?
KRAANNG
TOOT TOO
NOT ONE OF THE CREW, INDEED, SIMPLE SON OF TOIL, BUT RATHER A NIGHTMARE FROM WHICH THERE IS NO AWAKENING, AN UN-KNOWN TERROR THAT FILLS THE BATMAN AND A FABULOUS NEW ALLY--THE DEMON--WITH DEFEAT AND FEAR, WHEN THE NAKED CITY RESOUNDS TO THE CRY...
STORY BOB HANEY • ART JIM APARO
GOTHAM BAY, BE MY GRAVE!

A CASUAL SWIPE WITH A HAND THAT'S MORE LIKE A BEAST'S PAW, AND,...

NO! AIEEEEEEEE!

PART 1 "CITY OF FEAR!"

THEN, WITH PRODIGIOUS AGILITY, THE LIVING NIGHTMARE BOUNDS TO THE TUGBOAT WHEELHOUSE,...

I DON'T KNOW *WHAT* YOU ARE-- OR WHERE YOU CAME FROM-- BUT I'VE GOT MY *OWN* ANSWER RIGHT HERE IN MY HAND!

ARRGGH!

IT IS ONLY MINUTES LATER, AS A POLICE HELICOPTER WHIRLS OUT OVER THE HARBOR, A HIGH-FLYING EYE OVER THE NAKED CITY,...

THAT TUG'S GOING IN CIRCLES!

DOWN, ED!

AND WITHIN INSTANTS, GOTHAM'S FAMED GUARDIAN IS SWINGING DOWN ONTO THE AIMLESSLY CHURNING TUG,...

BATMAN! IT WAS AWFUL,... A HORRIBLE THING,... CAME OUT OF THE CAISSON!

THE *CAPTAIN*... BETTER SEE TO THE CAPTAIN!

THE *BATMAN* BOUNDS TO THE WHEELHOUSE, WHERE SPOKES WHIRL IDLY, THE MASTER HANDS THAT GRIPPED THEM STILL FOREVER...

GHASTLY! TORN AS IF BY SOME WILD BEAST!

SHORTLY...

HE BRUSHED YOU OFF THE HOOK AND WENT FOR THE CAPTAIN? THEN WHAT--?

THEN THAT... THING LEAPED OVERBOARD, AND SWAM TOWARD...

...THERE!

YES, THE END OF THOUSANDS OF MILES OF WATERY GAIETY AND EXOTIC STOPOVERS-- AND *ONE* TRAVELER WHO'S HEARTILY RELIEVED...

AT LAST, NO MORE FAT MATRONS TAKING UP MY TIME... NO MORE DUMB PARTIES WHERE I'VE GOT TO SMILE LIKE A HYENA!

TOOOOT

PURSER

JUST A BEAUTIFUL WEEK RELAXIN' IN GOTHAM--

AAAGGGHH...

3

HAPPY HOMECOMING WHISTLES DROWN OUT A DYING MAN'S LAST GURGLING GASPS... UNTIL, SOME TIME LATER...

I...I CAN'T LOOK--AND I'VE SEEN *PLENTY* IN MY TIME!

UNBRIDLED FEROCITY... WREAKED BY THE SAME THING THAT GOT THE TUGBOAT CAPTAIN!

BUT *WHAT* IS IT, COMMISSIONER? *WHERE* AND *WHEN* WILL IT STRIKE NEXT?

EFFECTIVE IMMEDIATELY, *BATMAN*, I'M PUTTING THE WHOLE CITY ON *EMERGENCY ALERT!*

SHORTLY, GOTHAM'S PARK ROW, A GLITTERING CANYON OF APARTMENTS AND TOWNHOUSES FOR THE RICH--AND THE *VERY* RICH...

AND IN *ONE* APARTMENT ALONG THIS CANYON, THAT OF *JASON BLOOD*, AN INDIVIDUAL OF EXTRAORDINARY BACKGROUND-- AND MYSTERY...

JASON, MY WOMAN'S INTUITION TELLS ME THERE'S SOMETHING BETWEEN YOU AND THIS AWFUL DEMON... *ETRIGAN!*

OF *COURSE* THERE IS, GLENDA! AS A PRO-FESSIONAL, REAL-LIVE DEMONOLOGIST, I'M VERY INTERESTED IN *ETRIGAN!*

AND I THOUGHT "WOMAN'S INTUITION" WAS *OUT*, NOW THAT WOMAN'S LIB IS IN-- HA! HA!

DON'T EVADE THE POINT! AND THESE PORTRAITS OF YOUR ANCESTORS, I'D *SWEAR* THEY WERE ALL OF *YOU*--!

④

NATURALLY, THEY'RE ALL "BLOOD" RELATIVES OF MINE--!

I MUST REDUCE BY CHEAP MOCKERY HER SUSPICIONS, FOR I TRULY AM ETRIGAN, THE DEMON, AND GREAT MERLIN IS MY MASTER!

BUT THIS SECRET SHE MUST NOT KNOW-- YET!

SUDDENLY, TWO WHO ARE AWARE OF JASON BLOOD'S AMAZING DOUBLE IDENTITY ARRIVE...

HARRY MATTHEWS! RANDU SINGH!

AW, EXCUSE US, JACE! TWO'S COMPANY... FOUR'S A DRAG! WE'LL COME BACK LATER!

OF COURSE, BUT FIRST WE MUST TELL JASON ABOUT THE... DEMON!

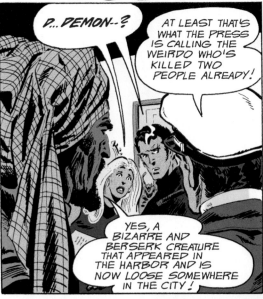

D...DEMON--?

AT LEAST THAT'S WHAT THE PRESS IS CALLING THE WEIRDO WHO'S KILLED TWO PEOPLE ALREADY!

YES, A BIZARRE AND BERSERK CREATURE THAT APPEARED IN THE HARBOR AND IS NOW LOOSE SOMEWHERE IN THE CITY!

WELL, WE ALL KNOW THERE'S REALLY ONLY ONE DEMON IN GOTHAM... THE REAL ARTICLE ... ETRIGAN! EH, JASON?

MAYBE HE AND THIS NEW ONE WILL TANGLE -- WHAT A CONCEPT!

SOMETIMES, HARRY, YOUR IDEA OF HUMOR IS A BIT STRAINED!

OKAY, SO I'M GOING... HEADING FOR MY LITTLE 30-FOOTER AT THE YACHT BASIN! WE SLAVING ADVERTISING EXECUTIVES HAVE TO UNWIND, YOU KNOW!

I... I'M LEAVING, TOO!

PERMIT ME TO ESCORT YOU, GLENDA!

GOODBYE, JASON...!

GOODBYE, GLENDA!... SEE YOU... SOON!

GO QUICKLY! I FEEL CERTAIN TELLTALE VIBRATIONS... A VERY IMPORTANT VISITOR IS NIGH!

5

JASON BLOOD WELL KNOWS WHAT COMES NEXT--A SHIMMER OF STRANGE LIGHT... A TINKLE OF BELLS... THE ODOR OF MAN-DRAKE ROOT--AND SUDDENLY MATERIAL-IZING, A DAZZLING, HAUGHTY FIGURE... *MERLIN! MERLIN, THE ENCHANTER... MERLIN, THE POWER!*

MASTER... GREAT FATHER!

AYE, MY DEMON! I SENSED A TROUBLE IN YOUR FIERY SOUL-- A ROT IN YOUR HEART WHERE ALL SHOULD BE FURY AND DEDICATION AGAINST THE DARK FORCES!

YOU SENSED TRULY, WISE ONE! THIS GIRL, GLENDA MARK, SHE PRIES AND PROBES AT MY SECRET LIFE... MY HEART! I VALUE HER HIGHLY --YET THIS BOND HAS A CERTAIN PRICE!

IT IS ALWAYS SO--EVEN A *DEMON* MAY BE BEWITCHED BY FEMALE POWER--BY LOVE!

BUT HEAR ME, *DEMON*--THESE FAILINGS AND LONGINGS ARE NOT FOR YOU--

FOR I HAVE CREATED YOU FOR A GREATER DESTINY THAN THAT OF CONSORTING WITH A MORTAL MAID!

I KNOW, MIGHTY MERLIN... BUT SOMETIMES THE CENTURIES OF MY DUTY SEEM SO *LONG*... MY CURIOUS AND UNIQUE LIFE SO *LONELY!*

SO BE IT! YOU ARE A CHOSEN ONE-- AND A BULWARK AGAINST ALL THAT MENACE GOOD! REMEMBER THIS-- FOR IT CANNOT BE CHANGED!

NOW I MUST GO! BUT ALSO FORGET NOT THAT I HAVE NEED OF YOU -- TOMORROW-- IN *TINTAGEL!** BE THERE!

AS YOU COMMAND, GREAT WIZARD!

*TINTAGEL: RUINS OF KING ARTHUR'S BIRTH-PLACE IN BRITAIN!

A TINKLE OF AN UNEARTHLY MELODY --AND JASON BLOOD IS ONCE AGAIN ALONE-- BUT...

YAAAAAHHHHH...

6

SEEING HIS BRASH FRIEND IN DEADLY DANGER, JASON BLOOD CHANTS WORDS WHICH PROBE DEEP WITHIN HIS BEING WHERE LIE THE ROOTS OF THE SUPERNATURAL...

AND, IN ANSWER TO THIS MYSTIC SUMMONS, ALL SIGNS OF JASON BLOOD VANISH, WHILE IN THEIR PLACE APPEARS...

HARRY... ATTACKED BY... THAT THING!!

LEAVE, LEAVE THE FORM OF MAN--! RISE THE DEMON, ETRIGAN!

...I, THE DEMON!

LET GO YOUR UNHOLY GRASP!

RIIIIIP

KWAAM

AGGGG!

THE DEMON'S ASSAULT WRINGS THE FIRST CRY FROM THE MAN-BEAST, AND IT LEAPS TO COUNTER-ATTACK...

CURSED THING-- IT HAS THE POWER OF A DOZEN STRONG MEN!

WHAAP

AND, AS THESE TWO INCREDIBLE CREATURES OF THE UNNATURAL WORLD CLASH, PART 1 ENDS-- BUT THE TITANIC BATTLE CONTINUES IN PART 2 ON NEXT PAGE FOLLOWING.

7

PART 2 "ENTER THE DEMON!"

HURLED WITH A FEROCITY THE LIKE OF WHICH HE HAS NEVER FELT BEFORE, *THE DEMON* FINDS HIMSELF ON A *NEW* BATTLEGROUND-- GOTHAM PARK-- BUT FACING THE SAME RELENTLESS FOE AS EARLY DARKNESS FALLS...

IT SPEAKS NOT-- BUT ITS FURY IS MOST ELOQUENT!

GATHERING ALL THE POWER SPAWNED BY HIS SUPERNATURAL BIRTH AS MERLIN'S CHAMPION, *THE DEMON*, EXPLODES...

THE THING FROM NOWHERE HITS THE CAROUSEL...

KRARUNCH

AND THE NEXT MOMENT-- LIKE A PROJECTILE FROM HELL...

TWA AM

NOW FROM THE STRANGE ENERGIES THAT BLAZE IN HIS VERY CORE, *THE DEMON* UNLEASHES...

DEMON-FLAME! LET IT CONSUME YOUR WRATH-- AND YOU BOTH!

8

BUT FOR PERHAPS THE FIRST TIME IN HIS ENCHANTED EXISTENCE, *DEMON* COMES TO A STUNNING REALIZATION...

IT BREATHES IT IN LIKE IT FEEDS ON FIRE ITSELF!

UNABLE TO HALT HIS ASTOUNDING ANTAGONIST'S ONRUSH, *DEMON* FINDS REFUGE ABOVE...

IT CAREENS OFF INTO THE GATHERING NIGHT!

I'LL FOLLOW!

BUT AS *DEMON* CHARGES OFF AFTER HIS QUARRY...

A NET-- ENTRAPPING ME?!

AND THE NEXT INSTANT, ANOTHER HUNTER OF THE NIGHT STRIKES!

CAUGHT THAT KILLER-THING!

LUCKY THIS ZOO NET WAS HANDY!

BUT...

WHAT--?? IT *ISN'T* THAT MAN-BEAST... BUT SOME *OTHER* NIGHTMARE--!

COMING UPON THE SCENE AT THIS CRITICAL MOMENT...

RANDU! BATMAN'S GOT *DEMON*!!

THEN, WE'D BEST THICKEN THE PLOT, HARRY-- *THIS WAY!*

LEAVE, LEAVE, ETRIGAN! RETURN THE FORM OF MAN!

9

AND BEFORE **BATMAN'S** AWED EYES...

HE... HE'S CHANGING INTO... **JASON BLOOD,** THE PROMINENT DEMONOLOGIST!?

WHY, THIS IS **FANTASTIC**--

--BUT **TRUE!** YOU AND WE TWO ARE THE ONLY MORTALS AWARE OF THIS AMAZING DOUBLE EXISTENCE!

HARRY MATTHEWS... RANDU SINGH--! WHY IN BLAZES ARE GOTHAM'S TOP HUCKSTER AND A FAMED U.N. DELEGATE INVOLVED IN ALL THIS?

SOON AS RANDU HAS ME FREE, YOU'LL KNOW EVERYTHING, **BATMAN!**

AND SHORTLY, BACK AT JASON'S APARTMENT...

SO, AS **DEMON,** YOU WERE CHASING THAT BEAST-THING?

YES, AFTER IT ATTACKED HARRY!

BLASTED CREEP RUINED MY YACHTING OUTFIT! GUESS IT DOESN'T DIG BOATING!

YOU AREN'T JUST JOKING, HARRY! EACH ONE IT ATTACKED WAS A MARINER-- OR SOMEONE DRESSED LIKE A SEAFARER!

THAT WOULD SEEM TO LIMIT ITS POTENTIAL VICTIMS, DON'T YOU THINK? BUT **WHY**--? WHY, UNLESS, SINCE IT CAME FROM THE RIVER ITSELF...

HMMM, MAYBE-- BUT MY DETECTIVE BAG DOESN'T CARRY THE ANSWER! THERE'S NO "RECORD" OR M.O. IN POLICE FILES ON DEMON-CREATURES!

THAT'S **MY** DEPARTMENT-- AND PERHAPS RANDU'S!

RANDU, OLD FRIEND, DO YOU THINK YOU COULD MAKE SOME CON- TACT OR SEARCH INTO THAT CREATURE'S ORIGINS OR IDENTITY WITH YOUR **ESP** POWER?

I CAN BUT HUMBLY TRY!

10

LATER, GOTHAM POLICE HEADQUARTERS...

OKAY, SO HE'S LIMITING HIS ATTACKS TO SEA-FARERS! I'VE GOT THE WHOLE WATER-FRONT BUTTONED UP TIGHT... TRIPLE PATROLS WITH RIOT GUNS!

AND THE REST OF THE CITY'S ON RED EMERGENCY WITH COPS EVERYWHERE!

BUT I FAIL TO SEE WHAT GOOD THIS *ESP* IDEA WILL DO!

PATIENCE, COMMISSIONER, AS RANDU SINGH CONCENTRATES ON THE POLICE-ARTIST'S SKETCH OF OUR MYSTERIOUS FOE...

NOW ACROSS THE MOST TENUOUS OF CONNECTIONS, THE REDOUBTABLE RANDU FOCUSES ALL HIS PSYCHIC POWER...

A SHIP... I SEE A SHIP...!

ANNIHILATING *TIME* AND *DISTANCE*, RANDU AMAZINGLY RELIVES THE EN-SUING EVENTS! SOMEWHERE WEST OF JAVA, 1883, AND A SHIP, OUT OF GOTHAM CITY PORT, HOVES-TO OFF A STARK VOLCANIC ISLAND, DESOLATE KRAKATOA...

JACK DOBBS, YOU ARE GUILTY OF KILLING MR. LARSEN, OUR FIRST MATE... AND, BY THE LAW OF THE SEA, YOU SHALL BE HANGED TOMORROW AT DAWN!

11

Panel 1 (dialogue): YOU'LL NEVER HANG JACK DOBBS, YOU SCUM -- AND I'LL DO TO YOU WHAT I DID TO LARSEN!

Panel 2 (caption): JACK DOBBS WAS RIGHT! BEFORE DAWN, KRAKATOA EXPLODES IN THE GREATEST NATURAL CATACLYSM OF MODERN TIMES...

SFX: WHAA-ROOOMM

THE SHIP VANISHES... BECOMES A CINDER-- AND ONLY THE IRON "BRIG" OR PRISON CABIN SURVIVES, TO SINK INTO A FIERY SEA...

SOMEHOW, JACK DOBBS SURVIVES, AND SOME TIME LATER, *ANOTHER* SHIP APPEARS...

THERE'S KRAKATOA-- SUBSIDING NOW! NO ONE IN THE AREA COULD HAVE LIVED THROUGH THAT HELL!

UNSEEN, WHAT HAD BEEN JACK DOBBS, COMMON MURDERER, BUT NOW CHANGED INTO SOMETHING STRANGE AND HORRIBLE, SLIPS ABOARD THE "LADY CLAIRE," HEADING HOME FOR GOTHAM CITY, HALF A WORLD AWAY...

IN THE NEXT FEW DAYS...

THERE'S SOMETHING *TERRIBLE* ABOARD, MATES ... SOMETHING DOING US IN *ONE BY ONE!*...

SEEK IT OUT -- *KILL IT!*

12

BUT WEEKS LATER... JUST OUTSIDE GOTHAM CITY HARBOR...

INCREDIBLE, A DESERTED SHIP SAILS HOME...HALF WAY'ROUND THE WORLD!

AYE, WE COULD FIND NOTHING AMISS-- EVERYONE JUST VANISHED!

BUT THE SEARCH HAS NOT BEEN THOROUGH ENOUGH TO FIND A SLEEP-ING FORM INSIDE A FALSE COMPART-MENT BELOW DECKS, WHICH SUDDENLY AWAKES...

LOOK! SHE'S SUDDENLY BEGUN TO SINK...LIKE A STONE!

MUST CUT OUR TOW LINE...!

NOW, A CENTURY LATER, A MAN RECOILS AT THE IMPRESSIONS FLOODING HIS MIND...

...THE CONTACT IS BREAKING... MY SENSES REEL!

EASY, RANDU, YOU'VE TOLD US MORE THAN ENOUGH!

WELL, BATMAN, YOU NOW HAVE A COMPLETE "POLICE RECORD FILE" ON JACK DOBBS, ALIAS THE KILLER-CREATURE!

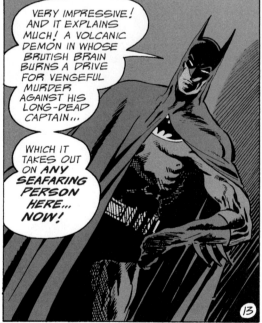

VERY IMPRESSIVE! AND IT EXPLAINS MUCH! A VOLCANIC DEMON IN WHOSE BRUTISH BRAIN BURNS A DRIVE FOR VENGEFUL MURDER AGAINST HIS LONG-DEAD CAPTAIN...

WHICH IT TAKES OUT ON ANY SEAFARING PERSON HERE... NOW!

13

WHEN THE "LADY CLAIRE" WENT DOWN, SHE MUST HAVE SUNK IN THE HARBOR MUD AND THE CREATURE WAS ENTOMBED ALIVE... ONLY TO BE RELEASED BY THE BRIDGE BUILDERS...

PROBABLY IN SOME SUSPENDED STATE! ITS VOLCANIC ORIGIN EXPLAINS WHY DEMON-FLAME NEVER FAZED IT!

WELL, GOOD DETECTIVE WORK WILL FIND IT-- AND DESTROY IT, IF NECESSARY!

I DOUBT IT, BATMAN! IT'S NOT EXACTLY MORTAL... THOUGH IT MAY HAVE AN ACHILLES HEEL! BUT WHAT--?

LEAVE IT TO US, BLOOD! AND DON'T GET ANY "DEMONIC" IDEAS--KNOW WHAT I MEAN?

ONLY TOO WELL! GOODBYE... FOR NOW!

BATMAN'S A GREAT CRIMEFIGHTER --BUT THIS KILLER MAN-BEAST IS... DEMON'S WORK!

YEAH, HE SURE WAS WARNING YOU TO BUTT OUT, JASON!

BRRRR, CREEPY! GOOD NIGHT FOR A MURDER!

YOUR JOKE IS GROSS, HARRY--BUT SUITABLE! WE BEST GET HOME!

SOMETIME LATER, GOTHAM'S WATERFRONT IS ALL BUT DESERTED, SAVE FOR A LONE MAN IN SEAFARING OUTFIT-- AND AS THE ARCLIGHT GLINTS ON THE GOLD STRIPES ON HIS SLEEVE...

OH, LIFE ON THE SEA... CAN BE HAPPY... AND FREEE!

(14)

BUT LIFE IN GOTHAM CITY CAN BE SHORT AND TERRIFYING THIS NIGHT, AS PART 3 PROVES ON THIRD PAGE FOLLOWING.

PART 3
"THE DERELICT FROM THE DEPTHS!"

A FRIGHTENED CITY BEHIND LOCKED DOORS... A LONE MAN, PERHAPS JUST OFF A SHIP, WALKING UNSUSPECTINGLY INTO IMMENSELY POWERFUL PAWS THAT CAN RIP AND TEAR AND DESTROY--!!

WHAT? THIS VICTIM DOES NOT GO DOWN-- DOES NOT CRUMPLE -- BUT FIGHTS BACK WITH CONSUMMATE SKILL AND LITHE POWER...

CHUK

I CAN USE HIS TERRIBLE STRENGTH AGAINST HIM... LIKE SO!

AND AS THE THING SPAWNED BY A CENTURY-OLD VOLCANIC ERUPTION TAKES A MOMENT TO PONDER THIS SURPRISE...

NOW, THAT I BAITED YOU OUT INTO THE OPEN...

...THIS TRAN-QUILIZER DART HAS ENOUGH SLEEP JUICE TO KAYO AN ELEPHANT!

HUH? BROKE-- LIKE A STRAW!?

MY SCHEME BACKFIRED-- BUT...

...GORDON... AND THE RIOT SQUAD... ARE BACKING ME UP... SHOULD BE HERE ANY INSTANT...

⑮

BUT SOME STREETS AWAY, COMMISSIONER GORDON HAS MET WITH A "SLIGHT" DELAY--SOME HOODS HAVE SEIZED ADVANTAGE OF THE CURFEW TO LOOT ARMS AND AMMO...

KRAK

GUNS • AMMUN

POW POW

TZING

BATMAN WILL HAVE TO WAIT! BESIDES, I'M SURE HE'S OKAY!

STARTING TO WEAKEN...THIS THING DOESN'T...

JASON BLOOD... MAYBE YOU WERE RIGHT... I NEED A DEMON TO FIGHT A DEMON!

JASON BLOOD? WHERE IS THE SERVANT OF MERLIN AND MASTER OF DEMONOLOGY? SHORTLY BEFORE...

"HISTORY OF GOTHAM CITY"? HARDLY A COLLECTION OF THE OCCULT, JASON!

YES AND NO, RANDU!

AH, HERE IT IS, THE STORY OF THE "LADY CLAIRE"...

AND SHORTLY AFTER...

THE GOTHAM MUSEUM...BUT IT'S LOCKED TIGHT AT THIS HOUR OF THE NIGHT!

GOTHAM M

YET I MUST GET IN, RANDU... AND THERE'S ONLY ONE WHO CAN DO THAT!

LEAVE, LEAVE THE FORM OF MAN! EMERGE THE DEMON, ETRIGAN!

MOMENTS LATER, A BIZARRE, POWERFUL FIGURE HAS BOUNDED TO THE MUSEUM ROOF-- THEN...

THEN, THE DEMON TAKES FROM A CERTAIN CASE ONLY ONE THING, A COIL OF ROPE...

16

MY *ESP* POWER SAYS *THE BATMAN* IS NIGH... AND IN MORTAL DANGER!

THEN WE MUST BE IN *TIME*, RANDU!

HASTEN, *DEMON*, FOR NOT FAR AHEAD, ANOTHER ASTOUNDING EVENT UNFOLDS...

YES, RELEASED FROM ITS LONG ENTOMBMENT BY BRIDGE BUILDERS' BURROWING IN THE RIVER MUCK, THE GOOD SHIP "LADY CLAIRE" RISES ONCE AGAIN, LIKE SOME NAUTICAL GHOST...

AND SOON, AS SOME UNNATURAL LONGING DRAWS THE MAN-BEAST BACK TO HIS OLD REFUGE, TWO OTHERS IN THIS AWESOME DRAMA FOLLOW...

AMAZING! IT MUST BE THE AIR PRESSURE FROM THE CAISSON PUMPS THAT INFLATED THAT OLD HULK--!

AYE, RANDU, AND THITHER FLY WE TO SAVE *BATMAN* AND PUT AN END TO THAT SPAWN OF EVIL WHO MENACES HIM!

MOMENTS LATER, *DEMON'S* FURIOUS FEET HIT THE MOULDERING DECK, AND...

HIM! HE WAS WAITING FOR ME--!

⑰

AND AS THE TWO MIGHTY DENIZENS OF THE NETHER WORLD ROLL IN COMBAT ON THE ROTTING BOARDS...

ONE GREAT EFFORT TO TOSS HIM CLEAR,... THEN THE ROPE WILL PLAY ITS DESTINED ROLE!

BUT AT THE VERY MOMENT VALIANT DEMON TRIES TO SHRUG OFF HIS TITANIC OPPONENT-- IN FAR-OFF TINTAGEL, IN A SECRET CAVE NEAR THE SOUNDING SEA...

ETRIGAN! I HAVE SUMMONED YOU--YOU APPEAR NOT! AS CHASTISEMENT, I SPEAK THUSLY --PERDU DEMONICUS ZRALL!*

* IN THE MYSTIC LANGUAGE OF THE ANCIENTS: LOSE THY DEMON'S POWER!

AND EVEN AS GREAT MERLIN SPEAKS, THOUSANDS OF MILES AWAY...

BY KRISHNA! DEMON'S CHANGING BACK TO JASON,...BUT NO ONE SPOKE THE MYSTIC WORDS--!

AS HIS NOW VASTLY MORE POWERFUL FOE SQUEEZES JASON'S LIFE'S BREATH FROM HIM,...

MERLIN!? IT MUST BE HE WHO DID THIS.! SOME-HOW I MUST TRY TO REACH HIS LONG-RANGE SORCERY WITH MY ESP WAVES!

AUDACIOUSLY, RANDU SINGH ATTEMPTS TO CONTACT AND INFLUENCE THE MIND OF THE IMMORTAL MERLIN...

WHAT IS THIS ? MY DEMON IN PERIL BY MY OWN DOING?!

I'M A PETULANT OLD FOOL !

REPLEVIN DEMONICUS ZRALL!*

AGAIN, ACROSS VAST SPACE...

* RETURN THY DEMON POWER!

18

REINCARNATED, *DEMON* SEIZES THE ODD COLLAR AROUND HIS FOE'S NECK...

SNAP

FOR THE FIRST TIME, THE FACE OF FROZEN WRATH SHOWS *FEAR*...

HAAAHAAAA

AS THE NOW TERRIFIED MONSTROSITY RACES FOR THE FAR RAIL-- AND PERHAPS FREEDOM...

IT IS ONLY A FEW MOMENTS LATER, WHEN...

DEMON... RANDU... THE MAN-BEAST... HAD ME... WHAT HAPPENED TO IT?

THERE HE IS!

MY GOD! BUT I THOUGHT IT WAS *INVULNERABLE* ...?

19

AYE, IT WAS INVULNERABLE TO ALL EXCEPT THAT *SPECIAL NOOSE*... THE SAME THAT ALMOST HANGED HIM LONG AGO!

IT ALONE HAD THE ENCHANTED POWER TO END ITS CURSED LIFE--!

NOW, MY TASK IS DONE! *BE GONE, BE GONE, ETRIGAN! RETURN THE FORM OF MAN!*

NOW, ONCE MORE, JASON BLOOD REPLACES *THE DEMON*...

YOU SEE, BESIDES JACK DOBBS HIMSELF, THE ONLY TRACE OF DOBBS' SHIP THE "LADY CLAIRE'S" CREW BROUGHT BACK WAS A *SPAR*... WITH A NOOSE ATTACHED... THE CAPTAIN'S LOG RECORDED IT!

WHEN THE DESERTED DERELICT REACHED GOTHAM CITY, THE NOOSE WAS FOUND IN THE CAPTAIN'S LOCKER BY ONE OF THE SEARCH PARTY! AFTER THE SHIP WENT DOWN, IT WAS PLACED IN GOTHAM MUSEUM!

BUT HOW DID YOU KNOW IT WOULD DE-STROY HIM?

HIS IRON COLLAR WAS THE CLUE -- IT HAD TO BE A DEFENSE AGAINST A WEAKNESS HE FEARED -- HIS ACHILLES "NECK", SO TO SPEAK!

OUR CONCLUSIONS WILL BE WRIT ON WATER -- IF WE DON'T LEAVE! THIS HULK'S SINKING!

AND SO, MOMENTS LATER...

THERE SHE GOES, BACK TO A MUDDY ENTOMB-MENT... AND WITH HER, THE MURDER-OUS SPIRIT OF JACK DOBBS!

YES, LIKE MUCH OF THE UNKNOWN, A THING BOTH TERRIFYING AND PATHETIC!

FAREWELL, JASON BLOOD, ALIAS *THE DEMON!* PERHAPS YOU'LL AGAIN RETURN TO THE PAGES OF *BRAVE & BOLD* -- AT SOME UNKNOWN TIME OF NEED!

FAREWELL, FOR NOW!

THE END.

20